Approaches to Discourse

Blackwell Textbooks in Linguistics

Approaches to Discourse

Deborah Schiffrin

BLACKWELL
Oxford UK & Cambridge USA

To David

Copyright © Deborah Schiffrin 1994

The right of Deborah Schiffrin to be identified as author
of this work has been asserted in accordance with the
Copyright, Designs and Patents Act 1988.

First published 1994

Blackwell Publishers
238 Main Street
Cambridge, Massachusetts 02142
USA

108 Cowley Road
Oxford OX4 1JF
UK

Library of Congress Cataloging-in-Publication Data

Schiffrin, Deborah.
   Approaches to discourse / Deborah Schiffrin.
    p. cm.—(Blackwell textbooks in linguistics)
   Includes bibliographical references and index.
   ISBN 0–631–16622–X.—ISBN 0–631–16623–8 (pbk.)
   1. Discourse analysis. I. Title. II. Series.
P302.S334 1994
410′.41—dc20   93–13359
                                    CIP

British Library Cataloguing in Publication Data
A CIP catalogue record for this book is available from the British Library.

Typeset in 10 on 12 pt Sabon by Pure Tech Corporation, Pondicherry, India
Printed in Great Britain by T. J. Press Ltd, Padstow, Cornwall

This book is printed on acid-free paper

Contents

Preface and Acknowledgments

Although discourse analysis is an increasingly popular and important area of study – both on its own and for what it can tell us about language, society, culture, and thought – it still remains a vast and somewhat vague subfield of linguistics. My goal in this book is to clarify the theories and methods of discourse analysis in such a way that it can continue to deal with a wide range of problems and phenomena of interest to linguists, sociologists, anthropologists, and psychologists, but can do so in a more systematic and coherent way.

The core of the book is a detailed description, application, and comparison of six different approaches to discourse analysis: speech act theory, interactional sociolinguistics, ethnography of communication, pragmatics, conversation analysis, and variation analysis. Although these approaches originated in different disciplines (and are relevant to broader topics within each discipline), they all attempt to answer some of the same questions: How do we organize language into units that are larger than sentences? How do we use language to convey information about the world, ourselves, and our social relationships?

Part I of the book provides an overview of the different approaches, outlines the plan of the book, and discusses difficulties in defining discourse – difficulties that are related to the currency of two different paradigms within linguistics. Part II provides a detailed discussion of each approach to discourse – one chapter for each approach. Included in each chapter is discussion of the work of scholars central to the development of the approach, i.e. the central ideas, concepts, and methods of each approach. Also included in each chapter is an extensive sample analysis illustrating how each approach handles specific phenomena and problems of discourse. Although the sample analyses begin with some of the same issues, problems, and data (centered on either question–answer sequences or referring expressions), they diverge sharply once the concepts and methods of each approach are applied (such that the different chapters also provide analyses of phenomena as diverse as participation frameworks, the organization of interviews, existential *there* sentences, and thematic constraints on pronouns). Part III compares approaches to discourse in a more systematic and abstract way: What does each approach assume about the relationships between structure and function, text and context, language and communication? Although these issues are quite different in some ways, they all require reconciliation of what is often defined as part of "language" with what is not typically defined as part of language. The final chapter searches for a possible synthesis among the approaches.

The issues discussed in this book have been ones that have long occupied my attention. When I was still a graduate student in linguistics at the University of Pennsylvania, one of the questions in my PhD exam noted the proliferation of perspectives interested in "language use," e.g. pragmatics, sociolinguistics, ethnolinguistics, and ethnomethodology. The question then asked us to compare these perspectives, e.g. did they focus upon the same problems, use the same methods of analysis, and so on. I passed the exam, but the question continued to haunt me. When I began teaching at Georgetown University, I found myself intermittently confronting similar questions through the courses that I taught. Although we sometimes ended up talking about some of the same phenomena (e.g. discourse markers) and issues (e.g. meaning) in different courses, our starting points (and often our final perspectives) were always strikingly different. In 1987, I was invited to teach a course at the Linguistic Society of America Institute, held that year at Stanford University: the Institute organizers suggested a course that would compare approaches to discourse analysis. This course was an exciting opportunity for me to explicitly work through some of the theoretical and methodological differences among approaches to discourse. About a year after the Linguistics Institute, Philip Carpenter (from Blackwell Publishers) approached me with an idea for a book comparing current approaches to discourse analysis. His proposal could not have been more finely timed to coincide with my own thinking. However, it is important to note that the way each approach to discourse analysis has been incorporated into linguistics has, not surprisingly, changed a great deal since I first became interested in discourse analysis. I expect the relationship between discourse analysis and the rest of linguistics to continue to change: I hope that this book will help people think about the way such change can proceed.

Many people have contributed, both directly and indirectly, to the ideas and the analyses in this book. Although such contributions are hardly limited to those who read preliminary drafts of my chapters, the latter include Ralph Fasold, Esther Figueroa, Michael Geis, John Gumperz, John Searle, Deborah Tannen, Sandra Thompson, and Peter Trudgill. None is responsible for the final form or content of the chapters. My students at Georgetown University have always been, and continue to be, a source of challenge and motivation: their contribution to this book has been invaluable. More recently, the opportunity to use a preliminary version of this book during a course that I taught at the University of California, Berkeley, and to be part of a reading group (on narrative analysis) provided me with yet other sources of challenge and motivation. Material support for preparation of much of the data and analysis reported here was provided by NSF grant BNS-8819845. A sabbatical from Georgetown and a year as a visiting scholar at Berkeley also provided the time and resources needed to complete the work.

Last, but not least, I want to thank my family, especially my husband Louis Scavo, for being a continual source of support and encouragement. Our son David has also contributed in immeasurable ways by giving me good reasons to take time off and for making that time off so much fun: it is to him that I dedicate this book.

The author and publisher gratefully acknowledge permission to reproduce extracts from the following: *Foundations of Sociolinguistics* (1974) by Dell Hymes. Reprinted by permission of University of Pennsylvania Press; *Principles of Pragmatics* (1983) by Geoffrey Leech. Reprinted by permission of Longman Publishing Group; *Structures of Social Action* (1984), edited by J. Maxwell Atkinson and John Heritage. Extract by Gail Jefferson. Reprinted by permission of Cambridge University Press and Gail Jefferson; *Discourse markers* (1987) by Deborah Schiffrin. Reprinted by permission of Cambridge University Press; *Talking Voices* (1989) by Deborah Tannen. Reprinted by permission of Cambridge University Press; *Linguistic Framing of Discourse* (1993), edited by Deborah Tannen. Extract by Deborah Schiffrin. Reprinted by permission of Oxford University Press; *Semiotica* (80), pp. 121–51 (1990). Extract by Deborah Schiffrin. Reprinted by permission of the publisher; *Pragmatics* 1/1: 71–106 (1991). Extract by Jack DuBois. Reprinted by permission of the author; *Language and Communication* 13/2: 133–6 (1993). Extract by Deborah Schiffrin. Reprinted by permission of the publisher.

Part I The Scope of Discourse Analysis

Since discourse analysis is one of the most vast, but also least defined, areas in linguistics, it is important to begin this book by commenting on the scope of discourse analysis. The two chapters in this introductory section do this in two different ways.

Chapter 1 addresses the vastness of discourse analysis by presenting an overview of the six approaches to be compared in the book: speech act theory, interactional sociolinguistics, ethnography of communication, pragmatics, conversation analysis, variation analysis. This selection seems to represent the diversity of approaches (from very different sources) that underlie contemporary discourse analyses. (Compare Taylor and Cameron's (1987) review of social psychological, speech act, exchange structure, Gricean pragmatic, and ethnomethodological approaches to discourse, or Potter and Wetherell's (1987) review of speech act theory, ethnomethodology, and semiology.) Chapter 1 introduces the approaches through examples illustrating issues that prompted scholars to begin to think about language as "discourse". It also outlines the general direction of the book.

Chapter 2 addresses the vastness of discourse analysis from another direction: how can we define discourse analysis in a way that captures it as a field of linguistics and differentiates it from other studies? I suggest in chapter 2 that two prominent definitions of discourse (as a unit of language larger than a sentence, as language use) are couched within two different paradigms of linguistics (formalist, functionalist).

1 Overview

1 Introduction

Discourse analysis is widely recognized as one of the most vast, but also one of the least defined, areas in linguistics (e.g. Stubbs 1983: 12; Tannen 1989a: 6–8). One reason for this is that our understanding of discourse is based on scholarship from a number of academic disciplines that are actually very different from one another. Included are not just disciplines in which models for understanding, and methods for analyzing, discourse first developed (i.e. linguistics, anthropology, sociology, philosophy; see van Dijk 1985), but also disciplines that have applied (and thus often extended) such models and methods to problems within their own particular academic domains, e.g. communication (Craig and Tracy 1983), social psychology (Potter and Wetherell 1987), and artificial intelligence (Reichman 1985).

The goals of this book are to describe and compare several different approaches to the linguistic analysis of discourse: speech act theory, interactional sociolinguistics, ethnography of communication, pragmatics, conversation analysis, and variation analysis. My aim is not to reduce the vastness of discourse analysis: I believe that at relatively early stages of an endeavor, reduction just for the sake of simplification can too drastically limit the range of interesting questions that can and should be asked.[1] Thus, I view the vastness of discourse analysis not as a weakness, but as a strength, and as a sign of interest and development. What I hope to do, however, is clarify the scope of discourse analysis in such a way that it can continue to deal with a wide range of problems and phenomena – but in a more systematic and theoretically coherent way.

Before describing the ways that I hope to accomplish this goal, I want to briefly introduce each approach with the help of a prototypical example from each perspective (section 2). I then go on to an overview of the book (section 3).

2 "Core" examples from different approaches to discourse

The examples in this section reveal some important similarities, and differences, among the approaches to be discussed in the book. I have chosen examples used by those scholars who were instrumental in developing an approach; sometimes these examples also reflected, or led to, controversy that motivated the development of theory and methodology within each approach. Since other kinds of data and other ways of presenting data (including methods of transcription and analysis) have developed within each approach, the examples here might not seem exactly like those from more recent literature representing the different perspectives, e.g. conversation analysts now pay much more attention to transcription than will be illustrated here. But rather than try to reflect current diversity within an approach through these examples, I want to reflect (at least in part) the most salient features, and the conceptual core, of each approach. Finally, as noted above, the examples here are from seminal works in each perspective: thus, they also suggest the sort of data that first prompted scholars to begin to think about language in a different way.

My presentation of approaches to discourse (part II of the book) begins with the *speech act* approach to discourse (chapter 3). Two philosophers, John Austin and John Searle, developed speech act theory from the basic insight that language is used not just to describe the world, but to perform a range of other actions that can be indicated in the performance of the utterance itself. For example, the utterance "I promise to be there tomorrow" performs the act of "promising." The utterance "The grass is green" performs the act of "asserting." An utterance may also perform more than one act, as illustrated in (1).

(1) SPEAKER: Can you pass the salt?
    HEARER: /passes the salt/

S's utterance *Can you pass the salt?* can be understood as both a question (about H's ability) and a request (for H to pass the salt to S). Although these two understandings are largely separable by context (the former associated, for example, with tests of physical ability, the latter with dinner table talk), this utterance has also been labelled an indirect speech act whose illocutionary force is an outcome of the relationship between two different speech acts (e.g. Searle 1975; compare the analyses in Clark 1979; Davison 1975; Ervin-Tripp 1976; Gordon and Lakoff 1975; Green 1975).

The speech act approach to discourse focuses upon knowledge of underlying conditions for production and interpretation of acts through words. In (1), we saw that words may perform more than one action at a time and that contexts (hypothetical contexts supplied along with hypothetical utterances) may help to separate multiple functions of utterances from one another. The literal meanings of words and the contexts in which they occur may interact in our knowledge of the conditions underlying the realization of acts and the interpretation of acts. Although speech act theory was not first developed as a means of analyzing discourse, particular issues in speech act theory (e.g. the problems of indirect speech acts, multifunctionality and context dependence illustrated in (1)) lead to discourse analysis. Speech act theory itself also provides a means by which to segment texts, and thus a framework for defining units that could then be combined into larger structures.

The approach to discourse that I am calling *interactional sociolinguistics* (chapter 4) has very diverse origins, for it stems from anthropology, sociology, and linguistics, and shares the concerns of all three fields with culture, society, and language. Some interactional approaches (especially those influenced by John Gumperz) focus on how people from different cultures may share grammatical knowledge of a language, but differently contextualize what is said such that very different messages are produced. Other interactional approaches (especially those influenced by Erving Goffman) focus on how language is situated in particular circumstances of social life, and on how it adds (or reflects) different types of meaning (e.g. expressive, instrumental) and structure (e.g. interactional, institutional) to those circumstances. (2) is an example (from Gumperz 1982a: 30) that illustrates the interactional approach.

(2) Following an informal graduate seminar at a major university, a black student approached the instructor, who was about to leave the room accompanied by several other black and white students, and said:
   a Could I talk to you for a minute? I'm gonna apply for a fellowship and I was wondering if I could get a recommendation?
   The instructor replied:
   b OK. Come along to the office and tell me what you want to do.
   As the instructor and the rest of the group left the room, the black student said, turning his head ever so slightly to the other students:
   c Ahma git me a gig! (Rough gloss: "I'm going to get myself some support.")

(2) is a report of an actual interchange. In addition to what is said (lines a, b, and c), the example itself includes the context of the interchange (e.g. the physical setting, social roles, relationship of speech to other activity) and other information about what participants are doing (e.g. the physical stance of the interactants). The example also replicates what is said in a way that reveals the use of a particular variety of speech. (Many of Gumperz's own examples, as well as other interactional analyses, rely upon a more precise transcription of linguistic, including prosodic, detail.) Gumperz's analysis of the utterance *Ahma git me a gig!* focuses upon how interpretations of the speaker's intent are related to different linguistic qualities of the utterance (e.g. phonological

and lexical variants) as well as the way the utterance is contextually embedded (e.g. what activities it follows, to whom it is directed). These interpretations are gathered by asking listeners (including, but not limited to, those present during the actual interchange) what they thought the speaker meant to convey, and relating those situated inferences to the means by which the speaker actually presented the utterance. As (2) thus illustrates, the interactional approach relies upon actual utterances in social context: the focus of analysis is how interpretation and interaction are based upon the interrelationship of social and linguistic meanings.

The *ethnography of communication* (chapter 5) is an approach to discourse that is based in anthropology, and it shares with much traditional anthropology a concern for holistic explanations of meaning and behavior. Much of the impetus for this approach was Dell Hymes's challenge to Chomsky's well known refocusing of linguistic theory on the explanation of competence, i.e. tacit knowledge of the abstract rules of language. What Hymes proposed instead was that scholarship focus on communicative competence: the tacit social, psychological, cultural, and linguistic knowledge governing appropriate use of language (including, but not limited to, grammar). Communicative competence includes knowledge of how to engage in everyday conversation as well as other culturally constructed speech events (e.g. prayer, public oratory). (3) is an example that illustrates the inclusive thrust of the ethnography of communication – so inclusive that cultural interpretation and difference permeates even what seems to be so basic a notion as what "counts as" communication. (This example, quoted from Hallowell 1964: 64, is cited in Hymes 1972a.)

(3)   An informant told me that many years before he was sitting in a tent one afternoon during a storm, together with an old man and his wife. There was one clap of thunder after another. Suddenly the old man turned to his wife and asked, "Did you hear what was said?" "No", she replied, "I didn't catch it." My informant, an acculturated [Ojibwa] Indian, told me he did not know at first what the old man and his wife referred to. It was, of course, the thunder. The old man thought that one of the Thunder Birds had said something to him. He was reacting to this sound in the same way as he would respond to a human being, whose words he did not understand.

Hymes (following Hallowell's discussion) uses this example to point out that even so fundamental a notion as "communication" cannot be assumed to be constant across cultures. Cultural conceptions of communication are deeply intertwined with conceptions of person, cultural values, and world knowledge – such that instances of communication behavior are never free of the cultural belief and action systems in which they occur. Other ethnographic analyses focus on how grammar itself reflects cultural knowledge and action systems (e.g. Ochs 1988; Schieffelin 1990); still others focus on communication through other verbal media (e.g. Feld 1982 on weeping) or even on the social distribution and meaning of silence (Basso 1972; Bauman 1974; Philips 1985; Saville-Troike 1982). Like the example in (3), such analyses depend upon extensive familiarity with speakers and with their culture. They also depend upon the analysis of what is particular about each act of communication – particular to a people, to a setting, and so on. Finally, they all seek to locate each particularity within a set of universally available possibilities, but at the same time, to build those possible generalizations from a representative collection of particular instances.

A *pragmatic* approach to discourse (chapter 6) is based primarily on the philosophical ideas of H. P. Grice. Grice proposed distinctions between different types of meaning and argued that general maxims of cooperation provide inferential routes to a speaker's communicative intention. Pragmatics is most concerned with analyzing speaker meaning at the level of utterances and this often amounts to a sentence, rather than text, sized unit of language use. But since an utterance is, by definition, situated in a context (including a linguistic context, i.e. a text), pragmatics often ends up including discourse analyses and providing means of analyzing discourse along the way. (4) is an example that illustrates the interplay between cooperation and inference so critical to a Gricean approach. (4 is from Grice 1975: 51.)

(4) A: Smith doesn't seem to have a girlfriend these days.
     B: He has been paying a lot of visits to New York.

Like the speech act example in (1), the prototypical pragmatics example is a constructed utterance in a constructed context. The issue driving the construction and analysis of (4) is the lack of obvious connection between A's *Smith doesn't seem to have a girlfriend these days* and B's *He has been paying a lot of visits to New York*. Grice points out that the lack of connection does not prevent us from trying to interpret B's utterance as cooperative at a level of understanding not readily available from the meanings of the words. What hearers do is supplement the literal meaning of utterances with an assumption of human rationality and cooperation: these allow B to infer that A has implicated that Smith has a girlfriend in New York. In other words, despite the lack of connection between A's and B's remarks, A implicates that which he must be assumed to believe (Smith has a girlfriend in New York) in order to maintain the assumption that he is following the maxim of relation (i.e. being relevant). Thus, what Gricean pragmatics suggests is that human beings work with very minimal assumptions about one another and their conduct, and that they use those assumptions as the basis from which to draw highly specific inferences about one another's intended meanings.

Conversation analysis (chapter 7) offers an approach to discourse that is also based in philosophy, but in the perspective known as phenomenology, associated with Alfred Schutz. Its underlying concerns were more extensively articulated by a sociologist, Harold Garfinkel, who developed the approach known as "ethnomethodology," and then applied specifically to conversation, most notably by Harvey Sacks, Emmanuel Schegloff, and Gail Jefferson. Conversation analysis (and ethnomethodology) differs from other branches of sociology because rather than analyzing social order *per se*, it seeks to discover the methods by which members of a society produce a sense of social order. Conversation is a source of much of our sense of social order, e.g. it produces many of the typifications underlying our notions of social role. Conversation also exhibits its own kind of order and manifests its own sense of structure.

The example in (5) is an exchange (a telephone call opening) that seems to violate a telephone rule that the person answering the phone is the one who talks first. As Schegloff (1972a) makes clear, however, (5) actually illustrates the workings of a deeper rule of sequencing in talk. (The example is from Schegloff 1972a: 356.)

(5) (Police make call)
     (Receiver is lifted, and there is a one second pause)
     POLICE: Hello.
     OTHER: American Red Cross.
     POLICE: Hello, this is Police Headquarters . . . er, Officer Stratton (etc.).

(5) is the only case in Schegloff's large corpus of telephone openings in which the Police (the party who had made the phone call) talk first. Although this case seems unusual, Schegloff uses it (treats it "seriously," p. 356) as the basis from which to search for a deeper formulation about telephone openings and about sequences in general. He ends up suggesting that (5) is a summons–answer sequence. The telephone ring resulting from the call made by the Police in (5) is a summons. A summons opens a conditional relevance for a second part of a sequence, an answer. Although a called party typically answers the telephone ring issuing the summons by saying *Hello?*, there is no such answer in (5): "Receiver is lifted, and there is a one second pause." The Police's "Hello" is thus a response to the "empty" answer slot: "Hello" redoes the summons. Far from being an anomaly, then, (5) reflects the regular operation of adjacency pairs in general and summons–answer sequences in particular: the sequencing of moves provides for a coordinated entry into the conversation, and for an orderly exchange of turns within the conversation.

As (5) illustrates, conversation analysis is like interactional sociolinguistics in its concern with the problem of social order, and how language both creates, and is created by, social context. Both approaches also focus on detailed analysis of particular sequences of utterances that have actually occurred. But unlike the interactional sociolinguistic willingness to judge participants' interpretation and intent with the help of contextual information, conversation analysts seek generalizations about context – and about social conduct and social life – *within* the progression of utterances themselves.

A *variationist* approach to discourse (chapter 8) stems from studies of linguistic variation and change. Both the initial methodology and the theory underlying such studies are those of William Labov. (Labov and Fanshel

(1977) have also applied a perspective to discourse that is more similar to speech act theory, i.e. "comprehensive discourse analysis.") Fundamental assumptions of variationist studies are that linguistic variation (i.e. heterogeneity) is patterned both socially and linguistically, and that such patterns can be discovered only through systematic investigation of a speech community. Although traditional variationist studies have been limited to semantically equivalent variants (what Labov 1972a calls "alternative ways of saying the same thing"), such studies have also been extended to texts.

An important part of the variationist approach to discourse is the discovery of formal patterns in texts (often narratives) and the analysis of how such patterns are constrained by the text. (6) is an example (from Labov 1972b: 387) that illustrates. (Since Labov's introduction to this example helps to illustrate the approach, I include this in 6.)

(6)   One of the most dramatic danger-of-death stories was told by a retired postman on the Lower East Side: his brother had stabbed him in the head with a knife. He concludes:
        And the doctor just says, "Just about this much more," he says, "and you'd a been dead."

Labov uses this extract as part of his discussion of the basic structure of narrative. The utterance being presented is a type of evaluation: the means by which narrators highlight different aspects of a reported experience as a way of revealing the point of the story. Although evaluations are sometimes separate sections of stories, they are also distributed throughout narrative and embedded within narrative clauses themselves. (Narrative clauses are typically event clauses that report "what happened.") Embedded evaluations rely upon deviations from the simple syntactic structure typical of a narrative clause. The evaluation in (6), for example, illustrates an evaluative device that Labov (1972b: 387) calls a comparator, a functional classification that includes "negatives, futures, modals, quasimodals, questions, imperatives, or-clauses, superlatives, and comparatives."

As illustrated in (6), a variationist approach to discourse utilizes some of the basic tools of linguistic analysis: it segments texts into sections, labels those sections as part of a structure, and assigns functions to those sections. This approach thus allows more context independence (i.e. a greater degree of autonomy for "text" in relation to context) than would be allowed, for example, in interactional sociolinguistics, ethnography of communication, or conversation analysis. An indication of this in (6) is Labov's willingness to discuss the evaluating clause as *separate* from the rest of the story – to treat it as an example of a structural unit and functional type that can be extracted from its story for comparisons with other evaluative devices. The variationist approach also integrates traditional linguistic categories into a framework of textual analysis.

In sum, the examples in this section revealed some important features of the approaches to be discussed in this book: what count as data, what problems and questions motivate analysis, how to address or resolve a problem. To oversimplify a bit, speech act theory focuses on communicative acts performed through speech: data are typically constructed utterances in hypothetical contexts that are chosen to illustrate the interplay between text and context that mutually informs production and interpretation of the acts performed through words. Interactional sociolinguistics focuses on the social and linguistic meanings created during interaction: although hearers draw inferences about speakers' intent (as in speech act theory and pragmatics), the inferences are considerably broader and more varied and they are based on a wide array of verbal and nonverbal cues that are part of cultural repertoires for signalling meaning (and can be discovered only through the collection of actual utterances). The ethnography of communication focuses on language and communication as cultural behavior: the status and significance of any particular act can be discovered only as part of a matrix of more general meanings, beliefs, and values that extend far beyond the knowledge of the grammar of one's language. Since such matrices pervade and organize a great deal of life within a particular society – and since they are culturally relative – the ethnography of communication requires extensive fieldwork within a community as well as comparisons between communities.

Pragmatics focuses on meaning, context, and communication of constructed utterances in hypothetical contexts. The communicative meaning of a particular utterance is derived through general assumptions about human rationality and conduct; together with the literal meaning of utterances, these assumptions are the basis from which to draw highly specific inferences about intended meanings. Conversation analysis focuses on sequential structures in conversation: the mechanics of conversation provide a basis through which social order (including a sense of "context") is constructed. Although conversation analysts are careful to transcribe the details of utterances, they pay little attention to linguistic categories of sound, structure, or meaning. Finally, variation theory focuses on structural categories within texts and the way syntactic structure (and variation) helps to define and realize those structures. Like the other approaches (except for speech act theory and pragmatics), variation analysis requires the close analysis of what is actually said. Although it pays close attention to linguistic structure, it relies less upon non-linguistic (contextual) detail than interactional sociolinguistics or ethnography of communication. In the next section, I describe in more detail how the rest of this book will develop the description of, and comparison among, the approaches that I have just introduced.

3 Plan of the book

Chapters 3 through 8 present the six approaches to discourse analysis just introduced – one chapter for each approach. Within each approach, I provide a general background with discussion of key issues and critical concepts. My description of each approach will focus primarily upon the work of scholars who have been most central to the development of that approach. However, because the approaches to be described have been so influential not only in discourse analysis, but also for the other domains that they more directly address (as noted above), a substantial body of work (supportive and critical, faithful and revisionist) has developed from the original insights upon which I mostly depend. I do not mean to slight these later works, and I make reference to them in the course of discussion of specific points. However, it is because the original works have spurred so much scholarly discussion and research that I want to take them as the source of the approaches to discourse to be developed in my own discussion.

3.1 Describing different approaches to discourse analysis

My first task in this book is the description of the six different approaches to discourse analysis noted above. Although these approaches often overlap in the work of particular scholars, we have already seen that they differ in several important ways. What underlies my decision to differentiate these six approaches is what I believe to be their most significant characteristic: they have very different origins.[2] The origin of an approach provides different theoretical and metatheoretical premises that continue to influence assumptions, concepts, and methods. For example, different origins may be responsible for different assumptions and beliefs about language – assumptions about the stability of linguistic meaning, the role of speaker intentionality, the degree to which language is designed for communicative purposes, and the contribution of linguistic meaning to interactive meaning.

Other differences that can be at least partially traced to different origins include beliefs about methods for collecting and analyzing data. For example, some approaches focus intensively on a few fragments of talk (e.g. interactional sociolinguistics), others focus on distributions of discourse items across a wide range of texts (e.g. variationists). Some require a great deal of social, cultural, and personal information about interlocutors and may use interlocutors as informants in analysis of their own talk (e.g. ethnography of communication); others assume an idealized speaker/hearer whose specific social, cultural, or personal characteristics do not enter into participant strategies for building text at all (e.g. pragmatics). Methodological differences such as these are due, partially, to different theoretical assumptions – assumptions that are based in the different origins noted above. If it is assumed, for example, that linguistic meaning is less important to interactive meaning than are sequential structures of talk, then an analyst would pay little attention to linguistic form and structure *per se* (e.g. as in conversation analysis). In short, no methodological preferences are reached in a vacuum: they are all the product of more general beliefs in what constitutes data and what counts as evidence and "proof."

Finally, how a perspective developed may continue to provide a set of different practical interests or ultimate goals in addition to (or even, instead of) the analysis of discourse *per se*. This may help us understand why particular findings are expressed in a certain manner (e.g. through abstract rules), interpreted in a certain way (e.g. in relation to cross-cultural communication), or seen as relevant to somewhat different issues (e.g. to semantics rather than linguistic variation).

Also included within each chapter is an extensive sample analysis showing how each approach can be applied to a specific problem. The sample analyses are quite detailed for several reasons. First, the approaches being discussed are supposed to *analyze* discourse (thus the label "discourse analysis," not "discourse theory" or "discourse studies"). It is important, then, to see how they can be applied to concrete problems and to translate the more general overviews within each chapter (and then in a more abstract, comparative mode, in part III; see below) into empirical tools. Second, on a more personal level, I believe that the best way to learn about something is to see how it works. It is in this spirit that I try to provide an account of how each approach proceeds (not so much what it finds, but how it goes about "doing" its finding) and I would encourage readers to do the same either through sample problems suggested at the end of each chapter or through problems of their own making. For these purposes, I strongly encourage readers who want to use this book as a "manual" to have available data of some sort (for suggestions, see appendix 1; some data samples are provided in appendix 3).

We will see that the sample analyses draw upon data in ways not always typical of the approaches being illustrated, e.g. I have never seen a Gricean pragmatic analysis of referring terms in a story (although this is what I present in chapter 6). I am intentionally relying upon the use of transcriptions of language use (see discussion of sociolinguistic interviews in appendix 1, also chapters 5 and 8), simply because I believe that the approaches to be discussed allow (indeed, demand) such data not only if they are to be seen as comparable, but if they are to be examined for signs of synthesis. The data that I use are primarily from sociolinguistic interviews. Elsewhere (Schiffrin 1987a), I have argued that sociolinguistic interviews provide data well suited to the different purposes of discourse analysis. We will have a chance to examine sociolinguistic interviews themselves as discourse – their status as a kind of "mixed genre," i.e. a mix of interview and conversation – in the ethnographic chapter, chapter 5. That chapter will also draw upon a small set of tape-recorded library reference interviews. Appendix 1 provides further discussion of how different corpora can provide data for the analysis of discourse.

In addition to drawing upon data in ways that may differ from the approaches being illustrated, I will also use discourse transcription conventions that may differ from those used by other approaches. Specifically, I will not adopt the transcription conventions used by most interactional sociolinguists for my analysis of data illustrating that approach (chapter 4); nor will I use those conventions used by conversation analysts (in chapter 7). Rather, I will use a single set of conventions in all the analyses, the one I use in my own work (e.g. Schiffrin 1987a), not because I believe that it is best (in fact, it provides no way to represent many of the qualities that can be represented by the others), but because I want to use one system throughout, and this is the one with which I am familiar. Readers interested in selecting a system for their own use, or in comparing different conventions, will find four different sets of conventions in appendix 2.

Each approach to be discussed adopts a slightly different view of discourse, and provides a different (sometimes radically different) way of analyzing utterances. Indeed, the term "discourse analysis" is not used by all of the perspectives to be discussed. Although variationist approaches do refer to discourse (or sometimes, text) analysis, pragmatics and speech act theory refer instead to analyses of "language in use" or "in context"; "conversation analysis" is a term used by scholars with an ethnomethodological orientation; interactional approaches refer to "interactional sociolinguistics"; ethnographic approaches share with pragmatics and speech act theory a focus on "language in use" or "in context" (although their conception of "use" and "context" differs from that of the philosophically based approaches). These differences in terminology do capture slightly different domains of interest (both analytical and theoretical). Finally, as noted earlier, not all the approaches to discourse to be reviewed explicitly concern themselves with discourse; even with those that do, there are often other wider (or overlapping) domains of interest. The broader topics to which discourse is seen as relevant have important influences on the way in which its analysis is approached.

3.2 Comparing different approaches to discourse

In addition to describing different approaches to discourse, I will also compare those approaches. I will try to facilitate a comparison among approaches in two ways: through the focus of my sample analyses in chapters 3 through 8 (section 3.2.1), and through the discussion of key concepts and assumptions in chapters 9, 10, and 11 (section 3.2.2).

3.2.1 Ongoing comparisons: comparing sample analyses

To enhance the comparative value of my descriptions of the approaches, I have decided to orient my sample analyses around two phenomena: (a) questions (and the sequences they initiated) to be analyzed in terms of speech act theory, interactional sociolinguistics, and ethnography of communication; (b) referring expressions (in referring sequences) to be analyzed in terms of pragmatics, conversation analysis, and variation analysis. We see not only that the different approaches provide different answers to some of the same questions, but that they highlight different facets of both questions and referring expressions.

An analogy may help. Imagine that we are trying out a number of different tools (a saw, a butter knife, a screwdriver, and a pair of scissors) to accomplish one particular task (we want to cut a piece of bread). We would probably learn not only about the tools, but also about the task that we are trying to accomplish (cutting) and the material that we are handling (bread). This analogy suggests that different analyses of referring terms (or questions) may tell us something about the analytical tools provided by the approaches themselves (e.g. pragmatics, speech act theory, etc.), and reveal something interesting about question–answer sequences and referring expressions. Those who expect to find exhaustive analyses of either phenomenon, however, will be disappointed: both are vast topics to which linguists have devoted a great deal of scholarly attention. Rather, what I try to do is find particular issues pertaining to either topic that can be understood through the approach being described in each chapter.

Notice, then, that not *exactly* the same problems or issues will be addressed in each chapter. Returning to my "breadcutting" analogy, for a moment, I noted above that we would learn about three things if we were trying different tools to accomplish one particular task: the task we are trying to accomplish, the material we are handling, and the tools we are using. One way of organizing this book would have been to keep the task completely constant, e.g. analyze the distribution of "there is" constructions (as in chapter 7), or keep the material completely constant, e.g. use a single episode for data. I felt, however, that this would have been difficult since different approaches define even what seems to be the "same" topic differently. (It also would have resulted in an overly redundant – and perhaps boring – set of chapters.) Indeed, even though we will see some of the same sample utterances reappear in different chapters as they are used and reused to make different points, I would maintain that even though the utterances might seem like the "same" examples, they should not necessarily be interpreted as the same "data." In the sample analyses, then, I decided to maintain some constancy (the two general phenomena) and allow some diversity (different aspects of the two general phenomena).

Although there are many other issues and problems that discourse analysts address in their research, I have chosen questions and referring expressions for several reasons. First, questions and referring expressions have both been said to be central concerns of discourse analysis. Question–answer sequences, for example, are a paradigm example of adjacency pairs (a construct central to conversation analysis (chapter 7)): adjacency pairs not only illustrate the sequential foundation of discourse, but play a key role in the view of discourse as fundamentally organized on a pairwise (two part) basis. Questions are also puzzling in and of themselves: some sentences that might be syntactically identified as questions are functionally not questions at all: one could not respond with just *Yes* to the syntactic question *Can you pass the salt?* (our earlier example 1) without being considered rude, making a joke, or having misunderstood. Similarly, some sentences that would not be syntactically identified as questions act like questions in that they "expect" an answer. A therapist's *I notice you're late again*, for example, is understood to demand an explanation (an answer) as certainly as *Why are you late again?* Examples such as these suggest not only that questions are difficult to define, but that what "counts as" a question (chapter 3) is strongly tied to the interactional (chapter 4) and institutional (chapter 5) contexts in which it is produced.

The study of referring expressions also plays a central role in forming some scholars' views of what discourse analysis is about: "the study of the functions of syntax and reference (e.g. matters of definiteness/indefiniteness) has come to represent, for certain linguists, the proper domain of discourse analysis" (Prince 1988: 166). One reason why discourse analysts are concerned with referring terms is that the processes by which expressions allow one to refer to an entity (person, thing, concept, etc.) in the universe of discourse involve not only speakers (their intentions, actions, and knowledge) but also hearers. Clark and Wilkes-Gibbs (1986), for example, speak of referring as a "collaborative process": they suggest that although a speaker can propose a referent, the identification of the referent needs to be seen as an outcome of speaker–hearer interaction (see also Martinich 1984: 161–2). Establishing a referent that a hearer can identify also involves what Green (1989: 47) calls "the cooperative exploitation of supposed mutual knowledge" – knowledge that is inferrable not just from our world knowledge (our "encyclopedic" knowledge), but from the information made accessible to us from both text (prior and current) and context.

There are other, more specific reasons why I have chosen these two particular areas of research as a basis for comparison among different approaches to discourse analysis. Question–answer pairs capture the syntagmatic thrust of discourse analysis (i.e. questions and answers are sequentially organized) and referring expressions capture the paradigmatic thrust of discourse analysis (i.e. speakers refer to an entity by choosing among various expressions). Nevertheless, analyses of both question–answer sequences and referring expressions also show that sequential location is interdependent with the options provided within a particular sequential slot. The context of a question has important bearings on how we ask and answer that question. The way we refer to something is influenced by where in a discourse we are making that reference, and whether a particular referring expression is an initial (or subsequent) mention of an entity.

3.2.2 *Concluding comparisons: assumptions and concepts*

In addition to the comparisons available through the descriptions and sample analyses themselves, other comparisons will be made towards the end of the book, following the specific descriptions of each approach. The main part of this concluding comparison will be centered on three issues that are central to discourse analysis and about which discourse analysts must make assumptions:

the relationship between structure and function, the relationship between text and context, and the nature of communication. I believe that these issues are critical to discourse analysis, and that all approaches take a stand (albeit often implicitly) on the relationship between structure and function, text and context, and discourse and communication, simply because these conceptual distinctions are all variants of the dichotomy between what is considered part of language and what is not (see chapter 2). We see that the approaches take surprisingly different positions on issues such as the interplay of structure and function (chapter 9), the degree to which text and context can penetrate one another (chapter 10), and the role of intention and intersubjectivity in communication (chapter 11).

My comparison among approaches also responds to more general issues in discourse analysis and what seem to be two developing needs. We already know a great deal about some very basic discourse phenomena, e.g. turn-taking, repair, topic organization, story telling, discourse markers, conversational inference and style. There now seems to be a need to move from empirical studies of how we use language to (a) the development of models and theories that help us organize our knowledge about how discourse works, and (b) links between our discourse models/theories and our models/theories of language in general. I believe that a less fragmented vision of discourse analysis may very well help us in these endeavors. The debate about structure and function in discourse (alluded to above), for example, could then be considered as one variant of the more general debate about the relationship between linguistic structure (the phonological and syntactic structures making up what is typically thought of as "grammar") and language use (the way people use grammatical resources to communicate with one another).

Given the wide variety of studies that are considered to be discourse analysis, is there any theoretical or conceptual unity to this inquiry? Are there similarities among approaches that override their differences? For example, one of the earliest discourse analysts, Zellig Harris (1951), proposed that the goal of discourse analysis is to discover how it is that discourse differs from random sequences. Many more recent analysts propose a surprisingly similar goal. Michael Stubbs (1983: 15) states: "People are quite able to distinguish between a random list of sentences and a coherent text, and it is the principles which underlie this recognition of coherence which are the topic of study for discourse analysts." It is important not only to know whether such a goal is shared by all discourse analytic approaches, but also to know whether strategies for accomplishing such a goal are shared: Harris, for example, confined his analytic methods strictly to formal patterns within the text, whereas Stubbs includes extensive information from outside of the text.

Chapter 12 is the concluding chapter. In addition to proposing some very general similarities among the approaches, I also try to utilize the two broad problems to which my sample analyses pertain in a still more general way. Questions are considered in chapters on speech act theory, interactional sociolinguistics, and ethnography of communication; referring expressions are considered in chapters on pragmatics, conversation analysis, and variation analysis. As I will make clear in chapter 12, the order of chapters, and thus the type of inquiry for each area of empirical focus, is not random: they reflect a transition (broadly speaking) from a focus upon the individual (whether the actions, knowledge, or intentions of a self) to a focus upon interaction (how self and other together construct what is said, meant, and done) to a focus upon the semiotic systems shared and used by self and other during their interactions (language, society, and culture). An ability both to build such transitions (from self to self/other to shared semiotic systems) into one's theory, and to allow and account for them in one's practice, is a crucial part of a discourse analysis that seeks to integrate what speech act theory, interactional sociolinguistics, ethnography of communication, pragmatics, conversation analysis, and variation analysis can offer, both individually and together, to the analysis of utterances.

Notes

1 Van Dijk (1985) shows that discourse analysis really has a rather long history – if one allows classical rhetoric to be considered as discourse analysis.
2 Despite basing my identification and selection of approaches primarily on historical factors, I also believe that my selection is representative of much of the work being done in discourse analysis today. Furthermore, other reviews (that are not as historically based) also differentiate largely the same approaches: Taylor and Cameron (1987), for example, compare social psychological, speech act, exchange structure, Gricean pragmatic, and ethnomethodological approaches to discourse.

2   Definitions of Discourse

1   Introduction

In chapter 1, I introduced six approaches to discourse analysis and outlined my plan for describing and comparing these approaches in parts II and III of the book. In this chapter, I consider three different definitions of discourse and introduce several basic issues that underlie the descriptions of, and comparisons among, the approaches.

Two paradigms in linguistics provide different assumptions about the general nature of language and the goals of linguistics (section 2).[1] These paradigms are sometimes differently labelled: what Newmeyer (1983) calls a formalist paradigm is similar to Hymes's (1947b) structuralist paradigm and to what Hopper (1988) calls *a priori* grammar; the functionalist paradigm is sometimes also called emergent (Hopper) or interactive (Mey et al. 1992). The two paradigms make different background assumptions about the goals of a linguistic theory, the methods for studying language, and the nature of data and empirical evidence. These differences in paradigm also influence definitions of discourse: a definition derived from the formalist paradigm views discourse as "sentences" (section 3), a definition derived from the functionalist paradigm views discourse as "language use" (section 4). A third definition of discourse attempts to bridge the formalist–functionalist dichotomy (section 5). The relationship between structure and function in general is an important issue that is related to other issues central to discourse analysis (section 6).

2   Formal and functionalist paradigms

Discourse is often defined in two ways: a particular unit of language (above the sentence), and a particular focus (on language use; see Schiffrin 1987a: 1).

These two definitions of discourse reflect the difference between formalist and functionalist paradigms. After briefly reviewing the two paradigms, I discuss discourse as structure (section 3) and discourse as function (section 4).[2]

Hymes (1974b: 79) suggests that the following qualities contrast structural (i.e. formalist) with functional approaches.

"Structural"	"Functional"
Structure of language (code) as grammar	Structure of speech (act, event) as ways of speaking
Use merely implements, perhaps limits, may correlate with, what is analyzed as code; analysis of code prior to analysis of use	Analysis of use prior to analysis of code; organization of use discloses additional features and relations; shows code and use in integral (dialectical) relation
Referential function, fully semanticized uses as norm	Gamut of stylistic or social functions
Elements and structures analytically arbitrary (in cross-cultural or historical perspective), or universal (in theoretical perspective)	Elements and structures as ethnographically appropriate ("psychiatrically" in Sapir's sense)
Functional (adaptive) equivalence of languages; all languages essentially (potentially) equal	Functional (adaptive) differentiation of languages, varieties, styles; these being existentially (actually) not necessarily equivalent
Single homogeneous code and community ("replication of uniformity")	Speech community as matrix of code-repertoires, or speech styles ("organization of diversity")
Fundamental concepts, such as speech community, speech act, fluent speaker, functions of speech and of languages, taken for granted or arbitrarily postulated	Fundamental concepts taken as problematic and to be investigated

Leech (1983: 46) suggests other ways that formalism and functionalism are "associated with very different views of the nature of language," including the following:

1 Formalists (e.g. Chomsky) tend to regard language primarily as a mental phenomenon. Functionalists (e.g. Halliday) tend to regard it primarily as a societal phenomenon.

2 Formalists tend to explain linguistic universals as deriving from a common genetic linguistic inheritance of the human species. Functionalists tend to explain them as deriving from the universality of the uses to which language is put in human society.

3 Formalists are inclined to explain children's acquisition of language in terms of a built-in human capacity to learn language. Functionalists are inclined to explain it in terms of the development of the child's communicative needs and abilities in society.

4 Above all, formalists study language as an autonomous system, whereas functionalists study it in relation to its social function.

At the risk of great simplification, we can say that functionalism is based on two general assumptions: (a) language has functions that are external to the linguistic system itself; (b) external functions influence the internal organization of the linguistic system. These shared assumptions contrast functionalism with approaches that are not concerned with how external processes impinge upon language (or view such a relationship as irrelevant to the goals of linguistic theory). They also contrast functionalism with the views of earlier linguists who largely restricted their analyses to functions *within* the linguistic system (e.g. Sapir's view that speech sounds are functionally organized did not go outside of language *per se*) and with the views of contemporary linguists who view functions as the role a category may play within a sentence (e.g. relational grammar: Perlmutter 1983) and/or as mathematical representations from names to values (e.g. lexical-functional grammar: Kaplan and Bresnan 1982).

Formalist views, on the other hand, argue that although language may very well have social and cognitive functions, these functions do not impinge upon the internal organization of language. Newmeyer (1983) captures these qualities in two defining characteristics: *autonomy* and *modularity*. First, autonomy (p. 2):

> the grammar of a language is characterized by a formal autonomous system. That is, the phonology, syntax, and those aspects of meaning determined by syntactic configuration form a structural system whose primitive terms are not artifacts of a system that encompasses both human language and other human facilities or abilities. (Emphasis in original)

The formal autonomy of the grammar, however, does not prevent intersection with other modules: surface features of phonology, syntax, and semantics can result from the interaction of the "formal grammar" module with other equally autonomous modules, each governed by its own set of principles. Such modules might include perceptual psychology, physiology, acoustics, conversational principles, and general principles of learning and concept formation. (See also Newmeyer 1991, and comments on that paper in Harris and Taylor 1991.)

Although scholars often articulate formalist/functionalist differences in terms that are mutually exclusive, Bates and MacWhinney (1982) suggest that differences within the functionalist paradigm bring functionalism either closer to, or further from, the formalist assumptions of autonomy and modularity. The most radical functionalist position, for example, would be that external functions (such as communicative concerns) define primitive categories, such that there would be no need to posit independently definable, autonomous grammatical categories (Bates and MacWhinney 1982: 188), e.g. DuBois's (1987) suggestion that ergativity is discourse based (also Hopper and Thompson 1980). A more conservative position would allow an interaction between form and function, such that external functions would work in tandem with the formal organization inherent in the linguistic system – influencing it at certain points in the system, but not fundamentally defining its basic categories. (This actually seems to be the position taken by Newmeyer (1983), although he presents his work as a strong defense of formal theory.)

Related to the difference in the degree to which external functions condition the system is a difference in the degree to which the linguistic system itself is open to functional influences. An extremely useful way of differentiating degrees of openness of the system is Bates and MacWhinney's (1982: 178–90) differentiation of four levels of correlation between form and function. The weakest correlation (a diachronic form–function relation) requires minimal assumptions about how open the system is to functional influence (and further suggests that certain points are only open for limited time periods, i.e. when in change). The strongest correlation (a form–function relation in adult competence) entails maximal assumptions about the openness of the system to functional influence.

The two definitions of discourse prevalent in the field reflect the differences between formalist and functionalist paradigms. After describing these definitions in the next two sections, I suggest an alternative definition that attempts to avoid some of the pitfalls of taking either a strong formalist or strong functionalist approach to the definition of discourse.

3 Discourse: language above the sentence

The classic definition of discourse as derived from formalist (in Hymes's 1974b terms, "structural") assumptions is that discourse is "language above the sentence or above the clause" (Stubbs 1983: 1). Van Dijk (1985: 4) observes: "Structural descriptions characterize discourse at several levels or dimensions of analysis and in terms of many different units, categories, schematic patterns, or relations." Despite the diversity of structural approaches noted by van Dijk, there is a common core: structural analyses focus on the way different units function in relation *to each other* (a focus shared with structuralism in general (e.g. Levi-Strauss 1967; Piaget 1970), but they disregard "the functional relations with the context of which discourse is a part" (van Dijk 1985: 4). Since it is precisely this relationship – between discourse and the context of which discourse is a part – that characterizes functional analyses, it might seem that the two approaches have little in common.

Structurally based analyses of discourse find *constituents* (smaller linguistic units) that have particular *relationships* with one another and that can occur in a restricted number of (often rule-governed) *arrangements* (cf. Grimes 1975; Stubbs 1983: chapter 5). In many structural approaches, discourse is viewed as a level of structure higher than the sentence, or higher than another unit of text. Z. Harris (1951) – the first linguist to refer to "discourse analysis" – claimed explicitly that discourse is the next level in a hierarchy of morphemes, clauses, and sentences. Harris viewed discourse analysis procedurally as a formal methodology, derived from structural methods of linguistic analysis: such a methodology could break a text down into relationships (such as equivalence, substitution) among its lower-level constituents. Structure was so central to Harris's view of discourse that he also argued that what opposes discourse to a random sequence of sentences is precisely the fact that it has structure: a pattern by which segments of the discourse occur (and recur) relative to each other.

Harris's approach sought to be a theoretical and methodological extension of linguistic structuralism, not only because it extended the notion of linguistic unit to another level, but also because it was methodologically dependent upon lower-level structural analyses for the identification of higher-level constituents: the constituents of discourse were morphemes and morpheme sequences (words, phrases) that were themselves identifiable through "any grammatical analysis" of a sentence (p. 1). In addition, the only type of structure admissible into analysis was what could be investigated by inspection of the data without taking into account other data, e.g. speakers, context, meanings. However, Harris's intention was that the regular recurrence of constituents would correspond to a semantic interpretation for the discourse – a hope that was quite consistent with the structural focus (at lower levels) on morphemes as sound/meaning correspondences.

Although structural approaches have been modified by Harris himself (e.g. Harris 1988) and by others (e.g. Grimes 1975; Polanyi 1988), what is still critical to structural views of discourse is that discourse is comprised of *units*. Although Harris's unit was the morpheme (and their combination into sentences), more recent approaches have identified the clause (e.g. Linde and Labov 1985), the proposition (e.g. Grimes 1975; Mann and Thompson 1988), or the sentence (see below) as the unit of which discourse is comprised. Some scholars also differentiate sources of "connectedness" within discourse and assign different roles to different units. Holker (1989), for example, suggests that the linguistic structures of an expression, including both form-based (morphological and syntactic) and meaning-based (referential and conjunctive) relations, create connexity and cohesion. (Coherence, however, would be a result of the interpreter's knowledge about states of affairs mentioned in a text.) Other structural approaches search for multi-based and/or diversified units: Polanyi (1988), for example, allows structures to be comprised of units as varied as sentences, turns, speech actions, and speech events.

Consistent with the definition of discourse as language "above the sentence," many comtemporary structural analyses of discourse view the sentence as the unit of which discourse is comprised. Yet several problems stem from the reliance of definitions and analyses on the smaller unit of "sentence."

One immediate problem is that the units in which people speak do not always seem like sentences. Research by Chafe (1980, 1987, 1992), for example, suggests that spoken language is produced in units with intonational and semantic closure – not necessarily syntactic closure. Some scholars also believe that the grammarian's focus on sentences stems from the value that we – as members of a literate culture – place on written language (Harris 1980; Hopper 1988). If we were to focus solely on spoken language, we would be more likely to view language in terms of intonation units that reflect not underlying grammatical structures, but underlying focuses of consciousness in which information is organized (Chafe 1987).

Support for this view is often found by examining the transcript of a stretch of speech and noting that the intonational breaks do not always correspond to syntactic boundaries. In (1), for example, we find chunks of speech that do not fit our traditional notions of sentencehood:

(1)   You can run a hou- whatcha- now whatcha you can- ran a house- you can run a house a- and *do* the job, which is important, y' can't y- a man can't do it himself, and a woman can't do it himself w- if y' want it to be successful. In most cases.

Of course it is possible to transcribe (1) in a way that would make it *look* more like a sentence, e.g. by applying editing rules to the non-fluencies and false starts (Labov 1966; but see Taylor and Cameron 1987: chapter 7). Nevertheless, one could still argue that the use of a transcription system that builds upon graphic punctuation symbols does not really capture the way words and expressions actually cluster together in spoken language (e.g. G. Brown 1977). Even more critically, one could argue that the use of such devices forces us to think of such chunks as sentences, rather than as providing an accurate representation of how speakers themselves produce language, e.g. as intonationally packaged foci of consciousness (Chafe 1987), as rhetorical amalgamations of clauses (Cumming 1984), in collaboration with interlocutors (Goodwin 1979). To reflect such concerns, some discourse analysts try to exclude from their transcription systems those conventions of punctuation (e.g. period, commas, capital letters) that are used in written language to indicate syntactic structure or closure, or to use such devices to capture aspects of speech production (see appendix 2).

The reliance on sentence as the unit of which discourse is comprised is theoretically problematic in other ways. Bloomfield (1933: 170) defined a sentence as "an independent linguistic form not included by virtue of any grammatical construction in some larger linguistic form." However, the view that discourse is a level of structure higher than sentences – more precisely, that discourse is a structure within which sentences are embedded – sometimes ends up challenging the view that sentences have grammatical autonomy and closure. Many analysts focus upon how syntactic properties of clauses or sentences contribute to (or, alternatively, are influenced by) higher-level structures of a text (e.g. Prince 1986; Ward et al. 1991). Interestingly, however, such analyses sometimes end up arguing that what, at first, seemed to be relatively static and stable properties of sentence grammar are really dynamic, emergent byproducts of the processes by which people organize information and transfer that information to another (e.g. Fox and Thompson 1990; Givón 1979; see also Goodwin 1979; Schegloff 1979a for proposals that sentences are interactionally constructed). In brief, some analyses end up challenging the very notion that sentences *are* what Bloomfield says they are: they challenge the notion that sentences are independent linguistic forms (for elaboration of this idea see Hopper 1987, 1988). However, if sentences have no existence outside of discourse – if they are created by discourse – then it is confusing (and perhaps even meaningless) to try to define discourse as something larger than the very thing that it creates, i.e. sentences.

Another consequence of the view that discourse is language above the sentence is that we may begin to expect discourse to exhibit a structure analogous to the sentences of which it is comprised – an expectation that may be unwarranted (Stubbs 1983: chapter 5). Take, for example, the sentence grammarian's use of the term "well formed" as it applies to structures. To illustrate, we can take Chomsky's well known example:

(2a)   Colorless green ideas sleep furiously.

Although this sentence is meaningless (in the usual sense of meaning, as sense and reference), it is syntactically well formed. In addition to being meaningless, however, (2b) is also syntactically deviant. (Examples and discussion are from Sells 1985: 3–4.)

(2b)   *Furiously sleep ideas green colorless.

Note that this distinction reappears even when the words do make conventional sense. Again, Sells's (1985: 3) examples:

(3c)   Revolutionary new ideas appear infrequently.
(3d)   *Infrequently appear ideas new revolutionary.

Sells (p. 4) makes the following important point:

the real syntactic truth underlying the contrasts in grammaticality seen above is that while some sequences of the form "Adjective-adjective-noun-verb-adverb" are syntactically well formed in English, sequences of the form "Adverb-verb-noun-adjective-adjective" are not.

Structure in this sense just does not seem to apply to discourse: it is simply not possible to contrast constituent strings of well-formed versus ill-formed discourse in the same way. One reason has to do with our inability to identify units of discourse in a way as clear cut (and mutually exclusive) as our ways for identifying constituents of sentences (e.g. chapter 3). As I discuss in Schiffrin (1988a: 257–9), a related point is that the types of structures identified by discourse analysts have not always been comprised of sentences, or indeed of language units *per se*, e.g. analysts have spoken of action structures and turn structures. Indeed, even units that *might* be defined linguistically are often viewed in terms of their consequences for the interaction between speaker and hearer. For example, even though a question–answer pair may be defined as a semantic sequence in which an incomplete proposition presented by one speaker is completed by another, such a definition is less relevant to the concerns of many discourse analysts than the fact that questions may be used to replicate (or negotiate) social relationships and status (e.g. chapter 5). A related point is that there are several different levels at which discourse analysts have identified structure. Some scholars have observed that entire encounters are framed and bracketed from each other at both their initiation (Collett 1983; Corsaro 1979; Godard 1977; Goffman 1974; Schegloff 1972a; Schiffrin 1977, 1981b) and termination (Schegloff and Sacks 1973). Others focus on how single turns at talk are sequenced (Sacks et al. 1974). Included between these extremes is a focus on topic structures (Brown and Yule 1983: chapter 3; Button and Casey 1984; Jefferson 1984; Keenan and Schieffelin 1976), and dialogic pairs (such as question–answer pairs). Because units such as encounters, topics, dialogic pairs, and turns are so different from each other in substance, however, it is not at all clear that they form the sort of hierarchical structures to which linguists are accustomed at other levels of analysis.

One way to try to get around some of the problems just noted is to adopt Lyons's (1977: 385, 387) distinction between system-sentence and text-sentence. System-sentences are "the well-formed strings that [are] generated by the grammar" (p. 387), i.e. they "are abstract theoretical constructs, correlates of which are generated by the linguist's model of the language-system" (p. 622). Text-sentences, on the other hand, are "context-dependent utterance-signals (or parts of utterance-signals), tokens of which may occur in particular texts" (p. 622). Lyons' distinction allows discourse to be comprised of text-sentences rather than system-sentences. And as Lyons (1977: 632) notes, "there is no reason to suppose that system-sentences, as such, play any role in the production and interpretation of utterances" (cf. text-sentences).

Defining discourse as text-sentences helps to capture the sorts of internal dependencies that we expect texts to have. In (4), for example, we see a variety of ways that the information presented in one sentence presupposes information in another (cf. Halliday and Hasan 1976; Lyons 1977).

(4a) ELLIPSIS

Jim: Where's the milk?

Karen: The milk is on the table.

(4b) NOMINAL ANAPHORA

I saw *that cat* the other day.

It was still wandering around without a home.

(4c) TEMPORAL ANAPHORA

We moved here *in 1982.*

We didn't even have jobs *then.*

(4d) REFERENCE

I saw *a robin* the other day.

It was *the first one* I saw this spring.

Viewing the sentences in (4) as text-sentences captures the idea that they are situated in a linguistic unit larger than themselves; furthermore, the fact that they are located in this way allows us to account for some of their internal properties.

Separating text-sentences from system-sentences also allows us to maintain a definition of system-sentences that is even more abstract than Bloomfield's definition. In 1957, for example, Chomsky viewed a sentence as a string of words with an abstract representation mapping sound to meaning; such a representation is derived in a certain way, i.e. generated by rules. Such a definition depends upon a theory of generative grammar: other definitions may be differently attuned to other theories of grammar. If we define discourse in terms of text-sentences, neither the theory dependency nor the level of abstraction of system-sentences is a problem for our definition of discourse. However, we may still end up returning to the problem of circularity noted earlier: defining discourse as comprised of just those constituents (text-sentences) whose definition actually depends on discourse.

We have seen thus far that viewing discourse as a unit above the sentence is not just a definition of discourse, but a way of leading to a particular type of analysis. Although this definition and the analysis to which it leads can be appealing, it also raises some problems. Let me briefly review these problems before turning to another definition of discourse. First, the view of discourse as a unit above the sentence allows one to focus quite easily upon how syntactic properties of clauses or sentences contribute to (or alternatively, are influenced by) higher level structures of a text (e.g. Linde and Labov 1975, Matthiessen and Thompson 1987), e.g. specific properties of sentences, such as word order or typotactic versus paratactic coordination, can be related to the properties of texts. Such analyses, however, often end up deriving the syntax of sentences from the properties of texts and the communicative goals of speakers. As noted earlier, it is somewhat circular to define discourse as something larger than the lower-level unit that it seems to create. Second, the structural view of discourse places discourse in a hierarchy of language structures, thus fostering the view that one can describe language in a unitary way that continues unimpeded from morpheme to clause to sentence to discourse. This view, however, attributes to discourse the kind of formal regularity often found at lower levels of linguistic description. (Taylor and Cameron 1987 suggest that this is one reason why formalisms may be generally attractive to those searching for patterns.) Thus, the extension of concepts from one level of linguistic description to discourse can actually *perpetuate* the view that discourse is parallel in "kind" to lower level linguistic constituents.[3] But as we noted earlier, this view might not be warranted: not only is it difficult to define a text as well-formed or ill-formed, but discourse structures are not always the sort of hierarchical structures to which linguists are accustomed at other levels of analysis.

Before turning to a functional view of discourse, let us take a sample discourse and see how we might find its structure. This will allow us to focus not just on the conceptual consequences, but also on some of the more specific analytical consequences of a view of discourse couched within a formalist paradigm. Let us consider a hypothetical exchange between two colleagues.

(5) JAN: (a) Are you free for lunch today?
     BARBARA: (b) I have to advise students all day.

(5) illustrates an easily recognizable and familiar discourse structure that we will be focusing upon in later chapters of this book: a question–answer pair. We can identify this as a structure because we know the units of which it is comprised ("question," "answer"), we know their relationship to one another (the question opens a proposition that the answer fills), and we know the order in which they must occur (question before answer). But how is it that we actually identify (a) as a question? What is the background knowledge that allows us to hear (or read) a string of words and come up with a label for those words? These are important questions: if we cannot come up with a way of identifying questions – of identifying the initial unit of which the structure is comprised – then we cannot go much further in our analysis of the relationship between the unit "question" and the unit "answer" (e.g. Selting 1992; also see discussion in chapters 3 and 5).

It seems to be quite easy to define (5a) *Are you free for lunch today?* as a question, simply because we can rely on purely formal clues typical of interrogative sentences, e.g. subject–verb inversion. The examples in (6), however, show that this process need not always seem so automatic, simply because it is not always easy to find exactly those criteria that allow utterances to be identified as questions.

(6) (a) You're free for lunch today?
     (b) Free for lunch today?
     (c) Lunch today?

Utterances (a), (b), and (c) in (6) are not questions by the syntactic criterion noted above. (6a), for example, is clearly a declarative, rather than interrogative, sentence. (6b) and (6c) cannot be unequivocally expanded to interrogatives: we cannot be certain of the fuller sentences underlying the elliptical forms. The fuller form for *Lunch today?* (6c), for example, could be a number of different interrogatives: *Are you free for lunch today?*, *Are you eating lunch today?*, *Do you want to eat lunch today?* Although these examples thus suggest the difficulty of relying upon syntax alone as a cue to utterance identity, they also suggest that we might be able to rely on intonation: note that (a), (b), and (c), are all represented as having final rising intonation – thought to be a frequent prosodic indicator of questions (see discussion in chapter 3).

The example in (7), however, suggests the reverse problem – for it is intonation, but not syntax, that fails to provide a consistent clue to the identity of the utterance as a question. (In keeping with many systems for transcribing conversation (see appendix 2) I am using a period (.) to indicate final falling intonation typical of what we might find with a declarative sentence.

(7)   Do you want to have lunch.

Thus, in (7), the word order is typical of interrogatives, but the intonation seems more typical of declarative sentences.

Finally, the utterances in (8) and (9) show neither the syntactic nor the intonational features typical of questions:

(8)   (a)   I want to ask if you're free for lunch.
      (b)   I was wondering whether you wanted to have lunch.

(8a) and (8b) might be called indirect questions and they do seem to "do" some of the same things as direct questions (with interrogative syntax), e.g. they elicit a particular kind of information from a respondent. But other utterances also seem to be directed toward the same purpose:

(9)   (a)   I'm hungry.
      (b)   Come eat.

Although (9a) and (9b) are clearly not questions according to either our syntactic or intonational criteria, the declarative statement in (9a) and the imperative in (9b) seem to accomplish some of the same things as the questions cited earlier, and could possibly be answered through the same range of responses.

These examples suggest that syntax and intonation are neither necessary nor sufficient criteria for the identification of questions. Although question–answer is an easily recognizable and familiar discourse structure, it turns out to be difficult to provide criteria allowing us to identify as questions all of the many different strings of words that we may intuitively think of as questions.

The problem is that if we cannot come up with a way of identifying the initial unit of which the structure is comprised, then we cannot go much further in our analysis of that structure.

To summarize: we have seen in this section that structurally based definitions of discourse lead to analyses of constituents (smaller units) that have particular relationships with one another in a text and that can occur in a restricted set of text level arrangements. They also try to extend methods of linguistic analysis that have been useful for other levels of linguistic description and/or to rely upon linguistic characteristics of clauses (or sentences) as clues to textual structures. We have also seen, however, that identifying structural constituents of discourse is often a difficult task. The next definition to be considered replaces what is basically a formalist thrust with a functionalist thrust: discourse is language use.

4   Discourse: language use

In section 2, I presented several ways that formalist and functionalist views of language differ, and in section 3, I discussed a view of discourse largely compatible with formalist assumptions about language. In this section, I consider a more functionalist view: "the study of discourse is the study of *any* aspect of language use" (Fasold 1990: 65). Another statement of this view of discourse is Brown and Yule's (1983: 1):

> the analysis of discourse, is necessarily, the analysis of language in use. As such, it cannot be restricted to the description of linguistic forms independent of the purposes or functions which these forms are designed to serve in human affairs.

As these views make clear, the analysis of language use (cf. Saussure's parole) cannot be independent of the analysis of the purposes and functions of language in human life. This view reaches an extreme in the work of critical language scholarship, i.e. the study of language, power, and ideology. Fairclough (1989: 23), for example, advocates a dialectical conception of language and society whereby "language is a part of society; linguistic phenomena *are* social phenomena of a special sort, and social phenomena *are* (in part) linguistic phenomena" (emphasis in original). In Fairclough's view, language and society partially constitute one another – such that the analysis of language as an independent (autonomous) system would be a contradiction in terms (see also Foucault 1982; Grimshaw 1981). Even in less extreme functionalist views, however, discourse is assumed to be interdependent with social life, such that its analysis necessarily intersects with meanings, activities, and systems outside of itself.

A definition of discourse as language use is consistent with functionalism in general: discourse is viewed as a system (a socially and culturally organized way of speaking) through which particular functions are realized. Although formal regularities may very well be examined, a functionalist definition of discourse leads analysts away from the structural basis of such regularities to focus, instead, on the way patterns of talk are put to use for certain purposes in particular contexts and/or how they result from the application of communicative strategies. Functionally based approaches tend to draw upon a variety of methods of analysis, often including not just quantitative methods drawn from social scientific approaches, but also more humanistically based interpretive efforts to replicate actors' own purposes or goals. Not surprisingly, they rely less upon the strictly grammatical characteristics of utterances as sentences, than upon the way utterances are situated in contexts.

Functional analyses may start from one of two directions, roughly paralleling the distinction made by linguists and anthropologists (e.g. Pike 1967) between etic and emic approaches. To take a relatively familiar example, compare phonetics and phonemics. A phonetic analysis provides all the possible distinctions (among means of articulation) irrespective of whether they are actually used in a particular language or a particular utterance. A phonemic analysis, on the other hand, provides only those distinctions that make a meaningful difference to speakers of a particular language (that produce semantically different strings of sounds).

Functional analyses of discourse that start from an etic direction delimit the functions served by a system (such as language or communication) and match particular units (such as utterances or actions) to those functions. An example of this kind of functional approach is Goffman's analysis of system and ritual conditions. Goffman (1981a: 14–15) proposes that conversational interaction requires two sets of conditions. System conditions (also called constraints, because they impose constraints on what can be said and done) center on the mechanical requirements of talk, e.g. a two-way capability for transmitting acoustically adequate and readily interpretable messages, feedback capabilities, contact signals, turnover signals, and so on. Ritual constraints, on the other hand, center on interpersonal requirements of talk: the management of oneself and others so as not to violate appropriate standards regarding either one's own demeanor or deference for another. Different ways of acting (including, but not limited to, verbal utterances) can serve system and/or ritual constraints (e.g. Schiffrin 1988b, on turn-initial particles), and when they do so we can say that they are serving the functional requirements of talk. Note that, if a particular way of speaking were to have a use undefined by the initial system, we might still discover it – but, unless we were to argue that we had missed a function, we would not be able to locate it in our system of functional requirements.

Many functionally based discourse analyses assume etic schemas more general than those devised specifically for conversational interaction. One such framework was proposed by Jakobson (1960). Jakobson differentiates six language functions that are identified through the way that utterances (cf. texts) can be related to different components of the speech situation (cf. contexts). I have adapted Jakobson's framework below – capitalizing the situational component and putting the corresponding function in brackets.

CONTEXT
[referential]

CONTACT
[phatic]

ADDRESSOR   MESSAGE   ADDRESSEE
[emotive]   [poetic]   [conative]

CODE
[metalinguistic]

Although others have proposed different functions (e.g. Halliday 1973), Jakobson's schema most firmly grounds language functions in the speech situation *per se*. Note that Jakobson's view of the speech situation includes language as just one of the components of a speech situation and as one of the foci of speech. That is, the basis for a metalinguistic function is the "code"; the basis for emotive and conative functions are addressor and addressee. Jakobson also makes the critical point that utterances do not have a single function: although a particular expression may have a *primary* function, it is most typical for it to be used to simultaneously realize different functions. *Do you know the time?*, for example, may have a phatic function (it opens contact), an emotive function (it conveys a need of the addressor), a conative function (it asks something of the addressee), and a referential function (it makes reference to the world outside of language).

The second direction available to functional analyses is a more emic direction: begin with how particular units (again, utterances, actions) are used and draw a conclusion about the broader functions of such units from that analysis. In other words, one would begin from observation and description of an utterance itself, and then try to infer from analysis of that utterance and its context what functions are being served. It is important to note that such inferences are not totally *ad hoc*: rather, they can be firmly grounded in principled schema as to what functions are available. But they do differ from more etic approaches because they are not as wed to the notion of system, and because they are more open to the discovery of unanticipated uses of language (see Hymes 1961).

Let us go on to see how a discourse analysis stemming from the functionalist view that discourse is language use might actually proceed. We can begin by returning to (5) from section 3.

(5) JAN: (a) Are you free for lunch today?
     BARBARA: (b) I have to advise students all day.

In addition to being identifiable as question and answer, we can recognize quite easily that the utterances in (5) are being used to realize certain functions, i.e. to try to accomplish interpersonal goals and to convey social and expressive meanings. Although we can suggest such goals and meanings quite readily, however, we might not be able to verify them without more knowledge of the context of the exchange, including such information as the relative status of, and relationship between, the participants, their setting, and their usual ways of interacting, as well as information about the conventional meanings of invitations to lunch. (For example, in some groups in American society, saying *Let's have lunch sometime* does not really "count as" an invitation to lunch.) We might find, for example, that Jan is pursuing a friendship, reciprocating for a prior offer from Barbara, and/or paying deference to Barbara's higher status. But in order to decide which (if any, or perhaps all) of these functions were being realized, we would probably need a good deal of information about the context of the exchange.

We have seen thus far that functional definitions of discourse assume an interrelationship between language and context. One problem stemming from this assumption is that it becomes difficult to separate the analysis of discourse *per se* from other analyses of language and context – even analyses that may really belong more in different areas of inquiry. I will illustrate through another example. (10) is from a sociolinguistic interview (Schiffrin 1987a; chapters 5 and 8 of this book); (10) also appears in Schiffrin 1988b.

(10) DEBBY: (a)   Yeh. Well some people before they go to the doctor, they'll talk to a friend, or a neighbor.
          (b)   Is there anybody that [uh . . .
      ZELDA: (c)   [Well:: well I guess-
      HENRY: (d)   [Sometimes it works.
          (e)   Because there's this guy Louie Gelman,
          (f)   he went to a *big* specialist,
          (g)   and the guy . . . analyzed it *wrong*.
          (h)   In fact his doctor didn't know,
          (i)   and the specialist didn't know.

We can informally characterize this exchange as one in which I am seeking information (a, b), and in which Henry tells me a story that provides the information that Henry thinks I am seeking. (Although space prevents me from including the entire story in (10), what is included in (e) to (i) is the story initiation.) The language used during this exchange might then be examined as to how it serves these functions.

When we focus on different aspects of what is said in (10), however, we find that there are many different ways to focus upon the language that is used *without* saying anything about the functional gloss just noted: a question-answer exchange in which the answer is a story. Let us focus first on my own utterances in (a) and (b):

DEBBY: (a) Yeh. Well some people before they go to the doctor, they'll talk to a friend, or a neighbor.

       (b) Is there anybody that uh . . .

We are fortunate, in some ways, that we can use my own knowledge (as the speaker) of what I was trying to accomplish with these utterances. Although my utterances could have a number of different communicative functions, what I wanted to find out was who Henry talks to about his problems – to whom he would complain, turn to for advice, if he didn't feel well. (As we will see, Henry acts upon an interpretation different from what I had intended.) I first describe the general situation in which I was interested (in a), and then assume that Henry can understand my elliptical question (in b) as asking for a specific instance of that general situation, i.e. whether there is anybody that he (as a member of the larger set of "some people") would *go to*.

The function that I have just described is most typically analyzed as part of speech act theory: the intended communicative force of an utterance can provide us with a way to categorize it as a particular speech act, e.g. as a "request". Performing actions through speech, or, to paraphrase Austin (1962), doing things with words, is certainly a function of language. The problem, however, is that speech acts may be (and often are) analyzed at a sentence level: in other words, an analysis of intended communicative functions need not say anything at all about discourse.

Let us take another aspect of (10) to illustrate how a focus on language use can take us in another direction. Although I did not include phonetic detail in my transcription of (10) above, I will now be more specific about how two words are pronounced: *there, this*. In saying *there* and *this* in (e), for example, Henry pronounces the initial consonants not as fricatives, but as affricates. These possible pronunciations join with a third – a stop – to form what has been called a sociolinguistic variable (Labov 1972a): an alternative way of saying the same thing (e.g. pronouncing the same word, producing the same phoneme), whose variants are used differently by people depending on who they are (e.g. social class, gender, age, ethnicity), where they are (setting), and how they are speaking (e.g. carefully, casually). Thus, given the particular distribution of these variants in the speech community in which Henry lives, we might interpret Henry's use of the affricate as a marker (Scherer and Giles 1979) of his social identity (male, lower middle class, who is speaking relatively casually). Put another way, we could say that the affricates have the social and interactional functions of displaying Henry as a particular kind of person engaging in a particular kind of interchange. Thus, these pronunciations have a great deal to do with the social identity and style of the speaker as someone who exists (and presents himself) within a particular constellation of social and cultural meanings – with contextual inferences resulting from what Henry says (e.g. chapter 4). However, they have little to do with the way what is said is used to fill the other functions I noted earlier – answering a question and telling a story.

I have been suggesting thus far that analyses stemming from a view of discourse as language use can be too inclusive: they can include sentence-sized units and phonological variation. I will take one other aspect of (10) to illustrate another way that such analyses can be too inclusive. Recall that, in (10), Henry complies with my request for information by telling a story about his friend Louie Gelman. Note that this is not the compliance that I had intended: rather than telling me who he talks to, Henry provides support for the general situation that I have described, i.e. he illustrates why talking to one's friends can be a better solution to medical problems than seeking professional help. Clauses (e), (f), and (g) focus on how Henry introduces some of the characters in his story (see chapters 6, 7, and 8).

HENRY: (d)   Sometimes it works.
        (e)   Because there's this guy Louie Gelman,
        (f)   he went to a *big* specialist,
        (g)   and the guy . . . analyzed it *wrong*.

Note, first, that *this guy Louie Gelman* is introduced as the object of an existential predicate "there is." This structure places a new referent (a referent about whom Henry cannot expect me to know anything) at the end of a clause, and predicates very little about the new referent except that he "exists." Crucial for our purposes here is that this information structure serves a communicative function. Of course this is not the function discussed earlier as "intended communicative force" or "display of social identity." Rather, we might say that this structure eases the transmission of information, i.e. it eases the hearer's understanding of a new referent.[4]

The order of words in (f) and (g) serves a similar function: it eases the hearer's processing of information by placing a new entity in the context of already assumable information. I show this below:

(e)   Because there's this guy Louie Gelman [NEW],
(f)   he [OLD = Louie Gelman] went to a *big* specialist [NEW],
(g)   and the guy [OLD = a big specialist] . . . analyzed it *wrong*.

We have already seen that in (e), *Louie Gelman* is new information in clause final position. "Louie Gelman" is next mentioned as *he* (in f) in clause initial position. This old information is then a background for the introduction of another new referent, "a big specialist", at the end of the clause. When "a big specialist" becomes old information, the referring term is definite and less specific (*the guy*) and in clause initial position. Thus, the old/new information order within a clause serves a communicative function, i.e. it eases the hearer's understanding of new information by placing it in the context of familiar information. Again, although this certainly contributes to our understanding of the functional design of word order within sentences (in fact, it allows us to view this as a text-sentence; see pp. 27–8), it has little to do with our intuitive gloss of the exchange as a question–answer sequence or with these clauses as a story initiation.

Before we go on, it is important to note that if we adopt a definition of discourse that is purely functional (e.g. analyze what Fairclough (1989) calls discursive practices), then what I have just described would certainly fall within the purview of discourse analysis. But is analysis of the phenomena noted above – pronunciation, speech acts, word order – really the analysis of how what Henry says serves the communicative functions I noted earlier – telling a story to provide an answer to a question? Such analyses seem, instead, to take us into areas of inquiry that have little to do with the functions just noted. My point here, then, is that although there are things we can say about (10) as language use, they do not all contribute to the function of Henry's contribution as an "answer" or a "story." Yet "giving an answer" and "beginning a story" seem to be functional glosses that contribute to our understanding of the communicative content of the utterances in (10): they give Henry's utterances an internal unity (grouping the utterances in one "turn" together) as well as an identity through which they are related to what I said initially in the exchange (they connect "turns" across speakers). In brief, these functions help us understand relationships "across," not "within," utterances.

There are some features and qualities of (10) that seem to bear more heavily on the way different utterances are related to one another. Observe first that Henry's story describes how different medical professionals wrongly diagnosed Louie until a neighbor was finally able to tell him what was really wrong; also, at the end of the story, Henry summarizes his point by saying that doctors can make mistakes. With this information about Henry's story in mind, let us re-examine the following section of (10):

(f)   he went to a *big* specialist,
(g)   and the guy . . . analyzed it *wrong*.
(h)   In fact his doctor didn't know,
(i)   and the specialist didn't know.

Several aspects of clauses (f) to (i) (the introduction to the story) prefigure the actions in the story, and the point being established through the story and made explicit through its summary. First is the contrastive stress on *BIG specialist* and *analyzed it WRONG*. This establishes a frame in which authority can be seen as wrong (Henry later states that *Doctors are not God!*) and thus makes Henry's point more salient.

Note, also, that Henry modifies a basic rule of narrative ordering (Labov 1972b): he does not always report events in the order in which they occurred. People typically visit their own doctors *before* consulting with a specialist. In (f) and (g), however, Henry reports his friend's encounter with the specialist and then mentions an encounter with *his doctor* (h). This deviation from temporal ordering is marked with *in fact* in (h): *in fact his doctor didn't know*. Modifying the reported order of events in this way has the discourse function of helping Henry enlarge the size or membership of the group of professionals who were wrong – thus adding to the overall point of his story.

Finally, the way Zelda begins to answer my question also hints at the overall point of Henry's story. I present this section again.

DEBBY: (a) Yeh. Well some people before they go to the doctor, they'll talk to a friend, or a neighbor.
       (b) Is there anybody that [uh . . .
ZELDA: (c)   [Well: : well I guess-

Zelda's *Well: :* had a high pitch and a final rise – an intonation often associated with uncertainty and doubt (Ward and Hirschberg 1988). We might say that this, too, has a discourse function: it conveys the attitudinal frame through which Zelda treats my proposition about whom people talk to when they're sick, and perhaps even Zelda's doubt about the wisdom of medical professionals.

As I have just illustrated, there are aspects of (10) that are relevant to key functions of the utterances (answering a question, opening a story) – functions that help utterances "fit" with other utterances. If we define discourse just as language use, however, there may be no way to legitimately separate questions about the functions that help us understand relationships across utterances from questions about the functions that are realized within utterances (e.g. speech acts, word order, phonological variation). Although this may be seen as a positive outcome if we are searching for ways to unify functionalism in general, it ends up removing a certain degree of autonomy from discourse studies as a particular branch of linguistics. Interestingly, it is this very synthesis that Tannen (1989a: 6) finds appealing about the definition of discourse as language *beyond the sentence*:

> Discourse – language beyond the sentence – is simply *language* – as it occurs, in any context (including the context of linguistic analysis), in any form (including two made-up sentences in sequence; a tape recorded conversation, meeting, or interview; a novel or play). The name for the field "discourse analysis," then, says nothing more or other than the term "linguistics": the study of language.

Despite the value of so integrative an approach, I believe that efforts to define discourse analysis as the study of language itself (as does Tannen) or to define discourse analysis as the study of language functions are more appropriate at later stages of theory building (e.g. when one wants to articulate a theory of language that accommodates discourse analysis) than at early stages of discourse analysis (e.g. when one wants to define what it is that one wants to study).

We have seen in this section that defining discourse as language use depends upon broader assumptions about the relevance of language to meanings, activities, and systems outside of itself. A corollary of this definition is that functionally based approaches view discourse as a socially and culturally organized way of speaking. Those functions are not limited to tasks that can be accomplished by language alone; rather they can include tasks such as maintaining interaction or building social relationships. Thus, functional analyses focus on how people use language to different ends: they are typically concerned less with the way people intend what they say to serve referential meanings (to convey propositional information), and more with the unintended social, cultural, and expressive meanings stemming from how their utterances are situated in contexts.

Although this inclusive view of the scope of discourse analysis is critical to the articulation of a linguistic theory within which discourse can fit, it also has the untoward effect of threatening to submerge discourse analysis within broader and more general analyses of language functions, without leaving a space within which discourse analysts can formulate a clear set of principles, goals, topics, and methods specific to their own enterprise. It makes no provision for analysis of the way the communicative content of an utterance contributes to our understanding of relationships across utterances, or, alternatively, for the way relationships across utterances help us understand the form, function, or meaning of a single utterance. Put most simply, it fails to make a special place for the analysis of relationships between utterances. Instead, a functionalist definition of discourse includes within its scope all language use: it provides no way to define discourse as different from other levels of language use (e.g. the use of sounds, words, or sentences). What we need to capture in a definition of discourse is the idea that discourse analysis imposes its own set of phenomena, its own problems and puzzles – and can discover its own regularities – in addition to those that it "inherits" from lower-level parts of discourse and those based in the way language is a social practice "determined by social structures" (Fairclough 1989: 17).

5 Discourse: utterances

In this section, I consider another definition of discourse: discourse is utterances. This view captures the idea that discourse is "above" (larger than) other units of language; however, by saying that utterance (rather than sentence) is the smaller unit of which discourse is comprised, we can suggest that discourse arises not as a collection of decontextualized units of language structure, but as a collection of inherently contextualized units of language use.

The main problem with this definition is that the notion of "utterance" is not really all that clear. For many linguists, utterances are contextualized sentences, i.e. they are context bound (as well as text bound). Hurford and Heasley (1983: 15), for example, make the following distinction:

A sentence is neither a physical event nor a physical object. It is conceived abstractly, a string of words put together by the grammatical rules of a language. A sentence can be thought of as the ideal string of words behind various realizations in utterances and inscriptions.

In Hurford and Heasley's framework, "Discourse analysis is fun" in (11a), (11b), and (11c) would all be considered one sentence, but different utterances:

(11a) Discourse analysis is fun.
(11b) Discourse analysis is fun.
(11c) BOB: I really like my linguistics courses.
       SUE: Oh I do too! Discourse analysis is fun.

The three occurrences of "Discourse analysis is fun" are three different utterances – three different instantiations of a single sentence. (11a) and (11b) are realizations of the sentence that share many aspects of a context: they both occur on the same page of the same book, and I am using them merely to make a point about utterances, without providing any more information about who, where, when, or how they may be found outside of this text. Despite this similarity, (11a) and (11b) are two different utterances: (11a) is the first appearance of the sentence, and (11b) is the second appearance (a repetition) of the sentence. What this means is a difference in the textual environment of (11a) and (11b). Finally, (11a) and (11b) both differ from (11c): although (11c) is also an illustration in a book, I have provided for it a hypothetical interactive context between two hypothetical interlocutors.

Before I go on to a problem with the view that discourse is "utterances" (stemming from the sentence–utterance distinction just illustrated), let me note the advantages of this view. First, defining discourse as utterances forces us to attend to the contextualization of language structure in a way going beyond Lyons's notion of text-sentence (pp. 27–8) to what we might call (following Lyons) context-sentence. Second, since this definition demands attention to more than one utterance, extended patterns and sequential arrangements automatically come under examination. Thus, defining discourse as utterances seems to balance both the functional emphasis on how language is used in context and the formal emphasis on extended patterns.

The main problem with this view of discourse is the definition proposed above of utterances – as realizations of sentences. Some linguists propose that sentences and utterances are radically different from each other, e.g. Fasold's (1990) belief that utterances need have no grammatical backing at all (they may or may not conform to grammatical principles) and sentences are abstract objects that may never actually "happen" or be realized. Others reverse the sentence-to-utterance mapping relationship to propose that sentences are "decontextualized" utterances. Figueroa (1990: 284), for example, claims the following: "all human actions take place within a particular spatio-temporal context; therefore whether one is introspecting about a sentence, whether one is reading a sentence, whether one is speaking, one is performing utterances." To extrapolate a bit from Figueroa, sentences are as contextualized as anything else that is the object of attention and intention; what complicates their consideration as utterances is that the context of a sentence is that of metalinguistic scientific discourse (see also Goffman 1981b). Thus, "the question for linguistic theory is . . . whether utterances are decontextualized either into an utterance type or sentence . . . or whether utterances are left contextualized" (Figueroa 1990: 284).

Regardless of these difficulties, the view that I will take in this book is that discourse can best be thought of as "utterances." I will view utterances as units of language production (whether spoken or written) that are inherently contextualized; whether (or how) they are related to sentences (or, in fact, to other units such as propositions, turns, or tone units) is an issue that will not explicitly enter into our discussion. A definition of discourse as "utterances" implies several goals of discourse analysis that underlie much of what follows in this book. First is what we might call syntactic goals, or more appropriately for discourse analysis, *sequential goals:* are there principles underlying the order in which one utterance, or one type of utterance, follows another? Second is what might be called *semantic and pragmatic goals:* how does the organization of discourse, and the meaning and use of particular expressions and constructions within certain contexts, allow people to convey and interpret the communicative content of what is said? how does one utterance (and the sequential relationship between utterances) influence the communicative content of another? Consistent with the differences between formalist and functionalist paradigms discussed earlier, the approaches to discourse analysis to be compared vary in terms of how deeply they pursue problems of sequential structure, and in terms of their willingness to delve into interpretations of meaning and use.

6 Summary: definitions, issues, and discourse analysis

I began this chapter with a brief description of two different paradigms underlying our conception of language (section 2). After comparing two different definitions of discourse stemming from these two paradigms – discourse as language above the sentence or clause (section 3), discourse as language use (section 4) – I proposed a third definition that sits at the intersection of structure and function – discourse as utterances (section 5).

The definitions of discourse that we discussed raise important issues that will help us understand the similarities and differences among the approaches to be presented in the rest of the book. Although I presented the structural (formalist) definition of discourse as separate from the functionalist one, I will suggest later in this book that actual analyses of discourse reveal an interdependence between structure and function (chapter 9). The distinction between structure and function also bears on two other issues that I discuss later. One is the relationship between text and context: structural definitions focus upon text and functional definitions upon context (chapter 10). Another is the way linguists view communication: structural definitions take a narrower view of communication than do functional definitions, and place a higher priority on the role of the code (cf. text) in communication (chapter 11). Although I discuss all three of these issues in general terms in relation to different approaches to discourse in part III, the sample analyses in chapters 3–8 (part II) will also show how different kinds of empirical analyses provide a basis for understanding these theoretically important issues.

Before closing this chapter, I want to make a slightly different point. I noted at the outset of chapter 1 that discourse analysis is one of the most vast, but also least defined, areas in linguistics. The availability of two different perspectives – stemming from two different ways of defining discourse – is partially responsible for the tremendous scope of discourse analysis. If we focus on structure, our task is to identify and analyze constituents, determine procedures for assigning to utterances a constituent status, discover regularities underlying combinations of constituents (perhaps even formulating rules for producing those regularities), and make principled decisions about whether or not particular arrangements are well formed. If we focus on function, on the other hand, our task is to identify and analyze actions performed by people for certain purposes, interpret social, cultural, and personal meanings, and justify our interpretations of those meanings for the participants involved. Dealing with either structure or function alone is thus a hefty task: but dealing with both can take us into two different analytical worlds that are often difficult to integrate.

The need to consider both text and context also increases the scope of discourse analysis. One obvious reason is that context can be tremendously broad and defined in different ways, e.g. mutual knowledge, social situations, speaker–hearer identities, cultural constructs. Another reason is that the text–context relationship is not independent of other relationships often assumed to hold between language and context (context as "culture," "society," or "interaction"). Yet, references to language "in" (or "and") context are far from neutral descriptions. Rather, any description of the language–context relationship veils tacit assumptions about the relationship between two different symbol systems and two different structures, e.g. their relative autonomy, the precedence of one over another, the way they impinge upon one another. Speaking of language *in* society, for example, assumes that language is a system both smaller than, and dependent upon, a broader matrix of social interactions and structures – thus making assumptions not only about how two systems impinge upon one another, but also about the very nature of those two systems. Such assumptions bear not only on our understanding of discourse, but on our understanding of language in general.

Notes

1 Compare Hopper's (1988) distinction between the A Priori Grammar Postulate and the Emergence of Grammar attitude.
2 I am by no means attempting a comprehensive review of all formal and functional approaches (a task that would require its own book). Rather, I am trying to take one or two typical (often classic) examples of each approach in order to show how they differ. Nor am I claiming that the characteristics that I present are shared equally by all representatives of structural or functional approaches. One criterion differentiating functionalists, for example, is the type of external function deemed important: in addition to (or as alternative to) a concern for social function (e.g. Halliday) and communicative function (e.g. Givón) is a concern for cognitive and perceptual function (e.g. Bates and MacWhinney, Kuno). Although these functions are associated with different perspectives (e.g. Halliday with sociolinguistics and Bates and Mac-Whinney with psycholinguistics) – and the influence they exert may be markedly different – what the perspectives share is an emphasis on the influence of factors outside of language on linguistic processes and structures. Thus, what I claim through the following discussion is that the assumptions made by formal and functional approaches are different: despite variation within structural approaches and within functional approaches, there is nevertheless greater variation between (than within) these two approaches.
3 The view that discourse is similar in kind to lower-level linguistic units leads to a tendency to view only grammatical units (sentences, clauses) as the building blocks of discourse, i.e. the hierarchy is comprised of units of "the same kind." In this sense, the view that discourse is propositionally structured can thus be quite different in some ways. Some analysts (e.g. Halliday and Hasan 1976) have proposed that the task of conveying meanings (semantics) is so different from the task of building sentences (syntax) that discourse is fundamentally different in kind than sentences. (Interestingly, however, Halliday and Hasan (1976: 2) still incorporate sentences into their view of text: although "a text does not *consist* of sentences; it is *realized by*, or encoded in, sentences.")
4 In addition to saying that a linguistic structure eases the transmission of information, we might also say that a structure in discourse (i.e. a sequence of referring terms in which a first-mention is explicit and indefinite, and a next-mention is inexplicit and definite) emerges because of constraints on the sequential flow of information: if a first-mention provides explicit information, a next-mention can provide considerably less information. (See discussion in chapter 5.)

Part II Approaches to Discourse Analysis

This part of the book discusses six different approaches to discourse analysis. None of the approaches takes as its sole object of inquiry "discourse" *per se*, and the broader topics to which discourse is seen as relevant have important influences on the way in which they approach the analysis of utterances. Speech act theory (chapter 3) focuses on communicative acts performed through speech. Interactional sociolinguistics (chapter 4) focuses on the social and linguistic meanings created during interaction. The ethnography of communication (chapter 5) focuses on language and communication as cultural behavior. Pragmatics (chapter 6) focuses on the meaning of individual utterances in hypothetical contexts. Conversation analysis (chapter 7) focuses on how sequential structures in conversation provide a basis through which social order is constructed. Variation theory (chapter 8) focuses on structural categories in texts and how form and meaning in clauses help to define text.

Each chapter in this part of the book provides a general background (critical concepts and key issues) of the approach, focusing primarily on the work of scholars central to the development of the approach. Each chapter also provides an extensive sample analysis, using data drawn primarily from sociolinguistic interviews (see appendix 1), to illustrate the methodology of each approach and its application to one of two concrete problems (question–answer sequences in chapters 3, 4, and 5; referring expressions in chapters 6, 7, and 8).

3 Speech Act Theory

1 Introduction

Two philosophers, John Austin and John Searle, developed speech act theory from the basic belief that language is used to perform actions: thus, its fundamental insights focus on how meaning and action are related to language. Although speech act theory was not first developed as a means of analyzing discourse, some of its basic insights have been used by many scholars (e.g. Labov and Fanshel 1977; see also chapter 8) to help solve problems basic to discourse analysis.[1] In addition, particular issues in speech act theory lead to discourse analysis, e.g. how an utterance can perform more than one speech act at a time, and the relationship between context and illocutionary force.

I begin in section 2 with an overview of the critical concepts and ideas introduced by both Austin (1962) and Searle (1969). I then use a sample discourse to discuss two different (but related) stages in the application of speech act theory to discourse analysis: how to identify utterances as speech acts (section 3.1); how to analyze sequences of speech acts (section 3.2). After exploring some of the issues raised by this analysis (section 3.3), I summarize the speech act approach to discourse (section 4).

2 Defining speech act theory

Speech act theory begins with the work of John Austin (section 2.1), whose ideas are expanded and incorporated into linguistic theory by John Searle (section 2.2). Searle's work also raises important questions concerning the inventory (and classification) of acts about which people know (section 2.3) and the way that a single utterance can be associated with more than one act (section 2.4). Although it is not initially proposed as a framework in which to analyze discourse, the issues with which speech act theory is concerned (meaning, use, actions) can lead to such an analysis (section 2.5).

2.1 Austin: from performative to illocutionary act

A series of lectures by John Austin in 1955, compiled in *How to Do Things with Words* (1962), is widely acknowledged as the first presentation of what has come to be called speech act theory. Austin's presentation seems intentionally argumentative and provocative: distinctions are proposed in the first few chapters that are then systematically dismantled in later chapters, such that the presentation of the theory by the end of the book is dramatically different from its presentation in the beginning of the book.

Austin begins by noticing that some utterances that seem like statements lack what is thought to be a necessary property of statements – a truth value. Not only do such statements not " 'describe' or 'report' " anything (p. 5), but "the uttering of the sentence is, or is a part of, the doing of an action, which again would not *normally* be described as, or as 'just', saying something" (p. 5; emphasis in original). Austin calls these *performatives* and distinguishes them from *constatives*, i.e. declarative statements whose truth or falsity can be judged. The following are examples of sentences (or utterances – the terms are initially interchangeable) that are performatives.

> I do (take this woman to be my lawful wedded wife) – as uttered in the course of the marriage ceremony.
>
> I name this ship the *Queen Elizabeth* – as uttered when smashing the bottle against the stern.
>
> I give and bequeath my watch to my brother – as occurring in a will.
>
> I bet you sixpence it will rain tomorrow.

The examples given all share several qualities. They all include a particular type of verb – a performative verb – that realizes a particular action (the action that the verb "names") when uttered in a specific context. Such a context can include setting (a marriage ceremony, writing a will), physical objects (a ship, legal documents), and institutional identities; it may also require a particular response (a bet requires what Austin calls "uptake"). Performatives require not only "the appropriate circumstances" (p. 13), but also the appropriate language: the performative verb in the above examples is in the present tense, each sentence has a first person subject, and the adverb *hereby* may modify any of the verbs (e.g. one can say "I hereby give . . ."). Thus, performatives meet certain contextual and textual conditions.

Austin goes on to classify the circumstances (the conditions) that allow utterances to act as performatives. He does so according to the circumstances themselves, and according to the consequence for a performative if the circumstance does not hold. As noted above, the circumstances allowing an act are varied: they include the existence of "an accepted conventional procedure having a certain conventional effect" (p. 26), the presence of "particular persons and circumstances" (p. 34), "the correct and complete execution of a procedure" (p. 36), and (when appropriate to the act) "certain thoughts, feelings, or intentions" (p. 39). An act can either misfire (not go through at all) or go through but, due to an abuse of the procedure, in a way that is not totally satisfactory. Appointing someone to office (i.e. saying "I appoint you") misfires if that person has already been appointed or if the speaker is not in the position to appoint anyone (p. 34). Likewise, saying "I bet you the race won't be run today" if more than one race was arranged (p. 36) causes the act of betting to misfire. So, too, saying "I bet you sixpence" will misfire and not be a "bet" unless you say "I take you on" or provide other words to that effect (p. 37). As noted above, other violations allow an act to go through, but in an "unhappy" or "infelicitous" (p. 14) way. Saying "I advise you to [do X]" without the requisite thought (i.e. if I do not think X is the course most expedient for you; p. 40), for example, does not void the performative of advice-giving: the act is still "advising" but it is infelicitous because one of the procedures has been abused. Thus, there is variation in both the circumstances allowing a felicitous performative and the way a performative can go wrong.

I noted above that Austin proposes distinctions in the first few lectures/chapters that are systematically dismantled in later sections. The distinction between constatives and performatives is one such distinction. Recall that constatives are declaratives whose truth could be judged; performatives are declaratives that "do" an action. By the end of the book, Austin proposes instead that all utterances have qualities that were initially seen as characteristic of constatives and performatives. The focus of attention is no longer sentences, but "the issuing of an utterance in a speech situation" (p. 139). All utterances perform speech acts that are comprised of a *locutionary act* (the production of sounds and words with meanings), an *illocutionary act* (the issuing of an utterance with conventional communicative force achieved "in saying"), and a *perlocutionary act* (the actual effect achieved "by saying").

Before discussing these three aspects of a speech act, I want to briefly go over the way the constative–performative distinction is collapsed. Basically, what Austin shows is that the conditions defining one type of utterance apply equally well to the other, and that neither type can be differentiated by formal clues. Thus, the dismantling of the constative–performative distinction can help to reveal Austin's view of two aspects of the conditions underlying speech acts: context (what makes an utterance "true" and "appropriate") and text (how what is said conveys what is done).

Consider the distinction between truth/falsity (applicable to constatives) and felicitous/infelicitous (applicable to performatives). Austin argues that performatives (as well as constatives) involve judgements of truth and falsity. Recall that certain conditions are necessary for a performative to be felicitous. These conditions are like statements that have to be true: saying that "certain things have to be so . . . commits us to saying that for a certain performative utterance to be happy, certain statements have *to be true*" (p. 45; emphasis in original). "I apologize," for example, implies the truth of certain conditions, e.g. it is true (and not false) that I am committed to doing something subsequently (p. 46). Similarly, implications thought to hold only for constatives hold for performatives as well. The entailment of one proposition (e.g. "The mat is under the cat") by another (e.g. "The cat is on the mat"), for example, is parallel to the way an underlying condition ("I ought") is entailed by a performative (e.g. "I promise"). Similarly, saying "I promise but I ought not" is as much of a contradiction as saying "it is and it is not" (p. 51). Thus, the conditions necessary for performatives to be felicitous have the same truth-based relationship with a performative utterance that constative statements have with other statements.

Just as performatives can be said to have truth conditions, so constatives may be said to meet felicity conditions. Take a statement that refers to something that does not exist: "The present King of France is bald." Austin argues that this is similar to someone purporting to bequeath an estate he does not own: both are void (i.e. they "misfire"), simply because both purport to refer to an entity (the King of France, an estate) that does not exist (pp. 20, 137). Constatives are also subject to the same specific kinds of infelicities that result in abuses of performatives. Recall that certain thoughts, feelings, or intentions may be part of the circumstances that allow a felicitous performative – such that an insincere "promise" would abuse the procedure of promising. Statements are also liable to sincerity abuses: saying "The cat is on the mat" if I do not believe that the cat is on the mat abuses a procedure in the same way as saying "I promise to be there," but not really intending to be there (p. 136).

We noted initially that performatives meet certain contextual and textual conditions. Now we have seen that the contextual conditions for performatives are not different in kind from those for constatives: both involve truth and falsity, both involve felicity and infelicity. It turns out that the textual conditions are not as different as initially suggested either. Although Austin initially grounded his analysis of performatives with a discussion of performative verbs (and he maintains this focus, to a certain degree, in his taxonomy; see section 2.3), he also raises the possibility that performatives can be realized without verbs (contrasting an explicit performative to a primary performative) and that not all types of performatives need verbs specialized to that task.

Let us briefly consider the distinction between explicit performatives (with the verb) and primary performatives (without the verb). Austin suggests that although performative verbs are neither necessary nor sufficient textual conditions for performative utterances, they do make explicit certain features of the speech situation (e.g. the actor, the action being undertaken). One outcome of this is that primary performatives may be ambiguous: saying "It is yours," for example, may be either an act of bequeathing ("I give it to you") or an acknowledgment that "it (already) belongs to you" (p. 62). A way to get around this problem is to suggest that primary performatives should be "reducible or expandible, or analysable . . . or reproducible" (pp. 61–2) to a performative formula (e.g. I hereby [verb] you that . . .).

Relying on the availability of a performative formula, however, does not solve all the problems of finding grammatical criteria (i.e. textual conditions) for performatives. The criteria themselves may be individually problematic: the use of the present tense, for example, need not always convey an action concurrent with the time of speaking (pp. 64–5). Nor can we be sure of the equivalence of primary and explicit performatives: "I am sorry" may not really be exactly like "I apologize" (p. 66). Finally, we may be able to do something through speech (e.g. insult), yet not have a performative verb by which to do it (pp. 65–6).

We have seen thus far that the constative–performative distinction cannot be maintained because both constatives and performatives involve truth and falsity; both are felicitous or infelicitous in relation to the conditions in which they occur; both are realized through a variety of forms that can be rewritten in terms of a performative formula. To put this more generally, we cannot find either contextual or textual conditions that support the constative–performative distinction. Thus, "to state is every bit as much to perform an illocutionary act as, say, to warn or pronounce" (p. 134). "Stating" is exactly on a par with "betting": "I state that he did not do it" is as much of an act as "I bet that he did not do it." Despite the collapse of the constative–performative distinction, performative verbs still play a key role in Austin's framework. Utterances whose act is not linguistically explicit (e.g. "He did not do it") may be made explicit through the use of a formula built upon a performative verb ("I state that . . .", "I argue that . . .", "I bet that . . ."). So pervasive is the resource for action provided by performative verbs that Austin suggests the existence of acts (and verbs) "of the order of the third power of 10" (p. 150) that can be discovered by "going through the dictionary" (p. 150). And so important is the speech situation (the context) in which these verbs are used (and acts are performed) that even the truth and falsity of statements is contextually bound: "in the case of stating truly or falsely, just as much as in the case of advising well or badly, the intents and purposes of the utterance and its context are important; what is judged true in a school book may not be so judged in a work of historical research" (p. 143).

I noted above that Austin segments the speech act itself into component acts – only one of which is the "act" typically spoken of in speech act theory. Three acts underlie the issuing of an utterance. A locutionary act involves the uttering of an expression with sense and reference, i.e. using sounds and words with meaning. This seems to capture the properties of the original constative group: the act "of saying something" (p. 100). An illocutionary act is the act performed "in saying" the locution (p. 99), such that what was said had the force (not the meaning) of that illocution. This level captures the acts initially viewed as performative: these acts are conventional in that they could be made explicit by a performative formula (p. 103). A perlocutionary act is the "consequential effects" (p. 102) of an utterance on an interlocutor, i.e. what is achieved "by saying" something. Since these three aspects of an utterance are all actions, they are all subject to the same kinds of failures – to "the ills that all action is heir to" (p. 105). Together, these acts produce a total speech act that must be studied in the total speech situation (pp. 52, 148): "the words used are to some extent to be 'explained' by the 'context' in which they are designed to be or have actually been spoken in a linguistic interchange" (p. 100).

2.2 Searle: from conditions to rules

Searle's (1969) *Speech Acts* builds upon Austin's work to propose a systematic framework by which to incorporate speech acts into linguistic theory. Searle also introduces several ideas that provide important ideas for the application of speech act theory to discourse (section 2.3 and 2.4), although he resists the idea that conversation is governed by constitutive rules (Searle 1989).

Searle (1969: 21) proposes that "the speech act is the basic unit of communication." Far from divorcing speech acts from the study of language, however, this view places speech acts at the very crux of the study of language, meaning, and communication; in fact, speech act rules are argued to be part of linguistic competence (see below). What allows the integration of speech act theory into linguistic theory is Searle's *principle of expressibility* (pp. 18–21): what can be meant can be said. This principle establishes that it is possible (in theory) for a speaker to come to be able to say exactly what she means either by increasing her knowledge of the language or by enriching the language (p. 19). Furthermore, all languages "can be regarded as different conventional realizations of the same underlying rules" (p. 39), comparable to the way a chess game is played in different countries, but still considered a game of chess. The principle of expressibility has several different consequences. Taken broadly, this principle moves nonliteral meaning, vagueness, ambiguity, and incompleteness out of the theoretical essence of linguistic communication (p. 20; cf. Gricean pragmatics; also chapter 11). Taken more narrowly, this principle has the consequence noted above: it brings together the study of speech acts, meaning, language, and communication. In Searle's own words, the principle of expressibility enables us to

> equate rules for performing speech acts with rules for uttering certain linguistic elements, since for any possible speech act there is a possible linguistic element the meaning of which (given the context of the utterance) is sufficient to determine that its literal utterance is a performance of precisely that speech act. (pp. 20–1)

Thus, viewing speech acts as the basic unit of communication allows Searle to explicitly associate speech acts with the study of language (its production, its interpretation) and meaning (both speaker meaning and linguistic meaning): "there are a series of analytic connections between the notion of speech acts, what the speaker means, what the sentence (or other linguistic element) uttered means, what the speaker intends, what the hearer understands, and what the rules governing the linguistic elements are" (p. 21).

I noted above that speech act rules are part of linguistic competence: language can be used for speech acts because people share rules that create the acts that say what is meant. Before describing how rules are responsible for the creation of acts (and how they incorporate both textual and contextual conditions), it is important to comment on the importance of rules within Searle's framework and on the type of rules important for speech acts.

Searle observes that "speaking a language is engaging in a (highly complex) rule-governed form of behavior" (p. 12). A methodological consequence of this is that linguistic characterizations do not report "the behavior of a group." Rather, they describe aspects of speakers' mastery of a rule-governed skill (p. 12) that can be obtained by relying heavily on the intuitions (and linguistic characterizations) of native speakers (p. 15). What such intuitions can provide are "idealized models" (p. 56) of the conditions that are necessary and sufficient for the utterance of a given sentence to be a successful, non-defective performance of a given act. The rules that are responsible for speech acts, however, are a special type of rule that Searle calls *constitutive*. In contrast to regulative rules (that regulate independently existing forms of behavior) constitutive rules "create or define new forms of behavior" (p. 33). The forms of the two types of rules reflect their different status: regulative rules are expressed as (or can be paraphrased as) imperatives, but constitutive rules are more definitional, e.g. "X counts as Y in context C" (p. 35).

Our discussion of Austin mentioned contextual conditions ("circumstances") and textual conditions (e.g. the availability of explicit performative formula) that allow an utterance to perform a certain illocutionary act. Like Austin, Searle's rules and conditions for speech acts draw upon both context and text: they also elevate intentions and other psychological states as conditions enabling a speech act, by assigning them their own type of rule (see below). Like Austin, Searle classifies conditions and rules according to their necessity for the act. But in contrast to Austin, Searle classifies different kinds of conditions (and rules) according to what aspect of text and context is focused upon in the condition or rule; the different conditions also overlap (partially) with the different components of a speech act.

Searle segments utterances into speech acts very similar to those proposed by Austin. The uttering of words (morphemes and sentences) is an *utterance act*. Referring and predicating are *propositional acts*. Acts like stating, questioning, commanding, and promising are *illocutionary acts*. Illocutionary acts are what is constituted by the rules noted above: in addition to being rule-governed, they are intentional, they have a name, and they are what the speaker (S) is doing, in relation to the hearer (H), with words. The consequences of illocutionary acts (the effects on actions, thoughts, beliefs of hearers) are *perlocutionary acts.*

As just noted, it is the illocutionary act that is subject to the conditions and rules so central to Searle's framework. The textual and contextual circumstances that allow speech acts to have an illocutionary force are categorized as different kinds of conditions; rules are extracted from the conditions. Because our sample analysis presents conditions for questions and requests (section 3), I will not present all the conditions for any one particular speech act here (Searle 1969: 66–7, presents the rules for requests, assertions, questions, thanks, advising, warnings, greetings, and congratulating). Rather, I will discuss the conditions in general terms, and in relation to the rules extracted from the conditions.

Propositional content conditions or rules are the most textual: they concern reference and predication (the propositional act). A propositional content rule for promises, for example, is the predication of a future act (A) by the speaker. Preparatory conditions or rules are varied: they seem to involve background circumstances and knowledge about S and H that must hold prior to (and may then be altered by) the performance of the act. A preparatory condition for promises, for example, concerns H's preference about S's doing of an act (A). The sincerity condition or rule concerns S's psychological state as it is expressed in the performance of an illocutionary act (e.g. S's intention, belief, desire). Finally, the essential condition or rule is what the utterance "counts as," i.e. the "point" of the act (Searle p. 59; also Searle 1979: 2–3). As the terminology "counts as" suggests, the essential rule is most critical to the creation of an act (i.e. the central constitutive rule). Thus, each rule focuses upon a slightly different aspect of what is said: the propositional content rule focuses only upon the textual content, preparatory rules focus upon background circumstances, the sincerity rule upon S's psychological state, and the essential rule upon the illocutionary point of what is said.

Just as Austin found some acts to be infelicitous (and to different degrees, i.e. misfires versus abuses), so Searle finds that different conditions or rules are more or less crucial to the non-defective performance of an act. As suggested above, the essential condition is critical. Whereas each condition or rule is individually necessary for the successful and non-defective performance of a given act, however, it is the set of conditions or rules that is collectively sufficient for such a performance (p. 54).

An earlier quote from Searle noted analytic connections between what the speaker means, what the sentence (or other linguistic element) uttered means, and what the speaker intends. Although speaker meaning and intention are sometimes separated from sentence meaning (see discussion of Gricean pragmatics, chapter 6), Searle argues that an analysis of illocutionary acts must capture "both the intentional and the conventional aspects" of meaning, and crucially, "the relationship between them" (p. 45) – a relationship that is sensitive to the circumstances of an utterance. Certain linguistic elements are viewed as illocutionary force indicating devices that provide conventional procedures (cf. Austin's mention of conventional procedures) by which to perform a given act. (Searle (p. 30) lists a variety of forms that function in this capacity: "word order, stress, intonation contour, punctuation, the mood of the verb and the so-called performative verbs.") But both conventional meaning (cf. text) and speaker intention can contribute to the circumstances in which saying something realizes a certain kind of doing.

In sum, Searle places the speech act at the center of the study of language, meaning, and communication: he proposes that "the basic unit of human linguistic communication is the illocutionary act" (Searle 1979: 1). Speech acts are performed through the use of conventional procedures and linguistically realized through illocutionary force indicating devices. They are enabled (i.e. created) by constitutive rules, the knowledge of which is part of our linguistic competence. Speech act theory thus analyzes the way meanings and acts are linguistically communicated. To summarize in Searle's words: "the semantic structure of a language may be regarded as a conventional realization of a series of sets of underlying constitutive rules, and . . . speech acts are acts characteristically performed by uttering expressions in accordance with these sets of constitutive rules" (p. 37).

2.3 Taxonomies of acts

Discovering the number, and categories, of illocutionary acts is an important part of speech act theory (Searle 1979: 1). The identity of an act is a product of the set of constitutive rules by which it is created. Since different acts may be similar to one another if they share particular rules, categorizing speech acts and speech act types can reveal relationships between rules, as well as relationships between acts. It is also important to know which acts can be created simply because speech acts are central to linguistic communication: knowing which speech act to perform (and the rules that govern it) is a crucial part of how speakers use language to communicate; likewise, knowledge of how to identify that act is critical to hearer understanding.

Although Austin (1962: chapter 12) proposes a classification of speech acts, Searle (1979) argues that Austin's taxonomy does not maintain a clear distinction between illocutionary verbs and acts; nor are the categories based on consistently applied principles. Searle relies upon taxonomic principles (that sometimes reflect the different types of conditions underlying speech acts) to build a two-tiered classification. He proposes five classes of speech acts: representatives (e.g. asserting), directives (e.g. requesting), commissives (e.g. promising), expressives (e.g. thanking), and declarations (e.g. appointing). Three main principles differentiate these classes. Other speech acts within these classes follow the same three principles, but are differentiated by less comprehensively applicable principles.

The most important principles are those that differentiate the five major categories of speech acts. The first taxonomic principle concerns the illocutionary point of the act: this is derived from the essential condition of an act (the condition that defines what the act "counts as"). The illocutionary point of directives (e.g. requests, orders, challenges, and dares), for example, is that they are attempts by S to get H to do A. The illocutionary point of commissives (e.g. promises, vows) is that they commit the speaker to some future course of action. The second principle is the way that words are fit to the world. Both commissives and directives are built upon a world-to-words fit: in making a promise, S undertakes to create a world first presented in the words; in making a request, S attempts to get H to create a world first presented in the words. Representatives (whose point is to commit S to something being the case), however, are built upon a words-to-world fit: insist, state, boast, and conclude, for example, are all based upon the way words are fit to a world that is "pre-existing" (in the sense that it is not being created by those words). The third principle is the expressed psychological state: this is derived from the sincerity condition. The psychological state expressed by representatives, for example, is "belief" (e.g. S believes that X). In contrast, the psychological state of directives is "want"; the psychological state of commissives is "intention."

The other principles discussed in Searle (1979) help to differentiate speech acts within the five broad categories noted above; they also reveal similarities (and differences) between specific speech acts that are not in the same general category. One principle concerns different strengths with which the illocutionary point is presented. For example, "insist" and "suggest" are both directives, just as "swear" and "guess" are both commissives: the former member of each pair is presented with more strength than the latter. Two additional principles are derived from the preparatory conditions of speech acts. The status of S and H bears differently on the illocutionary point: this principle would differentiate "proposal" from "command" even though both are directives. How the utterance relates to the interests of S and H is also derived from preparatory conditions: "boasts" (a type of representative) and "requests" (a type of directive) are similar because both have to do with S's interest; these would contrast with "congratulations" (a type of expressive) since that concerns H's interest. Another principle is based upon the propositional content condition: "differences in propositional content that are determined by illocutionary force indicating devices" (Searle 1979: 5). Thus, "prediction" differs from "report" because the former must be about the future, where as the latter can be about the past or present.

Although I will not discuss each principle underlying the taxonomy in detail, it is important to note that one principle concerns the availability of an illocutionary verb: for some acts, the corresponding illocutionary verb has a performative use; for others, it does not, e.g. "state" versus "boast." Illocutionary verbs can also mark aspects of an act other than their illocutionary point (e.g. "insist" marks the degree of intensity). These two points loosen the connection between verbs and acts so important to Austin. In so doing, they also extend the boundaries of what can count as an act: this makes it more difficult to define a closed set of language functions that can be encoded by illocutionary force indicating devices and realized by constitutive rules.

In sum, speech acts can be classified into groups and subgroups by a principled set of criteria. Communication relies upon shared knowledge of the name and type of a speech act: speaker and hearer share knowledge of how to identify and classify an utterance as a particular "type" of act, as a unit of language that is produced and interpreted according to constitutive rules.

2.4 Multiple functions and indirect acts

At the end of his article on a classification of illocutionary acts, Searle (1979: 23) points out that there are a limited number of things that we do with language: "we tell people how things are, we try to get them to do things, we commit ourselves to doing things, we express our feeling and attitudes and we bring about changes through our utterances." We have just seen that much of the 1979 paper is devoted to telling us how we make these functional discriminations among utterances. Taken up in other work is an observation made in the very last sentence of the article: "often, we do more than one of these at once in the same utterance."

How we do more than one thing at once with our words (i.e. the multiple functions of an utterance) is part of the important issue of indirect speech acts (Searle 1969). Searle's view of indirectness (like his taxonomy of speech acts) draws upon his analysis of the conditions underlying speech acts. An indirect speech act is defined as an utterance in which one illocutionary act (a "primary" act) is performed by way of the performance of another act (a "literal" act). Hearers are able to interpret indirect speech acts by relying upon their knowledge of speech acts, along with general principles of cooperative conversation (see Gricean pragmatics, chapter 6), mutually shared factual information, and a general ability to draw inferences.

Although I will not go through the inferencing of indirect speech acts in detail, I will take some brief examples to illustrate how Searle's view of indirectness arises from his speech act theory. Take, for example, the sentences "I hope you'll write a letter of recommendation for me" and "Would you be able to write a letter of recommendation for me?" Although both sentences are conventionally understood as directives (their "primary" act), they are also other acts: the former is a statement; the latter, a question. Both sentences, however, are understood as directives because the "literal" speech acts that they also perform (i.e. the statement, the question) focus upon a condition that allows directives to be performed (i.e. a rule that constitutes a directive). What the phrase "I hope you will do X" states is a speaker-based sincerity condition for requests, i.e. S wants H to do A. Likewise, what the phrase "Would you be able to do X?" questions is a hearer-based preparatory condition, i.e. H is able to perform A. It is by way of stating a sincerity condition, or questioning a preparatory condition, of directives that these sentences perform directives (their primary act).

The question of how we identify particular utterances as specific acts is of course one that we addressed before. This problem was noted by Austin: whereas performative verbs make explicit certain features of the speech situation, primary performatives do not, and thus may be ambiguous. Like Austin, Searle suggests a kind of trade-off between the contributions of textual and contextual information to our identification of speech acts: it is possible to perform an act "without invoking an explicit illocutionary force-indicating device where the context and the utterance make it clear that the essential condition is satisfied" (Searle 1962: 68). Thus, just as text (e.g. illocutionary force indicating devices) can assign an act a single identity, so too can context. But the question of how multiple identities are contextually assigned (or contextually separated) is not discussed at length in orthodox speech act theory.

In sum, an utterance can do more than one thing at a time. Some utterances have multiple functions because one act is being performed by way of another: these are called "indirect" speech acts. The conditions underlying speech acts provide an analytical resource for indirectness. That conditions can have this analytical function is possible because they have a critical role in our knowledge of speech act types. When more than one act is performed by a single utterance, the conditions for the two speech acts nevertheless have a systematic relationship to one another. Thus, it is relationships between underlying conditions that allow utterances to do more than one thing at a time.

2.5 Summary: meaning, use, and actions

We have seen in this section that speech act theory is basically concerned with what people "do" with language – with the functions of language. Typically, however, the functions focused upon are those akin to communicative intentions (the illocutionary force of an utterance) that can be performed through a conventional procedure and labelled (cf. that have a performative verb). Even within this relatively well-defined set of acts, the act performed by a single utterance may not be easy to discover: some utterances bear little surface resemblance to their underlying illocutionary force.

Despite the emphasis on language function, speech act theory deals less with actual utterances than with utterance-types, and less with the ways speakers and hearers actually build upon inferences in talk, than with the sort of knowledge that they can be presumed to bring to talk. Language can do things – can perform acts – because people share constitutive rules that create the acts and that allow them to label utterances as particular kinds of acts. These rules are part of linguistic competence, even though they draw upon knowledge about the world, including an array of "social facts" (e.g. knowledge about social obligations, institutions, identities), as well as knowledge about the grammar of language.

3 Sample analysis: questions, requests, offers

Now that we have discussed some of the key insights and concepts critical to speech act theory, let us see how it applies to discourse analysis. Speech act theory provides a framework in which to identify the conditions underlying the production and understanding of an utterance as a particular linguistically realized action. Utterances perform different acts because of their "circumstances" (Austin) and because of the knowledge that we have of the conditions and rules that constitute particular acts (Searle). We see in this section that our knowledge of the constitutive rules for acts provides a systematic framework in which we can not only identify relationships between different speech acts (e.g. understand how a threat differs from a promise), but also use a single utterance to perform more than one speech act at a time (section 3.1). We also see that this knowledge can be put to use as a way to understand sequential relationships between utterances (section 3.2).

Before beginning, it is important to note that although speech act theory began in philosophy (and relied upon hypothetical utterances), it has also been developed extensively in linguistics. We noted above Austin's (1962: 100) view that words "are to some extent to be 'explained' by the 'context' in which they are designed to be or have actually been spoken in a linguistic interchange." Yet many linguists (e.g. the collection in Cole and Morgan 1975) rely upon constructed utterances and hypothetical context as data by which to analyze speech acts. (In this sense, they are following Searle's (1969: 56) view that abstraction and idealization are crucial to systematization and theory construction.) Other scholars have relied upon actual utterances to try to answer the same sorts of questions concerning speech act conditions (e.g. Blum-Kulka 1987; Ervin-Tripp 1976), contexts (e.g. participant identity and relationship: Cherry 1990; Herbert 1990; Holmes 1989, 1990), modality (Pufahl 1988; Stubbs 1986), and categories (e.g. Halliday 1973, 1975; Labov and Fanshel 1977). Although these analyses sometimes considered speech acts in connected discourse, they did not apply their analyses to the sequential relationships between utterances themselves (but see Ferrera 1985; Labov and Fanshel 1977). Nor did they consider how utterances can define one another's speech act functions (but see Clark 1979; Schegloff 1987). If we want to consider speech act theory as an approach to discourse, however, we need to consider both of these issues: how speech act function contributes to sequential coherence, and how the speech act function of one utterance contributes to that of another.

As I noted in chapter 2, one focus of our sample analyses in this book is question–answer sequences. We begin in this section by analyzing how a single utterance fulfills the conditions of a question (section 3.1.1); we then go on to see that this same utterance also acts as a request (section 3.1.2) and an offer (section 3.1.3). This will help to illustrate how the underlying conditions of these different acts can be used to try to identify the functions of a specific utterance in talk. We then go on to analyze the utterances following the question/request/offer in terms of their relationship with the multifunctional utterance (section 3.2). This will allow us to see how the underlying conditions of acts have an effect on relationships between utterances, and on the sequential organization of talk.

The data that I use are an excerpt from an interaction among four people (Henry, Zelda, Irene, and Debby (myself)). At the time of the conversation, Henry and Zelda were in their late fifties, Irene was in her mid thirties, and I was in my mid twenties. Henry and Zelda are married; Irene is their next door neighbor and close friend. I was visiting Henry and Zelda's home for a sociolinguistic interview (see Schiffrin 1987a: 41–7; chapter 5 of this book). (1) occurs just after Henry, Zelda, and Irene have been discussing a recent funeral (of a teacher at their neighborhood school) that Irene and Zelda had attended. (1) also precedes the more formal beginning of our sociolinguistic interview.

(1)	HENRY:	(a)	Y'want a piece of candy?
	IRENE:	(b)	No.
	ZELDA:	(c)	^{z}She's on a diet.
	DEBBY:	(d)	^{z}Who's not on [a diet.
	IRENE:	(e)	[I'm on- I'm on a diet
		(f)	and my mother: [buys-=
	ZELDA:	(g)	[You're not!
	IRENE:	(h)	=my [mother buys these mints.=
	DEBBY:	(i)	[Oh yes I amhhhh!
	ZELDA:	(j)	Oh yeh.
	IRENE:	(k)	The Russell Stouffer mints.
		(l)	I said, "I don't want any Mom."
		(m)	"Well, I don't wanna eat the whole thing."
		(n)	She gives me a little tiny piece,
		(o)	I eat it.
		(p)	Then she gives me an[other,=
	HENRY:	(q)	[Was =
	IRENE:	(r)	=so I threw it out the window= =there a lot of people?=
	HENRY:		
	IRENE:	(s)	=I didn't [tell her. =
	HENRY:	(t)	[Was there=
	IRENE:	(u)	=She'd kill me.
	HENRY:		=a lot of people at the house?
	ZELDA:	(v)	All: the teach[ers.
	IRENE:	(w)	[A lot of teachers will- probably will all be there till late.
	HENRY:	(x)	Je:sus Christ.
	ZELDA:	(y)	All: the teachers.
	HENRY:	(z)	What a heartache

As I noted above, my initial focus is on the very beginning of (1): I use Henry's *Y'want a piece of candy?* to consider how speech acts are identified (3.1). In section 3.2 I turn to Irene's *no* (3.2.1), Zelda's *She's on a diet* (3.2.2), and Irene's story about her diet (3.2.3), in order to discuss speech act sequences.

There are two broad issues critical to the application of speech act theory to discourse; the analysis will be concerned with both. First is the identification of speech acts *per se*: how to identify an utterance as a particular speech act (3.1). Although identifying speech as action requires knowledge of the constituent rules for speech acts, it also depends upon an assumption that what is said can be "mapped onto" what is done – an assumption sometimes difficult to uphold given the fact that utterances may have multiple functions (chapter 2: pp. 33–8; also, recall the speech act view of this in section 2.4). The second issue is the sequential arrangement of speech acts: how an initial speech act creates an environment in which a next speech act is (or is not) appropriate (3.2). This issue bears centrally on discourse analysis simply because discourse (by definition) is comprised of sequentially arranged units, and because sequential regularities (sequences that fulfill our expectations) are a key ingredient in our identification of something as text.

Although I discuss these two issues separately, it will become clear that they are intimately related to each other: we cannot discover whether a particular string of utterances forms a "well-formed" sequence of acts unless we are reasonably certain of what actions those utterances are performing. Thus, despite the difficulty of making secure judgements about utterance–action correlations, this initial step is critical to the second issue with which we will be concerned, and ultimately, with the application of speech act theory to discourse. Put another way, identifying the speech act performed by an utterance is critical to the application of speech act theory to discourse: we need to know the units of a discourse before we can seek to discover, and explain, the principles responsible for their arrangements, i.e. the reason why some sequences seem coherent, but others do not.[2]

3.1 Identifying utterances as speech acts

In this section, I show how Henry's *Y'want a piece of candy?* can be identified as a question (3.1.1), a request (3.1.2), and an offer (3.1.3); a key part of my analysis is that these three acts are themselves intertwined (3.1.4).

Before we begin, note that we will be focusing on the *process* of identifying utterances as sequences of speech acts: I try to show the sorts of issues and problems with which a researcher might have to deal while doing a speech act analysis of discourse. Although this might seem laborious at times, it is important for two reasons. First, analyzing the process by which people identify speech acts is a critical part of speech act theory: thus, although uncovering bits and pieces of our knowledge (some of which might seem to be just "common sense") is tedious, this is exactly what speech act theory is concerned with.

Second, the way analysts try to resolve methodological problems stemming from analysis of this process forms a key part of the speech act approach to discourse analysis.

3.1.1 *"Y'want a piece of candy?" as a question*

We noted above that speech act theory defines underlying conditions (including considerations of speaker intent, desired outcome, and so on) that must hold for an utterance to be used to realize a particular speech act. These rules – and the felicity conditions they create – often require consideration of both what is said (its form, its meaning, how information is presented) and the context in which it is said. For example, since a promise is an obligation to undertake a future act that the hearer is assumed to want, one cannot enact a promise using a past tense verb; nor can that future act be one deemed harmful to the recipient – and this is a matter of social and personal value.

To identify *y'want a piece of candy?* as a question, we need to consider how particular conditions are both linguistically met and contextually satisfied. We begin with Searle's (1969: 66) rules for questions, and then consider how we might argue that Henry's particular utterance realizes those rules. Here are Searle's rules:

QUESTION

Types of rules

Propositional content	Any proposition or propositional function
Preparatory	(a) S does not know "the answer," i.e. does not know if the proposition is true, or, in the case of the propositional function, does not know the information needed to complete the proposition truly
	(b) It is not obvious to both S and H that H will provide the information at that time without being asked
Sincerity	S wants this information
Essential	Counts as an attempt to elicit this information from H

The rules above show that a question is constituted under the following conditions: the speaker lacks knowledge of a particular state of affairs (preparatory rule) and wants to gain that knowledge (sincerity rule) by eliciting information from the hearer (essential rule). We will go through these rules in more detail to see if *Y'want a piece of candy?* counts as a question.

Consider, first, that it would be helpful if *Y'want a piece of candy?* could be considered a reduced form of an interrogative: interrogative sentences are well suited to the function of questions. Because interrogatives are incomplete propositions, they fulfill Searle's first preparatory rule (the speaker lacks knowledge as to how to complete a proposition). The first preparatory rule also specifies two possible gaps in S's knowledge: S can lack either knowledge of the truth of a proposition or information needed to complete a true proposition. These two sources of propositional incompleteness parallel the syntactic and semantic difference between closed and open questions. Closed questions are those in which the subject noun phrase and verb auxiliary are inverted (e.g. *Does Andy want to go?*, *Is Betty there?*). Closed questions are propositionally incomplete due to a lack of knowledge as to whether a proposition is true (we don't know if "Andy wants to go" is true or not). What provides their completion is drawn from a closed set of options (e.g. *yes* or *no*) that fixes a positive or negative polarity, or allows an inference of confirmation or disconfirmation. Open questions also have subject/auxiliary inversion, but are initiated with a WH word (*who, what, when, which, how, where, why*) that specifies the source of their incompleteness. A question such as *who was there?*, for example, presents a proposition whose argument is not specified. Open questions are incomplete because the speaker lacks information sufficient for completion of a true proposition; in contrast to closed questions, their completion is relatively open-ended.

The form–function correlation between interrogative sentences and Searle's preparatory rule often leads to the view that interrogatives are the unmarked syntax for question asking (e.g. Geis 1989). This is important for our purposes: if *Y'want a piece of candy?* is an interrogative, it would then be fairly easy to say that it fulfills the preparatory rule for questions. Unfortunately, we cannot be sure that *Y'want a piece of candy?* is an interrogative. Although it may very well be a reduction of *Do you want a piece of candy?* (and thus an incomplete proposition), its surface syntactic form is a declarative sentence – a complete proposition that seems not to fit the preparatory condition of questions at all.

Note, however, that I have transcribed *Y'want a piece of candy?* with a question mark: this reflects its final rising intonation. In prior work (Schiffrin 1987a), I followed the practice of many scholars (e.g. Quirk et al. 1972: 386; Stenstrom 1984) and identified declarative sentences with final rises as questions. (See also Selting (1992), who argues that prosody is one system of constitutive cues for questions – sometimes the only distinctive cue.) Still other scholars have identified sentence fragments as questions even when a fuller interrogative form of those fragments is not unequivocally recoverable. Merritt (1976), for example, identifies the elliptical *Coffee to go?* and *Cream and sugar?* as questions, even though they are not clear reductions of any single fuller form (i.e. they can be expanded into a number of different interrogatives, e.g. *Do you have/can I buy coffee to go?*). Instead of depending on syntax as criterial for questionhood, such analyses seem to place more weight on final rising intonation.

Research on intonation suggests that final rising intonation may very well be an illocutionary force indicating device for some kinds of questions. Bolinger (1982), for example, suggests that final rises convey incompleteness (the first preparatory rule). Others suggest that final rises convey uncertainty in domains other than propositional knowledge, e.g. uncertainty about listener comprehension (Guy et al. 1986) or adequacy of a contribution to conversation (Lakoff 1975). Still others (e.g. Brown et al. 1980; Stenstrom 1984) suggest that final rises demand a response (the essential rule). Thus, some of the meanings that have been associated with final rises are compatible with the rules underlying questions.

Here I present some examples that support the idea that final rising intonation is an indicator of questions (cf. Geluykens 1988, 1989). All the examples suggest that final rises convey uncertainty (not propositional incompleteness) that may be interactionally motivated (e.g. by a prior question from H) and/or resolved (e.g. by an implicit or explicit acknowledgment from H). First is one of Guy et al.'s (1986) examples, along with a parallel interchange from one of my own sociolinguistic interviews:

(2) INTERVIEWER/H: (a) What's your name?
     INFORMANT/S: (b) Maria Martinetti?
(3) IRENE/H: (a) What's your name.
     DEBBY/S: (b) Debby Schiffrin?

In (2), the interviewer asks for the informant's name; in (3), these identities are reversed. S is the person upon whose utterance (2b, 3b) we are focusing; H is the person asking a prior question (*What's your name?*) and receiving the information that he has sought and that is being provided by S.

(2) and (3) both illustrate several important points about final rising intonation as an illocutionary force indicating device. Because final rises are used in these examples with information about which S does know (i.e. S's own name), the utterances *Maria Martinetti?* and *Debby Schiffrin?* do not seem like questions, i.e. they violate the preparatory rule of questions that S not know "the answer." However, there is uncertainty in this exchange – in fact, two sources of uncertainty. First, H does not know S's name: it is this uncertainty to which the propositional content of S's response is addressed. Second, although the propositional content of *Maria Martinetti?* and *Debby Schiffrin?* provides an answer to *What's your name?*, S cannot be certain how this information will be taken. In other words, it is not propositional content *per se* about which S is uncertain, but the adequacy of propositional content for H's needs (cf. the gloss "Is that what you meant?") or the adequacy of H's reception of the information (cf. the gloss "Did you get that?"). Note, finally, that S's response opens a third part of the exchange: it is up to H to let S know whether S's information is adequate for H's needs, i.e. to resolve S's uncertainty about the sufficiency of the response (Guy et al. 1986: 26). Thus, (2) and (3) suggest that intonation can serve as an illocutionary force indicat-

ing device based on the role of an utterance in an exchange – a role that supplements the contribution of propositional content to communicative function.[3]

The proposed function of the final rises in (2) and (3) can be related quite easily to the conditions underlying questions. We can restate what I just suggested above in terms of the rules for questions: S wants information about H's reception of information (the sincerity rule) that S does not have (the preparatory rule) and that S is attempting to elicit from H (the essential rule). Before returning to *Y'want a piece of candy?*, let me present several other examples also suggesting that final rising intonation can evoke the constitutive rules of questions.

(4) is from the opening portion of a phone call.

(4) Phone rings.
    CALLED: (a) Hello?
    CALLER: (b) Yeh, hi. This is Debby, David's mother?
    CALLED: (c) Oh hi . . . how are you . . .

Final rising intonation on *Hello?* (a) is suited to its dual function as answer to the summons provided by the phone ring, and, question as to who is on the other end of the line (Schegloff 1972). Similarly, final rising intonation with caller self-identification (*David's mother?* (b)) suggests its dual function as answer to the prior *Hello?* and attempt to elicit recognition of the self-identification. (Note that *David's mother?* follows a preliminary self-identification *Debby,* to which Called did not respond).

(5) is an example from a phone call in which I am providing my social security number to an insurance company agent. (Social security numbers are orthographically and conventionally, even when presented orally, broken up into three segments.)

(5) DEBBY: One two four?
    AGENT: Um.
    DEBBY: Three two?
    AGENT: Okay.
    DEBBY: Nine four six six.

In (5), I segment the sections of the number sequence and show by final rises on the first two segments that they are preliminary to completion of the full sequence. Prior to my continuation of the next segment, the recipient acknowledges receipt of each intermediate segment; the last segment has falling intonation.

A final example is (6):

(6) ZELDA: (a) The following year, his son, who ha- was eighteen years old just graduating from high school.

> (b)   Was walking through the em . . . the fountain, Logan Square
>   Library?
> (c)   Y'know that fountain?
> DEBBY: (d)   Yeh.
> ZELDA: (e)   Bare footed, and stepped on a- a bare wire.

In (6), Zelda is telling me a story about her neighborhood doctor (Schiffrin 1988b) and is fixing a location important to a key event in the story: she presents that identificatory information in (b) and (c) with final rising intonation to elicit my recognition of those locations prior to continuing her story.

Although some of the specific meanings of final rises in these examples differ, what they share is the following: S elicits from H a response concerning something (a referent, a proposition) that S has put forth in response to an inferred (or actual) "uncertainty" from H; S then pursues some other goal or activity that had been dependent upon H's receipt of the information put forth by S. Note that when expressed in these terms, the function of final rises comes very close to fulfilling the sincerity, preparatory, and essential conditions of questions. Final rising intonation marks S's uncertainty about how information provided to H will be taken: what S is questioning is not propositional content *per se*, but the adequacy of propositional content for H's needs. Thus, what S wants is information about H's reception of information (the sincerity rule) that S does not have (the preparatory rule) and that S is attempting to elicit from H (the essential rule).[4]

Let us return now to *Y'want a piece of candy?* I have just suggested that the intonation of this utterance realizes the preparatory, sincerity, and essential rules of questions. The propositional content of *Y'want a piece of candy?* also helps realize these same conditions: in speech act terms, we may say that both are illocutionary force indicating devices. Consider, also, the meaning of the verb *want*. Since verbs like *want* (*like*, *feel*) describe a state internal to the person of whom that state is predicated, being in a state of "wanting" cannot be verified by an examination of external evidence and cannot be something about which another person is certain. Furthermore, since a state like "wanting" is inherently subjective (and thus "knowable" only by its experiencer), assertions about that state are something to which its experiencer should respond. When S questions H's wants, then, it is up to H to either confirm or disconfirm the accuracy of those wants (cf. Labov and Fanshel 1977). Thus, *Y'want a piece of candy?* conveys S's lack of information (the first preparatory rule) and counts as an attempt to get H to provide that information (essential rule).

Note that we have moved from a discussion of S's uncertainty to ways to resolve that uncertainty. Once we begin to talk about H's responsibility to provide information to S, we have moved from the preparatory rule to the essential rule of questions – arguing, in effect, that *Y'want a piece of candy?* counts as S's attempt to elicit information from H. Thus, an expression of uncertainty *per se* does not tell us that *Y'want a piece of candy?* counts as an attempt to elicit information from H: people often express uncertainty about a state of affairs without trying to elicit information from another that will resolve that uncertainty. Rather, it is because it is up to H to confirm (or disconfirm) what S has said about her that *Y'want a piece of candy?* realizes both the first preparatory and the essential rules of questions.

We began our analysis of *Y'want a piece of candy?* by noting that we cannot be sure that this utterance is a reduced form of an interrogative sentence – an important consideration since it would be that form (an incomplete proposition) that would most easily allow us to argue that this utterance conveys lack of speaker knowledge. We then focused on other linguistic qualities of *Y'want a piece of candy?* – intonation, meaning – that seemed to converge as indicators of the same underlying rules. We argued that the final rising intonation of this utterance could be considered an expression of lack of speaker knowledge; this interpretation fit with the inherent uncertainty of predicating another's wants. We also argued that final rising intonation conveyed the speaker's desire to resolve uncertainty by appeal to the hearer; this interpretation fit with the essential rule for questions. Thus, our consideration of the linguistic qualities of *Y'want a piece of candy?* has ended up showing that Henry's utterance realizes one of the preparatory rules of a question (S does not know "the answer"), the sincerity rule (S wants this information), and the essential rule (it counts as an attempt to elicit this information from H).

One preparatory rule has not yet been considered: it is not obvious to both S and H that H will provide the information at that time without being asked (Searle 1969: 66). We really have no way of knowing for sure that Irene would *not* tell Henry that she wants a piece of candy if Henry did not ask her about this. We can guess that Irene might not tell Henry directly that she wants candy: she might not say *I want candy* simply because of the asymmetrical status or intimacy that such a statement implies. But we cannot be sure that Irene would not request that Henry give her candy ("Can I have a piece?") or hint that she would like candy ("That looks good"). Thus, all we can say is that *Y'want a piece of candy?* conveys Henry's desire (the sincerity condition, see below) that Irene provide information that she might not otherwise provide (the second preparatory condition).

Finally, we could also construct contextual arguments for the fulfillment of the felicity conditions. Recall that the sincerity condition underlying questions is that S wants this information (Searle 1969: 66). There are social and interactional reasons for arguing that Henry wants this information. First, it is considered impolite to eat candy without finding out if others also want some: candy is considered "a treat" in many middle-class American households that should be shared with others. Second, Henry and Irene are good friends who (despite open forms of competition: Schiffrin 1984a) build on each other's sense of well-being by not offending one another (e.g. not criticizing too harshly: Schiffrin 1985b), and by defending one another. Such a relationship is built upon a continued display of sensitivity to what the other wants and needs; thus, it is in the long-term interest of their relationship for Henry to continue to find out what Irene wants – in this case, whether she wants candy that he is eating.[5]

We have now examined Henry's *Y'want a piece of candy?* from several directions, and found linguistic clues that support our identification of this utterance as a question. Thus, we have relied primarily upon *how* something was said as a clue to the sincerity, preparatory, and essential conditions underlying questions.

3.1.2 *"Y'want a piece of candy?" as a request for information*

In addition to identifying *Y'want a piece of candy?* as a question, we might also identify it as a directive, specifically a request for information. Before we do so, however, it is important to note that requests and questions have a long and complicated relationship in speech act theory. Focusing first on their differences, note that *directives* (the larger speech act type of which requests are a subtype) differ from questions in an important formal way: the syntactic structure assumed to most directly manifest a directive is the imperative (e.g. *Come here*) whereas the basic syntactic structure for questions is assumed to be the interrogative. This form–function correlate, however, is not absolute. We saw in section 2.4 that many speech acts are performed by way of sentence structures other than those assumed to provide their most direct form: either declaratives (e.g. *I need water*) or interrogatives (e.g. *Can you pass the salt?*), for example, can be used with an intended directive force.[6] The problematic relationship between questions and requests is illustrated by the fact that one of the key puzzles in analysis of requests like *Can you pass the salt?* is how they are understood: does interpreting *Can you pass the salt?* as a request for salt require prior inference from an understanding of its linguistic meaning as a question about ability (2.4) or is it so conventionally used as a request that its interpretation bypasses identifying (and understanding) it as a question (Morgan 1975).

Many studies of directives have also shown that they are typically performed indirectly. Scholars often allow directness to be indicated not just by unmarked syntax (interrogatives for questions, imperatives for directives, declaratives for assertives), but also by the use of performative verbs. Given the latter criterion, it is quite clear that some directives do have a direct form: one can say *I request that you arrive by 9:00*, *I order you to pay your taxes*, *I warn you to stay away from there*. Regardless of which criteria of directness we apply, however, directives are realized as imperatives and through performative verbs only under fairly limited conditions, e.g. intimacy and/or expediency for the former (Brown and Levinson 1987; Ervin-Tripp 1976) in relatively formal, institutional, written modes of communication for the latter (Pufahl 1988). Thus, requests are typically performed in a number of very different (but also quite regular) ways (Ervin-Tripp 1976; Gordon and Lakoff 1975; Pufahl 1988; Searle 1975).

Let us now return to *Y'want a piece of candy?* to see how this question can also be a request. Again, let us start with Searle's (1969: 66) felicity conditions:

REQUEST

Type of rule

Propositional content	Future act A of H
Preparatory	(a) H is able to do A. S believes H is able to do A. (b) It is not obvious to both S and H that H will do A in the normal course of events of his own accord.
Sincerity	S wants H to do A.
Essential	Counts as an attempt to get H to do A.

The rules for requests should seem familiar: they are very similar to the rules for questions. Requests and questions share some of the same conditions:

Preparatory
    It is not obvious to both S and H that H will:

| do A in the normal course of events of his own accord
[request] | provide the information at that time without being asked
[question] |

Sincerity
    S wants:

| H to do A
[request] | this information
[question] |

Essential
    Counts as an attempt to:

| get H to do A
[request] | elicit this information from H
[question] |

This comparison shows that the preparatory, sincerity, and essential conditions for questions and requests are similar: since it is not obvious that H will provide information without being asked (preparatory condition for questions), or that H will do A in the normal course of events of her own accord (preparatory condition of requests), both questions and requests count as attempts to get H to do something (their essential conditions) that S wants (their sincerity conditions). The difference between questions and requests is that what a speaker wants through a question ("elicit information") is more specific than what a speaker wants through a request ("do A"). But what this suggests is that questions are one specific type of request: questions are attempts to get a hearer to do a certain A – to provide information (Searle 1969: 69). It is the provision of information that is the future act of H (the propositional content condition of the request). By fulfilling the conditions for a question, then, *Y'want a piece of candy?* fulfills the condition for a particular type of request.

In sum, we have seen in this section that *Y'want a piece of candy?* is both a question and a request. It enacts a request for Irene to undertake a particular verbal action, i.e. to provide information about whether she does or does not want candy. This is a future act (the propositional content condition) that will resolve Henry's uncertainty about what Irene wants (the preparatory condition for questions). We see in the next section that *Y'want a piece of candy?* has still another speech act identity: it is an offer.

3.1.3 *"Y'want a piece of candy?" as an offer*

Although I spent a great deal of time arguing that *Y'want a piece of candy?* is a question (3.1.1) and a request for information (3.1.2), I continue our sample analysis by proposing that it can also be identified as an *offer*, i.e. Henry is using the utterance to make something available to Irene.[7] In some ways this seems to be the action that is most conventionally identified with *Y'want a piece of candy?* Finding the speech act labels that people would typically use to categorize the illocutionary force of an utterance is important. Speech act analysts assume that interlocutors agree on the speech act performed by a particular utterance: this intersubjective agreement is a prerequisite to communication that is assumed to proceed through the reciprocal processes of producing and interpreting speech acts (Taylor and Cameron 1987: chapter 3; see chapter 11 of this book). Put most simply, it is by finding the "unit" into which an act fits – the unit intended by S – that H can present a next act.

But if "offer" seems to be the speech act most conventionally associated with *Y'want a piece of candy?*, why have we spent so much time showing that this utterance could be a question and a request? Here I propose that the function of *Y'want a piece of candy?* as an offer is intricately tied to its functions as question and request – such that we needed to understand this utterance as both question and request before we could understand it as offer. The relationship between question/request and offer also illustrates the application of important aspects of speech act theory to discourse: both the principles by which speech acts are classified (2.3), and the view that utterances are multifunctional because of relationships between their underlying conditions (2.4), can be incorporated into speech act applications to discourse. Finally, analyzing the multifunctionality of utterances helps to reveal the different response options made available by an utterance, and thus the possibility of underlying sequences bound by different functional relationships.

Before we begin, it is important to note a general difference between directives (the larger class of speech acts encompassing requests) and commissives (the larger class of speech acts encompassing offers): directives are attempts by S to have H do A; commissives are commitments from S to do A for H. Many utterances are requests but not offers: if I ask you to pass the salt, I have not committed myself to any action beyond using the salt in some way. But the asymmetry in who does what for whom that divides requests from offers can also disappear, such that many acts are simultaneously offers and requests (cf. Wierzbicka 1987: 190–7). Take, for example, the speech act "invitation." Although Searle (1979: 11) and Leech (1983: 217) view invitations as directives, they may also be analyzed as both offer and request: if I invite you to a party at my house, I am simultaneously offering you access to an event of which I am a sponsor and requesting access to your company at a future time (cf. Schiffrin 1981b: 239–40). Note, also, that Searle (1979: 11–12) assigns the same direction of fit (world-to-words) to both commissives and directives, noting that classifying speech acts would be simpler if they were really members of the same category (e.g. promises could be requests to oneself). (See also Leech's (1983: 206) suggestion that directives and commissives be merged into a "superclass.")[8]

We begin our analysis of *Y'want a piece of candy?* as an offer by noting the general conditions underlying commissives. Searle (1979: 11) defines commissives as "illocutionary acts whose point is to commit the speaker (. . . in varying degrees) to some future course of action." Commissives differ among themselves in terms of S's degree of commitment. When making a promise, for example, S undertakes an obligation to perform A in the future (essential condition); S also believes that H would prefer A being done to A not being done (preparatory condition; Searle 1962). When making an offer, however, the essential and preparatory conditions of promises do not hold. Furthermore, the reason the essential condition does not hold is because the preparatory condition does not hold.

The chart below reformulates the difference between promises and offers in terms of knowledge (as reflected in preparatory conditions) and commitment (as reflected in essential conditions):

Promise	Stage 1	Stage 2	Stage 3	Stage 4
Knowledge [preparatory]	S knows H wants A	⟶		
Commitment [essential]	S commits to do A	⟶		
Offer				
Knowledge [preparatory]	S does not know if H wants A	S finds out if H wants A	S knows H wants A	
Commitment [essential]				S commits to do A

This suggests that a key difference between an offer and a promise is the knowledge that S has about what H wants (the preparatory condition noted above). It also suggests that reducing S's uncertainty about H's wants can alter S's commitment to do A. Recall that uncertainty is a preparatory condition for questions and requests: thus, we might very well expect S to ask a question to find out what H wants before committing herself to do A. This is what I suggest at stage 2: S finds out if H wants A by requesting information from H. Given affirmation that H does want A, S's uncertainty is then reduced (stage 3) and S commits to do A (stage 4). This view of the difference between promises and offers allows us to see that questions (i.e. requests for information) can play a critical role in offers: they reduce uncertainty about whether H wants A, thus, potentially leading to a commitment to do A.

The relationship can be summarized in slightly different terms:

Act 1:   "S give H candy"
Offer   S intends act 1
Question   S does not know if H wants act 1
So Request   S wants H to do act 2: tell S if H wants act 1

This analysis suggests that we may paraphrase *Y'want a piece of candy?* as "I intend to give you candy if you want it." Note the important role of the conditional in the paraphrase: it is because S does not know if H wants candy (a preparatory condition of questions) that S wants H to tell S if H wants candy (a preparatory condition of requests). Once this uncertainty is reduced – with an answer to a question – S can undertake a commitment to do A for H. Thus, asking a question about the preparatory condition for promises (H prefers A to not A) can lead S to undertake an obligation to do A. We see in a moment that this relationship is reflected in the way people make offers.

The relationship between offers and requests described above suggests that people can make offers either with two separate utterances or with one utterance. The two-utterance possibility would occur if S were to elicit some go-ahead (e.g. approval, endorsement, confirmation) from H about the bene-fits of A for H, prior to committing to do A for H. Thus, the interchange in (a) and (b) of the hypothetical (7) could precede the offer in (c):

(7) CLIFF: (a)   Do you want help?
     DIANE: (b)   Yes.
     CLIFF: (c)   Well, here, let me help you then.

It seems, however, that speakers usually do not try to explicitly gain confir-mation that H wants A prior to offering A. The reason is what I have been hinting at above: questions can act as offers when they question (i.e. request information about) a preparatory condition of promises (H would prefer S's doing A to his not doing A and S believes this).

In order to see how the one-utterance possibility for offers works, we need to note yet another connection among the conditions underlying different speech acts. The preparatory condition of promises noted above (to simplify:

S believes that H wants A) has an interesting similarity with the sincerity condition of requests (S wants H to do A) and an important effect on indirect speech acts. Observe, first, Searle's (1975: 65, 72) suggestion that S can issue an indirect directive by stating that the sincerity condition obtains. This strategy accounts for the use of statements such as those in (8) to make requests:

(8) (a) I would like you to go now.
     (b) I want you to do this for me.
     (c) I'd rather you didn't do that anymore.
     (d) I wish you wouldn't do that.

Each of the utterances in (8) uses a verb that states (and thus fulfills) the sincerity condition for requests, i.e. S wants H to do A. Although a question about whether the sincerity condition obtains cannot issue a request, it is just such a question that can issue what we have been calling offers – just so long as we switch the role of subject and object. (9), for example, contains counterparts to (8) that I believe we would interpret as offers:

(9) (a) Would you like me to go now?
     (b) Do you want me to do this for you?
     (c) Would you rather I didn't do that anymore?
     (d) Do you wish I wouldn't do that?

The syntactic reversal between statement-based requests (in 8), and question-based offers (in 9), reflects the different roles played by S and H in relation to A – whether it is S or H who wants A. That is, what changes is our assumption about for whose benefit A is intended and who it is that wants A: the request seems to benefit S and the offer seems to benefit H. Note that this is entirely consistent with the different conditions underlying requests and promises. Whereas the sincerity condition of requests is that S wants H to do A, a preparatory condition of promises is that H would prefer (cf. want) S's doing A to his not doing A and that S believes this. Thus, stating that S would like A is a request because it states a speaker-based sincerity condition of requests; asking if H would like A is an offer because it questions a preparatory condition of promises. As we saw in the chart on page 73, the establishment of this preparatory condition (S's reduced uncertainty about H's wants) paves the way for S to undertake an obligation to do A.

Returning now to Henry's *Y'want a piece of candy?*, we see that this utterance is exactly parallel to the hypothetical "do you want X?" (8b). Not only does it question whether H wants A, but (as we see in a minute) it can receive a response appropriate to either a request for information or an offer. Multiple response possibilities provide important evidence in speech act theory: the availability of more than one response type shows that a single utterance performs more than one speech act. That one can respond to *Do you have the time?* by saying either *Yes, ten o'clock*, or just *Ten o'clock*, for example, indicates its potential understandings as either question or request (Clark 1979) (section 3.2 discusses the sequential effects of multifunctionality).[9] (10a) and (10b) show two different responses to *Y'want a piece of candy?*

(10a) S: Y'want a piece of candy?
       H: Oh yes.
       S: Here it is.
       H: [takes it] Thanks.
(10b) S: Y'want a piece of candy?
       H: [takes it] Thanks.

(10a) and (10b) illustrate that a respondent to *Y'want a piece of candy?* may choose between two alternative courses of action. The response in (10a) depends upon the literal meaning of *Y'want a piece of candy?* as a question (and request); the response in (10b) depends upon its primary (indirect) use as an offer. These two possibilities highlight the multiple speech act identities of *Y'want a piece of candy?*

In this section, we have seen that offers are commissives: S proposes a future A for H; S's uncertainty as to whether H wants A reduces S's obligation to do A. Although one way for S to resolve uncertainty is through a sequentially prior question that asks whether H wants A, it is also possible for S's question itself to act as an offer if the propositional content of the question focuses on the preparatory condition of a promise. Put another way, an offer can be a "primary" speech act (2.4) performed by way of a question (the "literal" speech act (2.4)) about H's desire for A; it is this question that allows S to find out whether A is what H wants before undertaking an obligation to do A.[10] Thus, when Henry says *Y'want a piece of candy?*, he is indeed making an offer to give Irene candy. However, his offer simultaneously questions Irene, requesting that Irene tell him whether she wants the candy.

3.2 Identifying speech act sequences

Built into the felicity conditions of questions, requests, and offers is a need for hearer response. Recall, for example, the essential condition of questions (an utterance counts as S's attempt to elicit information wanted from H) and requests (an utterance counts as an attempt to get H to do A). Similarly, offers require H to indicate interest in what A has conveyed a willingness to do. What this need for response suggests is that an analysis of a single utterance as a question, request, or offer leads naturally to an analysis of the utterance(s) that follow. Consistent with the notion that utterances perform speech acts, an analysis of succeeding utterances becomes an analysis of speech act sequences. As noted by Taylor and Cameron (1987: 58), however, "the question of how illocutionary acts are sequenced in actual episodes of connected speech is not one that looms large in the lives of philosophers. . . . For the analyst working with natural data, however, it is an issue on a par with that of classification/identification." Thus, although the identification of speech acts *per se* is central to the discourse application of speech act theory, and to speech act theory itself, the combination of speech acts into well-formed sequences is important only to discourse analysis.

Despite the sequential focus of this section, I begin again with the problem of identifying units, this time the second unit in a sequence. We see almost immediately that the "identification" issue differs dramatically for a unit in "second place," simply because the unit in "first place" provides information central to the identification of the next unit. We have just seen that *Y'want a piece of candy?* can be analyzed as three different speech acts: question, request, offer. This suggests that what follows *Y'want a piece of candy?* can also be classified in more than one way, such that the act performed in response to an offer is as multilevelled as the offer itself. I consider three responses: Irene's *No* (3.2.1), Zelda's *She's on a diet* (3.2.2), and Irene's story about her diet (3.2.3).[11]

3.2.1 Irene's "No": answer, compliance, and rejection

We saw above that Irene says *No* immediately after Henry's *Y'want a piece of candy?* It is relatively easy to identify *No* as an answer: although it is elliptical, we (as hearers and as analysts) rely on the content of the prior question to expand *No* and to understand that it provides the polarity left open by that question, thereby semantically completing the proposition. In addition to answering Henry's question, Irene's *No* also complies with Henry's request for information: Irene provides the information that she does not want candy. Finally, Irene's *No* also responds to Henry's offer of candy: she does not accept (she rejects) the offer of candy.[12]

Note, now, that the sequential consequences of our analysis would differ tremendously if we analyzed Irene's *No* only as an answer. The main difference is that question–answer sequences are structurally complete after the provision of their second part: despite the addition of other relevant material, e.g. an explanation for a negative answer, such material is not necessary for the sequence and the sequence is coherent on its own. If we analyze the sequence as having an initial request or offer, however, it is a little more difficult to argue for structural completion. Although *No* does comply with a request for information, either a positive or negative response alone seems incomplete. If Irene had said *Yes*, for example, she might then be expected either to wait for Henry to explicitly offer her candy, or to actually take the candy. And the *No* response seems to call either for a conventional marker of politeness (e.g. *no thanks*) or an explanation.

But why should Irene's *No* – which does supply the requested information and does respond to the offer – create a third slot in the sequence? Although many linguistically oriented speech act analysts have proposed answers to this question (e.g. Davison 1975; Green 1975), a more thorough account comes from more socially oriented analyses of politeness (discussed in chapter 4). We now go on to see what else actually does follow Irene's *No*.

3.2.2   Zelda's *"She's on a diet"*: expansion and account

After Irene says *No* to Henry's *Y'want a piece of candy?*, Zelda says *She's on a diet*.

(1)   HENRY: (a)   Y'want a piece of candy?
      IRENE: (b)   No.
      ZELDA: (c)   ^zShe's on a diet.

Our discussion of Zelda's remark will raise two sets of questions critical to applications of speech act theory to discourse analysis. First, what is the range of acts that can be performed through speech? Put another way, what is the overall inventory of acts for which utterances can be used and onto which utterances can be mapped? Questions such as these go to the very heart of speech act theory – for some of the acts that we discuss in this section are not those that would ordinarily be included in an orthodox speech act taxonomy that focused solely on those acts whose illocutionary force might be indicated by performative verbs (2.3). Rather, these are acts that are sequentially emergent: they arise only in relation to another prior act. The second set of questions concerns exhaustiveness: is everything that is said a realization of a speech act in a well-formed sequence? In other words, do we have to pack every utterance into a speech act that has a sequential relationship with other speech acts? This set of questions is also central to speech act theory: the assumption that the speech act is the basic unit of linguistic communication (2.2) leaves little room for communication by way of utterances that are not speech acts.

Here I will propose two different speech act identities of *She's on a diet* – the first more challenging to speech act theory than the second. Consider, first, the possibility that *She's on a diet* is an *expansion*: a sequentially dependent unit which adds information supplementary to a prior unit. Calling *She's on a diet* an expansion seems to capture the way that Zelda's remark develops, adds to, or follows up on (Coulthard et al. 1981) what Irene has said. But giving such a unit a place in a speech act sequence raises several concerns. Expansions are totally dependent on prior units, such that it would be difficult to state the rules for expansions independent of sequentially prior speech acts. Expansions are difficult to differentiate from other units in other ways: not only are there no clear criteria by which to identify them, but they do not meet Searle's necessary and sufficient conditions for a speech act.

Let me more fully explain these problems through some examples. Consider, first, that expansions need not be tied to answers: they may be expansions of virtually any other unit in a structure. Also in (1), for example, is a section where Henry repeats a question:

(q)   Was there a lot of people?
(t)   Was there a lot of people at the house?

Another way of looking at (t), however, would be to say that the addition of *at the house* to the initial question in (q) makes the question in (t) an expansion of the question in (q). But does this then mean that *all* additions are expansions? Does it also mean that *only* additions are expansions?

 (11) suggests that additions are neither necessary nor sufficient criteria for counting a remark as an expansion. (11) is also from one of my interviews.

(11)   DEBBY: (a)   Do you think there's much prejudice between like other
                              groups-
                    (b)   Other ethnic groups?
                    (c)   Other nationalities?

There are two changes in (11) that we might call expansions. First, if we view the change from *other groups* (a) to *other ethnic groups* (b) as an addition (simply because I have added *ethnic*), then we might call *other ethnic groups* an expansion. However, the change from (a) to (b) is the sort of addition often described as a self-repair (e.g. Schegloff et al. 1977). When a speaker repairs a word or expression, it is usually assumed that what is received by a listener as the message is the *replacement* itself (e.g. *other ethnic groups*), not the repairable (e.g. *other groups*) plus an addition (e.g. *ethnic*). But if it is only the repair that contributes to the message, we would probably not want to call *other ethnic groups* an expansion; instead, we might want to call it a replacement or even just a continuation (or completion) of the same prior unit (see e.g. Polanyi 1988). Thus, what the change from (a) to (b) suggests is that not all additions of lexical information are expansions.

 The second change to consider is from *other ethnic groups* (b) to *other nationalities* (c): this suggests that just as additions are not sufficient criteria for expansions, nor are they necessary criteria. "Nationalities" does not add lexical information to "ethnic groups"; nor does it supplement the semantic meaning of "ethnic groups."[13] But note how I intended this change: I was trying to clarify what I meant by *ethnic group*. Couldn't we therefore call the change from *other ethnic groups* to *other nationalities* an expansion of my meaning, i.e. an expansion of what I intended to convey?

 These examples have illustrated several problems. First, at a very general level, we can identify many different utterances as expansions – expansions of answers, expansions of questions – and see them all as having the same role. On a more particular level of analysis, however, this would be very misleading. The specific identity of an utterance as an expansion *of something* is intimately tied to the identity of that of which it is an expansion: a question expansion is thus as different from an answer expansion as a question is from an answer. Second is a methodological repercussion of allowing some units to be so dependent on, and non-autonomous from, what precedes them: our analysis of a single discourse unit rests critically on our analysis of its precursors in the text. Thus, if we are wrong in analyzing the status of an initial utterance, we cannot help but be wrong in analyzing the status of subsequent utterances. And our opportunities for being wrong thus multiply with each succeeding utterance.

Now that we have considered some problems with identifying *She's on a diet* as an expansion of an answer, let us turn to its possible function as an account – as an explanation for Irene's rejection of Henry's offer. Like expansions, accounts are relational: they provide reasons and/or motivations for some prior action that has been considered marked (e.g. inappropriate, impolite, insulting) in some way (Scott and Lyman 1968). Because they provide explanations, accounts are causally linked to prior actions, as if the person is saying "I did X because of Y." Zelda's *She's on a diet* acts as an account for a very simple reason. Our knowledge about candy and diets tells us that being on a diet provides a reason for not accepting candy: candy is fattening and diets don't allow fattening food; therefore, being on a diet is a reason for not accepting candy. Note, also, that the concept of "diet" is nicely fit to the content of Henry's asking about what Irene "wants": diets require people to forgo their more immediate "wants" (fattening food like candy) for the sake of their more long-term "wants" (losing weight).

To conclude: we can describe the sequential structure of (1) in two different ways: as a two-part sequence of S-question/H-answer with H's optional answer expansion, or we can see it as a three-part sequence of S-offer/H-rejection/H-account. Thus, our identification of *Y'want a piece of candy?* as multifunctional (question, request, offer) can lead us to see sequential completion after either a second act or a third act. In the next section, we show how Irene's *I'm on a diet* story provides another account.

3.2.3 Irene's "I'm on a diet" story: expansion and account

Although Zelda accounts for Irene's refusal of Henry's offer of candy, Irene also provides her own account, first by saying *I'm on a diet* in (e), and then by telling a story (e to u) about her diet:

IRENE:	(e)	=I'm on a diet
	(f)	and my mother ⌈buys-= ⌉
ZELDA:	(g)	⌊You're⌋ not!
IRENE:	(h)	=my⌈mother buys these⌉mints.=
DEBBY:	(i)	⌊Oh yes I am⌋hhhh!
ZELDA:	(j)	Oh yeh.
IRENE:	(k)	The Russell Stouffer mints.

```
          (l)   I said, "I don't want any Mom."
          (m)   "Well, I don't wanna eat the whole thing."
          (n)   She gives me a little tiny piece,
          (o)   I eat it.
          (p)   Then she gives me an other,=
HENRY:    (q)                       [Was  =
IRENE:    (r)   =so I threw it out the window=
HENRY:          =there a lot of people?=
IRENE:    (s)   =I didn't  tell her.   =
HENRY:    (t)            [Was there=   ]
IRENE:    (u)   =She'd kill me.
```

As I noted above, it is not merely saying *I'm on a diet* that provides an account, but Irene's entire story about her diet. Treating a story as a speech act raises important issues for the application of speech act theory to discourse – since it implies that an entire discourse unit can perform a speech act. (I consider consequences of this shift in unit size in section 3.3.) We will proceed by examining the content of Irene's story as a sequence of speech acts within the story world; we will also pay attention to how the story is linguistically tailored to the conversational world, i.e. as an account for the rejection of an offer.

Consider, first, how Irene opens her story:

I'm on a diet
and my mother buys- my mother buys these mints.
The Russell Stouffer mints.

The clause *my mother buys these mints* is not concurrent with speaking time: it shifts backward in time to locate an event as part of a previous experience (I comment on the use of the present tense below). Shifts in reference time often help to initiate a story world, separating it from an ongoing conversational world. Despite this shift, *my mother buys these mints* is syntactically connected with *and* to *I'm on a diet*; it is also presented in the same intonation unit. These linguistic connections link the first part of Irene's account (*I'm on a diet*) with the story told to expand that account. Note, also, that mention of *mints* establishes a cohesive tie with Henry's prior offer of candy.

The use of the present tense in *my mother buys these mints* is ambiguous: it can suggest either that buying mints is a repeated, habitual action or it can be a use of the historical present tense, a tense typically reserved for narrative events within the story world itself (Schiffrin 1981a). The latter interpretation is intruiging: it is a marked use of the historical present (since the HP is unusual in story abstracts) that could be said to have an evaluative, highlighting function, showing how critical buying candy is to later events. Introduction of the mints with the indefinite *these* can also be considered evaluative, but interestingly in a pejorative sense (Wright and Givón 1987), thus prefiguring

the disdain that Irene will show towards her mother's offer. Finally, the
addition of detail through *The Russell Stouffer mints* also draws attention to
the candy (Tannen 1989a: chapter 5). Use of a proper name to identify the
mints makes a claim about their "knowability" (i.e. they are recognizable; see
chapter 6). Postponing that name to the initial introduction of the mints
iconically marks that information as supplementary – a way of conveying
increased relevance (see chapter 6). Thus, the story abstract establishes a
cohesive tie with what Henry has just offered and reveals the centrality of the
candy bought by Irene's mother to the upcoming story events.

Although a story about a past experience can never really tell us what
actually happened during that experience, we can still interpret how a story –
as a version of the past – fits into a present conversational world. In other
words, we can examine Irene's story to see how Irene constructs a version of
her experience that fits her current conversational needs, i.e. that addresses a
current topic and accomplishes a current purpose.[14] A convenient way to see
how Irene accomplishes these goals is to dissect the story into actions – in
effect, to perform a speech act analysis on the events in the story (cf. Labov
1984). In addition to providing another application of speech act theory to
discourse, this analysis also provides further insight into offers and their
rejections. Thus the actions underlying Irene's reported experience are:

Actions in the story world

MOTHER:	Offer 1: S will do A	[unstated]	
IRENE:	Rejects Offer 1	I said, "I don't want any Mom."	(l)
MOTHER:	Explains Offer 1	"Well, I don't wanna eat the whole thing."	(m)
	does A	She gives me a little tiny piece,	(n)
IRENE:	Accepts Offer 1	I eat it.	(o)
MOTHER:	[no Offer 2]		
	does A	Then she gives me another,	(p)
IRENE:	Rejects A	so I threw it out the window.	(r)

Reactions to the story world

		I didn't tell her.	(s)
		She'd kill me.	(t)

Note that Irene's mother makes an offer (although it is not explicitly stated
in the story; see below). Irene rejects the offer (l), although the rejection is
ineffectual (the mother gives Irene the candy anyway (n)). Irene's mother then
repeats the act (p) without first offering to do so.

We spoke earlier of the conditions underlying offers, suggesting also that
offers contain implicit requests about whether H wants the A that S is making
available. Although Irene does not report her mother's offer of candy, I believe
we can infer that an offer was made (either verbally or nonverbally, e.g. by
holding out the box of candy). We saw earlier that a precondition for an offer
of goods is the availability of those goods to S: the fact that Irene reports

herself as addressing her mother (*I don't want any, Mom* (l)) suggests that her mother is the one with the available goods (the candy). We also saw that S cannot be sure that H wants A: we can infer that Irene's mother is S and that she is guessing that this is something that Irene might want. (Note the importance of the negative in *I don't want any, Mom*: negative statements typically imply a contrast with expectation; Givón 1979; Horn 1988.)

Additional evidence that Irene's mother has offered her candy is that Irene's mother then explains why Irene should take candy: *Well, I don't wanna eat the whole thing* (m). *Well* in (m) helps establish the sequential location of this utterance. More specifically, it is third in a sequence in which the initial move set up an option (an offer of candy), the second move deviated from that option (*I don't want any, Mom* (l)), and the third responds to the deviation (Schiffrin 1987a). Since Irene's mother does not want *the whole thing*, it seems reasonable that she would be trying to give candy away by offering it to Irene. A final reason to infer that an offer was made stems from our earlier observation that offers make goods or services available to another. Irene's mother actually *gives* Irene candy (*She gives me a little tiny piece* (n), *Then she gives me another* (p)). These are actions that physically realize exactly what an earlier offer would have made available.

After Irene's initial refusal of her mother's offer, Irene does accept the candy: *I eat it* (o). Note that Irene's mother has forced a compromise by appealing to Irene for help: *Well, I don't wanna eat the whole thing* (m) solicits Irene's help in preventing her from doing something that she herself does not want to do. (Irene's mother does not want to eat the whole thing because she does not want to get fat; but if she doesn't eat the whole thing, she may have to throw the rest away, thereby wasting the candy.) This appeal transforms the mother's offer into an act that will not *just* benefit Irene (recall that offers are beneficial to H, e.g. candy is supposed to taste good), but will also benefit the mother herself. If Irene does accept the candy, then, she can be seen to be putting aside her own best judgement in an effort to help her mother. And if Irene helps her mother, she can be seen as a good daughter – one who ignores her own reservations in order to comply with her mother's wishes.[15]

Because Irene's initial rejection of A was ineffectual, the mother's repetition of A (*Then she gives me another* (p)) has added social and personal implications. Irene reports that her mother just gives her the candy the second time around: S does A without asking whether H wants A and without trying to justify A. Irene does not attempt to reject this candy: rather, she avoids the need to do so by throwing the candy out the window (*so I threw it out the window* (r)). This action is important for it allows Irene to maintain the *appearance* of deference to her mother. That is, Irene manages to look as if she is doing what her mother wants, but she also maintains her own desire not to have her own wants (to stay on her diet) impinged upon. As Irene reports, there are consequences if her mother discovers this deception: *she'd kill me* (u). But it is precisely the fact that Irene is willing to risk these consequences that underline her seriousness about her diet and, thus, take us back into the conversational world in which her story provides an account for her refusal of Henry's offer of candy. Irene has gone to such great efforts to avoid eating candy – even to the extent of deceiving her mother – that she is not going to undo the product of those efforts just for Henry (see also Schiffrin, forthcoming).

Earlier I focused on the linguistic details of Irene's introduction of the candy into her story – details that established a cohesive tie with what Henry has just offered and showed the importance of the candy for the upcoming story events. Now that we have seen how a speech act analysis of the story world can help us interpret it as a speech act in the conversational world, it is worth noting again that the story is told in ways that help fit it into the conversational world. Note, for example, the alternation of tenses in which the main events are reported: preterite in (l), shift to historical present in (n), (o), and (p), then shift back to preterite in (r). The events reported in the historical present are those that provoke Irene's drastic action of throwing the candy out the window:

(n) She gives me a little tiny piece,
(o) I eat it.
(p) Then she gives me another,

Since it is the mother's persistence that creates the dilemma that Irene faces, these events are important for the point of Irene's story. The use of the historical present in (n), (o), and (p) also highlights these events not only in the story world, but in relation to the conversational world (Fleischman 1990; Schiffrin 1981a; Silva-Corvalan 1983): had Irene's mother not been so persistent, Irene would not have been forced to defy her mother. Thus, Irene will refuse an offer of candy despite persistent offers from her mother or from Henry.

In sum, Irene's story shows her sincere efforts to diet: the only time she accepts candy from her mother (even *a little tiny piece*) is when greater social and personal damage would be created by refusing candy. Irene's reported display of will and sincerity provides an account for why she has rejected Henry's offer of candy: Irene feels so strongly about her diet that she is willing to throw candy out the window, thereby deceiving her mother and facing the risk incurred by that rejection and deception (*she'd kill me* (u)).[16]

3.3 *Summary of sample analysis*

In sections 3.1 and 3.2 we considered the performance of several different acts through four chunks of speech: Henry's *Y'want a piece of candy?*, Irene's *No*, Zelda's *She's on a diet* and Irene's "I'm on a diet" story. To summarize:

Utterances		*Sequence 1*	*2*	*3*
Henry:	*Y'want a piece of candy?*	Question	Request	Offer
Irene:	*No.*	Answer	Compliance	Refusal
Zelda:	*She's on a diet.*	{Expansion}	Account	Account
Irene:	*I'm on a diet* + story	{Expansion}	Account	Account

This section summarizes and makes more general points concerning the utterance–act pairs (3.3.1) and the act sequences (3.3.2).

3.3.1 *Utterances and actions*

We began our application of speech act theory to discourse by analyzing relationships between utterances and actions: we showed how *Y'want a piece of candy?* is a question, request, and offer (3.1). We saw that the basis for our identifications of speech acts varied. In identifying questions, we relied largely upon linguistic clues. Requests and offers required that we try to judge communicative function. Instead of focusing just on the linguistic characteristics of utterances, we relied more upon our knowledge of the general background conditions necessary for an utterance to have a particular function (to count as a particular kind of action) and the applicability of those general conditions to particular circumstances. We also saw that identifying speech acts is complicated by the fact that utterances and speech acts need not have a one-to-one relationship. In analyzing how an utterance could perform more than one act simultaneously, we suggested that multifunctionality could arise (in part) from the way that underlying conditions for speech acts are themselves related to one another. We also saw that more than one utterance could figure in the performance of a single act, i.e. Irene's story served as an account. In brief, rather than "one form for one function" we found "one form for many functions" and "many forms for one function."

One-for-many and many-for-one relationships between form and function raise problems that affect the application of speech act theory to discourse analysis. Consider, first, problems stemming from "one form for many functions" relationships. Although the acts that we considered above (question, request, offer) are typical of those treated by philosophically oriented speech act theorists, many scholars who have taken a more social interactional approach to speech acts (e.g. Ciccourel 1980; Halliday 1975; Labov and Fanshel 1977; Schegloff 1987) have located acts quite unlike those that we have discussed. The relevance of their discoveries for the "one form for many functions" relationship is that these interactively embedded acts are often not performed alone, i.e. their identity is often dependent on the performance of another, simultaneously performed act. The challenges identified by Labov and Fanshel (1977: 93–7), for example, are second-order functions of repeated requests. Speech acts such as these raise problems: should we assign speech act labels to acts that emerge only as byproducts of other actions? Put another way, do we want to say that all of the many functions realized through a single utterance are speech acts? And do we then need to include all of these functions in the classificatory schema of speech acts assumed to be part of communicative competence? (Compare the taxonomies of those noted above, for example, to the taxonomies of Austin (1962) and Searle (1976), discussed in section 2.3.) How we answer such questions depends, of course, on how broadly we view speech acts: if we adopt Austin's relatively narrow view of speech acts, for example, then we cannot have a speech act without a performative verb (such a criterion would allow an act like "challenge" into the inventory, for example, but not an act like "tease"). Although these problems are not *created* by the existence of "one form for many functions" relationships, they are highlighted by them. Once we start finding multiple functions, we realize that not all of the many layers of functions that are realized through speech are as easily codified as those that have been more typically considered by speech act theorists, i.e. not all are first-order functions associated with communicative intentions.

"One form for many functions" relationships not only highlight problems already implicit in speech act theory, they also create new problems. For example, I suggested that *Y'want a piece of candy?* enacts three speech acts: question, request, offer. Questions, requests, and offers are intricately related to one another. Similar conditions underlie questions and requests: both count as an attempt to get H to do something that S wants; questions are a more specific attempt to get H to provide information that S does not have and that S wants. The question–request interdependence also arises because S's attempt to get H to tell him or her something ("I want you to do this: tell me if X") is based on the preparatory condition of questions, i.e. that S does not yet have information about X ("I do not know if X"). And offers may contain implicit requests that the hearer provide the speaker with information about the desirability of the act, thereby fulfilling the sincerity condition of requests.

Relationships such as these imply that a "one form for many functions" relationship may arise (at least partially) because of links among the acts (functions) themselves:

Utterance ⟶⟶ ⎡ act 1
                 ⎢ act 2
                 ⎣ act 3

Are other mappings also possible? For example, can a single utterance also be used to perform acts that are not themselves related? If so, then the mapping relationship might be more like this:

Utterance ⟹⟶ act 1
        ⟶ act 2
        ⟶ act 3

Such possibilities imply very different interpretive processes: the former, a single link between form and function, with links among related functions; the latter, multiple links between form and a number of independent functions. Thus, the existence of "one form for many functions" relationships not only forces us to consider links among different speech acts themselves, but also raises the possibility of different interpretive processes linking form and function.

The opposite mapping problem – "many forms for one function" – also creates dilemmas for the application of speech act theory to discourse. Complications can stem simply from the fact that it is discourse, rather than a single sentence, that is said to have a function. For example, we are used to the idea that a discourse itself has functions: stories are used for instruction (Heath 1982), for involvement (Tannen 1984), for self-aggrandizement (Labov 1972b; Schiffrin 1984b), for socialization (Gees and Michaels 1989). Furthermore, speakers may very well orient toward discourse level goals (e.g. thematic goals) even in the most minute details of individual utterances (e.g. Bamberg 1992). However, it need not follow that every linguistic feature or quality of that discourse serves the same, single function, or that every detail has a speech act function. Nor is it always easy to decide which particular discourse functions to assign to small details of utterances. Although we considered the historical present tense (HP) in Irene's story to have an evaluative function, for example, Wolfson (1979) has argued instead that it is the switch between the HP and the preterite that has a discourse function (to separate episodes). Finally, there is sometimes a circular quality to arguments about discourse function. Drawing again from our analysis of the HP in Irene's story, we claimed that events reported in the HP were being highlighted to relate the mother's persistence in offering Irene candy to Irene's defiance of her mother. We then claimed that, because it was this sequence of events that was being evaluated, it was this sequence that had a conversational relevance. But had other events been in the HP, we could just as easily have argued that it was those events that had conversational relevance for the central speech act function of Irene's story. *I threw it out the window* (r), for example, is central to Irene's account because it shows her willingness to defy her mother's repeated offers of candy.

Another problem stemming from "many forms for one function" relationships is that language rarely serves just a single function (Jakobson 1960; see chapters 2, 11). Thus, not only does a discourse itself probably have multiple functions (i.e. a "many forms for many functions" relationship), but there is also a good chance that individual utterances (or groups of utterances) within a discourse themselves perform acts. This suggests that we could conceivably end up finding hierarchies of speech acts, in which smaller speech acts would nest within more global speech acts, e.g. we might say that the clauses in Irene's story are all assertions (representatives) that build her account.

The most general lesson to be drawn from all these specific problems is that it is difficult to provide criteria allowing us to decide what counts (or doesn't count) as an instance of a speech act in such a way that other investigators would identify the act in the same way (see Kreckel 1981). This is often known, in social science research, as problems of validity and reliability: do our analytic categories correspond to similarities, and differences, among entities in the real world? Would others agree with our analytic categories and be able to discover them independently of our own efforts? Such problems are troubling to all research and can potentially occur at many stages of an analysis. Yet because the identification of utterances as actions is so important to later stages of speech act approaches to discourse – to describing relationships among units and combinations of units into larger patterns – trying to achieve validity and reliability at this first stage is especially important.

At the same time that we need to stress social scientific notions of reliability and validity, it is also important to note the inherent futility (and to some scholars, the foolhardiness) of trying to assign an understanding or function to an utterance with which all would agree (cf. chapter 4). Thus, despite our attempt to base our analysis of *Y'want a piece of candy?* on both the specific details of what was said and the general knowledge responsible for interpreting what was said as action, we cannot really be sure that we have "correctly" identified the speech act(s) performed by the utterance. Furthermore, we cannot really be sure of what we mean (or want to mean) by "correct." Many analysts shy away from grounding correctness in what speakers themselves would say they meant, i.e. the answer we would get if we were to ask Henry what he intended to do with his words. One reason for this is that different people tend to give very different answers to such questions. This discovery has led some to doubt the possibility of speech act taxonomies at anything other than the level of individual knowledge (Kreckel 1981; Taylor and Cameron 1987). Another reason is that the aim of linguistic inquiry (even one dealing openly with what sounds like psychological constructs of "wanting" and so on) is generally not seen as accounting for what someone "really means" (cf. Labov and Fanshel 1977). Rather, most analysts proceed in one of two directions. They may work backwards from what is said to infer what the possible meanings of those words could be and in which contexts. Or they may attribute a hypothetical intention to a speaker: if S wants to do/mean X, what are the possible ways that S might do so? (Bilmes 1985; Martinich 1984; Recanati 1987). Given such analytical routes, we might then say that a "correct" result is one that allows *Y'want a piece of candy?* to be used as question, request, and offer, provides a description of the conditions under which it may be so used, and explains why these are the conditions allowing these functions.[17]

3.3.2 Sequences of speech acts

In section 3.2 we showed how we could analyze sequences of speech acts: we viewed Irene's *No* as a rejection of Henry's offer, Zelda's *She's on a diet* as an account for Irene's rejection, and Irene's story (prefaced by *I'm on a diet*) as her own account for her rejection of Henry's offer. This analysis not only showed how our identification of an initial speech act defined our inventory of sequential possibilities, but it highlighted problems stemming from unit size and decisions about sequential appropriateness.

Let us focus first on the observation that, depending on how we identify an initiating speech act, the length of a sequence can differ. We saw that sequences initiated with a question can be closed with an answer, followed by optional expansions. Sequences initiated with a request can be closed with a compliance, although a non-compliance typically leads to an account (Davison 1975; Green 1975). Sequences initiated with an offer are similar to those opened with a request. Although they can be completed with a second part if that second part is an acceptance, refusals often lead to third parts, i.e. accounts. Thus, depending on how we identify an initial action, we end up with a different view of the expected length of the sequence initiated by that action.

It is important to note that more than mere sequence length is at issue here. What holds a question–answer sequence together – the basis for its coherence – is quite different from what holds an offer–rejection sequence together. Whereas question–answer coherence is based at least partially on propositional information, sequences initiated by offers are based on personal commitment toward action. If H accepts S's offer, S is committed to do A (and H is committed to allowing A to proceed); if H rejects S's offer, S has to alter a prior course of proposed action. The role played by personal commitment suggests that the reason why rejections to offers demand accounts has less to do with the constitutive rules of those speech acts themselves, than with what those rules imply about social relationships. Because speech act theory itself offers little to say about social relationships, I reserve discussion of the social coherence underlying speech act sequences for chapter 4. Here we can note, however, that the coherence of the offer–rejection–account sequence is grounded in the social meanings of these acts and their relationships to one another. This suggests that the basis for sequential coherence between speech acts can lie as much in the social and interactive world as in the cognitive world of speech act categories and rules.

4 Speech act theory as an approach to discourse

In this chapter, we discussed some of the central ideas of speech act theory as formulated by the philosophers Austin and Searle, and then applied these ideas to a particular set of speech acts in a discourse. In this concluding section, I briefly summarize how speech act theory provides an approach to discourse analysis.

The essential insight of speech act theory is that language performs communicative acts. In Searle's (1969: 21) words:

> The hypothesis that the speech act is the basic unit of communication, taken together with the principle of expressibility [whatever can be meant can be said], suggests that there are a series of analytic connections between the notion of speech acts, what the speaker means, what the sentence (or other linguistic element) uttered means, what the speaker intends, what the hearer understands, and what the rules governing the linguistic elements are.

Speech act theory, then, is basically concerned with what people "do" with language – with the functions of language. Typically, the functions focused upon are those akin to communicative intentions (the illocutionary force of an utterance) that can be labelled (cf. that have a performative verb) and realized in a single sentence. Even indirect speech acts (those that are performed "by way" of another act: Searle 1975) fall into this group: they are drawn from the same labelled taxonomy as direct speech acts.

Language can be used for speech acts because people share rules that create the acts: utterances "count as" successful and non-defective performances of speech acts when they fulfill certain conditions. The rules and conditions draw upon linguistic knowledge (e.g. the relationship between tense and the reference time of an event) and knowledge about the world (e.g. that people may be obliged to behave in certain ways) that allows certain linguistic devices to indicate illocutionary force. These two bodies of knowledge, and how they interact with one another, are assumed to be part of competence.

The conditions underlying and defining speech acts are central to speech act theory: they are the basis for the way we recognize and classify speech acts (and thus identify an utterance as a particular type of "unit") and for the way a single utterance can have more than one function (i.e. be more than one "unit"). Note that the knowledge that participants use in linguistic exchanges is thus relatively static knowledge: knowledge of what constitutes an act, what type of act it is, and whether more than one act is involved in its realization is brought "ready made" to each linguistic exchange. Yet such knowledge is also critical to the ongoing processes of communication: it is by identifying the units (acts) created by constitutive rules that communication proceeds. Although what happens during such an exchange can help to fulfill the conditions underlying a specific speech act, the circumstances of the actual exchange do not fundamentally define or alter those conditions.

In sum, by focusing upon the meanings of utterances as acts, speech act theory offers an approach to discourse analysis in which what is said is chunked (or segmented) into units that have communicative functions that can be identified and labelled. Although we can describe such acts in different ways (e.g. as realizations of constitutive rules, as the product of form–function relations, as the outcome of different textual and contextual conditions), the import of such acts for discourse is that they both initiate and respond to other acts. Acts specify (to a certain degree) what kind of response is expected: they create options for a next utterance each time they are performed, and thus provide a local, sequentially emergent basis for discourse. Since an utterance can also perform more than one act at a time, a single utterance creates different response options for a next utterance. Above I noted that what allows us to identify what others are doing is our relatively static speech act knowledge. This is not to say, however, that what we know about speech acts *prior to* any one particular linguistic exchange cannot alter the direction of an exchange. Recall that it is our speech act knowledge that allows us to infer not only that an interlocutor is doing something with words, but also that an interlocutor is doing more than one thing at once with words. Mappings between one form and multiple functions thus gives our exchanges a certain degree of flexibility: if we do not respond to one possible speech act interpretation of what someone has said to us, we may respond to another. This flexibility has an important analytical consequence: it means that a single sequence of utterances may actually be the outcome of a fairly wide range of different underlying functional relationships.

Exercises

1 People sometimes provide explicit speech act labels for their utterances: we might think of this as a metaspeech act, as the speech act of "defining," or as metapragmatics (cf. Lucy 1992). Below are examples of speakers using several different speech act labels.

(1) During a speech in which he was discussing the United States' reaction to the Iraqi take-over of Kuwait (October 1990), President George Bush said the following:
Iraq will not be permitted to annex Kuwait.
That's not a threat,
it's not a boast . . .
That's just the way it's gonna be.

(2) Parents of a three-year-old are discussing the new shoes they have just bought their son. Both parents had previously noted that because the shoes have a lot of laces, they will be hard to pull off the son's feet.
FATHER: (a)   You'll have to untie them.
MOTHER: (b)   Oh I know, it's okay.
FATHER: (c)   That's not a criticism, it's a reminder.
MOTHER: (d)   Oh no, I like the shoes!
FATHER: (e)   No, I mean you'll have to untie them.

For both of the examples, discuss the different conditions that would have to hold for each of the acts that are explicitly named. Are the conditions related to one another? Are there other labels that might have been assigned to these acts? (Consider, for example, what act is conveyed in Bush's statement "That's just the way it's gonna be.") What does the availability of multiple labels suggest about our organization of speech act knowledge and the way we use this knowledge during our communicative exchanges?

2 American children celebrate the holiday of Halloween by dressing in costumes and going around to their neighbors' houses to collect candy. After knocking on doors, and having the door opened, children say "Trick or treat."(Berko-Gleason and Weintraub (1976), discusses how children are socialized into this routine.) This formula is differently interpreted in different parts of American society and these different interpretations require different responses. The different interpretations are as follows:

(1)   Give me a treat.
(2)   Give me a treat, or I'll do a trick.
(3)   If you give me a treat, I'll do a trick.
(4)   Do you want a trick or a treat?

How would speech act theory explain these different interpretations? In what way does the syntactic structure of "Trick or treat" and its intonation (usually falling) convey these interpretations? (It may help to compare other "X or Y" utterances, e.g. "Coffee or tea.")

3 Presented below are several different examples of interactions. Each contains an utterance that can be interpreted as doing more than one speech act. (The target utterance in each case is marked with *.)

(1)   *CUSTOMER: (a)   Coffee to go?
       SERVER: (b)   Cream and sugar?
       CUSTOMER: (c)   Just cream.
       SERVER: (d)   /provides coffee/
       CUSTOMER: (e)   /pays/
(2)   CUSTOMER: (a)   Can I have an espresso?
       SERVER: (b)   You sure can!
                    (c)   /prepares coffee/
                    (d)   /provides coffee/
(3)   A commuter is at the Metro station with a $20 bill, and no fare card. She approaches a Metro employee.
       *COMMUTER: (a)   Do you know where I can get change for $20?
       EMPLOYEE: (b)   You'll have to go into a store or something
                    (c)   There are plenty outside of the station.
       COMMUTER: (d)   Well there's really nothing near by.
                    (e)   What should I do?
       EMPLOYEE: (f)   What you should do is check your money before you leave home, and make sure you have the right change.
       COMMUTER: (g)   Well I was really in a hurry and just didn't have a chance.
                    (h)   Anyway I thought I had it.
                    (i)   Couldn't you just give me change if you have it?
       *EMPLOYEE: (j)   Why don't you rely on the goodwill of your fellow riders?

(4) *LIBRARIAN: (a) Can I help you?
    PATRON: (b) Yeh maybe.
               (c) I'm uh- I've been working up in New York City in the theater doing acting and stage managing and one thing and another.
               (d) And I'm looking to try and get over to public relations which is why I'm down here.

(5) Professors A and B are colleagues at the same university. A is on leave in another city. B is in her university office, preparing for class. A calls Professor B on the phone: B tells A that she has a few minutes to talk. After spending a few minutes discussing an upcoming meeting, the following occurs:
    *PROF A: (a) Would you like to call me back?
    PROF B: (b) No that's okay, I don't have that much more to say.
    PROF A: (c) No, I meant use university money instead of mine!
             (d) I have some things I have to ask you.

(6) Father of a six-year-old is on the phone with "Grandmom."
    *FATHER: (a) Would you like to say hello to Grandmom now?
    CHILD: (b) No thank you.

(7) A and B are commuters on a daily train. A notices a newspaper on an empty seat next to where B is sitting.
    *A: (a) Is that your paper?
    B: (b) Yeh, but you can have it.

Identify the speech acts that are being performed in the target utterances. How does the context (including other utterances) influence your analyses? Are there other (hypothetical) sequences in which the target utterances could perform other speech acts? How would these sequences differ from the actual sequences? Finally, is multifunctionality of utterances ever an issue for interlocutors? Is multifunctionality solved (or exacerbated) by the fact that an utterance occurs in a sequence of other utterances?

Notes

1 Many scholars have already found speech act theory to be an important source of insight into discourse (e.g. Labov and Fanshel 1977; Sinclair and Coulthard 1975). Others have made observations similar to the essential insight of speech act theory, e.g. Halliday's (1978) thesis that language is the realization of meanings. But just as some have embraced the application of speech act theory to discourse, others have been more reluctant to transfer insights. Taylor and Cameron (1987: chapter 3), for example, have questioned the wisdom of relying so heavily on rules; Levinson (1983: chapter 5) has doubted the possibility of specifying mapping relationships between utterances and actions; Searle (1989) himself has suggested that discourse is more readily viewed in terms of speaker goals than felicity conditions and rules. Despite the interest and relevance of such a debate, it is important to note that I am neither endorsing nor criticizing the use of speech act theory for discourse analysis: rather, my goal is a neutral discussion of that application that can then be compared with the approaches created by other perspectives (part III).

2 Note that I am intentionally speaking of coherence rather than well-formedness. The question of well-formedness is a complicated one in discourse analysis (cf. chapter 2). As we will see in succeeding chapters, not all approaches (even all structurally derived approaches) hold the distinction between ill-formed and well-formed to be a valid one to apply to discourse. Replacing the notion of well-formedness with coherence not only allows for a more gradient view of sequential regularities, but it also gives interpretive processes a greater analytical role in the differentiation of sequences that "make sense" from those that do not.

3 Using intonation as a formal clue to the functional identification of *Y'want a piece of candy?* as a question, however, brings up still other dilemmas. First, intonation is not really linguistic *form*: Austin (1962: 74), for example, goes so far as to include it in a list of items illustrating the *context* of utterance production. Thus, we might be better off talking not of form *per se*, but in more general terms of *linguistic qualities* of an utterance. Second, it is extremely difficult to say that intonations have meanings that are independent of their contexts (e.g. Ladd 1978).

4 See chapter 5 for discussion of these questions as information-checking, rather than information-seeking, questions. The main differences are the scope of what is being questioned and the type of response sought: the information being sought is not the completion of a proposition, but reception of a referent or proposition; the response is not completion of a proposition but acknowledgment of information status.

5 Just as different forms of a single speech act may vary depending on social relationship, so different speech acts are differently associated with what some researchers have called the "social distance" variable. Wolfson (1988), for example, suggests that both compliments and invitations are less likely among intimates and strangers than among casual friends and acquaintances. Boxer (1993) suggests that indirect complaints (unlike compliments and invitations), on the other hand, are not equally likely among strangers and intimates.

6 Note, however, that depending on what is needed, by whom the need is felt, and to whom the need is expressed, the more specific directive force of a "personal need" statement can vary tremendously: *I need these letters typed by 3 p.m.* said by a boss to a secretary is more likely to be interpreted as an order (a relatively non-negotiable directive), whereas *I need a vacation* said by one spouse to another would receive quite a different interpretation.

7 Note that we need not interpret *Y'want a piece of candy?* as an offer, e.g. if Henry is not assumed to have candy available to him:

HENRY: Y'want a piece of candy?
IRENE: Yes.
HENRY: Well, it's in the living room.
         [or] Okay. I'll put candy on the shopping list.

An example we consider later has the same possibilities:

CLIFF: Do you need help?
DIANE: Yes.
CLIFF: Why don't you call the plumber then?

8 There are other relationships between directive and commissives that deserve consideration.

First, whether a single utterance serves as directive or commissive may depend on the social identities of speaker and hearer. "Let me come with you," for example, is an offer if said by a parent to a three-year-old child. But said by a three-year-old child to a parent who is about to leave the child with a babysitter, "Let me come with you" is clearly a directive. Although these different interpretations rest upon social identity, they also depend upon whom the act is deemed to benefit. In line with this point, some "let" statements have multiple functions whose beneficial value is not quite so clearcut: when a nurse tells a patient "Let's get dressed," for example, one might argue that both directive and commissive are being realized – and that both speaker and hearer will benefit.

Second, offers can be seen as pre-emptive versions of requests (Schegloff 1979b): instead of waiting for H to ask S to do A for H, S can present H with the option of actually doing A through an offer. Alternatively, H can try to elicit an offer of A from S, rather than request that S do A, e.g. through a "pre-request." Note that the view that S's offer allows H to avoid a request coincides with our cultural interpretation of offers as polite speech acts. By removing the need for H to make a request by making an offer, S makes it possible for H to avoid an act that is face threatening, i.e. H's request would restrict S's ability to decide upon his or her own next action (thus threatening one's negative face: Brown and Levinson 1979), as well as do an act that benefits H rather than S (Goffman 1971b). Put another way, by anticipating what another person wants, then one has allowed the other to avoid having to impose upon one's own course of action. Note that this reflects a general civic belief that "good citizens" are supposed to avoid self-interest (e.g. avoid making requests) and highlight altruism (e.g. make offers).

9 Note, also, that the request *Can you tell me the time?* can be easily analyzed as a request for a verbal action (the provision of the time) or a request for physical action (displaying one's watch to provide the time) – as indicated by the substitutability of *give* for *tell*.

10 The relationship between questions and offers can be posed in terms similar to the relationship between questions and requests, cf. discussions as to whether "can you pass the salt" is both question and request.

11 Two points. First, one issue that we will not address in this chapter is the fact that Zelda's *She's on a diet* is an account being offered *for someone else* (we consider this in chapter 4). To do so would require us to consider other actions even more abstract than question, request, and offer, e.g. giving solidarity, competing for the floor. I am avoiding such analyses here in conformity with the guidelines of fairly orthodox speech act theory, which focuses just on those speech acts whose intended communicative (illocutionary) function can be directly performed (e.g. through a performative verb) in a single utterance.

Second, we have already seen that *Y'want a piece of candy?* performs three acts, all of which can initiate a sequence. Note, also, that this utterance opens a side sequence (Jefferson 1972) that shifts the topic of the prior discussion (from a recent funeral to candy; see example (21) in chapter 5). This suggests that *Y'want a piece of candy?* initiates a new speech act sequence, rather than adds to or completes a prior speech act sequence.

12 Semantic dependency is a very general property of questions and answers: as Halliday and Hasan (1976) point out, ellipsis (i.e. recoverable deletions of text) is a common way to show cohesion (semantic ties) across clauses in discourse.

13 Ethnic groups are typically defined as subgroups within a culture or society that are differentiated by various complex criteria, including religious, ancestral, physical,

and/or linguistic characteristics. The importance assigned to ethnic distinctions, however, is often economically and socially determined.

14 The way stories are fit into conversations – in terms of turn-taking adjustments, topic, and so on – is an issue considered more by conversation analysts than speech act analysts. See e.g. Jefferson (1978).

15 Evidence that compliance with a parent's wishes is desired behavior (even for adult daughters and sons) is found elsewhere in my interviews with Irene, Zelda, and Henry. Henry, for example, boasts that his children "did what we wanted!" when they married within their own religion; Irene complains that children do not always "listen" nowadays. Zelda remarks that one of her daughters-in-law and her son followed her advice to call their in-laws "Mom" and "Dad"; she labels the situation with her other daughter-in-law (who does not call her "Mom") as a "sore spot" (see example (13) in chapter 8).

16 Note, also, that by reporting a deception, Irene alters the relationship she has with her audience: she creates a collusion and pulls the audience into a "secret." Elsewhere (Schiffrin 1984b), I have discussed how secrets create bonds of loyalty and solidarity: thus, the fact that Irene reveals a secret to Henry can be seen as a way to provide compensatory strength to their relationship – strength possibly threatened by her having turned down his offer.

17 We will meet these problems again in chapter 11 when we discuss communication and intersubjectivity, although we will discuss them there in relation to whether participants in an exchange agree on the meaning of what is said, rather than whether analysts of an exchange agree on its meaning.

4 Interactional Sociolinguistics

1 Introduction

The approach to discourse that I am calling "interactional sociolinguistics" has the most diverse disciplinary origins of those discussed in this book: it is based in anthropology, sociology, and linguistics, and shares the concerns of all three fields with culture, society, and language. The contribution to interactional sociolinguistics made by the linguistic anthropologist John Gumperz provides an understanding of how people may share grammatical knowledge of a language, but differently contextualize what is said – such that very different messages are produced and understood. The contribution made by the sociologist Erving Goffman provides a description of how language is situated in particular circumstances of social life, and how it reflects, and adds, meaning and structure in those circumstances. The ideas of both these scholars have been applied extensively within linguistics, e.g. by Brown and Levinson (1987), Schiffrin (1987a), and Tannen (1989a).

I begin in section 2 by presenting some of the concepts and ideas basic to interactional sociolinguistics. Despite the different disciplinary starting points of this approach, there are several basic beliefs about language, context, and the interaction of self and other that provide unity. My choice of a particular phenomenon upon which to base the sample analysis in section 3 stems from these central concerns: although I begin by focusing on the very same question–answer exchange discussed in chapter 3, I use that exchange as a way to consider how one particular self/other alignment ("speaking for another") serves as a discourse strategy and I show that different ways of contextualizing this strategy provide it with different interactional meanings. Section 4 summarizes the critical features of the interactional sociolinguistic approach to discourse.

2 Defining interactional sociolinguistics

In this section, I describe the basic ideas of interactional sociolinguistics. I begin with the work of Gumperz (2.1) and go on to Goffman (2.2); in section 2.3, I briefly summarize how the ideas of these two scholars can be combined.

2.1 *The contribution of anthropology: Gumperz*

In the introduction to his most recent collection of essays (*Discourse Strategies*), Gumperz (1982a: vii) states that he "seeks to develop interpretive sociolinguistic approaches to the analysis of real time processes in face to face encounters." After briefly describing some of Gumperz's work prior to the 1982a collection, I describe the concepts and methods that Gumperz has developed for the achievement of his goal.

Dil (1971) is a collection of Gumperz's essays through 1971: the dual focus of this volume – language and dialect diversity, language usage and social interaction – reflects the themes that continue (and become even more unified) in the 1982a collection. The research reported in Dil (1971) is all grounded in an assumption basic to social and cultural anthropology: the meaning, structure, and use of language is socially and culturally relative. The import-ance of this assumption is illustrated through studies focusing on a variety of different issues. For example, Gumperz's work in India – on regional and social language differences, on Hindi-Punjabi code-switching, and on linguistic convergence – focuses not just on linguistic structure, but also on how those structures become part of the verbal repertoires of interacting social groups. The three-part focus on language structure, use, and social groups also under-lies Gumperz's (Dil 1971: 114) classic definition of the speech community as "any human aggregate characterized by regular and frequent interaction by means of a shared body of verbal signs and set off from similar aggregates by significant differences in language usage."

Despite the social and cultural emphasis of Gumperz's early work, individual expression (what seems later to be seen as "strategy") also finds a place in this research. In his studies of code switching (Dil 1971), for example, Gum-perz defines two types of switching from one language variety to another. First is situational code switching: people may switch in accord with "clear changes in . . . participants' definition of each other's rights and obligations" (Dil 1971: 294). Second is metaphorical code switching: people may switch varieties within a single situation just to convey a different view of that situation and their relationship, such that "the language switch here relates to particular kinds of topics or subject matters" and is used "in the enactment of two or more different relationships among the same set of individuals" (Dil 1971: 295).

The connections among culture, society, individual, and code are developed in *Discourse Strategies*, the essays which (as noted above) seek to develop "interpretive sociolinguistic approaches to the analysis of real time processes in face to face encounters." In the first article of this collection, Gumperz (1982a: 12) points out the impact of structural linguistics (as formulated by Saussure (1959) and applied by anthropological linguists working with speakers of languages other than their own) on our understanding of culture and cognition: "structural analysis furnished empirical evidence for the contention that human cognition is significantly affected by historical forces. . . . What we perceive and retain in our mind is a function of our culturally determined predisposition to perceive and assimilate." Cognition and language, then, are affected by social and cultural forces: the way we behave and express ourselves in relation to a linguistic code and the underlying categories of the code itself are open to external influence. In order to understand these effects, what is thus needed is a "general theory of verbal communication which integrates what we know about grammar, culture and interactive conventions into a single overall framework of concepts and analytical procedures" (1982a: 4).

The theory of verbal communication proposed by Gumperz requires the addition of concepts and analytical procedures that build upon his earlier ideas about culture, society, language, and the self. One new construct is contextualization cue. As I explain in a moment, this is related to two other concepts: contextual presupposition and situated inference.

Recall Gumperz's (1982a: 12) observation that "what we perceive and retain in our mind is a function of our culturally determined predisposition to perceive and assimilate." One feature of modern, urban societies is their social and cultural heterogeneity, and one effect of such heterogeneity is that people from very different cultural and linguistic backgrounds come into contact with one another. Such contacts can lead to communicative difficulties precisely because of the fact that people's perceptions of similarities and differences in the world are culturally bound. As Gumperz notes, however, it is not just the core grammar of a language that exhibits such differences – despite the fact that grammatical (syntactic, phonological, semantic) differences in one's way of speaking are often the easiest to note. Just as pervasive a source of communicative difficulty are differences in what Saussure called the marginal features of language: "signalling mechanisms such as intonation, speech rhythm, and choice among lexical, phonetic, and syntactic options . . . said to affect the expressive quality of a message but not its basic meaning" (Gumperz 1982a: 16). Gumperz's studies of both interracial (blacks and whites in the United States) and interethnic (Indians and British in England) settings show that it is precisely differences in the marginal features of language that can cause misunderstandings, lead to the formation of racial and ethnic stereotypes, and contribute to inequalities in power and status.

The signalling mechanisms just described are what Gumperz calls contextualization cues: aspects of language and behavior (verbal and nonverbal signs) that relate what is said to the contextual knowledge (including knowledge of particular activity types: cf. frames; Goffman 1974) that contributes to the presuppositions necessary to the accurate inferencing of what is meant (including, but not limited to, the illocutionary force). Note how the two other constructs mentioned above (contextual presuppositions, situated inferences) are part of this definition. Contextual presuppositions are a type of assumed background knowledge that allows the inferencing (during the course of an interaction) of two levels of meanings that are themselves related. One level is the communicative activity type (cf. Hymes's speech event, chapter 5): whether one is teasing, lecturing, chatting, and so on. The second level is the particular illocutionary act that the speaker intends. Crucially, the interpretation of the illocutionary act (with the help of contextualization cues) is dependent on the use of the "frame" whose inference is also allowed by contextualization cues.

Let us take an example (from Gumperz 1982a: 147). The example illustrates the use of rising intonation as a contextualization cue.

TEACHER: James, what does this word say?
JAMES: I don't know.
TEACHER: Well, if you don't want to try someone else will. Freddy?
FREDDY: Is that a "p" or a "b"?
TEACHER: (encouragingly) It's a "p."
FREDDY: Pen.

The teacher's response (*Well, if you don't want to try someone else will*) indicates her interpretation of Freddy's *I don't know* not only in terms of its literal meaning, but also as an indication that Freddy did not wish to try to answer the question. Gumperz notes, however, that *I don't know* had final rising intonation, understood in the African American community of which Freddy was a member as conveying a desire for encouragement (cf. "I need some encouragement"). Thus we might say that the teacher did not retrieve the contextual presuppositions needed to accurately interpret Freddy's message from his use of rising intonation.

As illustrated in the above example, Gumperz's studies show that contextualization cues can affect the basic meaning of a message. To take another brief example: conversational code-switching (i.e. metaphorical switching) can be a contextualization cue because it "generates the presuppositions in terms of which the content of what is said is decoded" (Gumperz 1982a: 98) and in terms of which a hearer can infer a speaker's communicative intention. Although such cues are used habitually and automatically by members of a particular social group, they are almost never consciously noted or assigned conventional meanings: rather, they signal the speaker's implicit definition of the situation, and more importantly, how the propositional content of talk is to be understood.

As I noted above, when listeners share speakers' contextualization cues, subsequent interactions proceed smoothly. The methodological consequence of this is that one can discover shared meaning by investigating the process of interaction itself, i.e. by using the reaction that an utterance evokes as evidence of whether interpretive conventions were shared (Gumperz 1982a: 5). It is because contextualization cues are learned through long periods of close, face-to-face contact, however, that many people in modern, culturally diverse, socially heterogeneous societies are likely to interact without benefit of shared cues. And it is the analysis of misunderstandings between people from different groups – people who do not share contextualization cues – that can provide the most telling evidence that such cues are at work. Furthermore, such misunderstandings can have devastating social consequences for members of minority groups who are denied access to valued resources, based partially (but not totally) on the inability of those in control of crucial gatekeeping transactions to accurately use others' contextualization cues as a basis from which to infer their intended meanings.

We saw above that the individual entered Gumperz's earlier work primarily in social and expressive capacities – as a member of a social group, as the purveyor and creator of social meaning. In Gumperz's sociolinguistics of interpersonal communication, people have an added role: they have a cognitive capacity to make inferences. Contextualization cues are critical to this process, for they allow conversationalists to "rely on indirect inferences which build on background assumptions about context, interactive goals and interpersonal relations to derive frames in terms of which they can interpret what is going on" (Gumperz 1982a: 2). Also necessary to this process of situated inference is the maintenance of conversational *involvement* – since "we know that understanding presupposes the ability to attract and sustain others' attention" (Gumperz 1982a: 4). Thus, a general theory of discourse strategies must begin by: "specifying the linguistic and socio-cultural knowledge that needs to be shared if conversational involvement is to be maintained, and then go on to deal with what it is about the nature of conversational inference that makes for cultural, subcultural and situational specificity of interpretation" (Gumperz 1982a: 3).

Before summarizing, it is important to note that although some of Gumperz's concepts seem rooted in the individual (inference, involvement), these notions are actually grounded in a view of the self and what it does (e.g. make inferences, become involved) as a member of a social and cultural group and as a participant in the social construction of meaning. For example, Gumperz (1982a: 209) reformulates Hymes's (1974) concept of communicative competence in interactional terms, to include "the knowledge of linguistic and related communicative conventions that speakers must have to create and sustain conversational cooperation" (see also Gumperz 1985). And even in the complex question of speakers' internal differentiation of two linguistic systems, Gumperz (1982a: 99) argues that "effective speaking presupposes *socio-linguistically* based inferences about where systemic boundaries lie" and that "members have their own *socially defined* notions of code or grammatical system" (emphases added).

In sum, the key to Gumperz's sociolinguistics of interpersonal communication is a view of language as a socially and culturally constructed symbol system that is used in ways that reflect macro-level social meanings (e.g. group identity, status differences) and create micro-level social meanings (i.e. what one is saying and doing at a moment in time). Speakers are members of social and cultural groups: the way we use language not only reflects our group-based identity but also provides continual indices as to who we are, what we want to communicate, and how we know how to do so. The ability to produce and understand these indexical processes as they occur in, and are influenced by, local contexts is part of our communicative competence. As we see in the next section, the work of Erving Goffman also focuses upon situated knowledge, the self, and social context – but in different ways and with different emphasis.

2.2 The contribution of sociology: Goffman

Also contributing to the development of interactional sociolinguistics is the work of Erving Goffman. Although Goffman does not analyze language *per se*, his focus on social interaction complements Gumperz's focus on situated inference. Goffman places language (and other sign systems) in the very same social and interpersonal contexts that provide the presuppositions Gumperz finds to be an important background for the decoding of meaning. What Goffman adds is an understanding of the forms and meanings of those contexts that allows us to more fully identify and appreciate the contextual presuppositions that figure in hearers' inferences of speakers' meaning. Putting the work of the two scholars together, we can come up with a richly textured view of the contexts in which inferences about speakers' meaning are situated.

Goffman's sociology develops the ideas of several classic sociological theorists, and applies them to a domain of social life whose structural complexities had (before Goffman's work) gone largely unnoticed: face-to-face social interaction. Building upon the work of Emile Durkheim on social facts (1895), and primitive religion (1893), and the social psychologist George Herbert Mead (1934) on the formation of the self, Goffman argues that the self is a social construction or, more specifically, an interactive construction. One way of viewing the self as a public construction is through the notion of "face", i.e. "the positive social value a person effectively claims for himself by the line others assume he has taken during a particular contact." As Goffman 1967a: 5) notes, face is "something that is diffusely located in the flow of events in the encounter and becomes manifest only when these events are read and interpreted for the appraisals expressed in them." The maintenance of both self and face is built into the fabric of social interaction (e.g. "the maintenance of face is a condition of interaction, not its objective"; Goffman 1967a: 12; also pp. 7, 11, 39–40) and the complementary needs of self and other (Goffman 1963: 16; 1967b: 85). One contribution to the maintenance of face is interpersonal ritual, both avoidance rituals ("those forms of deference which lead the actor to keep at a distance from the recipient"; Goffman 1967b: 62) and presentational rituals ("acts through which the individual makes specific attestations to recipients concerning how he regards them"; Goffman 1967b: 71). Another contribution to the maintenance of face (and the presentation of self more generally) is the material resources made available through the social establishments and institutions in which people find themselves – resources that not only can be used to symbolize certain favored aspects of self (Goffman 1959) or to show distance from an institutionally allocated role (Goffman 1963), but can physically facilitate the division of self into a public character and a more private performer (Goffman 1959: chapter 3 on front and back regions).

Goffman's analyses of the relationship between interpersonal meanings and social structure are balanced by careful attention to both the symbolic value of what is said and done and the more abstract forms of social life (a duality that seems to be inherited from Georg Simmel's (1911) distinction between social form and meaning; see e.g. Goffman 1971a). It is in both form and meaning that we can find the sort of detailed attention to context that I noted above – detail that allows us to more fully understand the contextual presuppositions that figure in hearers' inferences of speakers' meaning.

Let me give two examples. We noted above Gumperz's point that situated inferences require interpersonal involvement, and that the maintenance of involvement requires that certain linguistic and sociocultural knowledge needs to be shared. Goffman's (1963: particularly chapters 3, 4, and 10) study of behavior in public places is relevant to Gumperz's concern with both the creation and the effect of involvement. What Goffman focuses on is the social organization of involvement; he describes the way different social occasions (and different phases of occasions) can create a wide array of expectations for the display of involvement (e.g. access rituals such as greetings require heightened involvement: Goffman 1971a; Schiffrin 1977), such that the very processes of both "being" involved and "showing" involvement are themselves socially situated. This is relevant for Gumperz's concern with involvement: since interactions impose their own rules of involvement, we must see those inferences that are based on involvement as also governed by broader rules of social engagement.

The second example concerns the contextual presuppositions that underlie hearers' inferences of speakers' meanings; here, let me focus on the notion of interpretive frame. One way of describing Gumperz' contextualization cues is as a framing device, i.e. they indicate the frame (e.g. serious, joking, business, chat) in which an utterance should be interpreted (cf. Tannen 1984, on meta-message). Goffman's (1974) work on frame analysis – the frames through which people structure experience – shows how the organization of framing activity is itself socially situated. Thus, again, we can see Goffman's work as providing an elaboration of the contextual presuppositions that people both use and construct during the inferencing process, and as offering a view of the means by which those presuppositions are externally constructed and impose external constraints on the ways in which we understand messages.

Before I close, it is important to note that Gumperz and Goffman have publically drawn upon each other's work – in ways that support the sorts of connections I am establishing here. Goffman's more recent work on the self (1974; 1979) builds upon his earlier (1959) division (between character and performer) to locate the self within a participation framework – a set of positions that individuals within perceptual range of an utterance may take in relation to that utterance. Goffman differentiates four positions, or participation statuses: animator, author, figure, and principal. Although these positions can be filled by different people, a single individual can also fill different participation slots: to simplify a bit, an animator produces talk, an author creates talk, a figure is portrayed through talk, and a principal is responsible for talk. Each position within a participation framework is associated with codified and normatively specified conduct (Goffman 1981a: 3), such that our recognition of shifts among animators, figures, authors, and principals is facilitated by our normative expectations about the conduct appropriate for each position. As I note in Schiffrin (1990c), however, the concepts of frame (Goffman 1974) and footing (Goffman 1981c) provide two additional links between participation frameworks and social interaction. Frames are the organizational and interactional principles by which situations are defined and sustained as experiences (Goffman 1974); footing concerns "the alignments we take up to ourselves and the others present *as expressed in the way we manage the production or reception of an utterance*" (Goffman 1981c: 128; my emphasis). As Goffman (1981c: 126–7) further notes, what indicates shifts in footing and alignment are not just the way we manage the production of an utterance, but also the kinds of devices identified by Gumperz as contextualization cues. This means that sociolinguists "can be looked to for help in the study of footing" (p. 128). But there is also help that sociolinguists can get from sociological analyses of footing: "if [sociolinguists] are to compete in this heretofore literary and psychological area, then presumably they must find a structural means of doing so . . . the structural underpinnings of changes in footing" (p. 128). Thus, what Gumperz adds to Goffman's dissection of the self is analysis of some of the devices that convey changes in footing, and a view of how these aspects of the production format of an utterance allow the situated inference of a new participant alignment. And, again, what Goffman's work adds to Gumperz's sociolinguistics of interpersonal communication is a more elaborated view (whether that elaboration is of meaning or form) of what "in" a context can provide a situated presupposition, and of the complex organizational and experiential frames that can be signalled through contextualization cues.

Two final points about Goffman's contribution to interactional sociolinguistics. First, although it may already be obvious from our discussion, Goffman's view of the self (like Gumperz's) is not grounded in individual psychology. Nor do psychological constructs (e.g. goals, emotions) enter Goffman's view of interaction. The study of interaction, for example, is a study not of motives, but of rules:

> to study face-saving is to study the traffic rules of social interaction; one learns about the code the person adheres to in his movement across the paths and designs of others, but not where he is going, or why he wants to get there. One does not even learn why he is ready to follow the code, for a large number of different motives can equally lead him to do so.

Second, Goffman makes a distinction between information that is given intentionally through language and information that is given off unintentionally through expression (Goffman 1959; 1963: 13–16). Yet, just as the distinction between core and marginal features evaporates once their significance as indicators of contextual presuppositions is recognized (Gumperz), so too does the analytical distinction between communication and expression evaporate in practice. Not only is it the case that "every linguistic message carries some expressive information, namely that the sender is sending messages," but "most concrete messages combine linguistic and expressive components, the proportion of each differing widely from message to message" (Goffman 1963: 16).

In sum, Goffman's focus on social interaction complements Gumperz's focus on situated inference: Goffman describes the form and meaning of the social and interpersonal contexts that provide presuppositions for the decoding of meaning. The understanding of those contexts can allow us to more fully identify the contextual presuppositions that figure in hearers' inferences of speakers' meaning.

2.3 Language, culture, and society as "situated"

Despite the different sets of interests reviewed above – one stemming from concerns about language and culture, the other from concerns about the self and society – there are two central issues underlying the work of Gumperz and Goffman that provide a unity to interactional sociolinguistics: the interaction between self and other, and context.

Gumperz's work focuses on how interpretations of context are critical to the communication of information and to another's understanding of a speaker's intention and/or discourse strategy; Goffman's work focuses on how the organization of social life (in institutions, interactions, and so on) provides contexts in which both the conduct of self and communication with another can be "made sense of" (both by those co-present in an interaction and by outside analysts). The work of both scholars also provides a view of language as indexical to a social world: for Gumperz, language is an index to the background cultural understandings that provide hidden – but nevertheless critical – knowledge about how to make inferences about what is meant through an utterance; for Goffman, language is one of a number of symbolic resources that provide an index to the social identities and relationships being continually constructed during interaction. Finally, both scholars allow language to have more active a role in creating a world than is perhaps suggested by the term "index": contextualization cues can alter not only the meaning of a message, but the participation framework of talk – such that both different intentions and different selves and others can be displayed through subtle changes in the way utterances are presented. Thus, the role of language in context, and the way it provides a path for self–other communication, is basically similar for both scholars.

As I illustrate in the sample analysis in the next section, the work of Gumperz and Goffman can be jointly applied to the meaning of utterances; the result is a richly textured view of the contexts in which inferences about speakers' meaning are situated.

3   Sample analysis: "speaking for another"

Interactional sociolinguists always draw upon naturally occurring interactions for data. Many scholars follow the tradition initiated by Gumperz and focus upon language used by speakers from different cultural backgrounds, often in institutional settings in which those backgrounds (and the difference in communicative style for which they may be responsible) have important long-term consequences (see, for example, the papers collected in Gumperz 1982b). Interactional sociolinguists also draw upon naturally occurring conversations among friends (Tannen 1984). Finally, interactional sociolinguists pay a great deal of attention to transcription of features of talk likely to serve as contextualization cues (see appendix 2).

The data used here are somewhat different: they are drawn from the same sociolinguistic interview that was the base for our speech act analysis. These data are well suited for the way that I illustrate an interactional approach, however: I recorded a good amount of speech from the participants, spent a number of years analyzing their discourse, and was myself a participant in the interactions (Schiffrin 1987a). Thus, I was able to incorporate contextual knowledge – necessary to interactional sociolinguistics – into my analysis.

Before I begin, I want to anticipate the direction the analysis will take. My initial focus is a single utterance from one speaker. At one point during an interview, Zelda said *She's on a diet* about Irene to Henry and me. Recall (chapter 3) that this utterance expands Irene's own answer (*No*) to Henry's question (*Y'want a piece of candy?*) and provides an account for Irene's non-compliance with Henry's offer. In contrast to the speech act analysis in chapter 3, I focus here on the participation framework created when Zelda makes a contribution relevant to Irene's exchange with Henry: in section 3.1,

I suggest that this utterance is an act in which one person "speaks for" another. Not only is this not the sort of act that would be discussed by speech act theorists, but the issues raised by an analysis of participation framework, and the methodology required to substantiate the interactional meanings of such acts relative to their participation framework, are quite different. In section 3.2, I contextualize the act of "speaking for another" as a way of uncovering its interactional meaning(s). We see that speaking for another can display at least two different participant alignments (3.2.1) within a particular sequence of interactional moves (3.2.2), and that these alignments are associated with gender identities (3.2.3). These analyses thus view speaking for another as a discourse strategy that is differently used by males and females to create either solidarity or distance. Speaking for another can also be said to serve as a contextualization cue through which participants signal identity and alignment. Finally, I briefly consider how this particular act is one of a "type" of acts whereby one person takes the role of another (3.3).

Note that I am intentionally not starting my analysis by focusing on either a particular linguistic form or problem. Rather, as noted above, I start by noticing a particular utterance (Zelda's *She's on a diet*) in an interaction. I continue by trying to uncover the situated meaning of this utterance through comparisons with other utterances and interactions.

At one level of analysis, the utterance to be focused upon has situated meaning as an account for a rejected offer issued through a question (chapter 3). But the characterization of *She's on a diet* in this chapter provides an analysis of the action sequence in which it is situated (i.e. question–answer–expansion, offer–rejection–account) from a perspective very different from that of speech act theory. Rather than focus on how individual acts are governed by autonomously functioning, static rules, we focus upon the social meaning of conduct (doing an act of a particular kind) and of the interaction that hinges upon such conduct. We see that who participates in an action sequence – and how they do so – is a matter of interactional significance at several different levels of analysis.

3.1 Speaking for another: "She's on a diet"

In chapter 3 we spent a great deal of time analyzing the speech acts in a particular interchange. I begin with a segment of that same interchange – Zelda's remark *She's on a diet* – reproduced as line (c) in (1) below:

(1) HENRY: (a) Y'want a piece of candy?
    IRENE: (b) No.
    ZELDA: (c) ^zShe's on a diet.
    DEBBY: (d) ^zWho's not on [a diet.
    IRENE: (e)   [I'm on-
        I'm on a diet

	(f)	and my mother [buys-=
ZELDA:	(g)	[You're not!
IRENE:	(h)	= my [mother buys these mints.=
DEBBY:	(i)	[Oh yes I amhhhh!
ZELDA:	(j)	Oh yeh.

In chapter 3, we said that *She's on a diet* is both an expansion (a sequentially dependent unit which adds information supplementary to a prior unit) and an account (an explanation for Irene's rejection of Henry's offer). Both expansions and accounts are relational acts: expansions add information to a prior act, and accounts provide reasons and/or motivations for a prior act that has been marked (e.g. inappropriate, impolite, insulting) in some way.

As noted above, I focus here on a very different aspect of Zelda's remark: its alteration of the participation framework of talk. Recall (2.2) that a participation framework is the set of positions which individuals within perceptual range of an utterance may take in relation to that utterance; in brief, the way that speaker and hearer are related to their utterances and to one another. Although the interactional meanings of speaking for another are by no means stable or determinate, there are some stable (and identificatory) features of this act. One key feature is that it involves three participant roles. We might label these roles using the relatively standard terms associated with the code model of communication (see chapter 11): a sender (who intends to send a message), a recipient (the intended target of the sender's message) and a spokesperson (who mediates in the transmission of the message from sender to receiver). But Goffman's analysis of participation framework allows us to be more specific about these roles. Since one person (the spokesperson) produces a message whose content is the responsibility of another (the sender), we might say that one person is acting as *animator* for another person who is in the *principal* role. Although we may still speak of B as the spokesperson, and A as the spoken-for, then, the ways in which the two parties can be said to be "speaking" involve very different notions of selfhood. The spokesperson draws upon the mechanical aspects of an animator; the spoken-for, the more moral aspects of a principal. Thus, when Zelda says *She's on a diet*, she is an animator for Irene's principal. Zelda is reporting something about Irene that Irene could have said herself (being on a diet is personal information) and to whose sentiments (or content) Irene is committed. Furthermore, Zelda's utterance is in a sequential position that Irene could have occupied herself (people often provide their own accounts when they reject an offer) and whose main relevance bears on the exchange between Irene and Henry (Irene has turned down Henry's offer).

In the next section, we see that the way *She's on a diet* alters the participation framework of ongoing talk is tied to the social relationship among participants (3.2.1), the social acts being performed (3.2.2), and the gender identities of participants (3.2.3).

3.2 *"Speaking for another" as situated meaning*

One of the key insights of interactional sociolinguistics is that meaning is situated (section 2). As shown by Bennett (1978) and Tannen (1989b), for example, the turn-taking structure during which one person's utterance (or part thereof) is simultaneous with another's can be labelled in two quite different ways: it can be labelled as "interruption" (with negative connotations) or "overlap" (with neutral or even positive connotations). Which label it receives (i.e. which meta-message is conveyed) depends on how that turn-taking structure is contextualized by speech activity, participant, and so on. "Speaking for another" is an act whose meaning is also interactionally situated. This section examines three different levels at which the meaning of speaking for another can be located. I begin with the temporary interactional alignments negotiated during talk in order to view speaking for another as a discourse strategy that is used to create either solidarity or distance (3.2.1).

3.2.1 *Alignments: "chipping in" or "butting in"?*

Speaking for another has little inherent meaning in and of itself: it can be interpreted in either a positive sense as "chipping in" or a negative sense as "butting in." The former gloss is consistent with an interpretation of this act as a display of positive politeness (Brown and Levinson 1987) and as a presentational ritual (Goffman 1967b): one shares so much with another that she is able to take her position in conversation (cf. "you know me so well you can read my mind!"). The latter gloss, on the other hand, is consistent with an interpretation of the act as a violation of negative face (Brown and Levinson 1987) and as a violation of an avoidance ritual: one is so invasive of another that she is unable to allow her to maintain her own position in conversation (cf. "you're always putting words in my mouth," "you don't let me get a word in edgewise"). Thus, speaking for another can be seen as either deferential or demeaning to the one being spoken for.

Here I will build upon interactional assumptions about social meaning to argue that Zelda's *She's on a diet* is both intended and interpreted in a positive way. Before we discuss the evidence for my belief, however, it is helpful to note some of the more general contextual factors that figure in such decisions – factors having to do with social relationship, social identities, speech act, and speech event (cf. chapter 5). (In section 3.2.3, we see some acts of "speaking for" among the same four participants that seem to be more intrusively interpreted as "butting in.")

Although space prevents us from a full examination of the interactive meanings of speaking for others, this act seems to be interpreted depending upon how the transfer of responsibility for speaking is achieved: does the spokesperson "take" responsibility or is it "given" to her? Sometimes the right to make such a transfer is institutionally allocated, such that its meanings can be partially derived from institutionally sanctioned roles that may either free one from the need to speak for oneself or force another to accede her own speaking rights. To take some simple examples, I recently received a phone call in which a receptionist, referring to her employer in the third person, said "Dr Robinson is calling you. He'll be with you in a moment." Part of the employee's institutionalized responsibility was thus to speak for another (her employer) who was freed from the need to speak for himself. In different circumstances, however, using a third party to initiate (or even sustain) a phone call for oneself can reflect quite differently upon the status of the spoken-for, as when, for example, parents arrange play dates for their children who do not yet have the communicative competence to do so themselves.

Even during institutionally based occasions of talk, however, the meanings of speaking for another can vary. Let us take a hypothetical example. Suppose that a person who has just immigrated to another country is filling out papers and answering questions during a gatekeeping encounter with authorities, and cannot understand enough of the indigenous language to answer a particular question from an interviewer. Another person (e.g. an official translator, an accompanying relative, or a passing stranger) may become a spokesperson. Participants' interpretation of this act can vary depending on how responsibility to speak for another was transferred, e.g. did the spokesperson offer to help or intervene, did the spokesperson agree to a request from another (either the interviewee or the interviewer), and so on. Participant point of view may also vary, e.g. the spokesperson may feel a sense of solidarity with the spoken-for person that is not at all shared. Thus, even a single act of speaking for another, performed by those in relatively institutionally allocated roles, can have a range of different meanings.

The range of interpretations that can hold for an act of speaking for another increases during conversation – when acts are bound not only (or not even) to institutional status and role, but to interactional positioning and participant footing. Because participant roles shift during conversation, the right to either take or abdicate responsibility for one's words also shifts. What this means is that the interactional meaning of speaking for another can be altered depending on current perceptions of alignments, such that speaking for another during a conversation can just as easily be positively or negatively glossed (as noted above). Furthermore, since social relationships are also reinforced (if not even created) during conversation, speaking for another during conversation can have not only local interactive meaning, but also broader implications about one's own (and the other's) rights, privileges, and responsibilities.

We are now ready to consider the interactional meanings of *She's on a diet.* I start with some information about the relationships among Henry, Zelda, and Irene. Full information of this sort (i.e. about social identities and relationships, and about the social, cultural, and individual meanings of actions) is available only through long-term participant observation in a community (the sort of methodology typical of the ethnography of communication; see chapter 5). Instead of that, I will offer here only knowledge that is based on my sociolinguistic fieldwork with Henry, Zelda, and Irene (a method of collecting data more typical of variationist approaches; see chapter 8) and knowledge of the social and cultural meanings of actions based on my own membership in a community roughly similar to the one in which Henry, Zelda, and Irene reside.

Zelda and Henry are married, and they display the closeness and loyalties of that relationship in their interactions, e.g. they frequently joke with and tease each other, they argue sociably (Schiffrin 1984a), they defend each other when challenged by a third person. Irene has lived next door to Zelda and Henry for more than fifteen years. The typical mode of interaction between Irene and Henry during my interviews was sociably combative: they playfully argued and insulted each other, but again rushed to one another's defense if report of a wrongdoing threatened the other's self-presentation or image (Schiffrin 1984b, c).

Most relevant to our current concerns is the relationship between Zelda and Irene. Zelda and Irene are close friends. Although Zelda is about twenty years older than Irene, both are mothers with three children each. Furthermore, although two of Zelda's children are married with their own children, Zelda's youngest daughter (a teenager) is a classmate of Irene's eldest son. Zelda and Irene have multiple opportunities for interaction, and multiple ways to relate to one another. One source of evidence for their relationship is what they say about one another. In (2), for example, Irene answered a question about her neighborhood by describing the advantages of having a neighbor like Zelda.

(2) Cause I – I like to know that in case I need something, like with Zelda, or: y'know she's been a big help t'me like since I'm workin' the kids – kids always here or in an emergency she's here t'get them or whatever until I can get there. So: I know I have a girlfriend that lives in Horhsam, and she doesn't know her neighbor on either side. Y'know? And I'm not that kind of person. Like in the wintertime, when you're snowed in and this and that, at least you can run next door, talk t'somebody if y'feel like you're gonna get closed in with the walls.

These comments reveal not only a closeness with, but also a dependence on, Zelda, e.g. *she's been a big help t'me*. Some of Zelda's comments about Irene (although not included here) also reveal the duality of their bond. For example, Irene helps Zelda shop for clothes for her teenage daughter: since Irene is younger, Zelda believes that she knows more about adolescent taste in clothing.

Let us now apply what we know about Zelda and Irene's relationship to the interactional meaning of Zelda's speaking for Irene. We saw above that Zelda and Irene are close friends based on their similarities (they are neighbors, mothers of adolescents) and on dependencies that stem partially from their differences (e.g. in age, experience, taste). In other words, Zelda and Irene are in a relationship of solidarity – but a solidarity that is based on both their similarities and their differences.

The participation framework created when Zelda speaks for Irene exhibits exactly the kind of shared responsibility and mutual dependence that is typical of Zelda and Irene's friendship. Recall that Irene has just turned down an offer of candy from Henry. By providing an account for Irene's rejection of Henry's offer (and by doing so before Irene's own account which actually repeats Zelda's), Zelda is creating a participation framework that mirrors (on a small scale) the more general bond that she shares with Irene. Just as Zelda "is there" to help Irene with her children or to provide company during snow-storms (see 2), so Zelda "is there" to help Irene soften the potentially threatening meanings created by her rejection of Henry's offer. Another way of saying this is that when Zelda says *she's on a diet*, her utterance serves the same general function as when she provides *a big help . . . in an emergency*. The difference is that the former displays solidarity on a micro-interactional level of talk relevant to an expressive domain of Irene's life (her relationship with Henry), and the latter displays solidarity on a macro-interactional level of rights and responsibilities relevant to an instrumental domain of Irene's life (her ability to manage both her career and her family).

It is important to note that Zelda's account is built upon the provision of information about Irene that may be essentially private information: being on a diet is something that one either has to observe about another or be told by that other (unless the diet has already resulted in a visible loss of weight). Thus, Zelda's account works by *revealing* information about Irene that had to be gleaned from a prior interaction and prior relationship (cf. Schiffrin 1984a). Although the revelation of information about another may actually threaten, rather than build, solidarity, I do not think this is the case here (cf. Besnier 1989). Indeed, because we know that Henry, Irene, and Zelda often use openly competitive forms of talk for positive ends, even an overtly negative gloss to *she's on a diet* might be reframed yet again: the ability to playfully violate an avoidance ritual (to bypass negative politeness) can attest to the strength of a relationship. Consider, also, that the information revealed by Zelda is essentially *positive* information about Irene: as typified by sayings such as "you can't be too rich or too thin," American culture values being thin.[1] Furthermore, being overweight is commonly interpreted as a lack of self-control. Thus, Zelda's account for Irene's refusal of the candy (and of course Irene's refusal itself) also portrays Irene in a positive way as someone who is "in control." Interestingly, these flattering portraits of Irene provide an implicit negative contrast with Henry – who (despite being overweight) is eating the candy.

Let us summarize how we have thus far analyzed the shift in participation framework created by Zelda's *She's on a diet*. After we identified *She's on a diet* as an instance of "speaking for," we observed some of the different possible interactional meanings of this way of speaking and the role of spokesperson. We viewed these meanings as not necessarily limited to Zelda's particular act, but more general meanings that were possibly applicable to Zelda's act. We proposed that Zelda's remark displays closeness and mutual dependency, and that it does so at two levels: the social relationship external to current talk, and the participation framework in current talk. Note that we said nothing about Zelda's intentions or goals: rather, we explained Zelda's remark by considering it as a way of speaking ("speaking for") that may be used with a person with whom one has a particular relationship (i.e. friendship). Thus, we moved from a particular utterance to the frameworks – or contexts – in which that utterance is embedded. Implicit in this procedure is a belief that it is the social contextualization of an utterance that motivates and explains its use. What are provided by context, then, are situated inferences about the meaning of an interactional move. Put another way, a particular utterance can act as a contextualization cue to the contextual presuppositions that inform and provide for its meaning and use.

But does such a procedure explain why Zelda says *She's on a diet* at this particular point in the conversation? And how do we know if our general explanation fits the particular relationship among Henry, Irene, and Zelda? In order to address this level of contextualized motivation, we need to consider the social meanings of rejected offers and to assess the meaning of a rejected offer for Henry and Irene in particular. In other words, we need to add another context to our consideration of the contexts in which *She's on a diet* is situated and interpreted.

3.2.2 Social actions: providing accounts for self and other

In chapter 3, we discussed how Zelda's *She's on a diet* and Irene's story about her diet both provide an account for Irene's rejection of Henry's offer of candy. But we had to defer our discussion of why accounts can supply a third part to offer–rejection sequences simply because the reasons have less to do with the constitutive rules of speech acts themselves than with what those rules imply about social relationships and social interaction. In this section, we illustrate how an interactional approach to discourse can help to explain the social coherence underlying this particular speech act sequence – thus suggesting that the basis for sequential coherence between speech acts lies in the social and interactive world in which speech acts are created. At the same time, we see that the social meanings of acts and their relationships to one another provide another context in which utterance meaning is situated.

In chapter 3, we said that offers are speech acts through which S makes A available to H. We also noted that S does not know for sure whether H wants A. Here I suggest that offers involve two kinds of "wants" with interactional and interpersonal consequences that can be remedied by accounts.

The first want is that H wants something: since offers are presumed to be for H's benefit, we can infer that S assumes that H might want the good or service being made available. As noted above, however, S has no guarantee that A is what H wants, and this means that S must guess about what H wants (chapter 3). The problem with this guesswork, however, is that guessing about what another wants means making assumptions about another's internal states. This can be a threat to H's negative face (Brown and Levinson 1987), to the desire that one's own needs and wants be unimpeded and unintruded upon. The second want is that S wants to do something for H (akin to a Searle sincerity condition). What this means is that when H rejects an offer, H is (in effect) saying that he does not want what S wants. This can be a threat to positive face (Brown and Levinson 1987), to the desire that others want the same thing that self wants.

Although guessing about another's wants never has a guaranteed outcome, that outcome can be improved with familiarity. But just as right guesses about what H wants (leading H to accept an offer) can thus reflect familiarity, wrong guesses about what H wants (leading H to reject an offer) can display a failed presumption of familiarity – that S does not know H well enough to guess about what H wants.[2] And this has two consequences. First, as already noted, S's guess about what H wants intrudes upon H's negative face. Second, by forcing H to reveal that what H wants is not what S wants, H is forced to threaten S's positive face.

I have suggested so far that rejected offers are threatening because of the vulnerability of opening one's wants to the other: rejected offers convey that H doesn't want what S wants, and that S was not able to guess what H wants. Thus, rejected offers are threats both to the self ("you don't want/like what I want/like") and to the self–other relationship ("I don't know you well enough to guess what you want/like"). These threats to the self and to the self–other relationship are mitigated by accounts: accounts can provide a reason independent of the offer itself as to why H does not want what S thinks he wants and why H does not want what S wants.

To return to Zelda's *She's on a diet* and Irene's "diet" story, Zelda and Irene both minimize the potential threat of Irene's rejection of Henry's offer. Interestingly, this remedial work ends up serving both Irene's and Henry's interactional needs and protecting their relationship with one another. By showing that Irene's rejection of Henry's offer was not due to a lack of respect for his values, the accounts both preserve Henry's values and allow Irene to reject them. Other analyses of the interactions among Henry, Zelda, and Irene show that this kind of mutually protective work is not at all unusual.

I have suggested thus far that rejections are potentially face-threatening: they threaten positive face by indicating that something found valuable by S is not similarly valued by H. But what about the meaning of rejected offers for Henry and Irene? Henry and Irene often argue with and insult one another playfully: they engage in interactions whose forms and meanings might threaten a relationship that was not firmly established through other bonds and threaten the selves of those not part of such a relationship (Schiffrin 1984c). This means that acts conventionally seen as face-threatening (e.g. rejected offers) might not threaten Henry and Irene and not need remedial work.

In this section, we have seen that the social meanings of acts can be formulated in terms of their interpersonal and interactional consequences, thus providing another context in which utterance meaning is situated. We see in the next section that speaker identity provides another facet of context in which interactional approaches situate utterance meaning: thus, speaking for another can be not only a discourse strategy by which to maintain solidarity, but also a contextualization cue that signals speaker identity and relationship.

3.2.3 *Micro- and macro-identity displays: alignments and gender*

In this section, we recontextualize *She's on a diet* yet again: we consider it within the context of who is speaking (male or female). In so doing, we will not only consider how speaking for another can display one's identity, but also how speaker identity provides another facet of context in which to discover utterance meaning. Our discussion will be helped by a brief comparison with other participant realignments among the same speakers.

Here is the relevant segment again.

```
(1)  HENRY:   (a)   Y'want a piece of candy?
     IRENE:   (b)   No.                           [I don't
     ZELDA:   (c)       ᶻShe's on a [diet.
     DEBBY:   (d)                   [Who's not on [a diet.
     IRENE:   (e)   =I'm on a diet
              (f)   and my mother [buys-=
     ZELDA:   (g)                  [You're not!
     IRENE:   (h)   =my [mother buys these mints.=
     DEBBY:   (i)       [Oh yes I amhhhh!
```

Note, first, that Zelda's *She's on a diet* is a remark said by one woman about another woman's diet. Although this utterance is directed to Henry, and not necessarily to me (another woman in the interaction), it becomes part of an ongoing interaction in which the women participants (me, Zelda, Irene) are engaged in a cooperative byplay, i.e. an interactively managed interlude, subordinate to talk about another topic, rather than an interactive focus itself (cf. Goodwin, forthcoming; Schiffrin, forthcoming). After Zelda's *She's on a diet*, I generalize the applicability of "diet" with a rhetorical question (*Who's not on a diet* (d)). Zelda's response (*You're not!* (g)) remedies the negative self-assessment that being on a diet implies (i.e. being overweight), but I persist in generalizing "diet" at least to myself (*Oh yes I amhhhh!* (i)). Overlapping this exchange between me and Zelda, Irene shifts from her own utterance (*I don't-* in (b)) to repeat the account offered by Zelda (*I'm on a diet* (e)). Irene's repetition leads into the story analyzed in chapter 3 – the story showing that she is so serious about dieting that she throws candy offered by her mother out the window.

What is important to note here is that Zelda has created a topic shift that is picked up by the two other women in the conversation – but not by Henry (this type of topic pursuit might also be characteristic of the ethnic style of the speakers; see Schiffrin 1984a; Tannen 1984). It might seem that this is a topic of more interest to the women, i.e. women are traditionally assumed to be more concerned than men with personal topics such as physical appearance (Aries and Johnson 1983), including their weight (but see below). And some studies have shown that women talk a great deal about food and diets: Deakins (1989), for example, found that the third most frequent topic of women executives at lunch was diets (see also Kipers 1987). Note, however, that Henry is overweight (more so than Irene), and elsewhere he talks about how thin he was when he was young, and how he plans to lose weight when he eats more fish over the summer (since fish is lower in calories than meat). Thus, we might expect Henry to avoid the topic of diet precisely because he *is* overweight and he is the one who *is* eating candy.

There might still be another explanation for the women's pursuit of the "diet" topic – one that centers on the way they display (and create) gender identities through the structuring of participation frameworks. That the differential construction of participation frameworks is a realization and reflection of gender is suggested by a variety of studies. Kalcik (1975), for example, suggests that women pursue topics of talk more interactively than men – that what one person proposes as a topic is progressively built upon by another. Cooperative topic building can easily be seen in terms of participation framework: it requires a joint alignment toward a focus of talk in which both addressor and addressee share the roles of animator and principal. Consistent with these findings is my own observation that Henry builds topics in ways less dependent upon others' active contributions (i.e. the listener places a relatively passive, supportive role) than either Irene or Zelda. Many of my questions to Henry, for example, were answered with lectures (Tannen 1990: 123–48): not only were Henry's turns at talk long with very few interruptions, but he imparted information, using traditional rhetorical devices, such as syntactic parallelism, to make a point. Studies of gender and dispute management can also be seen in terms of participation framework. Goodwin (1990), for example, shows that young African-American girls have remarkably different ways of managing group conflict than do boys: such differences revolve around the use of stories as a means by which to create and re-create participation rights both inside and outside of the group.

Returning to our example in (1), the findings noted above suggest that the way the *diet* topic is pursued by Zelda, Irene, and me – but not by Henry – is due not just to topic relevance or personal importance *per se*, but to women's conceptions of what interactional needs should be pursued at that moment in the conversation, and to the way that it is participation in talk itself that can meet those needs. Consider, for example, that my generalization of "diet" (d, i) and

Zelda's remark that I'm not on a diet (g) both work to minimize any one particular person's need to be on a diet. Thus, they function to minimize potential insults to weight (and physical appearance) and to build solidarity through positive politeness. Similarly, it is often noted that women attend more to maintaining solidarity during interaction than men (e.g. by avoiding conflict and minimizing threats) and that they focus more, in general, on the expressive implications of what is said than do men (e.g. Tannen 1990). Such observations are consistent with Gilligan's (1982) findings that instead of focusing on abstract principles and the impartial application of rules of right and wrong (the moral path followed by men), women emphasize human connections, caring, and the needs and situations of those affected by a problem.

(3) is a striking example of the different interactional paths – paths that seem to be gender related – that can be pursued by Henry and Zelda in my data.

(3) DEBBY: (a) Well, Irene, is there anybody around here that you would call a best friend?

    IRENE: (b) Now?

    DEBBY: (c) Yeh._z   hhhh

    HENRY: (d) ^zIn front of us?

    ZELDA: (e) No, we're not her [best friends, we're her=

    HENRY: (f)   [No! She's got a best friend.

    ZELDA: =neighbors!

    IRENE: (g) No, I [don't really think any *one person* I could say.

    HENRY: (h)   [=But she's [more of a friend to a person,=

    ZELDA: (i)   [She's not-

    HENRY: (j) =than a person is to her.   [Let's put it that way.=

    IRENE: (k)   ^zYeh. [T'be honest.

    HENRY: (l) =And it- [it   [Am I right or wrong?

    IRENE: (m)   [I think [I've-   I've
           been getting [hurt, too much lately.

    ZELDA: (n)   [Are you Irene?!

    DEBBY: (o)   Yeh.

    HENRY: (p) No but am I right or wrong Irene?

    (q) I could see [some damage! Yeh.=

    IRENE: (r)   [Yeh.   I feel I'm hurt.=

    HENRY: (s) =[See?]

    IRENE: (t) =[I   ] don't know how the other people feel.

Note, first, that my question in (a) follows the question–answer format of our interview (see chapter 5, section 3.3). The interchange between Henry and Zelda (d and e), however, alters this format of the interview since they both comment on the question, rather than allow Irene to answer the question (chapter 5, sections 3.3.1, 3.3.5). Henry then answers for Irene in what sounds like a supportive manner: *She's got a best friend* (f). He immediately uses his own assertion, however, to project an inequity between the way Irene treats others (positively) and the way she is treated by others (negatively): *But she's more of a friend to a person, than a person is to her* (h, j). Although Henry's comparison reveals more about Irene than she might otherwise prefer, Irene does agree with Henry (*Yeh. T'be honest* (k), *I think I've- I've been getting hurt, too much lately.* (m)). Note that once Irene herself reveals "trouble" (Jefferson 1980), Zelda immediately offers sympathy on a personal level with *Are you Irene?!* (n). But Henry uses Irene's revelation of *getting hurt* as a basis for the correctness of his own assessment: he uses it to pursue the validity of his own point (*No but am I right or wrong Irene?* (p)), to reaffirm what he himself has seen (*I could see some damage!* (q)), and to gain consensus about his point (*See?* (s)). Thus, whereas Zelda offers support based on the personal implications of what Irene has said, i.e. how the inequity affects Irene herself, Henry uses Irene's situation as a basis from which to buttress a more general assessment of her dilemma.

Thus far, I have suggested that Zelda's *She's on a diet* proposes an interactional alignment that is more typical of the stances taken by women than those taken by men. Above I noted that one way that gender is realized and reflected in talk is through the differential construction of participation frameworks. This suggests that we can further check this proposal about gender-related interactional differences by comparing participant realignments during same-gender talk to those created during cross-gender talk. In (4), for example, I have been asking Zelda, Irene, and Henry about their personal contacts in the neighborhood.

(4) DEBBY: (a)   How 'bout you Irene?
    IRENE: (b)   What?
    DEBBY: (c)   Who would you-=
    ZELDA: (d)   ᶻWho would you [discuss it with?
    DEBBY: (e)   =   =[if you had a hard day
           who would you complain to?
    ZELDA: (f)   Jayhhhhh

Irene (*What?* (b)) asks for clarification of the question I had initiated in (a). In (d), Zelda provides the clarification that Irene had requested from me. Zelda's contribution overlaps with my own expansion of the question (in c, e); note, also, how we both repeat the *Wh* portion of the question. In addition to sharing my questioning role, Zelda also shares Irene's answering role in (f) by providing *Jay* as a potential answer. Thus, Zelda speaks first for me and then for Irene – her adoption of the two roles reproducing the structure of the question–answer sequence.

(4) continues with Irene's answer building upon Zelda's answer:

    IRENE: (g)   Uh:: I don't know.
          (h)   Depending on what- what the problem really
             was, I might [talk] to a friend easier.
    DEBBY: (i)   [Yeh.]   ᶻYeh.

In (g) and (h), Irene states that she might *talk to a friend easier*; note that the implicit comparison is between *a friend* and Jay (Irene's husband, the person mentioned by Zelda). As Irene continues to compare herself to Zelda (and to Henry) in (j), however, Henry joins the talk:

IRENE:	(j)	=than to a- what- I'm not that family orientated.=
DEBBY:	(k)	Uhhuh.
IRENE:	(l)	=[Like they are.
HENRY:	(m)	[She should be. She's got a nice family.

We saw a moment ago that Zelda's remarks reproduced the structure of the ongoing discourse and allowed others to maintain their participant roles. Henry's assessment of Irene's claim (from (j) and (l) that she is not family oriented) in (m), however, shifts the participant alignment and forces others to fit their utterances into that framework. Rather than create a duality in the speaker role (a split between animator (the spokesperson) and principal (the spoken for)), Henry's assessment creates a split in the addressee role: by assessing what Irene has said *in her presence*, and addressing that assessment *to me*, Henry divides his audience into an addressed recipient (me) and an unaddressed recipient (Irene).

Henry's realignment of the audience has an outcome quite different from the inclusionary effect of Zelda's utterances. In one sense, Henry's remarks exclude Irene from the interaction; at the very least, from active participation in the dialogue that Zelda and I had initiated and maintained. Furthermore, since Henry's remarks offer a moral assessment of the content of Irene's answer, they open Irene to scrutiny from me – a relative outsider to their group (cf. 3). Thus, in one sense, Henry's remarks create a participation framework that can potentially separate co-participants from one another. In another sense, however, Henry's assessment draws Irene into interaction *with him*: although she is not formally addressed by his remarks (note the third person pronoun reference to Irene as *she*), she is certainly expected to hear what has been said about her. We can consider the effects of this in terms of Goffman's (1963) notion of information preserve and Brown and Levinson's ideas about politeness. Offering unsolicited advice about what is considered another's domain (e.g. closeness to family), particularly when what is said concerns what that other *should* do, is a violation of negative face – the sort of violation commonly called "not minding your own business" or "butting in." Thus, Henry does draw Irene into the interaction, but he does so by intruding upon her affairs and by forcing her to defend the management of those affairs.[3]

Consider what happens next:

ZELDA:	(m)	Well [she really- wait a minute she doesn't=
HENRY:	(n)	[She's got lovely children.
ZELDA:		=have any [sisters,
IRENE:	(o)	[I'm not talkin' about my children.
ZELDA:	(p)	_zRight.

HENRY: (q) Well you should make it so, it's good.
ZELDA: (r) Oh! C'mon!
IRENE: (s) Hen, I'm not you, Henry!
        (t) We've- we've had family problems where my husband and his brother were in business.
        (u) And at one time we were *very* close.
        (v) And now it's just hello, goodbye, how are you, and that's it.

Although Zelda's defense of Irene (*she doesn't have any sisters* (m)) continues the participation framework opened by Henry (note her third person reference to Irene), Zelda and Irene continue collaborating. Irene responds to Henry (*I'm not talkin' about my children* (o)) along the same lines as Zelda: both narrow Henry's reference to *family*. Zelda agrees with Irene's own defense (*Right* in p) even though Irene has bypassed the content of Zelda's defense. Finally, although Henry redirects his criticism to Irene herself (in q), Zelda continues to defend Irene by discouraging Henry's continued participation (*Oh! C'mon!* (r)). Despite Irene's and Zelda's collaboration, Henry's shift of the participation framework becomes dominant: Irene defends herself to Henry (*Hen, I'm not you, Henry!* (s)) but also orients that defense to me (in t to v). Thus, although Irene rejects the relatively passive role of the unaddressed recipient status, her defense still conforms to the participation framework created by Henry – simply because she defends herself relative to both her challenger (Henry) and the recipient of the words to whom the challenge was ostensibly addressed (me).

(3) and (4) have illustrated a difference in participant realignments predictable from previous scholarship on gender and discourse. Although both Zelda and Henry alter the participation framework, they do so in different ways: Zelda's realignment was more supportive and integrative; Henry's stance was more judgemental and divisive; in (4), Henry drew Irene into interaction by challenging her (an act requiring a defensive response) and by treating her as an unaddressed recipient (a position of relatively low status).

If the alignment differences just described for (1), (3), and (4) really are related to gender we would expect them to reappear during other exchanges – even those that do not involve speaking for another. Put another way, we might expect the same kind of interactional alignments to reappear with interactional moves other than the one with which we began our discussion. Suppose, for example, that instead of providing Irene's account by saying *She's on a diet*, Zelda had created a slot in which Irene would have to provide her own account, e.g. *Tell him why you don't want it* or *Henry doesn't know why you refused.* Fortunately, there were two interchanges in the same interview among these three participants that contain this alternative means of reorienting the content of another's talk: one person (either Zelda or Henry) prompts another (Irene) to produce (animate) what the prompter (as principal) had "in mind."[4] As we see, there are some striking differences in the division of responsibility for those realignments that seem to be predicted by gender – differences similar to those already seen.

First is an example of a realignment in same-gender talk:

(5)	DEBBY:	(a)	Yeh, who d'y'go bowling with?
	IRENE:	(b)	My next door neighbors.
		(c)	We have a team in the summer we bowl.
		(d)	Every summer [they- husband and wife-
	ZELDA:	(e)	[Tell her who you bowl with.
	IRENE:	(f)	Who we *bowl* with.
	ZELDA:	(g)	D- y'know the teams.
	IRENE:	(h)	Oh. Wha'd' y'mean [the kids?
	ZELDA:	(i)	[The kids.
	IRENE:	(j)	[Oh yeh, this year the kids have=
	HENRY:	(k)	[Kids. They have a very good thing.
	IRENE:		=their own team,
		(l)	[and they're . . . [they're eh . . . they're giving=
	DEBBY:	(m)	[Oh great!
	HENRY:	(n)	[They got a good thing going.
	IRENE:	(o)	=us a run for our money cause we- we're in first place and they're in second, and they're- they cheer everytime we lose a game.

The section to focus upon begins with Zelda's overlapping speech in (e): *Tell her who you bowl with*. This remark is (in the terms of ethnomethodologists; chapter 7) an other-initiated repair: by prompting Irene to provide a specific piece of information, Zelda is redefining something Irene has already said as "incomplete," i.e. as a repairable. By so doing, Zelda inserts herself into what has thus far been a question–answer exchange between me and Irene. Her role is somewhat like that of a monitor of the exchange: she is assessing the adequacy of the answer and prompting Irene to animate what she herself has "in mind" as a suitable answer to the question. In terms of participant alignments, then, Zelda is prompting Irene to animate the words for which she is principal.

Note, however, that Zelda repeats the content of my question (*who d'y' go bowling with?* (a)). This may account for Irene's repetition (in f) of what Zelda has asked for and her contrastive stress on *bowl*, i.e. if I had already asked about "bowling" why should Zelda also be asking about "bowl"? Following Irene's repetition of the slot that requires completion (the identity of "who you bowl with"), Zelda continues to prompt Irene: in addition to appealing to shared knowledge (with *y'know*; Schiffrin 1987a: chapter 9), she broadens the reference to *the teams*. In (h), Irene shows recognition with *oh* (Schiffrin 1987a: chapter 4) and becomes more explicit (she refers to *the kids*); however, she maintains Zelda's role as promptor of information – as one who has the "right" answer "in mind" – by asking for Zelda's confirmation (*Wha'd'y'mean the kids?*). Zelda has already begun to provide her own explicit meaning: *The kids* in (i) "latches onto" Irene's *Wha'd'y'mean*. In (j), Irene repeats the information given by Zelda: *Oh yeh* shows that she is inserting it into the slot created by Zelda's prompting. Note that Irene not only incorporates that information into her own contribution (*this year the kids have their own team*), but expands it into a brief narrative (j, l, o).

We have discussed (5) because it illustrates an alternative to speaking for another: rather than Zelda saying *Irene bowls with her kids*, Zelda prompts Irene to say this herself. Although it is Zelda's "idea" for Irene to include "the kids" in her answer, Zelda allows Irene to share responsibility for that information. In addition, Zelda brings Irene into the prompting process itself, such that they gradually build the mention of "the kids" together, each giving the other just enough to allow that other to maintain an active stance in the conversation. Thus, although Zelda prompts Irene to animate that for which she is principal, she also allows her to share responsibility for the words.

An effort to prompt another to speak is also illustrated in (6); again, Irene is being prompted to tell me something, but this time it is Henry who is doing the prompting. Prior to (6), I had been asking Irene whom she is friendly with; Irene is telling me about how infrequently she sees her childhood friends.

(6) IRENE: (a) I keep in touch with them, y'know I go to their affairs, but I don't *see* them that often. One lives in Jersey and one lives up in the Northeast.

DEBBY: (b) Umhmm.

HENRY: (c) Tell her about the [girl you were real close:,=

IRENE: (d)   [But-

HENRY: (e) =you were raised, and they got money, and they don't know y'.

IRENE: (f) Who? Barbara? Oh. Well . . .

HENRY: (g) Well she wants t'know!

ZELDA: (h) Yeh but she's friends with her.

IRENE: (i) I talk to her occa[sionally, but eh: she: she:=

HENRY: (j)   [Yeh but tell the way it is.=

IRENE: (k) =[has moved t'Brookside and they have a whole new=

HENRY: (l) =[She wants t'know. She wants t'know.

IRENE: =circle of eh: friends. Y'know.

Although it is important to consider how responsibility for information emerges interactively and sequentially, it is helpful to begin by comparing how Henry prompts Irene in (6) to how Zelda prompted Irene in (5).

Henry's prompts to Irene (6)	Zelda's prompts to Irene (5)
Imperative	Imperative
Tell her about "X"	*Tell her "X"*

Expands "X" (c) (e)
  Lists critical events
    (4 narrative clauses)
Externalizes need to tell about "X"
  Well she wants t'know! (g)
Imperative
  Yeh but tell the way it is. (j)
Externalizes need to tell about "X"
  She wants t'know. She wants t'know. (l)

Expands "X"
  Creates shared knowledge
    D- y'know the teams.
States "X"
  The kids.

Henry and Zelda both initiate their prompts with the imperative *tell her*; both make explicit what Irene is to say and to whom she is to say it. However, the way they pursue those prompts differs radically. In part, this difference has to do with what they are prompting Irene to say: Henry wants Irene to reveal what is potentially embarrassing information, i.e. an incident in her own history that ended "badly." (Recall that this was essentially the outcome of (4), in which Henry spoke for Irene concerning the importance of being close to family; recall also that that forced Irene to reveal her failed venture into a family business.) Following their imperatives, Henry and Zelda both expand what it is that Irene is to tell me. These follow-up strategies display differences that can be seen as gender related: by listing four events recapitulating the experience that he wants Irene to report, Henry is "telling" Irene the answer, i.e. transferring information to her; by prefacing the information with a marker of shared knowledge, Zelda is "helping" Irene with the answer, i.e. collaborating in the production of information. In effect, then, Henry allows Irene little more than a role as animator; Zelda, however, allows Irene to share in the principal role.

The prompting strategies diverge even further following the failure of the expansions to elicit the desired information. As we saw above, Zelda gives Irene the information – *The kids*. But Henry brings in an external justification for his persistent prompting: he couples a renewed imperative (*Yeh but tell the way it is.* (j)) with repeated assertions that I want the information that he is after: *She wants t'know*. Note, then, that Henry begins to *speak for me*: he uses me as an external validation for his own actions. Henry thus brings me back into the conversation, but with an altered role – as an addressed recipient – and the way he re-evokes this role alters the agenda from the one I had established to one that he is directing.

Let us compare Irene's responses to both Henry and Irene:

Irene's responses to Henry

Who? Barbara? Oh. Well . . . (f)
I talk to her occasionally,
but eh: she: she: has moved t'
Brookside and they have a whole
new circle of friends, y'know (i)(k)

Irene's responses to Zelda

Who we *bowl* with.
Oh. Wha'd'y'mean the kids?
Oh yeh, this year the kids
have their own team [continues]

Irene's responses to Henry's initial prompt show reluctance to provide what he is after. Note that her first response (in f) is formally similar to her response to Zelda: Irene asks *Who* and then offers a candidate identity (to Henry it is *Barbara?*, to Zelda, it was *we bowl with*). But following her recognition (*Oh*) that this is indeed the "story" that Henry wants, she displays what seems like reluctance to go on with *Well . . .*: it is here that Henry brings me into the prompting process with *Well she wants t'know!* Note, however, what happens when Irene presents her eventual story (filled with hesitation about how to formulate what happened):

IRENE:	(i)	I talk to her occa[sionally, but eh: she: she:=
HENRY:	(j)	[Yeh but tell the way it is.=
IRENE:	(k)	=[has moved t'Brookside and they have a whole new=
HENRY:	(l)	=[She wants t'know. She wants t'know.
IRENE:		=circle of eh: [friends. Y'know.
DEBBY:	(m)	[Yeh. Got snobbish.
HENRY:	(n)	Money makes a difference. Money's important=
DEBBY:	(o)	Yeh.
HENRY:	(p)	=to a lot of people. It's a status.

The information that Irene presents (in i and k) seems to be what Henry has been after – since Henry follows Irene's story with a statement of a more general theme (money changes people for the worse (n, p)) that he (a lower middle-class blue collar worker living near an affluent white collar suburb) has reiterated numerous times during our conversations. Yet Henry continues to prompt Irene during Irene's story: it is only after I present the "point" of the story (that Irene's friends became snobs after moving to a wealthier suburb (m)) that Henry states his own theme. Thus, Henry's prompting continues until he is sure that what he had "in mind" has not only been said (animated by Irene) but, also, that it has been "heard" in a way consistent with the general theme that he is putting forth.

  Observe, then, that Henry has done more than alter his footing in relation to Irene: he has shifted the structure of the discourse from a question–answer dialogue to a discussion of a general moral issue of which he is "in control" and to which he can orient his interlocutors. The continuation of (6) suggests that Henry is after still further restructuring:

HENRY:	(p)	[It's a status.
DEBBY:	(q)	[D'you-
	(r)	Yeh. Its: works in funny ways.
ZELDA:	(s)	Umhmm. That's exactly it. It [works in funny ways.
HENRY:	(t)	[D'you take a person for face value, or: or if they live in a big fancy house, does that make any difference to you?
DEBBY:	(u)	No. None at all.

HENRY: (v) Well that's the way it should be.
(w) You're a nice girl!

During Henry's restatement of his point (in p), I begin to ask Irene a question, i.e. to recreate the question–answer structure. I quickly adapt my remarks to Henry's theme, however, even building upon that theme in (r). Zelda supports my statement of the theme (in s) with agreement tokens and repetition. Although this is certainly the moral theme that Henry has initiated, Henry's interruption of Zelda (to ask me whether my own experience conforms to his view of what is right in t) rejects the collaborative nature of what Zelda and I have said to shift the participant structure still further from its earlier form. Recall that the interchange began with me asking Irene questions; Henry then evaluated Irene's answers, prompted Irene to shift her answers, and, finally, asked me questions and evaluated my answers. Thus, what the question–answer–evaluation sequence (in t through w) does is complete the restructuring of the participation framework to one in which Henry is "in charge."

We have seen in (6) that Henry prompts Irene to reveal potentially embarrassing information – information that is not exactly what I had requested, but information that allows Henry to state a general theme. We commented earlier that Henry allows Irene little more than a role as animator, and that his persistent prompting uses me as an external validator for his own actions. These strategies shift the discourse structure from one that I had established to one that Henry is directing: Henry's prompting continues until he is sure that what he had "in mind" has been said and "heard" in a way consistent with the general theme that he is putting forth. He also shifts the structure from one in which I ask questions to one in which I answer questions (and have my answers evaluated). Interestingly, the point that Henry is making is one that unifies us – Henry, Zelda, Irene, me – in a joint moral stance "against" another group. But the solidarity that is built is not only defined in opposition to another group (i.e. "we" are different from those who have more money because they reject us), it is also interactively constructed in a way that differentiates participant roles from one another and allows one speaker (Henry) to manage the way that others present and interpret information.

We began this section by proposing that Zelda's *She's on a diet* created a topic shift picked up by the two other women in the conversation and elaborated upon as a way of building solidarity through positive politeness. After noting that this interpretation was consistent with a great deal of work on gender and discourse, we compared some other participant realignments created during same-gender talk to those created during cross-gender talk. Our comparison showed that Zelda's realignments were inclusive and reinforcing, i.e. they seemed to allow participants to continue their prior (relatively active) roles; Henry's realignments were not only more divisive, but he also pursued them more completely, and they created more radical shifts in participant structure. Note that our interpretations have said nothing about participants' personalities (e.g. Zelda is being "kind") or intentions (e.g. Henry is "trying" to show Irene that he knows "what's best for her"); rather, we have tried to focus upon the interactional effects of what is said. Nor have we said, despite the seemingly cooperative nature of Zelda's actions (i.e. Zelda and Irene seem to share interactive goals) and the competitive nature of Henry's actions (i.e. Henry and Irene seem to have different interactive goals) that one alignment strategy reveals friendship and the other antagonism; rather, both sets of actions seem to reveal and create interpersonal involvement – the difference being in the means by which involvement is created (Tannen 1984).

Differences such as those just noted are consistent with prior work on gender and discourse (although they also show some of the more subtle ways that footing and alignment can be created, maintained, and shifted). However, it is important to note that not all realignments differ so dramatically by gender. Recall the example in which Zelda prompted Irene to tell me who she bowls with (5). Although I did not focus upon Henry's contribution in this exchange, let us examine it here:

(5) IRENE: (j)   [Oh yeh, this year the kids have] their own team,=
     HENRY: (k)   [Kids. They have a very good thing.]
     IRENE: (l)   [and they're . . .] [they're eh . . . They're giving us a=]
     DEBBY: (m)   [Oh great!   ]
     HENRY: (n)   [They got a good thing going.]
     IRENE: (o)   =run for our money cause we- we're in first place and they're
                    in second, and they're- they cheer everytime we lose a game.

As Irene incorporates Zelda's prompted information into her answer to me, Henry begins to evaluate Irene's response – much as he did in (3) and (6). Here, however, Henry's evaluations are positive, and perhaps because of this, they do not shift the participant structure at all. Rather, they are heard more as background support not only for Irene's bowling teams and for her family, but also for her stance in our conversation.

Consider, also, what happened prior to (5) – an exchange that I present below as (7).

(7) DEBBY: (a)   Does anybody here bowl?
              (b)   [D'you go bowling?
     ZELDA: (c)   [Yeh [she does.
     HENRY: (e)   [We used to.
     DEBBY: (f)   [Do you?
     HENRY: (g)   [She does.
     IRENE: (h)   [Yeh.

My initial question (*Does anybody here bowl?* (a)) is addressed to the group in general, but I quickly make it more specific and ask Irene if she bowls (*D'you go bowling?* (b)). While I am addressing my question to Irene, Zelda answers my first question about Irene: *Yeh she does* (c). I use Zelda's answer to continue to address Irene: rather than saying *Oh she does?*, for example, I bring Irene back into the question–answer format by asking for her confirmation with *Do you?* (f). Note that Henry also answers for Irene – *She does* (g) – but that he does so after reporting on his own situation (*We used to* (e)). Thus, we might interpret Henry's *She does* as a repetition of Zelda, and as an effort to join a framework that has shifted *before* his own utterance. Note, finally, that Irene also answers for herself: her *Yeh* (in h) follows my question to her and overlaps with Henry's answer about her (from g). In brief, Zelda, Henry, and Irene all provide the information that Irene goes bowling. Zelda and Henry both seem to be speaking for Irene: although there is a slight difference in the realignment among participants that their utterances create (simply because Zelda speaks for Irene *before* Henry does), there is nowhere near as dramatic a difference in realignment by gender as we saw in our other examples.

We began this section by noting that the exchange among Irene, Zelda, and myself might be (partially) due to gender-related notions of what is important to pursue in a conversation, and even more compelling, that the kinds of alignments taken up at various points in the conversation help display (if not create) gender identities. I supported this idea by discussing some ways that participant alignments seem to differ when shifts are created during cross-gender as opposed to same-gender talk, also noting some interchanges that illustrate less dramatic gender differences.

We need to be careful, however, not to generalize beyond the few examples that I have discussed here. The avoidance of any kind of generalization that is not based on case by case analysis is the methodological counterpart of the interactional sociolinguistic focus on situated meaning. Thus, if we wanted to be on firmer footing about gender and participant realignments, we would have to examine each realignment in detail: because each utterance (or exchange, or interaction) is situated in its own particular way, we would need to pay more careful attention to the ways that utterances (exchanges or interactions) differ from one another, as well as the ways that they are similar. Similarly, we might want to consider further what it means to say that someone is behaving in a particular "gender role": we might say, perhaps, that sounding authoritative and traditional is part of what it means to talk like a middle-aged man in lower middle-class Jewish American culture – not just to "act like a man." Note, finally, how our concerns have shifted. We began (3.2.1) by discussing participant roles (sender/principal, spokesperson/animator, recipient). We then discussed how an understanding of self–other relationships adds to our ability to account for speech act sequences (3.2.2). Now we have discussed the way interactional alignments reveal more stable participant identities, such as gender.

3.3 *"Speaking for another" and taking the role of the other*

In previous sections, we situated the meaning of a single utterance, *She's on a diet*, in several different ways: as a participation framework within the micro-structure of an interaction, as a socially motivated account within a sequence of acts, and as a gender-based involvement strategy. Our means of analysis included comparing the particular utterance *She's on a diet* with other utterances whose text and context were similar in some ways, but different in others.

Trying to locate a behavior in relation to other behaviors – to that with which it is similar in some ways, but different in others – is important, for one might very well argue that we cannot really understand what a phenomenon *is* without also understanding what it is not. (Of course comparing two entities that are totally different from each other would not give us a very good idea about what gives either one an identity: we need some shared quality to make such a comparison meaningful.) We can also compare behaviors at a more abstract level of analysis. What can help us here is a higher-level construct that allows us to more systematically discover both the similarities and the differences between the two entities in relation to each other and that construct. This sort of classificatory procedure is common in interactional sociolinguistics: for example, Goffman (1974) helps us understand the shared (and unshared) features of requests and apologies by considering them both as remedial acts (acts that circumvent violations of the other). Similarly, Tannen (1984) proposes that telling personal stories and asking rapid, overlapping questions are both high involvement strategies; Brown and Levinson (1987) suggest that "y'know" and compliments are both positive face strategies.

In this section, we consider speaking for another as part of two higher-level analytical constructs that are themselves related to each other: speaking for another is an act in which one person *takes the role of another*, and taking the role of another is itself a way of *showing sequential coherence*.

Let us begin by recalling one of Goffman's observations critical to the analysis of discourse: when two (or more) people come together, they not only respond to the institutional and interactional orders in which they find themselves, but they are also co-constructors of those orders. The entry of language into this relationship is especially pervasive, simply because a current-utterance creates a range of potential contexts to which a next-utterance can respond. It is easy to see how the context-reflecting and context-creating role of language can locate utterances as part of a particular institutional order. Consider, for example, the utterance *Drink?* When said by a bartender to someone sitting at a bar, we understand *Drink?* as an offer to sell something (or as a directive to place an order) in a particular kind of service encounter. We also know that an appropriate response might be *Michelob*, but not *No thanks, I'm not thirsty*. Because *Drink?* would not be understood as an offer to sell a drink in other contexts (e.g. during a dinner party) or among different participants in the same setting (e.g. if said by one customer to another), *Drink?* reflects its institutional setting. It also helps to create an interpretation of the setting as one in which a service encounter is taking place in a way that other utterances might not.

Utterances can also reflect and create the particulars of an interactional order. If we take Irene's refusal (*No*) of Henry's offer of candy (*Want a piece of candy?*) as a current-utterance, we can imagine a number of different next-utterances from Henry.

(8) HENRY: Want a piece of candy?
     IRENE: No.   current-utterance]
     HENRY: (a) Oh c'mon.   next-utterances ⌐
           (b) There's nothing wrong with it!
           (c) Suit yourself.
           (d) Just testing you! I know you're on a diet.
           (e) What?
           (f) I didn't hear you.
           (g) What time did the teachers leave?
           (h) Y'know I bought this candy at that new place in the mall, and when I was there /continues/ ⌐

The utterances in (8) select different aspects of Irene's *No* as a basis for response, and in so doing, they provide an interpretive context for the utterance pair. Some utterances in (8) are clearly linked to the prior offer–refusal sequence itself (a to d), whereas others are tied to more mechanical and general aspects of language production (e and f); still others provide the prior offer–refusal pair with an additional sequential identity, e.g. as a side sequence (g) or as a lead into a new topic (h). As I noted above, what is important about this range of responses (and certainly more could be added; see Goffman 1981b: 68–70, on which this example is modelled) is that each next-utterance selects a slightly different aspect of the current-utterance as a basis from which to respond. In so doing, it provides an interpretive context in which not only the next-utterance, but the entire utterance pair can be understood. Put another way, a next-utterance is a slot in which a speaker can both respond to, and create, a *prior* context. Although this mutually constituting relationship – just the sort of codependency between self and context that I noted above – might seem to constrain interactants, it also gives them a tremendous creative potential to lead interactions in a number of different directions (accounting, perhaps, for some of the topic fluidity that is often associated with conversation; e.g. Dorval 1990).

One reason why the self/context codependency is important for discourse analysis lies in the notion of sequential coherence. The utterances in (8) reflect not just the variety of ways that a current-utterance can be understood, but a variety of different frameworks for understanding talk – as actions (a to d), as language production (e, f), as topic structure (g, h). What makes all of the utterances in (8) interpretable as sequentially coherent is the availability of different interpretive frames for talk – different ways of contextualizing what is said. Put another way, each framework provides a different basis for understanding how one utterance follows another – a different resource for sequential coherence. (Note that we may easily express this in either Gumperz's or Tannen's terms: the different utterances are contextualization cues pointing to, or meta-messages about, different interpretive frames.)

Another resource in the repertoire being described is the participants in talk themselves: self and other. Let us take the self first; some different ways that the self can become a resource, again, for Henry's next-utterance, are illustrated in (9):

(9) (a) Yeh, I shouldn't have any either.
     (b) Right, I forgot you're on a diet.
     (c) Oh- I meant fruit.
     (d) It really annoys me when you don't take candy.
     (e) I admire your will power.

As (9) illustrates, a next response can be a comment about one's own action (a, b), a self-repair (c), or a personal sentiment (d, e). Just as the self can be a resource for response, so too, can the other; (10) illustrates some ways – roughly parallel to those in (9) – that the other can be a basis for Henry's next-utterance:

(10) (a) You never accept my offers.
      (b) You're on a diet again.
      (c) Did you say no?
      (d) You're stubborn about that diet.

Just as a response can focus upon the self in relation to an action, so too can it focus upon the other (a, b); similarly, a response can be either a self repair or an other repair (c), or offer an assessment of the self or other (d).

Although it might seem that self and other provide interchangeable alternatives as a focus for a next-utterance, the interactional repercussions of using the other as a resource for response are quite different. One way of expressing this difference is in terms of Brown and Levinson's notion of face: using another's words can theaten the other's negative face wants (i.e. not to be imposed upon). Thus, as we saw in our earlier examples, the way an other-based response is treated depends, in part, on what is said about the other: although negative assessments of the other (as in some of Henry's comments about Irene) are treated as violations, positive assessments (as in some of Zelda's comments about Irene) may actually reinforce positive face wants.

Thus far in this section, we have proposed two analytical constructs that are themselves related to each other. We began by considering resources for sequential coherence, then considering the use of self or other as a particular resource. Speaking for another is an act that fits into both these constructs: it is one way of providing sequential coherence by drawing upon the other as a resource for a next utterance. What differentiates it from other such acts is, first, that it is an act that emerges during a three-party interaction – in which a spokesperson animates the words of another (a principal) to an addressed recipient. More critically, speaking for another displays an interpersonal stance in which a spokesperson not only *uses* the other as a basis for a next-utterance, but enters into the other's perspective to issue a next-utterance from that other's point of view. Thus, speaking for another is a way of "taking the role of the other."

Although not often discussed as an explicit part of interactional sociolinguistics, the notion of taking the role of the other is critical to the foundations of interactional sociolinguistics because it is critical to the process of interaction itself. Learning the specific cluster of behaviors normatively expected of one who occupies a particular social position (Goffman 1961) is critical to the process of socialization into a specific community. As argued by George Herbert Mead (1934), this process is made possible by the symbolic resources provided through language and evidence of shared meanings provided during communication. To oversimplify a great deal, we learn the standards of normative behavior by observing how others respond to us, anticipating another's response, and incorporating a kind of generalized response into our own repertoire of actions and meanings. Although this process is critical to the emergence of communicative competence (as well as the development of a self), it hardly ends once we are socialized. Not only is much of what we say explicitly or implicitly oriented toward reception by a hearer, but we often continue to display an awareness of norms and standards in the way we use language and the way we interact with others. And speaking a language is itself a process that requires *symbolically* putting oneself in the other's place in order to know how to tailor one's information (syntactically, semantically, and pragmatically) so that it will be comprehendable to that other. What speaking for another thus represents is the ritualization – the formal display – of a process that is at the very crux of social interaction: speaking for another can be seen as the linguistic submersion of the self in the interactive process itself.

3.4 Summary of sample analysis

We began this section by focusing on a single utterance said by Zelda about Irene to Henry and me: *She's on a diet.* At one level of analysis, this is an utterance that accounts for a rejected offer issued through a question (chapter 3). Here we characterized this utterance as a quite different act: one person "speaks for" another. We situated the meaning of this act in several ways: as a display of participant alignment, gender identity, interactional frames, and as a means of building sequential coherence through taking the role of the other. Each effort to uncover situated meaning depended upon a comparison with other utterances and interactions with which it is both similar and different, and upon a movement from a particular utterance to more general frameworks – or contexts – in which that utterance was interactively and socially embedded. Implicit in this procedure was a belief that it is the contextualization of an utterance that motivates its use: the contexts in which an utterance occurs explain why it occurs there.

Note, also, that context allowed us to sidestep the attribution of motivation to participants. Our sample analysis was, in some ways, an attempt to explain why a speaker produced a certain utterance at a certain point in time. Asking why someone does something can lead us into a search for explanations of human conduct – a domain of inquiry that linguists are probably not prepared (or eager) to enter. Interactional sociolinguistics tries to avoid imputing intentions (or any internal motivations or goals) to speakers. Rather than say, for example, that Henry wanted to "dominate" the others in conversation, we can say that Henry reoriented the participation framework in ways that maintained his active role as animator and principal. What this approach thus uses to account for why someone says or does something is not the construct of "motivation," but "discourse strategy": a wide range of expressions, features, and so on – e.g. politeness (Brown and Levinson 1987) and repetition (Tannen 1990) – are said to serve as techniques (i.e. strategies) suited to the fulfillment of very broad interpersonal goals (e.g. face wants, involvement). In Goffman's (1967a: 13) terms, we may say that these strategies serve as "traffic rules of social interaction . . . the code the person adheres to in his movement across the paths and designs of others." Thus, just as Henry's way of speaking reoriented the participation framework, Zelda's way of speaking ("speaking for" Irene) served as a strategy for interpersonal solidarity and involvement. Note, then, that interactional sociolinguistics does not necessarily explain how a way of speaking conveys a specific intention – although it can seek to explain how a way of speaking serves a broad interactional goal. Furthermore, because the nature of that goal is interpreted according to the contexts in which something is said, what interactional sociolinguistics does is ground motivation in context – such that both the meaning and the motivation of an utterance are contextualized.

We also noted that we need to be careful not to generalize beyond the few examples that we have discussed here: since each utterance (behavior, interaction, encounter, and so on) is itself situated in a particular way, a generalization can be developed only through detailed attention to the contexts of each particular case. The particularities of each case, however, did not prevent us from trying to view that case in terms of higher level analytical constructs: we viewed speaking for another as a way of taking the role of another, which itself, is a resource for sequential coherence (cf. Goffman (1971) and Schiffrin (1977), who viewed greetings and farewells as a type of access ritual, and access rituals, in turn, as a type of supportive interchange). (Contrast the ethnomethodological avoidance of such constructs; chapter 7.)

In sum, each context of an utterance has a crucial analytical role in interactional sociolinguistics. Considered along with the relatively observable contexts of what was said before and what is said next are the more abstract contexts of the place of an utterance in a repertoire of ritual interchanges, face-saving strategies, or resources for sequential coherence. All are sources of meaning for what is said and evidence for what is done in talk.

4 Interactional sociolinguistics as an approach to discourse

We have seen in this chapter that interactional sociolinguistics provides an approach to discourse that focuses upon situated meaning. Scholars taking this approach combine the ideas of the anthropologist John Gumperz and the sociologist Erving Goffman. What Gumperz contributes to this approach is a set of concepts and tools that provide a framework within which to analyze the use of language during interpersonal communication; Gumperz views language as a socially and culturally constructed symbol system that both reflects and creates macro-level social meaning and micro-level interpersonal meanings. Speakers use language to provide continual indices of who they are and what they want to communicate. The work of Erving Goffman also focuses upon situated knowledge, the self, and social context in a way that complements Gumperz's focus on situated inference: Goffman provides a sociological framework for describing and understanding the form and meaning of the social and interpersonal contexts that provide presuppositions for the interpretation of meaning.

We applied the ideas of Goffman and Gumperz to a particular utterance, trying to uncover its situated meaning and to see how that meaning contributed to the processes and outcome of interaction. We analyzed *She's on a diet* in several different ways: we began with its location in an action structure (similar to those we discussed in chapter 3) and then went on to consider its role in a participation framework within the micro-structure of an interaction and as a gender-based involvement strategy. These analyses viewed speaking for another as a discourse strategy used by males and females to realize different interactional goals – as a contextualization cue through which participants signal identity and alignment. (Note that in viewing the social function of contextualization cues at a micro-level of status and power, we are extending Gumperz's view that these cues signal status and power at a macro-level of social relations.) Finally, we also considered how "speaking for another" is one way of taking the role of the other, and how this, in turn, is a resource for sequential coherence.

There were still other contexts in which we could have situated the meaning of "speaking for another." As Goffman's work shows, for example, all interactive activity is socially organized at multiple levels: all utterances are situated within contexts such as "occasions," "situations," or "encounters" that not only provide structure and meaning to what is said, but may themselves be organized by what is said (e.g. Goffman 1963). What Gumperz stresses is the interpretive importance of contexts, including, of course, the occasion in which an utterance is produced. Contextualization cues provide information allowing participants to interpret the meaning of what is said; one way that they do so is to locate an utterance within an interpretive frame identifying an encounter as a particular kind of occasion or situation. Thus, another source of contextual meaning – and interpretations based on that meaning – is the overall structure of an occasion (see chapter 5).[5]

Our means of analysis included comparing the particular utterance *She's on a diet* with other utterances whose text and context were similar in some ways, but different in others. Although much of our discussion focused on inter-actions other than that in which *She's on a diet* occurred, we always selected (and analyzed) those interactions in terms of what they could contribute to our understanding of *She's on a diet*.

Our overall effort also depended upon a movement from a particular utterance to more general frameworks – or contexts – in which that utterance was interactively and socially embedded. Implicit in this procedure was a belief that it is the contextualization of an utterance that motivates its use: the contexts in which an utterance occurs explain why it occurs there. Consistent with this belief, we tried to identify different aspects of contexts, the organiz-ational and interpretive role of contexts, and the contextualizing role of different ways of speaking (i.e. as contextualization cues or meta-messages).

In sum, interactional sociolinguistics views discourse as a social interaction in which the emergent construction and negotiation of meaning is facilitated by the use of language. Although the interactional approach is basically a functional approach to language, its focus on function is balanced in import-ant ways. The work of Goffman forces structural attention to the contexts in which language is used: situations, occasions, encounters, participation frame-works, and so on, have forms and meanings that are partially created and/or sustained by language. Similarly, language is patterned in ways that reflect those contexts of use. Put another way, language and context co-constitute one another: language contextualizes and is contextualized, such that language does not just function "in" context, language also forms and provides context. One particular context is social interaction. Language, culture, and society are grounded in interaction: they stand in a reflexive relationship with the self, the other, and the self–other relationship, and it is out of these mutually constitutive relationships that discourse is created.

Exercises

1 Analyze the excerpt in appendix 3 (or any other of your own choosing) in terms of participant alignments, footing, and contextualization cues.

- What kind of interaction is going on? What makes it sound like a hostile (or sociable: Schiffrin 1984a) argument? A lecture? A friendly discussion? An interview? Anything else?
- What aspects of the utterances (e.g. contextualization cues) signal shifts in participation structure? For example, when and how are the interlocutors cooperating? Competing? Why do alignments seem to shift, and how do they do so?
- Are there contextual presuppositions that are necessary to make sense out of what is being said? If so, how is the importance of these presuppositions conveyed?
- What social and interactional identities are relevant to the interaction? How are these identities being managed through the discussion?

2 Encounters are often bracketed by relatively straightforward interactional rituals (i.e. greetings) which first open a period of interpersonal access (see Goffman 1967; Schegloff 1972a; Schiffrin 1977) and then close that period of access (Schegloff and Sacks 1973). Yet the exchange below seems to combine parts of both an opening and a closing.

Professor A is in her office preparing for class (the door is open) when Professor B walks by.
A: (looking into the hallway) Hi.
B: (walking by without stopping) Hi.
A few minutes later, B is in his office and A walks by.
A: (walking by without stopping) See you.
B: Hi.
    On your way to class?
A: Cool, calm, and collected!

How would you explain this interaction? Under what circumstances can such an exchange occur?

3 Everyday stories provide useful data for an interactional perspective: one can analyze not only how the story is situated in an ongoing social interaction (e.g. Jefferson 1978; Ochs et al. 1991; Schiffrin 1984b) but also how social interactions within the experience being recreated create a story world (e.g. Labov 1981; chapter 3 of this book). One linguistic device used to report social interaction in narratives is quoted speech, or what Tannen (1989: chapter 4) calls constructed dialogue: the storyteller animates the voices of characters in the story. Apply an interactional analysis to the reported interactions (including constructed dialogue) in the "I was robbed" story in chapter 6 of this book or to a story that you have collected. For example, what social actions and interactions are reported? What participation frameworks and alignments are created within the story world? How does the story world justify the speaker's telling of the story in the ongoing interaction?

4 Linguists often speak of some of the same words and expressions as discourse markers and interjections, even though these groups of items are defined differently. Discourse markers are sequentially dependent expressions that optionally initiate utterances (Schiffrin 1987a). Interjections are forms that occur "predominantly as minor sentences, entering into few or no constructions other than parataxis" (Bloomfield 1933: 176ff.). But some terms (e.g. oh)

are said to be both discourse markers and interjections, and some analysts view both sets of items through a single functional lens (e.g. Goffman's 1981e analysis of response cries). Use an interactional sociolinguistic approach to identify and analyze the discourse markers and interjections in a sample of data. Compare the interactional functions of these expressions to the function of *mmhmm, ummm,* and other vocalizations that fill conversational space without contributing referential meaning.

Notes

1　Note, also, the constant stream of new diet books and the prevalence in our culture of food-related neuroses. Interestingly, however, there are also opposing values, e.g. the association between weight and prosperity (I have heard portly men described as prosperous looking) or the idea that we have "to fatten up" to be healthy.

2　Such familiarity can be based on either personal or positional knowledge about the other: for example, personal knowledge might allow me to make a decent guess about what my father wants for dessert (thus leading me to offer him something that he is not likely to reject); positional knowledge might allow an employee to make a good guess about what kind of accommodations an employer wants on a business trip (thus leading an employee to offer a choice of hotels likely to contain a place that is appropriate).

3　Note that the role of *should* (a modal of obligation) is critical here, for it invokes Henry as an authority about Irene's own affairs. We can see the importance of *should* quite easily by imagining that, instead of saying *She's on a diet*, Zelda had said either *She should be on a diet* or *You shouldn't take it*. Regardless of whether reference to Irene is third person (as an unaddressed recipient) or second person (as an addressed recipient), we would interpret Zelda as invoking authority – and as being as intrusive as Henry. Similarly, if instead of saying *She should be*, Henry had just said *She used to be* and then gone on with his description of Irene's family, we would be more likely to interpret Henry as building solidarity with Irene.

4　Efforts by one speaker to prompt another to provide information can be seen as ritualized displays of more instrumentally motivated clarification requests. Instead of B asking A for clarification about what A has said, B tries to get A to provide self-clarification in a way consistent with B's notion of what is "correct." Both the ritualized and instrumental versions of this move reveal the division of interactional responsibility and control that Ochs (1985) calls an "expressed guess" strategy.

5　In Tannen's work, the contextualizing role of occasions and situations can be conveyed in terms of frames (i.e. structures of expectations) or meta-messages (Tannen 1979; Tannen and Wallat 1986): utterances are not only framed by occasions and encounters, they may themselves convey meta-messages about the initiation, continuation, alteration or closing of a frame. Similarly, contextualization cues may be said to provide meta-messages about how to contextualize or frame an utterance (Tannen 1984).

5 The Ethnography of Communication

1 Introduction

The ethnography of communication is an approach to discourse that is based in anthropology and linguistics. As we see in this chapter, this approach is the most encompassing of all those considered. Not only does it focus upon a wider range of communicative behaviors than the other approaches, but built into its theory and methodology is an intentional openness to discovery of the variety of forms and functions available for communication, and to the way such forms and functions are part of different ways of life. In addition, the ethnography of communication is not an approach that can "simply take separate results from linguistics, psychology, sociology, ethnology, as given, and seek to correlate them" (Hymes 1974a: 20, fn.6). Rather, it is an approach that seeks to open new analytical possibilities (by finding new kinds of data and asking new questions) and to propose new theories. It seeks to do so by analyzing patterns of communication as part of cultural knowledge and behavior: this entails a recognition of both the diversity of communicative possibilities and practices (i.e. cultural relativity) and the fact that such practices are an integrated part of what we know and do as members of a particular culture (i.e. a holistic view of human beliefs and actions).

The key figure responsible for the development of the ethnography of communication is Dell Hymes. After describing the basic assumptions and concepts of this approach (section 2; see also Saville-Troike 1982), I apply it to discourse by focusing on one particular speech act – questions – in two different varieties of a speech event – interviews (section 3). Section 4 summarizes the ethnographic approach.

2 Defining the ethnography of communication

Although the ethnography of communication was developed by Hymes in a series of papers written in the 1960s and 1970s (many of which are collected in his 1974 *Foundations in Sociolinguistics: An Ethnographic Approach*), the roots of this approach reach back to Edward Sapir's (1933) movement away from the study of sociocultural form and content as "product" toward their study as "process" (Hymes 1974a: 20, fn.6). Also important was the emphasis of the Prague School of linguistics (e.g. Mathesius 1924) on the penetration of language structure by function. A more contemporary impetus for the ethnography of communication as a particular mode of inquiry stemmed from Hymes's observation of theoretical and methodological difficulties in two different fields: anthropology and linguistics. After explaining how some of the central assumptions and constructs of the ethnography of communication stem from both of these fields (2.1), I outline the methodology of this approach (2.2) and note its relation to other approaches to discourse (2.3).

2.1 *"Communication" in anthropology and linguistics*

The ethnography of communication builds a single integrated framework in which communication has a central role in both anthropological and linguistic studies. Although I explain this role by discussing each field separately, we will see that the key concepts and methods intentionally bring together the two separate starting points, building an interdependence between them.

Linguistics and anthropology are disciplines whose data, problems, methods, and theories are often seen as clearly distinct from one another. However, one area in which both fields share an interest is "communication." Since language is the central means by which people communicate with one another in everyday life (see chapter 11), understanding communication is an important goal for linguists. The understanding of communication is also important for anthropologists: the way we communicate is part of our cultural repertoire for making sense of – and interacting with – the world. As Hymes observed, however, anthropologists often ignore language as cultural behavior and/or knowledge, neglecting the ways that language is a system of use whose rules and norms are as integral a part of culture as any other system of knowledge and behavior (e.g. kinship, or political, systems). Thus, the status of linguistic communication as a grammatical system that is used for communication and that is part of culture – and a framework for analyzing it as such – was surprisingly neglected prior to Hymes's work.

We noted above that anthropologists often pay little attention to language as cultural behavior and/or knowledge. Note that I have assumed here that "behavior" and "knowledge" are both "part of" culture. It is important to point out, however, that it is not always easy to find agreement among anthropologists as to what comprises "culture" or the locus of "culture" itself (Kroeber and Kluckhohn 1952, for example, review over fifty definitions of culture). The view that Hymes seems to adopt is that culture is a system of ideas that underlies and gives meaning to behavior in society (cf. Keesing 1974). (As we see in a moment, however, this does not preclude the possibility that behavior and knowledge can be analytically separated.) Culture thus comprises a general "world view": a set of assumptions and beliefs that orient and organize the way people think, feel, and act.

However, not every aspect of culture – not every part of our cognitive "blueprint" – needs to be shared (i.e. known) by all members. "To restrict the concept of the cultural to something shared to the limits of a community is an arbitrary limitation on understanding, of both human beings and the cultural" (Hymes 1974a: 20, fn. 6). The possibility of differential knowledge is also implied in Hymes's (1973) point that members of a culture may have available to them different forms, and be differentially comptetent in, the way they draw upon a communicative repertoire (or the parts of the repertoire from which they choose). Thus, one can differentiate the ability to engage in a particular meaningful behavior from the fact of that behavior itself: "what is distinctively cultural, as an aspect of behavior or of things, is a question of capabilities acquired or elicited in social life, rather than a question of the extent to which the behavior or things themselves are shared" (Hymes 1974a: 20, fn. 6). But, as noted above, neither knowledge nor behavior has to be available to, or realized by, every member. Freeing both knowledge and behavior from a "sharedness" requirement allows almost any piece of knowledge (or any behavior) to be part of culture:

> The frequency and spread of a trait is important, but secondary, so far as concerns the criterion for its being a product of cultural behavior, as having a cultural aspect. A sonnet, for example, is such a product, whether or not it goes beyond a desk drawer, or even survives the moment of completion. (Hymes 1974a: 21, fn. 6)

Thus, neither knowledge nor behavior need be completely replicated to be part of culture. (Compare Hymes's (1972: 54) definition of a speech community as "a community sharing rules for the conduct and interpretation of speech, and rules for the interpretation of at least one linguistic variety." See also his (1984) discussion of linguistic problems in defining the concept of "tribe.")

We have suggested thus far that language is a system of use whose rules and norms are an integral part of culture. We also noted that the locus of culture is knowledge. Thus, we might say that language use in speech situations, events, and acts (2.2) helps realize the cultural norms that underlie the way we act toward one another: culture is continually created, negotiated, and redefined in concrete acts between persons who are participating in some kind of interactive situation (cf. Geertz 1973; Malinowski 1978; Ochs 1988). Thus, the way we communicate with each other is constrained by culture (simply because it is a part of culture), but it also reveals and sustains culture. From an analytical standpoint, an analysis of the patterns that are formed when we communicate thus contributes to our understanding of culture. Language use is also a type (and a part) of social behavior in many different institutional realms (e.g. political, economic, religious, family) that are themselves bound to culture. Thus the norms that guide communication also reflect, and help constitute, social institutions.

Hymes argues that ethnographers can analyze communicative patterns using the traditional method of anthropological research: participant observation. By participating in a wide range of activities endemic to the life of a particular group of people, one attempts to replace one's own way of thinking, believing, and acting with a framework in which what is done by the members of another group starts to seem "expected" and "natural." The challenge faced by an anthropologist is thus, in some ways, similar to that faced by any neophyte: an anthropologist has to learn what native members already know about how to "make sense" out of experience. Although ways of speaking (and more generally, communicating) are clearly part of this knowledge, recognition and analysis of those patterns (as noted above) were not often goals of anthropological fieldwork. It is this that Hymes sought to rectify.

Linguists ignored the study of communicative patterns and systems of language use for reasons quite different from those of anthropologists. Chomsky's (1957, 1965) reformulation of the goals of linguistic theory excluded the analysis of performance (cf. de Saussure's "parole"), focusing theoretical interest instead on competence, i.e. tacit knowledge of the abstract rules of language (cf. de Saussure's "langue"). Rather than concentrate linguistic theory on competence, Hymes proposed that scholarship focus on communicative competence: the knowledge governing appropriate use of grammar. Knowledge of abstract linguistic rules is included in communicative competence. But also included is the ability to use language in concrete situations of everyday life: the ability to engage in conversation, to shop in a store, to interview (and be interviewed) for a job, to pray, joke, argue, tease, warn, and even to know when to be silent. Furthermore, the study of language in use – the study of how we *are* communicatively competent – contributes "in an empirical and comparative way [to] many notions that underlie linguistic theory proper" (Hymes 1974a: 20; also Hymes 1981), simply because it is not easy (either theoretically or methodologically) to separate areas of language that are insulated from cultural and social processes, from those that are vulnerable to such processes (Ochs 1988: 3).

We noted above that the ethnography of communication builds a single integrated framework in which communication has a central role in both anthropological and linguistic studies, such that key concepts and methods bridge the two separate starting points. One such concept is communicative competence: knowledge of grammar and knowledge governing appropriate use of grammar. The methods for studying communicative competence are also integrative (2.2). The ethnography of communication shares with much traditional anthropology a concern for holistic explanations of meaning and behavior, i.e. explanations that locate particular behaviors (including, but not limited to, utterances) in a wider framework of beliefs, actions, and norms. Also shared with anthropology is an emphasis on how meanings and behaviors need to be understood in an analytical framework in which comparisons establish not only what is different in different cultures (i.e. the "diversity" noted on p. 143), but also what is potentially the same. The discovery of universals, however, is based only upon the ethnographic discovery of particulars: "one cannot only generalize the particularities, but also particularize the generalities" (Hymes 1974a: 9).

The particularities that ethnographers discover are particularities of language use. However, in keeping with the partial linguistic heritage of the ethnography of communication, these particularities also reside in linguistic form and structure itself: the form of a message (and the rules governing that form) is as critical to interpretation of particular functions as its content (Hymes 1972b: 59). One way that Hymes makes this point is by referring to Ernst Cassirer's (1961: 99) analysis of the necessity for art of "two fundamental factors, which constitute the whole of the work only by means of their union and interpenetration." Hymes (1981: 9) suggests that "interpretation that excludes speech falls short, as would treatment of painting that excluded paint."[1] And speech is to be analyzed as linguistic structure within a relativistic (i.e. "emic" (2.2)) and holistic (i.e. "ethnographic") mode of inquiry:

> The essential method . . . is simply persistence in seeking systematic co-variation of form and meaning. The spirit of the method is "structural" in the sense of Sapir's linguistics, "emic" and "ethnographic" in the sense of concern for valid description of the individual case. (Hymes 1981: 10)

2.2 *Methodology: an etic grid for ethnography*

We noted above that ethnographers of communication analyze communicative patterns using the method of participant observation: a key goal is to learn what members of a culture know about how to "make sense" out of experience and how they communicate those interpretations. To this end, Hymes proposed a methodology by which to discover "what counts" as communicative events. The methodology is based on the distinction between "emic" and "etic." Linguists studying the sound system of an unfamiliar language try to discover phonemic patterns (i.e. what sounds are "meaningful" in a particular language) with the help of a phonetic classification (i.e. what sounds are physically possible). So, too, one can discover communicative units with the help of a classification system that dissects communication into the components of which it may be potentially comprised. One can then also discover communicative patterns (e.g. a systematically differentiated inventory of events) formed by interrelationships among components.

The classificatory grid that Hymes (1972b) proposed is known as the SPEAKING grid: each letter is an abbreviation for a different possible component of communication.

S   setting   physical circumstances
    scene   subjective definition of an occasion
P   participants   speaker/sender/addressor
                         hearer/receiver/audience/addressee
E   ends   purposes and goals
                         outcomes
A   act sequence   message form and content
K   key   tone, manner
I   instrumentalities
                         channel (verbal, nonverbal, physical)
                         forms of speech drawn from community repertoire
N   norms of interaction and interpretation
                         specific proprieties attached to speaking
                         interpretation of norms within cultural belief system
G   genre   textual categories

The SPEAKING grid can be used to discover a local (i.e. culturally relative) taxonomy of communicative "units" that are "in some recognizable way bounded or integral" (Hymes 1972b: 56). The largest such unit is the speech situation: the social occasion in which speech may occur (e.g. meals). Although speech situations may provide the setting or scene in which speech occurs, they are not themselves governed by a single set of rules. The next unit is the speech event: "activities, or aspects of activities, that are directly governed by rules or norms of the use of speech" (Hymes 1972b: 56). The smallest unit is the speech act: although Hymes (1972b) does not explicitly define this, his examples include acts that can be defined through their illocutionary force (chapter 3; e.g. commands, greetings), as well as those that cannot be so defined (e.g. jokes). Although discourse is important to all the units, it seems to be the speech act level that is most fundamental to the local, turn by turn management of discourse: "Discourse may be viewed in terms of acts both syntagmatically and paradigmatically: i.e., both as a sequence of speech acts and in terms of classes of speech acts among which choice has been made at given points" (Hymes 1972b: 57). Finally, the larger units in the set embed the smaller: a party is a speech situation; a conversation during the party is a speech event; a joke within the conversation is a speech act (Hymes 1972b: 56).

2.3   *Summary: the integration of diversity*

In chapter 2, we used Hymes's (1974b) comparison between structural and functional approaches in linguistics as a way of differentiating two definitions of discourse analysis. The ethnography of communication falls squarely within the functionalist paradigm: in fact, we might take Hymes's presentation of this paradigm as the presentation of core premises of the ethnographic approach. I present these features again here:

1 Structure of speech (act, event) as ways of speaking.
2 Analysis of use prior to analysis of code; organization of use discloses additional features and relations; shows code and use in integral (dialectical) relation.
3 Gamut of stylistic or social functions.
4 Elements and structures as ethnographically appropriate.
5 Functional (adaptive) differentiation of languages, varieties, styles; these being existentially (actually) not necessarily equivalent.
6 Speech community as matrix of code-repertoires, or speech styles ("organization of diversity").
7 Fundamental concepts taken as problematic and to be investigated.

As indicated in these features, the ethnography of communication is reluctant to assume a closed set of language functions that apply equally to all languages and all speech communities (3, 5): rather, diversity is assumed, and the limits of diversity are explored. Similarly, it is categories of language use, e.g. acts, events, not language structure, that have theoretical priority: language use itself is patterned and structured (1) and these regularities are central to one's discovery of properties of the linguistic code (2). As noted above, what *can* be assumed is diversity: structures and functions are relative adaptations to different cultural systems (4, 5); a single speech community is itself an "organization of diversity" (6). (The nature of such diversity, of course, needs to be empirically discovered before any generalizations can be proposed.) Note, also, that even the concepts that seem most fundamental – text, context, structure, function, communication – are "problematic" and in need of investigation (7). (It is because of this that the ethnographic approach can encompass (or even redefine) the other approaches to discourse discussed in this book; see below). Hymes (1974a: 9) summarizes functionalist assumptions in this way:

> primacy of speech to code, function to structure, context to message, the appropriate to the arbitrary or simply possible; but the interrelations always essential, so that one cannot only generalize the particularities, but also particularize the generalities.

Consider, also, that the ethnography of communication is the most integrative approach of those considered in this book: this reflects the fact that culture itself encompasses or embraces a totality of knowledge and practices. Thus, an ethnographic approach to discourse in general (and to questions in particular; section 3) can combine speech act and interactional approaches within a larger framework of inquiry. (I consider its relationship to the other approaches yet to be discussed – pragmatics, conversation analysis, variation analysis – in chapter 12.) Constitutive rules – knowledge of the conditions by which we recognize a speech act – are part of our cultural knowledge, as are the principles by which we organize our interactions and display our identities.

Since our knowledge of what words and meanings are appropriate for a given time, place, purpose, and so on is cultural knowledge, the use of contextualization cues to convey the contextual presuppositions of an utterance displays our communicative competence as a member of a certain culture and situates us in a particular web of beliefs and actions specific to that culture.

It would be misleading, however, to think that an ethnographic approach to discourse just adds a new component ("culture") to the basic material of speech acts and interactional sociolinguistics. Rather, to paraphrase Durkheim on the *sui generis* nature of society, an ethnographic approach creates a whole that is greater than the sum of its parts: it *seeks to define* the basic notions of the other approaches to discourse simply because it views all phases and aspects of communication (from the cognitive to the political) as relative to cultural meanings (e.g. Sherzer 1983). We see in the next section some of the ways that this approach applies to the analysis of questions.

3 Sample analysis: questions as speech acts in speech events

We saw in section 2 that the ethnography of communication is an approach to discourse that studies communicative competence. It does so by discovering and analyzing the patterns (structures) and functions of communicating that organize the use of language (in speech situations, events, and acts) in the conduct of social life. This section applies the ethnographic approach to the analysis of one particular speech act (questions) in two varieties of a speech event (interview).

We considered questions in earlier chapters from the point of view of speech act theory (chapter 3) and interactional sociolinguistics (chapter 4). In chapter 3, we discussed the felicity conditions underlying questions, beginning with the issue of how we might recognize a particular utterance (*Y'want a piece of candy?*) as a question. We also considered how a single utterance might enact more than one speech act (question, request, and offer) and how more than one utterance (e.g. a story) could realize a single speech act. Finally, we considered the way speech acts could be sequentially located and sequentially defined. Our approach in chapter 4 was quite different. Although we discussed the same utterance (*Y'want a piece of candy?*), our initial focus was on the way that utterance was responded to and how those responses were situated in a participation framework. We then went on to consider how a particular way of speaking displayed social identity and the more general implications of a particular interactional move ("speaking for another"). The broader issues raised by speech act and interactional approaches also differed. The speech act approach led us to consider issues such as the following: the role of speech act knowledge in communication, the multifunctionality of utterances, the functional basis of discourse structure. The interactional approach raised other issues: how utterances both reflect and create context, how "much" context (and what "kind of") context is used in interpreting the social meaning of an utterance, how utterances are potential indicators of social meaning.

Although we will not begin with the same utterance (*Y'want a piece of candy?*) here, our sample analysis in this chapter will provide yet another framework within which this utterance (and others that are functionally similar) could be considered: as a speech act within a speech event; more specifically, as a question within an interview. After briefly using the SPEAKING grid to describe two variants of the "interview" speech event (3.1), I illustrate some of the ways that questions are normatively situated within these speech events and related to their communicative properties: questions during interviews at a library reference desk (3.2); questions during sociolinguistic research interviews (3.3). The analysis goes well beyond discussion of the form, meaning, and use of questions themselves. Although I did not do ethnographic fieldwork, I try to reflect aspects of the ethnographic approach by drawing upon my own knowledge as a "native" informant who has participated in and observed both kinds of interviews. My descriptions preliminary to the analysis of the questions themselves thus try to reveal the circumstances surrounding, and perhaps accounting for, the normative meanings of those questions as particular types of verbal behavior. A result of this method is that we will see how ethnographers might address some of the same issues considered earlier: the relationship between form and function in questions (cf. chapter 3), and the contextual meanings of questions and responses (cf. chapter 4). Thus, we will see how the form–function relationship realized in single utterances is related to specific aspects of context. The systematic analysis of context as a framework within which form meets function is an important feature of the ethnographic approach, since as Hymes (1972a: xxviii) observes, form is not a reliable indicator of illocutionary force: "one and the same sentence, the same set of words in the same syntactic relationship, may now be a request, now a command, now a compliment, now an insult, depending upon tacit understandings within a community." Section 3.4 summarizes the sample analysis.

3.1 Interviews as speech events

Interviews are a speech event with which many people in American society have become familiar: "Interviewing has become a powerful force in modern society. Starting almost from birth, we are confronted by questions posed by educators, psychologists, pollsters, medical practitioners, and employers, and we listen to flamboyant interviewers on radio and television" (Briggs 1986: 1). Although all interviews may very well share some common core – the core that allows them all to be understood as different variants of the same speech event – they also differ among themselves. Interviews that serve a gatekeeping function (Erickson and Schultz 1982), for example, are asymmetric speech situations during which a person who represents a social institution seeks to gain information about the lives, beliefs, and practices of people outside of that institution in order to warrant the granting of an institutional privilege. In other interviews (e.g. survey research interview, opinion polls), an institutional representative still seeks information from and about outsiders, but that information will be taken back to members of the institution, with no direct or lasting effect on the lives of those who have provided the information. Interviews broadcast to a radio or television audience have additional (or alternative) functions (e.g. entertainment) that create quite different constraints on what is said, e.g. to have the guest talk to the audience about things the audience wants to know (*SF Focus*, July 1992). Despite differences such as these, questions are central to the information-gaining function of all interviews.

The central role of questions for interviews makes interviews a convenient speech event in which to locate an analysis of questions. The centrality of questions for interviews, however, does not mean that one can analyze questions from interviews by extracting them, as a group unto themselves, from the interviews in which they were asked. The multifaceted relationship between utterances and their contexts in general means that a great deal of information about questions and answers would be lost if one considered them as a dialogic pair isolated from surrounding actions and beliefs. As Briggs (1986: 104) suggests, "the interview must be analyzed as a whole before any of its component utterances are interpreted." The questions asked in interviews, then, cannot be interpreted apart from analysis of the interview itself.

Earlier we noted that systematic attention to, and analysis of, context is one of the most critical parts of an ethnographic approach to discourse. We also noted that a convenient way to "segment" contexts from one another (as units of analysis) is in terms of speech acts, speech events, and speech situations. These are all units that ethnographers analyze, and they can all be classified according to Hymes's SPEAKING grid (2.3). In the rest of this section, I illustrate the use of the SPEAKING grid as a heuristic by which to describe two types of interviews (the speech event) in which questions (the speech act) occur.

Table 5.1 uses Hymes' SPEAKING grid as a way of discovering the communicative features and qualities that underlie our knowledge of how to participate in two types of interviews and our identification of two events as certain "kinds" of occurrences. Although I do not comment in detail on each component from table 5.1 in the analyses, I will draw upon this grid when discussing questions in each interview in later sections. I focus particular attention on the ACT SEQUENCES and their relation to PARTICIPANTS and ENDS. (In all discussions to follow, I use capital letters to highlight the status of components from the SPEAKING grid.) Since questions are a key part of interviews, we can also examine questions themselves as a way of understanding the structure of the speech events in which they are used. At the same time, we will learn a great deal about questions because we will see how they are used by participants whose identities are relative to a particular speech event, to the goals defined by that speech event, and to the other acts accomplished during that speech event.

Table 5.1 Communicative components of different interviews

	Reference IV	Research IV
SETTING	IVee's workplace (desk)	IVee's home (kitchen, l.r., d.r.)
PARTICIPANTS	IVer: patron	IVer: researcher
	IVee: librarian[2]	IVee: researched
ENDS	overt	overt/covert
	complementary	some complementary
	IVer/ee lacks information	IVer lacks info
	IVee/er gives info	IVee gives info
ACT SEQUENCE	opened by either	opened by IVer
	IVer: makes query	IVer: requests info
	IVee: requests clarification	IVee: provides info
	IVer: provides clar	IVee/IVer: requests clar
	IVee: resolves query	IVer/IVee: provides clar
	recycles	recycles
	rearranges	rearranges
	range of acts: narrow	range of acts: varies; partially controlled by IVer
	closure by both depends on resolution of query; closure is final	closure by either depends on compliance with negotiated time constraints; closure is temporary
KEY	narrow range	medium range
INSTRUMENTALITIES	verbal/nonverbal; physical materials	verbal, maybe physical materials
NORMS	interaction is based on need for information	interaction is based on need for information
GENRE	narrow range	medium range

3.2 Reference interviews

American public libraries typically have departments that specialize in "reference material": relatively technical information, or information of interest to a specialized audience, that is stored in formats (e.g. encyclopedias, manuals, specialized journals, archives, computer disk) not always available outside of the library setting. Public access to such materials is often controlled by a specially trained librarian (a "reference librarian") who is posted at a specific desk ("reference desk").

Interactions during which the reference librarian (L) increases the access of a library user (often called a "patron," P) to specific reference materials are called "reference interviews." These interviews arise because libraries regulate access to reference material in several different ways. The most restrictive regulation on materials is physical: the reference material can be kept at the reference desk itself. In such cases, P must ask L for use of the specific material. Even when such materials are physically accessible – when they are in the generally available, circulating sections of the library known as the "stacks," for example – P may need help locating material. The asymmetric distribution of knowledge between L and P also regulates P's access to reference material. When P is not familiar enough with either the reference materials or the format of a particular set of materials to locate information pertaining to a particular topic, P has to ask L for help not just in locating a source of material, but also in identifying the appropriate material in which to search. Finally, L may also offer P help in actually formulating a specific need – in making a query – in a way that is appropriate to the resources available in the library.

The reference interview is the shorter and more focused of the two types of interviews to be considered here. As noted in table 5.1, the range of ACTS, the KEY, and the GENRES are all relatively narrow. Both L and P direct their talk toward resolution of the problem(s) brought to the desk by P: the goal (ENDS) of each participant is mutually known. Although more specific goals (based upon different amounts of information about either the informational need or the library resources) temporarily diverge from the main goal during the course of the interview, these specific goals are all subordinate to the main goal.

As suggested above, it is P who has a particular need and L who can fulfill that need. This complementary distribution of needs and abilities suggests that several different kinds of speech acts might occur during a reference interview – speech acts through which P makes his need known to L and through which L draws upon her abilities to fulfill that need. Even when both participants use what we might think of as the "same" speech act, the use of that speech act varies according to participant. As we see in a moment, the questions in reference interviews are explicitly geared to the event-based roles of participants and their complementary goals: P seeks to gain information and L seeks to provide that information. Thus, although both participants ask questions, the form and function of their questions reflect their roles and the goals defined by those roles.

In the next sections, I turn from the description of reference interviews as speech events to the analysis of questions within these speech events. I draw upon fifteen audio-taped interviews from the reference desk of a public library to show that there are three kinds of questions in reference interviews: questions that make offers, issue queries, and request clarification about queries. I begin by discussing the questions used to initiate reference interviews (3.2.1): L's question makes an offer; P's question opens a query. I then discuss the main query driving the exchange and the supporting (and subordinate) requests for information (3.2.2); both of these acts can be realized through questions. Section 3.2.3 summarizes.

3.2.1 Opening the interview

The opening portions of reference interviews are similar to the openings in service encounters (Merritt 1976).[3] After P (cf. customer) makes L aware of his presence (e.g. by establishing eye contact) at the reference desk (cf. service post), either party can verbally open the encounter: L can ask a question that offers help or P can ask a question that initiates a query. (Note that I use the term "query" rather than request for information so that I can reserve the term "request" for more specifically defined speech acts.) We will see that the function of initiating questions clearly establishes the institutionalized roles of L and P.

(1) illustrates L's initiating offers and P's responses to those offers.

(1) Librarian asks initial question
(A) L: (a) May I help you?
     P: (b) Sure.
         (c) Um if I don't find an indication in the card catalog of which
              branch the book is to be found,=
     L: (d) ^{z}Uh huh.
     P: (e) =what do I do next.
(B) L: (a) May I help you?
     P: (b) Yes.
         (c) I'm looking for . . . Fanny Mae, and Fanny Mac?
         (d) And Freddie Mac, regulations. (Federal) banks.
     L: (e) Okay.
(C) L: (a) Can I help you?
     P: (b) Yeh maybe.
         (c) I'm uh- I've been working up in New York City in the theater
              doing acting and stage managing and one thing and another.
         (d) And I'm looking to try and get over to public relations which is
              why I'm down here.
     L: (d) Okay.

Each reference interview in (1) is verbally opened by an utterance (*May/can I help you?*) that is conventionally understood as an offer. But notice that these opening utterances also seem like questions, both syntactically (they are interrogatives) and intonationally (they have final rising intonation). This multifunctionality raises some of the same issues that we discussed in chapter 3: there we used speech act theory to propose a functional relationship between questions/requests and offers. We also pointed out, however, that these acts could be independent. Some analyses of indirect speech acts, for example, argue that interrogatives may be requests for action without also being "literal" questions: *Can you pass the salt?*, for example, seeks action rather than information about ability. Other interrogatives that seem like questions fall short on other underlying conditions: rhetorical questions (Athanasiadou 1991), for example, seek no verbal response or action response from others at all; nor do they address situations about which speakers lack information. Similarly, not all offers are questions; not all questions are offers.

Because not all interrogatives actually seek information from a respondent, it is important to ask whether *May/can I help you?* actually functions as a question. In chapter 3, we analyzed multifunctionality by finding relationships among the conditions for each individual act – arguing that a single utterance might perform several acts if the rules for constituting those acts were similar in some way. An ethnographic way of addressing multifunctionality supplements the speech act approach by relating knowledge about speech acts to knowledge about speech events, and by finding evidence in participants' behavior for the communicative norms and understandings being proposed through the more abstract and general analysis.

In order to see whether *May/can I help you?* is both offer and question, let us begin by reviewing what we learned in chapter 3 about offers. In our discussion of *Y'want a piece of candy?*, we noted that a speaker (S) who makes an offer does not necessarily undertake an obligation to perform an act (A), simply because S cannot be certain that the hearer (H) finds A to be in his best interest. We proposed that some offers issued as interrogatives question the preparatory condition of promises (that H would prefer A to be done) and allow S to check on whether A is something that H does indeed want or need. Such an assessment is critical to the likelihood that what is being offered will actually end up being provided.

Although offers like *Y'want a piece of candy?* focus on H and explicitly ask about hearer-based conditions (H's needs or wants), other offers focus on S and explicitly state or ask about speaker-based conditions. Saying *I want to help you*, for example, would be an offer that states a speaker-based preparatory condition, i.e. S wants to do A for H. Offers can also be issued by *questioning* a speaker-based preparatory condition – questioning S's ability to do what H needs or wants. (Note the similarity with requests that question a hearer-based preparatory condition, i.e. requests can question H's ability to do what S wants.) Thus, offers may be made when it is uncertain that H wants A, or when it is uncertain that S is able to do A.

To paraphrase what I have suggested thus far, offers may be made when one (or both) of two conditions are uncertain: H may want (or not want) A, S may be sure (or unsure) that she can do A. Since both of these circumstances affect the likelihood that S will undertake an obligation to do A (and thus that A will actually be provided for H), it is reasonable for S to try to reduce uncertainty before actually committing to do A. The strategy that we discussed in chapter 3 was for S to question the hearer-based condition in order to learn whether H wants A ("Do you want A?"). As noted above, an alternative strategy is for S to question the speaker-based preparatory condition that S is able to do A ("Can/may I do A"). This question elicits information from H that will allow S to know whether or not she can do A: as we see later, H's response to this question can provide S with a description of what would constitute "doing A." Since it is just this information that will allow S to assess her ability to do A, H's answer can affirm the speaker-based preparatory condition and allow S to go on to undertake the obligation to do A.

The discussion above suggests that *Can/may I help you?* does have a specific question function as well as act as an offer. This question function rests partially on the root and epistemic meanings of the modals *can* and *may*. The root meanings of *can* and *may* have to do with ability (e.g. "I can/may [be able to] lift that chair – it's not that heavy"); the epistemic meanings have to do with possibility and permission (e.g. "You can/may have that dessert only if you eat your vegetables"). These meanings work together when S asks H whether S can (or may) do A for H. Consider two hypothetical responses to the offer being considered:

(1′) L: Can/may I help you?
      P1:   Maybe, but you look like you're pretty busy already.
      P2:   Maybe, but I'm looking for something that's marked "lost" in the card files.

The hypothetical responses from P1 and P2 both convey uncertainty about whether L can really provide help, i.e. they define this help as a "possibility" but not a certainty. The contingent nature of the "help," however, arises for different reasons. Consistent with the root meaning of *can* or *may*, the response from P1 raises doubts based on L's ability to carry through with the offer. Although these doubts reduce the likelihood that A will be possible (the epistemic meaning), the source of that assessment is L's ability (the root meaning, and a speaker-based preparatory condition of offers). Although the response from P2 also raises doubts about the likelihood of A, these doubts rest upon P's own assessment of his needs in relation to available (or un-available) resources, and are thus less bound to the root meaning of *can* or *may*.

I have suggested thus far that the question form of *Can/may I help you?* is aimed toward the reduction of uncertainty: by questioning a speaker-based preparatory condition that S is able to do A, *Can/may I help you?* allows H to provide S with information that bears either directly or indirectly on S's ability. We might wonder, however, why S would offer A without being sure that she *is* able to do A. It is here that an understanding of the particular speech event can help: the likelihood that a particular act can actually be provided is relative to the circumstances of the speech event in which it is either offered or requested. We can make some simple comparisons to illustrate that the provision of acts known as "help" is more guaranteed for some acts, and in some kinds of public service encounters, than others. If one asks a museum guard for help in finding the exit, for example, it is virtually certain that that help can be provided. But other acts fall outside of one's expectations about what typically occurs in a specific type of encounter, e.g. asking a museum guard for help in finding a particular postcard in the museum shop. The status of still others is somewhere in between, e.g. asking a museum guard for help in finding a particular painting in the museum.

The reference librarian is similar to the "in between" example just noted. Recall that the reference librarian is posted at a particular location from which she is supposed to help P. Note, however, that L really has no information about the specific needs of any patrons who approach her desk – even though it is this information that she needs in order to try to provide help. By asking *Can/may I help you?*, then, L is requesting that P provide her with information about what she needs so that she will be able to try to provide what her job has trained her to do, i.e. help locate information. Thus, the ability of L to actually fulfill the offer depends upon knowing the kind of help that P is seeking.

The analysis thus far suggests that the question form and intonation of L's initial offer contributes to its speech act function in the interview. This suggestion was based not only on our understanding of speech act conditions, but on the linguistic meaning of the utterance (e.g. the modals) and our contextual knowledge of a particular speech event. This multifaceted approach is consistent with the ethnographic belief that the function of an utterance resides in its "text" (i.e. its form and meaning) and its "context" (i.e. knowledge of the circumstances of a speech event), a relationship that is itself mutually constitutive (chapter 10).

An ethnographic perspective also seeks evidence for a particular analysis within participants' conduct: how do participants themselves display knowledge of communicative norms and understandings? Two aspects of the form and content of P's responses suggest that P treats *Can/may I help you?* as both question and offer.

First, P's response to L may address the literal meaning of *Can/may I help you?*, i.e. the actual ability of L to "help" P. Although some patrons just respond with *Yes* (as in b in 1B) or just describe the sort of help they need (as I note in a moment), other responses are more informative. Compare (1A) and (1C):

(1A) L: (a) May I help you?
      P: (b) Sure.
(1C) L: (a) Can I help you?
      P: (b) Yeh maybe.

Sure and *Yeh maybe* differ along a scale of certainty – the former conveying more certainty that L is able to help P than the latter. That P's responses to L's *Can/may I help you?* can convey such differences suggests that P may bring a general notion of what kind of help can be reasonably expected to a reference interview and compare his own particular needs to what he thinks L can provide. Focus for a moment on (1C). P's *Yeh maybe* anticipates a problem with the upcoming query, e.g. it is atypical, inappropriate, difficult to convey. These doubts are also conveyed in the way P goes on to formulate his query: *Yeh maybe* is followed by an unusually detailed description of P's previous job and his move from New York, neither of which is directly relevant to his query itself. (Note that P later states his uncertainty very directly: *I don't quite know how to phrase my question.*) Thus, by conveying relative uncertainty that L is able to help P, P is responding to the "question" meaning of *Can/may I help you?*, i.e. P interprets this utterance as a question about L's ability (the root meaning) to provide "help."

Second, P may respond to L's offer by issuing a query. In all the examples in (1), P's affirmation (line b in 1A, 1B, and 1C) is followed immediately by his query (lines c).[4]

(1) (A) L: (a) May I help you?
          P: (b) Sure.
              (c) Um If I don't find an indication in the card catalog of which branch the book is to be found /conts /
     (B) L: (a) May I help you?
          P: (b) Yes.
              (c) I'm looking for . . . Fanny Mae, and Fanny Mac? /conts /
     (C) L: (a) Can I help you?
          P: (b) Yeh maybe.
              (c) I'm uh- I've been working up in New York City /conts /

It is important to note that P begins a query without L having to elicit a query more explicitly. That is, the following sequence does not occur:

L: May I help you?
P: Yes.
L: Tell me what I can do.
P: I'm looking for . . .

Notice, however, that L's ability to provide help depends upon knowing what kind of help – what specific information – is needed by P. The queries from P in (1) either state information that P needs (B) or lead into a request for information (A, C). This information has to be provided by L for P if L's offer is to be actualized, i.e. if S is to commit herself to doing A for H. Thus, by describing the kind of "help" that P needs, P is responding to the "offer" meaning of *Can/may I help you?*, i.e. P interprets this utterance as an offer from L to do A for P.

Not all reference interviews open with an initial question from L. The examples in (2) show that sometimes it is P who can ask the first question in a reference interview.

(2)   Patron asks initial question
(A)   P: (a)   Hi I'm in the business section looking for something on mutual
                   funds ratings?
            (b)   Now I don't even know where to start . . .
            (c)   could you help me?.
(B)   P: (a)   Yes. Can you tell me where I might find a numismatic catalog
                   and if it can be taken from the library for a couple of days?

After recognition tokens (*Hi* (A), *Yes* (B)) acknowledging L's implicit availability, P uses questions as part of his query about specific information in the
library, e.g. the interrogative forms (*Could you help me?*, *Can you tell me
where*). P's queries also include other forms that fulfill the felicity conditions
of both questions and requests. For example, first person statements about
what P seeks (e.g. *I'm looking for* (A)) fulfill a preparatory condition of
questions (S lacks knowledge) and the sincerity condition of requests (S wants
A). P's queries in (2) also provide information about what is being sought:
something on mutual funds ratings (A), *a numismatic catalog* (B). P may also
provide information about his own knowledge (*I don't even know where to
start* (A)) that states a preparatory condition of questions. (See section 3.1.2
in chapter 3 for discussion of the relationship between questions and requests.)
Finally, as noted above, P also asks questions that seek L's help (*Could you
help me?* (A), *Can you tell me* (B)): these questions not only realize the
essential condition of requests, but they compensate interactionally for L's lack
of an explicit offer and open the way for L to actually begin to offer help.
    In this section, we have seen two ways that participants in reference inter-
views use questions to initiate the body of the interview: L may ask a question
that offers help, P may ask a question that makes a query. Because the
questions used by L and P have different functions in the interview, the options
for realizing these functions differ. Rather than ask *Can I help you?*, for
example, L may use a nonverbal signal of openness to interaction (e.g. raised
eyebrows; Ekman 1979). And rather than use a question to make a query, P
may use a number of other request forms that also open a phase of joint
formulation and clarification of the reference material being sought (as discussed in the next section). Note, finally, that the functions of the initiating
questions examined here clearly establish the asymmetric roles of the participants: P solicits a service (P wants information) and L provides a service (L
gives information). Despite this global asymmetry in participant role, the
devices for formulating and eventually satisfying a query are more symmetrically distributed on a turn-by-turn basis. In the next section, we examine the
way P and L work together to formulate and satisfy a query.

3.2.2 *The query: how it is issued, clarified, and satisfied*

The formulation and satisfaction of a query are the main ENDS of the reference interview: P's query seeks information and it is up to L to help P find

that information.[5] The query thus has a central role in organizing the NORMS by which the ACT SEQUENCE is constructed. We saw in section 3.2.1 that although the query does not initiate the encounter, it is the query to which the initiation of an interview leads. We see in this section that questions from L and P work towards local clarification of the query (on a turn-by-turn basis) and global resolution of the query (at the level of the entire speech event): L and P use questions to issue, clarify, and try to resolve the query. Our discussion will also note that questions are not necessary to the formulation of a query: other forms can be used for some of the same ENDS.

I begin with an example in which P uses a statement to request a specific item that is then provided by L.

(3) P: (a) I would like the um Mansfield Chart stock chart.
     L: (b) [gives it to P]

The statement in (a) is a query even though it does not use a question form to ask for information. Since P knows specifically what he wants and where he can find it (at L's desk), he can use a standard request form (i.e. state a sincerity condition of requests; see chapter 3, p. 71) to seek that item from L. Because L can give P the requested item, there are no requests for clarification of the query and the query is satisfied.

In (4), P also knows what he wants but is less familiar with either its location or rules about its use. P phrases his query (in a) as a question (*can you tell me*) that asks about L's ability to satisfy the query (i.e. questions a preparatory condition of requests; see chapter 3, p. 71).

(4) P: (a) Yes. Can you tell me where I might find a numismatic catalog and if it can be taken from the library for a couple of days?
     L: (b) Is numismatics coins?
     P: (c) Yeah.
     L: (d) Yes there- we do have some circulating books.
         (e) It would be on the second floor
         (f) and the call number for the coin books is 737.
         (g) There's a stairway to the left of the front door and there's someone up there who can help you find . . .
     P: (h) Thank you.
     L: (i) You're welcome.

Instead of immediately providing P with the requested information, L checks the meaning of *numismatics* (b), proposing a definition of *numismatics* immediately following the query. After P affirms the meaning of numismatics with *Yeah* (b), L provides both pieces of information requested by P: the location (*where I might find . . .* (a)) and how to reach it (d to g), and the fact that some are *circulating books* (d). Although this information does not address the particular item being sought (*a numismatic catalog* (a)), it tells P how he *might find* (a) that item himself. Thus, L satisfies P's query (d to g), but requests (b) and receives (c) clarification of the query before doing so.

P can also check the formulation of the query or request clarification of his own query; the outcome of these acts may involve work from both P and L. In (5), P both offers and requests from L clarification of his own query. (5 continues an earlier example (1C).)

(5) L: (a) Can I help you?
    P: (b) Yeh maybe.
        (c) I'm uh- I've been working up in New York City in the theater doing acting and stage managing and one thing and another.
        (d) And I'm looking to try and get over to public relations which is why I'm down here.
    L: (e) Okay.
    P: (f) Uh what I'm trying to find out is a source of PR firms, and related sorts of things that would be interested in people that deal in the media.
        (g) In other words in the- I don't quite know how to phrase my question . . .
        (h) in the sort of technical end of the image making end of it . . .
        (i) the people who deal in commercials in television, radio, that end of it.
    L: (j) Straight public relations?
    P: (k) Yeh that's a great- that's a good place to start.

After giving reasons for his query (c, d), P presents his query (f) as a request that presupposes a need for help (through the pseudo cleft *what I'm trying to find out*) and states what he needs in very general terms (*a source of PR firms, and related sorts of things*) that are relevant to himself and his own previously stated qualities (*that would be interested in people that deal in the media*). In (g), P begins to rephrase his own query (*in other words*) and conveys uncertainty about how to make the query (*I don't quite know how to phrase my question . . .*). He then offers a reformulation of his query that modifies the item for which he is searching: *in the media* is rephrased as *in the sort of technical end of the image making end of it . . . the people who deal in commercials in television, radio, that end of it* (h, i). L also reformulates the item being requested (*Straight public relations?* (j)). When this reformulation is acknowledged by P (*Yeh that's a great- that's a good place to start* (k)), the query is resolved.

(6) is another example in which P opens the query to reformulation from L. The reformulation here is facilitated by a question-like feature: rising intonation. (We already discussed the relationship between rising intonation and questions in section 3.1.1 of chapter 3.)

(6) P: (c) I'm looking for . . . Fanny Mae, and Fanny Mac?
        (d) And Freddie Mac, regulations.

       (e) (Federal) banks.
L: (f) Okay.

In (c), P uses a "question-like" intonation on one part of his query (*Fanny Mac?*): this intonation opens a possible turn transition space in which an item, whose information status is uncertain, is opened to interactional scrutiny (see chapter 3, section 3.1.1, and chapter 7, section 3.1.2). Such a device can be used if P himself is uncertain about how to identify a referent: note that what follows *Fanny Mac?* (i.e. *Freddie Mac* (d)) can be interpreted as a self-repair. Rising intonation can also be used if P is uncertain about L's recognition of the referent or prior use of the referent as a next-mention (chapters 6–8). We might thus call the utterance produced with this intonation contour an information check, as in section 3.3.2 of this chapter. The important point here, however, is the interactional function of this intonation within the reference interview itself. *Fanny Mac?* opens the way for L to begin her own turn in a number of fairly constrained ways: L can ask for clarification, show recognition of, or provide, the information being sought in the query. When L does not begin her own turn, however, P continues his turn: P continues to formulate the query (d, e) until L recognizes what P is seeking and takes responsibility for fulfilling the query (*Okay* (f)).

    Both P and L use rising intonation in (7). Here the initial part of P's query is followed by P's direct request for help and a question: L later questions P's formulation of the query.

(7) P: (a) Hi I'm in the business section looking for something on mutual
                 funds ratings?
           (b) Now I don't even know where to start . . .
           (c) could you help me?
    L: (d) That exact title is what you're looking for?

Although P's query in (7) is issued through a request form (i.e. *I'm looking for* (a) states the sincerity condition), P also presents the item for which he is looking (*mutual funds ratings?*) with rising intonation. When L does not offer any verbal acknowledgment or recognition, P continues with another request format that states his own need more directly (*Now I don't even know where to start . . .* (b)). When P then asks for help, *could you help me?* (c) realizes the essential condition of requests. It is after P directly asks L for help that L checks P's formulation of the query: *That exact title is what you're looking for?* (d) facilitates the resolution of the query by putting the terms of P's query into a category (i.e. "title") that can be searched within the library resources. L's use of rising intonation with this question transfers responsibility back to P, thus showing again that P and L jointly share in the overall ENDS of the speech event, i.e. solving the query.

    Our examples thus far have suggested that P can use a variety of forms – questions, statements, phrases with rising intonation – to elicit L's help in

formulating, and thus resolving, a query. (8) is another example of joint work
from both P and L (note that 8 follows 3).

(8)   P: (c)   Uh okay do you have the latest Forbes Magazine?
         (d)   In September they put out a $_z$
      L: (e) ^{z}Mutual fund.
      P: (f)   [Yeh.
      L: (g)   [Yeh.

In (8), P asks a direct question about a particular item (*Do you have the latest
Forbes Magazine?* (c)). When L does not respond, P adds information about
the item (*In September they put out a* (d)) that begins to clarify and explain
the item. It is then that L shows her recognition of what is being sought:
Mutual fund (e) is latched onto P's supplemental information. The accuracy
of this description is noted by P (*Yeh* (f)) just as L affirms (*Yeh* (g)) that this
magazine is available. Thus, P and L work together to reformulate the query:
even though P does not create a turn transition space (e.g. through rising
intonation) in which L can respond to the query, P's own clarification is
completed by L.

The examples have illustrated several aspects of the use of questions to issue
queries. First, queries can be issued without questions: they can be issued as
requests made through declarative statements (3). Second, questions can have
different roles within queries: questions can occupy an entire query (4) or they
can be part of a query (8). Third, question-like features can also serve functions within queries: rising intonation allows P to check on whether the
information being provided can allow L to begin satisfying the query (6, 7);
it also allows L to check on a possible resolution of the query (line j in 5).
Fourth, L tries to satisfy the query even while it is being issued: L proposes
refinements of the query (with or without rising intonation: compare 5 and 7
to 8), asks for clarification (through a question (4)), and marks recognition of
the information being sought (5). Finally, the examples above show that
although L may ask for clarification from P (e.g. 4), and P may begin to offer
his own reformulation of a query (e.g. 5), P and L also work together to
reformulate (and thus resolve) a query (5 to 8).

We have seen in this section that two levels of questioning activity facilitate
the formulation and satisfaction of the query in reference interviews. First,
questions and question-like features figure in the formulation of the query
itself. P presents a query using either question forms or request forms that are
clear realizations of Searle's conditions for felicitous questions: the speaker
lacks knowledge of a particular state of affairs (preparatory rule) and wants
to gain that knowledge (sincerity rule) by eliciting information from the hearer
(essential rule). Second are the clarification sequences. In order to provide P
with information, L may have to seek information about the query or redefine
P's query in terms compatible with the organizational schema used by the
library to organize reference materials.[6] P may also reformulate his own query

under several different circumstances: when P himself anticipates L's need for further specificity or recategorization; when L shows a need for more information (perhaps by withholding a response at a turn-transition space). Thus, questioning facilitates the reformulation and resolution of the query on a turn by turn basis, and on the level of the speech event itself.

3.2.3 Summary: questions in reference interviews

Patrons and librarians use questions for three different specific ENDS in reference interviews: questions from L make offers, questions from P issue queries, and questions from both L and P seek clarification (cf. check the formulation) of the query. The chart below summarizes the question–answer sequences in reference interviews. Note that this chart is not meant to illustrate all possible arrangements of questions or their functions; nor is it an exhaustive description of all speech acts and functions in reference interviews. Question–answer sequences that are subordinate to others have indices indicating their subordination (e.g. question-2a) and the fact that they are also next-questions (e.g. question-3).

L:	question-1	[offer]
P:	(answer-1	[accepts])
	question-2	[begins query: seeks information]
{L/P}:	question-3/2a	[seeks clarification of q-2] or [checks information in q-2]
{P/L}:	answer-3/2a	[provides clarification of q-3/2a] or [confirms information in q-3/2a]
L:	answer-2	[resolves query: provides information]

This chart shows that questions can be used to offer help and thus prompt the query, to issue the query, and to reformulate the query (as either L or P seeks clarification of, or checks the information in, P's query) as a way of facilitating the resolution of the query. Requests for clarification and information checks open a sequence subordinate to the main query. Furthermore, regardless of who requests clarification or checks information from whom, the floor belongs to L following the provision of clarification or confirmation of information: L uses the reformulated query as a basis from which to resolve P's query. Thus, questions play a critical role in reference interviews: P enters a reference interview with the explicit goal of seeking information and both P and L use questions as a way to find that information.

We began our discussion of reference interviews by using Hymes's SPEAKING grid to describe the communicative components comprising this speech event. By way of conclusion, we can relate the questions in reference interviews to these communicative components. Questions in reference interviews are distributed among participants in ways that reveal both asymmetric and symmetric PARTICIPANT roles. We noted a global asymmetry underlying the entire interview: P solicits a service and L provides a service. We also noted, however, that the clarification sequences that help to formulate and eventually satisfy a query are symmetrically distributed. This allocation of acts to actors suggests a more collaborative effort than might be suggested by the term "interview" (see section 3.4). This symmetry could also reflect the fact that L and P share ENDS (and both know that they do so). And the sharing of goals could help to account for the ACT SEQUENCE: a series of questions and answers, interchanged between participants, that work cumulatively toward fulfilling the main task of the interview.

3.3 Questions in sociolinguistic interviews

This section focuses upon questions in another variety of interview: sociolinguistic research interviews. Sociolinguistic interviews have some features typical of an interview. One important feature is their ENDS: since one person (a sociolinguist, S) seeks to gain specific information from another (a respondent, R), the structure of activities and the expectations for behavior revolve, at least partially, around a desire to resolve an asymmetrical distribution of information. These ENDS are similar to those of other interviews. This similarity is important, for as Cameron et al. (1992: 13) point out: "interaction between researcher and researched does not produce some anomalous form of communication peculiar to the research situation and misleading as to the nature of 'reality'. Rather such interaction instantiates *normal* communication in one of its forms." Thus, to rephrase the point from above in the terms of Cameron et al., we can say that "interviews" are one of the forms of 'normal' communication to which sociolinguistic interviews are similar (see also Wolfson 1976).

As noted earlier, one of the goals of the ethnography of communication is to discover the communicative features or qualities that underlie our identification of particular events, encounters, or situations as certain "kinds" of occurrences. Since questions are a key part of interviews, we can examine the questions in sociolinguistic interviews as a way of understanding at least part of the structure of this particular speech event – perhaps the part that is most "interview" like. And at the same time, we will learn something about questions by seeing how they are located in a particular configuration of actions and beliefs that differs from other varieties of the same speech event. We will see that what influences the form and function of questions in sociolinguistic interviews are the following communicative components: PARTICIPANTS, ENDS, ACT SEQUENCE, and GENRE. Just as we described the general circumstances of reference interviews before focusing on questions within those interviews, so too will we briefly consider these components before discussing NORMS for questions in sociolinguistic interviews.

Let us start by considering (in fairly general terms) the PARTICIPANTS. Goffman (1961: 323) divides occupations into two broad categories: "Specialized occupational tasks can be divided into two categories, one where the practitioner 'meets the public' through his work, a second where he does not, performing it only for the established members of his work organization." Goffman's categories provide a base from which to discuss different types of interviewers. The division noted above minimizes the importance of the activity *per se* and maximizes the importance of the audience to whom the activity is directed. Although all interviewers "meet the public," the results of such meetings are not always directed toward the needs and wants of that particular public in either an immediate or long-term sense. In one sense, of course, sociolinguistic researchers are often very involved in interpreting the meanings and intentions of their respondents: such involvement is a critical part of trying to obtain certain kinds of responses from informants. But the primary goal (END) of a researcher's interview is nevertheless the production of knowledge for other researchers – for the established members of a work organization (in Goffman's terms).

The information that researchers seek to gain through a research interview depends largely on the theories, hypotheses, issues, and problems current in their field, as well as a varied collection of (sometimes implicit) methodological assumptions about the nature of data and its means of analysis. The information sought in a sociolinguistic interview, for example, is information that is interesting to sociolinguistic theory, practice, and application, e.g. information about phonological, grammatical or discourse patterns, language and social attitudes, and ways of life in a community. Researchers' knowledge can also serve the public (both the segment of the public interviewed and a larger public): researchers can become advocates for public causes or empower the public to become advocates for their own causes.[7] But, as noted above, the intended and actual products of a research interview are not geared toward the public with whom they are meeting, but toward other researchers. This contrasts sharply with the ENDS of reference interviews: librarians' goals are limited to the interview itself, i.e. to help a patron find information.

Another difference between sociolinguistic interviews and reference interviews concerns the degree to which the interviewer's goals are shared with the interviewee. Not all of S's goals are explicitly shared with R. This is because of what Labov (1972e) calls the "observer's paradox": linguists want to observe how people use language when those people are not being observed (or are not aware of being observed). Although S often tells R of an interest in language, this interest is often put in terms of broader social and cultural issues (issues that are consistent with sociolinguistic interests in general). Sociolinguists do not share many of their more specific goals with their informants: they do not tell informants that they want them to speak in different styles, that they want to hear the pronunciation of a particular sound in different phonological environments, that they want them to tell narratives of personal experience. This asymmetric knowledge of the ENDS of a sociolinguistic interview differentiates them from reference interviews and also has an effect on the questions asked. As seen earlier, the fact that librarian and patron share a goal (and both know that they share a goal) helps to account for the ACT SEQUENCE: a series of collaborative questions and answers that work cumulatively toward fulfilling the main task of the interview (resolving a query). The asymmetric knowledge of ENDS also bears on the overall structure of the sociolinguistic interview as a speech event, and on the ways that questions are used during the interview.

A brief consideration of some of the ways in which sociolinguists achieve their goals suggests still other differences between the two speech events being considered. In keeping with the sociolinguists' goal of obtaining a variety of different speech styles, for example, both S and R are encouraged to introduce topics and to shift topics away from an already loosely structured agenda (Labov 1984). One effect of this is a sometimes explicit avoidance of the question–answer format and fixed topic structure typical of many institutional interviews. Rather than follow what can be called a "serial" format (asking a set of questions whose order is predetermined by an interview agenda), for example, S often uses what can be called a "stepwise" format (cf. chapter 7) in which S's next-question is based on a topic initiated by R's answer to a prior-question. Another effect of the intentional loosening of constraints on the maintenance of topic is that sociolinguistic interviews allow a variety of exchange types besides question–answer sequences, and permit a number of different genres, e.g. stories, descriptions, and arguments. As I noted at the outset of this book, sociolinguistic interviews provide most of the data used for the sample analyses in this book, e.g. the exchanges in chapters 3, 4, and 7, the story in chapter 6, and the lists in chapter 8. This fluidity in ACT SEQUENCE helps to produce an important difference in terms of how questions relate to the overall structure of the interviews in which they are asked: whereas reference interviews are centered on the joint resolution of a single query (or series of queries), sociolinguistic interviews seek to integrate the asking and answering of questions within other kinds of talk.

Above I noted that S and R are both encouraged to avoid the question–answer format and fixed topic structure typical of many interviews. It is important to note, however, that this "encouragement" comes from different sources and in different guises. Sociolinguists are taught how to conduct loosely structured interviews (e.g. in courses in field methods, through practice with interview modules) and they use their knowledge to guide the way they themselves speak and the way R speaks. Sociolinguists, for example, often talk about how to "get" people to tell stories or how to "elicit" stories; similarly, it is believed that casual speech can be increased by "allowing" people to introduce topics that may seem "tangential" to the topic proposed by S (Labov 1984). During an interview, S transforms these goals into interactional practices that often have the desired results. By intentionally altering (e.g. supplementing or even avoiding) formats that are explicitly constrained only by S, however, S is often forced into another kind of position of control: S monitors the speech of another for reasons that are not at all known to interlocutors, e.g. to elicit one form of speech rather than another, to allow (rather than try to prevent) the saying of something. And this means, again, that the ENDS of the interview – even the local, utterance-by-utterance goals of participants – are quite different for S than for R.

Different orientations towards speech and towards participation in a speech event may differentiate the social meaning of participants' utterances more radically than we might expect. One of the goals of my own interviews, for example, was to record people's pronunciation of the vowel [æ] in the word "planet." To this end, I found that asking people if they thought there was life on other planets did not always produce the desired token, i.e. people could just say "yes" or "no." I built upon my observations that my respondents often completed one another's sentences, however, to ask the question in the following way: "Do you think there's life on other . . ." My respondents would then use the word "planet" to fill in my question, usually going on to discuss their beliefs as well. This question, then, certainly had multiple meanings and functions for me – not all of which were shared by my interlocutors. Thus, formally equivalent productions of what seems to be the same utterance may have very different interactional meanings depending upon the speaker.

Finally, it is important to note that sociolinguistic interviews can be seen as mixed GENRES. In my own work, for example, I sometimes refer to my interviews as "interviews" *per se*. The direction of my analyses, however, has always assumed that they reveal interactional patterns shared with conversations as well (e.g. Schiffrin 1984a, b, 1987a). Because the term "genre" concerns the formal characteristics of texts more than the situational understandings supplementing text types (cf. chapter 8), however, I will refer to sociolinguistic interviews as "mixed" or "hybrid" speech events, rather than genres (but see Bauman and Briggs 1990; Briggs and Bauman 1992). Classifying sociolinguistic interviews in this way (part institutional talk, part conversation) can suggest an underlying duality in sociolinguists' sense of what is going on during such an occasion, i.e. in their definition of the situation as one based on power and/or solidarity.

As further support for this duality, consider the way sociolinguists talk about what goes on during an interview. People whose language is being researched are often referred to as informants: people who "give" information about language to one with less information about that language. The one to whom information is given is one who is assumed to have the power to gain such information. But sociolinguists' use of the term "consultant" rather than "informant" (Guy 1992) suggests a different status and role: here the researched party is either an expert from whom one seeks advice or an equal with whom one jointly pursues information. Descriptions of how different speech activities are located within the interview can also rely upon an assumption of an asymmetric power distribution, e.g. the goals noted above of "getting" people to tell stories or "allowing" people to introduce their own topics. But other talk about interviews suggests a sense of cooperation that emerges from solidarity and affiliation – definitions of the situation more allied with conversation. Sometimes such a sense of cooperation is intentionally fostered by the researcher. In asking questions about another's educational level, sociolinguists are often told to phrase the question as *How many years of school did you manage to finish*? Since the factive verb "manage" implicates that the subject *tried* to finish school (but may have been prevented from doing so), this question seeks to reduce a probable status discrepancy between the educational levels of S and R; one might also argue that this question assumes that both parties value education. The hybrid status of sociolinguistic interviews is also reflected in the variety of relatively monologic genres (stories, descriptions, arguments) that arise during interviews. The forms and meanings of questions from different participants during different parts of the interview also help to provide for the sense that sociolinguistic interviews are comprised of more than one type of speech event.

I have suggested thus far that there are several properties of sociolinguistic interviews that influence the types of questions asked and their functions in the interview: PARTICIPANTS, ENDS, ACT SEQUENCE, GENRE.[8] The analysis to follow is organized around who asks what kinds of questions. We noted earlier that the interview replaces one's everyday roles with the institutionally structured roles of interviewer and interviewee (cf. Briggs 1986: 2). These roles influence the mode of questioning available to participants (Goody 1978), such that not all modes are equally available to interviewer and interviewee. However, it is not only role relationships themselves that influence questions: the degree to which role relationships are externally defined influences the ability of questions to define a relationship (Goody 1978: 39). When roles are clearly defined (e.g. customer and server in a service encounter, patron and reference librarian in a reference interview), role expectations bias the interpretation of any questions asked. But when roles are weakly defined (e.g. two strangers sitting next to one another in an airplane), the mode of questioning itself can help to establish a role relationship.

In what follows, I will have space for only a relatively brief discussion of who asks what questions, and how this distribution of questions is related to the speech event. Space also prohibits an analysis of all the questions in a single sociolinguistic interview (comparable to our analysis for reference interviews). Not only are sociolinguistic interviews often fairly long (typically more than an hour), but their form and content vary depending on a number of factors: social characteristics of S and R, number of participants (e.g. more than one R) and their relationship, first or later interview with informants, early or later section of the interview. The discussion here is based on the questions in ten sociolinguistic interviews carried out by the same researcher (Anne Bower): the informants were working-class, Irish American or Italian American men and women, ranging in age from early twenties to mid seventies. I also draw upon observations from seven interviews in which I was the researcher and the informants (described in my earlier work, e.g. Schiffrin 1987a) were lower middle-class, middle-aged (mid thirties to early sixties), Jewish American men and women.

I begin with a mode of questions used primarily by sociolinguists (3.3.1) and go on to questions used by both sociolinguists and informants (3.3.2, 3.3.3).[9] I then consider the relationship between questions and participants in different phases of the interview (3.3.4). After a brief summary of the use of questions in sociolinguistic interviews (3.3.5), I summarize the entire sample analysis (3.4).

3.3.1 *Information-seeking questions*

The mode of questioning conventionally associated with an IVer's role is *information-seeking questions*. These questions are straightforward realizations of Searle's felicity conditions for questions: the speaker lacks knowledge of a particular state of affairs (preparatory rule) and wants to gain that knowledge (sincerity rule) by eliciting information from the hearer (essential rule). The overwhelming majority of information-seeking questions are asked by S. S typically uses questions to seek either information about general topics ("What kinds of games did you play as a kid?") or specific information (e.g. "How did you play jacks?"). The information elicited by an information-seeking question may be related to prior discourse. Suppose S asks a general question about games, R responds by listing a number of games, including "jacks," and then S asks how R played jacks. Both of S's questions would be considered information-seeking questions – even though the second question pursued a topic opened by R's answer to the first question.

I suggested earlier that sociolinguistic interviews define roles for participants that influence the mode of questioning available to them. But the way that participants sometimes adopt the mode of questioning conventionally associated with the other's position suggests that they try to redefine those roles, and thus that the participant roles in sociolinguistic interviews are less rigid than those in reference interviews.

When R does ask S information-seeking questions, the questions often have unexpected effects (i.e. the "outcome" aspect of ENDS (2.2)). First, R's information-seeking questions can lead to interchanges that seem less like interviews than conversations. (As noted in appendix 1, we can think of conversations as sociable (rather than task-driven) speech events with relatively fluid boundaries between topics, flexibility in allocation of turns and participant roles.) Second, R can adopt the role of S and ask questions to another R. I illustrate each of these possibilities below.

Consider, first, how R's questions help alter our interpretation of an activity. They can be part of interchanges that seem less like interviews than conversations.[10] Let us compare (9) and (10). (9) is a segment from one of my interviews in which I ask information-seeking questions.

(9) s: (a) Is the- are there ever block parties on this block?
    R1: (b) No.

S: (c)   No?
R2:   (d)   Ump um.
S: (e)   Did you ever go to a block party any[where?
R3:   (f)   [No.
R1:   (g)   Years ago, yeh.
S: (h)   Did you ever go to one?
R2:   (i)   No.
S: (j)   They're supposed to be fun. I've never been to one.

(9) seems very "interview" like, perhaps to an extreme since the only responses elicited by my questions are monosyllabic affirmations or denials. Note, also, that I introduce and continue the topic, and that my questions select the next-speaker, such that I am exercising control over who speaks when.

(10) is from a later interview with one of the same speakers (R3, identified here just as R). In addition to noting R's questions, I note certain features that seem more typical of a conversation than an interview. Prior to (10), R had been telling S about her twin grandsons. Included were two short stories about children's language, a topic that R had initiated. One story focused on what the twin grandsons call each other; the other on what another grandchild calls her. (10) begins as R ties the two topics together by anticipating what the twins (when they can talk more) will call her.

(10)   R: (a)   So probably my other ones will call me that.
              (b)   I think Grandmom's nice.
       S: (c)   I think it's nice too.
       R: (d)   I like it.
       S: (e)   Yeh. I [call my-
       R: (f)   [Does your baby talk?
       S: (g)   Uh: he doesn't t- [say my name yet.
       R: (h)   [Oh.
       S: (i)   Um . . . he: makes a lot of noises!
       R: (j)   Yeh.
       S: (k)   And he has a very deep voice [for his age=
       R: (l)   [Does he?!
       S: (m)   =hh yeh it's really funny t'hear him!
              (n)   Because he's so little, y'know, and his voice is deep,
              (o)   it sounds like it's coming from an older person.
       R: (p)   Right.
       S: (q)   And uh:
       R: (r)   He'll probably have a deep voice.
       S: (s)   Yeh I bet he will.
              (t)   Well my brother has a deep voice.
       R: (u)   Oh.
       S: (v)   And so does my father.
              (w)   He took- he knows mama, y'know and [cat.=

R: (x)   [Yeh.=
S: (y)   =[They have a cat.
R: (z)   =[Oh that's goo:d!
S: (aa)   =And um: I guess there are [more words than=
R: (bb)   [That's very good!
S: =I can recognize y'[know in all those noises.
R: (cc)   [Yeh: right. Right.
     (dd)   The mother knows what- what d'you [call=
S: (ee)   [Yeh.
R: =*your* grandmother?
S: (ff)   Well one I called um Nanny, and the other I call Grandma.

(10) is a section that seems less like an interview and more like a conversation. We can see this not only by observing R's questions (f, l, dd; to be commented on below) but in the way R and S manage the topic of talk and negotiate speaking rights.

After R's coda to her stories about her grandchildren (*So probably my other ones will call me that* (a)), S and R occupy three turns (b to d) mutually evaluating the name *Grandmom*. This brief sequence neither adds nor explicitly seeks new information; rather its use of repetition creates interpersonal involvement (Tannen 1989). S and R then *both* begin to follow up on the general topic of language in the family, although in different ways. After still another acknowledgement (*Yeh* (e)) of the evaluation, S begins to position herself as "grandchild" to report what she calls her grandmother (*I call my-* (e)). R seeks to position S as an adult (rather than child) by asking *Does your baby talk?* (f). ("Your baby" here refers to S's nephew, whom S had previously mentioned as "my brother's child.") The first part of S's response (*Uh: he doesn't t-* (g)) to R's information-seeking question about S's relative provides the information sought by R. The second part (the repair to *say my name yet*) also ties that information to the more local topic of what children call adults – the topic just pursued by R. In lines (h) to (p), S elaborates on her response while R provides continuers that neither claim a turn for R, nor motivate S to offer R a turn (Schegloff 1981): R's information checking question (*Does he?!* (l)) works here as a continuer. This same distribution of speech continues in (r) to (cc), even though the topics shift slightly. R's next question (*What d'you call* your *grandmother?* (dd)) continues the pattern in which S provides information sought by R, although it switches the topic back to what S had begun to initiate with *I call my-* (e).[11] Thus, R's questions open and maintain a phase of the interview in which R and S add to a jointly pursued topic. It is because of this joint allocation of participant rights that (10) seems less like an interview and more like a conversation

Recall Goody's observation that a mode of questioning can help define a role relationship when roles are not strongly defined by institutional norms. Roles clearly help define normative expectations and obligations for participants in a sociolinguistic interview: who expects what kind of behavior from whom is clearly a key part of participants' definition of the interview. But who asks whom questions can define not only the capacity in which one person is acting towards another, but also the situation of which those actions are a constituent part. In (9), S's questions conformed with normative expectations about the role of an interviewer. But in (10), R's questions in (f), (l), and (dd) allowed S and R to jointly pursue and collaborate on a topic of talk. Thus, R's questions help to alter participants' interpretation of the ongoing activity.

The second way that R uses information-seeking questions arises in multi-party interviews: one R adopts the role of S and asks questions to another R. One of my own informants, for example, sometimes paraphrased my questions for me (Schiffrin forthcoming, and 1992a; also chapter 4). In (11), I am asking R1 (Irene) with whom she discusses her problems. Another informant, R2 (Zelda), is also present, but she is not explicitly addressed in this particular interchange. (This is example (4) in chapter 4.)

(11) s: (a) How 'bout you Irene?
      R1:   (b) What?
      s: (c) Who would you-=
      R2:   (d) Who would you [discuss it with?
      s: (e) =   [if you had a hard day who would you
                  complain to?
      R2:   (f) Jayhhhhh
      R1:   (g) Uh:: I don't know.
            (h) Depending on what- what the problem really was, I might talk
                 to a friend easier.

S's question (*How 'bout you Irene* (a)) is clearly addressed to R1. It is R1 who asks for clarification (*What?* (b)) and S who begins to provide clarification (*Who would you-* (c)). But as S continues in her own questioning role (*if you had a hard day who would you complain to?* (e)), R2 also takes S's role as questioner (*Who would you discuss it with?* (d)). As R1 continues in her own role to provide an answer (g, h), R2 also takes R1's role as respondent (*Jayhhhhh* (f)).

Although R can temporarily adopt S's questioning role, too overt and pro-longed adoption of this role can be rejected as behavior inappropriate for an interview. In one of my own interviews, for example, a wife commented on her husband's repeated questioning to me by reminding him that *she's inter-viewing you!* In the example in (12), R asks S a question that S answers, but S then reworks the participant structure so that she is the one asking the question. Prior to (12), S and two respondents had been wondering what happened to someone who had been present.

(12) s: (a) Maybe he's a ghost.
      R2:   (b) Yeh, did you have any experiences in ghosts?
      s: (c) Oh, yeh.

	(d)	That was one thing I did want to ask you.
R3:	(e)	As a ghost?
R1:	(f)	[I bet you were never a ghost.
S:	(g)	[As a ghost hh.
	(h)	Like, for instance, in some families, there's somebody that has dreams that come true.
R2:	(i)	Yeh.
S:	(j)	Or, y'know, a family that, y'know, there's somebody that dreams something and it *means* that something's gonna happen.
	(k)	Like the Irish are big for that.
	(l)	I wonder, like, did you ever dream that you felt (something) [for anybody in your family?
R1:	(m)	[Uh: well, uh, before my mother died. I . . . uh /continues/

After S jokingly comments that *Maybe he's a ghost* (a), R2 proposed this as a new topic of talk by asking S if she had *any experiences in ghosts* (b). S's *Oh, yeh* does not answer R's question in the sense that it affirms an experience with ghosts. Instead, *Oh, yeh* acknowledges the topic of the question, such that S explicitly formulates the topic in terms of a question that she wanted to ask (*That was one thing I did want to ask you* (d)). Although this topic is temporarily treated in a joking key (e to g), S then resumes with a straightforward request for information about ghosts (h to l) and dreams to which R1 responds. S later comments to R2 (the one who asked the question in (b)) that she would *be a good coworker*.

We have observed thus far that information-seeking questions are used primarily by S: when they are used by R, they help to create a change in activity (or genre) or they are adaptations of S's questions that are directed to another R. These restrictions on the use of information-seeking questions by R, however, do not mean that R does not ask questions. As we see in the next sections, there are two types of questions that both S and R ask.

3.3.2   Information-checking questions

One type of question asked by both S and R is the information-checking question. Information-checking questions may have a variety of forms: interrogative sentences, tag questions in which the tag is a subject-aux inversion with reversed polarity (e.g. "You can do it, can't you?"), particle like tags (e.g. "see?," "y'know?") at the end of a declarative statement, particles with rising intonation (e.g. "really?," "oh?," "right?"), rising intonation on a declarative statement or part of a statement (see chapter 3, section 3.1.1). Largely because of the meaning associated with final rising intonation (again, see chapter 3, section 3.1.1), information-checking questions fulfill the sincerity, preparatory, and essential conditions of information-seeking questions. The main quality differentiating information-checking from information-seeking questions is the scope of what is being questioned and the type of response sought: the information being sought is not the completion of a proposition, but reception of a referent or proposition. These features also create different turn-taking consequences: whereas information-seeking questions always select a next-speaker, information-checking questions either serve in a back channel capacity (Duncan 1972) or allow a current speaker to continue pending receipt of acknowledgment or recognition.

Although both S and R use information-checking questions, the way they do so is quite different. The chart below suggests how S and R use these questions. (As previously, in section 3.2.3, subordinate question–answer sequences have indices indicating that they are next-questions and that they are subordinate to prior questions. The table does not illustrate all possible arrangements of the act being considered.)

Information-checking questions from S
S: question-1   [seeks information]
R: answer-1   [provides information]
S: question-2/1a   [information-check]
R: answer-2/1a   [affirms information]
      answer-1

Information-checking questions from R

S: question-1   [seeks information]
R: answer-1   [provides information
        question-2/1a   [information-check]
S: answer-2/1a   [affirms information]
R: answer-1   [provides information]

Although information-checks and their responses can always be seen as subordinate to a main sequence, the participation status occupied by S and R differs when they use these questions. S typically uses information-checks to address some aspect of what R has said; R uses them to address some aspect of his own talk. In other words, S uses these questions to check her own reception of another's talk, and R to address another's reception of his own talk. Note, however, that what information-checks from both S and R are directed to is S's reception of talk; also, regardless of who asks an information-checking question, what follows is R's answer.

(13) illustrates how one particular form of S's information-checking questions (an affirmative particle with rising intonation) can be situated in a sociolinguistic interview as a turn-continuer (Schegloff 1981).

(13)   S: (a)   Well, like did you have a team when you were goin' to school
                  on a little league, or-
       R: (b)   Oh yeh. [We used to-]

s: (c)   [Really?]
R: (d)   = yeh, I play- I was on an organized I was five years old when
          I was on my first organized baseball team.

During R's answer (*Oh yeh* (b)) to S's question (*did you have a team* (a)), S
asks *Really?* (c). R's response treats *Really?* as a yes–no question about his
own prior response (*Oh yeh* (b)) that had affirmed the existence of a team.
But in addition to answering *yeh*, R begins a long list of the different teams
that he was on (example 25 in chapter 7). Thus, S's question (*Really?* (c))
prompts R to expand his own answer to S's prior information-seeking question
(*did you have a team* (a)).

The next examples illustrate how R's information-checking questions check
on R's own talk. We also see that they may be issued through a greater variety
of forms than S's information-checking questions. In (14), R's question is a
full interrogative that checks S's familiarity with a specific referent.

(14) s: (a)   Who was your favorite star? [Or-
      R: (b)   [Oh, uh, Wallace
                 Reed, I guess.
           (c)   Do you remember readin' about him?
      s: (d)   Uh huh. I- I like old films, I've watched a lot.

After providing an answer (*Oh, uh, Wallace Reed, I guess.* (b)) to S's question
(*Who was your favorite star?* (a)), R checks on S's reception of the answer,
i.e. S's familiarity with the referent, in (c), *Do you remember readin' about
him?*

In (15), R is describing a particular ball game (*Error*) and the type of ball
used for the game.

(15) R: (a)   And what we used to do we used to, we used to play it with a
                 golf ball . . . Right?
           (b)   You ever know what a golf ball, how fast it come back to you
                 off of the brick wall?
      s: (c)   I can ima[gine.
      R: (d)   [Anyway, it could shoot back.
           (e)   We used to throw 'em all at the brick wall, and you hadda
                 catch it.

R first uses the tag *Right?* (a) to check on S's reception of *a golf ball*. After
receiving no verbal response, R switches to a *you know* question (Schiffrin
1987a) to check on S's knowledge of the properties of that referent (*You ever
know what a golf ball, how fast it come back to you off of the brick wall?*
(b)) before using it in his description. S's acknowledgment of the properties
(*I can imagine* (c)) overlaps with R's restatement of the properties (*Anyway,
it could shoot back* (d)). R then returns to his description of the game (e), this

time referring to "a golf ball" pronominally (see discussion of this referring pattern in chapters 6 and 8).

Information-checking questions allow R to check the reception not only of referents, but also of propositions that contribute to the point being developed. In (16), R is contrasting the attitudes of children today with those of her own youth.

(16)   R: (a)   They don't respect their parents as much as *we* did.

              (b)   Now, if my mother got sick, we all got sick with her . . . Y'know?

      S: (c)   Right. Yeh.

      R: (d)   Today, the children can't say the same thing.

After arguing in general terms about children's current attitudes (*They don't respect their parents as much as* we did (a)), R gives a specific example (*Now, if my mother got sick, we all got sick with her . . .* (b)) illustrating how she and her siblings shared her mother's problems. R checks this example with *Y'know?* After S's acknowledgment (*Right. Yeh* (c)), R completes her comparison (d).

So far, we have seen how various forms allow R to check S's receipt of different amounts of information, i.e. of referents (14), properties of referents (15), and propositions (16). When information is being packaged and presented for a particular interactive purpose during an interview, the same kinds of forms can check on how that information suits the purpose defined by that particular interactional slot. In (17), two pieces of information (in e and i) fill a clarification slot.

(17)   R: (a)   I never drank so much- so many sarsaparillas in all my life. hh

      S: (b)   What's a sarsaparilla? I've heard about 'em, [but uh-   ]

      R: (c)   [What's that?]

      S: (d)   Wh- what *is* a sarsaparilla?

      R: (e)   Oh:, it's something on the order of uh cream soda.

      S: (f)   Oh, oh.

      R: (g)   Y'know?

      S: (h)   Yeh.

      R: (i)   And it's- uh pretty near the same: uh taste, I think.

In (17), S initiates a clarification sequence (*What's a sarsaparilla?* (b)) that occupies several turns. After R's *what's that?* (c) requests a repeat that S provides (*Wh- what is a sarsaparilla?* (d)), R provides clarification (*something on the order of uh cream soda* (e)). Although S marks her receipt of the new information (*Oh, oh* (f); Schiffrin 1987a), R checks that reception with *Y'know?* (g). Following S's affirmation (*Yeh* (h)), R then continues his clarification by describing a slightly different feature of the drink (i) in a new intonation and information unit. Thus, the information-checking *Y'know?* in

(17) marks a transition between two pieces of information that occupy a single interactional slot, i.e. the provision of clarification.

The information-checking question in (18) also has a transitional role, but to a new interactional slot within a sequence. (18) is from a section of a sociolinguistic interview in which informants are asked about their familiarity with regional lexical variants. Sections such as these are typically comprised of either two-part question–answer exchanges or three-part question–answer–evaluation sequences. In (18), S asks whether R ever heard of *a baby cab* (a).

(18)   s: (a)   Did you ever hear of a baby cab?
       R: (b)   I've *heard* of it.
            (c)   I don't know,
            (d)   I- I- I think uh England uses that?
            (e)   Some [country anyway.
       s: (f)   [Yeh.

After offering one answer (*I've HEARD of it* (b)) and conveying uncertainty (*I don't know* (c)), R offers a possible location where *baby cab* is used: *I- I- I think uh England uses that?* (d). S's acknowledgment of the information as a proposed answer overlaps with R's continuation of her answer (*Some country anyway* (e)). Note that the answer is accepted despite continued uncertainty about its veracity: not only does R become more vague (*some country*) but the use of *anyway* implicates that *England* may not be right. S then goes on to a new question.

We have seen in this section that S and R use information-checking questions to check some aspect of ongoing talk: S typically checks her reception of R's talk, and R checks S's reception of his own talk. R regains the floor after S: R either acknowledges that S's reception is sufficient and then continues (as in 13), or S acknowledges adequate reception of what R has said and then R continues (as in 17). At first glance, this allocation of speaking rights seems to contrast with that achieved by information-seeking questions: whereas S's information-seeking questions select a next-speaker, R's information-checking questions allow a current speaker to continue. Note, however, that both question types create a slot in which it is R who continues talking: just as R is the next speaker after S's information-seeking questions, both S's and R's information-checking questions return the floor to R. As we see in the next section, the turn-taking consequence of clarification-questions is similar to that of information-seeking and information-checking questions.

3.3.3 Clarification-questions

Although clarification-questions are used by both S and R, their locations and functions differ according to participant status. The chart below shows the participant distribution of clarification-questions. Three features of this chart

enable comparison with the chart on page 159 (showing clarification sequences in reference interviews): the clarification-questions are listed in terms
of question–answer sequences; subordinate question–answer sequences have
indices indicating that they are next-questions that are subordinate to prior
questions. Again, the chart does not illustrate all possible arrangements of the
act being considered.

Clarification-questions from R
S:　question-1 [seeks information]
R:　　question-2/1a [seeks clarification of question-1]
S:　　answer-2/1a [provides clarification of question-1
R:　answer-1 [provides information sought by question-1]

Clarification-questions from S
S:　question-1 [seeks information]
R:　answer-1 [provides information sought by question-1]
S:　　question-2/1a [seeks clarification of answer-1]
R:　　answer-2/1b [provides clarification of answer-1]
　　answer-1 [provides information sought by question-1]

As shown, R typically seeks clarification of a question from S; S typically seeks
clarification of an answer from R. When R seeks clarification of S's question, the floor is nevertheless returned to R after S's clarification, so that R
can provide an answer to S's question. When S seeks clarification of R's
answer, then R's clarification continues the answer initiated earlier. Thus, the
completion of either sequence returns the floor to R. This further suggests that
although the clarification requests from R clearly serve his own needs – since
they facilitate the provision of the answer – they also provide a space for
exactly what S wants, i.e. continued speech from R.

　The next examples illustrate the distribution just noted – how clarification-
questions are situated in sociolinguistic interviews and how their functions
depend upon who does the asking. In (18), R requests clarification of S's
question; the distribution is reversed in (19).

(18)　S:　(a)　And your wife's passed on, right?
　　　R:　(b)　Pardon me?
　　　S:　(c)　Your wife has passed on?
　　　R:　(d)　Is my wife what?
　　　S:　(e)　Is your wife passed on, she's passed away, right?
　　　R:　(f)　Oh, my wife's dead?
　　　S:　(g)　Yeh.
　　　R:　(h)　Yeh, that's why I- I have a room here /continues/

(18) contains multiple clarification-questions from R (b, d, f). Each request
makes more explicit guesses (Ochs 1985) about what is being asked by incorporating more information from S's clarifications (c, e) of her initial question

(a). The entire clarification sequence is embedded in the question–answer exchange (a, h) and facilitates the provision of an answer.

Although it is S who requests clarification in (19), the clarification sequence is similarly embedded in the question–answer exchange, and again it is geared toward getting a clear formulation of an answer from R.

(19) R: (a) There was- there was one person up the street,
          (b) he was a number writer,
          (c) and he owned a car.
      S: (d) A number writer?
      R: (e) A number writer.
      S: (f) What's that?
      R: (g) Well, a number writer, um, man that uh- /continues/

Following R's description of *one person up the street* (a to c), S requests clarification of one part of that description (*A number writer?* (d)) with an echo question (Christian 1973). When the echo question format of S's request is treated only as a "non-hearing" (i.e. it receives only repetition of *a number writer* (e) from R), S asks more directly for clarification (*What's that?* (f)) and R provides clarification (beginning in g). Thus, although it was S who requested clarification in (19), that clarification results in an answer from R (g) that also supplements the informational content of R's prior answer (a to c).

(20) is a slightly more complex example with several clarification sequences.

(20) S: (a) What did kids do on dates?
          (b) When you were [growin' up.
      R: (c)   [When I was younger?
      S: (d) Yeh.
      R: (e) [Clears throat] Excuse me.
          (f) It would either be like maybe going bowling
          (g) And then take in- like you stop, uh, like for a soda or something.
      S: (h) Uh huh.
      R: (i) Or a movie.
          (j) Or the *biggest* thing was the dance.
      S: (k) Like where'd you go for dances?
      R: (l) Schools.
          (m) Like [your schools used to-
      S: (n)   [High schools?
      R: (o) Eh, eh, no, grade schools.
      /R continues/

The first clarification sequence in (20) is subordinate to S's question *What did kids do on dates?* (a). As S begins to modify this question with clarifying information (*When you were growin' up* (b)), R also requests clarification of

S's question (*When I was younger?* (c)). After S provides clarification (*Yeh* (d)), R answers the question from (a). In answering the question, R mentions *the dance* (j). S then asks a question whose focus is much more local than that of her earlier question about what *kids* did *on dates* (a): *Like where'd you go for dances?* (k) asks specifically about the prior referent *the dance* (j) and its answer clarifies that referent (*schools* (l)). The next question from S is also local and could be said to seek further clarification of the referent: S asks *High schools?* (n) and R answers *Eh, eh, no grade schools* (o).

To summarize: we saw earlier that information-seeking questions from S, and information-checking questions from both S and R, allow R to continue talking. Clarification sequences seem to have a similar turn-taking consequence: regardless of who requests clarification from whom, the floor belongs to R after completion of a clarification sequence.

3.3.4 *Questions, participants, ends, and act sequence*

We have seen thus far that some questions during sociolinguistic interviews are asked primarily by S (information-seeking questions) and some are asked by both R and S (information-checks, clarification-questions). All of these questions can create participation structures that replicate the more global structure and participatory norms of an interview: one person seeks information, one person provides information. As noted earlier, however, sociolinguists and their informants can also temporarily trade or alter the roles assigned by the interview structure: one way that informants do so during a multiparty interview is by adopting the questioning strategies of the interviewer.

Interviewing more than one person at a time has a general methodological advantage for sociolinguists: it increases the likelihood that informants will shift styles, thus providing important data on phonological variation (Labov 1972c). Multiparty interviews also mean that a greater number of interactive roles – and genres – become available for each participant. Although members of a family or friends who are being interviewed together may talk just to S (i.e. they may do no more than separately answer S's questions, as in 9), they often talk to one another about other matters, or they may construct joint responses to S's questions that lead to other speech activities. Thus, multiparty interviews may reveal a greater variety of genres (conversation, argument, discussion) than individual interviews.

(21) illustrates the use of questions in a multiparty interview: it highlights not only the way different PARTICIPANTS use questions to create an ACT SEQUENCE relative to different ENDS, but also the way a mode of questioning can help differentiate phases of the speech event. (21) also contains the question discussed in chapters 3 and 4, *Y'want a piece of candy?* To maintain consistency with our previous use of this example, I use personal names instead of S (Debby) and R (Henry, Irene, Zelda).

Before I present (21), it is important to note that ongoing with the physical activities of setting up our interview was a discussion about the unexpected death of a teacher from the neighborhood school; in fact, this was the main topic of our talk prior to the beginning of the interview itself. (Because the conversation about the teacher had been in progress before I turned the tape recorder on, I do not have a record of it and cannot include it in (21).) I was planning to start this interview with a word list: one of the most formal sections of an interview during which informants read a list of words (targeted for study because of the phonological environment they provide for a particular sound).

(21) HENRY: (a)   Y'want a piece of candy?
      IRENE: (b)   No.
      ZELDA: (c)   ^zShe's on a diet.
      DEBBY: (d)   ^zWho's not on [a diet.
      IRENE: (e)   [I'm on-
                      I'm on a diet
               (f)   and my mother [buys-=
      ZELDA: (g)   [You're not!
      IRENE: (h)   =my [mother buys these mints.=
      DEBBY: (i)   [Oh yes I amhhhh!
      ZELDA: (j)   Oh yeh.
      IRENE: (k)   The Russell Stouffer mints.
               (l)   I said, "I don't want any Mom."
               (m)   "Well, I don't wanna eat the whole thing."
               (n)   She gives me a little tiny piece,
               (o)   I eat it.
               (p)   Then she gives me an[other,=
      HENRY: (q)   [Was =
      IRENE: (r)   =so I threw it out the window=
      HENRY: =there a lot of people?=
      IRENE: (s)   =I didn't [tell her.=
      HENRY: (t)   [Was there=
      IRENE: (u)   =[She'd kill me.
      HENRY: =[a lot of people at the house?
      ZELDA: (v)   All: the teach[ers.
      IRENE: (w)   [A lot of teachers will- probably will all be
                      there till late.
      HENRY: (x)   Je:sus Christ.
      ZELDA: (y)   All: the teachers.
      HENRY: (z)   What a heartache.
      ZELDA: (aa)   And that Miss DiPablo? She was d- she must be her very
                      best friend. She was there. She said she was with her all:
                      week. She must be stayin' at her house!
      IRENE: (bb)   Probably.

ZELDA:	(cc)	[With-
DEBBY:	(dd)	[Did it happen today?
IRENE:	(ee)	[Saturday.
ZELDA:	(ff)	[No:
DEBBY:	(gg)	Oh, oh.
HENRY:	(hh)	[Damn shame.
IRENE:	(ii)	[All right, let's go.
HENRY:	(jj)	All right.
DEBBY:	(kk)	Okay, who wants to go first?
ZELDA:	(ll)	Oh: I'll go first.
DEBBY:	(mm)	Okay.
ZELDA:	(nn)	I better get my glasses.
DEBBY:	(oo)	Okay.
IRENE:	(pp)	Well I'll go first, then.
DEBBY:	(qq)	Okay.
IRENE:	(rr)	What am I su- just read-
DEBBY:	(ss)	Just read them. Umhmmm.

The interchange in (21) can be clearly divided into two phases: a pre-interview phase (a to ii); a lead-in phase (ii to ss) that makes a transition to the word list reading in the interview. These two phases are characterized by radically different topic structures and participant orientations. (21) also contains eight questions, repeated below:

(a)	HENRY:	Y'want a piece of candy?
(d)	DEBBY:	Who's not on a diet.
(q)	HENRY:	Was there a lot of people?
(t)	HENRY:	Was there a lot of people at the house?
(aa)	ZELDA:	And that Miss DiPablo?
(dd)	DEBBY:	Did it happen today?
(kk)	DEBBY:	Okay, who wants to go first?
(rr)	IRENE:	What am I su- just read-

The functions of these questions are related to the phases of the speech event in which they occur.

Let us take the pre-interview phase first. It is here that Henry offers Irene candy (*Y'want a piece of candy?* (a)), Irene refuses (*No* (b)), Zelda provides an account for the refusal (*She's on a diet* (c)), and Irene tells a story further accounting for her refusal (c to u). My rhetorical question (*Who's not on a diet* (d)) establishes solidarity through positive politeness (chapter 4, p. 117). Henry's questions (*Was there a lot of people?* (q), *Was there a lot of people at the house?* (t)) overlap with Irene's story to initiate a return to the main topic (the teacher's death). Irene and Zelda jointly answer Henry's question (v, w, y). Henry evaluates the situation (x, z). Zelda's *And that Miss DiPablo?* (aa) is an information-checking question concerning a new referent.

The pre-interview talk has a relatively fluid topic organization: three topics (candy, diets, the teacher) cross cut one another with none overtly reinforced by participants. In addition, turn selection (who speaks when) is, for the most part, a matter of self-selection (chapter 7), such that the participant roles of speaker and hearer are relatively available to any party. The five questions in the pre-interview phase have a range of different functions. Henry's first question (*Y'want a piece of candy?* (a)) is simultaneously an offer and request that opens a three-part exchange (see chapter 3). My question (*Who's not on a diet* (d)) is part of a gender-specific byplay about "diet." Henry's next two questions (*Was there a lot of people?* (q), *Was there a lot of people at the house?* (t)) return the discussion to the topic prior to "candy" and "diet." Zelda's question (*And that Miss DiPablo?* (aa)) is an information check that introduces a new referent into talk about "the teacher" (see chapters 6, 7, and 8). Thus, questions have a range of functions in this phase of the interview: this lack of functional rigidity matches the fluid topic and turn organization noted earlier.

The structure of the lead-in phase is in dramatic contrast to the pre-interview phase just discussed. Critical to the shift in topic and participant structure is Irene's *All right, let's go* (in ii). Note, however, that prior to this I have asked a question (*Did it happen today?* (dd)) that overlaps Zelda's elaboration of a referent (Miss DiPablo) pertinent to the ongoing discussion (aa, cc). My question reflects an asymmetry in information: I am seeking information that I do not have. Thus, it reveals my status as an outsider to the topic, and displays a participation framework more typical of an interview. Irene's answer (*Saturday* (ee)) fits the interview structure simply because it does no more than provide the information that I had requested. (Zelda's response *No:* is more evaluative.) It is after Irene's answer to my question that Irene says *All right let's go*, noted above as critical to the lead into the interview itself. Irene's topic pre-closing (*all right* in (ii); Schegloff and Sacks 1973) overlaps Henry's evaluation (*Damn shame* (hh)). Irene follows her pre-closing with a directive (*let's go*) that makes explicit not only that there is an agenda (we are gathered together for a purpose) but that it is time to start attending to that agenda. Thus, Irene's *all right, let's go* does lead into the interview. However, this relatively global transition in interactional structure has been eased by a prior question–answer exchange that conforms to the norms and participant structure of an interview: S seeks information from R.

In the remainder of the lead-in phase (ii to ss), topic and participation framework are explicitly directed toward starting our agenda. My question (*Okay, who wants to go first?* (kk)) opens a series of short turns through which participants negotiate the specifics of who is to do what when (i.e. begin reading the words in the word list). The topic of each turn is narrowly constrained toward the goal of getting us started with the task: Henry agrees with the proposed transition (*All right* (jj)), I agree and offer others the opportunity to self-select the order in which they will do the task (*Okay, who wants to go first?* (kk)). I continue to allow the others latitude in the way they plan to fulfill the task: my repeated *okay*'s (mm, oo, qq) transfer responsibility to the others to take the next action (Merritt 1976), whether that action is Zelda offering to go first (*Oh: I'll go first* (ll)), Zelda saying she needs her glasses (*I better get my glasses* (nn)), or Irene offering to go in Zelda's place (*Well I'll go first, then* (pp)). Once it is decided that Irene goes first, responsibility for instructing the others in performance of the task is clearly transferred to me: Irene's question (*What am I su- just read-* (rr)) about what she is supposed to do places me in a directive role. Thus, what gives this segment its status as a lead-in phase is that both topic and participation are oriented toward making a transition to the main agenda: the topic is task-driven and participation rights are allocated and relatively circumscribed by the nature of the task.

We have seen in this section that questions have different functions in different phases of the interview. Just as the mode of questioning may alter our sense of role relationships and our identity of the speech event as "interview" or "conversation," so too can it help to create different phases of an interview and organize the flow from one interview activity to another.

3.3.5 *Summary: questions in sociolinguistic interviews*

We have focused here upon three types of questions used during sociolinguistic interviews: questions primarily from S seek information, questions from both S and R check the information being provided and request clarification. Although the distribution of these modes of questioning generally supports the norms of the interview structure, participants also exploit these conventionalized expectations as ways to alter their role relationships and their definition of the situation.

Like the reference interviews discussed in section 3.2, the norms underlying the use of questions during sociolinguistic interviews are most influenced by the ENDS and PARTICIPANTS of the speech event. Since the specific ends and participants of sociolinguistic interviews differ from those of reference interviews, however, the distribution and social meaning of questions also differ between the two speech events. Despite differences in the specific research goals of sociolinguists, one relatively consistent goal is to record a great deal of speech from an informant. S's information-seeking questions clearly support this goal. Information-checking questions and clarification-questions also support this goal: they all allow R to return to, or maintain, a turn at talk. The goals and participant identities specific to reference interviews produced not only different forms and functions of questions (offers and collaboratively reformulated queries), but also an important difference in the relationship between questions and the overall ACT SEQUENCE of the interview. Reference interviews are centered on the joint resolution of a single query (or series of queries). Sociolinguistic interviews integrate the asking and answering of questions within other kinds of talk, including talk that can seem less like interview than conversation.

3.4 Summary of sample analysis

We noted earlier that the ethnography of communication is the most integrat-ive approach of those considered thus far: it can combine other approaches within a larger framework of inquiry into cultural knowledge and the social and linguistic practices for which it provides. Our analysis of the ways in which a speech act (question) can be used during a speech event (interview) thus illustrates cultural knowledge of language structure and function, the latter broadly enough construed to include how language functions as a resource through which to organize social interactions and enact social roles. But as also noted earlier, it is misleading to view an ethnographic approach to discourse as just the addition of a new component ("culture") to the basic material of other approaches. Rather, an ethnographic approach seeks to define the basic constructs of other approaches (along with its own constructs) as aspects of communication whose identities and interrelationships all reflect particular cultural meanings. In keeping with the idea that an ethnographic approach seeks culturally relative definitions of the basic "stuff" of communica-tion, let us summarize our sample analysis by considering how this approach can add to our knowledge of questions as speech acts.

Most scholars who study questions find them difficult to define, and they often note a number of criteria (syntactic, intonational, lexical, semantic, functional) by which to do so. Applying the criteria to actual utterances is complicated not just because of the multiple criteria themselves, but also because the criteria themselves seem to fluctuate in importance: what seems important to recognition of a question in some instances is not important in others.

Interactional and contextual criteria for questions are not operationally failsafe either. Goody (1978: 26), for example, suggests that "the *direct* illo-cutionary force of all questions is the elicitation of a response – but not necessarily a verbal response" (cf. Lund 1984). Broadening the notion of response to include a cognitive change in information state without verbal recognition of that change would allow many information-checking devices to pass as questions (as in the examples in section 3.3.3). But the identification of responses that are not manifested verbally (or nonverbally, e.g. through a head nod) is difficult for discourse analyses that rely for data upon naturally (rather than experimentally) occurring communicative events.

Context further complicates the identification of an utterance as a question. Although participant identity and setting clearly influence the interpretation of utterances as questions, for example, the degree to which these contextual parameters have an influence can vary. Even something so basic as the responsi-bility for deciding upon meaning can be unevenly distributed among partici-pants. McHoul (1987) suggests, for example, that the way a hearer interprets an utterance is more critical to its function (e.g. the interpretation of an interrogative as question or warning) than the speaker's intention. But even this distribution is culturally relative, reflecting deeply held cultural assumptions about responsibility for knowledge and the ability of one person to interpret another's thoughts and feelings (DuBois 1987; Duranti 1988; Ochs 1985).

We have identified in our analysis a greater variety of utterances as questions than might be included in either a straightforward speech act analysis or by reliance upon formal clues alone. We incorporated many aspects of Searle's analysis of questions in doing so: we spoke repeatedly of how utterances fulfilled preparatory, sincerity and/or essential conditions of questions. But we also added different aspects of context to our analysis of the utterances that we called "questions." Perhaps more importantly, we did so in a way that built upon an underlying assumption that communicative events themselves are organized and that their properties have systematic effects on constituent acts.

Let me be more specific about the methodology. We first described the communicative properties of events. What is it like for people to participate in a reference interview? What understandings underlie participation in a sociolinguistic interview? We then used some relatively traditional means of defining questions to choose some utterances to focus upon. We tried to discover how different communicative properties of speech events would define the function of those utterances and how they did so. By considering the utterances within the overall communicative organization of the speech event, we found that all the utterances that we called "questions" shared a general function: they all sought a response that facilitated the transmission of information in line with the overall goal of the speech event. Note that this function was not something we presumed initially: we did not begin with a definition of questions that assumed their goals to be so neatly attuned to the overall goal of the speech event.

The communicative properties best differentiating types of questions both within and across speech events were PARTICIPANT, ENDS, and (to a lesser degree) ACT SEQUENCE. Thus, who says what, why, and when, explains a great deal about questions in interviews. This analysis of context allowed us not only to identify a group of utterances that share a function, but to reveal the more subtle differences among those utterances. We might pursue this still further to propose a contextually motivated taxonomy of speech act functions – one that seeks to show the similarities and differences among questions themselves, as well as between questions and other utterances. Although the questions discussed all seek a response facilitating the transmission of information, there are some important differences among them: how much participants can presume about each other's knowledge, the kind of response being sought, the way a response facilitates information transmission. Differences such as these can serve as heuristics by which to define different types of questions.

Some approaches to discourse would seek to support the kinds of trends described here with quantitative analyses that compare the number of question types asked by different participants in different locations (both within and across speech events). Our discussion has proceeded as if such analysis is a possible next step in an ethnographic approach: I presented examples of each question type as if they were always mutually exclusive categories and as if each utterance filled just one question function. An ethnographic approach to discourse, however, does not assume either the mutual exclusivity of categories or the monofunctionality of an utterance. These, too, are subject to variation depending upon context. The following example suggests that although information-seeking questions, information-checking questions, and clarification-questions can be separately realized by different utterances, their functions can also overlap in a single utterance or be difficult to discriminate. In (22), S asks three questions.

(22) S: (a)   So are most of the guys that hang in your crowd uh what, Italian, Polish, Irish?
      R: (b)   Indians . . .
      S: (c)   Indians?
           (d)   You had everybody, huh?
      R: (e)   Yeh.

S's question in (a) is the easiest to categorize. *So are most of the guys that hang in your crowd uh what, Italian, Polish, Irish?* seeks new information: R had been describing his crowd, but said nothing about their nationalities. The questions in (c) and (d) are more difficult to categorize. S's question (*Indians?* (c)) can be interpreted either as a request for clarification or an information check (since *Indians* (b) is a surprising addition to this list of ethnic identities). These two question types can be especially difficult to tease apart because the categories "information-check" and "clarification-question" are not necessarily mutually exclusive: one reason why people might check their reception of another's utterance (information-check) is that it is unclear to them (clarification-question). This is not to say, however, that these two categories cannot be differently defined in principle: information-checks can be addressed either to one's own talk ("Do you understand what I mean?") or to another's talk ("Do I understand what you mean?"), whereas clarification-questions can be addressed only to another's talk simply because they presume a lack of understanding in what another has said.

The categorization of S's question *You had everybody, huh?* (d) in (22) is also difficult, but for slightly different reasons. Like S's *Indians?* (c), the question in (d) is semantically dependent on prior talk. But in addition to being identifiable as an information check, *You had everybody, huh?* can be identified as an information-seeking question that builds a stepwise topic transition (chapter 7) in which S's question (d) builds on a topic initiated by R's answer (b) to a prior-question (a). Thus, here the data themselves do not allow a clear formulation of criteria by which to differentiate question types.

The discrimination of question types gets even more complicated if we try to identify the same types of questions across speech events. In several sections

(3.2, 3.3.2, 3.3.3), we discussed examples in which questions were issued through rising intonation on single lexical items:

(6)   P: (c) I'm looking for . . . Fanny Mae, and Fanny Mac?
(13)   S: (a) Well, like did you have a team when you were goin' to school on a little league, or-
        R: (b) Oh yeh. [We used to-]
        S: (c)   [Really?]
(15)   R: (a) And what we used to do we used to, we used to play it with a golf ball . . . Right?
(19)   R: (a) There was- there was one person up the street,
            (b) he was a number writer,
            (c) and he owned a car.
        S: (d) A number writer?

Despite the formal similarity of these questions, we identified each one as slightly different: *Fanny Mac?* (6) opened a turn-transition space for joint reformulation of the query, *Really?* (13) and *Right?* (15) were information-checks, *A number writer?* (19) was a request for clarification. Although all these functions may very well be related to one another at one level of analysis, the differences captured through their divergent descriptions reflect important differences in the way they are situated in the speech event. For example, in our discussion of (15) in section 3.3.2, we said that R uses this type of utterance to check on S's reception of a proposition or referent and to provide a slot in which S can request clarification if that reception is deemed problematic. The function of *Fanny Mac?* (6, in section 3.2) is similar, but it is tailored more specifically to the overall goal of the query: if L does find P's formulation of the query adequate (i.e. L does not need to request clarification), L can resolve the query by providing the information being requested. Thus, although we might very well call *Fanny Mac?* in (6) an information-check, this would ignore its more situated meaning within the reference interview. Ignoring differences such as these would ignore the way speech act identity is embedded in speech events – a source of contextual variability that is crucial to the ethnographic approach to discourse. Note, however, that the level of specificity with which we discussed the function of specific utterances that we called "questions" (and utterances that we labelled as different types of questions) makes it difficult to draw conclusions about questions in general.

There are several points to draw from these examples before going on to the next issue. First, categorizing questions may be difficult because the categories themselves are not necessarily mutually exclusive: this is a major obstacle to quantitative comparisons. Second, the discrimination of question types may depend on semantic relationships across clauses. Information-seeking questions can be semantically independent of prior talk, but information-checks and clarification requests cannot. Thus, the degree to which the information in a question is semantically tied to a prior proposition helps to determine its question type. What an ethnographic perspective might point out is that participants' expectations for semantic continuity between propositions might vary in different speech events – such that what seems like an information-seeking question in one speech event would not seem like one in another. Third, a form that serves as one mode of questioning in one context may not do so in another. The most general point, then, is that both types and tokens of questions (and other speech acts) can be contextually relative and can benefit from systematic analysis of communicative contexts. (I return to this point in chapter 9.)

Consider, finally, that our sample analysis suggested that an ethnographic approach to questions in interviews required consideration of how questions fit into the interview itself, and thus an analysis of the interview as a speech event. We described two different types of interviews and the questions asked within them: we saw that the form and function of these questions were intricately tied to the communicative structure of the different interviews. This interrelationship between speech act and speech event suggests that speech acts stand in a reciprocal relationship with speech events – both analytically and in our own ways of thinking and knowing about communication. Thus, an ethnographic approach to discourse might also use findings about a speech act (questions) to learn about a speech event (interviews) and posit knowledge of this relationship as part of our communicative competence. To this end, one would also need to examine more general cultural beliefs about transmission of information, norms for interactions between strangers, and behavior in public and private social establishments (e.g. library versus home), for these (and other) beliefs also underlie the way we use language to question and be questioned in interviews.

4 An ethnographic approach to discourse

We have seen in this chapter that an ethnographic approach to discourse seeks to discover and analyze the structures and functions of communicating that organize the use of language in speech situations, events, and acts. Knowledge of these structures and functions is part of our communicative competence: what we say and do has meaning only within a framework of cultural knowledge. The ways that we organize and conduct our lives through language are thus ways of being and doing that are not only relative to other possibilities for communicating, but also deeply embedded within the particular framework by which we – as members of our own specific communities – make sense out of experience.

Although an ethnographic approach provides an analysis of language, it views language as but one part of a complex pattern of actions and beliefs that give meaning to people's lives. Consistent with this assumption, our sample analysis did not just focus on questions within different types of interviews, but on the goals, settings, participants, and other acts that constituted (and were constituted by) the speech events. Similarly, we also noted that the questions themselves contributed to the definition of the speech event "interview." Thus, "talk is always *constitutive* of some portion of reality: it either makes something already existing present to (or for) the participants or creates something new" (Duranti 1988: 225).

Exercises

1 Analyze the following example of a library reference interview through an ethnographic perspective.

L: (a)   Yes. Can I help you?
P: (b)   Is there a way that I can find out where in periodicals this
          periodical is. . . .
    (c)   Archives in [Pathology and Laboratory Medicine.
L: (d)   [Pathology. ^{z}Yeh.
[6 seconds]
L: (e)   Okay.
    (f)   Um, there's a listing under Archives of Pathology.
    (g)   It said it was called the Archives of
          Pathology$_z$ and Laboratory Medicine=
P: (h) ^{z}periodical?
L: (i)   from nineteen twenty six to twenty eight?
    (j)   [But now it's
P: (k)   [This is just their March issue-$_z$
L: (l) ^{z}Now it's just called the Archives of
          Pathology, according to *this*.
    (m)   It's . . . I'd- when- that could be wrong or this could be wrong
    (n)   I don't know which.
    (o)   Uh it's at the Georgetown Medical School Library and at the
          George Washington . . . University, Medical Library, and at
          Howard's Medical Library.
P: (p)   Okay,
    (q)   I'm going to be going to G. W. tomorrow.
    (r)   Would that be- is that the main library, or is it a separate [li-
L: (s)   [There's
          a separate library.
    (t)   Are you going on the subway? [Be-
P: (u)   [I'm going to a class at-at-at uh
          George Washington so . . .$_z$
L: (v) ^{z}The- the medical school is when you
          come up the escalator,
    (w)   it's immediately to your right.

(x)   You have to turn right,

(y)   and then, turn left to go into the building,

(z)   but, when you come up the escalator it's the building.

(aa)   It says Medical School.

P: (bb)   Okay. So it's in the medical school and it's=

L: (cc) ^{z} And=

P: =[not in the library.$_{\rceil}$

L: (dd)   =[it's ju- ^{z} Yes. And I'm just checking to- it does say open
           to the public . . . the Medical School Library.

P: (ee)   So I can just go in and use it.

L: (ff)   Uhhuh.

P: (gg)   Thank you very much.

2 Suppose you were setting out to do an ethnography of communication in your own culture. What speech situations and events would you try to tape-record? Why?

3 Tape-record a session either in a classroom where English is being taught as a second language, or in a classroom where a foreign language is being taught to native English speakers. How are the assumptions of an ethnographic approach to discourse reflected in the teaching strategies used in the classroom (or in the textbooks)? If they are not reflected, how might they be? If the students are having particular difficulties, how might they be explained in ethnographic terms?

4 Although the sample analysis in this chapter focused upon question–answer sequences, the ethnography of communication can also offer a rich contextual framework for the analysis of pronouns (e.g. Hanks 1990) and other referring terms. For example, what cultural assumptions are revealed by the use of the vague pronoun *they*, or the expression *a colored guy*, in the "I was robbed" story presented in chapter 6? In what other speech situations are the same referring terms used? Or consider the referring expressions in the sample data in appendix 3: e.g. who are the different *they*'s? How are they woven not only into the communicative structure of the argument (e.g. participants, goals) but also into the cultural themes underlying the argument?

5 Collect fifteen to twenty examples of service encounters. Use the etic grid to compare the communicative structure of these speech events (including, but not limited to, the use of questions) with the interviews discussed in this chapter. Alternatively, tape-record and transcribe examples of other interviews (e.g. on television talk shows, news interviews) and compare their communicative structure (and their question–answer sequences) to reference interviews and research interviews.

Notes

1 Although Hymes is using Cassier's point in relation to the speech used during Native American verbal art, I believe that the same point applies to all communicative events.

2 Since P is the participant in need of information, and L is the one who supplies information, P can be seen as the IVer and L the IVee. This role designation clearly

predicts the distribution of acts among participant: P presents a query (often through a question) just as an IVer in a research interview (3.3) requests information (often through questions). However, an alternative to the division of interactional work noted in table 5.1 is to suggest that P and L both function as IVer and IVee. Since L is in an institutionalized role that provides access to, and control over, information that P needs, we might compare L's role to that of a doctor (or a job counselor) who conducts an intake interview with a patient (or a client) so as to make a diagnosis (or assess the other's needs or abilities). It is in this sense that we can say that L is interviewing P so as to more precisely assess what it is that P (as IVee) needs. This designation of participant role interacts with the classification not just of events as interview or not (e.g. we might prefer to think of parts of this speech event as more like a "consultation" between expert and novice (Jacoby and Gonzales 1991) than like an "interview"), but also with our underlying ideas of occupational relations and obligations. Thus, an analysis of questions might help us build a more exact taxonomy of speech events whose main goal is the seeking of information. Similarly, we might find that although reference interviews are not prototypical interviews, they are more "interview" like than sociolinguistic interviews (3.3) since their central goal (resolution of a query) is a macro-level realization of an information-seeking question.

3 Reference interviews share some features with service encounters, e.g. the server (cf. the librarian) may ask a series of questions about the product being considered for purchase. Responses to such questions, however, do not guarantee that the customer in a service encounter will actually make a purchase; the two speech events also differ in that the reference interview is an exchange of information, whereas the service encounter is a potential economic transaction that can benefit the server.

4 Note that *yes* from P need not be interpreted as an affirmative response to a question. *Yes* is used not only when responding to requests, but also when accepting responsibility for the next move. For example, a graduate student taking her oral PhD exams once responded *yes* to a WH question (*What is the difference between . . .*) and then proceeded to give the substantive answer – thus accepting the responsibility for answering the question prior to actually providing the information.

5 In some ways, a query is very much like a question: P's purpose in making a query is to elicit information from L which he does not have, but which he presumes L to have. I discuss this in section 3.4.1. Note also that although space prevents discussion of other evidence of the centrality of the query, it is helpful to note the following: if an interview is interrupted (e.g. by a phone call to L), participants return to consideration of the query; if the query cannot be satisfied, alternative help is offered (cf. the provision of "accounts" when requests cannot be met or offers are rejected; chapter 3, pp. 78–84); new queries are structurally separated from one another and independently managed.

6 A common complaint among reference librarians concerns the patron's formulation of a query in terms that are too general (e.g. "do you have books on foreign languages?") to allow resolution within the organizational schema of library materials. Compare the need of physicians to "translate" patients' descriptions of their own physical conditions into terms that can be interpreted as "symptoms" and understood in relation to a physiological model of the body and the schemas through which diseases and syndromes are defined.

7 See Cameron et al. (1991) for arguments to this effect. *Language and Communication* volume 13, no. 2 (April 1993) is devoted to discussion of the social and political role of research interviews.

8　These properties are not only related to the form and meaning of utterances within an interview: they are also interrelated with one another. The sociolinguist's role as "interviewer," for example, emerges from the goals of the interview and allows greater control of its act sequence.

9　I do not include informants' questions to each other. My impression is either that these questions duplicate the interview framework (e.g. when one informant takes the role of the interviewer to replay the interviewer's question to another informant) or that they are questions that are outside of the interview frame itself (Schiffrin 1992a).

10　Compare the use of politeness forms that are conventionally used in one social setting, or for one social relationship, as a strategy through which to alter the meanings of another setting or relationship (Ervin-Tripp 1976).

11　Although we cannot be sure that the informant had even attended to the interviewer's pre-empted description – let alone completed it in the way S intended – it is important to note that this kind of effort to create both local and global cohesion by drawing from others' contributions is what I often find myself doing when trying to be conversational during an interview.

6 Pragmatics

1 Introduction

Pragmatics is another broad approach to discourse: it deals with three concepts (meaning, context, communication) that are themselves extremely vast and unwieldy. Given such breadth, it is not surprising that the scope of pragmatics is so wide, or that pragmatics faces definitional dilemmas similar to those faced by discourse analysis. Levinson (1983), for example, devotes an entire chapter of his pragmatics textbook to the problem of definition, and he finds none that successfully limit the scope of the field as well as represent it as a unified scholarly endeavor.[1] A consequence of this breadth is the need to devote more space to discussion of how pragmatics can provide an approach to the specific discourse problem considered by our sample analysis (referring sequences) than is necessary for the other approaches to discourse being discussed.

This chapter focuses on one particular type of pragmatics – Gricean pragmatics – not only because some other definitions of pragmatics cover much of the same ground as discourse analysis, but because this theory has become "the hub of pragmatics research" (Fasold 1990: 128). In section 2.0, I describe the philosopher H. P. Grice's ideas about speaker meaning (2.1) and the cooperative principle (2.2). After some general points about the application of Gricean pragmatics to referring terms (section 3), I use one particular discourse to suggest how Gricean pragmatics provides an approach to discourse analysis (section 4). Note that the sample analysis in this chapter begins the second focus of the analyses in this book: referring terms. I concentrate on the way the Gricean maxims of quantity and relevance explain the sequential alternation between referring terms, particularly the use of indefinite/definite, and explicit/inexplicit referring terms. These sequences reveal patterns, and raise issues, to which we return in chapters 7 and 8. Section 5 summarizes the pragmatic approach.

2   Defining pragmatics

Pragmatics was defined by Morris (1938) as a branch of semiotics, the study of signs (but see Givón 1989: 9–25, for discussion of its earlier roots). Morris (p. 81) viewed semiosis (the process in which something functions as a sign) as having four parts. A sign vehicle is that which acts as a sign; a designatum is that to which the sign refers; an interpretant is the effect in virtue of which the sign vehicle is a sign; an interpreter is the organism upon whom the sign has an effect. Put another way, something is a sign of a designatum for an interpreter to the degree that the interpreter takes account of the designatum in virtue of the presence of the sign (p. 82). In Morris's own terms: "Semiosis is . . . a mediated-taking-account-of. The mediators are *sign vehicles*; the takings-account-of are *interpretants*; the agents of the process are *interpreters*; what is taken account of are *designata*" (p. 82; emphasis in original).

In addition to defining different aspects of the semiosis process, Morris identified three ways of studying signs: *syntax* is the study of formal relations of signs to one another, *semantics* is the study of how signs are related to the objects to which they are applicable (their designata), *pragmatics* is the study of the relation of signs to interpreters. Thus, pragmatics is the study of how interpreters engage in the "taking-account-of" designata (the construction of interpretants) of sign-vehicles.

Contemporary discussions of pragmatics (although not viewed within the behaviorist framework of Morris) all take the relationship of signs to their users to be central to pragmatics. In the rest of this section, I describe Gricean pragmatics: a contemporary version of pragmatics which focuses on meaning in context, but expands both the "sign" and the "user" ends of the sign–user relationship. I discuss two central concepts of Gricean pragmatics: speaker meaning (2.1) and the cooperative principle (2.2).

2.1   *Speaker meaning*

The first concept important to Gricean pragmatics is *speaker meaning*. As we will see, speaker meaning not only allows a distinction between two kinds of meaning (and hence, a division between semantic and pragmatic meaning), it also suggests a particular view of human communication that focuses on intentions (chapter 11).

Grice (1957) separates non-natural meaning (meaning-nn) from natural meaning. Natural meaning is devoid of human intentionality, as in, for example, *Those spots mean measles*. Non-natural meaning is roughly equivalent to intentional communication (but see below): Grice's example is *Those three rings on the bell (of the bus) mean that "the bus is full"* (p. 53). A critical feature of meaning-nn is that it is intended to be recognized in a particular way by a recipient. As Grice (p. 58) states: " 'A meant-nn something by x' is (roughly) equivalent to 'A intended the utterance of x to produce some effect in an audience by means of the recognition of this intention'." Implicit in this definition of meaning-nn is a second intention – the intention that a recipient recognize the speaker's communicative intention. Pursuing Grice's example of *three rings on the bell*, we might say that for the three rings to have meaning-nn, it is sufficient for the bus riders to recognize that the conductor (or whoever caused the three bells to ring) intended the effect of the bells (i.e. "the bus is full") to be produced by their recognition of his intention. (See Recanati 1987 for discussion of whether such recognition is necessary and sufficient.)

Strawson (1964: 155) separates not two, but three, intentions in Grice's formulation. In Strawson's terms, to mean something by x, S must intend the following:

(a) S's utterance of x to produce a certain response r in a certain audience A;

(b) A to recognize S's intention (a);

(c) A's recognition of S's intention (a) to function as at least part of A's reason for A's response r.

We can view these intentions as cycling back upon one another: intention (c) is that intention (b) function as at least part of the reason for the fulfillment of intention (a). It is only when the three intentions are activated that an individual is acting as a communicator; it is only when the three intentions are realized that communication has occurred. Thus, to convey a speaker meaning, a communicator makes manifest (displays) the sort of reflexive intention described above.

Where does semantic meaning enter into Grice's framework? That is, how are the stable senses of words (their literal, conventional meanings) related to speaker meaning? (See Grice 1968.) Certainly a person may intend to communicate by the words "Sam is a boy" precisely the conventional understandings associated with those words; in Grice's terms, a speaker may intend to create in a hearer a recognition of the intention to convey that proposition about the world, i.e. about Sam's identity. But what if someone states *Boys will be boys*, or *Sam is Sam*? If we were to focus just on the meanings that these utterances have by virtue of their conventional meanings, then we would be able to do little more than identify them as tautologies. Yet speakers routinely use such utterances to mean considerably more than what is conveyed by their semantic meanings (but see Fraser 1988; Ward and Hirschberg 1991; Wierzbicka 1987).

What Grice's framework does is allow speaker meaning to be relatively free of conventional meaning; in fact, the critical insight of Grice's meaning-nn for our purposes is that what the speaker intends to communicate need not be related to conventional meanings at all, and not conventionally "attached" to the words being used. Thus, as we discuss in section 2.2, speaker-meaning need not be code-related, i.e. it may be inferred through processes quite different from the encoding and decoding processes assumed by the code model of communication (chapter 11). But how do speaker-meanings arise? We will find an answer to this question when we discuss the next concept critical to Gricean pragmatics: the cooperative principle.

2.2 The cooperative principle

In order to understand the cooperative principle (CP), it is helpful to first describe Grice's view of logical meaning in relation to natural language. Our discussion will also focus on the concept of implicature: an inference about speaker intention that arises from a recipient's use of both semantic (i.e. logical) meanings and conversational principles. Because implicatures are related to semantic meaning, the "sign" remains important in meaning-nn. But because implicatures are also dependent on conversational principles, "context" mediates the sign–user relationship.

Grice (1975) is concerned with the relationship between logic and conversation (in fact, "Logic and conversation" is the title of the paper). As Grice explains, natural language utterances do not seem to convey the same meanings that corresponding logical propositions would:

> It is a commonplace of philosophical logic that there are, or appear to be, divergences in meaning between, on the one hand, at least some of what I shall call the formal devices – ~, $\land$, $\lor$, $\supset$, (x), $\exists$(x), $\int$(x) . . . and, on the other, what are taken to be their analogs or counterparts in natural language – such expressions as *not*, *and*, *or*, *if all*, *some*, or (*at least one*), *the*. (Grice 1975: 41)

For example, the utterance *I went to the store and I put gas in the car* might be represented as "P & Q" (in which "P" represents the proposition in the first clause, and "Q" the second). But the interpretation of the utterance is broader than that which would rest upon the logical meaning of the connective "&". The logical meaning of "&" can tell us, for example, that "P & Q" is true only if both P and Q are true. We typically understand such an utterance, however, as conveying temporal sequence (I went to the store before I put gas in the car). Grice differentiates such understandings from logical meanings by saying that logical meanings are part of what someone "says": to "say" is "closely related to the conventional meaning of the words (the sentence) he has uttered" (p. 44). The broader interpretations are what someone "implicates" (although he reserves discussion of the meaning of "implicate" until after his discussion of conversation; see below). This distinction allows Grice to propose that natural language expressions really do not diverge from the formal devices of logicians. Rather, the added meanings that seem to appear in utterances are *implicatures*, and they are due to rules and principles of conversation; more precisely, to the *cooperative principle* underlying communication.

In order to support his proposal, Grice (p. 45) makes several initial observations about conversation:

> Our talk exchanges do not normally consist of a succession of disconnected remarks, and would not be rational if they did. They are characteristically, to some degree at least, cooperative efforts; and each participant recognizes in them, to some extent, a common purpose or set of purposes, or at least a mutually accepted direction . . . at each stage, *some* possible conversational moves would be excluded as conversationally unsuitable. (emphasis in original)

Going on from these initial and very general observations, Grice (p. 45) proposes a general principle which participants will be expected to observe: "Make your conversational contribution such as is required, at the stage at which it occurs, by the accepted purpose or direction of the talk exchange in which you are engaged." This principle is labelled "the cooperative principle" (CP) and it consists of four more specific maxims (p. 46):

Quantity:
1 Make your contribution as informative as is required (for the current purposes of the exchange).
2 Do not make your contribution more informative than is required.

Quality
Try to make your contribution one that is true.
1 Do not say what you believe to be false.
2 Do not say that for which you lack adequate evidence.

Relation: Be relevant.

Manner:
Be perspicuous.
1 Avoid obscurity of expression.
2 Avoid ambiguity.
3 Be brief (avoid unnecessary prolixity).
4 Be orderly.

It is important to note that these maxims (indeed, the CP in general) derive not from the nature of conversation *per se*, but from the fact that talking is "a special case or variety of purposive, indeed rational, behavior" (p. 47). We will see in a moment that it is these principles that provide a basis for the inference of implicatures: the CP and its attendant maxims allow speakers to lead their hearers to interpretations of their communicative intent (speaker meaning) that go beyond the logical meanings of what they "say." Note that since such principles are not principles of conversation – indeed, not even principles of language use – they do little to return us to the "sign" side of the sign–user relationship so central to Morris's pragmatics. But when we take a closer look at the way hearers arrive at implicatures, we will see that this inferencing process includes a hearers' interpretation of what a speaker "says," and thus builds upon semantic meaning.

A crucial feature of implicatures is that they must be capable of being calculated by a hearer. Grice (p. 50) describes the process as follows:

> To work out that a particular conversational implicature is present, the hearer will rely on the following data:
> (1) the conventional meanings of the words used, together with the identity of any references that may be involved
> (2) the CP and its maxims
> (3) the context, linguistic or otherwise, of the utterance
> (4) other items of background knowledge
> (5) the fact (or supposed fact) that all relevant items falling under the previous headings are available to both participants and both participants know or assume this to be the case.

Given this basic process, implicatures can be created in one of three ways: a maxim can be followed in a straightforward way, a maxim can be violated because of a clash with another maxim, or a maxim can be flouted. I illustrate each below.

Let us begin with our earlier example *I went to the store and I put gas in the car* to show how implicatures can be calculated in a straightforward way. We have already said (consistent with (1) above) that when I present this utterance, I "say" something, and that what I "say" has conventional meaning, including the meaning of the logical connective "&". We also suggested that an implicature of temporal order is created, i.e. that I went to the store before I put gas in the car. How does this happen? We see from Grice's description that we need to make a general assumption that both I and my hearer know the CP and its maxims (2 above) as well as the context (linguistic or otherwise) of the utterance (3 above) and other items of background knowledge (4 above). Given these assumptions, we might say that an implicature of temporal order arises from the Manner maxim "Be orderly," i.e. it is orderly to present events in the order in which they occur, from the Manner maxim "Be brief," or from the Quantity maxim, i.e. it is not necessary to present temporal information about events if that information can be inferred iconically (from the order of clauses in the text). Whichever maxim is responsible for the implicature, it is important to note that the implicature arises without my hearer assuming that I have violated a maxim: the implicature can be inferred under the assumption that I am following the maxims in a straightforward way.

Although conventional meaning is said to be part of what must be known for the calculation of implicatures, it does not seem to play that central a role in implicatures that arise when the maxims are followed in a straightforward way. Nor is it that important when an implicature arises from a clash between maxims (Grice's second possibility). Let me provide Grice's example (p. 51).

A: Where does C live?

B: Somewhere in the South of France. (Gloss: There is no reason to suppose that B is opting out; his answer is, as he well knows, less informative than is required to meet A's needs. This infringement of the first maxim of Quantity can be explained only by the supposition that B is aware that to be more informative would be to say something that infringed the maxim of Quantity, "Don't say what you lack adequate evidence for," so B implicates that he does not know in which town C lives.)

It is the third possible route toward implicatures that shows most clearly the role of conventional meaning: a flouting of the maxims. Grice (pp. 52–6) explains that people can say things that seem to violate one or more of the maxims, e.g. one can violate the Quantity maxim by presenting less information than seems to be required, the Quality maxim by saying things which seem to be false.[2] When this occurs, however, hearers still assume that a speaker is following the general CP; thus, they find an interpretation of the violation that allows them to preserve this assumption of cooperation. It turns out that some maxim violations are apparent only because of semantic problems – and it is here that we can see the role of conventional meaning most clearly in the calculation of implicatures. Grice's example of metaphor, which flouts the maxim of quality, provides the clearest illustration:

> Examples like *You are the cream in my coffee* characteristically involve categorial falsity, so the contradictory of what the speaker has made as if to say will, strictly speaking, be a truism; so it cannot be THAT that such a speaker is trying to get across. The most likely supposition is that the speaker is attributing to his audience some feature or features in respect of which the audience resembles (more or less fancifully) the mentioned substance. (p. 53)

Thus, hearers would not know that a maxim had been violated – and not search for an implicature – if they did not first know that the semantic properties of "human" (evoked by the pronoun *you*) exclude the possibility of also being "liquid" (*cream*).[3]

In this section, I discussed implicatures in relation to the CP and its maxims. Before closing, let us recall (from section 2.1) that the independence of meaning-nn from the linguistic sign *per se* freed the study of speaker meaning from the sign–user relationship (the focus of Morris's pragmatics). We have just seen that implicatures rest primarily on a principle of communication – the cooperative principle – rather than principles of language *per se*: implicatures allow us to account for how people convey messages not provided through the stable semantic meaning of their words. But we have also seen that the process by which speaker-meaning is inferred includes within it the interpretation of conventional meaning. And because conventional meaning plays a role in hearers' inference of speaker meaning, the linguistic sign (the code) also has a role in Gricean pragmatics (see chapter 11).

3 Referring terms: pragmatic processes in discourse

Gricean pragmatics provides a way to analyze the inference of speaker meaning: how hearers infer the intentions underlying a speaker's utterance. It is not intended as an approach to the analysis of discourse, i.e. to sequences of utterances. In the remainder of this chapter, however, I show how the CP can help define the way information from one utterance contributes to the meaning of another utterance, thereby contributing to our knowledge of relationships between utterances.

Our sample analysis in section 4 focuses on the organization of referring terms in a narrative. Before beginning this analysis, I introduce several terms to be used in section 4 and in the other chapters (7 and 8) dealing with similar issues (3.1). I also present brief examples suggesting the importance of the maxims of quantity and relation (3.2), motivate a discourse analysis of referring sequences (3.3), and comment on methodology (3.4).

3.1 *Referring as a pragmatic process in discourse*

Although reference and referring terms have been analyzed through many different perspectives in philosophy and linguistics, scholars often view the process of referring to entities in the universe of discourse as pragmatic – simply because it is a process involving speakers, their intentions, actions, and knowledge. Givón (1989: 175), for example, states that:

> Reference in a Universe of Discourse is already a *crypto pragmatic* affair. This is because every universe of discourse is *opened* ("established") – for whatever purpose – by a *speaker*. And that speaker then *intends* entities in that universe of discourse to either refer or not refer. And it seems that in human language it is that *referential intent* of the speaker that controls the grammar of reference. (emphasis in original)

Similarly, Searle (1969: chapter 4) views referring as a speech act, governed by conditions similar to those governing the performance of actions such as promises or requests (see chapter 3). Clark and Wilkes-Gibbs (1986) go still further to speak of referring as a "collaborative process": they suggest that although a speaker can propose a referent, the identification of the referent needs to be seen as an outcome of speaker–hearer interaction (see also Martinich 1984: 161–2). Some particular types of reference are especially dependent on mutual knowledge: Clark and Murphy (1982), for example, argue that definite reference (reference to an entity with the expectation that the hearer will be able to make a similar identification; see below) depends critically upon mutual knowledge, beliefs, and suppositions (see also Clark and Marshall 1981). Thus, as seen from both the speaker's and the hearer's point of view, the process by which expressions refer to an entity can be seen as pragmatic: "the mechanism by which referring expressions enable an interpreter to infer an intended referent is not strictly semantic or truth-conditional, but involves the cooperative exploitation of supposed mutual knowledge" (Green 1989: 47).

Note, however, that Grice himself does not consider reference in detail. Grice includes "the identity of any reference that may be involved" (1975: 50), along with the conventional meanings of words, as part of the information relied upon in the calculation of a conversational implicature. This exclusion of reference from the domain of pragmatics suggests that the identity of a referent is not inferred through use of the CP (cf. Clark 1975). It is also faithful to Morris's (1938) view of semantics as the study of how signs are related to the objects to which they are applicable, and pragmatics as the study of the relation of signs to interpreters. Yet, Grice's discussion also suggests that specific maxims (e.g. quantity and relevance) constrain the speaker's *choice of referring terms* – an effect that can be more easily reconciled with the view that reference is a relationship between language and an entity in one's (mental) discourse model (Green 1989; Webber 1979; see also Kronfeld 1990). I return to this point in sections 3.2 and 4.

Viewing referential processes as pragmatic is important not just for the general reasons sketched above, but also because it may help us account for distributional differences between *definite* and *indefinite* forms, and *explicit* and *inexplicit* forms. Referring terms that are definite are noun phrases with the definite article *the*, possessives, pronouns, names, titles; those that are indefinite include noun phrases with the indefinite article *a*, with quantifiers, and with numerals. Indefinites can also be the predicates in existential *there* sentences (but see Bolinger 1977; Ziv 1978; also chapters 7 and 8). This distributional restriction is important since some forms (e.g. *this*: Prince 1978) can be used for both definite and indefinite reference.

Although it is relatively easy to formally differentiate referring terms that are definite from those that are indefinite, it is not as easy to define their functional differences, i.e. to reveal the conditions under which different terms can be appropriately used. Referents are often introduced into discourse with terms that are indefinite and explicit (e.g. *a woman I work with*) and continued with terms that are definite and inexplicit (e.g. *she*). The reasons for this distribution can be conveyed in pragmatic terms. Definite forms are often said to indicate S's intention to refer to a single entity that can be specifically identified by S, and that S expects H to be able to identify from whatever clues (textual, contextual) are available (Ariel 1990; Green 1989: 46).[4] Indefinite forms, on the other hand, are said to indicate "the fact that the term is being introduced into the discourse for the first time – and without any *speaker's presumption of hearer's familiarity*" (Givón 1989: 179, emphasis in original).[5]

The explicitness of referring terms can also be viewed in pragmatic terms. Whereas definiteness has to do with S's assumption that H will be able to identify a single, specific entity to which S intends to refer, explicitness has to do with the presentation of information that actually enables H to correctly identify a referent, i.e. the lexical clues that allow H to single out whom (or what) S intends to differentiate from other potential referents. (In this sense, explicitness is similar to informativity.) Definiteness and explicitness can easily crosscut one another. For example, I can use all of the following (and more) definite descriptions to refer to the same person: *my husband, Louis, Dr Scavo, the man I live with*. These are all more explicit than the indefinites *an adult I live with, someone I met in college*. The definite *he*, however, is *less* explicit than the indefinites just given. Note, finally, that the explicit–inexplicit distinction is more continuous than discrete: *someone I met in college* is more explicit than *someone I knew when I was younger*, but less explicit than *someone I met in my third year of college*; *he* is less explicit than any of the above expressions, but more explicit than zero anaphora.

We have seen so far that the process of referring may be seen as pragmatic, simply because it is a process involving speakers, their intentions, actions, and knowledge. Similarly, both definiteness and explicitness can be defined in pragmatic terms. Definiteness is concerned with S's intentions and assumptions about what H can be expected to know. Explicitness is partially motivated by S's cooperative intentions, i.e. information is presented to enable H to identify an intended referent.

3.2   A preliminary Gricean analysis: quantity and relevance

Differences in both definiteness and explicitness among referring terms can be associated not just with pragmatics in general, but with the Gricean maxims of quantity and relevance. As I noted above, for example, I may refer to the very same person in numerous ways: definite descriptions (*my husband, Louis, he, Dr Scavo, the man I live with*) and indefinite descriptions (*an adult I live with, someone I met in college*). Although I may intend each expression to refer to the same person, they are not all equally suited to the task of helping you identify that person. For example, use of the referring expression *someone I met in college* may very well be accurate, but it is not explicit enough. Not only do I know a great deal more about the person to whom I intend to refer than where we met, but because I met many people in college, this description would not allow you to uniquely identify who it is that I am talking about.

This problem can easily be cast in Gricean terms. Although *someone I met in college* adheres to the maxim of quality, it violates the *maxim of quantity*: I have not provided you with information sufficient for your task of selecting from the set of referents "people I met in college" the one particular entity to whom I intend to refer. Thus, the various ways that we may refer to someone are ordered in terms of how much information they supply about that person and about our relationship with that person.

Equally important as the quantity of information conveyed in a particular referring term, however, is the relevance of that information (cf. Kronfeld's (1990) distinction between functional and conversational relevance). Here I will consider an example that will allow us to begin to address not only paradigmatic, but also syntagmatic, choices among referring terms. During a sociolinguistic interview, a middle-aged woman (Sue) was talking about her high school friends. She stated the following:

(1) SUE: (a) I always wanted to marry an Italian guy.
    IVER: (b) How come?
    SUE: (c) I just wanted to.
          (d) And I said it.
          (e) And I did.

Although Sue did marry *an Italian guy* (*And I did* (e)), her statement in (a) of her wish to do so is referentially opaque: we do not know whether she intends to refer to a specific "Italian guy" who she wants to marry, or to anyone who meets the description "Italian guy." Because Sue has been talking about a period of time (high school days) *prior to* her acquaintance with any Italian guys, however, we can use this background knowledge to infer that Sue does not have one specific "Italian guy" in mind. When the evoked time period of Sue's discourse switches in (e) to *after* her marriage – *and I did* (e) – we understand that there is one specific "Italian guy" whom she has married.

When Sue goes on to describe how her husband's family viewed his marriage to her (since her family is part Italian and part Irish) she explicitly brings her husband into the discourse. In (2), Sue is describing how her sister-in-law married someone who was not completely Italian:

(2) SUE   (a) So she was the oldest daughter.
         (b) And she broke the ice for me like she said.
         (c) Y'know, for Tony, my husband.
    IVER: (d) How did you meet Tony?

In (c), Sue mentions her husband in two ways: his name (*Tony*) and his kin relationship (*my husband*). Thus, (1) and (2) have supplied three descriptive resources for a next-mention: ethnicity, name, relationship.

Although the referring term (*Tony*, a proper noun) used by the IVer in (d) (*How did you meet Tony?*) identifies a specific person, let us see how Sue refers to Tony in her answer to the IVer's question. (3) presents the section of a narrative describing the first time Sue met Tony:

(3) (a) So anyway, this real dark looking, gangster looking guy, comes out the door,
     (b) and he looked like an old man to me.
     (c) And he looked like a gangster.

Sue's description of her first encounter with Tony uses a referring expression (*this real dark looking, gangster looking guy*) that is explicit, but much less restrictive than the expressions (*Tony, my husband*) that she used earlier. (There are many more people who can fit into the category of "real dark looking, gangster looking guys" than into the category of "my husband.") Note, however, that the shift in time frame and in information state alters the descriptive categories that are available for reference. Sue's description in (3a) matches the quantity of information that she then had about Tony. It is also relevant to her first meeting with Tony (or at least to the impression she wants to convey about that meeting). Thus, the shift in time frame creates a scenario to which a referring term can (or even, must) be both informationally appropriate and relevant.

Our discussion of the way Sue mentions her husband in (2) and (3) illustrates that relevance can be as important a pragmatic constraint on referring terms as quantity of information. In (3), relevance shifted along with information quantity: *this real dark looking, gangster looking guy* is consistent with S's knowledge – her quantity of information – about Tony at that time. Relevance can also figure in the choice of a referring term even without a shift in quantity. In Schiffrin (1988b), for example, I discuss a narrative told in response to a question I had asked about local availability of medical help. Despite her knowledge of explicit information about a particular doctor (e.g. his name), my respondent refers initially to *a neighborhood doctor who we use* – simply because it was that categorization that was relevant to my prior question.

So far, we have seen that referring terms convey different quantities of information and can be more or less relevant to ongoing discourse. I have also noted that quantity and relevance may work together (or separately) to constrain referring terms. In the sample analysis in section 4, we see in more detail how the maxims of quantity and relation work relative to information provided in other utterances, thereby influencing both paradigmatic and syntagmatic choices within referring sequences. Before we do this, however, it will be helpful to view referring not just as a pragmatic process, but also as a sequential process.

3.3 *Referring as a discourse process*

Referring may be seen as a sequential problem. Rather than analyze referring terms *per se*, we may analyze *referring sequences*: how is reference initiated?

How is reference continued? This shift in perspective is important primarily because it allows us to view reference in terms familiar to discourse analysis. In chapter 2, we saw that discourse analysts often focus on sequential patterns, e.g. of clauses, moves, actions. This is because discourse creates syntagmatic options: what occurs at one point in time (in one slot in a sequence) constrains the options (and selection of an option) at a later point in time (in a later slot in the sequence). Discourse is frequently noted to be constrained in this way. The occurrence of what is heard as a question in [slot 1], for example, constrains the way a remark in [slot 2] will be heard, i.e. as an answer (see chapters 3, 4, 5, and 7). Research on referring terms in discourse reveals the existence of similar kinds of expectations about sequences of referring terms: a particular referring term in [slot 1] constrains what terms will occur in [slot 2] and, even further, the way a sequentially next term, e.g. a pronoun, will be interpreted. Such research has focused a great deal of attention not only on characterizing the slots in which particular terms appear, e.g. in terms of paragraph, rhetorical, or story structure (Fox 1987; Tomlin 1987), or in terms of recency and accessibility (Ariel 1990; Givón 1989), but also on accounting for why particular expressions are suited for use in different slots. Thus, referring terms exhibit a dependence across clauses that can be seen as similar to other sequential dependences in discourse.[6]

Focusing on referring sequences also allows us to clearly differentiate *first-mentions* of a referent (cf. [slot 1]) from *next-mentions* (cf. [slot 2]). As noted earlier, first-mentions are often indefinite noun phrases (e.g. *a* + NP) and explicit (e.g. nominals rather than pronominals). Next-mentions may be definite and less explicit (e.g. pronouns rather than nominals). The main functional factor underlying this distribution is information status (cf. Chafe 1974, 1976, 1980, 1987) and accessibility (Ariel 1990). A first-mention evokes an entity that may be new to H or that H cannot be assumed to currently have in consciousness. A next-mention evokes an entity that need not be assumed to be new to H: H might either have that entity in consciousness or be able to retrieve it from memory.

In sum, some very different questions can be asked depending on the discourse location of a referring term. For first-mentions, for example, we may ask how it is that H identifies new entities. Does S provide assistance by tying a new entity to information that is already either situationally or textually evoked (Prince 1981)? How is the specific formulation of such references sensitive to different aspects of physical or social context (e.g. Schegloff 1972b; Sacks and Schegloff 1979)? Our questions are quite different for next-mentions. How does S provide sufficient information to guide H toward identification of a referent even if a referring term is very inexplicit (e.g. a pronoun or even zero anaphora)? Alternatively, why would S use a referring term that provides more than enough information for identification of a referent?

Now that we have motivated the analysis of referring terms in relation not only to pragmatics, but to discourse analysis in general, we should be ready to present a more detailed Gricean analysis of referring sequences. However, there is just one more issue to mention: a methodological issue.

3.4 The importance of method and data

Before going on to apply Gricean pragmatics to some of the issues raised above, it is important to make some observations about method and data. Although I am applying Gricean pragmatics to discourse, the application that I propose does not always adhere to the typical methodology of Gricean analyses. As we discussed above, the disciplinary origins of Gricean pragmatics are in philosophy. Contemporary pragmatics is certainly a part of linguistics (Levinson 1983), but it is part of a linguistics that takes as data a hypothetical sentence, adds to it a hypothetical context, and calls it an utterance (e.g. Cole 1981). However, if we want to use Gricean pragmatics as an approach to a discourse analysis that is committed to analyzing how people actually use utterances to communicate with one another, then we need to make the sorts of adjustments that I will be making in this section (cf. Levinson 1983: chapter 6; Schiffrin 1987b). Most importantly, rather than rely on constructed sentences that are treated as if they are contextualized utterances, we must use actual utterances that have been produced by speakers in contexts. Such a shift in data can have far-reaching effects on Gricean pragmatics itself.

Although I do not discuss the effects of using actual utterances on Gricean pragmatics in general (but see Schiffrin 1987b), some effects will become apparent in my analysis. The decision to base my illustration of Gricean pragmatics on the referring terms in one story means that the analysis is guided in large part by the referring sequences that are in that story. Thus, rather than propose relatively abstract relationships between maxims and try to find examples that substantiate (or refute) those relationships (e.g. Horn 1985b), we will try to use the maxims to help explicate particular uses of referring terms in particular utterances in one particular story. This is not to say that such an analysis might not end up influencing our understanding of abstract relationships between different maxims. But this is not what guides the analysis. Rather, what guides the analysis is an effort to resolve problems that stem from concrete observations about language use.

4 Sample analysis: referring sequences in narrative

The sample analysis in this section is based upon the referring expressions in one particular discourse – a narrative. After presenting the narrative (4.1), I show

how the maxims of quantity and relevance help to account for the referring sequences in this particular discourse (4.2). I summarize in section 4.3.

4.1 The data

Stories are useful texts in which to analyze referring sequences. In telling a story, a speaker constructs a story world in which a limited number of entities act and interact with one another in a defined location and for a limited period of time. In addition, although stories are situated within conversations, a story world can be somewhat independent of that world and can involve distinct time (and information state) shifts away from that world. This means that referents not yet textually evoked may have to be introduced and made relevant to domains that are not currently relevant to the conversation *per se.* Thus, stories offer the opportunity to find referring sequences in which new referents are introduced and continually used in a particular framework to which they are relevant.[7]

The story on which I focus is quite long, and I will be drawing from different sections of it to make various points. For these reasons, it will help to see it as a whole before we begin its analysis; I present it as (4). Lines in the narrative itself (the story world) are alphabetized; others are numbered.

(4) IVER: Have you ever been robbed?
     GARY: I was robbed. At night.
     IVER: When was this?
     GARY: I guess about six or eight weeks ago.
     IVER: How'd it happen?
     GARY: (a)   I picked up a fare [1] at Board and Elm.
              (b)   He [1] was a colored guy.
              (c)   He [1] flagged me down.
              (d)   So I wasn't- it was late at night.
              (e)   It was around one thirty in the morning.
              (f)   And I was gonna turn it [1] down.
              (g)   So I figured, y'know, I'd pick him [1] up anyway.
              (h)   But then two friends [2] came out.
              (i)   So they [?3] said, "We're only going right around the corner more or less," y'know. "Could you take us up?"
              (j)   They [?3] gave me an address.
              (k)   They [?3] said, "We'll get- show you how to get there."
              (l)   So it was maybe only three blocks away,
              (m)   so they [?3] said- I think they [?3] gave me an address that's at the center of the block,
              (n)   and there was a small light on at the house. /Mhm./
              (o)   So I pulled up,
              (p)   I turned on the light,

	(q)	and the guy he [?1] grabbed me from the back of my head
	(r)	and [?1] put a gun to it.
		Andhh uh,
IVER:		Jesus.
GARY:	(s)	I had about fifty dollars in my sock
	(t)	and I had about nine dollars on me.
	(u)	So I gave 'em [?3] the nine dollars
	(v)	and they [?3] wanted more.
	(w)	So they [?3] took my wallet.
	(x)	I didn't want to give them [?3] the money.
	(y)	So then the guy up front he [?4] stuck a gun on my temple, asking for more money.
	(z)	They [?3] were gonna, y'know, shoot me.
	(aa)	So I gave them [?3] the rest of the money.

IVER:	(1)	In your sock, [right
GARY:	(2)	[Yeh.
IVER:	(3)	If you hadn't pulled out the money in your sock, do you think they [?3] would've looked?
	(4)	Do they [?3] know you keep it here?
GARY:	(5)	No.
	(6)	But, from what other cab drivers [5] told me,
	(7)	[5] said I probably would've been shot.
IVER:	(8)	Oh, Gary
GARY:	(9)	That's what they [5] *tell* me.
	(10)	Maybe they're [5] doin' it to scare me.
	(bb)	But, I gave 'em [?3] the money.
	(cc)	Like I figured-
	(dd)	I didn't really get upset.
	(ee)	I wasn't scared.
	(ff)	I wasn't scared till after it was all over with.
	(gg)	At the time I don't think- it never even-
	(hh)	all I thought of was Diane and the baby.
IVER:		Su:re.
GARY:	(ii)	And uh, I gave the guy [?4] the money.
IVER:		Of course.
GARY:	(jj)	And they [?3] said- well, they [?3] ripped out the radio cabinet,
	(kk)	they [?3] ripped the microphone out of it.
	(ll)	So I went- I backed down the street,
	(mm)	and I found a cop [6] right around the corner.
IVER:		Jesus.
GARY:	(nn)	And uh, then when-
	(oo)	y'know, I told the cop [6] what happened.
	(pp)	He [6] said, "All right, get in your car and go back onto Broad Street. I'll meet you up there."

(qq) Cause they [6a] were trying to pick people up for identification.

(rr) That's when it hit me.

(ss) My leg started jumpin' up and down.

(tt) I just couldn't control my nerves.=

IVER: [Jesus.]

GARY: (uu) =[But] then the whole time I was-
         I- I didn't even get scared or upset.

(vv) And I- I- maybe I thought subconsciously if I would've been scared or shown that I'd have been scared, then I probably would've been hurt.

(ww) Maybe they [?3] would've gotten jumpy.

(xx) Y'know, and . . .

The referring terms to be discussed have bracketed numbers to index the referents and to help trace their mentions through the text. Some expressions (e.g. *they*) are ambiguous; these have question marks preceding their indices. Although it would be useful to be able to use Gricean pragmatics to resolve referential ambiguity, this sample analysis has a more limited goal: show how Gricean principles provide an interpretive basis for the various referential possibilities that can be inferred and for the referring sequences that they would create. This limitation follows Grice's (1975: 50) view that "the identity of any reference" is part of the information relied upon to calculate implicatures; "identity" (and more generally, how signs are related to the objects to which they are applicable, Morris's view of semantics) is not itself a product of implicature. (But the view that reference is a relationship between language and an entity in one's "mental/discourse model" more readily allows the use of Gricean pragmatics for reference itself.) Although I proceed for now as if each expression has a clear referent, I discuss the ambiguity of several terms in the appropriate sections and the general problem of ambiguity in section 4.4.

My analysis focuses on each human referent with a continued existence in the story. These are listed below with the location (first-or next-mention) of each referring term, whether the terms are indefinite (Indf) or definite (Df), explicit (Ex) or inexplicit (Inex), and the referring terms used for each referent. To avoid confusion, I use single quotation marks to distinguish my identificatory uses of expressions as referents from the specific realizations of those referents, e.g. the referent 'cop' may be realized as *a cop*, *the cop*, or *he*.

First mention   Next mention
Referent 1 'passenger'
Indf/Ex   Df/Inex   Df/Ex
a fare (a)   *he* (b, c), *it* (f), *him* (g), 'zero' (r)   *the guy he* (q)

Referent 2 'two friends'
Indf/Ex   none
two friends (h)

Referent 3 'they'
Df/Inex   Df/Inex
they (i)   *they* (j, k, m, u, v, w, z, jj, kk, ww) *them* (u, x, aa, bb)

Referent 4 'guy up front'
Df/Ex   Df/Ex
the guy up front he (y)   *the guy* (ii)

Referent 5 'other cab drivers'
Indf/Ex   Df/Inex
other cab drivers   (6) 'zero' (6) *they* (9) *they* (10)

Referent 6 'cop'
Indf/Ex   Df/Ex   Df/Inex
a cop (nn)   *the cop* (oo) *he* (pp)

Referent 6a 'cops'
Df/Inex   none
they (qq)

This chart shows that some of the referring sequences in (4) fit a common pattern in which first-mentions presuppose less about the ability of hearers to identify a referent than do next-mentions. First-mentions of 'other cab drivers' and 'cop' are indefinite and explicit; next-mentions of these same referents are definite and inexplicit. The chart also shows other referring sequences that are less typical. Next-mentions of 'cop' alternate between explicit (*the cop*) and inexplicit terms (*he*). And whereas referent 3 ('they') is mentioned only pro-nominally (*they*) regardless of location, referent 4 ('guy up front') is mentioned only nominally (*the guy up front he*, *the guy*). Still other referents ('two friends', 'cops') are evoked only once, the former explicitly (*two friends*), the latter inexplicitly (*they*). Finally, it is also important to note the complex referent 'passenger' (that can be metonymically evoked as *it*) and that referents 6 ('cop') and 6a ('cops') are linked by a relationship of inclusion. Since full discussion of each referring sequence would occupy too much space for our current purposes, I devote most of what follows to those sequences raising problems that can be best addressed by a Gricean approach to discourse analysis.

4.2 The analysis

We see in this section that the maxims of quantity and relation work together in a very general way to guide H's interpretation of S's referential intention. We will use the story in (4) as a source of information (the quantity maxim) to which successive referents in the story are relevant (the relation maxim). Thus, we will see how referring terms are fit to the information presented in a text, and made relevant to that information. Although my discussion is centered on first- and next-mentions in (4), I try to point out the more general applicability of Gricean pragmatics for analyses of referring sequences.

4.2.1 Referent 1: 'passenger'

The referring expressions used for referent 1 raise several important issues. The first issue concerns the labelling of the referent as 'passenger' and the use of the word *fare* to evoke that referent. A 'passenger' is a person who acts in a particular capacity within a particular situation: a 'passenger' pays a fee to travel. Cabdrivers' passengers are sometimes called "riders" and what they pay is a "fare." Thus, the referent 'passenger' combines two conceptually related entities: a 'person' and a 'fare'. It is this relationship that allows the word *fare* to be used to evoke the referent 'passenger'. More specifically, saying *fare* to evoke 'passenger' is allowed by the conceptual relationship known as metonymy: we use one entity (a fee paid) to refer to another (a person who pays the fee) to which it is related (Lakoff and Johnson 1980: chapter 8). The general relationship between 'fare' and 'passenger' is one in which an object used ('fare') stands for its user ('passenger'). An example of this from Lakoff and Johnson (1980: 38) is "The sax has the flu today". The particular relationship between 'fare' and 'passenger' is one in which the user is a source of the object (the fare) and transmits that object to a recipient (the cabdriver). A similar relationship would hold if a salesperson said "The cash and carries always need help to their cars," or a newspaper delivery person said "The weeklies are behind again." In these hypothetical examples, *the cash and carries* would evoke the people paying cash and carrying their own merchandise (rather than waiting for its delivery); *the weeklies* would evoke the people paying each week (rather than each month) for their newspapers.

As we noted in the chart above, referent 1 is introduced as an indefinite explicit noun (*a fare*) and its next-mentions (*he, it*) are definite. This distribution raises three other issues. First, why is the first-mention of "passenger" an indefinite explicit noun (*a fare*) and why are its next-mentions definite inexplicit pronouns (*he, it*)? Second, why do the next-mentions switch between *it* and *he*, i.e. why isn't the metonymic *it* always used to evoke the person who pays a fare? Third, why do the referring expressions used for "passenger" (*he/him* (b, c, g), *the guy he* (q), and 'zero' (r)) vary in explicitness? I consider each issue in turn.

Consider, first, how Gricean pragmatics might explain the definiteness or indefiniteness of first-mentions. Although first-mentions are typically indefinite, it is well known that background information can allow a first-mention to be definite (Prince 1981; Brown and Yule 1983: 186). In Gricean terms, information (quantity maxim) can allow a hearer to infer the existence of a referent by providing a framework within which the existence of such a referent is expected (relation maxim). As (5) illustrates, background information can be textually presented.

(5) I went back to school.
    The truant officer came after me.

In (5), the textual mention of 'school' is informative enough to allow us to assume that a particular entity ('truant officer') is in (i.e. "exists" in) a particular setting ('school'). Background information can also be situationally provided: if one or more interlocutors are near a school, for example, one might use a definite description for a first-mention of a number of entities typically relevant to that setting.

Let us return to (4): the first-mention of 'passenger' is indefinite, not definite. A Gricean analysis might explain this in terms similar to those just suggested: first-mention of 'passenger' is not definite because Gary did not present information (nor was such information contextually available) that would allow his hearer to expect (i.e. find relevant) the existence of such an entity. To be more concrete, 'passenger' was neither textually anchored (e.g. Gary did not mention a phone call from a dispatcher) nor situationally anchored (e.g. Gary was not receiving instructions from a dispatcher).[8] We can suggest, then, that first-mentions are indefinite if neither prior text nor context provides information sufficient for S to assume that H can expect an entity to be relevant enough to have an existence. (Compare discussion of 'guy up front' (4.3.4) and initial definites in chapter 8, section 3.2.2.)

Although 'passenger' is not anchored in prior text or context, its first-mention is not without any relevance at all: 'passenger' is anchored to the speaking situation, to a prior topic of talk, and to the story topic (cf. DuBois 1980; Prince 1981). In saying *I picked up a fare*, Gary makes *a fare* (the metonymic reference to 'passenger') relevant to himself and his own reported action. Since the speaker is assumed present during an act of speaking, the link between 'passenger' and 'I' anchors the referent to the speaking situation. Other information in the clause relates the referent to both prior and upcoming topics. Earlier in the interview, Gary had been talking about 'tough neighborhoods'. Since *Broad and Elm* is an area of town known to be relatively dangerous, Gary's location of 'fare' at this intersection is relevant to that prior topic, as well as the threat that he will face. Finally, notice that Gary begins his story with an event (*I picked up a fare*) that is critical to what happens later in his story. Had Gary not picked up *a fare* (an action about which he had doubts: *I was gonna turn it down* (f)), he would not have been robbed. Thus, although 'passenger' is not anchored in prior text or context, its multiple relevancies (to the speaker himself, to a prior topic of talk, and to later story events) are conveyed through information within the same clause in which it is introduced.

Gricean pragmatics can also help explain the use of the lexical item *fare* (rather than, for example, *a robber*, *someone*, or *a guy*) for the first-mention. The general topic being discussed prior to Gary's story was cabdriving. First-mention of *a fare* situates the story as a type of experience relevant to this topic, and as an encounter with someone who occupies an occupationally defined position. *Fare* is also matched in terms of quantity and relevance to what Gary knew when the experience itself began to unfold.[9] Stories routinely move speakers to a prior information state at which they did not know what they came to know at later points in the story world. Story tellers often present what they know later (time 2) as unknown to them when they are situated earlier in the story world (time 1). This shift in temporal perspective also creates a different world in which entities are inferrable as relevant (cf. our discussion of *this real dark looking, gangster looking guy* in 3).

Mention of 'passenger' continues in the story as *it* (f). This use of the pronoun *it* is not surprising: having introduced *a fare*, Gary has provided information sufficient to allow his hearer to identify a referent without repetition of the explicit noun. Furthermore, we can easily find an explicit, textually accessible antecedent for *it* (see e.g. Ariel 1990; Chafe 1974, 1980; Clancy 1980; Givón 1989; Wong 1990). But as I noted above, both *a fare* and *it* are metonymic references to 'passenger'. Rather than continue to use metonymy to evoke this referent, Gary more frequently evokes 'passenger' as *he* (b,c) *him* (g), *the guy he* (q) and 'zero' (r). As noted earlier, this variation raises two additional issues: the switch between *it* and *he*, and the difference in explicitness among *he*, *the guy he*, and 'zero'.

Consider the *he/it* alternation first:

(a)   I picked up a fare at Broad and Elm.
(b)   He was a colored guy.
(c)   He flagged me down.
(d)   So I wasn't- it was late at night.
(e)   It was around one thirty in the morning.
(f)   And I was gonna turn it down.
(g)   So I figured, y'know, I'd pick him up anyway.

One possible explanation for why Gary uses *it* in (f) rather than *he* lies in the notion of information state noted above and the relevance of different descriptions for different information states. Immediately prior to (f), Gary had provided descriptive background information (*late at night* (d), *around one thirty in the morning* (e)) relevant to his first encounter with 'passenger' as a potential job. This embedded orientation (Labov and Waletsky 1967) suggests a narrative shift in information state during which Gary defines the relevance of 'passenger' not as a person *per se*, but as a job, i.e. a source of money. Thus, using *it* as a next-mention for 'passenger' during an embedded orientation coincides with the textual relevance of this referent as a job-related category.

Although we are illustrating the application of Gricean pragmatics to discourse by focusing on the referring sequences in one particular story, a Gricean approach would also try to find evidence in sequences from other texts. Note, then, that Gary uses a metonymic *it* ('fare' stands for 'passenger') whenever the most relevant identifying category is job rather than person related. (6) is from another conversation:

(6) (a) Like, this one colored lady I picked up yesterday.
     (b) She's a schoolteacher.
     (c) She lived in- well, a nicer part of Germantown.
     (d) Over towards Mount Airy.
     (e) And we were talkin'.
     (f) It was a long fare
     (g) so we were talkin' for a while.
     (h) And she told me . . . [continues]

In (6), Gary is telling a story about *this one colored lady* (a). His next-mentions alternate between *she* (b, c, h) and *it* (f). *She* evokes the referent in personal terms: 'she' does human actions (*she lived* (c), *she told* (h)), 'she' has an identity outside the world of cabdriving (*she's a schoolteacher* (b)). Notice that although it would be infelicitous to use *it* in any of these utterances (e.g. *It's a schoolteacher* (b)), either *it* or *she* can be used as the subject of *was a long fare* since this defines the referent in relation to a job (as in our earlier comments on metonymy.) *It* in Gary's story in (4) is similar: *it* is situated in an earlier point in the story world when the most relevant identifying category for 'fare' is not person, but job.

Another next-mention of 'passenger' in Gary's story is a definite nominal *the guy he* (q). What seems to motivate the explicitness of this particular term is the displacement of this referent from the text (Ariel 1990: chapter 2; Brown and Yule 1983: 183). Textual displacement can be described in Gricean terms. After talking about referent 1 (through both explicit and inexplicit forms), Gary introduces new referents ('two friends' (h) and 'they' (i to m)) that became the focus of the narrative action (4.3.2, 4.3.3). It is only when Gary arrives at the destination that 'passenger' is again given a more central role:

(o) So I pulled up,
(p) I turned on the light,
(q) and the guy he grabbed me from the back of my head
(r) and put a gun to it.

As noted above, the entity most relevant to the story prior to the collective referents ('two friends' 'they') was 'passenger'. But once the collective referents enter the story, the relevance of 'passenger' is temporarily suspended. Because the relevance of this referent can no longer be textually or contextually assumed, Gary uses a referring term (*the guy he* (q)) that presents enough information to bring it back into the story. As noted above, we can thus explain the effect of displacement on referring terms in Gricean terms: when an individual referent loses its relevance (its identity) in a collectivity, that relevance can be reinstated with an explicit next-mention. More generally, what can compensate for a temporary loss of textual relevance is a highly informative lexical item.

Evidence for this explanation is a sequence from another text. In (7), Gary is describing his family and uses explicit nominals to individuate them:

(7) IVER: (a)   Did you have older brothers and sisters and stuff?
    GARY: (b)   I have an older brother and a younger sister.
            (c)   Like we're all two years apart.
            (d)   So like my brother he's gonna be twenty six,
            (e)   and I'll be twenty four in August.
            (f)   He'll be twenty six three days after me
            (g)   and my sister, she just turned twenty one.

Gary introduces his siblings in (b) with indefinites; more specifically, in existential predicates in which the siblings are related to him (i.e. *I have*; see chapters 7 and 8). A collective referent *we* follows in (c). Then, when Gary returns to his description of the individual members of the group, he initially differentiates them using *my brother he* (d) and *my sister, she* (g) rather than just pronouns. Thus, again, when an individual referent loses its relevance in a collectivity, that relevance can be reinstated with an explicit next-mention. (Another example like this is *the guy up front he* (4.3.3).)

Finally, it is important to note that Gary also uses a zero pronoun for 'passenger' in (r):

(q)   and the guy he grabbed me from the back of my head
(r)   and put a gun to it.

Such uses seem to be syntactically and textually constrained, e.g. they occur with verbs that are conjoined or in clauses with close textual antecedents (e.g. the use of 'zero' for 'other cab drivers' in line 7 in this story (4.3.5)). Zero pronouns, however, can also be explained in Gricean terms consistent with those proposed for *the guy he*. Above, I suggested that a temporary suspension of relevance in the text can lead to a greater amount of information in the referring term. Here I am suggesting the opposite: maximal relevance in prior text can lead to minimal information in a next-mention slot (cf. Ariel 1990: chapter 6).

We have concentrated in this section on the referent 'passenger'. We saw that *a fare* is a referring expression that is metonymically related to the entire referent through a relationship of "object used" to "user." We also saw that referent 1 is made relevant to the speaker and his topics of talk within the same clause in which it is introduced. We explained the alternation between mentions of 'passenger' as *it* and *he* in terms of relevance and quantity. We suggested that explicit next-mentions (*the guy he*) can compensate for suspended relevance and that inexplicit next-mentions ('zero') are allowed under conditions of maximum relevance. On a procedural note, we applied a set of general principles to some specific utterances: we used those principles to try to explain the selection of different options within and across those utterances.

The principles not only explained what occurred in a particular sequential slot in a text (i.e. first-mention, next-mention), they also drew upon prior text as a source of information (the quantity maxim) to which referents in the story are relevant (the relation maxim). We also provided some other examples that supported the explanations being proposed. Although slightly different problems arise with the next referents to be discussed, we can use the same general procedure to address these referents.

4.2.2 Referent 2: 'two friends'

The first (and only) mention of referent 2 is as *two friends*. The main importance of this referent in the story is to be part of the later 'they', a collective referent comprised of 'passenger' and 'two friends' (but see section 4.2.3).

Like the initial reference to 'passenger', 'two friends' is introduced in relation to an entity assumed to be more familiar and already accessible. This is because the lexical item *friend* is inherently tied to another entity (i.e. friends are friends "of" somebody), in this case to the textually evoked 'passenger'. Thus, again, the speaker presents in his text a certain amount of information that allows a new referent to be heard as relevant to already familiar information, in this case to a prior character in the story.

4.2.3 Referent 3: 'they'

Referent 3 is the most problematic in the story, and it raises several difficult issues that concern not just reference, but pragmatics in general, e.g. whether hearers are able to recognize speakers' referential intentions, the potential vagueness and shifting meaning of pronouns, and the importance of discourse structure for pronoun interpretation. The basic problem with referent 3 is that it is so inexplicit that we cannot be sure to whom *they* is intended to refer. This inexplicitness also makes it difficult to know whether *they* is a first-mention of a new referent or a next-mention of a prior referent – both possibilities to be considered below.

One possibility is to consider 'they' broadly as 'passenger' and 'two friends'. If we do so, then *they* in (i):

(i) So they said, "We're only going right around the corner more or less," y'know. "Could you take us up?"

is a first-mention, just as *they* in (j), (k), (m), (u), (v), (w), (z), (jj), (kk), and (ww), and *them* in (u), (x), (aa), and (bb), are next-mentions. Although so inexplicit a first-mention as *they* might seem somewhat unusual, we could argue that more explicit information about who comprises the group has actually already been given and that *they* is a *containing inferrable* (Prince

1981). Indeed, as a previous example showed, referents may be introduced individually and then collectively: after mentioning 'an older brother' and 'a younger sister' in (7), Gary added yet a third (implicit) referent (himself) to the entire sibling group (*we*). Thus, given explicit introduction of its separate members, a first-mention of a collectivity can be an inexplicit pronoun. In this sense, we may see *they* in Gary's story as evoking a referent that is anchored in the prior text. Indeed, we could even use the maxims of relation and quantity to explain the tendency for *they* to be used to include as many relevant individual referents as are informationally available.

An obvious alternative to this broad interpretation of 'they' is that *they* is co-referential with just *two friends*. Not only would this follow a common pattern (first-mention is indefinite and explicit; next-mention is definite and inexplicit) but it also adheres to the well-established tendency for pronouns to be co-referential with the most recent semantically compatible nominal. Note that *two friends* immediately precedes the first occurrence of *they*:

(h)   But then two friends came out.
(i)   So they said /continues/

A problem with the narrow interpretation of *they* as just 'two friends', however, is that it conflicts with our knowledge about Gary's experience, i.e. we know that there were three people in Gary's cab. Why would Gary talk about only two of these people – especially given the role that all three play in the robbery?

Gricean pragmatics provides still another direction from which to approach the referent of *they*. Rather than puzzle over which interpretation of *they* is what the speaker intended, we may ask about our inability as hearers to settle upon the exact referents evoked by *they*. Although we might take this inability as incompatible with the Gricean view of communication in which the hearer's goal is to recognize speaker intentions, we might also view the speaker's use of vagueness as intentional and as strategic to his purposes. Furthermore, we can express this in terms completely consistent with the Gricean view of communication and implicatures: if the use of *they* violates the maxim of quantity because it is informationally insufficient for hearer recognition of a referent, we need to nevertheless assume the constant underlying operation of the cooperative principle and try to discover why the quantity maxim has been violated.

One reason for the violation of the quantity maxim might be to allow *they* to have a membership – to evoke referents – that fluctuates according to its relevance to the story. This would allow us to see the vagueness of *they* not as a communicative failure, but as a communicative resource (cf. the CA treatment of seeming violations: Schegloff 1972a, and chapter 7 in this book). With this in mind, let us examine the different uses of *they* in the story.

Observe, first, that none of the actions predicated of *they* as a collectivity can possibly be actions that were performed by the specific group as a collectivity with no internal differentiation among members. All the verbal actions – the constructed dialogue (Tannen 1989: chapter 4) – are presented as group actions:

(i)   So they said, "We're only going right around the corner more or less,"
       y'know. "Could you take us up?"
(j)   They gave me an address.
(k)   They said, "We'll get- show you how to get there."
(l)   So it was maybe only three blocks away,
(m)   so they said- I think they gave me an address that's at the center of the
       block

Use of *they* with constructed dialogue suggests not a "choral" presentation of
speech (Tannen 1989: chapter 4) but, rather, that individual responsibility for
what was said is less important than the presentation of the actual dialogue.
Similarly presented are physical actions in which the group is agent of the
action:

(v)   and they wanted more.
(w)   So they took my wallet.
(z)   They were gonna, y'know, shoot me.
(jj)   And they said- well, they ripped out the radio cabinet,
(kk)   they ripped the microphone out of it.
(ww)   Maybe they would've gotten jumpy.

or the group is recipient of Gary's actions:

(u)   So I gave 'em the nine dollars
(x)   I didn't want to give them the money.
(aa)   So I gave them the rest of the money.
(bb)   But, I gave 'em the money.

Again, the use of *they* here suggests that individual responsibility for what was
said and done is less important than the conduct itself.
   Despite the numerous collective referring terms, the group is broken apart
at the most pivotal points in the story: the actions that physically threaten
Gary. It is the event reported in (q) that actually initiates the robbery and leads
Gary to realize that he is being robbed:

(q)   and the guy he grabbed me from the back of my head
(r)   and put a gun to it.

(I have already discussed *the guy he* (q) as a next mention of 'passenger'
(4.3.1).) It is after Gary gives into the demand for money (u, v) that the
robbery is physically intensified:

(y)   So then the guy up front he stuck a gun on my temple, asking for more
       money.

Note that two different people are involved in the events reported in (q) and (y). They are explicitly differentiated from one another not in terms of their earlier introduction as referents (e.g. *one of the two friends, the fare I origin-ally saw*), but in physical terms relevant to the pivotal events in the story: the location of the three men in the cab is relevant to the physical threats felt by Gary, i.e. whether a gun is put either at the back or the side of his head. (I discuss *the guy up front he* in the next section.) Finally, although Gary does use a pronoun in reporting his response to the demands for money, he also does so with a more explicit *the guy*:

(aa)   So I gave them the rest of the money.
(bb)   But, I gave 'em the money
(ii)   And uh, I gave the guy the money

I discuss these alternative next-mentions in the next section.

Thus far I have suggested that explicit next-mentions separate individuals in the group when those individuals are performing actions particularly relevant to – even pivotal to – the reported experience. This, in turn, supports the idea that *they* is an intentionally inexplicit reference to the passengers in Gary's cab. We can phrase this in Gricean terms: the inexplicitness of *they* is an intentional violation of the maxim of quantity motivated by the communicat-ive goal of tailoring the relevance of actors and actions to the details of a reported experience. In Gary's story, *they* was thus used to portray a group as an undifferentiated collectivity rather than a set of individuated members.

Before we turn to the next referent, it is important to note that Gary uses the pronoun *they* for several referents: it seems to be co-referential with 'other cab drivers' (4.2.5) and it establishes a collective identity for 'cop' (4.2.6). I discuss the way these other uses of *they* textually intervene with Gary's continual reference to the three people in the cab in sections 4.2.5 and 4.2.6.

We have seen in this section that *they* can be argued to have a narrow interpretation ('two friends'), a broad interpretation ('passenger' and 'two friends'), or a vague interpretation that violates the quantity maxim, but allows referents to shift according to their relevance for the story. The value of Gricean pragmatics for this analysis was not necessarily to choose the right interpretation from among these options, but to explain the principles provid-ing an interpretive basis for the various options. Note, again, that our applica-tion of the principles depended upon viewing the text as a source of information to which referents in the story are relevant.

4.2.4   Referent 4: 'guy up front'

I mentioned 'guy up front' in the previous section as a referent who was individuated from the collective 'they'. Both first- and next-mentions of this referent are definite and explicit: *the guy up front he* and *the guy*. Before discussing this sequence it is important to note why I have inferred that these are mentions of a single referent. Prior text provides us with information allowing us to infer that *the guy* (ii) is a next-mention of 'the guy up front'. The action 'ask for money' (y) is linked to 'give money' (ii) as a request–compliance pair (chapter 3, p. 3.1.2). Since people usually comply with a request by directing an action to the person who has issued the request, we interpret *the guy up front he* (y) and *the guy* (ii) as the same referent.

Let us consider the first-mention:

(y)   So then the guy up front he stuck a gun on my temple, asking for more money.

Since *the guy up front* is understood as part of the previously mentioned collectivity 'they', the initial definiteness is not surprising. In Prince's (1981) terms, this first-mention is a contained inferrable, i.e. a member of a previously mentioned set. We motivated the explicitness of this expression in terms of its heightened relevance to the experience in the previous section.

The next-mention is part of a reported action that responds to the threat from 'the guy up front':

(ii) And uh, I gave the guy the money.

Since this event is central to the story – it is Gary's unwilling concession to the robbery and the resolution to the complicating action – it might not be surprising to find a definite explicit noun here rather than a pronoun. Furthermore, this next-mention is also textually distant from the first-mention.

'Giving money', however, is an action that has already been reported twice in the story with *them*. Although I discussed these mentions of 'they' in section 4.2.3, it is important to note them again during our discussion of 'guy up front' – simply because they co-occur with what seems to be the same event.

(aa) So I gave them the rest of the money.
(bb) But, I gave 'em the money
(ii) And uh, I gave the guy the money

The questions that we need to address are: (1) Why does Gary switch between *them* (and its variant *'em*) and *the guy* in different reports of the same event? (2) How can Gricean pragmatics explain those alternations?

Earlier we saw that quantity violations may serve the goal of relevance (4.3.1). By checking the sections of text in which the event 'give money' is reported with different referents, we may be able to discover whether *the guy* (ii) and/or *them* (aa, bb) are quantity violations motivated by relevance. Procedurally, then, we will again be relying upon text as a source of information and relevance.

The event 'give money' is first reported in (aa):

(y)   So then the guy up front he stuck a gun on my temple, asking for more money.

(z)   They were gonna, y'know, shoot me.

(aa)   So I gave them the rest of the money.

Gary gives the money to *them* (aa), not to *the guy*. These two referents convey links with two different antecedent events: whereas *them* links 'give money' with the just mentioned group threat (*They were gonna, y'know, shoot me* (z)), *the guy* would have linked 'give money' with the prior event (*the guy up front he stuck a gun on my temple, asking for more money* (y)). Thus, *they* in (aa) helps portray the event 'give money' as an outcome of Gary's evaluative inference of what would have happened to him (he would be shot (z)), not as an outcome of what was done to him (y). In this sense, we might say that *them* is an informationally adequate expression that serves a goal of relevance because it establishes a relationship with a prior event.

The next report of 'give money' follows the interchange between Gary and the IVer; it returns to the story frame itself:

(bb)   But, I gave 'em the money

It is surprising that *'em* is used here. *'Em* seems to violate what scholars (e.g. Givón 1992) think of as distance and clarity constraints: not only was the last mention of this referent eight clauses earlier, but since those other clauses used *they* for a different referent ('other cab drivers' (4.3.5)), the use of *'em* in (bb) is potentially ambiguous. Thus, *'em* seems to be a quantity violation because it gives too little information. Although we suggested that quantity violations giving too *much* information were a way of lexically compensating for a suspension of textual relevance, it is unclear whether too little information can also serve relevance. Note, however, that we might interpret *But, I gave 'em the money* (bb) as a way of returning the discourse to a non-adjacent focus. *But, I gave 'em the money* (bb) paraphrases the event *So I gave them the rest of the money* (aa), which was the last story event to be mentioned – the most recent story event before the evaluative digression with the IVer. Furthermore, this paraphrase is initiated with *But,* which establishes a global link in the discourse (Schiffrin 1987a). Thus, the repetition of the same referring term – despite its informational shortcomings – might also figure in the return to the story frame.

It is in the third report of 'give money' that Gary uses *the guy*. What precedes this is an evaluation of the experience:

GARY: (cc)   Like I figured-
        (dd)   I didn't really get upset.
        (ee)   I wasn't scared.
        (ff)   I wasn't scared till after it was all over with.
        (gg)   At the time I don't think-it never even-

(hh)   all I thought of was Diane and the baby.
IVER: Su:re.
GARY: (ii)   And uh, I gave the guy the money

Note that (ii) continues the narrative action initiated in (y):

(y)   So then the guy up front he stuck a gun on my temple, asking for more
      money.
      [evaluative digression from narrative sequence]
(ii)   And uh, I gave the guy the money

As I indicate in the excerpt, the two events in (y) and (ii) are interrupted by
an exchange with the IVer (which functions as an external evaluation: Labov
1972b; see chapter 8) and by Gary's own report of his feelings (also evaluative). Despite this interruption, we understand these two actions as sequentially tied together as request and compliance: (y) *So then the guy up front he
stuck a gun on my temple, asking for more money* reports a demand from a
particular person for money; (ii) *And uh, I gave the guy the money* reports
compliance with that particular demand. Thus, despite the interruption of this
sequence, we understand these two actions as sequentially tied together in an
act sequence (cf. chapter 3). Note, also, that Gary continues his story after
this event: *I gave the guy the money* is the first event to return to the
temporally sequential events making up the complicating action of the story
(ii to pp). Thus, we may explain the explicit reference to *the guy* in (ii) as a
way of making apparent a non-adjacent sequential tie (cf. Fox 1987) that
reinstates a prior textual focus. Note that this is similar to our suggestion that
repetition of the pronoun (from aa to bb) established sequential relevance:
quantity is linked to the need to show relevance. But because we said that *the
guy* was overinformative (and *'em* was underinformative) it is only *the guy*
that illustrates the trade-off between textual relevance and lexical information
noted earlier: an informative referring term can compensate for a temporary
loss of textual relevance.

4.2.5   Referent 5: 'other cab drivers'

'Other cab drivers' follows a typical pattern of indefinite/definite and ex-
plicit/inexplicit mentions. Like other indefinite first-mentions discussed (4.2.1,
4.2.2), an introduction is made in relation to the speaker himself:

(6)   But, from what other cab drivers told me

Other cab drivers includes the speaker as a member of the group "cab drivers"
(i.e. he could not have felicitously said *other truck drivers*). Nor would the use
of generic *cab drivers* be related to the speaker in the same way. In addition,

'other cab drivers' is introduced in terms of their actions toward the speaker, i.e. they *told me*.

During our discussion of 'they' (and the use of *they* as next-mentions) in section 4.2.3, I mentioned that Gary also uses *they* as a next-mention for 'other cab drivers'. Here I will return to a question that was implicit in that section: can a speaker use *they* to evoke different referents without causing confusion about which entity is being mentioned? This question is important because the third person pronouns (*they, 'em*) in the adjacent clauses (10, bb) could evoke two different referents, i.e. 'cab drivers' and 'they' (the robbers):

IVer: (3)   If you hadn't pulled out the money in your sock, do you think
                 they would've looked?
        (4)   Do they know you keep it here?
GARY: (5)   No.
        (6)   But, from what other cab drivers told me,
        (7)   said I probably would've been shot.
IVer: (8)   Oh, Gary.
GARY: (9)   That's what they *tell* me.
        (10)   Maybe they're doin' it to scare me.
        (bb)   But, I gave 'em the money.

Although it is clear that *'em* (bb) is a next-mention of the robbers, *they* in *Maybe they're doin' it to scare me* (line 10) is less easily interpreted. By labelling this line with a number rather than a letter (p. 204), I am obviously implying that *they* is a next-mention of a referent not involved in the story events, i.e. 'other cab drivers'. But *they* in line 10 is problematic because it has another possible antecedent: referent 3, the 'they' who robbed Gary. This interpretation would require not only a more distant antecedent for *they* (prior to the introduction of 'other cab drivers'), but also a different interpretation for *doin'* and *it*, i.e. as the threatening actions in the story.

In the Gricean analysis illustrated thus far in this section, we have viewed text as a source of information in relation to which referring expressions establish (or convey) relevance. To solve the problem of the seemingly ambiguous 'they' in line 10, then, we can examine the section of text in which *they* is used to see whether the quantity and relevance of information presented in that text leads to an interpretation of *they* as 'other cab drivers'.

Let us take a closer look at the text in which *Maybe they're doin' it to scare me* is embedded. The IVer's question (*Do they know you keep it here?* (line 4)) asks about what the robbers ('they') knew about where Gary kept his money. It is during Gary's answer to this question that Gary introduces 'other cab drivers' and then reports what *they* tell him: *But, from what other cab drivers told me, said I probably would've been shot* (lines 6, 7). Notice that Gary's initial mention of 'other cab drivers' (6) is clearly demarcated from the story *per se*: he opens the segment in which they are introduced with *but* followed by a pause. Despite the temporary nature of this referent, its relevance to Gary's interchange with the IVer is high enough to allow a zero subject in line 7 (cf. section 4.2.1).

Although *they* in *Maybe they're doin' it to scare me* (line 10) seems ambiguous, the text itself suggests that *they* is a next-mention of 'other cab drivers'. When people contrast what someone says with what he "really means," they may do so by stressing the verb *say*, e.g. "He *said* he was sorry but he didn't really mean it." This is exactly what we see in lines 9 and 10:

GARY: (9)   That's what they *tell* me.
       (10)   Maybe they're doin' it to scare me.

The contrastive stress on *tell* in line 9 suggests a contradiction between what the cab drivers say and what they "mean" (their intentions). The continuation of the present tense from line 9 to line 10 also suggests that these actions are contrastively paired.

We noted earlier that the digression about 'other cab drivers' was opened by *But,*:

(6)   But, from what other cab drivers told me,

Gary returns to the story frame by again using *But*, this time with a repetition of the last story event from (aa):

(aa)   So I gave them the rest of the money.
(bb)   But, I gave 'em the money.

The fact that Gary pauses after *But* in both line 6 and (bb) is important. *But,* marks a global (non-adjacent) contrast, rather than a local contrast with a proposition in a just-prior clause (Schiffrin 1987a). More specifically, *But,* in line 6 opens a digression from the story frame, and *But,* in (bb) closes that digression from the story frame. *But,* also brackets referents inside and outside of the story world: *they* in *Maybe they're doin' it to scare me* is outside of the story world (i.e. 'other cab drivers') and *'em* in *But, I gave 'em the money* is clearly a next-mention within the story world.

I have argued thus far that a referring term that is potentially ambiguous – *they* in line 10 – is a next-mention of 'other cab drivers'. But I also suggested earlier that the very next use of *they* is a next-mention of a different referent (referent 3, the robbers). The reason *they* can be next-mentions of two different referents is that the speaker provides clear discourse boundaries that separate the story being told (the story world) from the interchange with the IVer (the conversational world). These same boundaries separate the two uses of *they*, such that one use of *they* (relevant to the conversational world) can be a next-mention of 'other cab drivers' (referent 5), and the other use of *they* (relevant to the story world) can be a next-mention of 'they' (referent 3, the robbers). Thus, the explicit demarcation of the conversational from the story world allows Gary to evoke referents in both worlds without using explicit referring terms to do so. In Gricean terms, what happens is a kind of trade-off between information provided in a text and information provided in a referring expression itself: when discourse provides information sufficient to the identification of a specific world in which an entity can be found relevant, then discourse is a source of informativeness that can offset the inexplicitness (and potential ambiguity) of a referring expression.

4.2.6   *Referents 6 and 6a: 'a cop' and 'cops'*

The final referent is 'a cop', introduced (again) in relation to the speaker:

(mm)   and I found a cop right around the corner.

It is the speaker who found *a cop*, and furthermore did so in a location defined in relation to his own physical location (*right around the corner* rather than, e.g. at Broad and Lee). Next-mentions of 'a cop' are definite: first, a nominal (*the cop*) and then a less explicit pronoun (*he*).

'Cops' are also evoked collectively as *they* (qq). Note that this use of *they* precedes the use of *they* as a next-mention of referent 3, the robbers (ww). But we see here, again, that discourse boundaries can help to separate these potentially ambiguous referring terms from one another. In this case, however, the basis for the discourse boundary between the two successive uses of the referring term *they* (in qq and ww below) is temporal.

GARY: (nn)   And uh, then when-
        (oo)   y'know, I told the cop what happened.
        (pp)   He said, "All right, get in your car and go back onto Broad Street. I'll meet you up there."
        (qq)   Cause they were trying to pick people up for identification.
        (rr)   That's when it hit me.
        (ss)   My leg started jumpin' up and down.
        (tt)   I just couldn't control my nerves.
IVER: [Jesus.
GARY: (uu)   [But then the whole time I was-
             I- I didn't even get scared or upset.
        (vv)   And I- I- maybe I thought subconsciously if I would've been scared or shown that I'd have been scared, then I probably would've been hurt.
     (ww)   Maybe they would've gotten jumpy.

Gary concludes the events of his narrative by reporting his encounter with *the cop* (oo, pp) and the motivation underlying their action (qq). Gary then evaluates his experience by tying it to the time of that encounter (*that's when it hit me* (rr)) and comparing his reaction *after* the actual robbery (rr to tt) to the way he felt during the robbery itself (uu to xx). Note how Gary clearly differentiates the two time periods: the period during which Gary reports the crime begins with *that's when it hit me* (rr); the return to the period of the robbery itself is noted with *but then the whole time* (uu). So, again, we see that by clearly separating different worlds – here, different temporal worlds – Gary can use discourse information to separate the different referents of two inexplicit referring terms: *they* evokes 'cops' in one time period, *they* evokes 'robbers' in another time period. Put another way, discourse provides enough information to allow Gary to evoke two different referents with a single inexplicit referring term.

4.3   Summary: referring sequences, relevance, and quantity

I have been suggesting in this section that one way that Gricean pragmatics applies to discourse analysis is by providing a description of the pragmatic conditions during which different referring terms are interpreted. The maxim of quantity helps to guide H toward information that can provide clues about the identity of a referent. The maxim of relation leads H to search for the relevance of a particular referent. Although the maxims do similar work for both first-mentions and next-mentions, the sequential location of a referent (first-mention, next-mention) influences the source of information in relation to which it is interpreted. A first-mention is interpreted relative to textually and contextually provided background assumptions about shared knowledge: first-mentions are relevant to information based in H's knowledge of context (including general background knowledge about other entities in the world). Next-mentions draw upon an additional source of information, i.e. information that has been textually grounded (including, but not limited to, information available through a first-mention). Next-mentions are thus relevant to information based in H's knowledge of both text and context.

We can gain more insight into the contribution of Gricean pragmatics to discourse analysis by going over how the referring sequences in Gary's story in (4) are sensitive to the maxims of quantity and relation. Although I will state some of our findings in relatively general terms, it should be kept in mind that these suggestions are based on a very small amount of data, and that they are meant more to illustrate the way Gricean pragmatics would approach the analysis of referring sequences than as a definitive Gricean analysis of reference.

Let us consider first-mentions first. Referents were introduced in ways relevant to surrounding information. Initial definites (e.g. *they, the guy up front*) were relevant to previously presented (or assumable) information, i.e. they were used when the speaker could assume a hearer's ability to use text (or context) to infer the existence and relevance of a specific referent. Initial indefinites were a more varied group: although most of these (*a fare, other cab drivers, a cop*) were relevant to information presented in the same clause, one initial indefinite was relevant to prior textual information.

Next-mentions were likely to be definite and less explicit than first-mentions. This suggests – in line with virtually all other work on referring terms – that the pragmatic conditions underlying next-mentions differ from those underlying first-mentions. But Gricean pragmatics also provides a description of next-mentions similar to that for first-mentions. Thus, we can say that subsequent definites occur under pragmatic conditions very similar to those for initial definites, i.e. when a referent can be interpreted as relevant to already accessible information. The only difference, of course, is that the information to which a referent is relevant has already been textually encoded, i.e. it is the prior mention of the referent in the text itself. Prior textual information also allows next-mentions to be inexplicit. In brief, textual encoding of a referent creates background relevant to a subsequent definite referent and provides the information allowing subsequent reference to be inexplicit.

The next-mentions in Gary's story also suggest that quantity and relevance can act together to define the pragmatic conditions underlying the interpretation of different referring terms.[10] We found one example of quantity and relevance working together in a relatively straightforward way: the alternation between *he* and *it* as next-mentions for 'passenger' (4.2.1). *He* and *it* convey different information: *it* relies on a metonymy between 'passenger' and 'fare', *he* and *it* provide different information about gender and animacy. However, both *he* and *it* follow the quantity maxim. Their difference lies in the *way* they follow that maxim: they select information according to which identificatory category (person versus job) is relevant to a particular event in the story. In brief, we might say that these inexplicit forms alternated according to different conceptions of what was relevant.

Other referring sequences in Gary's story suggested that quantity *violations* can be explained in terms of the maxim of relation. Recall our discussion of explicit next-mentions. We explained the use of *the guy he* (q) for 'passenger' and *the guy* (ii) for 'guy up front' in terms of a trade-off between lexical informativeness and suspended relevance. Explicit next-mentions can thus be viewed as a violation of the quantity maxim designed to show relevance.

Another example suggesting that quantity violations are related to relevance was the use of *they* for three different referents ('passenger' and 'two friends', 'other cab drivers', 'cops') without reinstatement of the referent through a more explicit term. These adjacent uses of *they* with different referential intent also violate the maxim of quantity although in a different direction: not enough explicit information is presented in the referring term itself to allow the differentiation of referents. Despite this violation, we said that *they* was interpretable as three different referents, simply because the adjacent uses were clearly demarcated from one another by structural markers (discourse markers, temporal markers) that defined different subunits of the text. Thus, what separated these inexplicit and potentially ambiguous forms from one another was the clear presence of discourse boundaries that defined different frames of relevance for adjacent occurrences of the inexplicit form *they*. Put another way, what compensated for the lack of lexical informativeness was an increase in explicitness at the discourse level, specifically the marking of different discourse worlds to which each referent of *they* could be found relevant.

A final example of how quantity violations were motivated by the need for relevance is the way *they* served as first- and next-mentions of a collective referent ('passenger' and 'two friends' (4.2.3)). We saw that it was not always clear to whom the inexplicit pronoun *they* was intended to refer. One way to interpret this vagueness is as an intentional violation of the maxim of quantity – a violation allowing the speaker to allow different members of a collectivity to be relevant to different portions of the narrative action.

Although *they* as a collective referent raised the issue of ambiguity most clearly, there were also other expressions about whose referents we were somewhat uncertain. Recall that I identified both *the guy he* (q) and 'zero' as next-mentions of 'passenger' (4.2.1):

(q) and the guy he [?1] grabbed me from the back of my head
(r) and [?1] put a gun to it.

However, it is also possible that *the guy he* and 'zero' are not meant to evoke 'passenger' at all – but one of the *two friends* (4.2.2) who had just been mentioned. Although it would be useful to be able to use Gricean pragmatics to resolve referential ambiguity, the goal of this sample analysis was more limited: I have tried to show how Gricean principles provide an interpretive basis for the various referential possibilities that can be inferred.

Consider, however, another way of viewing referential ambiguity in a Gricean framework. Recall that the quantity maxim stated the following:

1 Make your contribution as informative as is required (for the current purposes of the exchange).
2 Do not make your contribution more informative than is required.

Rather than view unclear cases like *the guy he*, and ambiguous expressions like *they*, as violations of the quantity maxim, we might view them as informationally appropriate to the purposes of the exchange. Consider, for example, if Gary had been telling his story to the *cops* he finds. The purposes of an exchange with the police would be quite different: rather than describing a dangerous experience, Gary would be reporting a crime (with possible legal ramifications) and would thus need to be specific about who did what. Information about exactly who *put a gun* to his head (r) and who *stuck a gun* to his temple (y) would be critical to that purpose. What I am suggesting, then, is that the referential ambiguity in Gary's story need not be seen as a violation of a maxim at all: the vagueness might be perfectly well suited to the purposes of the story.

This raises a broader question about the application of Gricean pragmatics to language use. We noted earlier (3.4) that linguists using a Gricean perspective often analyze utterances that are hypothetical sentences in hypothetical contexts. The use of actual utterances, however, forces us to attend to the actual situations in which language is used – situations that include speakers and hearers, whose needs, goals, and wants are tailored to a particular socially and culturally defined communicative situation (see chapters 4 and 5). Just as cross-cultural analyses of Gricean pragmatics suggest that the Gricean maxim of quantity may be sensitive to culturally specific (and variable) ideas of how much information is appropriate (Keenan 1979), so analyses of different communicative situations within one culture might suggest that how much information we provide is tailored to our socially based conceptions of what our interlocutors need for the purposes of our social exchange. To this end, it is important to note that all the uncertain cases that we discussed were clustered within the complicating action of Gary's story: it is in this section that establishing the precise identity of who did what is less critical to the point of the story than establishing the danger of the experience.

To conclude: the maxims are general principles of communication; their application to specific conversational or linguistic phenomena is an outcome of the way they are used by a hearer to infer speaker meaning. When the maxims are applied to a referential problem (i.e. what inferences can a hearer draw about the speaker's referential intention upon hearing a particular referring term?), the work they do is very general. The quantity maxim leads hearers to search for information, i.e. the amount of information in a text, the amount of information in a description itself. The maxim of relation leads hearers to use information in a certain way, i.e. to find its relevance to the rest of the text and to the context in which it is situated. The maxims of relation and quantity do not themselves provide a hearer with the identity of a speaker's intended referent; rather, they lead a hearer toward information and provide a means of using that information to help hearers infer a speaker's referential intention. It is these pragmatically based choices that help create sequential patterns of referring terms and are thus partially responsible for different discourse structures.

5   Gricean pragmatics as an approach to discourse

In this chapter, we described Grice's ideas about speaker meaning and the cooperative principle (section 2) and then applied these ideas to a particular problem: we used the CP (specifically, the maxims of quantity and relevance) to describe the conditions under which people use different expressions to communicate referential intentions in discourse (section 4). We concluded by saying that referring sequences are the outcome of pragmatically based choices concerning the provision of appropriate quantities of information in relevant ways, and thus that discourse structures are created (in part) by the cooperative principle.

We saw that Gricean ideas about information quantity and relevance (cf. Horn 1985b; Levinson 1983, 1987; Sperber and Wilson 1986) can help solve problems of utterance interpretation that hinge on assessing the contribution of various kinds of contexts to such interpretations. The application of the CP to discourse leads to a particular view of discourse and its analysis: discourse as a text whose contexts (including cognitive, social, and linguistic contexts) allow the interpretation of speaker meaning in utterances. What Gricean pragmatics thus provides is a set of principles that constrains speakers' sequential choices in a text and allows hearers to recognize speakers' intentions by helping to relate what speakers "say" (in an utterance) to its text and contexts.

Although I more fully discuss the assumptions of a Gricean approach in relation to several key issues in discourse analysis in chapters 9, 10, and 11, it is important to briefly foreshadow those points here. The approach that Gricean pragmatics offers to discourse analysis is based in a set of general principles about rationally based communicative conduct (the CP) that tells speakers and hearers how to organize and use information offered in a text, along with background knowledge of the world (including knowledge of the immediate social context), to convey (and understand) more than what is said – in brief, to communicate. The operation of these principles leads to a particular view of discourse structure in which sequential dependencies – constraints imposed by one part of a discourse on what occurs next – arise because of the impact of general communicative principles on the linguistic realization of speaker meaning at different points in time. Our analysis of referring sequences suggested, for example, that the textual and contextual information provided in an initial position [slot 1] in a discourse serves as a background by which to judge how much information is appropriate in a next position [slot 2], as well as the relevance of that information for [slot 2]. The operation of the cooperative principle in one part of a discourse thus helps to define options in another: it is this functionally based interdependency that helps to create the sequential regularities characteristic of discourse and that allows people to use both text and context as a resource by which to communicate with each other. Thus, what Gricean pragmatics offers to discourse analysis is a view of how participant assumptions about what comprises a cooperative context for communication (a context that includes knowledge, text, and situation) contribute to meaning, and how those assumptions help to create sequential patterns in talk.

Exercises

1   Although Gricean pragmatics highlights the cooperative assumptions that we bring to conversations, not all verbal interchanges seem cooperative (e.g. Grimshaw 1990). The sample data in appendix 3, for example, contain some exchanges that seem overtly hostile, and others that seem more competitive than cooperative. After identifying what seem like the non-cooperative parts of the interchange, describe how Gricean pragmatics could account for these sections.

2   Many scholars have supplemented or altered Grice's cooperative principle. Examples of neo-Gricean work can be found in Horn (1985a, b), Lakoff (1973), Leech (1983), Martinich (1984), Recanati (1987), and Sperber and Wilson (1986); see also the special issue of *Brain and Behavior* 1989. After reading some of the works just noted, apply both Grice's framework and those suggested above to the following data (or other data of your own choice).

(1)   Professors A and B are colleagues at the same university. A is on leave in another city. B is in her university office, preparing for class. A calls Professor B on the phone: B tells A that she has a few minutes to talk. After spending a few minutes discussing an upcoming meeting, the following occurs:

PROF A: (a)   Would you like to call me back?
PROF B: (b)   No that's okay, I don't have that much more to say.
PROF A: (c)   No, I meant use university money instead of mine!
          (d)   I have some things I have to ask you.

(2)   A and B are commuters on a daily train. A notices a newspaper on an empty seat next to where B is sitting.

A: (a)   Is that your paper?
B: (b)   Yeh, but you can have it.
     [or] No, you can have it.

3   We often infer that two propositions are related to one another even when that relationship is not explicitly stated (e.g. Halliday and Hasan 1976; Thompson and Mann 1987). In the following pairs of sentences, for example, we are likely to infer some relationship between the two propositions even though none is explicitly stated.

(a)   I stopped at the bank on the way home from work.
      I withdrew $200.
(b)   It rained last night.
      The rabbit got wet.
(c)   I went into the kitchen.
      The cookies burned.
(d)   Jay was in the hospital last week.
      He needed emergency surgery.
(e)   My father fell on the ice.
      He broke his leg.

(f)   Our neighbors must be on vacation.
      Their newspapers are piling up.

After identifying the possible relationships between the propositions in the
above sentence pairs, use the Gricean maxims to account for the inferred
relationships. How did you decide between the relevance of one maxim rather
than another? Suppose you were to add the connectives *and, then, so, because*
to each of the above examples. How could you integrate the Gricean analysis
of inferred relationships into descriptions of the meanings of these different
connectives? How do the inferences supplied through the use of the connectives differ from those available without connectives?

4   A shampoo that is intended to remove head lice has the following short
text in large, bold letters on the bottle:

A Single Application
● Kills Lice & Their Eggs
● Prevents Reinfestation

Given this amount of information, what interpretation(s) could a consumer
draw about the amount of shampoo to apply and the frequency of use?
   The box containing the shampoo repeats the same text, again in large bold
letters, on the front; the text is centered on the box. The box front also notes,
in smaller letters at the bottom, that it is a Family Pack with two bottles. What
inference about amount and frequency could this information evoke?
   Now consider information presented on each bottle, and on the back of the
box.

A sufficient amount should be applied to saturate hair and scalp. . . . A single
application is sufficient.

Does this text evoke the same interpretation(s) about the amount of shampoo
to apply and the frequency of use? How can Gricean pragmatics explain the
alternative interpretations? How could this product labelling be clearer?

Notes

1   What Levinson terms the "continental" view of pragmatics is more similar to what
    Americans call "sociolinguistics" and "discourse analysis." Research in this vein is
    represented in the journals *Pragmatics* and *Journal of Pragmatics*.
2   The central theoretical role played by "violations" stems from the level of generality
    at which the principles are defined. Compare the discussions of interactional
    strategies in chapter 4 and local rules in chapter 7.
3   Levinson (1983: 147–62) discusses alternative theories of metaphor. See also Lakoff
    and Johnson (1980) and Lakoff (1987), whose dependence on the framework known
    as "cognitive linguistics" defines the relationship between semantics and pragmatics
    quite differently than does the formal semantics perspective assumed by Grice.
4   Exactly how identifiable an entity must be, however, is not clear. DuBois (1980:
    233), for example, counts a reference as identifiable "if it identifies an object close

enough to satisfy the curiosity of the hearer" (see also Grimes 1975; Kronfeld 1990). Donnellan (1978) and Klein (1983) also argue that one can refer to entities with a definite pronoun without knowing their identity.

5   Although our analysis refers to both definites and indefinites, I am using these terms to refer to categories that are actually much narrower: definites and indefinites that are both *referential* and *specific*. Donnellan (1966: 198) describes the differences between using expressions attributively and referentially:

A speaker who uses a definite description attributively in an assertion states something about whoever or whatever is the so-and-so. A speaker who uses a definite description referentially in an assertion . . . uses the definite description to enable his audience to pick out whom or what he is talking about and states something about that person or thing.

(1a) and (1b) illustrate the attributive–referential distinction for definites; (2a) and (2b) for indefinites.

   (1a)   Definite, Attributive
          The vandals who burned the books should go to jail. Whoever would do
          such a thing should be punished, and I hope that's what happens when
          they eventually find out who did it.
   (1b)   Definite, Referential
          The vandals who burned the books should go to jail. I hope that's what
          the judge decides when he hears their case today.
   (2a)   Indefinite, Attributive
          I never saw *a two-headed person*.
   (2b)   Indefinite, Referential
          There was *a two-headed person* at the circus who was the hit of the
          whole show.

Both definite and indefinite expressions can be used either specifically or non-specifically. (3) illustrates the specific–non-specific distinction for definite forms; (4), for indefinite forms.

   (3a)   Specific definite
          Last night *the cat* knocked our trash can over.
   (3b)   Non-specific definite
          The cat is an animal that often acts as a scavenger.
   (4a)   Specific indefinite
          Every night *a cat* knocks our trash can over. It must be hungry.
   (4b)   Non-specific indefinite
          Every night *a cat* knocks our trash can over. They've become real
          scavengers lately.

In both (3a) and (4a), the speaker seems to have in mind a specific cat that can be identified; this assumption does not seem to hold for either (3b) or (4b).

As I stated earlier, I will refer in what follows to definites and indefinites – although what I mean by this is referential, specific indefinites and definites.

6 Although space prevents me from a comprehensive review of other analyses of referring terms (or reference in general), I try to build on the insights of other approaches and to note some compatible concepts and tools from other perspectives – most notably, from the information flow perspective (Chafe 1976, 1987; DuBois 1987; Givón 1979, 1983, 1984; Prince 1981). However, fuller discussion of how Gricean pragmatics compares to other approaches to discourse is reserved for the conclusion of the book.

7 Much of the literature on referring in discourse makes use of narrative as a type of discourse in which referring must be accomplished (see e.g. Givón 1992). Arguments for the theory of emergent grammar (Hopper and Thompson 1980, 1984) also seem to assume that narrative is the basic form in which lexical categories, like nouns and verbs, and clause relationships are to be found.

8 Not all relevant textual or contextual information, however, allows the use of a definite noun phrase for initial reference. Gary had been talking about "tough neighborhoods" in the conversation prior to his story, and he mentioned that much of his knowledge about the city came from *driving a cab* to different locations and *picking up people*. Rather than pursuing either of these issues, however, he continued to talk about different city neighborhoods, and it was this topic that led to the IVer's question *Have you ever been robbed?* Because driving a cab and picking up people had been mentioned, we might have expected these activities to provide enough information to allow an initial definite reference (*the fare*) for "passenger". But perhaps because these activities had a subordinate role in relation to Gary's main topic (they were mentioned only to explain how he acquired his knowledge of different neighborhoods), they were not sufficient to warrant the assumptions needed for an initial reference to *the fare*. Compare the use of initial definites for referents 3 (4.2.3) and 4 (4.2.4).

9 Note also that even though Gary knew when he was telling the story (and indeed, knew when he was grabbed and had a gun put to his head (q)) that his fare was "a robber," it is not surprising that he did not introduce his story by saying *I picked up a robber at Broad and Elm*. If he had, his hearer might very well have wondered about why Gary would do such a thing – a question that does not at all come to mind if he picks up a fare.

10 The relationship between quantity and relevance has been the focus of recent work in pragmatics. Key to much of the discussion is the second part of Grice's quantity maxim – which essentially places an upper limit on quantity. I repeat both parts: "Make your contribution as informative as is required (for the current purposes of the exchange). Do not make your contribution more informative than is required." Horn (1985b: 12) notes that the second quantity principle is "essentially akin to Relation (what would make a contribution more informative than required, except the inclusion of material not strictly relevant to and needed for the matter at hand?)." Levinson (1988), however, argues that relevance does not really concern information at all (for him, it has more to do with "timely helpfulness in relation to interactional goals"). Levinson (1988) suggests instead that the second quantity principle is a principle of informativeness: from the speaker's end, this is a maxim of minimization ("say as little as necessary"); from the recipient's end, this is a maxim of maximization ("amplify the informational content of the speaker's utterance, by finding the most specific interpretation, up to what you judge to be the speaker's m-intended point"). In short, for Horn, the upper limit on information quantity is akin to relevance (i.e. too much information would not be relevant); for Levinson, the upper limit pushes the speaker to say less and the hearer to interpret more.

7 Conversation Analysis

1 Introduction

Conversation analysis (CA) offers an approach to discourse that has been extensively articulated by sociologists, beginning with Harold Garfinkel who developed the approach known as ethnomethodology (influenced by the phenomenology of Alfred Schutz), and then applied specifically to conversation, most notably by Harvey Sacks, Emanuel Schegloff, and Gail Jefferson. Conversation analysis differs from other branches of sociology because rather than analyzing social order *per se*, it seeks to discover the methods by which members of a society produce a sense of social order. Conversation is a source of much of our sense of social order, e.g. it produces many of the typifications underlying our notions of social role (Ciccourel 1972). Conversation also exhibits its own order and manifests its own sense of structure.

CA is like interactional sociolinguistics in its concern with the problem of social order, and how language both creates and is created by social context. It is also similar to the ethnography of communication in its concern with human knowledge (cf. our discussion of communicative competence in chapter 5) and its belief that no detail of conversation (or interaction) can be neglected *a priori* as unimportant. All three approaches also focus on detailed analysis of particular sequences of utterances that have actually occurred. But CA is also quite different from any of the approaches discussed thus far: CA provides its own assumptions, its own methodology (including its own terminology), and its own way of theorizing.

I begin in section 2 with an overview of CA assumptions and methods, as well as some of its key findings and concepts (see also Goodwin and Heritage 1990; Heritage 1989; Wootton 1989; Zimmerman 1988). Section 3 is a sample analysis that focuses upon the way a particular construction (that I call "there + BE + ITEM") helps to solve some recurrent problems of talk. Since one of the problems addressed by this construction has to do with how people mention and recognize referents (i.e. the ITEM noted above), this sample analysis also continues and amplifies our concern with referring sequences. Section 4 summarizes.

2 Defining conversation analysis

Since CA is derived from ethnomethodology, it is important to very briefly discuss this sociological perspective before discussing CA. Although I cannot possibly hope to do justice to this field (see Button 1991; Garfinkel 1967; Heritage 1984a; Turner 1974), I will try to present some key ideas that can be connected to the assumptions, methods, and findings of CA.

Garfinkel's term "ethnomethodology" was modelled after terms used in cross-cultural analyses of ways of "doing" and "knowing." Ethnobotany, for example, is concerned with culturally specific systems by which people "know about" (classify, label, etc.) plants. Garfinkel (1974: 16) states that he used the term "ethno" for the following reason: " 'Ethno' seemed to refer, somehow or other, to the availability to a member of common-sense knowledge of his society as common-sense knowledge of the 'whatever'." The "whatever" encompassed by ethnomethodology is not a specific body of knowledge about one domain (e.g. plants). Rather it is the "ordinary arrangement of a set of located practices" (p. 17). What ethnomethodology is thus concerned with is: "a member's knowledge of his ordinary affairs, of his own organized enterprises, where that knowledge is treated by us as part of the same setting that it also makes orderable."

The above quotes suggest that uncovering what we know is a central concern for ethnomethodology. They also suggest that knowledge is neither autonomous nor decontextualized; rather, knowledge and action are deeply linked and mutually constitutive. (I suggest below that this has an important bearing on the study of language.) Much of Garfinkel's research reveals that participants' understandings of their circumstances provide for the stable organization of their social activities. Such understandings, however, are not ready and waiting apart from human activity: participants continually engage in interpretive activity – and thus reach understandings – as a way of seeking order and normalcy during the course of their everyday conduct. Furthermore, the sense of order that emerges is displayed through ongoing activity that provides a practical basis, and a sense of intersubjectivity, through which further activity can be sustained. Social action thus not only displays knowledge, it is also critical to the creation of knowledge: one's own actions produce and reproduce the knowledge through which individual conduct and social circumstance are intelligible.

The link between knowledge and action has an important bearing on the study of language. Ethnomethodological research avoids idealizations, arguing instead that what members produce are "typifications": categories that are continuously adjusted according to whether the anticipation of an actor (an anticipation on which the actor's own conduct was based) is confirmed by another's actions. The anticipations to which actors orient, and to which actions are held accountable, can be formulated in terms of interactional rules (or systems), i.e. "a detailed texture of institutionalized methods of talking to orient to" (Heritage 1984a: 292). These methods provide actors with "cognitive bearings" that are essential to their ability to "make continuous sense of their environments of action" (Heritage 1984a: 292).

Language (and action through language) is no less a situated product of rules and systems than other typifications. Although language is the medium through which common-sense categories are constituted, the meaning and use of a particular term (and thus the boundaries of a category) are nevertheless indeterminate and negotiable. The relationship between words and objects is as much a matter of the world of social relations and activities in which words are used, as of the world of objects that is being "named." Put another way, the meaning of a particular utterance (including the sense of particular descriptive terms) is indexical to a specific context and purpose. The contextualization of language in these ways allows its entry into the mutually constitutive relationship between action and knowledge: speakers produce utterances assuming that hearers can make sense out of them by the same kind of practical reasoning and methodic contextualizing operations that they apply to social conduct in general. It is these methods and operations that allow actors to "proceed on the basis that their experiences are 'identical for all practical purposes' " (Heritage 1984a: 60). Furthermore, it is because actors succeed in using the sequential progression of interaction to display their understandings of its events and rules that the shared world that has been jointly achieved is publicly available for analysis (Taylor and Cameron 1987: 104).

Although specific CA analyses do not always acknowledge their ethnomethodological heritage, some of the key ideas in CA can be related to the ideas briefly noted above. The focus of CA on conversation, for example, arises out of the ethnomethodological distrust of idealizations as a basis for either social science or ordinary human action. Sacks (1984) argues that many idealizations in social science produce general concepts that have only a vague and indeterminate relationship with a specific set of events. Since it can be difficult to decide whether a specific event supports a generalization, this distance between "type" and "token" hinders the development of a cumulative body of knowledge. (By the same line of argument, CA distrusts linguistic categorizations of the functions of particular words or expressions: such categorizations may be generalizations that do not at all reflect the specific uses of an item; see section 4 and chapter 10.) Sacks chose to work on conversation in an effort to remedy the idealizations of sociologists. He wanted to: "handle the details of actual events, handle them formally, and in the first instance be informative about them in the direct ways in which primitive societies tend to be informative, that is, that anyone else can go and see whether what was said is so"

(Sacks 1984: 26). Tape-recorded conversation thus provided data that could be available for many analysts and subjected to many analyses. Again, in Sacks' words: "I could get my hands on it and I could study it again and again . . . others could look at what I had studied' (Sacks 1984: 26).

The goals and beliefs that I have just described continue to influence CA. CA focuses upon the details of actual events: analysts record conversations that occur without researcher prompting (cf. our discussion of sociolinguistic interviews in chapters 5 and 8). Analysts also produce transcriptions of events that attempt to reproduce what is said (both linguistic details such as pronunciation and nonlinguistic details such as inbreaths) in ways that avoid presuppositions about what might be important for either participants or analysts themselves (e.g. Jefferson 1989; see appendix 2).[1] Similarly, analysts avoid positing generalizations about what participants "know": the focus, instead, is on specific events that occur during the conversation. And in keeping with the relationship noted above between action and knowledge, the events that are focused upon are said to reflect and realize practical knowledge.

The CA treatment of context is also ethnomethodologically based. We noted above that utterances are indexical: this indexicality locates utterances not just in a world of social relations (more on this in a moment), but in a world of other utterances. Furthermore, each utterance in a sequence is shaped by a prior context (at the very least, and most typically, the immediately prior utterance) and provides a context for a next utterance (again, for a very next utterance). In Heritage's (1984a: 242) terms, "the significance of any speaker's communicative action is doubly contextual in being both *context-shaped* and *context-renewing*." This notion of context as being both retrospective and prospective can be seen as yet another way that meanings (and knowledge) are continually adjusted and sequentially emergent.

Although CA assumes that utterances always have contextual relevance for one another, not all aspects of context are assumed to have so constant a relevance. We noted above that the indexicality of utterances locates them in a world of social relations. However, CA transcripts of talk pay little attention to social relations and to what other approaches call "social context," e.g. social identities of participants, setting, personal attributes, and so on. By intentionally ignoring what are often assumed to be static features of a social world (e.g. the occupation of a participant), CA reflects yet again the ethnomethodological avoidance of premature generalizations and idealizations. Social identity (setting, and so on) is viewed instead as a category of social life and conduct that is subject to locally situated interpretive activity: the relevance of a social identity can be no more presumed to hold across different times and places than can the relevance of a one second pause (on the latter, see Jefferson 1989). As Schegloff (1987a: 219) points out:

> the fact that they [social interactants] are "in fact" respectively a doctor and a patient does not make those characterizations *ipso facto* relevant . . . their respective ages, sex, religions, and so on, or altogether idiosyncratic

and ephemeral attributes (for example, "the one who just tipped over the glass of water on the table") may be what is relevant at any point in the talk. . . . That is, there should be some tie between the context-as-characterised and its bearing on "the doing of the talk" or "doing the interaction".

As Coulter (1989: 103) says, "it is only within organizations of sayings and doings that assignably 'personal' attributes are made manifest" (see also Schenkein 1978). Thus, although CA is an approach to discourse that emphasizes context, the relevance of context is grounded in text.

Now that we have discussed some of the basic ideas of ethnomethodology and their reflection in CA, let us turn to some of the specific methods and findings of CA. Heritage (1984a: 241) lists three assumptions of CA: (a) interaction is structurally organized; (b) contributions to interaction are contextually oriented; (c) these two properties inhere in the details of interaction so that no order of detail can be dismissed, *a priori*, as disorderly, accidental, or irrelevant. The latter two assumptions have already been discussed above; the assumption of structural organization will be discussed in a moment in relation to adjacency pair organization. Consistent with the CA avoidance of premature generalization and the ethnomethodological focus on action as the locus of knowledge, CA views the empirical conduct of speakers as the central resource out of which analysis must develop (Heritage 1984: 243). Furthermore, what is said provides not only the data underlying analysis, but also the evidence for hypotheses and conclusions: it is participants' conduct itself that must provide evidence for the presence of units, existence of patterns, and formulation of rules. To this end, CA searches for recurrent patterns, distributions, and forms of organization in large corpora of talk.

We noted above that the CA view of interaction is a structural view. One such structure is the adjacency pair: a sequence of two utterances, which are adjacent, produced by different speakers, ordered as a first part and second part, and typed, so that a first part requires a particular second part or range of second parts (Schegloff and Sacks 1973: 295–6; also Schegloff 1972a). We saw an example of an adjacency pair in chapter 1: a summons–answer sequence. There we noted that a telephone ring is a summons; a summons opens a conditional relevance for a second part of a sequence, an answer. When an answer is not forthcoming, it is heard as officially absent, such that a summons can be reissued and/or an account offered for its absence. The summons–answer adjacency pair not only has structure in and of itself, it also provides for a coordinated entry into, and an orderly exchange of turns within, the conversation. Conversational closings also depend upon two-part sequences that provide for coordinated exit from turn exchange (Schegloff and Sacks 1973). Thus, adjacency pairs are organized patterns of stable, recurrent actions that provide for, and reflect, order within conversation. Their sociological importance is that they provide a normative framework for actions that is accountably implemented (Heritage 1984a: 249). Their linguistic importance is that they provide an environment in which inferences about relevance can be assigned across utterances (cf. Gricean pragmatics, chapter 6) and a sequence in which expectations about form and meaning can be specified across utterances.

Adjacency pairs also reflect the local nature of conversational structure. So pervasive is the pairwise organization of talk that a next-utterance need not be explicitly tied to a prior utterance: rather, adjacency itself can provide a basis for assumed relevance (cf. Gricean pragmatics, chapter 6). Sacks (1971: lecture 4, 11–12) points out the importance of next-position:

> There is one generic place where you need not include information as to which utterance you're intending to relate an utterance to . . . and this is if you are in Next Position to an utterance. Which is to say that for adjacently placed utterances, where a next intends to relate to a last, no other means than positioning are necessary in order to locate which utterance you're intending to deal with.

From a speaker's point of view, next-position thus offers a location in which to find the recipient's analysis of the utterance – to see whether an anticipated response is confirmed. From a recipient's point of view, next-position offers an opportunity to reveal aspects of the understanding of prior talk to which own talk will be addressed. (Recall the context-shaping and context-renewing features of utterances.) Thus, next-position is a crucial location for the building of intersubjectivity: each next turn provides an environment in which recipients can display many understandings, including problematic understandings (i.e. misunderstandings) that lead to "third position repair" (Schegloff 1992).

Although conversation typically proceeds in a pairwise fashion, there are also ways that a pair can be expanded, before its initiation (see Schegloff 1980; Levinson 1983: 345–64, on pre-sequences), after its completion (see Fox 1987: 23–8, on post-elaborations), or even during its creation (see Jefferson 1972, on side sequences). That such modifications are specifically constructed *as* modifications shows the robustness of the adjacency pair organization for participants themselves (recall the need to find evidence for patterns within participants' own talk; but see Tsui 1989). Finally, although the first part of an adjacency pair defines a slot for the second, more specific preferences within that slot can be structurally indicated. A preference for agreement (rather than disagreement) with an assessment, for example, can be indicated by a lack of structural marking (Pomerantz 1984), i.e. no qualifiers, prefaces, pauses, or accounts. Consistent with the focus on structure (and the reluctance to posit psychological states that are not empirically grounded in conduct; Pomerantz 1990), preferences are seen as *structural* preferences defined on the basis of the skewed distribution of forms and behaviors. (But see discussion in Bilmes 1988; Taylor and Cameron 1987: 109–15).

The pervasiveness of local organization in talk is also revealed in the CA analysis of turn-taking (Sacks et al. 1974). A central problem underlying talk is what might be called a "distribution" problem: how do speakers allocate turns at talk? How do they know during what period of time one will be expected to speak and the other obliged to be silent? How does one person know when to end speaking, and another when to begin speaking, with minimal gap and minimal overlap between turns? Note that some of these problems arise from empirical observation of talk, e.g. the minimal gap/overlap problem.

CA offers a solution to these (and other) problems centered on turn exchange – a solution whose operation is demonstrable in actual talk. The solution is "a basic set of rules governing turn construction, providing for the allocation of a next turn to one party, and coordinating transfer so as to minimize gap and overlap" (Sacks et al. 1974: 12). The rules are locally managed in that they apply to all possible points of turn exchange:

1 At initial turn-constructional unit's initial transition-relevance place:
   (a) If the turn-so-far is so constructed as to involve the use of a "current speaker selects next" technique, then the party so selected has rights, and is obliged, to take next turn to speak, and no others have such rights or obligations, transfer occurring at that place.
   (b) If the turn-so-far is so constructed as not to involve the use of a "current speaker selects next" technique, self-selection for next speakership may, but need not, be instituted, with first starter acquiring rights to a turn, transfer occurring at that place.
   (c) If the turn-so-far is so constructed as not to involve the use of a "current speaker selects next" technique, then current speaker may, but need not, continue, unless another self-selects.
2 If, at initial turn-constructional unit's initial transition-relevance place, neither 1(a) nor 1(b) has operated, and, following the provision of 1(c), current speaker has continued, then the rule-set (a)–(c) reapplies at next transition-relevance place, and recursively at each next transition-relevance place, until transfer is effected (Sacks et al. 1978: 12).

Central to the rules is "transition-relevance place" – a location at which the rules may apply. Such places reflect the existence of various "unit types" (sentential, clausal, phrasal, and lexical constructions) through which a speaker may construct a turn. Included within that construction is a projection of unit type and, thus, its possible completion point. The rules above operate recursively upon the completion of successive unit types, thus providing one important motivation for recipients of talk to continue attending to that talk.[2] Note, finally, that the exchange of turns is as critical to the emergent architecture of intersubjectivity and accountability built through talk as are adjacency pairs (Heritage 1984a: 254–60; Atkinson and Heritage 1984: 7). It is the exchange of turns that provides for "next-position," and thus for the emergence of sequentially ordered displays of understandings to which actors are mutually accountable – not only in conversation, but presumably in other interactions as well (Greatbatch 1988).

In sum, CA approaches to discourse consider the way participants in talk construct systematic solutions to recurrent organizational problems of conversation. The existence of those problems – and the need to find such solutions – arises out of the ethnomethodological search for members' knowledge of their own ordinary affairs, knowledge that reveals and produces a sense of order and normalcy in everyday conduct. Since the sense of order that emerges is publicly displayed through ongoing activity, one can examine the details of that activity for evidence of its underlying order and structure – searching not just for evidence that some aspect of conversation "can" be viewed in a certain way, but that it is viewed that way by participants themselves (Levinson 1983: 318–19).

3 Sample analysis: "there + BE + ITEM"

We noted above that CA approaches to discourse consider how participants in talk construct systematic solutions to recurrent organizational problems. Among the many problems that are solved are opening and closing talk, turn taking, repair, topic management, information receipt, and showing agreement and disagreement. Solutions to such problems are discovered through the close analysis of how participants themselves talk and to what aspects of talk they themselves attend: CA avoids positing any categories (whether social or linguistic) whose relevance for participants themselves is not displayed in what is actually said. Analysts have demonstrated that aspects of talk as varied as particles (Heritage 1984; Pomerantz 1984), error correction (Jefferson 1974), laughter (Jefferson 1979), silence (Jefferson 1989), and syntactic structure (Ford and Thompson 1986; Goodwin 1979) are relevant to the ongoing management of conversation.

The sample analysis in this section considers how a single device addresses several problems of conversational management. In order to do this, we need to locate all occurrences of the device in a corpus of talk, and search for recurrent patterns of use (sequentially based distributions) in the data, showing that what are hypothesized to be sequential expectations are actually oriented to by participants. In so doing, we will be showing that sequential expectations and structures solve certain organizational problems: these solutions may also raise (or be applied to) other problems (Levinson 1983: 326).

The device considered is a linguistic construction – the existential *there* construction. Analyses of this construction have often noted that it presumes very little in the way of new, semantically complex information at the beginning of the sentence, but focuses a great deal of information at the end of a sentence. The information focused upon need not be assumed to be shared with the hearer: indeed, this "newness" is what motivates its location at the end of the sentence and its introduction by material that imposes few processing demands upon the hearer.

(1) is an example of an existential *there* construction used by a library patron (P) to open a query during a reference interview with a librarian (L) (see chapter 5). The *there* construction focuses the item for which P is searching.

(1) P: (j)   There used to be a monthly report that comes from S- Securities
              Exchange Commission . . . on insiders' transactions=
     L: (k)   Uh huh
     P: (l)   =and many years ago you used to carry it
          (m)   and I haven't seen it in a long time.

The query is opened with *there used to be*: this predicates nothing but the existence (prior to speaking time) of what we will call an ITEM. P's description of the ITEM being queried includes a great deal of information within the noun phrase: when the publication comes out (*monthly*), its source (*Securities Exchange Commission*), and its topic (*insiders' transactions*). When P continues to add information about this ITEM (when it was carried (l), her own knowledge of its availability (m)), however, the ITEM is evoked through the pronoun *it*. Thus, the existential *there* construction in (1) initiates a referring sequence (chapter 6) in which a first-mention is indefinite and explicit (*a monthly report . . .*) and the next-mention is definite and inexplicit (*it*).[3]

I hope to have suggested thus far that focusing on the existential *there* for our CA sample analysis will allow us to consider some of the same questions raised in our earlier discussion of referring terms and referring sequences: how are referents introduced? How do first-mentions differ from next-mentions? What the CA approach adds to this discussion is an analysis of the way a particular construction that seems to do referential work is integrated into the systems through which participants organize talk. In still broader terms, the CA approach can reveal how referring sequences are part of the mechanics of conversation.

We noted earlier that CA research (especially when initiated and pursued by sociologists) typically pays little attention to linguistic structure *per se*.[4] In keeping with this practice, I will not refer to the focus of our analysis as existential *there* constructions, but as "there + BE + ITEM" constructions. This descriptive label allows us to ignore what have often been seen as structural and semantic differences among different surface forms of this construction. Consider the examples in (2).

(2a)   There's the old ladies from the home.
(2b)   And there was him- there was him- my brother and the dog, Prince.
(2c)   There's a little boy down here I'd say he's eight, not no more.
(2d)   And then there's the Jewish section, too.

Although I will use the label "there + BE + ITEM" construction to describe the uses of "there" illustrated in (2), examples like these have been identified by linguists as different constituents of grammatical structure, and the four sentence types have been said to derive from different underlying syntactic structures (e.g. Erdmann 1976). These distinctions would not typically be discussed by CA, and we, too, will disregard them for now. (In section 4, however, I consider some of the advantages and disadvantages of this terminology.) Thus, in all the examples in (2), whatever information is relevant to the noun following the copula will be considered an ITEM: *the old ladies from the home* (2a), *him, my brother, the dog, Prince* (2b), *a little boy down here I'd say he's eight, not no more* (2c), and *the Jewish section* (2d).

I noted above that the CA approach can reveal how referring sequences – first-mentions and next-mentions of an ITEM – are part of the mechanics of conversation. We see in this analysis that "there + BE + ITEM" constructions address two problems of conversational management: the sequential mention of individual ITEMS and the organization of ITEMS into larger topics. The solutions offered by "there + BE + ITEM" for the former problem intersect with two other mechanisms of conversational organization: adjacency pairs (3.1) and turn-taking (3.2). The way "there + BE + ITEM" addresses problems of topic management is an outgrowth of its use with mention-pairs, but the work of the construction at the topic level is less dependent on other systems of conversational management (3.3). The means of presenting the analysis that I have chosen highlight the CA view of conversational structure and the ways that a device can be reflexive of that structure. This presentational style also allows us to continue our focus on referring sequences. However, we will also note separately how "there + BE + ITEM" can be used for first-mentions, next-mentions, and only-mentions of a referent outside of the adjacency pair organization (3.4).

Before we begin, I want to briefly compare the upcoming analysis to the Gricean pragmatic analysis and highlight the main features of the CA approach. In chapter 6, we used the maxims of quantity and relevance to explain the use of definite/indefinite and explicit/inexplicit referring terms in a story. At first, a CA approach to first-mentions and next-mentions might seem similar to the pragmatic approach: both locate referring as something a speaker *does* within a communicative setting. However, CA turns the pragmatics approach around: rather than posit generally applicable abstract principles that are used to explain specific utterances, CA seeks to discover general principles from specific patterns of speaking. The CA search for patterns is also a distributional method of analysis. Although this is rarely explicitly acknowledged as part of a CA procedure, this kind of "item and arrangement" (Hockett 1958) procedure is actually fairly typical (Bilmes 1990; Levinson 1983: 295). Above I noted that I will present the analysis of "there + BE + ITEM" in relation to adjacency pairs and turn-taking. However, I did not assume prior to the analysis that these aspects of conversational organization were related to the construction. Rather, the importance of adjacency pairs and turn-taking emerged after I had located all instances of "the item" ("there + BE + ITEM") and tried to identify the environments in which it was used. In what follows, then, what I characterize is the sequential "arrangement" of the item in relation to (and independent of) other sequentially definable units, both within and across turns.

Discovering the sequential patterns in which a construction is integrated leads CA to ask more general questions about both the construction and the conversation. What does the distribution of a construction reveal about how participants manage tasks of conversation? Are the tasks being managed part of a broader problem of conversational management that is being systematically addressed by a single device? By asking these questions, CA tries to identify the very same problems that participants themselves – rather than linguists or other outside observers – address when they enter into a conversation.

3.1 "Mentions," "There + BE + ITEM," and adjacency pairs

Since conversation typically proceeds in a pairwise fashion, a basic means of conversational organization is the two-part adjacency pair sequence (section 2). The pairwise system can also undergo modification, however: a pair can be expanded before its initiation, after its completion, or even during its creation. These extensions of the adjacency pair organization support the idea that adjacency pairs are central to sequential implicativeness.

This section considers how first- and next-mentions of an ITEM presented in "there + BE + ITEM" are related to adjacency pair organization. "There + BE + ITEM" is found in two types of question/answer (Q/A) pairs: Q/A pairs that are structurally independent of surrounding talk (3.1.1); Q/A pairs embedded in surrounding talk, as either pre-sequences or insertion sequences (3.1.2).

3.1.1 "There + BE + ITEM" in independent Q/A pairs

This section begins with several examples of "there + BE + ITEM" in the first parts (questions) of Q/A pairs. These examples suggest that "there + BE + ITEM" in questions projects the form and content of answers, such that the second part of the Q/A adjacency pair displays its conditional relevance to the first. I begin with examples (3 to 6) that show that "there + BE + ITEM" in a question can project on to the first utterance in an answer, thereby immediately displaying the conditional relevance of the answer for the question. Other examples (7 and 8) illustrate how "there + BE + ITEM" in a question can project an organizational basis for the entire answer. We also note briefly that "there + BE + ITEM" can be used in the second parts of Q/A pairs (but see section 3.3).

(3) and (4) illustrate the simplest way that "there + BE + ITEM" in a question can project onto an answer. The format projected by the question onto the answer is just the question form itself, i.e. the unknown polarity conveyed by a yes/no question form.

(3) IVEE: (a) Fact, I never hung on the corner in my life,
           (b) I never set in a bar in my life.
→ IVER: (c) Yeh? Was- was there a corner bar or a tap room that your
                dad went to?
   IVEE: (d) Oh, yeh hhhh.

In (a) and (b), the IVee has been describing her teenage activities. The Iver (through a stepwise topic transition; see section 3.2) then asks *was there a corner bar or a tap room that your dad went to?* (c). The IVee's answer builds upon the question function itself with its *yeh* response: the existence of "a corner bar or a tap room" is unknown and *yeh* establishes that existence.

(4) is similar to (3), but it illustrates that an answer can be constructed with a negative (i.e. X does not exist) as well as an affirmative (i.e. X does exist) token.

(4) → IVER: (a) Were there any social functions that the church had that
                  you kids went to?
     IVEE: (b) Not me, no.

(5) illustrates how "there + BE + ITEM" can project slightly different material onto the format of the answer. In (5), it is "there + BE" that constitutes the answer.

(5) → IVER: (a) So there were a lot of mills around here in the old days.
     IVEE: (b) There was.
     IVER: (c) Wow.
     IVEE: (d) But not no more. [Yeh.]
     IVER: (e)   [What] happened to 'em? Did they close
                  down, or-
     IVEE: (f) Well, yeh, they w- they moved away or they moved to
                  Can- some moved to Canada, some moved down south.

In (5), it is "there + BE" from the question in (a) that is repeated (*There was*) in (b). Note that the ITEM itself has not been mentioned in any of the answers in the examples considered thus far: in (5b), for example, the IVee does not say *there were mills*. However, ellipsis of the ITEM is a source of internal evidence that participants "know" what they are talking about.[5] Furthermore, the ITEM in (5) is subsequently mentioned pronominally (*they*) in both the IVer's questions (*What happened to 'em? Did they close down?* (e)) and the IVee's own further descriptions (e.g. *they moved away* (f)).

(6) shows that the use of "there + BE + ITEM" as a first-mention in a question can project multiple formats onto an answer. Prior to (6), the IVer

and IVee have been discussing Irish parties; the topic of "drinking" has come up (see 3.2). (Note that IVee-1 is hard of hearing, and her niece (IVee-2) is acting as a spokesperson in this section of the interview; see chapter 4, and chapter 5, pp. 168–9)

(6) IVEE-1   (a) Oh, they used to get feeling good and a lot of them did get drunkhhhh I won't deny thathh

  IVER: → (b) Was there ever any trouble?

  IVEE-2:   (c) Was there ever any trouble?

  IVEE-1   (d) Hm, yes, there was, sometimes:,

        (e) but uh they used to squash it down pretty good y'know.

        (f) There'd always be somebody there that would watch for trouble,

        (g) you'd always have somebody to take care of anybody that would get into trouble.

  IVER   (h) Uh huh.

  IVEE-1:   (i) But she always had very nice parties and they always came back to them, like if- she had another one herself, and Irish dances and stuff like that.

Following the IVer's question *Was there ever any trouble?* (b) and its repetition by IVee-2 (d), IVee-1's answer builds upon all the components of the "there + BE + ITEM" format of the question in *Hm, yes, there was, sometimes* (d). *Yes* affirms the existence of "trouble" (fixing the polarity of the question *per se*), *there was* restates the "there + BE" component, and *sometimes* modifies the existence of trouble *per se*. Following this initial part of her answer, the IVee modifies "trouble" with a disclaimer ((e) *but uh they used to squash it down pretty good*) that introduces a new ITEM *they*. "There + BE + ITEM" in (f) provides a next-mention of "they" that specifies the capacity in which "they" is relevant to "trouble": *somebody there that would watch for trouble*. Further specification is given in (g): *somebody to take care of anybody that would get into trouble*. IVee-1 then returns to the topic of "parties" (i).

Thus far, we have concentrated on how "there + BE + ITEM" in a question can project onto the first utterance in an answer – thereby immediately displaying the conditional relevance of the answer for the question. The next two examples illustrate how "there + BE + ITEM" in a question can project an organizational basis for the entire answer. Since space prevents lengthy consideration of both examples, I will be brief with (7) and provide more detail for (8).

(7) IVER: (a) → Do you think there's a difference between kids gettin' married *now* and when you got married?

  IVEE: (b) Well, to me, when we got married, we got married *for* love.

        (c) Today, they don't even know when they're *in* love.

In (a), the IVer asks whether *there's a difference* between X (*kids gettin' married* now) and Y (*when you got married*), i.e. she asks for a comparison. Although the ITEM in this question is relatively complex, all three parts of it (*a difference*, *kids getting married* now, and *when you got married*) provide an organizational format for the answer. In (b), the IVee begins with a repetition of the time frame *when we got married* and a description of what happened at that time (a reason for marriage). The contrast in (c) follows the same format: first the time frame (*today*), then a description of a different reason for marriage. Although I do not include it here, the rest of the answer expands this format, as the IVee alternates between time frames (*today* versus *in my days*) and their described features.

   (8) is an example of an answer that builds extensively upon the "there + BE + ITEM" format in the question. In (8), an IVer is asking three informants about the population on the block. The initial question in (c) *Are there any old folks livin' on this block?* is prefaced by *but gettin' back to*, showing that the IVer is returning to a prior topic, i.e. *the people on this block*. The collectivity ("any old folks") in the "there + BE + ITEM" question in (c) is dissected in the answer in ways that show that the people (mentioned in the answer) are included in the larger collectivity (mentioned in the question). (Compare our discussion of group and individuating referents in chapter 6, pp. 213–14.)

(8) IVER:	(a)	But gettin' back to the people on this block,
	(b)	so it's mostly kids, right?
→ (c)		Are there any old folks livin' on this block?
IVEE-1:	(d)	Yes,=
IVER:	(e)	^{z}Like older people.
IVEE-1:	(f)	=all down this street [( )
IVEE-2:	(g)	[There's a couple.
	(h)	There's um . . .
IVEE-1:	(i)	There's [three.
IVEE-3:	(j)	[That kook hangin' out the window.
IVEE-2:	(k)	Yeh. [That's-
IVEE-1:	(l)	[( ) you don't like him ( )?
IVEE-2:	(m)	[Kids call him Uncle Ed? Hh.
IVER:	(n)	[What's that address?
IVEE-2:	(o)	That his name?
IVEE-3:	(p)	Uncle Ed, ( ) Uncle Ed.
	(q)	I'll break his jaw.
IVEE-2:	(r)	Then there's one woman here, crippled or whatever,=
IVER:	(s)	^{z}Mhm.
IVEE-2:	(t)	=you want to call her. She's-$_{z}$
IVEE-3:	(u)	^{z}Delirious.
	(v)	She just walks around the street with a walker?=
IVER:	(w)	Mhm.

IVₑₑ-3:	(x)	=She'll stop any car comin' down the street, too.
IVₑₑ-2:	(y)	(No,) [hh she's not. Hh.
IVₑₑ-3:	(z)	[Tell you her whole life history.
IVₑₑ-2:	(aa)	She gets you to come in her house and-=
IVₑₑ-3:	(bb)	Fix her ( ).
IVₑₑ-2:	(cc)	=read her mail for her and-
IVₑR:	(dd)	Hh, oh, bless her heart.
	(ee)	She really sounds lonely.
IVₑₑ-2:	(ff)	And then there's a- another couple up the street who never come out.=
IVₑR:	(gg)	Uh huh.
IVₑₑ-2:	(hh)	=And, God forbid you parked your car in their pavement and they're- they're out there ready to throw bricks at you and, they call the cops . . .
IVₑR:	(ii)	What's- what's that address?
IVₑₑ-2:	(jj)	I don't know the address.

[TAPE ENDS]

The IVer's question (*Are there any old folks livin' on this block?* (c)) uses a "there + BE + ITEM" format: she asks about the existence of a particular type of person ("old folks") in a particular location ("on this block"). Following an initial affirmation token (*yes* in (d)), IVee-1 alters the locational description of *old folks livin' on this block* (c) to *all down this street* (f). This description is overlapped by an affirmation from IVee-2 (*There's a couple* (g)): IVee-2 repeats "there + BE" and describes the referent numerically as a "couple". Thus, both IVee-1 and IVee-2 answer the question affirmatively, but in different ways: IVee-1 with *yes*, IVee-2 with repetition. In addition, both IVee-1 and IVee-2 build a description of the referent, but again they do so differently: IVee-1 provides locational information, IVee-2 provides numeric information.

In (h), IVee-2 initiates another "there + BE + ITEM" construction that is not completed. IVee-1 then does a post-position other-repair (Schegloff 1992) of IVee-2's numeric description, switching from *there's a couple* (g) to *there's three* (i). Recall that the IVer's question about whether there are *any old folks* contained a first-mention that focused not just on existence, but on quantity (through *any*). Here we have seen that this question is followed by two next-mentions that similarly focus on existence (through "there + BE") and on quantity (*couple, three*).

Thus far, I have noted four features of this example: the IVer's question incorporates a "there + BE + ITEM" format, both IVee-1 and IVee-2 answer the question affirmatively, both IVee-1 and IVee-2 build a description of the referent, both IVee-1 and IVee-2 initiate "there + BE + ITEM" constructions as extensions of their initial answers.

"There + BE + ITEM" is also used for mentioning ITEMS in the answer. Recall that the ITEM first-mentioned in the question is *any old folks* (c). The first member of the group of *three* old folks (i) is introduced in (j): *That kook hangin' out the window.* Although IVee-3 does not explicitly say that *that kook* is one of the "three old folks," that membership is sequentially inferrable. Because *that kook* follows a numeric specification (*there's three* (i)), it is interpreted as an enumerated item, i.e. as "counting as" one of the "three old folks." Compare, for example, picking cakes out at a bakery. If I say "I'll take three. That chocolate cake . . .", the salesperson would understand "chocolate cake" as the first item on my three part list. Further evidence that *that kook* is intended as a specific member of the group of "three old folks" is the way it is followed by a next member of the group. In *Then there's one woman here* (r), "one woman" is introduced with *then* (see chapter 8; also Schiffrin 1992b). By establishing "one woman" as a second member of the group of "three old folks" – as "next" in the list – *then* retroactively establishes the prior ITEM (*that kook*) as first in the list. Again, consider the bakery example. If I continued the order for cakes by saying "then the coconut," the way I introduced "coconut" would retroactively fix the identity of the previously mentioned "chocolate cake" as a member of the list. In addition, the indefinite article *one* (in *one woman here*) is a numeric mention of the ITEM: this displays a sequential tie with *three* (i).

The third member of the group of "old folks" is introduced in (ff): *And then there's a- another couple up the street who never come out* (ff). This ITEM is also established as part of the group of *old folks livin' on this block* (c) in several ways. In addition to using *then* and "there + BE + ITEM," IVee 2 uses a numeric descriptor (*another*) that establishes *another couple* as subsequent in a list, and a locative (*up the street*) that establishes their presence *on this block* (c). Thus, the mention of a third ITEM in the answer also reflects a contingency upon the "there + BE + ITEM" format in the question.

In sum, (8) illustrates that the use of "there + BE + ITEM" in a question can project the form and content of an answer well beyond its first utterance. *Any old folks livin' on this block* is the ITEM in the question introduced through "there + BE + ITEM." The first specification of this ITEM (as *three*) was also through "there + BE + ITEM." Following the initial member (*that kook*) of the list of "three old folks" were two other entries also in the "there + BE + ITEM" format: *Then there's one woman here, crippled or whatever, And then there's a- another couple up the street who never come out.* All the ITEMS mentioned in the answer were understood as members of the general ITEM introduced through "there + BE" in the question. Thus, "there + BE + ITEM" in a question can project an organizational basis for an entire answer, thereby allowing a speaker to provide a continual display of the conditional relevance of the answer to that question.

We have seen in this section that first-mentions through "there + BE + ITEM" can occupy the first part of a question/answer pair. We have also seen some ways that "there + BE + ITEM" can project the second part of a question/answer pair. Discussion of the dependency between first-mention through "there + BE + ITEM" and next-mention of that ITEM is reserved until section 3.3.

3.1.2 *"There + BE + ITEM" in embedded Q/A pairs*

"There + BE + ITEM" creates a first-mention in another kind of Q/A adjacency pair: Q/A pairs that are structurally and topically dependent on surrounding talk as either a presequence (Levinson 1983: 345–64; Schegloff 1980) or insertion sequence (Jefferson 1972; cf. chapter 5, pp. 159, 170). This dependency is reflected in the location of the next-mention of the ITEM in relation to the first-mention. Instead of projecting a next-mention within the Q/A pair itself (i.e. in the answer), the first-mention created by the "there + BE + ITEM" format in the first part of the pair projects a next-mention in post-pair talk.[6]

(9) illustrates "there + BE + ITEM" in a variant of the *then there's X* list format (Schiffrin 1992b; also chapter 8), acting here as a pre-sequence. Since this presequence attends to problems in prior talk, we will also need to discuss the talk leading up to the use of "there + BE + ITEM."

(9)	IVer:	(a)	Well, you said you'd go dancin' and then go to oyster saloon.
		(b)	Where did you all dance?
	IVee:	(c)	On Second Avenue.
	IVer:	(d)	Well- at a ballroom or a dance hall?
	IVee:	(e)	Well, what they called a dance hall.
	IVer:	(f)	Yeh.
	IVee:	(g)	McKenzie.
	IVer:	(h)	McKenzie?
	IVee:	(i)	McKenzie.
	IVer:	(j)	Ah.
→	IVee:	(k)	Then there was one on Main Street right down uh Main and Parker?
	IVer:	(l)	Uh huh.
	IVee:	(m)	That was Rap's.
		(n)	And they had them, all around.
		(o)	Wherever there was a dance goin' on and they used to sell tickets.

Let us start with the IVer's question: *Where did you all dance?* (b). This question can be interpreted in two ways: asking for location or asking about a type of place (Schegloff 1972b). The IVee's answer displays the former understanding: *On Second Avenue* (c). The IVer then asks a question displaying the latter understanding: *ballroom or a dance hall?* (d). Note that this question can be sequentially interpreted in one of two ways. *Ballroom or a dance hall?* (d) can be a next-turn other-initiated repair to (b), implying that the IVee misheard *where* in (a) as a question about a street name rather than a place type. Alternatively, *ballroom or a dance hall?* (d) can be a post-elaboration, i.e. a question initiating a second adjacency pair that seeks information about the information given in the first (Fox 1987; 23). Regardless of which interpretation reflects participants' actions, the IVee selects a member of the category "place type" from the disjunction *ballroom or a dance hall?* (d), marking its descriptor (the place type, *dance hall* (e)) as a term used by others but not by herself (*what they call* (e)). She then self-confirms it (*yeh* (f)) and states the name of the dance hall (*McKenzie* (g)).

Note, however, that *McKenzie*, the name of the dance hall (g), is also problematic. After the IVee provides this name in (g), the IVer issues a next-turn response that repeats the answer with rising intonation (*McKenzie?* (h)). (We could also use the terms of chapters 4 and 5 to call this a request for clarification or information-check.) The IVer's questioning repetition is followed by the IVee's own repetition of *McKenzie* (i). Put another way, the IVer's *McKenzie?* (h) offers the IVee an opportunity for an other-initiated self-repair. The IVee's repetition of *McKenzie* (i) shows that the opportunity for repair can be bypassed.

The "there + BE + ITEM" construction in (k) (*Then there was one on Main Street right down uh Main and Parker?*) opens a presequence to mention of the next dance hall (*Rap's* (m)). This pre-sequential introduction is, in part, a consequence of the just noted uncertainty about *McKenzie*. Note that *Then there was one on Main Street right down uh Main and Parker?* is offered prior to a specification of the next dance hall by name (*That was Rap's* (m)). When issued with a terminal rise (as in k), *then there's X* opens a pre-sequence in which what is being questioned is the other's knowledge about the existence of X. (Compare discussion of information-checking questions in chapter 5, (3.3.3).) This use of "there + BE + ITEM" can be reissued until it is followed by a recognition token (*yes, right, um*). Thus, *uh huh* (l) in the second part of the embedded Q/A pair closes the pre-sequence prior to the use of the ITEM in a next-mention (*that was Rap's* (m)).

Then there was one on Main Street right down uh Main and Parker? (k) also attends to an earlier problem from prior talk: the dual understanding of "where" as calling for either a place category (ballroom or dance hall) or a specification of physical location. By saying *Main Street right down uh Main and Parker*, the IVee re-establishes physical location as the proper understanding of "where."

We have just seen "there + BE + ITEM" used in a pre-sequence completed prior to the specification of the ITEM in an identificatory frame. More can be said about an ITEM following its first-mention in a "there + BE + ITEM" pre-sequence. In (10), for example, two people being interviewed are about to do what is called a minimal pair test. The IVer is interested in whether Philadelphians can perceive differences between two vowels that are very close in pronunciation (i.e. near-mergers, Labov et al. 1991). To this end, one person will read a word (e.g. "merry") and another person will guess whether the reader is trying to say the word "merry" or the name "Murray." (10) occurs when an IVee (IVee-1) who is familiar with the test is telling another IVee (IVee-2) who is new to the test how she should announce which word she thinks is being read by IVee-3 (referred to in 10a, b as Barb).

(10) IVER: (a)   Barb, you read them.
    IVEE-1:   (b)   Yeh, you read 'em, Barb.
                     (c)   Now you ha-
          →   (d)   now there's a guy's named Murray, right?
    IVEE-2:   (e)   Yeh.
    IVEE-1:→   (f)   And there's merry Christmas, right?
    IVEE-2:   (g)   Yeh.
    IVEE-1:   (h) ^{z}Now you gotta tell her which [m^ri] she's sayin'.
                     (i)   The guy's name or Christmas.
                     (j)   Go ahead.

In (d), IVee-1 uses the "there + BE + ITEM" format with a final rise (on the tag *right*) to first-mention *a guy's named Murray* as a way for IVee-3 to announce her identification of IVee-2's intended meaning. After IVee-2's information receipt (*yeh* (e)), IVee-1 uses the same format to mention *merry Christmas* as the announcement procedure for the alternative interpretation of IVee-2's intended meaning. Both of these first-mentions are preliminary not just to the description of the minimal pair test, but to the actual use of the terms "guy" or "Christmas" as ways to identify IVee-2's intended meaning during the enactment of the test. Following the completion of both Q/A pairs, IVee-1 summarizes the use of the terms (*Now you gotta tell her which [m^ri] she's sayin* (h), *The guy's name or Christmas* (i)) and opens the test itself (*Go ahead* (j)). Thus, the "there + BE + ITEM" format in (10) creates first-mentions in a pre-sequence to an activity that relies on next-mentions.

In addition to providing a first-mention in a pre-sequence, "there + BE + ITEM" can provide a first-mention in another kind of embedded Q/A pair: an insertion sequence. In (11), "a school" (subsequently referred to during a story illustrating the problems of forcing schools to bus students for racial balance) is introduced with "there + BE + ITEM."

(11) IVEE: (a)   And this is what the thing is.
               (b)   They get in,
               (c)   and i- what's it- what's it bein' done for?
    IVER: (d)   Yeh.
               (e)   That's right.
    IVEE: (f)   There- I'll tell you.
        →   (g)   There's a school down in my mother's town, right?
    IVER: (h)   Right.
    IVEE   (i)   Strictly colored.
               (j)   It's the *newest* school in North Beach.
               (k)   It was all colored.
               (l)   And because of this law of integrating,
               (m)   these colored children had to go to this white school,
               (n)   which they didn't want.

In (a), (b), and (c), the IVee presents generalizations that both follow from her prior points (about educational inequalities) and project further development of those points. After beginning what sounds like a "there + BE + ITEM" format in (f), she self-interrupts with *I'll tell you* (see section 3.2) before completing the construction as *There's a school down in my mother's town, right?* (g). The tag *right?* makes explicit that this first-mention is seeking recognition and that it is not an end in and of itself. This dependency is also shown by the IVer's response (*right* (h)) and by the fact that the IVee continues her description of the school (i to k) after the IVer's recognition. All of the next-mentions of the school are inexplicit and definite: ellipsis in (i), *it* in (j) and (k). In addition, the description of the school in (g) and (i) through (k) allows the IVee to use *these colored children* in (m) as a referring term for children who attended the school, without mentioning the school another time.

We have seen in this section that "there + BE + ITEM" opens a mention in the first part of an embedded Q/A pair (either an insertion sequence or pre-sequence). The next-mention does not occur within the adjacency pair itself (i.e. not in the answer, the second part of the pair), but in post-pair talk that follows what does occupy the second part of the pair (i.e. recipients' acknowledgment). This is a distributional difference that is defined in relation to units of conversational structure.

3.1.3 Summary: "there + BE + ITEM" in adjacency pairs

In this section, we discussed the use of "there + BE + ITEM" for first-mentions in questions (the first part of an adjacency pair) and the way this construction projects the form and content of answers (the second part of an adjacency pair) and post-pair talk. We also saw that "there + BE + ITEM" can provide for ITEMS in answers.

The occurrence of first- and next-mentions through "there + BE + ITEM" in adjacency pairs is not surprising. Since the first part of an adjacency pair creates a slot for the second part, first- and next-mentions have ready-made conversational slots into which they can be fit (see also Fox 1987). Nor is it surprising that "there + BE + ITEM" can project a construction format onto the second part of the Q/A pair. The adjacency pair structure provides a slot in which a second part is sequentially implicative on the first: what is said in the first part will be pursued in the second part, and will be assigned an identity based on the identity of the first part. The projectability of "there + BE + ITEM" from the first part to the second part is thus an extension of this conditional relevance between the two parts.

When "there + BE + ITEM" opens a mention in the first part of an embedded Q/A pair, however, the next-mention does not occur within the adjacency pair itself, but in post-pair talk. The relationship between the location of a next-mention of an ITEM (in an answer or in post-pair talk) and the autonomy of the Q/A pair is an important distributional difference. In independent Q/A pairs, Q opens a slot for A and the provision of A completes the Q/A pair. Thus, the projectability of "there + BE + ITEM" in Q extends only to A. In dependent Q/A pairs, however, Q itself is sequentially implicative upon prior talk. Thus, the contingency that Q opens is not confined to an upcoming A, but extends into surrounding talk. The use of "there + BE + ITEM" in pre-sequences and insertion sequences also highlights a more general CA point about talk. Any aspect of talk can be sequentially implicative in two directions: utterances respond to prior talk and create contingencies for further talk; that is, they are both context shaped and context renewing (section 2).

3.2 "There + BE + ITEM" and the organization of a turn at talk

Our discussion of the use of "there + BE + ITEM" in adjacency pairs allowed us to focus on several ideas critical to CA: the importance of sequential structure and implicativeness in talk, how the distribution of a specific construction is related to the pairwise organization of talk, how a specific construction is distributed across turns in talk. This section focuses on another major source of conversational structure and organization: the exchange structure created by the need to take turns. The use of "there + BE + ITEM" is sensitive to the management of individual turns and how these turns are designed for a recipient: we find a preference for "there + BE + ITEM" to occupy one turn-constructional unit, and to be located in a turn-internal position. Although this section illustrates the CA method in a way similar to that just considered (again, we are locating a linguistic device in conversational structure), the constraint imposed by the turn exchange system is very different from that imposed by the adjacency pair system.

Let us start by observing that almost all of the examples in the corpus of sixty "there + BE + ITEM" constructions considered here were produced under a single continuous intonation contour. Note that the cases that are intonationally continuous include not only those with a few words and no syntactically defined turn-transition spaces (as in 12 below) but also those that are longer and that span syntactically defined turn-transition spaces (as in 13 below):

(12)   There's three.
(13)   There's always something to do in a home where there is a family.

That speakers produce – under one continuous intonation – even those tokens of "there + BE + ITEM" cases that extend past syntactically definable turn-transition spaces suggests a preference for "there + BE + ITEM" to be *a single turn-constructional unit*. In other words, an example like (14) can be produced as it actually was, without an intonational break:

(14)   because there was homes over through there that I knew like from a
       kid.

Or it can be produced with intonational breaks marking the syntactically
definable turn-transition spaces:

(14′) because there was homes, over through there, that I knew, like from a
       kid.

The fact that such utterances are routinely produced under one continuous
intonation (as in 14) suggests a preference for "there + BE + ITEM" to be
issued as a single turn-constructional unit.

CA typically finds further evidence for a preference system by comparing
preferred structures to those thought to be dispreferred: dispreferred structures are usually structurally marked in some way (Pomerantz 1984). Let us
examine some examples of "there + BE + ITEM" that are *not* intonationally
continuous to see if they are structurally differentiated from the others in
a way that suggests that they are, in fact, dispreferred. The following are
examples, from the data considered thus far, that are intonationally discontinuous.

(1)   (j)   There used to be a monthly report that comes from S- Securities
            Exchange Commission . . . on insiders' transactions /Uhhuh/ and
            many years ago you used to carry it and I haven't seen it in a long
            time.
(8)   (r)   Then there's one woman here, crippled or whatever, /Mhm./ you
            want to call her. She's- /Delirious./

These intonationally discontinuous "there + BE + ITEM" constructions are
multiple turn-constructional units in particular sequential contexts that make
interactive use of the boundaries between those units. I discuss these examples
below, highlighting the way the possible turn-transition points are interactively fit and recipient designed.

The intonational discontinuity in the example from the library reference
interview stems from the way the utterance is designed for reception by a
particular participant, i.e. a librarian. (The fact that the utterance *is* designed
for a librarian is of course part of our knowledge about the particular speech
event, although the term "speech event" is not used in CA.) We noted in
chapter 5 that patrons open an informational query for librarians' response in
multiple locations. Likewise, librarians often begin to reformulate patrons'
queries at the first possible location at which they achieve some recognition
of what is being sought. In (1), the patron pauses after having provided some
key pieces of information about the ITEM being sought: its frequency (*a
monthly report*) and source (*that comes from S- Securities Exchange Commission*). This pause is thus an opportunity for the librarian to display her

recognition – if possible – and to satisfy the query. When that recognition is not provided, the patron continues her description of the ITEM. Thus, the "there + BE + ITEM" in (1) is designed for a particular recipient (a librarian): the intonational discontinuity at the turn-transition spaces facilitates the provision of a next appropriate action.

The next example, (8) from this chapter, is also recipient designed, but in quite a different way. In (8), each part of the "there + BE + ITEM" construction is a separate turn-constructional unit that figures in the negotiation of participant rights in the conversation. Put another way, the interactive work accomplished by the intonational breaks in (8) is geared to the turn-taking mechanism itself and the way that different participants have already established their rights to speak. We can best see this by reviewing earlier portions of (8) from a turn-taking perspective:

(8) IVER   (c)   Are there any old folks livin' on this block?
    IVEE-1:   (d)   Yes,=
    IVER: (e) ^{z}Like older people.
    IVEE-1:   (f)   =all down this street [(   )
    IVEE-2:   (g)   [There's a couple.
              (h)   There's um . . .
    IVEE-1:   (i)   There's [three.
    IVEE-3:   (j)   [That kook hangin' out the window.
    IVEE-2:   (k)   Yeh. [That's-
    IVEE-1:   (l)   [(   ) you don't like him (   )?
    IVEE-2:   (m)   [Kids call him Uncle Ed? Hh.
    IVER: (n)   [What's that address?
    IVEE-2:   (o)   That his name?
    IVEE-3:   (p)   Uncle Ed, (   ) Uncle Ed.
              (q)   I'll break his jaw.

Three people are participating in the provision of an answer: they latch onto one another's talk (e), repair (i), and overlap with one another. The intonationally discontinuous "there + BE + ITEM" construction not only continues this interactive pattern, but reflects the specific way of participating in which IVee-2 has already been engaged. Note that IVee-2's contributions – at least up until this point – are not attended. IVee-2's *there's a couple* (g) is corrected by IVee-1's *there's three* (i) when IVee-2 (in what sounds like the beginning of a list) closes herself off (*There's um . . .* (h)). IVee-2 (*Yeh. That's-* (k)) is interrupted by IVee-1 (*you don't like him* (l)). IVee-2 (*Kids call him Uncle Ed?* (m), *That his name?* (o)) twice questions the name of someone who has been mentioned. IVee-3 uses IVee-2's information about *Uncle Ed* (in (p)), but ignores the way IVee-2 had sought recognition of that information through questioning intonation (m, o; see chapter 5, pp. 156–7). Thus, IVee-2 is accorded less status as an authority about the block and is less likely to be "heard" as someone who can provide an answer.

It is within this interactive context that the intonationally discontinuous "there + BE + ITEM" occurs:

(8) → IVEE-2: (r) Then there's one woman here, crippled or
                 whatever,=
     IVER: (s)   ^zMhm.
     IVEE-2: (t) =you want to call her. She's-
     IVEE-3: (u)   ^zDelirious.

The pause after *here* in (r) brackets the introduction of *one woman here* from its continued description in a way that allows the allocation of participation rights through the turn-taking distribution system to continue in the pattern already established, i.e. another participant can take over either to amplify or repair what has been said. When no such transfer of speaking rights occurs after *here*, IVee-2 continues. IVee-2 pauses again after *or whatever*, as the IVer issues a continuer (*Mhm*). Note that when IVee-2 *does* continue (*you want to call her* (t)), she is interrupted again by IVee-3, who completes the description of *one woman* as *Delirious* (u). Thus, the multiple turn-constructional units created by intonationally discontinuous "there + BE + ITEM" in (8) is a way by which participants create or replicate participant speaking rights.

Turn-constructional units in "there + BE + ITEM" also allow recognitional work in descriptions. Before illustrating this, however, it will help to look briefly at (15) to see how turn-constructional units can accumulate toward a recognizable description of a location – but only pending receipt of each unit cumulative to that description.

(15) IVEE: (a) Did you ever ride in Grays Ferry Road?
             (b) It runs like past Shunk Avenue?
             (c) On one side is the uh Naval Home.
     IVER: (d) Right.
             (e) There's a wall there.
     IVEE: (f) Big d- high wall?
     IVER: (g) Uh huh.
     IVEE: (h) (It) would come up around the-
     IVER: (i) I think I've even seen that.
     IVEE: (j) Yeh, that's the Naval Home.
     IVER: (k) Yeh.
     IVEE: (l) Well, they-   I think they're talkin' about=
     IVER: (m)   Yeh.
     IVEE: =doin' away with that.

In (15), an IVee is describing what is going to be done with a particular place (*the Naval Home* (c)): *I think they're talkin' about doin' away with that* (l). Prior to that description, recognition of the location of the place is achieved through a series of descriptors (each a separate turn-constructional unit offered by the IVee) that is coupled with a series of receipt markers (from the IVer).

(16) is similar, but here it is the turn-constructional units within an intonationally discontinuous "there + BE + ITEM" construction that build a cumulative description of a location pending a receipt marker.

(16) IVEE: (a)   There's a few pockets in West Philadelphia that are- is white.
             (b)   I think there's still J- there's uh s- a small Jewish section,
             (c)   of around uh S- Springfield Avenue,
             (d)   say,
             (e)   like [Fiftieth and Springfield or=
      IVER: (f)   [You're right.
      IVEE: =something.
                          ᶻThat's right.
      IVER: (g)

The IVee uses "there + BE + ITEM" to present both a general category (a) and a specific category member (b): after introducing *a few pockets in West Philadelphia that are- is white* (a), he specifies a member of the set of "white neighborhoods" (*a small Jewish section* (b)). Although the general category is presented in one turn-constructional unit, presentation of the specific category member is comprised of multiple turn-constructional units. In (b), the two separate qualities ("Jewish," initiated as *J*-, and "small," initiated as *s*-) are linked as *a small Jewish section* prior to a turn-transition point. Note, however, that this turn-transition space is marked with "continuing" intonation. Locational information is provided about *a small Jewish section* in two further turn-constructional units. The first unit offers a description *of around uh S- Springfield Avenue* (c) that also has "continuing" intonation, receives no continuer from the IVer, and then is made tentative with another turn-constructional unit *say* (d). The next description is overlapped by the IVer's recognition markers. Thus, (16) illustrates that "there + BE + ITEM" can be an intonationally discontinuous description when it is "added on to" pending the receipt of recognitional tokens.

Finally, (17) illustrates a multiple turn-constructional use of "there + BE + ITEM" in which a temporal *when* clause is intonationally separated from the "there + BE + ITEM" mention.

(17) IVEE: (a)   This was an Irish neighborhood at one time.
             (b)   Years and years ago.
      IVER: (c)   Right around here, huh?
      IVEE: (d)   Yeh. [This area-
      IVER: (e)   [(   )
      IVEE: (f)   Oh, yeh.
      → (g)   There was Jewish and Irish and Polish up this street, when
             we moved in.
      IVER: (h)   Mhm.
      IVEE: (i)   And then as uh, well, now I'm talking about forty years ago,
             Ada.

IVER: (j) Mhm.

IVEE: (k) And then I'd say in about two or three years, it started getting strictly Italian.

    (l) The neighborhood had changed.

In (17), the IVee has been describing the ethnic composition of her neighborhood (*this was an Irish neighborhood* (a)) in the past (*years and years ago* (b)). She continues that description but shifts to another time period *when we moved in* (g). The "there + BE + ITEM" format describes the ethnic composition of the neighborhood (*There was Jewish and Irish and Polish up this street*) at a point in time that differs from the prior time period mentioned. Thus, the intonationally separated "when" clause is part of a larger description of "who lived here when" (Ford 1993); it need not be seen as part of the ITEM *per se*. (Note that the IVee continues to move through time with her description, shifting next to *in about two or three years* [past the time they moved in] *it started getting strictly Italian* (k).

Thus far, I have shown that "there + BE + ITEM" shows a preference for intonational packaging as one turn-constructional unit. This preference is indicated not just by the frequency of "there + BE + ITEM" constructions occurring under one continuous intonational contour, but by observations about the particular locations of multiple turn-constructional versions of "there + BE + ITEM."

Another way that "there + BE + ITEM" is fit to the turn-taking system of conversation is through its positioning in relation to turns themselves: "there + BE + ITEM" shows a preference for turn-internal position. I show this preference in two kinds of examples. First are examples in which turn-initial "there + BE + ITEM" is a repairable (18, 19, 20). Next are examples in which turn-internal "there + BE + ITEM" is repaired-to from some other first-mention construction (21, 22, 23).

Beginning with (18), we see a turn-initial use of "there + BE + ITEM" that is self-interrupted, such that its completed version ends up in turn-internal position. (18 was discussed earlier as 11.)

(18) IVEE: (a) And this is what the thing is.

        (b) They get in,

        (c) and i- what's it- what's it bein' done for?

    IVER: (d) Yeh.

        (e) That's right.

    IVEE: (f) There- I'll tell you.

  → (g) There's a school down in my mother's town, right?

    IVER: (h) Right.

In (18), the speaker self-interrupts (*There-* (f)) to insert a pre-announcement (*I'll tell you* (f)). She then completes the "there + BE + ITEM" construction in (g) as a recognitional (with *right?*), and goes on to embed an announcement

(cf. a point) in a story about students at the school just first-mentioned by
"there + BE + ITEM." Thus, (18) suggests that a turn-initial "there + BE +
ITEM" construction may be self-interrupted to check on the recognitional
status of an ITEM and/or to allow a suspension of turn-taking rules so as to
secure a turn space long enough for an activity in which next-mentions are
embedded.

Several other examples in which turn-initial "there + BE + ITEM" is self-
interrupted suggest similar reasons for moving this format away from turn-initial
to turn-internal locations. In (19), for example, the speaker's self-interruptions
and intonational breaks (a to c) are geared toward mentioning an ITEM (or
ITEMS) that his interlocutor could recognize (and show recognition of) *before*
he relies upon those mentions for a next-description:

(19) IVEE: (a) Well, there's uh certain sections, where-
           (b) now like in-
           (c) oh, I guess you, y'know,
      → (d) in the newspapers there's a Catholic high school,
           (e) Saint Thomas Moore out there,=
      IVER: (f) Yeh.
      IVEE: (g) =in West Philly.
           (h) And they were sayin' it's the ideal situation.

Note that the ITEM in the "there + BE + ITEM" construction in (a) is *certain
sections*. The ITEM in the next "there + BE + ITEM" construction (d) is *a
Catholic high school* that is named and physically located in a way that is
progressively specified (from *out there* (e) to *in West Philly* (g)). Note, also,
that the location (*West Philly* (g)) of the second-mentioned ITEM (*Saint
Thomas Moore*) is a specification of the first-mentioned ITEM (*certain sections* (a)): in the IVee's continuation of his turn (not included above), this
location becomes the focus of a long description. Thus, again, it looks as if
turn-initial "there + BE + ITEM" does not secure a turn space sufficient for
an extended description.

(20) is similar: what is interesting here is that the movement of "there + BE
+ ITEM" away from turn-initial position is also a movement to a floor that
is free from competing talk.

(20) IVER: (a) Like what, for instance?
           (b) I bet you could tell some really good stories.
      IVEE: (c) Hh I've had a lot happen to me, but-
      IVER: (d) Well, [roll 'em out, cause this is- [this=
      IVEE: (e)   [Well, there's-   [Y'know,=
      IVER: =[is your chance.
      IVEE: (f) =[there's-
      → (g) a couple weeks ago there was just a cab driver was
             shot.

Observe, first, that when reintroducing *there's* from (e) in (f), the IVee replaces *Well* with *Y'know*. This is a switch to a device that is more geared toward getting the floor than responding to a prior utterance (Schiffrin 1987a). More critically, the IVee does not complete – or even restart – the "there + BE + ITEM" mention for the third time (*a couple weeks ago there was just a cab driver was shot* (g)) until competing talk has ended. When the IVee finally does have the floor, the temporal adjunct *a couple weeks ago* precedes the "there + BE + ITEM" construction and the first-mention of *a cab driver*. The preposing of the temporal adjunct is evidence that the IVee has secured a turn (Ford 1993).

In the excerpts thus far, we have said that speakers' repairs *from* turn-initial "there + BE + ITEM" suggest a preference for this construction to be turn-internal. These excerpts also suggest that a reason for this preference is to guarantee a turn long enough for extended descriptive use of the ITEM first-mentioned by "there + BE + ITEM." This guarantee does not seem to be provided by "there + BE + ITEM" itself.

The same preference is shown by a somewhat different set of examples. (21), (22), and (23) show that turn-internal "there + BE + ITEM" can be repaired to form some other turn-initial (but interrupted) construction. These examples also show that even ITEMS that are background to a different topic of talk are turn-internal.

In (21), an IVer has asked an IVee about a childhood rhyme (a). The name of the rhyme becomes a source of extensive discussion.

(21) IVER: (a) Do you remember um a rhyme that went "doggie diamond?"
       IVEE: (b) Yeh. [Yeh.
       IVER: (c)   [Was it a game, or was it a rhyme . . .?
       IVEE: (d) No, that was just a rhyme.
              (e) See, remember- uh we used to call-
      → (f) in them days uh there were men,
              (g) they were kinda half witted people.

The IVee begins with no more than a recognition token (*Yeh* (b)) to the IVer's initial question (*Do you remember um a rhyme that went "doggie, doggie, diamond?"* (a)). Upon repetition of this token, the IVer asks another question (*Was it a game, or was it a rhyme . . .?* (c)) that pursues the topic of the first. The IVee's answer (*No, that was just a rhyme* (d)) does not initially expand the topic. In (e), however, the IVee does begin to expand the topic by invoking recognitional work on the part of the IVer with *See, remember*, and *we used to call*. Both of these beginnings are self-interrupted to a "there + BE + ITEM" construction prefaced by a time adjunct (*in them days uh there were men* (f)). What the IVee introduces with the "there + BE + ITEM" construction (*men, they were kinda half witted people* (f, g)) seems to have little to do with the topic opened by the IVer. Although space prevents me from presenting the entire exchange relevant to the rhyme, the *men* introduced in (f) actually are important because their job was to pick up dog droppings (the dog "diamonds" of the rhyme). Thus, without knowing about these men, the IVee's explanation for the name of the rhyme will make no sense.

The analysis of (21) offered thus far suggests that *See, remember- uh we used to call-* (e) is what Polanyi (1978) calls a true start: it is a repairable designed specifically as something to be repaired from. (I explore the relationship between repairs and "there + BE + ITEM" further during discussion of next-mentions in section 3.4.) Rather than information designed to "stay on the floor" in and of itself, the function of such a start is to gain the floor in order to create a turn space long enough for presentation of another piece of information (i.e. to suspend the relevance of turn-transition spaces for turn exchange). Thus, the true start used by the speaker in (21) can create the same result (turn-internal "there + BE + ITEM") as the repairs from turn-initial "there + BE + ITEM" in (18), (19), and (20).

I present (22) and (23) very briefly just to support the generality of the repair format suggested in (21). In (22), the "there + BE + ITEM" construction is, again, repaired-to.

(22) IVee: (a)   We used to play cowboys and Indians.
      IVer: (b)   Oh, [really?
      IVee: (c)   [I remember that when I was about- I guess I was about four or five.
      IVer: (d)   Geez, that's ( )
      IVee: (e)   [And we used to-
   → (f)   there's a lamppost in the one alley over on Hope Street.
      IVer: (g)   Uh huh.
      IVee: (h)   And we used to pretend we'd make like a little fire there.

In (22), the IVee switched from *And we used to* (e) to *there's a lamppost in the one alley over on Hope Street* (f). The ITEM introduced by the "there + BE + ITEM" construction in turn-internal position serves as the location of different games being described. After receiving recognition of that item (the IVer's *Uh huh* (g)), the IVee returns to her true-start from (e) to expand the description of the game in a way that incorporates the ITEM just introduced: *And we used to pretend we'd make like a little fire there* (h).

In (23), an IVee is comparing the skills required for different kinds of sports.

(23) IVee: (a)   Where hockey you can have-
   → (b)   there- there's- there is a guy he's about five two, and maybe not even that tall.
      IVer: (c)   Yeh.
      IVee: (d)   And he- he was one of the best players for the Montreal Canadians for years.
      IVer: (e)   Huh.
      IVee: (f)   See, now that- that's a sport where you *have* to be good to play.

After saying that basketball is not *a fair sport* (because people who are tall have an unfair advantage), the IVee brings up *hockey* (a). The "there + BE + ITEM" construction is, again, repaired-to turn-internally: *there- there's- there is a guy he's about five two, and maybe not even that tall* (b). The ITEM first-mentioned in that construction is important for the "hockey" part of the comparison between basketball and hockey (d): it provides a concrete example supporting the general value of hockey (f).

To summarize this section: I have shown two ways that "there + BE + ITEM" is fit to the turn-taking system of conversation. First, "there + BE + ITEM" shows a preference for intonational packaging as one turn-constructional unit. We indicated this preference not just by frequency ("there + BE + ITEM" typically occurs under one continuous intonational contour), but also by observations about the particular sequential locations of multiple turn-constructional versions of "there + BE + ITEM." Second, "there + BE + ITEM" shows a preference for turn-internal position. We indicated this preference by showing that turn-initial "there + BE + ITEM" is repaired-from (it is a repairable), and that turn-internal "there + BE + ITEM" is a repaired-to. Both repair formats suggest the same reason for the turn-internal preference: to locate "there + BE + ITEM" in a turn in which current-speaker has already secured the time needed for extended descriptive use of the ITEM first-mentioned by "there + BE + ITEM."

3.3 *"There + BE + ITEM" and topic organization*

In previous sections, we considered "there + BE + ITEM" in relation to first- and next-mentions of an ITEM within adjacency pairs and turns. Conversations, however, may cover more than just one ITEM at a time. Furthermore, even when there are extended discussions of a single ITEM, such discussions might not exhaust the boundaries of the conversation itself, i.e. people talk about more than one ITEM during a single conversation. These observations suggest two additional problems that must be resolved by conversationalists: the organization of talk about multiple ITEMS and the management of transitions between multiple ITEMS.

In this section, we discuss how "there + BE + ITEM" can help to manage these problems. I focus on the role of "there + BE + ITEM" in what Sacks (1972: 15–16) calls stepwise topic transitions:

A general feature for topical organization is movement from topic to topic, not by a topic-close followed by a topic-beginning, but by a stepwise move, which involves linking up whatever is being introduced to what has just been talked about, such that, as far as anybody knows, a new topic has not been started, though we're far from wherever we began.

Stepwise topic transitions may be built in several ways. Although Sacks's description of this movement from topic to topic does not require lexically explicit transitions, it is possible to linguistically mark a stepwise transition, e.g. through repetition (or anaphora) and a metalingual link (as in "Speaking of that reminds me of [topic 2]"). Less explicit transitions can lack clear markers or rely upon inferred category relationships between topics. A discussion of houses [topic 1], for example, can become a discussion of split-level houses [topic 1a]; a discussion of split levels [topic 1a] can become a discussion of bungalows [topic 1b]. Despite the different kinds of topic relationships possible – with or without explicit markers of linkage – all these examples accomplish a transition by mentioning topics without explicitly opening or closing those topics.[7]

Before we consider "there + BE + ITEM" in relation to topic, it is important to make a procedural point. CA assumes a methodological dependency between how analysts pose problems and how they discover solutions. The past sections have been considering "managerial" problems of talk to which people must attend and the way the sequential location of a specific construction in conversational structure offers solutions to those problems. Although a particular conversation analysis can begin with consideration of a single problem, analysis of what a device seems to offer a "solution for" can also reveal other problems of talk to which people attend – simply because what serves as a solution for one problem of talk may be applicable to another problem as well. Although we are introducing in this section a new problem (talking about different topics) with what seems to be a new solution (stepwise topic transitions), our analysis of "there + BE + ITEM" in relation to this problem and solution can build upon what we have already learned. We saw earlier that "there + BE + ITEM" could be sequentially implicative in two directions: it could respond to prior talk and create contingencies for further talk. Stepwise topic transitions are themselves a means of sequential organization that works both retrospectively and prospectively: they link up whatever is being introduced to what has just been talked about (Sacks 1972: 15–16). Thus, we might expect "there + BE + ITEM" to allow stepwise topic transitions – simply because both build upon the same type of sequential implicativeness.

We start with (24), an example in which topic 1 ("relief") is explicitly provided prior to topic 1a ("soup houses"), and topic 1a-x ("a place up on Francis Avenue"). Topics 1 and 1a-x both enter talk through "there + BE + ITEM."

(24) → (a)   I mean, in them days there was no such thing as rel- as relief.
      (b)   You had to make a livin', y'know.
      (c)   And they had free soup houses.
  → (d)   There's a place up on Francis Avenue here, oh about three miles up.
      (e)   That's still in existence yet.
      (f)   They se- they go in there and they make- give you soup, for free.

The speaker begins with a "there + BE + ITEM" construction that notes the non-existence of "relief" (topic 1). After stating an alternative to "relief" ((b) *You had to make a livin', y'know*), he states that one type of assistance was "free soup houses": *And they had free soup houses* (c). Although "free soup houses" (topic 1a) is a set member of the larger category "relief" (topic 1), it is also a category that can itself be further specified. This is precisely what happens in (d) through (f): the speaker first-mentions a specific soup house (topic 1a-x) with the "there + BE + ITEM" format (d), and then provides two properties of that soup house (e, f). Thus, "there + BE + ITEM" introduces topic 1 ("relief") and helps shift from topic 1a ("soup houses") to the more specific topic 1a-x ("a place up on Francis Avenue here").

Although space prevents us from discussing the next example in full, (25) illustrates the role of "there + BE + ITEM" in handling complex topic connections among more than one ITEM at once.

(25) IVER: (a) Yeh. Well, like did you have a team when you were goin'
                  to school or a little league, or-
      IVEE: (b) Oh yeh. [We used to- yeh, I play- I was on an=
      IVER: (c)   [Really?
      IVEE: (d) =organized- I was five years old when I was on my first
                  organized baseball team.
             (e) I was six years old when I was on my first organized
                  *foot*ball team.
             (f) And I was seven years old when I first got in my soccer league.

After beginning to answer the IVer's question (*Well, like did you have a team when you were goin' to school or a little league, or-*) with several repairables (b, d), the IVee instead expands his answer with a list organized around two topics. Topic 1 is "age": the list is organized chronologically (*I was five* (d)/ *six* (e)/ *seven* (f) *years old when . . .*). Topic 2 is "sport": the list is comprised of the teams on which the IVee played different sports ("baseball" (d), "football" (e), "soccer" (f)). Note that these two topics are related: the general category of "age" provides a time frame within which each sport/organized team is introduced (i.e. "I was YEARS OLD when SPORT").

In (g), the speaker typifies himself (*I was the type of kid that . . .*) by bringing together topics 1 and 2 ("age" and "sport") and linking them with a new one that exemplifies the *type of kid* he was. It is here that we find "there + BE + ITEM."

(g) I was- I was the type of kid that when I turned seven years old, there
     was not a day in the week I wasn't playing some kinda sport on some
     kinda team.

In (g), topic 1, "age" (*when I turned seven years old*), and topic 2, "sport" (*playin' some kinda sport on some kinda team*), continue. What is added by

"there + BE + ITEM" is topic 3, "day": *there was not a day in the week.* . . .
Thus, the "there + BE + ITEM" format in (g) provides a first-mention of a
new topic ("day in the week") that is linked to the prior topics of "age" and
"sport." It is in this sense that it makes explicit a stepwise topic transition:
from topic 1, "age," and topic 2, "sport" (d, e, f), to topic 3, "day" (g). The
IVee then continues the list exactly as projected by the "there + BE + ITEM"
format: he describes further subtopics of both topic 2 ("sport") and topic 3
("day") within a subtopic of topic 1 ("age", *seven years old*):

(h)   I used to play football on Sundays,
(i)   Saturdays was my soccer night,
(j)   I used to play Mondays and Wednesdays was my basketball,
(k)   eh: it was Tuesdays and- what is it.
(l)   Mondays and Thursdays was basketball

Thus, schematically, the list is continued exactly as projected by the "there
+ BE + ITEM" format:

Topic 1 "age"
Topic 1a "seven years old"
  Topic 2 "sport"   Topic 3 "day"
  Topic 2a football   Topic 3a Sundays
  Topic 2b soccer   Topic 3b Saturdays
  Topic 2c basketball   Topic 3c Mondays, Thursdays

Following an insertion sequence (not discussed here), the IVee closes his list
as follows:

(t)   I used to always, I- I was playin' sports every day.

The list thus concludes with the topics that had previously been jointly
presented in the "there + BE + ITEM" construction (g) and expanded in the
list.

We have discussed (25) in some detail to show that "there + BE + ITEM"
can contribute to the management of several ITEMS at once. In (25),
the speaker linked the prior topics of "age" (*turned seven*) and "sports"
(*some kinda sport on some kinda team*) with a new topic "day in the week."
Thus, "there + BE + ITEM" linked ITEMS from prior talk (i.e. treating them
as next mentions) with an ITEM important to upcoming talk (i.e. a first-
mention).

In sum, our discussion of "there + BE + ITEM" in the management of topic
has shown that this construction can help organize larger sequential transitions between different ITEMS that serve as topics in talk. Our discussion has
also illustrated the CA dependency between the posing of problems and the
discovery of solutions. Although we introduced a new problem (talking about

different topics) and what seemed to be a new solution (stepwise topic transitions), we also noted that the use of "there + BE + ITEM" with topics might be able to build upon the fact that "there + BE + ITEM" could be sequentially implicative both retrospectively and prospectively. Since stepwise topic transitions build upon the same type of sequential implicativeness, it is not surprising that "there + BE + ITEM" allows stepwise topic transitions. Thus, although a particular conversation analysis can begin with consideration of a single problem, analysis of the way a device offers a solution can also tell us something about other problems of talk to which people attend.

3.4 *"There + BE + ITEM" and the organization of mentions*

We have seen thus far that "there + BE + ITEM" constructions address two problems of conversational management: the organization of mentions (first-mention, next-mention) of an item and the organization of topic. First- and next-mentions are related to two other mechanisms of conversational organization, adjacency pairs and turn-taking. Although our focus on adjacency pairs and turn-taking highlighted the CA view of conversational structure and the integration of a device into specific structures, it is also important to note that "there + BE + ITEM" can organize first and next-mentions *independently* of the adjacency pair organization. On a procedural note, we will again see how the solutions provided by "there + BE + ITEM" can be applied to slightly different problems of conversational management.

I begin with examples showing that "there + BE + ITEM" can provide first-mentions (outside of the adjacency pair structure) that project a variety of next-mentions and do some of the same recognitional work as was accomplished in embedded question/answer pairs. These examples also illustrate the referring sequences familiar to us from chapter 6: first-mention is indefinite and explicit, next-mention is definite and inexplicit.

Let us begin with (26). The IVer has asked about gangs, and the IVee begins her answer by mentioning her girlfriends (a).

(26) IVEE: (a) We did have uh three or four or five girl friends, but uh like that . . .

           (b) Like I say, we had, a radio.

    IVER: (c) Yeh.

    IVEE: (d) So we danced at home, and different girls' houses if we didn't have: any place to go.

           (e) You'd uh:, go maybe one girlfriend's house an' you'd dance: in the parlor, or so like that.

  → (f) Or else if uh if there's a couple boys in the neighborhood that you *did* talk to,

           (g) you bring them in.

After describing activities with her girlfriends, the IVee offers an alternative activity in (f). This alternative (*you bring them* [boys] *in*) hinges on the existence of *a couple boys in the neighborhood that you* did *talk to* (f) – the ITEM first mentioned in the "there + BE + ITEM" format. Note the lengthy description in the first-mention of the ITEM: a syntactically complex description that crosses a syntactically, but not intonationally marked, turn-transition space (after *neighborhood* in (f), section 3.2). The term used in the next-mention is truncated: *them* (g).

(27) is similar to (26) in that the ITEM first mentioned in the "there + BE + ITEM" format receives an immediate next-mention. It differs, however, because it is a short ITEM (*a ferry run*), and because it is issued as part of a self-repair.

(27)   IVEE: (a)   So uh they liked to go away for them- that two days, y'know,
                 (b)   and that-=
         IVER: (c)   Yeh.
→ IVEE: (d)   =and then there used to be a ferry run and that-
                 (e)   just for uh twenty cents it would take you all the way down to what they call Billingsport.
         IVER: (f)   Twenty cents, (yeh).

In (a), the IVee is describing how people used to go away for summer weekends. *And that* in (b) is self-interrupted and replaced by *then there + BE* and the ITEM *a ferry run* (d). Although the IVee reissues *and that* after "there + BE + ITEM," *and that* is self-interrupted yet again and followed by a description of where *it* (a truncated mention of "the ferry run") will *take you* (e).

Note that it is difficult to say whether *that* (b) is a first-mention of "ferry run" that is repaired to a more typical indefinite, explicit first-mention (*a ferry run*). If this is the case, then it looks as if "there + BE + ITEM" can do remedial work in the organization of referring sequences by providing a slot for a first-mention that will allow a recipient to achieve recognition of the ITEM. Next-mention *it* (c) can then be definite and inexplicit.

(28) illustrates that a first-mention in a "there + BE + ITEM" format need not be lexically explicit to project a truncated next-mention. It also suggests that "there + BE + ITEM" can be used to accomplish recognitional work similar to that achieved in a presequence or insertion sequence (3.1.2). In (28), the speaker is describing the time he almost fell off a roof.

(28)   (a)   And the ladder gave way.
        (b)   And it was a slanty roof.
        (c)   And I'm rollin' and rollin'
        (d)   and somehow or other I- I managed to grab the edge of the roof
        (e)   and there happened to be-
        (f)   it was a good pla- it was-

→ (g) there- there was a what' cha call them in there, y'know?
   (h) And I could hold onto it.

Like the "there + BE + ITEM" mention in (27), the first-mention in (28) also
follows self-interruptions – here, interruptions that display difficulty in finding
a description of the item on *the edge of the roof* (d) that the speaker grabbed.
The first-mention (in g) ends up being formulated as a non-specific item (*a
what' cha call them in there*) that seeks recognition with *y'know?* and thus
accomplishes some of the same recognitional work that "there + BE + ITEM"
did with pre-sequences. Use of the "there + BE + ITEM" format with *a what'
cha call them in there* and *y'know* resolves the descriptive difficulty, such that
the speaker then returns to his narration of how he saved himself from falling
off the roof with a truncated reference to what saved him: *I could hold onto
it* (h).

   (29) also suggests that "there + BE + ITEM" first-mentions can do recognitional work, and that such work can be tailored to a recipient's informational
need.

(29) IVEE-1: (a) Yeh, I think I'm goin' down- downtown tonight and see
                      the-
   → (b) y'know, the- the- there is such a team in Philadelphia as
                      the Flyers.
      IVEE-2: (c) How're you gonna get in, [Butch?=
      IVER: (d)   [I've heard of the Flyers.
      IVEE-2: (e) =That's gonna cost you ninety dollars a seat.
      IVEE-1: (f) No, I'm gonna- they- they have the cable downtown,
                      down in South Philly.

In (a), IVee-1 announces his plans for *tonight*, but self-interrupts with a
recognitional (*y'know*) and a "there + BE + ITEM" first-mention of *such a
team in Philadelphia as the Flyers* (b). This first-mention is not intended to
help IVee-2 identify who is being spoken about. Not only are the two IVee's
close friends (who know one another to be familiar with the Flyers), but
IVee-2's response (he questions the feasibility of the plans (c, e)) makes
clear that he knows who the Flyers are. Rather, the "there + BE + ITEM"
first-mention is intended for the IVer. The IVer's receipt of the information
(*I've heard of the Flyers* (d)) acknowledges the ITEM not as new knowledge *per se*, but as knowledge that can now be used in the course of understanding IVee-1's announcement about his plans. Thus, "there + BE + ITEM"
is a way not only of identifying the ITEM as a first-mention, but also of
making the subsequent use of an ITEM (in a later description, not included
here) recognizable to someone who cannot be presumed to be part of the
category of person who would typically know the ITEM. The "there + BE +
ITEM" format does both these tasks by providing a spot for first-mention of
an ITEM.

So far we have seen that "there + BE + ITEM" can produce first-mentions outside of the adjacency pair structure. Such mentions vary in length, specificity, and detail; in the terms used in chapter 6, they are indefinite and explicit. The next-mentions projected are relatively truncated; in the terms of chapter 6, they are definite and inexplicit. We have also been suggesting that the first-mentions presented through "there + BE + ITEM" can help a specific recipient achieve recognition of an ITEM.

"There + BE + ITEM" can also provide for next-mentions outside of the adjacency pair structure. Like the first-mentions just discussed, these mentions seem to do repair work for an ITEM whose recognition is potentially troublesome to a recipient. In (30), for example, the IVer has asked if the IVee knows what a Father, Son, and Holy Ghost house is. The IVee's answer begins in (a).

(30) IVEE: (a)   That's three- has three rooms on top of one
                 another. Right?
      IVER: (b)   ᶻhhhh ᶻYou're right! That's the sign of an old
                 Philadelphian, somebody [who=
      IVEE: (c)   [Yeh.
      IVER: (d)   =knows what one of [those are.
      IVEE: (e)   [I like- I was in one.
      IVER: (f)   You were?
      IVEE: (g)   Yeh.
      IVER: (h)   Where?
      IVEE: (i)   A girlfriend of mine, downtown somewhere.
            (j)   She m- uh got married and she moved into one.
            (k)   One room here and then it's one room on the second floor
                  and one room on the top.
      IVER: (l)   Yeh, that's right.
      IVEE: (m)   So she used her downstairs as her parlor.
      IVER: (n)   Uh huh.
      IVEE: (o)   Her second-
      → (p)   there's only three rooms [like] y'know.
      IVER: (q)   [Yeh.
      IVEE: (r)   The second story of the room was her bedroom and the
                  third room was her bedroom.
      IVER: (s)   Where did she cook? Where did she cook?

The initial definition of a Father, Son, and Holy Ghost house is in (a): *That's three- has three rooms on top of one another*. The IVee then identifies the three rooms (k): each mention of a room is a member of the set "three rooms." She then begins to describe what each room is used for (*So she used her downstairs as her parlor* (m)) but self-interrupts the description of the second room (in o) to repeat the general category *there's only three rooms* (p) in a recognition seeking format (*like y'know*) prior to the description of the second and third stories/rooms (r).[8]

Before going on to the next use of "there + BE + ITEM" (for only-mentions), it is important to note that some of the "there + BE + ITEM" examples already discussed suggest that "there + BE + ITEM" can do remedial work in the organization of referring sequences. I repeat the relevant examples. In one group of examples, a speaker initiates a first-mention, which is then repaired-to as an ITEM in "there + BE + ITEM." (As noted earlier, we cannot be sure of the referential status of *that* in line (b) in (27) – such that *a ferry run* may be a first or next-mention.)

(6) (e) but uh they used to squash it down pretty good y'know.
     (f) There'd always be somebody there that would watch for trouble
(27) (b) and that-
     (d) and then there used to be a ferry run and that- just for uh twenty cents it would take you all the way down to what they call Billingsport.
(29) (a) Yeh, I think I'm goin' down- downtown tonight and see the-
     (b) y'know, the- the- there is such a team in Philadelphia as the Flyers.
(30) (o) Her second-
     (p) there's only three rooms like y'know.
     (q) The second story of the room was her bedroom and the third room was her bedroom.

(6), (29), and (30) are examples in which "there + BE + ITEM" provides a next-mention (a repaired-to) for a prior mention (a repaired-from). (Recall our uncertainty about 27.) The first-mention in each case is definite (*the-* (29a), *her second* (30o)) and possibly inexplicit as well (*they* (6), *that* (27)). The ITEMS in "there + BE + ITEM" that are repaired to are all indefinite and explicit.

In the second type of example, the speaker self-interrupts before first mention of an item in a "there + BE + ITEM" format:

(22) (e) And we used to-
     (f) there's a lamppost in the one alley over on Hope Street.
     (h) And we used to pretend we'd make like a little fire there.

In (22), the speaker repeats and completes the self-interrupted *And we used to* from (e) in (h), after using "there + BE + ITEM" to first-mention *a lamppost in the one alley over on Hope Street* (f). This continuation *after* "there + BE + ITEM" suggests a need to have provided information that would allow hearer recognition of the location of *there* (i.e. the location of the game in (h)). The use of "there + BE + ITEM," then, seems to provide a slot in which to mention an ITEM in a way that is recipient designed for recognition of that ITEM.

The remedial use of "there + BE + ITEM" just suggested helps make sense out of its use for only-mentions, i.e. when a speaker uses "there + BE + ITEM" to mention an ITEM just once. As we see, an only-mention can be inserted into a sequence in a backgrounded capacity: "backgrounding" might be seen as a way that a speaker anticipates a hearer's lack of recognition or familiarity with an ITEM, i.e. a type of pre-emptive repair.

In (31), for example, "there + BE" introduces an ITEM during a list. The ITEM, however, is not in and of itself a category member in the list (see chapter 8). A speaker is describing how her mother was *a very good neighbor*. After listing five activities engaged in by her mother, the speaker lists a sixth.

(31) (a) And if there was sickness in any of the homes
     (b) she was always there ready to help.
     (c) She was a very good neighbor,
     (d) everybody loved her, really did, I mean that.

The activity *she was always there ready to help* (b) continues the list of the mother's typical activities. The "there + BE + ITEM" presented prior to that activity provides a background condition motivating that particular activity: it is the presence of *sickness in any of the homes* (a) that motivates the mother's *help*. Because familiarity with or recognition of this background condition cannot be presumed, we might say that introducing it prior to continuation of the list pre-empts a need for later repair. Once the mention of "sickness" has served this function, "sickness" is not mentioned again; rather, the speaker closes the list with a repetition of what each listed activity established, i.e. *she was a very good neighbor* (c).

(32) shows that "there + BE + ITEM" can be used to insert background ITEMS in lists of events that are interpreted as having occurred successively in time. In (32), the speaker is describing her mother's activities during a wake for a deceased relative and uses "there + BE + ITEM" to mention an item relevant to those events.

(32) (a)   When he died, my mother had all the clay pipes: and the tobacco,
     (b)   and she bought all different brands of cigarettes,
     (c)   and you laid them around.
     (d)   So as: your friends came in,
   → (e)   there was someone to take them upstairs and give them a shot.
     (f)   And then they'd go downstairs
     (g)   and then they'd s-
     (h)   y'know, each person come in would get a shot of whiskey.

The events in (32) are a list of activities comprising "a wake": they are presented as "one-after-another" events in "a story." Interspersed with the story events are several background conditions (*when he died* (a), *as: your friends came in* (d)) that provide a temporal framework for the events. The "there + BE + ITEM" format also provides a background condition for an event – not a temporal condition, of course, but an existential condition: a person (*someone to take them upstairs*) is present to facilitate a next activity ("have a drink") in the wake by giving participants *a shot* (of whiskey). The speaker continues to another event (which itself follows a return to *downstairs* (f)), but self-interrupts to restate the general circumstance from (e) as an event *per se* without explicit mention of the "someone" who would facilitate it: *y'know, each person come in would get a shot of whiskey* (h).

(31) and (32) suggested that "there + BE + ITEM" can insert only-mentions into lists of events in which the only-mentioned ITEM serves in a background capacity. (33) is an example in which an only-mentioned ITEM provides background for an important event. The speaker is telling about a childhood fight.

(33)　(a)　So the next thing I know I'm standing out front
　　　(b)　and she comes up
　　　(c)　and she happened to say something very foul about my mother
　　　(d)　and that just drew the line.
　　　(e)　With that I went up the playground
　　　(f)　and all the neighbors-
　　　(g)　I had a viewer-
→　(h)　uh like y'know there was so many people up there like you might've thought Cassius Clay was fighting or somebody, y'know.
　　　(i)　And uh, my Aunt Betty came up and got me.

The story events are in (a) through (e). Following these events, the speaker offers three possible descriptions of an audience to the fight. First is *all the neighbors* (f). This is self-repaired to *I had a viewer* (g), which, in turn, is reformulated not only in a recognition seeking format ("like y'know X, y'know"), but in a "there + BE + ITEM" format to *like y'know there was so many people up there like you might've thought Cassius Clay was fighting or somebody, y'know* (h). Despite the length and complexity of this ITEM, it is not used again in the story: rather, the speaker returns to the events themselves to continue the story.

In sum, "there + BE + ITEM" can be used in a variety of ways that are independent of the adjacency pair structure (3.1.1). This construction can introduce first-mentions that project a truncated next-mention. It can also be used for next-mentions and only-mentions of an ITEM. When used for next-mentions, "there + BE + ITEM" may serve as a recipient designed repair. When used for only-mentions that are backgrounded to other talk, "there + BE + ITEM" may pre-empt the need for repair.

3.5 Summary: "there + BE + ITEM"

Our sample analysis has examined how "there + BE + ITEM" fits into two conversational systems, adjacency pairs (3.1) and turn-taking (3.2). We have also examined the role of this construction in topic management and in the organization of mention pairs (i.e. referring sequences) outside of adjacency pairs. Thus, we have ended up considering several different facets of conversation together: referring sequences, question/answer pairs, turn-taking, and topics. That the analysis of "there + BE + ITEM" led us to consider these different tasks suggests not just something about the construction itself (i.e. one construction can serve different tasks), but more generally about conversational management: conversationalists need to manage multiple problems simultaneously.

That one construction can fit the resolution of simultaneous tasks also suggests that these tasks themselves might be related to one another, having more in common than is sometimes thought. Take, for example, the recognitional work achieved by the turn construction of "there + BE + ITEM." We saw that "there + BE + ITEM" is packaged as a single turn-constructional unit as a way of leading a recipient toward recognition of an ITEM. We also saw, however, that "there + BE + ITEM" is a multiple turn-constructional unit when used in repeated attempts to accomplish recognition of an ITEM. The location of "there + BE + ITEM" in an insertion pair is also geared toward hearer recognition. This suggests that the task of helping a hearer identify a referent has a systematic bearing on how turns are constituted and exchanged and on how (and when) adjacency pairs are embedded in ongoing talk. Thus, by explicating the distribution of a construction in conversation, we have gained insight not only into how that construction contributes to the sequential progression of talk, but also into how different tasks, and different systems, are related to one another.

We can also consider what a CA analysis of "there + BE + ITEM" contributes to our understanding of referring sequences. Although referring sequences in general are not pairs that are as tightly organized as adjacency pairs, we have seen that "there + BE + ITEM" does project a next "slot" in several ways: the form and content of an answer can reflect the prior "there + BE + ITEM" construction in the question; a next-mention can be truncated (definite and inexplicit) in the second parts of adjacency pairs or in post-pair talk to an embedded adjacency pair. We have also seen that a next-mention through "there + BE + ITEM" may serve a remedial purpose, or that a first-mention may pre-empt the need for remedy.

As noted above, however, referring sequences are not pairs that are as tightly organized as adjacency pairs. Referring sequences are often produced by one person, thus violating the two party requirement. Furthermore, a speaker may very well refer just once to an entity, with no "noticeable gap" produced upon the absence of a second mention. Also distinguishing referring sequences from adjacency pairs is that the constraint to continue a referring sequence can vary depending upon the format of the first-mention. *Y'know X?*, for example, allows a first-mention of X that seems to unconditionally project a second mention of X (cf. discussion of information checks in chapter 5, pp. 169–73). Thus, in (34), it would be surprising if the item brought into discourse by *y'know* was not subsequently used in the discourse:

(34) ZELDA: (a) Y'know, that eh orthopedic doctor?
              (b) Y'know that took care of Henry when he had his back?
              (c) Problems?

Although not included in (34), Zelda goes on to use the referent "that ortho-pedic doctor that took care of Henry when he had his back problems" in a short narrative. Thus, as I noted above, the *y'know X?* format carries with it an expectation that X will be mentioned again and will be used in some way in the discourse. (See Schiffrin (1987a: 285) for a description of this exchange structure. Schiffrin (1987a: 267–89) also discusses how the *y'know X?* format involves the hearer in the interactive recognition of an entity.) In contrast to the way *y'know X?* projects a second mention, other ways of mentioning an entity may very well be heard as an only mention. (35) illustrates *the X* as an only mention.

(35) And I happened to look and there the blood was comin' out of the horse's leg, y'know, and then, the foot.

In (35) – which is a climactic moment in a story about the cavalry – there are three items that are mentioned once and only once: "the blood," "the horse's leg," and "the [horse's] foot."

In sum, what a CA approach contributes to our knowledge of referring sequences is the following. Referring is an interactive process that is inter-meshed with other structures of talk: first- and next-mentions are located relative to adjacency pair structure and turn-taking constraints. Linguistic constructions are used in ways that allow a recipient to recognize an item (i.e. a referent) at the same time that other conversational tasks are being pursued and accomplished. Finally, referring terms are sequentially implicative, but in a looser sense than adjacency pairs.

4 Conversation analysis as an approach to discourse

We have seen in this chapter that a CA approach to discourse considers the way participants in a conversation construct systematic solutions to recurrent organizational problems of talk. It discovers such solutions through the close analysis of the sequential progression of talk. By focusing on the way "there + BE + ITEM" allows first-mentions, next-mentions, and only-mentions – in relation to adjacency pairs, turn-taking, and topic management – we have seen not only how attention to the sequential progression of talk can reveal the distribution and interactional functions of a conversational phenomenon (both within and across turns), but also how such attention can suggest interdependent relationships among tasks (functions) and among solutions (systems). Thus, although I began with a single construction in relation to a single problem (i.e. referring), the way the problem seemed to be solved by the construction led to discussion of other problems and other systems of talk.

It is in this sense that the order in which I presented examples of "there + BE + ITEM" was actually more important – in a methodological sense – than it might have seemed. I presented each example (and set of examples) as both a response to and a prompt for another example (and set of examples): different ways of presenting examples might have suggested a different mode of organization in the data. Far from seeking to impose an external "outsider's" organization on the data, however, I would argue that this attention to order in the data was actually quite the opposite: an attempt to arrange instances of talk in a way that would reveal the "natural" and "correct" arrangement of items in the sequential and distributional (cf. syntagmatic and paradigmatic) patterns with which speakers themselves work. Put another way, my sequential presentation of data in this chapter tried to mirror the way conversational phenomena (items, constructions) are themselves patterned *for speakers*. This is yet another reflection of the use of talk as a resource for the discovery and definition of particular problems and their solutions ("rules," "systems," "connections among systems," "functions") from the participants' point of view.

Consider, also, that traditional terms of linguistic analysis played almost no role in my sample analysis. As noted initially, "there + BE + ITEM" has been considered quite widely by linguists as existential *there*, i.e. the use of *there* with a copula predicates existence of a referent (often an indefinite NP). (See Erdmann (1976) for an extensive review and Hannay (1985) for an analysis in functional grammar.) Despite the lack of attention to grammar, CA analyses of discourse can have an important bearing on our understanding of grammar (e.g. Ford 1993; Ford and Thompson 1992; Fox 1987; Goodwin 1979; Schegloff 1979a). Existential *there* sentences are right branching constructions that can focus a great deal of information (recall the length and syntactic complexity of some of the ITEMS) at the end of the sentence. This might be said to serve particular communicative problems very similar to those addressed in our account. Put another way, we might say that the syntactic qualities of existential *there* sentences arise from the problem (discussed in our analysis) of trying to get another to achieve recognition of a first-mention. The interactional packaging of existential *there* sentences as multiple turn-constructional units (with each unit adding another syntactic constituent) might be motivated by the need to achieve recognition of an ITEM in a way that provides its own opportunity for the confirmation of intersubjectivity at each syntactic (also, each informational and possibly intonational) juncture (cf. Schegloff 1992).

I also noted initially that, consistent with the CA approach, I referred to "there + BE + ITEM" in a way that presumed very little about linguistic structure. Before we close this chapter, it will be helpful to compare three different types of "there" that CA would not differentiate: demonstrative, adverbial, and pronominal (see also Freeze 1992). By so doing, we will be able to assess the strengths and weaknesses of the CA practice of ignoring language structure.

(36) illustrates demonstrative *there*. The IVee had been talking about his time in the cavalry (a, b), and had interrupted himself to greet some acquaintances who passed by (c). In (d), he identifies the acquaintances who he has just greeted with a *there* construction. (36 was 2a.)

(36) IVEE: (a)   And uh, but, you couldn't do nothin'.
             (b)   See, what happened when that cavalry was there-
             (c)   Hello there.
             (d)   There's the old ladies from the home.=
     IVER: (e)   [I figured this.
     IVEE: (f)   [=All these women who we've talked to?
     IVER: (g)   Yeh.
     IVEE: (h)   They all know me because I- I do errands for them.
             (i)   Those that can't get out, y'know?

There in (36) is a demonstrative that has a *deictic* function: the referent to which it points ("the old ladies from the home") is situationally present and *there* locates it at a relative distance from the egocentric locus of the speech event (i.e. the speaker himself). More generally, *there* is a spatial deictic that occupies the distal end of a proximal–distal axis: *there* contrasts with *here* to indicate distance from the speaker's current location (e.g. "I worked there" would indicate that "there" is not the speaker's current location). Notice that demonstrative *there* in (36) introduces a first-mention as a definite explicit noun phrase (*the old ladies from the home* (d)); next-mentions are pronominal (*they* (h), *those* (i)). Notice also that the IVee "points" to a situationally present referent *after* he has already greeted them (*Hello there* (c)) – after they have become salient in the interaction. As we also noted, the IVee continues to identify these referents for the IVer. This sequential location is similar to that already seen for existential *there* sentences (e.g. in 3.4).

Adverbial *there* in (37) also has a locational meaning. (Because *there* does not physically situate the referent in the immediate here and now, however, uses such as this are not typically seen as deictic.) Here is the fuller context: (37) is from a story in which the speaker (an adult) is telling about how his brother (as a child) had discovered some treats that his mother had hidden from the children. (37 was example 2b.)

(37) (a)   So, my mother went out,
     (b)   and my brother says, "I gotta search around here."
     (c)   So he went upstairs in the bedroom
     (d)   and there he found them hid.

 (e) You know, she had hid them.
→ (f) And there was him- there was him- my brother and the dog, Prince.
 (g) They got on the bed and he was goin' to the dog, "One for me and one for you."

The brother's search for the treats begins in (c) as he travels *upstairs in the bedroom*; this location is marked by an adverbial *there* in (d). *There* in (f) – the case of interest – is also a marker of location, indicating where (in the bedroom) the brother discovered his other brother and the dog. Thus, both cases of *there* in (37) are *locational adverbs*: they convey the location of a situation, i.e. an action ("he found them" in (d)) and a state ("my brother and the dog were at X" in (f)). Notice, again, that although the first-mentions in (f) are definite noun phrases (*him, my brother, the dog, Prince*), the next mentions are less explicit (*they*). And again, there is a repair from a less explicit *him* to a more explicit *my brother* within the *there* sentence itself.

 (38) illustrates the case of "there + BE" that has been said to differ most dramatically from those with the locational meaning. In (38), the speaker is telling a story that reports on the behavior of some neighborhood boys. The general point of the story is to complain about the parents of those boys – since the parents are nowhere to be found during the disturbing incident being reported. (38 was example 2c.)

(38) (a) They wouldn't take-
  (b) They got one little boy over there-
  (c) now these are boys about fourteen, thirteen, fourteen.
→ (d) There's a little boy down here
  (e) I'd say he's eight, not no more.
  (f) I seen 'em cornering him over there about four of them.
  (g) On the lady's: step in the corner.
  (h) He was cryin'
  (i) and they were spittin' on him.

The basic idea underlying the type of "there" in (37d) is that it is not a locative: the construction "there + BE + [indef] NP" asserts the *existence*, rather than the location, of an entity. (Important – but not absolutely critical – to the identification of this type of "there" is that the NP is an indefinite noun phrase (see discussion of definiteness and indefiniteness in chapter 6, pp. 198–9; cf. Abbott 1993; Rando and Napoli 1978; Ward and Birner 1993; Ziv 1982). It is this case of "there" that has been called not just existential, but expletive (Fillmore 1968), pronominal (Erdmann 1976), and presentative (Hannay 1985).

 Since "there" can be used in a sentence that asserts existence of an entity (in particular, as an indefinite NP), it is often suggested that "there + BE + [indef] NP" is a very useful way to introduce a referent into discourse. That is, because "there + BE + [indef] NP" predicates very little about an entity other than its existence, it is an efficient way to provide information about something about which hearers cannot be assumed to have prior knowledge (cf. the definition of indefinites) in a separate chunk of talk (idea or tone unit: Chafe 1992) without also forcing hearers to immediately make use of that entity in a more elaborated way (e.g. as someone doing something). Furthermore, by placing a weak predicate ("be") prior to what is often a long and highly informative noun phrase, "there + BE + [indef] NP" creates a word order in which last position is reserved for what Firbas (1964) calls the rheme, i.e. new information with the highest degree of communicative dynamism.

Returning to our example in (37d), we can see that this is exactly what happens here: a new entity ("a little boy down here") is introduced, to which subsequent reference is then brief, inexplicit, and definite (a pronoun in e, f, h, and i). Note, also, that the referent is introduced with a lengthy predicate (*a little boy down here*) followed by a brief independent clause (*I'd say he's eight, not no more*) that further modifies the description (he is not just *little* but *eight, not no more*); it is also a repair of an earlier introduction in (b) *They got one little boy over there-*.

I have discussed here uses of "there" that are demonstrative (deictic, 36), adverbial (37), and pronominal (38). The demonstrative and adverbial uses are typically said to occur in locative sentences, the pronominal *there* in existential sentences. Although it seems relatively easy to differentiate the uses just noted, there are some cases that are less clearcut. (39) illustrates.

(39) IVer: (a) What- what would it be mostly around here?
       IVee: (b) Oh, combination Irish:,
               (c) Irish and there-
       → (d) and then there's the Jewish section, too.
               (e) There's no Jewish people right in this area, either.
               (f) I guess it's just Irish, Polish,
                     all the leftovers, from Italian and Jewish.

After having been asked *what it would be around here* (i.e. what ethnic groups would live here) in (a), the IVee lists Irish (b), Jewish (d), and Polish (f). In (38d), "there" in *and then there's the Jewish section, too* seems to be existential despite the definite NP, simply because the existence of a new entity is being predicated. In other ways, however, "there" seems to have a locational meaning and thus to be adverbial: although the IVer asked about *around here*, the speaker is listing sections in the physical space designated by "around here," and could be seen as travelling (on an imaginary tour) through her neighborhood. (Note, also, that the "there" construction in (e) denies the existence of a Jewish section right in *this area*: this might be seen as a "weak locative.") In still another way, the "there" construction in (d) can be said to be locative in a kind of metaphorical way in a discourse world, i.e. to locate an item *as an item* being enumerated as part of a list comprised of a set of such items (cf. Bolinger 1977; Lakoff 1987: 462–582). This is also suggested by the addition of *then* as a list marker (chapter 8), i.e. the self-repair from *there* (c) to *and then there* (d).

Although CA would not compare different uses of *there*, I have done so to suggest some of the strengths and weaknesses of the CA practice of ignoring language structure. One weakness is that syntactic and semantic differences such as those suggested here are ignored by calling all cases of "there + BE" the same construction. Recognizing the existence of different cases of *there*, however, actually gives us more of an appreciation for how the different uses seem to crosscut one another (i.e. 39). This might then be said to challenge syntactic and semantic classifications that assume mutually exclusive structures and functions. My discussion has hinted at an underlying shared function of these constructions in talk with a similar consequence for next-mentions. Not only did each use of a *there* construction allow a truncated next-mention, but each use located an entity (in some way) and did so in a sequence that required recognitional (and some remedial) work on the part of the hearer. A CA analysis that examines all *there* constructions, but also classifies them according to conventional syntactic and semantic categories, might be able to best explicate the functional basis of the structural categories.

Just as traditional linguistic analyses not explicitly mentioned by CA can actually be related quite nicely to the results of CA analyses, so, too, we find that terms and concepts not explicitly mentioned can be said to underline such analyses and to be part of the implicit assumptions and procedures of CA. Although I discuss these terms and concepts in chapters 9, 10, and 11, it is worth giving an example here. As I have repeatedly said, CA is an approach to discourse that works from "what is said": more specifically, it takes what is said as the source of observations, of evidence, and of explanations. This dependence on what is said makes CA an approach to discourse that is strongly bound to *text*. This is not to say, however, that people are assumed to *communicate* only on the basis of what is said at a particular moment in time. As ethnomethodologists make clear, what is said is not only indexical of a larger social world (as it simultaneously creates and re-creates that world), it also cannot be understood without the taken-for-granted assumptions that we bring to (and reconfirm with) our utterances. Nevertheless, it is text that remains central to CA procedures when applied to talk: text is the way our taken-for-granted worlds are discovered. Put another way, text is the route to our discovery (as analysts, as participants) of the *contexts* that text creates and by which it is created.

Consider a final point about the CA approach to discourse that emerges from our analysis of "there + BE + ITEM." We have analyzed the distribution of "there + BE + ITEM" in several different environments: adjacency pairs (independent, dependent), turns, topics, and mention-pairs. Although we discussed the use of "there + BE + ITEM" in each of these environments separately, it should be clear that we actually used our observations about the construction in one environment to inform our analyses of another. We noted, for example, that "there + BE + ITEM" can do recognitional work in embedded question/answer pairs: this was an inference about the function of the construction based on observations about its sequential distribution in relation to particular units of conversational structure. When we found that the same construction occurred in a quite different environment – for first, next, and only-mentions outside of adjacency pairs – we nevertheless tried to explain this set of occurrences in terms of the functions already identified from our previous analyses. CA is reluctant to assign either meaning or function to a form apart from a thorough investigation of how that form is sequentially embedded in actual talk. Once a function is found in one environment, however, it is reasonable to see whether that same function can be applied to other tasks. We thus related our knowledge that "there + BE + ITEM" could do recognitional work in embedded Q/A pairs to other sequences – finding the same kind of function. We made a similar point through our discussion of the relationship between "there + BE + ITEM" and stepwise topic transitions: since "there + BE + ITEM" could be retrospectively and prospectively implicative in embedded Q/A pairs, it was not surprising that this structural ability could be applied to stepwise topic transitions. Thus, the CA reluctance to assign meaning or function to a construction might better be seen as a reluctance to assign a meaning or function that has been taken out of context, i.e. decontextualized.

Exercises

1 Analyze the turn-transitions in a five-page sample of spoken data. What turn-taking rules apply and where do they apply? (For example, do certain speakers select others more frequently? Do some speakers self-select more than others? Where is self-selection likely?) Which instances of overlapping speech are interruptions, and by what criteria did you identify them as interruptions? Upon what linguistic qualities (e.g. syntax, semantics, pragmatics, intonation) of an utterance do current-speaker and next-speaker seem to rely as a guide to the identification of turn-transition spaces?

2 Our CA sample analysis differentiated independent from embedded question/answer pairs. What are the sequential differences between these two locations? Can these differences be related to the linguistic (syntactic, semantic, pragmatic) structure of questions?

3 Pre-sequences are utterances that prefigure a more focused upon speech action, e.g. a pre-announcement such as *I have to tell you something* prefigures an announcement (Terisaki 1976); a pre-question such as *Can I ask you something?* prefigures a question (Schegloff 1980). Using a corpus of conversational data, try to identify the interactional work that is accomplished by different pre-sequences.

4 Telephone openings are summons–answer sequences that help to set up the exchange structure of a phone conversation, as well as provide an environment for speaker–hearer recognition (Godard 1977; Schegloff 1972a, 1979a).

Tape-record twenty to thirty phone openings in either a single setting (e.g. a home) or several settings (e.g. home, business). What is the typical sequence of steps? How are relationships between the caller and the called party (e.g. their social identities, level of familiarity, intimacy, power differences) revealed in the openings? (Helpful readings include Godard 1977; Robert 1992; Sifianou 1989.)

5 Conversation analysts rely upon both phone conversations and face-to-face conversations as data, without explicitly assessing the possibility that these two different channels of communication may influence (or be displayed in) what is said. Tape-record several exchanges on the phone and several during face-to-face interactions. If possible, try to record roughly comparable speech events from both sources, e.g. a friendly chat, requesting information from a public service, complaining about an insurance policy or the quality of a service. How are the different channels of conversation reflected in the turn-taking and adjacency pair organization of the exchanges? Are there other differences, e.g. in pause length, in use of discourse markers, in openings and closings, that may be related to the channel difference? (This exercise may also be applied to comparisons across spoken and written modalities, or to comparisons across speech situations.)

6 Our sample analysis in this chapter focused upon *there is* constructions. Examine the sequential location of this construction in a different corpus. After comparing the results of the two analyses, assess the relationship between sentence structure and discourse function in conversation analytic terms. (Helpful work to read might be Ford 1993; Fox 1987; Goodwin 1979; Schegloff 1979b.)

Notes

1 CA transcripts do not always use traditional orthography or spelling, depending instead on what has been called "eye dialect" to replicate the way people speak. Jefferson (1984: 348), for example, provides the following transcribed line:

   I thought that was pretty outta sight didju hear me say are you a junkie.

   A key feature of this system is that phonetic details (e.g. associated with rapid speech rules, voicing (*surprise* might be transcribed as "surprize"), and so on) are represented orthographically. The use of "eye dialect" has been criticized by linguists (e.g. Macauley 1991; Preston 1982).

2 A key issue in the organization of turns centers on the identification of turn-constructional units and the parameters (e.g. intonational, syntactic, semantic) that underline their identification (see Ford and Thompson 1992). This issue intersects with the identification of the basic linguistic units used by speakers in spontaneous conversation.

3 Although CA research has not focused extensively on referring terms (or on problems of reference), much has been said that is relevant to these issues. CA research relevant to referring sequences includes the following. Schegloff (1972b) discusses how ways of formulating location reflect participant decisions about membership: for example, how one selects from among alternate place descriptions such as "65-year-old house,"

"Silver Spring," "Washington," "the East Coast," "the US" reflects speakers' categorization of hearer. Sacks's (1972b) discussion of membership categories touches on the attribution of relationships between referents: when we hear a sequence like "The baby cried. The mommy picked it up," for example, we understand "the mommy" to be the mother *of* the baby. Schegloff and Sacks (1973) point out, in their discussion of minimization in reference, that our referring terms provide the least amount of information needed for recognition by another. General ethnomethodological views on the indexicality of meaning (Garfinkel 1967) are also relevant to reference: e.g. the inherent contextual basis of all meaning is exemplified by the referential vagueness of an utterance like "it is nice." Most recently, Fox (1987) has shown that alternation between nominal and pronominal reference not only follows sequential constraints, but also helps to create such sequential structures. Conversation analysts (e.g. Sacks 1972) have also discussed topic in talk, i.e. how participants accomplish "talking about something."

4 Linguists who are interested in how syntactic structure emerges from discourse, however, sometimes combine CA techniques with syntactic analysis (e.g. Ford 1993; Fox and Thompson 1990).

5 Prince (1981) and Halliday and Hasan (1976) offer different perspectives on the relationship between ellipsis and recoverability of information.

6 Note also that the questions in embedded Q/A pairs are yes/no questions about existence with no subject–auxiliary inversion, i.e. they are *there's X?* but not *is there X?* In this sense, they are more similar to try markers or information-checking questions (chapter 5, section 3.3.3); see also our discussion of rising intonation with declarative sentences in chapter 3 (pp. 65–8).

7 Definitions and analyses of "topic" within linguistics are not consistent, partially because of the conflation of the notion of topic with information status: topic is often seen not only as "what we are talking about," but also as "what we are familiar with," i.e. given information (Schiffrin 1992c). By the former definition, the ITEM introduced by "there + BE + ITEM" can certainly *become* a topic – although it is unlikely to be a topic at the time of mention. Furthermore, if the ITEM is a first-mention, the latter criterion (its familiarity to hearer) cannot be assumed.

8 Note that the IVee's mention of two bedrooms (in line r) is apparently a mistake and is treated by the IVer as an opportunity for other-initiated self-repair. The interaction continues, but is interrupted (when another person enters the room) before the self-repair can be completed:

IVER: Where did she cook? Where did she cook?
IVEE: On the second floor. That was her-
IVER: ᶻHer bedroom and kitchen, huh?
IVEE: No, no. See you have three- like- [there's=
IVEE: [No, come on in, it's OK.
IVEE: =three rooms.
       Oh, did you get your new shoes, hon?
       Oh, they're cute.
IVER: Hey, those look pretty good.

8 Variation Analysis

1 Introduction

The variationist approach to discourse is the only approach discussed in this book whose origins are solely within linguistics. This approach stems largely from studies of variation and change in language: fundamental assumptions of such studies are that linguistic variation (i.e. heterogeneity) is patterned both socially and linguistically, and that such patterns can be discovered only through systematic investigation of a speech community. Thus, variationists try to discover patterns in the distribution of alternative ways of saying the same thing, i.e. the social and linguistic factors that are responsible for variation in ways of speaking.

Both the initial methodology and the theory underlying such studies are those of William Labov (who has also developed a speech act approach to discourse; chapter 3). Although traditional variationist studies have been limited to semantically equivalent variants (what Labov calls "alternative ways of saying the same thing"), such studies have also been extended to texts. It is in the search for text structure, the analysis of text-level variants and of how text constrains other forms, that a variationist approach to discourse has developed.

After an overview of variation analysis in relation to discourse in section 2, I present a sample analysis that focuses upon a particular discourse unit, the list, in section 3. My sample analysis takes two directions. First, I compare the structure of lists to the structure of narratives (3.1). Second, I analyze linguistic variation within lists, focusing here upon referring terms and sequences (3.2). These two directions show that variation analysis provides a two-pronged approach to discourse, one that focuses upon texts *per se*, and one that focuses upon how texts constrain other variants (3.3). Section 4 summarizes.

2 Defining variation analysis

As I noted above, the variationist approach to discourse is the only approach discussed in this book whose origins are solely within linguistics. Although the linguistics in which it is grounded is "socially realistic" (a term used by Hymes 1974d: 196), Labov resists the term sociolinguistics "since it implies that there can be a successful linguistic theory or practice which is not social" (1972f: xiii). Furthermore, although social factors (e.g. social stratification) are considered in actual analyses, and in more general formulations of patterns and explanations of distributions, the influence of sociology (its assumptions, concepts, and theory) was not heavily incorporated into early studies of language variation and change. Thus, the influence of linguistics pervades the variationist approach to discourse. (But see sections 2.2 and 2.3.)

Many of the problems addressed by variationists are problems familiar to linguists in general, e.g. the problem of linguistic change. Other problems that prompted the development of variation analysis required solutions whose analysis exceeded the theoretical and/or methodological tools of descriptive linguistics (e.g. free variation) or dialectology (e.g. urban dialects). Discourse also presents problems for linguistic analysis; as we see below, solutions to these problems are both inside (and outside) traditional linguistics.

We see in this section that variationists search for units in (and of) discourse that bear systematic and patterned relationships to one another. After describing the variationist approach to "units" in discourse (2.1) and the ways that units have "relationships" with one another, including methods for analyzing those relationships (2.2), I turn to a brief consideration of data collection (2.3). We will see that despite its linguistic heritage, many aspects of the variationist approach to language differ quite dramatically from traditional (and formalist) linguistics. Section 2.4 summarizes.

2.1 Units in discourse

Labov (1972b; Labov and Waletsky 1967) provided a systematic framework for the analysis of oral narrative – a framework that illustrates quite well the variationist approach to discourse units. As I discuss in a moment, this framework defines a narrative as a particular bounded unit in discourse, and it defines parts of narrative as smaller units whose identities are based on their linguistic (syntactic, semantic) properties and on their role in the narrative. Labov's interest in narrative, however, arose not just out of a search for discourse units *per se*, but also out of a set of social and political concerns stemming from the notion of verbal deprivation:

The notion of verbal deprivation . . . leads its sponsors inevitably to the hypothesis of the genetic inferiority of black children that it was originally designed to avoid. The most useful service which linguists can perform today is to clear away the illusion of verbal deprivation and to provide a more adequate notion of the relations between standard and nonstandard dialects. (Labov 1972a: 201–2)

Labov argues that the sort of verbal behavior used as evidence for verbal deprivation is hardly due to a genetic deficit, but to regular sociolinguistic factors operating upon a white adult and black child in an asymmetrical interview situation (p. 207). The verbal behavior found in narratives of personal experience, however, is quite different: far from being impoverished, narratives reveal that "the black English vernacular is the vehicle of communication used by some of the most talented and effective speakers of the English language" (Labov 1972b: 396).

I have introduced narratives in this way not only to show one way that variation analysis is socially realistic (recall our comment on p. 283), but also to lead to an understanding of why narratives have provided so fruitful a source of data for analysis: narratives are a discourse unit with a fairly regular structure that is largely independent of how they are embedded in surrounding talk. (Their methodological value is further noted in section 2.3.) Although I describe part of this structure during our sample analysis (to provide a comparison with lists (3.1)), I also do so here to highlight the variationist view of discourse units.

Narratives have a linear structure in which different sections present different kinds of information. Each section has a different function within the story. In addition, each section is comprised of different types of clauses whose syntactic and semantic properties contribute to their identity as units within the story, and to their function. Narratives are opened by an abstract, a clause that summarizes the experience and presents a general proposition that the narrative will expand. Orientation clauses (typically with stative predicates) follow the abstract: they describe background information such as time, place, and identity of characters. The main part of the narrative is comprised of complicating action clauses. Each complicating action clause describes an event – a bounded occurrence in time – that is understood to shift reference time, i.e. it follows the event immediately preceding it, and precedes the event immediately following it. Evaluation pervades the narrative: speakers can comment on events from outside of the story world, suspend the action through embedded orientation clauses, and report events that themselves indicate the significance of the experience. Speakers can also modify clause syntax as a way of revealing the point (cf. general proposition) of the story. Finally, the story is closed by a coda – a clause that shifts out of the past time frame of the story to the time frame of current talk.

In addition to the narratives providing data in chapters 3 and 6, we saw an example from a narrative in chapter 1, repeated here:

One of the most dramatic danger-of-death stories was told by a retired postman on the Lower East Side: his brother had stabbed him in the head with a knife. He concludes:

> And the doctor just says, "Just about this much more," he says, "and you'd a been dead." (Labov 1972b: 387)

The utterance presented above is an example of an evaluation. I noted in chapter 1 how this example is derived from the tools of linguistic analysis: not only is it classified linguistically (as a "comparator" that is realized by different linguistic forms), but it is a labelled segment of a text that has a function in relation to other sections. Despite this functional interdependence, variationist approaches allow a textual segment more autonomy relative to its sequential location in a specific story than would be granted in explicitly contextualizing approaches like interactional sociolinguistics (chapter 4) or the ethnography of communication (chapter 5), or in more sequentially based approaches like conversation analysis (chapter 7). As we noted in chapter 1, an indication of this in the example above is Labov's willingness to discuss the evaluating clause as separate from the rest of the story – to treat it as an example of a structural unit and functional type that can be extracted from its story for comparisons with other evaluative devices.

Although narrative clauses can be extracted from their text and compared for analytical purposes, units (clauses) within a particular narrative are also defined in relation to one another. As noted above, for example, an abstract is a generalization that prefigures the point of the story; a complicating action clause is defined according to its temporal relation to an adjacent clause. A particularly striking example of this text-internal dependency is that the function of a clause can change depending upon its location in the story. A clause such as "she was only eight years old" presented prior to the complicating action would be a descriptive background clause (part of the orientation). The same clause embedded in the complicating action would be evaluative – serving to suspend the action prior to a point of resolution.

I have been suggesting that variationists view the structure of narrative as largely independent of surrounding talk: narratives are autonomous textual units whose internal parts stand in systematic relationships with one another. Furthermore, as we note in section 2.2, narrative structure can create an environment within which different linguistic forms are variable ways of saying (or doing) the same thing. Although narratives are thus units that can be studied apart from the immediate textual or interactional contexts in which they are told, they are not independent of personal meanings and significance. In fact, it is the personal value of an experience for the story teller that is responsible for evaluative structure in narrative, and hence for the way that narratives "command the total attention of an audience in a remarkable way, creating a deep and attentive silence that is never found in academic or political discussion" (Labov 1972b: 396). The telling of stories is also sensitive to the social context (e.g. interactional setting, speaker identity) in which they are told. Recall Labov's argument that the notion of verbal deprivation is due to regular sociolinguistic factors operating upon a white adult and black child in an asymmetrical interview situation. Social context operates upon displays of verbal competence in general – such that "an average middle class speaker [may be] enmeshed in verbiage, the victim of sociolinguistic factors beyond his control" (Labov 1972c: 214). Thus, although narrative structure is independent of surrounding talk, narratives are nevertheless personally meaningful and their means of production is socially anchored.

Consider, also, that although narrative structure might seem to be found at a relatively surface level of analysis, other texts have structure beyond what is revealed in the utterances themselves. Analyses of apartment descriptions (Linde and Labov 1975), for example, reveal that text structure can be modelled on spatial perceptions and physical structure. Although not often considered part of variation analysis *per se*, Labov's analyses of ritual insults in Black English Vernacular (Labov 1972d), and of therapeutic discourse (Labov and Fanshel 1977), are built on some of the same abstract premises as variation analysis. The analyses just noted seek to be explicit about the speech act relationships between spoken utterances. The premise underlying such analyses is that coherence in interaction cannot be understood from the surface linguistic form of utterances, but has to be found at an underlying level of actions and reactions (see also Labov 1981). To this end, Labov and Fanshel (1977) propose an extensive speech act analysis of discourse termed "comprehensive discourse analysis." The meaning of what is said is expanded with the help of background knowledge, including social information about participants' rights and obligations: the result of such expansions is a set of propositions (somewhat like underlying thematic statements). Propositions are, in turn, related to speech actions: "how the speaker meant to affect the listener, to move him, to cause him to respond, and so forth" (Labov and Fanshel 1977: 59). Mapping rules relate expanded meanings to utterances ("what is meant" and "what is done" to "what is said"); sequencing rules connect abstract speech actions (at the level of "what is done").

The abstract speech actions focused upon by comprehensive discourse analysis and the linguistic variables focused upon by Labovian variation analysis (see below) seem very different at first. Labov proposes, however, that coherence depends upon a complex hierarchical organization that "is plainly derived from the linguistic analysis of phonology and grammar" (Labov and Fanshel 1977: 350). Whereas linguistic variables form a set of closed options (again, see below), however, speech actions do not – simply because of their contextual dependence (Labov and Fanshel 1977: 358).

I have suggested in this section that variationists extend beliefs about language structure to the analysis of texts: the variationist approach to narratives treats them as relatively autonomous textual units within which smaller parts are linguistically defined and systematically related to one another. One way that personal identity enters into the study of discourse units is in relation to the evaluative structures used to convey the personal significance of an experience. Social context is also part of the study of discourse units, since the setting in which a story is told allows (or inhibits) the display of linguistic competence. Finally, social context enters into the construction of speech actions and the formulation of speech act rules.

2.2 Variable relationships in discourse

Although the narrative is an example of a textual unit, it is important to note that variationists typically focus upon other units of analysis that are not text sized. As Labov (1972a: 188) observes:

> It is common for a language to have many alternate ways of saying "the same" thing. Some words like *car* and *automobile* seem to have the same referents; others have two pronunciations, like *working* and *workin'*. There are syntactic options such as *Who is he talking to?* vs. *To whom is he talking?* or *It's easy for him to talk* vs. *For him to talk is easy.*

One of the main tasks in variation analysis is to discover constraints on alternative realizations of an underlying form: such constraints (that can be linguistic and/or social) help determine which realization of a single underlying representation appears in the surface form of the utterance. Consider, briefly, the alternation noted above between *working* and *workin'*; more precisely, between the velar and apico-velar nasal. This alternation is constrained both linguistically and socially. The use of *in'* is more frequent in progressives and participles than in gerunds – reflecting different patterns of historical development (Houston 1989). *In'* is also more frequently used by working class than middle class speakers and by men than women; all speakers use *in'* more than *ing* when they are speaking casually instead of carefully (Labov 1972c; Trudgill 1974).

Since variationists try to discover patterns in the distribution of alternative ways of saying the same thing, i.e. the social and linguistic constraints on linguistic variation, an initial step in variationist studies is to establish which forms alternate with one another and in which environments they can do so. Constraints are then proposed in line with different hypotheses that may propose a variety of different explanations for a given phenomenon, ranging from the physiology of articulation to processing considerations to social or biological universals. Variationist approaches compare different explanations by searching for data that confirm (or cast doubt upon) the co-occurrences predicted by each explanation. Although this is not, of course, a goal unique to variationists, variationist approaches add the strengths (and limitations) of quantitative analysis to such efforts. Quantitative analyses require definitions of the variants (all the different possible realizations of an underlying type, i.e. a closed set), a classification of factors in the environment with which those variants may be associated, and a comparison of the frequencies and probabilities with which different variants co-occur with different factors.

As noted above, the discovery of patterns in the distribution of linguistic variants requires an obvious first step: establish which forms alternate with one another (are "the same") and in which environments they can do so. Labov (1972a: 188) intends "sameness" to be defined narrowly "by some criterion such as 'having the same truth value'." This restriction has made it challenging (and, for some, theoretically problematic) to extend the notion of variable to levels of analysis beyond the phonological. Morphological and syntactic forms, for example, convey meanings that may or may not be neutralized in different discourse environments (Sankoff 1988). Forms that are semantically distinctive in one environment may not seem so in another – although it is difficult to say whether residues of those meanings remain with each occasion of use and whether they are exploited for textual and/or pragmatic purposes (Lavendera 1984). Finally, wedding the notion of "semantic" equivalence to truth value assumes a relatively narrow view of semantics that not all variationists (e.g. Lavendera 1978) and not all linguists (e.g. Bolinger 1977) are eager to accept. The narrow view of semantics concerns a level of referentiality associated with abstract sentence-types; the broader view of semantics concerns a level of actual utterances in specific contexts (Silverstein 1976; cf. our discussion of formalist and functionalist definitions of discourse in chapter 2). For reasons such as these, some variationists have suggested replacing the requirement of semantic equivalence with functional equivalence (cf. Myhill 1988). By the latter criterion, generalizing tags with obvious semantic differences – tags like *and whatever, or something, etcetera* – would be considered variants (Dines 1980). As noted above, discussion of these issues considers whether discourse neutralizes (Sankoff 1988) or builds upon (Lavendera 1978) meaning-related differences in syntactic form. (See also Labov 1978; Lefebvre 1989; Romaine 1981.)

The search for variants in discourse inherits many of the problems of the search for syntactic variants (e.g. Schiffrin 1985a; Vincent 1983). There are additional problems. One stems from the status of discourse as a linguistic unit *per se*. Texts do not seem to have the same kind of internally constrained, externally bounded structure as sentences (Schiffrin 1988a). This makes it difficult to define the theoretical status of discourse variants. They are not alternative realizations of a single underlying form or representation (as one could argue for phonological, morphological, or syntactic variants); nor do they occupy a "slot" (a phonological segment, a syntactic constituent) in a grammar or set of grammatical rules. Analyzing variation within a discourse unit (such as the narrative, section 2.1) whose structure is relatively easy to delineate partially obviates the need to make such a decision about grammatical status, i.e. one can analyze alternative forms that appear within specific slots in a narrative structure.

Note, finally, that the way one analyzes distributions across social groups in a speech community may also be altered by a reliance on functional equivalents: the form that one segment of a community uses to realize a specific function may not be identical to the form used by another segment of the community. Thus, formally distinctive, but functionally equivalent, forms can be differently distributed among speakers in a community (Sankoff and Thibault 1981).

We have seen in this section that an important unit of analysis for variationists is the linguistic variable. Incorporated into the definition of the variable as a unit is an empirically grounded relationship between surface forms of utterances: different ways of saying the same thing are grouped together as alternative realizations of an underlying form only because they stand in an "equivalence" relationship to one another (either a referential or functional equivalence).

2.3 *Locating vernacular speech in a community*

Variationists assume that the social context of speech influences the use of speech – so much so that very different judgements about verbal competence (and community members' judgements about social status) may be made depending upon the particular sample of speech to which one has access (2.1). Social context has a still deeper importance for variationist studies. Because linguistic analysis is based upon what people say, rather than upon linguists' intuitions of grammaticality and appropriateness (cf. the comparison between formalist and functionalist paradigms in chapter 2), it is critical to have access to a sample of speech that provides data adequate for analysis. When people know that their language is being observed and/or judged, however, they may alter their ways of speaking toward socially prestigious forms and/or toward forms more like those of their interlocutors. What variationists thus seek is a mode of speech called the vernacular. The vernacular is the variety used when speakers pay minimum attention to speech (Labov 1984: 29; what Labov 1972e calls "casual style"); it is also that mode of speech acquired in pre-adolescent years (Labov 1984: 29). The highly regular character of the vernacular is a result of the lack of attention to speech, and the fact that the linguistic rules acquired early in life appear to be "more regular than those operating in more formal 'super-posed' styles that are acquired later in life" (Labov 1984: 29).

In addition to needing speech representing the vernacular, variationists also need speech representing a range of styles (because people often shift their pronunciation of sounds that are undergoing change when they shift styles) as well as a large volume of high-quality recorded speech from different members of a speech community (to facilitate analysis of the social distribution of linguistic forms). The technique traditionally used to collect data with these qualities is the sociolinguistic interview (Labov 1984: 32–42). Sociolinguistic interviews are a mixed genre of talk (chapter 5). One way in which they differ from other interviews is that they encourage topic shifting and group interactions among people present. Another difference is that respondents are encouraged to tell narratives of personal experience. This is not only because narratives reveal community norms and styles of personal interaction, but also because speakers regularly shift toward the vernacular when telling a story (Labov 1984: 32). Thus, narratives have another value for variationists apart from their status as discourse units: the search for the vernacular within a sociolinguistic interview is believed to be greatly facilitated when a respondent tells a story.

In sum, variationists require data that allow the discovery of the highly regular rules of language and the social distribution of variants governed by those rules. This type of data – a variety of language termed the vernacular – emerges only during certain social situations with certain interactional conditions. One such condition is when a speaker tells a narrative of personal experience. Thus, the same discourse unit that is useful for variationists because of its regular textual structure (2.1), and because it enables the definition of environments in which to locate specific linguistic variants (2.2), is also useful as a source of vernacular speech in which patterns of linguistic variation and change may be discovered.

2.4 Summary

The variationist approach to discourse is based within a socially realistic linguistics. In some ways, linguistics clearly pervades the variationist approach to discourse. Although other approaches to discourse (e.g. conversation analysis, chapter 7) also search for units and posit regular relationships (e.g. sequential relationships) between units, for example, the variationist approach defines those units in ways that incorporate their linguistic properties. Furthermore, a discourse unit such as the narrative is seen as more autonomous from its immediate interactional context than would be the case for interactional, ethnographic, or conversation analytic approaches – approaches sharing their disciplinary origins with sociology and anthropology. However, the variationist approach also differs from traditional linguistics in many ways. Variationists collect data to obtain samples of the vernacular; they never rely just upon their intuitive judgements about grammaticality or use constructed examples to test a hypothesis (but see Rickford 1990). Variationists use quantitative methods of analysis to test hypotheses about constraints on the distribution of forms within connected speech; these methods differ markedly from those of formal linguists.

A variationist approach to discourse is thus a linguistic approach that considers social context under certain methodological and analytical circumstances. Although a discourse unit such as the narrative is sensitive to the social context in which it is told, and its point is grounded in the speakers' values and subjective experience, the structure of a story can be analyzed apart from the way it is locally situated (cf. Schiffrin 1984b). Variationist analyses of discourse other than narratives show a similar separation between language and social life – a reluctance to mesh them as two mutually constitutive systems (cf. interactional sociolinguistics, ethnography of communication, conversation analysis). For example, variationist analyses of two-party discourse (in which speakers exchange turns) rely more upon considerations of social meaning and context than do analyses of narratives. Although Labov (1972e: 252) proposes that the "fundamental problem of discourse analysis is to show how one utterance follows another in a rational, rule-governed manner," he also notes that "there is no formal basis in sentence-grammar to explicate our reaction" to many everyday exchanges as coherent and well formed (Labov 1972d: 299). In analyses of exchanges such as the following:

A: Are you going to work tomorrow?
B: I'm on jury duty.

Labov locates coherence at a level of actions and reactions, but he does so in a way that adds social context to methods and concepts borrowed from linguistic analysis. Labov (1972d) and Labov and Fanshel (1977: chapter 3), for example, propose rules that connect actions and meanings to words. This is a major task of discourse analysis and should be pursued in formal terms: "Linguists should be able to contribute their skill and practice in formalization to this study . . . formalization is a fruitful procedure even when it is wrong: it sharpens our questions and promotes the search for answers" (Labov 1972d: 298). Variationist formalizations of discourse rules include social information with linguistic primitives because discourse is an area "of linguistic analysis in which even the first steps towards . . . rules cannot be taken unless the social context of the speech event is considered" (Labov 1972e: 252). Thus, a variationist approach to discourse is a linguistically based approach that adds social context to analyses of the use of language.

3 Sample analysis: the "list" as text

The sample analysis in this section focuses upon a particular discourse unit, the list. In section 2 we saw the importance of discourse units for variation analysis: they reveal discourse structure, provide an environment in which to define constraints on linguistic variants, and can be a site for the study of the vernacular. Most variationist attention to discourse units has focused on narratives (cf. Horvath 1987; Linde and Labov 1975). But it is also important to find another type of discourse with regular forms and functions. My discussion of lists suggests that lists are descriptive structures that center on categories and category members (3.1). Although we have already discussed the structure of narratives, I use narrative structure as a backdrop for the discussion of lists. This is meant not only to elucidate the structure of lists, but also to suggest that comparing textual structures (variation across text types) is as much an application of variation analysis as is comparing forms and structures within texts (variation within a text type). The former level of comparison can contribute not only to what we know about text level variation (e.g. the distribution of predicate types across clauses (3.1.3b)), but also, even more fundamentally, to our understanding of how it is that we (as members of a speech community) attribute to a particular string of utterances an identity as an instance of one genre rather than another.

I also illustrate variation analysis by analyzing variation within a text type: referring terms within lists (3.2). This is meant to illustrate the latter focus noted above: the analysis of variants within a text type. Specific problems pertaining to referring terms have already been posed in the sample pragmatic (chapter 6) and conversation analyses (chapter 7). We see in this chapter how variationists might address some of the same questions concerning the distribution of definite/indefinite, and explicit/inexplicit referring terms (chapter 6), as well as more general questions concerning first-mentions and next-mentions (chapter 7). To maintain continuity with the sample analyses in the previous chapters, it would help to be able to begin our analysis with referring terms themselves. However, the analysis of variation within text depends on a prior understanding of that text itself: indeed, the formulation of text-specific constraints (which is a key part of a variationist approach to referring terms) requires this. Our discussion of lists themselves will also help us see how the list is a discourse unit that is especially relevant to our understanding of reference and referring expressions.

Before I begin, it is important to comment on the data to be used and the methodology. Variationist studies of discourse face some of the same methodological requirements as variationist studies of phonology and syntax. As noted earlier, such studies proceed by identifying variants and different features of their linguistic environment that are hypothesized to constrain (either favor or disfavor) particular variants. These hypotheses are then supported (or refuted) with the help of quantitative analysis. Each step of this process requires a corpus whose size is sufficient to its goals. Not only does one need to find "enough" of each variant, but the features used to categorize a linguistic environment cannot be so narrow that the environment is subdivided into groups too small for meaningful comparison. The same holds for social categories: studying the distribution of a phonological variant in a speech community requires a selection of informants who adequately represent the differences in social status and role (e.g. social class, gender, ethnicity, and so on) that are meaningful in that community. One also needs a number of cases sufficient for the application of statistical tests of significance. Unfortunately, it is never simple to say how many cases are "enough." Rather, the answer to this question depends on the number of variants being analyzed and the complexity of the constraints, i.e. the number of "factors" into which social and linguistic environments are divided. Regardless of exact numbers, the point is that the method of analysis requires a relatively large corpus that encompasses both linguistic and social heterogeneity. Many variationists have found that such a corpus is best provided through sociolinguistic interviews in a community (2.3; also chapter 5, section 3.3).

Finally, let me briefly look ahead to some general features of the variationist approach that I will illustrate. As I noted above, I begin by comparing two text types (lists and narratives): I then focus on variation in referring terms in lists. These analyses reveal several assumptions that variationists make about discourse. First, text is built from linguistic constituents that can have formal and functional relations to one another. Second, although text is comprised of smaller units, the coherence underlying the text is based on the way those units are related to one another at other levels of analysis. Third, analyzing the distribution of variants within texts is a way to discover differences among texts, as well as features of texts themselves. Finally, limiting the study of linguistic variants to a particular text type whose structure is familiar allows the relatively precise identification of textual constraints. It also permits a view of sentence and discourse as interdependent systems.

3.1 Linguistic variation across text types

One of the most basic differences between narratives and lists is that narratives tell what happened and lists describe a category. This difference bears on both the content of what is said and its function in discourse. Before I discuss several differences between narratives and lists that stem (at least partially) from the fact that telling about an experience differs from describing a category, however, it will be helpful to present an example of a list to show one way that the form of a list can be explicitly related to the organization of a category (3.1.1). I then discuss some specific linguistic differences between lists and narratives stemming from the difference noted above: the unit of a list is an entity (a "list-item") rather than an event (3.1.2), lists build descriptive rather than temporal and evaluative structures (3.1.3). Section 3.1.4 summarizes what is revealed here about the variationist approach to text structure: text is built from linguistic constituents that have formal relations to one another.

3.1.1 An example of category organization in a list

I suggested above that the focus of lists is on a descriptive category and its members. Lists present a collection of items that can be classified as "the same" in some ways, but "different" in other ways. The "sameness" of the items justifies their inclusion in a single class, and the differences between them separate them into subclasses. Just as "sameness" is criterial to inclusion in the *category* that unites a list, so too, are "differences" criterial to segmentation into the *subcategories* that divide a list.

I begin with an example of a list that reveals, in an unusually explicit way, the organization of the category being described. (1) is also a "good" example of a list. Although variationist approaches to discourse also analyze texts that are not "good" representatives of a particular text type, they often begin with examples that display the full text structure in as clear a way as possible. Specific differences that appear in other examples (e.g. different clause ordering, elaboration or reduction of specific parts) are then seen not as aberrations, but as motivated variations of the "basic" structure.

(1) is a list of "race tracks around here." What is shared is the general identity of the places named (each is a "race track around here") and what is different is the particular location (*around here*) and identity of each race track.

(1) IVer: (a) Racing's big around here, isn't it?
     IVee: (b) Yeh.
     IVer: (c) Yeh.
     IVee: (d) Well, you got uh, Jersey.
            (e) You got . . . Monmouth
            (f) and you got Garden State.
            (g) Y'got Atlantic City.
     IVer: (h) Mhm.
     IVee: (i) And then uh here you got Liberty Bell.
            (j) And they're building a new one up in Neshaminy.
     IVer: (k) That's right. [I've never seen that, though.
     IVee: (l)   [And uh . . . you got Delaware.
            (m) And of course, if you want to re- be- really go at it you can go up to New York.=
     IVer: (n) Mhm.
     IVee: (o) =You got Aquaduct
            (p) and you got Saratoga
            (q) and you have that Belmont, y'know.
            (r) I mean like uh . . .

The list in (1) is prompted when an IVer makes a general assertion (*Racing's big around here*) to which a tag *isn't it* (requesting confirmation, or at least hearer uptake) is appended. The IVee's list of specific "race tracks around here" can thus be seen as specifying (or supporting) the IVer's generalization through cumulative instances. In sequential terms, the list provides a response (confirmation) to the prior request for confirmation.

Let us focus here on what (1) tells us about lists as linguistic reflections of category members. In a moment, I will present a diagram in which the category and subcategories are labelled in ways showing their hierarchical relationship to one another. Although this step is not absolutely critical to variationist approaches to discourse, it reveals several variationist beliefs about text. First, it suggests that just as narratives can reveal the speaker's organization of a world apart from language – a world of experience – so too can lists. Second, it suggests that the order in which people present information (e.g. narrative events, list-items) is an important source of information about text itself. This order is assumed to be motivated in some way, and discovering that motivation can help to reveal the source of underlying coherence. A related belief is that texts have a structure beyond what is revealed in the utterances themselves. Labov and Waletsky (1967), for example, diagrammed displacement sets that were based on temporal relations between events, but also suggested the functional identity of clauses. Similarly, Labov (1972d) and Labov and Fanshel (1977) sought to be explicit about the speech act relationships between spoken utterances: they argued that coherence in interaction cannot be understood from the surface linguistic form of utterances, but has to be found at an underlying level of actions and reactions.

Let us thus examine (1'). This diagram labels the subcategories (list-items) in the order in which they were presented in (1). It also shows their categorical relationships to one another. On the far right are the line numbers from (1) that correspond to each item.

(1') The structure of (1)

X	Racing around here	(a)
X1	Racing in New Jersey	(d–g)
X1a . . .	Race tracks in New Jersey	(e–g)
X2	Racing here [in Pennsylvania]	(i, j)
X2a . . .	Race tracks in Pennsylvania	(i, j)
X3/X3A	Racing in Delaware/race track in Delaware	(l)
X4	Racing in New York	(m–q)
X4a . . .	Race tracks in New York	(o–q)

Three levels of structure appear in (1'). The highest (most general, superordinate) is the category itself: "racing around here." The next level of structure is the states (New Jersey, Pennsylvania, Delaware, New York). The lowest level of structure is the particular race tracks in the states. (Despite their difference in level of subordination, both the states and the race tracks are list-items.)

(1) reveals an iconicity between the order of clauses in the text and category structure. Note, first, that the order of items in (1) is iconic. As shown in (1'), the order in which each race track is mentioned matches the hierarchical relationships between items being listed: the category X1 ("race tracks in New Jersey") is presented prior to the subcategories X1a ("Monmouth"), X1b ("Garden State"), and X1c ("Atlantic City"). X2 ("race tracks in Pennsylvania") and X4 ("race tracks in New York") are similarly presented. The one apparent exception is X3/X3a. From the way this category is presented (*And uh . . . you got Delaware*) it is impossible to tell whether the speaker intends to mention the state "Delaware" as X3 (cf. *you got uh, Jersey* as X1) or the

"race track in Delaware" as X3a (cf. *you got Garden State* as X1b). This referential ambiguity, however, may in itself be iconic simply because there is a race track in Delaware that is called Delaware race track. (In addition, the "race track in Delaware" (X3a) is the only race track in the state of the type (horse, not harness, racing) being listed here, such that X3 cannot be instantiated beyond X3a.) Thus, just as *you got* is used to introduce two levels of subcategory (X1 or X1b), so too can the lexical item *Delaware* evoke a state or a race track.

The way that items are introduced in the list is also iconic. Many of the list-items are introduced in the same way (*you got* + ITEM in d, e, f, g, i, o, p) regardless of their category level. Such repetition is iconic simply because the introduction of different items through a single predicate structure is a linguistic reflection of their coexistence in a common conceptual realm. Similarly, the means of introducing a list-item diverges from the *you got* pattern when an atypical item is mentioned: a race track that has not yet been built (*And they're building a new one up in Neshaminy*) and race tracks in New York further from the speaker's home than the others (*And of course, if you want to re- be- really go at it you can go up to New York*). The deviations from the *you got* pattern in (1) may be seen as reflections of the peripheral (versus core) status of these racetracks as examplars of the category "race track around here": the one not yet built is not yet a "race track"; the one in New York is not quite "around here." Note, also, that *Belmont* is introduced in a way (*you have* and as *that Belmont*) that marks its special status (Belmont is a nationally known race track, a place where major races, comparable to the Kentucky Derby, are run). Thus, it is not only repetition itself that is iconic, but the interplay between repetition and innovation: the list-items introduced through one structure share a categorical status (as core members) and the items introduced through different structures have different categorical statuses (as peripheral members).

Although lists are iconic in the ways noted above, it is important to note that not all aspects of lists are linguistic reflections of categorical organization. For example, we might expect each separate item in a list to be syntactically and/or intonationally packaged as a separate unit. We do find an example of this in (1) when a higher-level list-item is mentioned separately from its subcategories: X1 ("New Jersey") is introduced in its own independent clause and its own intonation unit as *Well, you got uh, Jersey* (d). But there are also counterexamples: X2 ("Pennsylvania") is introduced pronominally as *here* in the same clause and the same intonation unit as X2a ("Liberty Bell"), *And then uh here you got Liberty Bell* (i).

(1) has illustrated one way that a list is a linguistic reflection of categories and categorical organization. I turn now to a discussion of more general characteristics of lists (contrasting them briefly with narratives) in order to suggest that lists are a discourse level realization of a descriptive category in which the cumulative presentation of category members (list-items) instantiates the general category.

3.1.2 Units of lists are entities

In this section, I compare the basic units of lists (entities) to the basic units of narratives (events). This comparison reflects yet another variationist assumption about text: text is comprised of smaller units that form a configuration which is based on the way those units are related to one another.

Whereas the basic syntactic unit of a narrative is a clause with temporal juncture, i.e. an event that moves reference time forward (2.3), the basic unit of a list is an entity, i.e. anything of which something may be predicated (individuals, sets, propositions; Webber 1979). (One type of entity may very well be an event, and people may list events rather than tell about them in stories (see 3.1.4c)). Evidence that lists are segmented into entities is that items are introduced into lists in ways that focus on entities *per se*, rather than on what may be predicated about those entities. One common way to introduce an entity into a list is to use a right-branching construction in which semantically weak (and given) information precedes semantically new information (the list-item itself). We already saw an example of this in (1) in which the core members of the "race tracks around here" category were all introduced with *you got* + ITEM; we also discussed the use of "there + BE + ITEM" for the introduction of both first-mentions and second-mentions in lists in chapter 7. Constructions of this type include not only *you got* and *there is*, but other possessive verbs (*have, got*) with either first person (*I/we*) or third person (*they/(s)he*) pronouns: such constructions focus upon the entity itself, rather than a predication about the entity.

Another way to focus upon entities in a list is through ellipsis: the presentation of an item with no surrounding information at all. Since it is the item alone that is presented, ellipsis is a striking illustration of how lists reduce the need to predicate something about each individual item: rather, any properties of the item that need to be known to merit its inclusion in the list are assumed (or presupposed) from shared knowledge about what category is being described.

The type of ellipsis allowed in lists differs sharply from that allowed in narratives. Whereas narratives may very well have numerous intonation units that lack NP subjects (regardless of whether we see these as verb chains having undergone subject deletion or as conjoined verbs), lists may have numerous intonation units that lack predicates. (2) illustrates two variants of list ellipsis.

(2) IVer: (a) Well, was this a big Irish neighborhood when you were a kid, [growin' up? Really?
    IVee: (b)   No. [Just um
            Irish, German, and Jewish.
    IVer: (c) This neighborhood.
    IVee: (d) Yeh, mhm.

(e)   Irish, German, and Jewish.
IVER: (f)   Mhm, yeh.
IVEE: (g)   In fact, there's a Jewish woman the first house here.
IVER: (h)   Been there a long time?
IVEE: (i)   She's still there, yeh.
        (j)   Since I was a kid.
IVER: (k)   Yeh?
IVEE: (l)   And then there was a Jewish family next door.
  → (m)   Then us.
  → (n)   Then Jewish,
  → (o)   then Jewish.
IVER: (p)   What did they do?

(2') presents the structure of (2). Although I exclude *then us* (m) from ('), note how an external physical structure (here, the physical structure of houses on a block) can impact upon list structure (cf. Linde and Labov 1974).

(2') Structure of (2)

X	Ethnic groups in the neighborhood	
X1-[T1]	A big Irish neighborhood [then]	(a)
X1-[T1]	Irish	(b)
X2-[T1]	German	(b)
X3-[T1]	Jewish	(b)
X3a-[T2][T1]	A specific Jewish woman [now] and [then]	(g)
X3b-[T1]	Jewish family	(l)
X3c-[T1]	Jewish	(n)
X3d-[T1]	Jewish	(o)

[T1] and [T2] are time indices

Two types of ellipsis are illustrated in (2). The ellipsis in *Irish, German, and Jewish* (b, e) is very typical of short three-part) lists in which entities are themselves short (NPs) and not elaborated upon. What is important for our purposes here is that nothing is predicated of the entities themselves: rather, their mention is sufficient to their inclusion as members of a category. The second type of ellipsis illustrated in (2) is less typical. *Then* + ITEM (*then Jewish* (n, o) is potentially extendable into lists that include more than three items, and that allow a great deal to be said about each item *after* its introduction into the list. Here the entity being listed is prefaced by a sequential marker that marks the progression of the items through discourse time (see (3.1.3a)), and perhaps also the progression of houses down the block (see Linde and Labov 1975, on tours). Although these forms of ellipsis differ, the point here is that they both allow mention of the entity itself, with no supporting proposition, and nothing overtly predicated about the entity. Furthermore, we understand the entities to be category members even without overt indications of their status in relation to the category.

In sum, the basic unit of a list is an entity. Evidence for this is the way entities are introduced into lists, either by constructions that syntactically and semantically focus upon an entity or by elliptical mentions that allow a focus upon the entity as a "next item" without any overt predication about that entity.

3.1.3 Information structures

This section continues the variationist approach to text, but rather than focus upon the basic building blocks of a text type (events or entities: 3.1.2), I focus upon the information structures that are formed through clauses in the text. We noted earlier that the focus of lists is on a descriptive category and its members: lists present a collection of items that can be classified as "the same" in some ways, but "different" in other ways. Although there are numerous analyses of spoken narrative from both linguistic and literary perspectives (e.g. Chatham 1978; Fleischman 1990; Sheldon 1988), virtually all scholars agree that narrative is concerned with experience. To oversimplify, narratives tell about something that happened to someone. The experiences upon which narratives focus can include a circumstance that the narrator himself or herself had an active role in bringing about or a problem for which the narrator sought a resolution. Thus, narratives frequently "tell about" what happened to a human being – a human who can take an agentive role in bringing about a particular change in circumstance.

This general difference between lists and narratives extends to the information structures that prevail in these text types. We see in this section that narratives and lists both build two types of information structures – temporal (3.1.3a), and descriptive (3.1.3b) – although the text types do differ in terms of which information structure is dominant. The speaker's subjective involvement in recounting an experience, however, means that narratives also build evaluative structures (3.1.3c).

One way to see how lists and narratives rely upon different information structures is to compare the function of different linguistic items in both structures. Notice that this reveals another variationist assumption about discourse analysis (one to be pursued at length in section 3.2): syntactic and semantic differences among linguistic items are sensitive to text structure. In addition to analyzing such differences *within* one text type (as we do in section 3.2), one may analyze such differences *across* text types (as we do here). The direction pursued here is also consistent with the view of text that we noted earlier: text is a structure by virtue of its particular configurations of "lower level" linguistic forms. Thus, we can discover differences among text types by examining how linguistic forms themselves fit certain distributional patterns.

a Temporal structure
The Labovian view of narrative defines temporal structure as the criterion central to the definition of narrative (2.3): temporal information (what

occurred when) is inferred largely from the sequential presentation of two event clauses in discourse. Put another way, the interpretation of narrative rests largely upon the assignment of reference time (the time period in relation to which something can be assumed to have happened; Reichenbach 1947) to events: it is the linear presentation of event clauses in narrative that typically allows one to assume that reference time shifts from one event to the next (but see Dry 1983; Ehrlich 1990; Fleischman 1990). The temporal structures of lists, however, are not typically structures that are concerned with reference time. Rather, the time relations in lists are textual relations between items presented successively in the discourse itself, i.e. a matter of textual rather than propositional structure.

We noted above that one way to see the difference between the two text types is to compare the function of different linguistic items in both structures. *Then* in narrative is linked primarily to reference time (even when it marks global changes in episode; Segal et al. 1991). (3) illustrates. (I have chosen a stative clause from narrative, simply because stative predicates are so common in lists.)

(3)   (a)   And then, and uh, you rode twenty miles one way
  → (b)   and then uh there was an old deserted ranch house there
     (c)   and that's where I- we used to meet the other fellow comin' from the other direction.

Rode twenty miles in (a) is an achievement predicate (Vendler 1967); *was* in (b) is a state (part of an existential predicate, used frequently in lists; see pp. 302–4). Although "an old deserted ranch house" is assumed to exist *prior to* the speaker's mention of it, we interpret its existence in relation to the speaker's prior action, i.e. we infer that he observed the house only after he *rode twenty miles* (the distance noted in (a)). In this sense *there was an old deserted ranch house* is almost like an achievement, as if the speaker had noticed the house, or realized that it was there, and is conveying this observation to the hearer (cf. Dowty 1986: 50). *Then* plays a central role in evoking this interpretation: *then* provides both an ending point for the achievement and a starting point for the state. Note, also, that the clause position of *then* in narrative clauses has a dramatic effect on reference time, such that clause-final *then* in (3b) would continue rather than shift reference time (Schiffrin 1990b, 1992b).

The use of *then* in lists is quite different. *Then* in lists is always clause-initial, a restriction consistent with its function. That is, the clause-initial position of *then* reflects its use as a discourse level marker of temporal succession that is based on the S-occurrence of *then* (in initial position) rather than the VP-occurrence (in final position; Ernst 1983; Schiffrin 1992b). *Then* in lists has temporal meaning only as a discourse marker (Schiffrin 1987a: chapter 8): it shows progression not through reference time (events, states), but through discourse time. *Then* in (4) illustrates. A sociolinguistic interviewer has asked whether any policemen live in the respondent's neighborhood.

(4)   There's a cop up the next block.
      There used- there was a cop over here.
      He's retired.

The speaker begins by listing two members of the set "policemen around here." Following the two list-items, the speaker describes policework in general – a section not included above – and then adds another entity to the list:

Then uh, there are a couple uniform cops around here somewhere.

Then establishes a return to the list. Despite a fairly extensive description pertinent to the more general topic under discussion (that is not part of the list *per se*), *a couple uniform cops* is clearly the next list item. Note that the use of the stative predicate "be" with each list-item establishes a descriptive structure (3.1.3b). In sharp contrast to *then* in the narrative (*then uh there was an old deserted ranch house there* (3b)), however, *then* with stative predicates in lists does not shift reference time. *Then* in lists has meaning only as a discourse marker that marks the sequential progression of items through discourse time.

In sum, the temporal structure of a narrative is central to its identity as a discourse unit and to its semantic interpretation; temporal structure in the propositional sense, however, has little relevance to the structure of lists. An indication of this difference is that *then* in narrative is a marker of reference time whose clause position can alter our interpretation of what happened when; *then* in lists is a marker of text sequence, i.e. the "next item in the list."

b Descriptive structure

Another informational difference between narratives and lists concerns their descriptive structures. Description in narratives is typically assigned to a background "orientation" function (Labov 1972b). The identification of who was present, where something happened, and when it happened often prefaces the narrative action itself. Such information is typically assumed to endure throughout the time of the story world, such that changes in background states need to be explicitly noted.

Narrative orientation may also be embedded within the complicating action, and here it may have a descriptive and/or evaluative function. In (5), for example, the speaker interrupts his narration to describe physical features of a location. (5 presents the clauses prior to the story excerpt in 3).

(5) → (a) See, every five miles they had a little stone.
     → (b) Say on one side was Mexico and the other side was the United States. Y'know?
        (c) And then, and uh, you rode twenty miles one way

Clauses (a) and (b) are restricted background clauses (Labov 1972b): static descriptive situations relevant for a limited period of time in the reported experience. The states in (5) also serve as landmarks (Psathas 1979): they are locations that the speaker uses as a base from which to orient a next action (in c). Thus, the embedded orientation clauses in (5) have a limited relevance in the story: they are pivotal locations for a next-action that returns to the temporal structure of the story. Although not illustrated here, I noted that some embedded orientation clauses have an evaluative function in narrative (3.1.3c). Thus, although the information itself may be a static description (i.e. a stative predicate that does not move forward in reference time), it can also have a secondary function of conveying the significance of certain events for the point of the story.

Description in lists plays a very different role. Since lists are themselves text level category descriptions, it is not surprising that stative predicates (such as "have" (5a) and "be" (5b)) are the main verb types used to build the descriptive structure of a list. What such predicates provide are just what lists need: descriptions of situations that are assumed to hold for an unspecified period of time (with no beginning or ending points), or items that are assumed to have stable conceptual identities. Put another way, part of what makes a text into a list is the use of predicates representing situations that can serve as continuing instantiations of a given category.

Consistent with the different functions of description in the two text types is a different pattern of active and stative predicates. As I noted above, stative predicates in narrative either precede active predicates (we see a specific example below, as 8) or are inserted within a sequence of active predicates (as we saw in 3). The distribution of active and stative predicates in lists, however, is quite different.

(6) is a section of an example (seen in full as 8 in chapter 7). An IVer asks some teenage friends (two females, one male) whether *there* (are) *any old folks livin' on this block*. The section in (6) reverses the distribution of active and stative predicates typical in narratives: rather than a stative or two inserted into a sequence of active predicates which comprises the complicating action, the statives in (6) provide the skeletal organization of the list, with active predicates adding supplementary information about each item.

(6) → IVEE-2: (r)   Then there's one woman here, crippled or
                    whatever,=
        IVER: (s) ^{z}Mhm.
        IVEE-2: (t)   =you want to call her. She's-
        IVEE-3: (u) ^{z}Delirious.
                (v)   She just walks around the street with a walker?=
        IVER: (w)   Mhm.
        IVEE-3: (x)   =She'll stop any car comin' down the street, too.
        IVEE-2: (y)   (No,) [hh she's not. Hh.
        IVEE-3: (z)   [Tell you her whole life history.

IVEE-2: (aa) She gets you to come in her house and-=
IVEE-3: (bb) Fix her ( ).
IVEE-2: (cc) =read her mail for her and-
IVER: (dd) Hh, oh, bless her heart.
         (ee) She really sounds lonely.
→ IVEE-2: (ff) And then there's a- another couple up the street
         (gg) who never come out.=
IVER: (hh) Uh huh.
IVEE-2: (ii) =And, God forbid you parked your car in their pavement
         (jj) and they're- they're out there ready to throw bricks at
               you
         (kk) and, they call the cops . . .

Two list-items are introduced here with stative predicates: *Then there's one woman here, crippled or whatever* (r) *And then there's a- another couple up the street who never come out* (ff). Following its introduction into the list, each referent is described with active predicates (v, x, z, aa, cc; ii-kk). Note, also, that the two active predicates (*parked your car* (ii), *call the cops* (kk)), and the stative predicate (*they're out there* (jj)) form a short temporal sequence embedded within the list structure.

(7) is a slightly more complicated example: the speaker presents two intersecting lists that are differentiated by predicate type. An IVee (an elderly woman) is answering a question from an IVer about *where* a young man would have taken a young lady when they were dating long ago. The IVee begins her response by saying that there were *not many places* to go (because the Depression reduced everyone's income). What she presents, instead, is a list that is partially responsive to the focus of the IVer's question (a list of "places"), but also an intersecting list of "what dates used to do" (a list of "activities"). We see that the former list uses stative predicates, and the latter list active predicates.

(7) IVEE: (a) We did a lot of walking. /Hh./
     IVER: You could go a long way walkin', no kidding.
     IVEE: Yeh. Mhm.
     IVER: Walkin' and talkin' I bet.
     IVEE: Yeh. That's all you could do.
                 I mean uh he, uh he wasn't workin' at the time.
                 And to get a job I mean, oh, it was- it was awful.
     IVER: Was it very difficult?
     IVER: Yeh, terrible.
          (b) And uh, every once in a while we'd stop and get a soda,
               y'know, or something like that.
     → (c) And then- they- they always had these little um ice cream
               parlors around, /Uh huh/ which they don't have today.
          (d) You go in, y'know,

(e) and you sit at a table

(f) and- and uh you can get yourself a soda or a dish of ice cream or something like that, y'know.

→ (g) In fact we even had a bakery.

(h) You can go in there

→ (i) and they had tables.

→ (j) And they had the homemade ice cream.

(k) You could get a big dish of ice cream for a dime.

After a short description of activities ("walking" (a), "stop and get a soda" (b)), the IVee introduces a place ("ice cream parlors" (c)) that has a pivotal role in the list. Note that immediately prior to *ice cream parlors*, the speaker had self-corrected from *then*. This self-correction suggests that the speaker was about to continue the list of activities from (a) and (b): in fact, she does return to the activities after specifying a location ("ice cream parlors") for one of those activities. But the specification of "place" (*they always had these little um ice cream parlors around* (c)) has a dual role in the list. As already noted, mention of "ice cream parlors" provides the locational frame in which the IVee can elaborate a previous item ("stop and get a soda" (b)) from the "activity" list initiated in (a). This elaboration is facilitated by repetition: the repetition in (f) of *get a soda . . . or something like that* from (b) ties the two mentions of the "activities" together; *a dish of ice cream* (f) also ties the "activity" to the specific location *ice cream parlor* (c). But mention of "ice cream parlors" also provides a first-item in a list of "places" (that continues with "a bakery" (g)). Thus, by initiating a list of "places", "ice cream parlors" also shifts focus back to the IVer's question about *where* people would go on dates.

Note that the distribution of predicate types in (7) helps to separate the different intersecting lists from one another. Not surprisingly, the items in the "activities" list are all event clauses with active predicates ("walk" (a), "stop and get" (b), "go in" (d, h), "sit" (e), "get" (k)). The items in the "place" list (and in a subordinate "things in the place" list) are all statives (all are "have" (c, g, i, j,). Thus (7) shows, again, how the distribution of predicate types in lists differs from that in narratives: whereas only active predicates can comprise a narrative, either active or stative predicates can comprise a list.

Still another way to see the difference between description in narratives and lists is to contrast the use of the same syntactic construction in both types: existential *there* constructions (chapter 7). Example (8) (already seen as 11 in chapter 7) shows the use of an existential predicate in the orientation to a narrative.

(8) IVEE: (a) And this is what the thing is.

(b) They get in,

(c) and i- what's it- what's it bein' done for?

IVER: (d) Yeh.

(e) That's right.

IVEE: (f) There- I'll tell you.
→ (g) There's a school down in my mother's town, right?
IVER: (h) Right.
IVEE: (i) Strictly colored.
(j) It's the *newest* school in North Beach.
(k) It was all colored.
(l) And because of this law of integrating,
(m) these colored children had to go to this white school,
(n) which they didn't want.

"There's + ITEM" in (b) is used in a turn-position in which the referent focused upon is guaranteed a slot in which to be described: prior to the introduction of *a school* in (b), the speaker self-repaired from *there* to a pre-announcement *I'll tell you* that secures the floor for her story. The tag *right?* also makes explicit that the speaker is seeking recognition of this item as preliminary to its further use in the story. Although the school is described in more detail (i-k) prior to the story, the school does not figure in the narrative action itself: rather it remains background information in the story that allows the speaker to talk about what happened (i.e. the narrative action) to the children who attended the school.

The background function of existential *there* in narratives can also be seen when this construction serves as an embedded orientation. (9) is a section of a long narrative in which a cabdriver tells about being robbed (the narrative discussed in chapter 6). In the section of the story reproduced here, the speaker interrupts the complicating action to describe the destination to which he is sent.

(9) (l) So it was maybe only three blocks away,
(m) so they said- I think they gave me an address that's at the center of the block,
→ (n) and there was a small light on at the house.
(o) So I pulled up,
(p) I turned on the light,
(q) and the guy he grabbed me from the back of my head
(r) and put a gun to it.

Lines (l) through (n) present material that is backgrounded to the complicating action. In (n), *there is* introduces one particular feature of the destination being described, *a small light on at the house*. The light introduced in (n), however, has no further role in the story. In fact, when the speaker returns to the complicating action of his story, he turns on a different light (*I turned on the light* (p)) – the light in his cab – after reaching the destination (o). It is surprising that the same lexical item "light" appears in two different clauses. Not only is it used with different referential intentions, but *there is* often introduces an item that is then treated as an accessible referent (e.g. conveyed as a definite) in subsequent clauses (see chapter 7). But it is precisely because this sequence is unexpected that it is so instructive. What is introduced by the existential predicate is in a backgrounded descriptive section of the story – a section structurally and functionally segmented from the complicating action that does not play an important role in the story.

There is has a much different role in lists than it does in narratives. In (10), an IVer asks about children's relationship with an absent father.

(10) IVER: (a) Have any of the kids ever expressed a desire to see him?
     IVEE: (b) No.
          (c) No, they never did.
          (d) I mean like uh, they never asked about daddy or where did daddy go or-
    → (e) I mean like, there was me
    → (f) and there was my father
    → (g) and there was my cousins.
          (h) And the kids were pretty well occupied.

The list of items in (10) begins in (e) with *there was me*, continues in (f) with *there was my father* and ends in (g) with *there was my cousins*. All the items in the list are definite descriptions (see 3.2.2c). The same kind of structure – the same string of existentials – occurs with indefinites.

(11) (a) There's uh, there's string bands,
     (b) there's brigades,
     (c) there's comic divisions,
     (d) there's- y'know, there's quite a few divisions.

The existential predicates in (10) and (11) contrast sharply with the existentials in the narratives in (8) and (9). Rather than being used to introduce background (a character, a place, etc.) prior to a text, the entities introduced by *there is* are central to the text.

We have seen thus far that narratives build temporal structures and lists build descriptive structures; use of the temporal marker *then*, and the distribution of active versus stative predicates, reflect these different structures. We see in 3.1.3c that there is still another difference between narratives and lists: narratives do not just report, they also evaluate, experience.

c Evaluative structure

Narratives and lists differ in the degree to which human subjectivity guides the productive processes underlying the speech activity itself. Stories are often said to be constructions of an experience, rather than representations of a reality (e.g. Bruner 1990). A story teller's active involvement in the creation of an experience pervades the story telling process: speakers may impose their own subjectivity on what happens at a variety of levels, e.g. what to report (or leave out), the relevance (or irrelevance) of specific occurrences, temporal and causal relations between events, and so on (see e.g. Bamberg 1991; Bamberg and Marchman 1991; Slobin 1991, for cross-linguistic views at the syntactic level). The telling of a story is also intersubjectively guided. A story is a reconstruction of an experience, told at a specific time, in a specific place, to a specific audience for whom the storyteller seeks to demonstrate the validity of a general claim (e.g. about oneself, one's experience, or the world). Put another way, a story seeks to establish an intersubjectively agreed upon point (a point which may involve the audience as co-author: Duranti 1988; Ochs et al. 1991).

Members of a category seem slightly less immune to individual subjectivity: some categories may even have members whose qualities justify their inclusion in the category independent of an "observer's" subjective view of those qualities. Rosch (1978), for example, emphasizes that categorization is structured according to perceived structure and function in the world: naturally occurring groups of attributes may be non-arbitrarily related to particular functions. Rosch also points out that categorization is structured by a principle of cognitive economy that defines a "basic level" of categorization whose concepts are among the first to be learned, the most commonly used, and are labelled with short, structurally simple words (see also Berlin et al. 1974; Berlin 1976; Downing 1980; Rosch 1973; Rosch et al. 1976). This is not to say, however, that categorization is totally "independent of who is doing the categorizing and on what basis" (Lakoff 1987: 50). The specific details of categorization can vary across individuals, subgroups, and cultures, and can change over time (Kay 1975; MacLaury 1991); some studies also find that different strategies are used to place objects into categories (e.g. Reed 1972). Despite such variation, however, categorization seems to be a less subjectively guided process than narration: the involvement of the self seems less likely to pervade the "logical" processes underlying category membership than the "narrative" processes underlying memory of experience (cf. Bruner's 1986 use of the terms paradigmatic versus imaginative).

Speakers' involvement in the reconstruction of what happened has an important consequence for the language used in story telling; so, too, the relative lack of involvement in category reconstruction has a consequence for the language used in list making. I suggested above that subjective involvement is geared partially toward making a point through a story. The point of a story is indicated through what Labov calls evaluation (2.3). Evaluative structures in stories are often deviations from textual norms (Polanyi 1979), e.g. from simple clausal syntax (Labov 1972b) or from unmarked tense forms (Fleischman 1990; Schiffrin 1981a; Silva-Corvalan 1983; Wolfson 1979), but a variety of other means are also used for expressive purposes, e.g. prosody, repetition, and direct quotes (see also Bauman 1986). Thus, evaluation pervades not only the processes whereby "what happens" becomes part of one's experience, but also the processes whereby an experience is situated in the "here and now," the "why," and the "to whom" of its telling.

Although lists are also situated and can also be used to make a point, the evaluation of items in lists is fundamentally different from the evaluation of events in narratives. Evaluation is central to the task of reconstructing an experience and to the task of embedding a story in an interaction. Although evaluation in lists may very well figure in the interactive function of the list, it is less crucial to the internal construction of a list *per se*. More generally, evaluation is required and pervasive in a story (e.g. Polanyi 1979, 1985), but optional and minimal in lists. These points are important because when the items in a list are proposition-sized (e.g. event clauses), a list seems more like a narrative than we might expect.

The next examples have two purposes: to show how lists themselves (not their specific items) can have an evaluative function in discourse (cf. Johnstone 1983; Rains 1992); and to differentiate lists of events from narratives.

(12) is a relatively simple example showing that list-items may be enumerated to make a point. The speaker (a 70-year-old woman) has been comparing the relatively easy housework of nowadays to the time when she was a housewife and found housework to be demanding.

(12) (a) But to *me*, eh: I always found something to do.
      (b) There's always something to do in a home where there is a family.
           /Um hm./
      (c) There is such things as closets to clean out
      (d) and drawers to clean out
      (e) and curtains to sew
      (f) and windows to do
      (g) and, and dishes to do
      (h) and cooking to do
      (i) and you t- name it
      (j) and scrubbin' to do
      (k) there's always *is* constantly something to be done if you want a
           nice, clean home.

The accumulation of items (of "things to do") in (12) provides evidence for the general claim that *there's always something to do in a home* (b): each list-item provides a specific instantiation of the indefinite NP *something to do* (b). None of the items are highlighted as more central to the general experience of housekeeping than any others: rather, it is the fact that such tasks can be enumerated without differentiation that provides the constancy underlying the claim that there is *always something to do*.

(13) is another list in which the speaker supports the validity of a general claim by enumerating specific instances. It is slightly more complicated than (12), however, because each specific instance is itself evaluated as a way of legitimizing it as support for the claim. Prior to (13), the speaker had been complaining that her younger daughter-in-law does not call her "Mom." The speaker states that the only solution to this problem is to *start in the beginning*

(of the in-law relationship (a)), and she presents evidence that this is the appropriate solution.

(13) (a) And you have to start in the beginning.
      (b) Now my daughter in law *did*.
      (c) My older daughter in law from the very beginning she said Mom,
      (d) so she's used to it.
      (e) Mom and Dad.
      (f) See it does m- it's only a name!
      (g) And Ron- we told Ronny *too*,
      (h) in the beginning, you call- if you can't say Mom and Dad, call them by their first name.
      (i) But call them *some*thing.
      (j) Not "uh:::::"
      (k) And she's an intelligent girl
      (l) and she's a *nice* girl.
      (m) She gives us the biggest respect.
      (o) And she's really nice.
      (p) I like her very much.
      (q) It's just that she can't say it.
      (r) Now I remember when I first got married,
      (s) and *I* was in that situation.
      (t) And eh the first- like the first . . . few times, I wouldn't say anything.
      (u) And my husband said to me "now look it isn't hard, just say 'Mom'."
      (v) He says, "And I want you to *do* it."
      (w) And I *did* it.
      (x) And I got *used* to it.

The list-items in (13) are the specific people who adhered to the general rule *you have to start in the beginning* (a): "older daughter in law" (b to f), "Ronny" (the speaker's son (g to j)), and the speaker herself (r to x). We can summarize the members of the list as follows:

(13′) The categories in (13)
  X   "people who did the right thing"
  X1   "my older daughter in law"   (b–f)
  X2   "my son Ronny"   (g–j)
  X3   "myself"   (r–x)

Although the items above constitute the categories in the list itself, there is clearly more in the discourse than just the three items in (13′). In addition to defending the person who has done the wrong thing (the daughter in law who does not call the speaker "Mom" (k to q)), the speaker establishes for each list-item the validity of its membership in the list. One way that she does so is to tie each list-item to the general claim through repetition or paraphrase of a critical part of the claim. In (a), the speaker states that the behavior has to occur in *the beginning* of the in-law relationship. The behavior of each person mentioned is indexed to the appropriate time: the older daughter-in-law to *the very beginning* (c), the son to *the beginning* (h), the speaker herself to when she *first got married* (r). People in the list are also presented in ways that highlight their role either in the comparison with the daughter-in-law who behaved inappropriately, or in the collection of people who behaved appropriately. The older daughter-in-law's behavior (b to f) contrasts with that of the younger one. This is shown through contrastive stress (*did* (b)) and ellipsis ("did [call me 'mom']"). Ronny (g to j) and the speaker herself (r to x) are additions to the descriptive set being built in support for the claim about appropriate behavior. This is shown through contrastive stress on *too* (g) when Ronny is first mentioned, and on *I* (s) when the speaker mentions herself. Still another way that the speaker in (13) shows that the list-items support her general claim is the use of devices that are similar to narrative devices in both form and function. The speaker uses, for example, a meta-comment that functions like an external evaluation (*See it does m-it's only a name!* (f)) of the older daughter-in-law, reported speech (to the son (h to j) and from the speaker's husband (u, v)) that functions like an internal evaluation, and reported actions (w, x) that are temporally sequenced in relation to the constructed dialogue.

Before going on to more general points about the role of evaluation in lists and narratives, it is important to summarize our discussion of (13). (13) is a list in which the accumulation of items substantiates a claim about the world. The list-items mentioned ("older daughter-in-law", "Ronny", "I") would be part of the list with or without the devices just discussed, i.e. repetition, contrastive stress, meta-comments, and reported actions. It is in this sense that evaluation in the list in (13) is not internal to the construction of the list itself. Rather, what evaluative devices do in (13) is legitimate the use of each specific instance as support for the general proposition being put forth in the interaction: they are part of the ongoing construction of the list as evidence for the speaker's claim.

Thus far we have treated the list-items in (12) and (13) as entities that are no different from the entities considered in earlier examples: (12) is a list of "things to do," (13) is a list of "people." There is another way, however, to consider the entities in these lists. Since the basis for the inclusion of "people" in the list in (13) is their behavior, for example, we might categorize (13) in terms of propositions. Each list-item could be said to be an event clause in which the predicate "called mother-in-law 'Mom' " has a succession of different arguments ("older daughter-in-law", "Ronny", "I"). Rather than be a list of people as in (13'), then, (13) would be a list of propositions about people. Similarly, the list-items in (12) can also be recast as propositions, e.g. as instantiations of stative predicates "there is X to do."

When list-items are syntactically and semantically defined as clause-sized propositions, rather than as NP-sized referents, temporal order can play a greater role in the construction of lists than previously indicated. This is because events that do follow a particular temporal trajectory in the speaker's experience may very well be presented in terms of that trajectory. When this happens, a list of events might seem very much like a story. But as I suggest in the next examples, it is only when those events are evaluated that we begin to interpret the discourse as story-like.

In (14), an IVer asks an IVee about his *first job*. This descriptor becomes a subcategory in a list of 'jobs' in which the jobs are temporally ordered. I include time indices in the left margin.

(14)	IVER:		Well, hey, do you remember your first job?
			The first job you had?
	IVEE:	(a)	The first job.
[T(1a)]		(b)	I think my first job,
		(c)	*one* of my first,
		(d)	I must've been about ten years old.
X1		(e)	I used to stock the shelves in a grocery store.
		(f)	I used to work eight hours on a Saturday for two dollars. Hh.
	IVER:		Oh, what slave labor.
	IVEE:		Yeh.
[T(1b)]		(g)	Well, I think as I got older,
X2		(h)	I was a janitor in a cleaners.
		(i)	Not any- well, /Uh huh./ I cleaned up
		(j)	and made hangers up for the-
		(k)	put the plastic on the hangers
		(l)	and the cardboard on the hangers
		(m)	and the paper around the hangers you put in your suit jackets.
[T(1)]	IVER:		Then, that's when- you were a kid, [right?
	IVEE:		[Yeh.
[T(2)]	IVER:		And, so, did you work when you were in high school?
X3	IVEE:	(n)	Well, I was a short order cook in a hoagie shop.
	IVER:		Oh, really?
			Jesus, you've had a checkered career, haven't you?
	IVEE:		Hh. /Hh./
X4		(o)	I was- I was a busboy at a country club while I was in school.
X5		(p)	I was a dishwasher, /Uh huh/ for a pancake house.
		(q)	They had dishwasher
		(r)	then you were a busboy. /Yeh./
		(s)	Half the night you wash dishes,
		(t)	the other half you cleaned the tables up.

IVER: (u) Did you like bein' a short order cook at a hoagie-
factory?

Most of the jobs are formulated as stative predicates, i.e. *I was* + "job title":
I was a janitor in a cleaners (X2 in h), *I was a short order cook in a hoagie
shop* (X3 in n), *I was-I was a busboy at a country club while I was in school*
(X4 in o), *I was a dishwasher, for a pancake house* (X5 in p). The one job
not formulated as a stative is X1: *I used to stock the shelves in a grocery store*
(e). This deviation from the pattern reflects the non-prototypical nature of the
job: not only is there no conventionally used nominal (e.g. *shelf stocker*) for
this job, but the speaker stocked shelves as a child (a period in life during
which people do not have what we think of as a "real" job). Underlying the
presentation of jobs is a collaboratively built temporal organization – an
organization that is all the more notable because it involves shifts in reference
time between stative predicates (see Dry 1983; Schiffrin 1992b) that are not
typically temporally ordered in lists (see 3.1.3c). It is the IVee who initiates
the temporal structure: after his description of his first job (b to f), he moves
forward in time (*Well, I think as I got older . . .* (g)) to describe his next job
(h to m). This temporal framework is picked up by the IVer's proposal that
these jobs be grouped together as part of a certain stage of life: *Then, that's
when- you were a kid, right?*. The IVer then pursues this more global, episodic
structure of jobs by asking about a second stage (*And, so, did you work when
you were in high school?*) during which the next jobs are understood to have
occurred.

Notice that there is more information presented in this list than just names
of jobs. The IVee and IVer, however, diverge in terms of what kinds of
information they add. The IVee adds information relevant to his descriptions
of the jobs *per se*: he describes the tasks that comprised the jobs in terms that
continue the list format. The IVer (in addition to the temporal information
noted above), adds evaluative information: after evaluating the job herself
(*Oh, what slave labor*), she proposes an evaluation for the IVee to consider
(*Jesus, you've had a checkered career, haven't you?*) and finally directly asks
the IVee to evaluate a job (*Did you like bein' a short order cook at a hoagie-
factory?*). That the IVer proposes shifts in stance – shifts that are not pursued
by the IVee – is important for my point about the difference between lists of
events and stories. The IVee is presenting a list in which the main focus is not
so much his participation in the job, but the type of job *per se*. Thus, the
subcategories in the list are not the speaker's relationship to the jobs, but the
jobs themselves:

X1   stock the shelves in a grocery store
X2   a janitor in a cleaners
X3   a short order cook in a hoagie shop
X4   a busboy at a country club
X5   a dishwasher for a pancake house

The IVer's evaluative comments, on the other hand, seek to open a different kind of speech activity – more akin to story telling – in which what is central is not the categories of an experience, but a person reacting to an experience. (This effort is consistent with the goals of sociolinguistic interviewing; see section 2.3, also chapter 5.) Thus, (14) illustrates that a sequence of temporally ordered events provides material for two very different speech activities: lists (which categorize experience) and stories (which evaluate experience). Put another way, although both stories and lists can have constituents that are temporally ordered, it is evaluation that differentiates the two: evaluation is required and pervasive in a story, but it is optional and minimal in lists.

The same point is illustrated by (15) and (16). Both are reports (from a single speaker) about where she lived, and in both, events are marked (sometimes with *then*) as temporally successive.

(15) (a) Well, I was born at 22nd and em . . . tsk . . . oh I forgo- well I think it's 22nd and Lanham.

(b) And um . . . and uh I grew up really, in the section called Larkspur.

(c) And then, I went into the service, for the two years,

(d) and then, when I came back, I married . . . I-I-I got married.

(e) And then I lived at uh 51st and Lyle. Which is West Ph- it's right off of 51st and Granite Avenue. That's where I lived.

(f) And then we moved here.

Except for some embedded descriptive material concerning specific locations (a, e) and an event ("getting married") that creates a natural juncture (i.e. people usually move from their parents' home when they are first married), the speaker lists the places in which she lived in the order in which she lived there. Nothing is said about how the speaker experienced life in any of the places: there is no evaluation of any of the locations. In (16), the same speaker (in a later interview) provides more details about life at *51st and Lyle*. (This is example (44) in Schiffrin 1987a: 249.)

(16) (a) We lived there for two weeks without water, or gas.

(b) We had electricity.

(c) And it was wonderful that we could wake up in the morning, and play the radio, and do what we want.

(d) Because this landlord- landlady was terrible.

(e) And then we lived there for five years,

(f) and *we* bought a triplex across the street.

Like (15), (16) contains a sequence of temporally ordered events: *We lived there for two weeks without water, or gas* (a) precedes *we lived there for five years* (e), which precedes *and WE bought a triplex across the street* (f). These events, however, are interwoven with descriptions and evaluations. What was good about living at 51st and Lyle is presented as a short list: *it was wonderful that we could wake up in the morning, and play the radio, and do what we want* (c)). These good qualities compensated for what was bad (*without water, or gas* (a)) to make life at 51st and Lyle a better place to live than their former home (where the *landlady was terrible* (d)). Not only is this location thus evaluated from the speaker's point of view, but even the demarcation of time is evaluative. As noted above, reference time moves forward in (e), *we lived there for five years*. What shifts from (a) to (e), however, is not location: rather, it is the qualities of that location (presumably the home had water and gas after the two-week period ended) and thus the speaker's experience of that location. Thus, even the temporal demarcation of events – the temporal structure of the sequence – is evaluatively motivated.

I have suggested in this section that the relative necessity and pervasiveness of evaluation is important to the distinction between narratives and lists, and even more critical to the distinction between narratives and lists of events. We noted earlier that the basic unit of a list is an entity: anything of which something may be predicated (individuals, sets, propositions). Now we are seeing that lists whose items are propositions do the same kind of categorical work as other lists: they predicate of each proposition a group membership, such that a next-proposition is understood as an instantiation of the same general category as prior propositions. When the reference time of one situation (whether event or state) is understood to end prior to the time that another begins (as in 14 and 15), a list of events may begin to seem very much like a narrative – but a narrative without evaluation (i.e. a report). The difference, however, is that events in a narrative work together to make a point about oneself or one's world: the events in a narrative are linked together through an evaluative structure. Lists of events, on the other hand, have a cumulative effect: events are added together as separate instances and it is their accumulation itself that substantiates a generalization.

3.1.4 Summary: variation across text types

In this section, we have compared the text structure of narratives and lists: narratives tell what happened and lists describe a category. This basic difference is related to differences in the basic unit of the two text-types (event versus entity) and in the relative importance of different information structures (temporal and evaluative versus descriptive). The comparison of text-types is a key part of a variationist approach to discourse: it contributes not only to our knowledge of text level variation (e.g. in the distribution of predicate types across clauses) but also to our understanding of how it is that we attribute functional identities (and labels) to strings of utterances. And this, in turn, can allow a more systematic analysis (again, from a variationist perspective) of how text-types are socially situated, e.g. how linguistic differences in the stories told (or lists constructed) reflect the different situations in which texts are used.

The discussion in this section has also helped to make more general points about variationist approaches to discourse. Texts are built from linguistic constituents that have formal relations to one another: these relationships help to reveal the basis for coherence within the text. The comparison of what seems like the "same" linguistic item (or the "same" information structure) is key to the discovery of these relationships. Notice that this comparison reveals another variationist assumption about discourse analysis: syntactic and semantic differences among linguistic items are sensitive to text structure both within and across text types. We have also seen that what seem like the very same linguistic units (e.g. *then*, existential *there*, stative predicates, event clauses) have radically different functions depending on the text-type in which they occur. Although this dependency illustrates the point made earlier (text-types are built from linguistic units), it also helps to make a point fundamental to variationist approaches to discourse: one cannot assume that syntactic difference (or equivalence) is always associated with functional difference (or equivalence) in text. I expand upon this point in section 4.

3.2 *Variation within text*

Now that we have illustrated the variationist approach to discourse by comparing text-types, we turn to another direction taken by variationists: variation within a single text-type. Although our focus is still linguistic variation, the locus of that variation shifts from text-type *per se* to lower level forms (e.g. syntactic, morphological) whose distribution can be discovered either generally in discourse, or more specifically in particular text-types. For example, one might analyze coordinate and subordinate markers either in general, or in specific text-types, e.g. arguments, stories. Limiting one's study of linguistic variants to a particular text-type has both methodological and theoretical advantages. A methodological advantage is that we can use our knowledge of the structure of a text-type to define the linguistic environments in which formal alternations are possible (what Labov calls the "envelope of variation": 2.3) and to define different features of those environments as variable constraints on the occurrence of the formal alternants (2.3). A theoretical advantage is further understanding of the functions of formal variants in discourse: how variation both reflects and realizes particular textual structures. Our discussion of predicate types in section 3.1.2, for example, showed their different distribution in narratives and lists, suggesting that statives function as background clauses only in narrative. Form–function correlations such as these allow us to approach textual structure from two complementary directions: the way a particular text-type contrasts with another text-type (as we saw in section 3.1), and the way a particular text-type is internally constituted by combinations of structures and meanings both within and across its sentences.

The focus in this section is variation in referring terms in lists. Specific problems pertaining to reference and referring terms have already been posed in the sample pragmatic (chapter 6) and conversation analyses (chapter 7). In this section, we see how variationists might address some of the same questions. Before I begin this portion of our sample analysis, it is important to note that the list is a discourse unit that is especially relevant to our understanding of reference and referring expressions. We have already discussed referring terms in another text-type (a story, chapter 6) and mention-pairs in other discourse sequences (e.g. question/answer pairs, chapter 7). Like other texts, lists also allow the analysis of sequential relationships between "mentions" of an item. Lists present a clear set of items whose relevance begins and ends not only in the list itself, but also at specific junctures within the list. These features help us to identify sequential constraints on referring. Lists are also a closed discourse unit in which a group of conceptually related entities is brought into focus for a hearer: a new referent is brought into discourse, used for a while, and then dropped. Rather than becoming agents involved in the actions of a reported experience (as in narrative), it is the entities themselves that are the focus of talk – such that we might expect to find constraints on informativeness that are quite different from those in narrative. In addition, it is well known that reference to entities is sensitive to the structural junctures and transitions within texts (e.g. Fox 1989): in lists, such junctures are category based.

Lists allow another view of referring expressions – a view that stems from the way lists display categorical organization, or, more generally, from the relationship between discourse and conceptual categories. Conceptual categories are intimately tied to choices between different referring terms. To take a brief example, in the story analyzed in chapter 6 we noted that the speaker alternated between *he* and *it* when referring to "a passenger" (i.e. a person paying a fee to travel). We suggested that this alternation reflected two different ways of situating "a passenger": the former in a world of people, the latter in a world of occupational roles and identities. It is precisely such conceptual worlds (or, more accurately, pieces thereof) that are presented in lists.

Getting a view of conceptual worlds through discourse has an important bearing on our understanding of referring sequences. Virtually all analyses of pronouns in discourse assume that pronouns can be used when a more precise understanding of a referent (or in pragmatic terms, recognition of a speaker's referential intention) is available (or inferrable) from context (see Kronfeld's (1990) concept of functional relevance). We saw in chapter 6, for example, that speakers may initially mention an entity with a definite noun phrase if they can assume that a hearer has information sufficient to allow recognition of that specific entity. Although one source of such information is prior text, a critical part of accessing a referent is drawing inferences based not only upon what is said, but also upon what is assumed to be known about the world (e.g. Ariel 1990). The knowledge upon which such inferences depend can very well be knowledge about category organization. Prince's (1981) "containing inferrables" (a type of given information), for example, are defined in relation to set membership. Clark and Haviland's (1977) view of "bridging" is similar: an entity such as "beer" is considered given information if it can be considered a member of a group of "picnic supplies." Since it is precisely the organization of category members that lists can help to reveal, lists may help us learn how categories allow the inferences underlying the use of particular referring expressions (e.g. definite noun phrases). Put another way, lists are a means by which a speaker uses discourse to convey an organization of a category; category membership is, in turn, an extremely important notion in our understanding of how referents are accessed.

In the next two sections, I consider constraints on variation in referring terms within lists. I begin with a very general factor, not limited to lists *per se*, that constrains definiteness and explicitness of list-items: order of mention (3.2.1). I then turn to how text-specific factors that arise from the organization of lists themselves constrain referring terms in lists (3.2.2).

3.2.1 *A general discourse constraint: order of mention*

Since a key interest of discourse analysts is sequential patterns, it is not surprising that many analyses of referring terms in discourse focus upon referring sequences (see discussion in chapter 6). Two general patterns emerge from such research: one concerning definiteness; the other, explicitness. First-mentions are often indefinite noun phrases; next-mentions are often definite. The second sequential pattern concerns explicitness: first-mentions are typically more explicit (i.e. full nouns) than next-mentions (pronouns).

Variationist approaches to discourse seek to add precision to generalizations such as those noted above (about what "often" or "typically" occurs) through quantitative analyses: variationists count the number of times a particular variant appears and compare that with the number of times that the variant could have appeared in a particular linguistic environment (2.2). This procedure is repeated for each linguistic environment in which the alternation can be found. Variationists actually avoid statements about typical patterns unless they are based on frequency counts and evaluated by statistical tests of significance.

Table 8.1 counts the number of definite referring expressions (compared to indefinites) in both first- and next-mentions of items in lists. I include here just those list-items that were mentioned more than once. Consistent with the notation used in our diagrams of the hierarchical organization of list-items, I will use (X) as the general category underlying the list, (X1 ... *n*) as the subcategories (the list-items), and so on, in subsequent discussion. Tables 8.1 and 8.2 do not differentiate mentions of list-items by level (e.g. X1 versus X1a); nor do they include mentions of X itself.[1]

Table 8.1 Referring sequences and definiteness in lists

	First-mention	Next-mentions	Total
Indefinite	23	0	23
Definite	9	74	83
Total	32	74	106

As table 8.1 shows, referring sequences in lists follow a general definiteness pattern similar to that noted for referring sequences in other discourse: 72 percent (23/32) of the first-mentions, but none of the next-mentions, are indefinite.

Referring sequences in lists also show the same general explicitness pattern as sequences in other discourse. Table 8.2 shows the relationship between order of mention (first-mentions versus next-mentions) and explicitness, going from most explicit (full noun phrases) to less explicit (pronouns, zero pronouns).

Table 8.2 Referring sequences and explicitness in lists

	First-mention	Next-mentions	Total
Full NP	32	10	42
Pronouns	0	61	61
Zero	0	3	3
Total	32	74	106

Table 8.2 shows that 100 percent (32/32) of the first-mentions are full noun phrases, but only 13 percent (10/74) of the next-mentions are full noun phrases. Note, also, that none of the next-mentions of $(X1 \ldots n)$ are more explicit or more informative than their first-mentions. This is not to say, of course, that more information cannot be added about a list-item after its first-mention. But rather than being added by more explicit referring terms, such information is always added in a construction (e.g. a predicate nominal) that links the information to a pronoun.

The list of "old folks living on this block" (6) was an example of both patterns seen above. Rather than present the entire example again, I just present the referring terms here as (17).

(17) Referring expressions from example (6)

First-mention	Next-mentions
that kook hangin' out the door	him/his (4 times)
one woman here	she/her (12 times) "zero"
another couple up the street	they/their (3 times)

The first-mentions are both indefinite and more lexically informative (i.e. explicit) than next-mentions: "kook" is evaluative, "woman" is gender-specific, and "couple" provides information about number. Reference to each entity is also textually bound, i.e. (X1) is not mentioned again after (X2 ... *n*) is introduced (see 3.2.2b).

As we discussed in section 2.2, variationist approaches do not always seek to explain individual cases that might be seen by others as violations of a categorical constraint. This is because variationists assume that constraints operate in a probabilistic fashion: one expects to find less then perfect complementary distributions and heterogeneity at both social and linguistic levels of analysis. Nevertheless, it is still important to know the boundaries of variation, i.e. to know in what environments (if any) realizations of language structure are categorical. The more precise one can be about constraints on variation, the more one can use variation studies to compare and evaluate competing hypotheses and explanations for empirical observations. In addition, heterogeneity and variability play an important role in sociolinguistic theory: language variation is related to social identity, language variation both reflects and creates language change, and so on. Finally, the possibility that one constraint interacts with (e.g. supplements, cancels) another raises important questions about whether formalist assumptions of autonomy and modularity of language are justified (chapter 1).

Reasons such as these lead variationists to try to explain as much variation within a particular realm as possible. Thus, we might try to explain why the constraints in tables 8.1 and 8.2 are not categorical: there were 9/32 definite first-mentions and 10/74 explicit next-mentions. A number of different strategies for explaining variation within a particular realm are available: identifying new types of constraints (either internal or external to the language system), analyzing the operation and possible intersection of multiple constraints. In our discussion of referring expressions in chapter 6, we made several observations about initial definites that may help explain the "atypical" cases in tables 8.1 and 8.2. We noted that first-mentions could be definite if hearers have accessible to them information that can be used as a conceptual framework within which to locate a referent. It is this factor that accounts for the nine initial definites in table 8.1. Note, however, that the source of accessibility underlying these initial definites was due to different contextual parameters, only some specific to lists. Some initial definites were referents anchored to the speakers themselves, e.g. speakers always began lists about their relatives by anchoring the person occupying a particular kinship role to themselves with a first person possessive pronoun (e.g. *my grandmother, my older brother*). Other initial definites were proper names whose referent is assumable as part of shared knowledge, e.g. the name of a country or state. Recall from (1), for example, that the speaker named the states with race tracks without first introducing the states as indefinites (e.g. "There's a state around here called New York"). As noted earlier, other initial definites in lists were inferrable (either textually or as containing inferrables: Prince 1981) from the general category underlying the list: I discuss these in section 3.2.2.

The approach to atypical cases that I pursue here is to find constraints arising from the particular text-type serving as the locus of variation. I show how variation in referring sequences in lists is due to the structure of lists themselves by drawing upon observations from our earlier discussion (3.1) and trying to identify features of lists with enough precision to make quantitative comparisons of referring expressions in different textual environments – comparisons that can then be used to evaluate different hypotheses about the organization of referring expressions in talk.

3.2.2 *Constraints specific to lists*

Although mentions of list-items form referring sequences much like those in other discourse, mentions of list-items also vary in ways that arise from the list organization itself. We saw in section 3.1 that lists focus on a general category (X) and its members (X1 ... n). A speaker presents items that share a common attribute and are inferrable as part of a collection: the cumulative presentation of such items in talk reflects their similarity and their shared category membership. Although category members are partially the same, they are also partially different from one another.

Constraints on variation in referring terms stem from the categorical structure of lists. Evidence that the language used in lists is sensitive to categorical structure is provided in table 8.3. Table 8.3 shows that *and* is used with coordinate relationships between category members (regardless of their level, e.g. X1 and X2, X1a and X1b), but not with subordinate relationships (going either up a level (X1a to X1) or down a level (X1 to X1a)).

Table 8.3 Connections between list-items

	Subordinate	Coordinate	Total
And	1	35	36
"Zero"	15	5	20
Total	16	40	56

Table 8.3 shows that although *and* links coordinate level relationships between categories (e.g. X1 and X2), it rarely links subordinate relationships between a category and subcategory (e.g. X1 and X1a): 87 percent (35/40) of the coordinate relationships are linked by *and*, compared to only 6 percent (1/16) of the subordinate relationships. Thus, the categorical relationships between list-items establish structurally differentiated boundaries and transitions within lists that are linguistically reflected. We see in the next subsections that variation in referring terms is constrained by these structural boundaries. I begin by suggesting that lists provide environments for referring expressions that are at least partially segmented from surrounding discourse (3.2.2a); this suggestion further justifies the idea that the referring sequences in lists are

sensitive to constraints stemming from the text-type itself. I then focus on how the general category (the "sameness") in lists constrains referring expressions (3.2.2b). I conclude the analysis by defining thematic and recency constraints within lists and comparing their effects on referring terms (3.2.2c).

a Inside and outside of lists

Lists provide environments for referring expressions that are at least partially segmented from surrounding discourse. One way to see this is to find an example in which an item is mentioned both before and during a list. If lists are relatively closed discourse units, we might find that mentions of an item prior to the inception of the list have little sequential effect on mentions of that item within the list.

Let us consider (18). (18) begins as an IVer asks a question about the IVee's in-laws:

(18) IVER: (a) Did you ever live with your in-laws after you got married?
      IVEE: (b) Eh: no, I didn't.
             (c) We had- well, they lived on the first floor:
             (d) they owned this eh triplex.
             (e) And eh my mother in law and father in law lived on the first floor,
             (f) and my sister in law and her husband lived on the second,
             (g) and we lived on the third.
             (h) And it was a very good arrangement because we- we had our own: um apartments.

The item to focus upon in (18) is "in-laws." "In-laws" is first mentioned outside the list in the IVer's question (*Did you ever live with your in-laws after you got married?* (a)). "In-laws" is then treated as a next-mention (an inexplicit definite *they*) as the IVee begins her answer to the question (*they lived on the first floor* (c), *they owned this eh triplex* (d)). The answer requires an explanation of a particular kind of house which is introduced as *this eh triplex* (d). It is the living arrangement in the triplex that becomes the general category underlying the list: what is listed is the occupants of different floors in the triplex. Recall that "in-laws" had previously been treated as old information: its next-mention was *they* in (c) and (d). Within the list, however, "in-laws" is introduced in terms relevant to the list itself: *And eh my mother in law and father in law lived on the first floor* (e) establishes "in-laws" as occupants of the first floor of the triplex. Central to my point is that "in-laws" is also brought into the discourse as if it were new information: it is mentioned through explicit full nouns. Thus, an item previously used in the discourse is *treated* as a first-mention once it enters the list.

Although lists can open environments for reference that differ from prior discourse, it is not quite so clear that their environments for reference end once the list closes. One reason for this is that lists do not end as neatly as they begin (cf. Labov's (1972b) point that the endings of narratives are less clear-cut than their beginnings; also Schiffrin 1984a). Another reason is that lists can intersect with other discourse units whose boundaries may or may not coincide with those of the list (see (23) in 3.2.2c) What this means is that it is not always easy to know when a person has temporarily left a list and will return to that list, or when a person closes a list. Furthermore, speakers themselves may not have a clear idea of when their list will end simply because the mention of one item may remind them of another.

b Category constraints

We saw above that lists open a new environment for referents. An important characteristic of such an environment is the presence (either stated explicitly or assumed implicitly) of a general category (X) in relation to which other referents (X1 . . . *n*) are understood. In this section, we see how the underlying presence of such a category constrains referring expressions (to X and to X1 . . . *n*) within lists.

We noted earlier that first-mentions can be definite if speakers can assume hearers' accessibility to a conceptual framework within which to locate a referent. Since the category underlying a list provides just such a framework, the referential existence of first-mentions can be inferred in relation to that framework – hence, some definite first-mentions in lists.

(19) illustrates list-items whose referents can be inferred to be specific members of an assumed collectivity (cf. Prince's containing inferrables), i.e. "family members." (Note that these list-items were not included in tables 8.1 and 8.2 because they were mentioned only once.) In (19), definite NPs are the focus of the existential predicate *there is*. (19 was seen earlier as 10.)

(19) IVER: (a) Have any of the kids ever expressed a desire to see him?
      IVEE: (b) No.
              (c) No, they never did.
              (d) I mean like uh, they never asked about daddy or where did daddy go or-
              (e) I mean like, there was me
              (f) and there was my father
              (g) and there was my cousins.
              (h) And the kids were pretty well occupied.
              (i) I mean like,
      IVER: (j) Yeh, it sounds like they were busy.

The IVer's question about whether the IVee's children ever missed their father (the parents are separated) is responded to with a list of people who kept *the kids . . . pretty well occupied: me* (e), *my father* (f), *my cousins* (g). Each of these list-items is presented as the focus of the existential predicate *there was*. Although such constructions are often said to require indefinite NPs, it has also been noted that lists are an exception to this generalization. Hannay

(1985), for example, describes enumerative uses of existential predicates in which entities are understood as particular cases, i.e. members of a sometimes implicit set (see also Rando and Napoli 1978). Definite NPs in *there is* constructions thus present an entity that is thought to be of interest not so much because it itself exists, but because it exists as some member of a larger set. In (19), *me*, *my father*, and *my cousins* are presented as members of the implicit set "family members": their existence is relevant to the category being described. Put another way, each definite description is presented as an example that fills a specifying role.

The category (X) underlying a list constrains references to individual list-items (X1 . . . *n*) in ways other than definiteness. (20) illustrates that the lexical informativeness of first-mentions can be constrained by the implicit category unifying the list. (20 is a summary of 6; I include only the first-mentions.)

(20) IVER: (c)   Are there any old folks livin' on this block?
        . . .

     IVEE-3: (j)   That kook hangin' out the window.
        . . .

     IVEE-2: (r)   Then there's one woman here, crippled or whatever, you
        . . .   want to call her.

     IVEE-2: (ff) And then there's a-another couple up the street who never
                     come out.

The information provided about each list-item is relevant to the IVer's question, which not only prompts the list but also provides the general category underlying the list. Although two unifying factors ("age" and "location") are made salient in the question *Are there any old folks livin' on this block?* (c), only "location" continues to explicitly unify the list-items, first in the general affirmative response *all down this street* (f) and then in first-mentions of list-items: *the window* (j) is a boundary between the privacy of home and the public nature of the street; *here* (r) and *up the street* (ff) are relative to the speaker's own location on the block. Thus, each mention of (X1 . . . *n*) is made relevant to the category (X) of which it is a member.

The category (X) underlying a list constrains mentions not just of subcategories (X1 . . . *n*), but also mentions of the category (X) itself. The next example illustrates the salience (cf. the topic accessibility; Givón 1983a) of the category (X) in the list. This example will also help us begin to compare two constraints on pronouns: recency versus thematicity (see Clancy 1980; Grimes 1978; Tomlin 1985). Finally, it will suggest the importance of subcategory boundaries within a list.

(21) IVER: (a)   That's right, I'm- slowly getting your family straight here
                    [hh. It's-
     IVEE: (b)   [hhhOh, when my mother died, they u-

	(c)	this is funny,
	(d)	she had forty five great grand- forty-five grandchildren, and over: twenty-five great grandchildren.
IVER:	(e)	Holy [Mackerel.
NEICE:	(f)	[Now it's more than doubled.
IVEE:	(g)	Oh, it's doubled since she died, I think she's must had about fifteen more born since she died.
NEICE:	(h)	More than that.
IVEE:	(i)	What, in ten years?
NEICE:	(j)	Su:re.
IVER:		Wow.
IVEE:	(k)	[Well, I know I'm losing track myself.
NEICE:	(l)	[I had two, ^{z}I had two,
	(m)	Susie had two,
	(n)	Peggy had two,
	(o)	Cathy had one,
	(p)	Teresa had *three*,
	(q)	Patsy had two more since she died. *Three* [more.
IVEE:	(r)	[Three. Uh:
NEICE:	(s)	And then there's a lot of other ones in the family.

(21′) highlights the categorical structure of (21). The reference to "my mother" (who is a key part of the category) crosses subcategory boundaries:

(21′) Categorical structure of (21)

X	"my mother's descendants"	
X1	"my mother's descendants born before she died"	
X1a	forty-five grandchildren,	
X1b	over: twenty-five great grandchildren.	(d)
X2	"my mother's descendants born after she died" Oh, it's doubled since she died, I think she's must had about fifteen more born since she died.	(g)
X2a	I had two,	
X2b	Susie had two,	
X2c	Peggy had two,	
X2d	Cathy had one,	
X2e	Teresa had three,	
X2f	Patsy had two more since she died.	(q)

(X) in (21) is "mother's descendants." The descendants are differentiated according to their time of birth in relation to the mother's life: X1 are those "born before she died," X2 are those "born after she died" (g). After noting those born "before she died" (*forty-five grandchildren, and over: twenty-five great grandchildren* (d)), the next subcategory "mother's descendants born after she died" (X2) is introduced: *it's doubled since she died* (g). Note that in introducing X2, "mother" is evoked by *she*. The use of a pronoun here is not surprising: "mother" is still a very salient (and recent) referent, and there are no competing antecedents (Clancy 1980; Givón 1983a).

The pronoun in *Patsy had two more since she died* (q) – in which *she* evokes "mother," not "Patsy" – is surprising. Note that a long list of descendants born *since she died* is presented: these are subcategories of X2. It is within the first-mention of one such subcategory (X2f *Patsy had two more since she died*) that "mother" is mentioned again. The pronominal reference to "mother" as *she* is especially striking here, given both the distance between *she* and the explicit mention of "mother" (*my mother* (b)) and the other intervening referents. Thus, this use of *she* seems to violate what scholars (e.g. Givón 1983a; Tomlin 1987) have called a recency constraint. What *she* in (23) seems to suggest, instead, is the operation of a thematic constraint: an entity that plays an important textual role (cf. in the text topic; Schiffrin 1988b) remains an accessible topic even if not mentioned recently. Put another way, although the antecedent of *she* in (q) is certainly across structural (i.e. subcategory) boundaries, it is still located within an open focus space (Grosz 1981; Sidner 1986) simply because the referent is the category underlying the list itself.

Although the competition between recency and thematic constraints is hardly confined to lists, lists provide an especially clear source of data in which to evaluate these two constraints. Thematicity is particularly easy to identify: the general category (X) underlying the list is thematic. Recency can also be easily identified, but more importantly, our understanding of recency can be supplemented: the presence of clear structural boundaries between subcategories (e.g. X1 and X2) allows us to consider recency not just in terms of the number of clauses intervening between a pronoun and its antecedent, but also in terms of the location of successive mentions of a list-item (e.g. X1) relative to the mentions of other items (i.e. the subcategory boundaries) in the list.

Table 8.4 provides a quantitative view of a thematic constraint in lists: it compares next-mentions across subcategory boundaries depending upon whether next-mentions evoke the category itself (X) or a subcategory (X1 . . . *n*). In other words, table 8.4 compares next-mentions of (X) to next-mentions of (X1) when (X2) precedes that next-mention. A thematic constraint predicts that next-mentions of (X) can be less explicit because they are higher on a scale of topic accessibility (Givón 1983a, b, c) than next-mentions of (X1 . . . *n*).

Table 8.4 Category level and next-mentions across subcategory boundaries

	Next-mention is of		
	Category (X)	Subcategory (X1 . . . n)	Total
Pro/"zero"	11	0	11
Full NP	0	6	6
Total	11	6	17

As table 8.4 shows, 100 percent (11/11) of the next-mentions of (X) are pronouns. This is in sharp contrast to the distribution of pronouns for next-mentions of (X1 . . . *n*): no pronouns at all were used for next-mentions across subcategory boundaries. This difference supports the idea that the general category whose specific members the list instantiates is thematic in the list. Put another way, the focus space of a general category (X) never closes as long as the list continues; the focus spaces of the subcategories (X1 . . . *n*), on the other hand, open and close during the course of the list.

Before I go on to supplement the data from table 8.4 with data that reveal more about the importance of subcategory boundaries, let me summarize thus far. We have seen three ways in which the category being described in a list can influence mentions of items in a list: first-mentions of (X1 . . . *n*) can be definite because they are all members of a general category (X); lexical information ties mentions of (X1 . . . *n*) to (X); pronouns can have antecedents that cross subcategory boundaries when they evoke the category (X) underlying the list. In 3.2.2c we see that just as the category (X) influences referring terms in a list, so too do differences among subcategories (e.g. the difference between (X1) and (X2)).

c Subcategory constraints

Just as the overall unity of a list (the category) is reflected in its referring terms (3.2.2a), so too are the differences and boundaries between subcategories. We saw earlier that if a next-mention of a list-item (X1) is after another list-item (X2) has been mentioned, then the next-mention of (X1) is a full noun. Table 8.5 presents these data again, but contrasts them with next-mentions *within* subcategory boundaries, i.e. next-mentions of (X1) before (X2) is introduced.

Table 8.5 Next-mentions within and across subcategory boundaries

	Cross boundaries	Do not cross boundaries	Total
Pro/"zero"	0	64	64
Full NPS	6	4	10
Total	6	68	74

Table 8.5 shows that 92 percent (68/74) of the next-mentions are within subcategory boundaries; 95 percent (64/68) of these are pronominal or "zero".

Table 8.5 also shows that 8 percent (6/74) of the next-mentions have antecedents that cross subcategory boundaries, i.e. return to a list-item (X1) after another list-item (X2) has already been discussed. All six next-mentions are full nouns: five of these appear in descriptive structures whose sequential organization is quite different from the lists considered thus far. After discussing these five cases, I briefly comment on the one other case.

All the lists discussed so far in this chapter can be called depth-before-breadth lists. List-items and descriptive material about those items are together in the text; each list-item (X1) is completed prior to the introduction of a next list-item (X2).

> X1 . . .
> X2 . . .
> X3 . . .

In this structure, speakers provide "depth" to the list (information about (X1)) before adding "breadth" to the list by mentioning (X2). Notice that pronominal next-mentions can be clearly linked with a single unambiguous antecedent in this structure, simply because no new list-items are introduced until description of the prior item is complete. Not only is (X1) closed before mentioning (X2), but list-items are not typically returned to once they are closed. Thus, in the depth-before-breadth list structure, references to list-items typically do not cross subcategory boundaries.

Lists can also be presented in a breadth-before-depth structure: speakers provide "breadth" to the list (they first mention (X1), (X2), and (X3)) before providing much information ("depth") about each item.

> X1
> X2
> X3
> X1 . . .
> X2 . . .
> X3 . . .

In this structure, each list-item is presented prior to its elaboration. This means that speakers return to prior list-items (e.g. to X1) cyclically and they cross the subcategory boundaries of other list items (e.g. X2 and X3) to do so. (22) illustrates. The IVee is describing what is known in Philadelphia as a "father, son, and holy ghost" house. (This was example (30) in chapter 7.)

(22) IVEE: (a) A girlfriend of mine, downtown somewhere
             (b) she m- uh got married and she moved into one.
X1   (c) One room here
X2   (d) and then it's one room on the second floor
X3   (e) and one room on the top.
      IVER: Yeh, that's right.
X1   IVEE: (f) So she used her downstairs as her parlor.
      IVER: Uh huh.
X2   IVEE: (g) Her second,
X   (h) there's only three rooms [like,] y'know.
      IVER: [Yeh.]
X2   (h) The second story of the room was her bedroom
X3   (i) and the third room was her bedroom.

The IVee in (22) begins by mentioning all three list-items as indefinite full nouns: (X1) is *one room here* (c), (X2) is *one room on the second floor* (d), (X3) is *one room on the top* (e). She then provides more information about them in the same order in which they were introduced. Note that although she provides that information as predications about the list-item, she also explicitly labels each list-item again: (X1) *her downstairs* (f), (X2) *the second story of the room* (h), (X3) *the third room* (i).

As noted earlier, five of the six explicit next-mentions of list-items across subcategory boundaries are in breadth-before-depth lists. The one remaining example is (23). We noted earlier that lists can be environments for reference that differ from surrounding discourse, but that it is not always easy to establish when a list ends. (23) is an example in which a speaker embeds several narratives into a list, and references to entities move between the list structure *per se* and the narratives. In (23), the speaker lists his jobs in temporal order (3.1.3a) and tells stories that explain his transition from job to job. Although space prevents presentation of the whole discourse, I include a mention of a "job" (X2 at time 2) that is within a narrative and does not cross subcategory boundaries, as well as the next-mention of primary interest: mention of a "job" (X1 at time 4) within a narrative that crosses subcategory boundaries.

(23)   X1/T1   Mostly what happened was I was-I worked there as a metal polisher,
       X2/T2   and then I went to a loom company that was cuttin' looms. For about six months.
               [describes illnesses]
               All right, I was workin' for them about six months.
               [doctor forbids him to go back to work]
               [argument with supervisor: he's fired]
       X3/T3   And I went and got a job right over here at Baxter and Kelly's makin' uh plush materials.
               [describes problem with second job]
       X1/T4   So I went back to metal polishing.

In (23), the speaker describes how he went from metal polishing (X1 at time 1) to a loom company (X2 at time 2) to making plush materials (X3 at time 3) and then back to metal polishing (X1 at time 4). When the speaker mentions a work place currently in focus in the list, the referring term is pronominal even if a long description intervenes between the first and next-mentions: he mentions "the loom company" as *them* in *All right, I was workin' for them about six months.* Although not included above, the speaker mentions *Baxter and Kelly's makin' uh plush materials* (X3 at time 3) after a story but within the same subcategory description, and again uses a pronoun to do so. Note, however, that when "metal polishing" (X1) is mentioned again (at time 4) it is evoked through a full noun: *So I went back to metal polishing.* This difference shows, again, that list-items can be treated as given information (and be evoked through pronouns) only if a new subcategory has not been introduced.

We have seen thus far that pronominal next-mentions of list-items (X1 . . . *n*) typically have antecedents within their own subcategory boundaries: the only exceptions are when the referent evoked by the pronoun is the thematic category (X) itself. Next-mentions of list-items (e.g. X1) that cross subcategory boundaries (e.g. after mention of X2) are full nouns.

Recall, however, that some next-mentions of (X1 . . . *n*) are explicit nouns even though their first-mentions are not across subcategory boundaries: 4 out of 68 of the referring expressions *within* subcategory boundaries were full nouns (table 8.5). All four of these next-mentions had evaluative functions in their lists (3.1.3). (24) illustrates.

(24)   IVEE: (a)   But- see, years ago, every neighborhood had its own little,
                     uh stores,
               (b)   y'know, corner stores and everything,
               (c)   which the supermarkets knocked out of [commission.
       IVER: [No kidding.
               That's right.
       IVEE: (d)   And there were little restaurants,
               (e)   that you don't find today.
       IVER: Well, like-
       IVEE: (f)   See, H and H come in and knocked all the little restaurants
                     out of business.
       IVER: Well, that's really a shame.
       IVEE: (g)   Yeh. Right. Progress is ba:d.

The list in (24) is part of a discussion of differences between the past and the present: the speaker is listing the types of establishments (*little stores* (a), *little restaurants* (d)) that are no longer in her neighborhood. The speaker's attitude toward change is not only summarized at the end of the list (*Progress is ba:d* (g)): it is conveyed through the description and evaluation of list-items themselves. In (a) through (c), *the supermarkets* (c) are portrayed metaphorically (Lakoff and Johnson 1980) as antagonists who *knocked* the little stores (X1) *out of commission*. The first-mention of *little restaurants* (X2) is evaluative. The repetition of *little* (from *little, uh stores* (a)) in (d) (*little restaurants*) and the intonationally separate adjunct (*that you don't find today*) both prefigure the powerless position, and fate, of the restaurants; *that you don't find today* (e) also ties (X2) to the comparison underlying the list. The next-mention of "little restaurants" (X2) is a full noun *all the little restaurants* (rather than the pronominal *them*) that is also evaluative. Not only does the speaker increase the generalizability of this example with *all*, but the explicit next-mention of (X2) – repeating *little restaurants* from the first-mention – conveys that the fate of the restaurants is part of a repeated pattern, thus also contributing to the generalization.

To summarize: we have focused here upon how referring terms in lists reflect differences among subcategories. Specifically, we have seen that the presence of subcategory boundaries constrains the use of pronouns, i.e. pronominal mentions of list-items have antecedents within the section of the list describing that list-item itself. Put another way, the alternation between pronouns and full noun phrases in lists is constrained by the way different sections of the list are segmented from one another. Thus, just as the overall descriptive unity of a list is reflected in its referring terms (3.2.2a), so too are differences among the parts of a list.

3.2.3   *Summary: variation within text*

In this section, I have illustrated how variationist approaches to discourse analyze variation within text. I focused on variation in referring terms in lists. We saw that referring terms in lists reflect the category structure underlying a list. The alternation between pronouns and full noun phrases in lists is constrained by category level and subcategory boundaries – by the way different units in the list are related to, and segmented from, one another. Such findings drew upon our knowledge of the structure of lists (3.1) to define possible constraints on referring terms and to analyze variation in referring terms under different structural conditions.

4   The variationist approach to discourse

I noted at the outset of this chapter that the variationist approach to discourse stems from quantitative studies of linguistic change and variation. Although such analyses typically focus on social and linguistic constraints on semantically equivalent variants, such an approach has also been extended to texts. In this chapter, I illustrated extensions at two different levels of analysis: comparing text types (3.1) and analyzing variation within text (3.2). I did so to show not only that variationist approaches to discourse can take two directions, but that there is an important relationship between these two directions: our comparison between text-types provided valuable information about different types of textual structure, and thus information about discourse constraints on grammatical variation that are specific to particular text types.

In section 3.1, we identified and compared the textual structures of narratives and lists. We saw that the basic unit of narrative is the event; the basic unit of lists is the entity. The primary information structures of narratives are temporal and evaluative; the primary information structure of lists is descriptive. Such comparisons reflect the variationist tendency to speak of discourse in terms similar to those used by structurally oriented linguists: "units" are akin to constituents; "information" is propositional in nature (despite the fact that propositions may themselves have evaluative interpretations); "structures" are syntagmatic and paradigmatic arrangements of units in recurrent patterns. Texts are thus built from linguistic constituents that have formal relations to one another: these relationships help to reveal the basis for coherence within a text (or across turns in an interaction: Labov 1972d; Labov and Fanshel 1977).

Comparing text types also contributes to our knowledge of variation in text structure *per se*. Recall that we depended upon variation in the distribution of specific linguistic forms (e.g. temporal markers, stative predicates) across text-types as a source of information *about* those text-types. We began these comparisons thinking that we were comparing the "same" linguistic form, just in different linguistic environments. Our results showing how syntactic and semantic differences among linguistic items reflect (and help realize) text structure, however, suggest that what seemed the same *at a sentence level* is really very different at a *text* level. *Then*, existential *there*, stative predicates, and event clauses all have dramatically different functions depending on the text-type in which they occur. Although such differences clearly illustrate the interdependency between sentence and text, they also raise an important issue about *referential* and *functional* equivalence.

We noted earlier (section 2) that variationists try to discover patterns in the distribution of alternative ways of saying the same thing, i.e. the social and linguistic factors that constrain linguistic variation. Thus, an initial step in variationist studies is to establish which forms alternate with one another. We also saw that applying variation analysis at a discourse level has sometimes required loosening the criterion by which alternating forms are grouped together from referential equivalence to functional equivalence. Although I am not advocating the use of one criterion over another, what I am suggesting is that the adoption of any kind of *formal* basis for identifying equivalents (whether it is referential or syntactic) does not allow us to ignore functions: in fact, it may end up highlighting functional variability at another level of analysis. This result is the converse of what happens when we begin with functional equivalents and find that a great variety of different forms can serve similar functions. In our discussion of library reference interviews in chapter 5, for example, we discussed the different forms and devices (interrogative or declarative statements, rising intonation) that patrons could use to accomplish a single function (i.e. issue a query). Thus, regardless of the locus of analysis from which variationists initiate a study of variation in and of discourse, they may end up at a destination quite different from the one anticipated – and may find that they reached that destination using a rather surprising path.

In section 3.2 we focused on referring terms as linguistic variants within texts: we analyzed how such variants are constrained by both general features of discourse and particular features of the text type. After noting a general discourse tendency for first-mentions to be indefinite and explicit (cf. chapter

6), we concentrated on how referring sequences are sensitive to the particular structure of lists. Put another way, we analyzed how formal variants within lists (nouns versus pronouns) are constrained by the descriptive structure of the list.

Limiting the study of linguistic variants to a particular text-type – as we did – has both methodological and theoretical advantages that point out the importance of taking a two-pronged approach to variation in discourse. By focusing on referring terms within a discourse whose structure we had just described, we were able to use our knowledge of that structure to identify the linguistic environments in which formal alternations were possible, and to define different features of those environments as constraints on variation among formal alternants. We saw, for example, that the distribution of full nouns and pronouns was constrained by the location of an item in the hierarchical structure of a list. We interpreted this constraint as evidence that pronouns can be constrained by thematicity, as well as by recency. Efforts to relate the findings of variation analysis to other issues and controversies within linguistics are not unusual: variationists often form their hypotheses and use their findings to address the adequacy of an explanation, or try to find evidence that will help resolve particular problems or decide among competing solutions for those problems.

The way variationist approaches to discourse compare different possible explanations is by searching for data which confirm (or cast doubt upon) the co-occurrences predicted by each explanation. Although this is not, of course, a goal unique to variationists, variationist approaches add the strengths (and limitations) of a quantitative paradigm to such efforts. Quantitative analyses require definitions of the variants (the different possible realizations of an underlying type), a classification of factors in the environment with which those variants may be associated, and a comparison of the frequencies with which different variants co-occur with different factors. In our analysis in (3.2.2b), for example, we defined the variants as pronouns and nouns, we identified environments in terms of categorical structure (i.e. as next-mentions of items at different levels of category structure), and we compared the relative frequencies of pronouns and nouns according to their location in the categorical structure of the lists in which they occurred. Quantitative procedures depend upon certain assumptions about the relationship between text and context that limit the range of discourse variation to which they can be applied, and the way that such variation can be interpreted.

Although the quantitative thrust of variationist approaches to discourse has the advantages suggested above, it also limits the amount of attention paid to particular cases, concentrating instead upon general trends and patterns. Variationist approaches do not always seek to explain the cases that seem to violate a general pattern: this is consistent with the belief that constraints operate in a probabilistic fashion (one expects to find less then perfect complementary distributions) in response to both synchronic and diachronic pressures in social life and language structure. (Inherent variability plays a tremendously important role in both sociolinguistic and linguistic theory; to oversimplify a bit, language variation is related to both social identity and language change.) This does not mean, however, that it is not important to know the boundaries of variation. The more precise one can be about constraints on variation, the more one can use variation studies to compare and evaluate competing hypotheses about social life and language structure. A number of different strategies for explaining variation within a particular realm are available: identifying new types of constraints (either internal or external to the language system), analyzing the operation and possible intersection of multiple constraints. The approach illustrated here was to find constraints on referring sequences in lists that were due to the structure of lists themselves, and to make quantitative comparisons of referring expressions in different list environments – comparisons that could be used to evaluate different hypotheses about the organization of referring expressions in talk.

Finally, although variationists can also focus upon interactional and situational variation in texts, this was not a direction pursued in our sample analysis. Note, however, that such analyses would be built upon – and incorporate – studies such as those provided here. The comparison of text-types and the analysis of textual constraints on variation both allow more systematic analyses of how text-types are socially situated: they first "factor" out how particular features of a text are linguistically, rather then socially, motivated.

Exercises

1 Collect versions of the same story (or the same list) in different modalities (e.g. a shopping list that is spoken and written) and different situations (e.g. a story told to a friend and to a family member). How do the text structures vary in ways that might be due to modality and situation? Are there any syntactic variants that seem to appear in one modality/situation but not the other?

2 Thematic and recency constraints can be compared in text types other than lists. Using a written text as data (e.g. a short story, an expository text, a recipe, a newspaper article), analyze how thematicity and recency constrain pronominal/nominal variation in the text.

3 Recipes are a form of written discourse that combine features of both lists (the ingredients necessary to make a certain dish) and narrative (steps for making the dish are typically presented in temporal order). Collect ten to fifteen recipes for the same dish (e.g. pie crust, meat loaf) from a range of cookbooks intended for different audiences (e.g. novice to expert). Analyze the textual structure of the recipes in terms of the two text-types noted, as well as the features that do not seem to conform to either text-type. Identify text-level variants (e.g. in the order in which ingredients are listed) and clause-level variants (e.g. in the use of referring terms, adverbial clauses, conjunctions). Do the textual structures and/or the variants seem to be related to the different audiences to which the recipes are directed? If not, what might be responsible for the differences that you found? (Note: The same exercise can be applied to other procedural texts in which instructions are given in a comparable format.)

4 Texts can be identified by a number of different criteria, discussed in work such as Bauman and Briggs (1990), Biber (1988), Briggs and Bauman (1992), Enkvist (1991), Ferguson (1983), Horvath (1987), and Virtanen (1992). Compare the criteria used in this chapter to differentiate lists from narratives to the criteria proposed in some of the above-mentioned references. What other criteria might have been used to differentiate lists from narratives? How can we evaluate the principles underlying a text typology? What is the value of constructing text typologies, and can this goal be accomplished?

5 Research by Ellen Prince (Prince 1984, 1985) and Gregory Ward (Ward 1990; Ward et al. 1991) has examined how principles derived from Gricean pragmatics influence the use of syntactic variants. After reading one or two selections from each of these authors, assess the compatibility of the Gricean and variationist approaches, either by focusing on a specific construction in your own data sample or by reanalyzing the referring sequences in chapters 6 and 8 of this book. (You might also include referring sequences from the data in chapters 4, 5, and 7.)

6 The constraints on referring terms discussed in this chapter have been largely structural constraints, defined according to the location of a "mention" in a text. However, we also noted some exceptions to the structural patterns that seemed to be evaluatively motivated. Some of the constraints considered in other chapters (adjacency pair, cooperative principle) might also be considered evaluative: they arise from the way a speaker weaves together the need to make a "mention" recognizable to a hearer with a subjective point being made by a text and by the role of a referent within the text. Analyses by Duranti (1984), Maitland and Wilson (1987), Muhlhausler and Harré (1990), and Varenne (1984) pursue this line of inquiry more thoroughly. Using some (or all) of the referring sequences considered in chapters 7–9, the data in appendix 3, or any other data of your choice, consider referring sequences from an evaluative (non-structural) perspective.

Notes

1   Variation analyses often check the statistical significance of quantitative distributions. However, I have not done so in this chapter: the extremely skewed distributions (i.e. the contrast between cells with a very low percentage of tokens and those with a high percentage of occurrences) seem to be sufficient to my claims in this chapter.

Part III Conclusion

We began this book by observing that discourse analysis is widely recognized as one of the most vast, but also one of the least defined, areas in linguistics. We saw in previous chapters that one reason for this is that our understanding of discourse is based on scholarship from a number of academic disciplines that are actually very different from one another. The chapters in part II have not only reviewed six different approaches to discourse, but illustrated how these approaches address some important issues bearing on the production and interpretation of utterances as both linguistic and social practice.

In this final part, I compare approaches to discourse in a more systematic and abstract way that I hope will enable us to consider them not just as tools for analysis, but as possible candidates for theories of discourse. My discussion is grounded in three issues that discourse analysts face: the relationship between structure and function, text and context, utterances and communication. Although these issues are quite different in some ways, they all require reconciling what is often defined as part of "language" (or at least, part of a linguistic system) with what is not typically defined as part of language. Many scholars are comfortable making such a distinction in principle, but find it difficult to maintain such a distinction in practice. The three issues on which my comparison is centered all obscure the borders between different analytic domains, and are thus partially responsible for the vastness of discourse analysis.

9 Structure and Function

1 Introduction

Discourse has often been viewed in two different ways: a structure, i.e. a unit of language that is larger than the sentence; and the realization of functions, i.e. as the use of language for social, expressive, and referential purposes (chapter 2). Despite the diversity of structural approaches, structural analyses all focus on the way different units function in relation to each other: they disregard "functional relations with the context of which discourse is a part" (van Dijk 1985: 4). Since it is precisely the relationship between discourse and the context of which discourse is a part that characterizes functional analyses, it might seem that the two approaches have little in common.

All the approaches discussed in this book, however, incorporate both structure and function into their analyses. After describing how approaches starting from structure lead to function, and vice versa (section 2), I compare the approaches more explicitly in terms of how they relate individual utterances to structures holding across utterances (section 3). We will see that all the different approaches to discourse analysis try to bridge or somehow combine the two analytical worlds of structure and function: not only do the types of structures analyzed in discourse lead to the identification of functions, but the types of functions analyzed in discourse are linguistically realized in ways that create structures (section 4).

2 Structure and function in discourse analysis

Whereas some approaches to discourse begin from structure and lead to function (2.1), others take the opposite route (2.2). Approaches that are theoretically oriented toward either structure or function, then, actually end up combining structure and function in practice.

2.1   From structure to function

I discuss two approaches in this section: conversation analysis (2.1.1) and variation analysis (2.1.2). Although both begin with structure (but at a different location within "text"; chapter 10), both also bring function into their means of analysis.

2.1.1   Conversation analysis

One of the central assumptions of conversation analysis (CA) is that interaction is structurally organized. Rather than posit generalizations about structure apart from the details of specific events, however, it is participants' conduct itself that must provide evidence for the presence of units, existence of patterns, and formulation of rules. To this end, CA searches for recurrent patterns, distributions, and forms of organization in talk. One structure discovered in talk is the adjacency pair: a sequence of two adjacent utterances produced by different speakers, and ordered as a first part and second part. Adjacency pairs are also "typed" so that a first part requires a particular second part or range of second parts.

In addition to analyzing structure, CA also seeks to discover the solutions that people construct for recurrent organizational problems of social life. One such problem is the exchange of turns at talk. This "distribution" problem is resolved by the operation of a series of ordered rules that operate at turn transition locations. One might say, then, that turn-taking rules have the function of allocating turns at talk.

The description of turn-taking rules (and other devices, see below) as having a "function" might seem as though CA is an approach to discourse that is explicitly structural *and* functional. Because CA derives functions from sequential structures and regularities that hold across utterances, however, CA does give structure a more central methodological importance than function. Whatever can be established as serving a function – linguistic devices, rules, a one second silence (Jefferson 1989), laughter (Jefferson 1984) – serves that function only by virtue of its sequential arrangement with other parts of talk. CA tries to uncover patterns in the way participants use particular terms or devices through a distributional method of analysis akin to a method used in structural linguistics whereby items are "arranged" in relation to one another. In our sample analysis in chapter 7, for example, we characterized the sequential "arrangement" of a linguistic construction (although the construction was characterized without consideration of its linguistic structure as "there + BE + ITEM") both within and across turns, and in relation to (and independent of) other sequentially definable units (questions, answers, topics). Thus, the distrust of generalizations that are neither empirically grounded nor appliable to specific events extends to the analysis of functions within CA. What CA finds to be an antidote to premature generalizations about function is the recurrence of an item in a particular slot in a sequential structure. Put another way, CA analyses of sequential structure provide a methodological resource for the derivation of function.

I noted above that CA assumes a structural framework at the level of relationships between utterances, rather than linguistic structure. Note that this does not preclude linguistic structure from serving a function in a text – a function derived (as just noted) from recurrent observations about its location in sequential structure. Just as my discussion of the "functions" of "there + BE + ITEM" in chapter 7 was based on its sequential location, so too I suggested that an understanding of the functions of different types of "there" (demonstrative, adverbial, pronominal) could be based on observations about sequential structure. Thus, even the CA discovery of the functions of language structure is based on sequential distribution of a form in relation to conversational structure.

In sum, CA is a structural methodology for the analysis of talk. The sequential regularities and patterns that it discovers, however, reveal how specific features of talk are used by participants to accomplish tasks that are central to the organization of talk, i.e. how they function to create solutions for recurrent problems of talk.

2.1.2 Variation analysis

Although variation analysis also searches for structure, the means by which it does so, the structures that it discovers, and the units within those structures all differ from CA. Discourse structure for variationists is found in texts defined as either primarily monologic (e.g. narratives, lists) or dialogic (e.g. question–answer or request–response sequences). In the former case, structure is found within a discourse unit whose external boundaries and internal relationships define an autonomous unit that is largely independent of how it is embedded in surrounding talk (cf. Goodwin 1984; Jefferson 1978). In the latter case, structure is found at a level of underlying actions and reactions that are related to one another through sequencing rules, and that are related to utterances through rules of production and interpretation (see section 2.2.1 on speech act theory).

The variationist view of linguistic variables also builds upon the notion of structure. A linguistic variable is part of a system of interrelated parts: it is a set of linguistic realizations defined in relation to a single underlying form or representation that occupies a "slot" (a phonological segment, a syntactic constituent) in a grammar. Furthermore, the linguistic environment by which variables are constrained is a structured environment: "factors" are segments of text that themselves can have different values and impact upon the occurrence/non-occurrence of the variable. Recall, for example, our analysis of textual constraints on referring terms (chapter 8): we tried to identify features of lists with enough precision to make quantitative comparisons of referring expressions in different textual environments. To this end, we found that the distinction between categories and subcategories, and the presence or absence of category boundaries between first-and next-mentions of a list item, constrained the explicitness of a referring term (full noun versus pronoun). Thus, factors in the linguistic environment create textual constraints on which variants are dependent.

I have been suggesting so far that the structure assumed by variationists is both syntagmatic and paradigmatic. Descriptions and comparisons of different text-types focus upon syntagmatic structure, and analyses of textual constraints on variation focus on paradigmatic structure. Thus, variationists assume discourse structure in terms similar to those used by structurally oriented linguists: "units" are similar to constituents, "information" is propositional in nature, "structures" are syntagmatic and paradigmatic arrangements of items in recurrent patterns.

When we consider the locus of variation a bit more closely, however, we see that function also enters into variationist approaches to discourse. Variationists have to establish which forms are in alternation with one another. Doing this at a discourse level has sometimes led analysts to shift from a requirement of referential equivalence to one of functional equivalence. As I noted in chapter 8, however, the locus of analysis from which variationists begin a study of text-related variation may not be the point at which they end such a study. The adoption of a referential basis for identifying equivalents does not allow us to ignore functions: in fact, it may end up highlighting the functional constraints (and thus functional differences) at another level of analysis. This result is the opposite of what happens when we begin with functional equivalents.

Let us consider this point in a bit more detail in relation to referring terms. A variationist analysis of referring terms can define equivalence either referentially or functionally. Depending upon one's definition of equivalence, the forms upon which one would focus would be quite different. Analyses of referential equivalents would begin by focusing upon the different forms used to realize the same referential intent. An example from chapter 6 (presented here as 1) illustrates. Sue is describing how her sister-in-law married someone who was not completely Italian:

(1) SUE: (a) So she was the oldest daughter.
             (b) And she broke the ice for me like she said.
             (c) Y'know, for Tony, my husband.
     IVER: (d) How did you meet Tony?

A bit later, Sue is describing how she met Tony, and she uses two other expressions that have the same referential intent:

(2) (a) So anyway, this real dark looking, gangster looking guy, comes out the door,

   (b) and he looked like an old man to me.

   (c) And he looked like a gangster.

(1) and (2) contain four different referring expressions that all realize the same referential intent: *Tony, my husband, this real dark looking, gangster looking guy,* and *he* are alternative ways of conveying a single entity to which Sue intends to refer. Note, however, that the referring terms vary in terms of their functional relevance (see discussion in chapter 6). What a variationist approach would do is operationalize the functional differences among these expressions as constraints on their use (along with whatever structural constraints also seemed to be important).

Analyses of functional equivalents, on the other hand, focus on the realization of a single function. Although such analyses might begin by focusing upon a single form that would realize a variety of different referential intents, they also broaden their focus to other forms that fill the same function. The indefinite description "this X" (used as first-mention), for example, has been said to have a particular function: it displays a negative evaluation of a referent (it is pejorative) that will become a topic of next talk (Prince 1978; Wright and Givón 1987). One of the examples above, *this real dark looking, gangster looking guy* (3a), used "this X" in a way that seems consistent with this function. (Note that if we want to consider "this X" as a first-mention in (2), we can do so only if we consider it in relation to the shift in information state accompanying entry into a story world; chapter 6, p. 210.) Not only is *this real dark looking, gangster looking guy* an unflattering description (which continues in the next lines of the story), but, consistent with others' predictions, this referent becomes a topic of next talk: the focus of the story initiated with (2) is how a romantic relationship evolved, such that the referent is a topic at both sentence and text levels (Schiffrin 1988b). (3) is another example: a speaker uses "this X" while complaining about the demands of the church.

(3) (a) And in September, the beginning of October, they have this block collection.

   (b) And you are supposed to give twenty-five dollars.

   (c) Each family is supposed to give twenty-five dollars.

   (d) Well, they- I used to give whatever I could afford, before.

   (e) And now, "Well, Father, if I catch you, fine. If not, sorry about that."

Since *block collection* is being viewed negatively – and is the text topic underlying the next few utterances – this would be another example in which "this X" realizes the suggested function. The distribution of "this X" would be checked in all other texts in a sample to see whether it is a referring expression whose uses are functionally equivalent – even though different tokens of this referential type would of course be realizations of equivalent referential intents. Pursuing this a bit further, one could then examine the distribution of "this X" by different speakers (their social characteristics), in different text types, different modalities, and different registers.

Although a functionally based analysis of "this X" could continue in the way suggested above, it would also have to identify other forms that might serve one (or more) of the same functions as "this X" (e.g. "this one X," "one X"). But once we do this, we are back to the study of formal variants – not formal variants that are referentially equivalent (since they would probably be used to evoke different referents), but formal variants that are functionally equivalent. Thus, as I noted in chapter 8, regardless of the locus of analysis from which variationists begin a study of text-related variation, they may end up at a destination quite different from the one anticipated, and find that they reached that destination using a path that they may have wanted to avoid.

Thus far, I have been suggesting that the variationist focus on structure leads to an analysis of function. I want to also suggest that the sorts of structures (both within and across clauses) that might be considered by variationists can serve text-level functions. This interdependency also forces an analysis of both structure and function.

In chapter 2, we discussed an example in which a speaker (Henry) used five clauses to introduce the main characters of a narrative. I present this example here as (4):

(4) (e) Because there's this guy Louie Gelman,
     (f) he went to a *big* specialist,
     (g) and the guy . . . analyzed it *wrong*.
     (h) In fact his doctor didn't know,
     (i) and the specialist didn't know.

Note that the introduction of these characters is critical to Henry's story: before Henry can use his story to make a general point about doctors (*doctors are not God!*), he has to introduce the characters whose experience and interaction with one another provide a specific instance of this general point. The old/new information structures in clauses (e), (f), and (g) provide this introduction.

(e) Because there's this guy Louie Gelman [new],
(f) he [old] went to a *big* specialist [new],
(g) and the guy [old] . . . analyzed it *wrong*.

By placing new information in the context of familiar information within each clause, Henry facilitates the introduction of characters important to the point of his story. Thus the information structure within the clauses serves the text-level function of introducing the characters whose experience is central to the story.

Structures across the clauses in (4) also facilitate the general point to be made by the story. Clauses (e) to (g) above mention two referents, twice each. The first-mentions and next-mentions form referring sequences, presented below:

	First-mention	Next-mention
Referent 1	this guy Louie Gelman	he
Referent 2	a *big* specialist	the guy

Referent 1 is evoked initially through an indefinite NP (*this guy*) and a proper noun (*Louie Gelman*); its next-mention is a pronoun (*he*). Referent 2 is evoked initially through an indefinite noun (*a big specialist*); its next-mention is a definite noun (*the guy*). Sequences such as these recur throughout discourse: indeed, the clauses in which we can find dependencies between referring terms need not even be adjacent to one another. These distributional regularities suggest that speakers construct sequences even apart from these that we intuitively identify and label as particular chunks of discourse (e.g. answer, story). The point here, however, is somewhat different. The referring terms in (4) shift from explicit to inexplicit, from indefinite to definite. These shifts reflect the incorporation of the referents into a story world. Put another way, one reason why Henry can go on to make the point of his story is because the characters central to that point have been structurally embedded in the story world. Thus, a text-level function is allowed by structures that hold across clauses.

We can make a similar point by considering temporal structures across clauses. Formal analysts often try to model temporal interpretation in discourse, taking into account how different linguistic forms and meanings within clauses influence temporal interpretations across clauses (e.g. Dowty 1986; Dry 1981, 1983; Fleischman 1990; Hinrichs 1986; Kamp and Rohrer 1983; Partee 1984; Webber 1988). We noted in chapter 2 that a modification of the basic rule of narrative ordering – in which reference time shifts with each complicating action clause – helps Henry make the point of his story: Henry reports his friend's encounter with a specialist before the friend's temporally prior encounter with his own doctor. Henry's deviation from a temporal order in which time moves forward can certainly be formally represented – but it is not formally motivated. Rather, the shift back in reference time has the discourse function of helping Henry increase the membership of the group of professionals who was wrong, adding to the overall point of his story.

In sum, variationists begin with structure: they search for structure within monologue and dialogue, they assume that the underlying form whose different realizations constitute a variable are part of the structure of language, and they assume that variants are structurally constrained. Yet they are also led to analyses that build upon an interdependency between structure and function: analyses of textually constrained variants veer between structure and function, and analyses of text-level functions reveal that these functions can be fulfilled by structure within and across clauses.

2.2   From function to structure

This section discusses approaches to discourse that begin with function and end up incorporating structure into their analyses: speech act theory (2.2.1), ethnography of communication (2.2.2), interactional sociolinguistics (2.2.3), and pragmatics (2.2.4).

2.2.1   Speech act theory

Speech act theory begins by grounding its units of analysis in a system outside of language (in speaker intention and action, in our knowledge of constitutive rules), but its application to discourse leads to a structural approach in which units are sequentially arranged in certain patterns. The units focused upon by speech act theory are a relatively small subset of language functions: communicative actions that can be realized in a single sentence, labelled by a particular culture, and often performable with a verb naming the act, e.g. promise, thank, offer, hint, regret, conclude. As Searle (1979: 22) notes:

> If we adopt illocutionary point as the basic notion on which to classify uses of language, then there are a rather limited number of basic things we do with language: we tell people how things are, we try to get them to do things, we commit ourselves to doing things, we express our feeling and attitudes and we bring about changes through our utterances.

Speech acts are discovered by examining texts and contexts (chapter 10): conditions underlying the realization of a particular act are both linguistically met and contextually satisfied (see also section 2.2.3). These conditions are the basis for the way we classify speech acts (and thus identify an utterance as a particular type of "unit"), for the way a single utterance can have more than one function (i.e. be more than one "unit"), and ultimately, for the patterns formed by the use of utterances as acts during social interactions.

There are several reasons why the functional thrust of speech act theory noted above leads to discourse structure. We saw several examples in chapter 3 of speech acts that were definable only sequentially: answers, expansions, and accounts. This means that identifying the speech act function of an utterance often requires looking at where it occurs in relation to other utterances, i.e. its location in what is assumed to be an orderly arrangement of other units. To take a simple (hypothetical) example, compare the role of *yes* in (5a) through (5c):

(5a)   S: Do you want to go to the movies tonight?
      H: Yes.
(5b)   S: That's a beautiful view.

H: Yes.

(5c) S: Do you promise you'll be there?

H: Yes.

In (5a), the function of *yes* is answer to a question; in (5b), agreement with an assessment; in (5c), making a promise. Since each of these functions is obviously dependent upon the preceding act, we must conclude that the speech act functions of *yes* in (5) result from its location in a discourse structure defined through the functional identity of the first constituent in that structure. Other approaches (e.g. conversation analysis) that have reanalyzed speech act sequences suggest that the effect of structure on speech act function is even more penetrating than we have suggested: there are numerous occasions where the illocutionary force of an utterance – the very bedrock of speech act theory – may not even be clear until it is *followed by* another utterance. Such structures thus have a retrospective effect on the identity of a prior utterance, such that some speech act categories depend on what precedes and/or what follows the utterance in which they are realized.

The multifunctionality of utterances can be accommodated in the speech act view of structure. Since an utterance can perform more than one act at a time (have more than one function), a single utterance creates different response options for a next utterance. This gives our exchanges a certain degree of flexibility: multiple interpretations of X can lead to multiple possibilities for responding to X. In analytical terms, this means that whatever sequence results may be the outcome of very different underlying functional relationships. It also means that whatever structure results is comprised of only one of a range of (possibly) very different functional units.

In sum, speech act theory leads to the discovery of well-formed sequences of discourse. This outcome is exactly what is aimed for by structural analyses – despite the fact that the structures are functionally (and contextually) based.

2.2.2 Ethnography of communication

The ethnography of communication is a functional approach to discourse: language is always constitutive of some portion of social and cultural life, either indexing a prior reality, or creating a new reality, for participants. The meanings and functions of language are personal, social, and cultural functions that mesh with other systems of actions and beliefs. Consistent with the comparative and relativistic premises of this approach, however, little can be assumed about such functions: it is up to ethnographers to discover both the range of and ways of realizing such functions.

What allows language functions to mesh with context – and to be discovered through contextual analyses – is the fact that context itself is not random and disorganized: rather, context has a communicative structure built from a variety of communicative components that co-occur and alternate with one another. In our sample analysis of questions in chapter 5, for example, we added different aspects of context to our analysis of particular utterances in a way that built upon an underlying assumption that the organization of communicative events has a systematic effect on (helping to define the function of) constituent acts. We ended up suggesting that all the utterances that we called "questions" share a general function: they all seek a response that facilitates the transmission of information in the speech event. And this suggested that the smaller "units" of an ethnographic analysis (e.g. the utterances used to realize speech acts) may be mutually constitutive with the larger units (e.g. the speech events) in which they occur.

The procedure that I have just sketched suggests an intentional interdependency between structure and function: the communicative structure of a speech event reveals the function of constituent acts, and the function of the act itself contributes to the structure of the event. Thus, an analysis of the structure of a speech event can end up revealing how that structure accommodates the functions realized by the event. Put more generally, "the recognition of social function brings recognition of new structure, transcending conventional compartments" (Hymes 1974c: 150).

The interdependence between the communicative structures of context and the function of individual utterances can be put to further use in relating structure and function: systematic analysis of communicative contexts can help to explain the multifunctionality of utterances. We spent a great deal of time in chapter 3 discussing how *Y'want a piece of candy?* could serve as three speech acts (question, request, offer), and in chapter 5 discussing how *Can/ may I help you?* could serve as two speech acts (question, offer). In both discussions, I noted that the interpretation of an utterance as an offer depends on S's belief that A (the act) would benefit H and that S is able to do A. What counts as beneficial and within the realm of S's ability, however, is contextually relative, and rests partially upon S's assessment of H's goals in a speech event. One reason why we assume that a patron in a library can understand a librarian's *May I help you?* during a reference interview as an offer, for example, is because we know that the patron has come to the librarian's desk for help and that the librarian expects to be able to provide help. Similarly, during one of my sociolinguistic interviews, I interpreted a question addressed to me by an informant when her husband entered the room, *You want Henry to talk more for you?*, as an offer to get her husband to talk. This was consistent with my knowledge that one of my goals during that interview was to record people's talk and with the informant's definition of the situation and her expectations of her own role and responsibilities.

Although the point that the fulfillment of felicity conditions is contextually bound (and thus contextually relative) may seem obvious, it helps to explain why other questions about H's wants are not offers. The hypothetical examples in (6) suggest some other functions served by such questions.

(6a)   You want a new car? You have to work for it.

(6b)   You want to stay here for vacation or go away?
(6c)   You want to get the phone? I'm in the shower.

None of the questions in (6) are offers by S to provide A for H. (6a) functions like a conditional sentence (cf. "if you want a new car . . . ", Schiffrin 1992c), not an offer by S to buy H a car. (6b) seems to be a straightforward information question. (6c) acts as a request. In brief, the interpretation of A as beneficial and possible depends on situational parameters. Thus, analyzing the interdependence between contextual structures and utterance functions can help us disentangle multiple functions of utterances from one another.

The analysis of the communicative structure of contexts so important to an ethnographic approach to discourse can lead to still another way of relating form and function: the identification of functional alternatives. An ethnographic approach makes no more assumptions about the mapping between form and function within a sentence than it does within discourse. One consequence of this is that a tremendous variety of different forms may serve the same interactional function. The formal properties of an utterance may very well be compatible with its functions: we can sometimes use sentence meaning and structure as clues by which to identify function (e.g. our analysis of offers as questions in reference interviews in chapter 5, section 3.2.1). But the functions of other utterances seem to be independent of their forms. For example, a librarian's opening offer in a reference interview may be interchangeable with eye contact, a patron's query in a reference interview may be issued as a statement, a request for clarification can be made by repetition (with or without rising intonation). Although these alternatives can all substitute for questions, they can do so only within very specifically defined act sequences and settings.

Another example illustrates that functional alternatives can also depend upon participant. Take requests for clarification from a researcher and an informant during sociolinguistic interviews. A researcher's requests for clarification are functionally similar to information-seeking questions that build on an informant's answer to a prior question as a way of progressing from one topic to another in a stepwise fashion (chapter 7). But an informant's requests for clarification are more similar to informants' own information-checking questions: both help to tailor the informant's answer to the researcher's expectations and knowledge. Again, the general point is that a systematic analysis of the communicative structure of context helps analysts to define functional alternatives.

It is important to note that the discovery of a cluster of different forms that fulfill a similar function has a consequence not just for the analysis of how specific acts are realized, but also for the analysis of discourse organization itself. As we noted above, functional equivalents are defined only relative to particular contexts. The discovery of contextually defined alternatives suggests the existence of higher level functions that provide for "slots" in still other sequential structures. To return to the reference interview for a moment, we can very well identify question–answer sequences within that interview, but we can also identify a structure of query–resolution that encompasses almost the entire reference interview. In some ways, a query is very much like a question: a patron's purpose in making a query is to elicit information that he does not have, but which he presumes the librarian to have. But a query realizes these question functions at a discourse level, such that other utterances (which also serve speech act functions) are pressed into service at a higher level of analysis.

To summarize: I have been suggesting that an ethnographic approach to discourse finds the function of a specific unit (e.g. a speech act) by locating that unit within a context that is partially structured as another unit (i.e. speech event). Thus, the function of an utterance is intricately tied to the communicative structure of speech events.

2.2.3   *Interactional sociolinguistics*

Interactional sociolinguistics is also a basically functional approach to discourse that incorporates structure into its analyses. Like other functional approaches, interactional sociolinguistics focuses upon language use: it is concerned not just with the way people intend language to serve referential meanings, but also with the social, cultural, and expressive meanings stemming from how utterances are situated in contexts. One of the key tasks of the interactional approach is to describe the contexts in which language is used, and to relate the meanings and specific functions of an utterance to those contexts. The range of functions allowed-by interactional sociolinguistics includes illocutionary force, but it is also more inclusive than most of the other approaches discussed: face strategies, the creation of involvement, and the realignment of participants can all be seen as functions. (Note that these functions are more interactively and interpersonally situated than need be the case in ethnographic analyses.) The willingness to allow so wide a range of functions (and multiple functions of a single utterance) is in keeping with the theoretical belief in the importance of context and its methodological counterpart of progressive contextualization: the addition of more information about the contexts (both general and specific) in which a single form occurs allows us to identify more functions of that form.

Note, however, that the discovery of functions – even those that are highly contextualized – has an effect on structure. We can make this point by returning to a hypothetical example from chapter 2, presented here as (7):

(7)   JAN: (a)   Are you free for lunch today?
        BARBARA: (b)   I have to advise students all day.

Jan's *Are you free for lunch today?* can have a number of functions – all grounded in contexts – other than a questioning function. We noted (in chapter 2) Jakobson's (1960) differentiation of a conative function from an emotive function, according to which aspect of the situation (addressee, addressor) was the focus of speech. Jan's utterance can be said to function as a display of solidarity with Barbara (a conative function) and to display gender identity (an emotive function) by using a conventionalized form of indirectness to check on the other's availability. Although these functions seem to have little to do with structure, they do set limits upon what follows next in the interaction. If *Are you free for lunch today?* is heard as a display of solidarity, for example, it would be considered impolite to provide a negative response by just saying *no* (cf. chapter 3, pp. 77–8 and chapter 4, p. 113–15). A more appropriate response would draw from the same functional repertoire: make a counter offer for lunch (e.g. *How about Friday?*), show appreciation (by saying *thank you*), or provide a reason for non-availability (e.g. *I have to advise students all day*). Thus, the linguistic realization of contextualized interpersonal functions sets up expectations about what comes next – expectations that act as a cognitive foundation for sequential structure.

It is also important to note that some interactional sociolinguistic studies do concern themselves explicitly with structure, e.g. with the "traffic rules of social interaction" (Goffman 1967a), participation structures (Goffman 1981a), or patterned exchanges of moves (Goffman 1971a, b). (Since moves are similar to speech acts that are sequentially located and sequentially relevant, I compare such structures to speech act structures in section 3.) Some interactions may thus have structures that can be both indexed (cf. the role of contextualization cue) and constructed by particular utterances.

Before we close this section, it is important to comment on the importance of the term "interaction" in interactional sociolinguistics. Discourse is inherently an interactive activity in which what one person says and does is both response to past words and actions, and input to future words and actions. The focus on interaction gives interactional sociolinguistics a more elaborated view of participant role, identity, and relationship than the other approaches discussed. It also provides another way that structure and function enter into this approach. We noted in chapter 4 that much of what we say is oriented toward reception by a hearer: speaking a language is a process that requires symbolically putting oneself in the other's place in order to know how to tailor one's information (syntactically, semantically, and pragmatically) so that it will be comprehendable to that other. Sequential structures in talk are based not just upon the communicative functions of linguistic expressions *per se*, but also upon the emerging set of understandings that participants gain through the give and take of interaction – through the process of orienting toward the other person. As critical to the construction of coherence as speaker intention (cf. speech act theory, pragmatics), then, is the reciprocity of perspective between self and other: each builds upon what the other has said to offer a meaning that the other can adapt, and to which the other can respond. In effect, then, the structure of interaction arises from the same "chain of ceremony" that is responsible for the maintenance of self and other: "individuals must hold hands in a chain of ceremony, each giving deferentially with proper demeanor to the one on the right what will be received deferentially from the one on the left" (Goffman 1967a: 85). That is, each utterance in an interaction receives part of its meaning from what another person *offered before*, and gives part of its meaning back to that other person to use in what *comes next*: it is from this chain of self/other reciprocity that the structure of interaction emerges. Language enters into this reciprocity: because of its contextualizing, indexical functions, language stands in a mutually constitutive relationship with the self, the other, the self/other relationship, and the contextualized meanings that are continually negotiated during interaction.

2.2.4 Pragmatics

Functional explanations of language build on the very basic idea that language has functions by finding explanations for language structure in systems outside of language itself. By this criterion, Gricean pragmatics is a functional approach to language (Levinson 1983: 97): its main constructs are located outside of language *per se* in speaker meaning (i.e. speaker intention) and rational principles of human communication (i.e. the cooperative principle). Although communication between people is based partially on shared knowledge of structural representations and stable meanings in a linguistic code (i.e. a text; chapters 10 and 11), communication also depends upon a cognitive ability to use context to make inferences. As Sadock (1985: 141) puts it, "many of what were conceived of as essentially inexplicable structural facts of language are really reflections of the fact that natural language is used by real speakers in real contexts to accomplish real goals." But rather than go into detail about what is involved in human communication (as Sadock would suggest, the real goals of "real speakers in real contexts"), Grice posits as the underlying basis of conversation a general cooperative principle, and as the underlying basis of the CP human rationality itself. Consistent with the functionalist idea of searching for explanations for language structure in systems outside of language itself, Gricean analyses rely upon the CP and its attendant maxims for explanations of language structure.

Since Gricean pragmatics is not concerned with discourse *per se* (the "inexplicable structural facts" for which it provides functional explanations are usually syntactic or semantic), we have to search a bit for its impact on discourse level structures. One example we have already seen comes from our analysis of referring sequences. In chapter 6, we used the maxims of quantity and relation to describe referring sequences: a particular referring term in [slot 1] constrains what terms will occur in [slot 2], and, even further, the way a sequentially next term will be interpreted. Our analysis showed that the maxims of quantity and relevance constrained the choice between definite and indefinite, and explicit and inexplicit, mentions of a referent: thus, pragmatic constraints were partially responsible for different discourse structures.

Another example of how the Gricean approach to discourse structure is functionally grounded comes from the more traditional discourse analytic concern with question/answer structure. As we discussed in earlier chapters, different approaches to discourse analysis view the source of coherence between question and answer (what allows an utterance following a question to be heard as an answer?) very differently. Speech act theory, for example, finds sequential coherence to stem from well-formed structures of speech acts. Conversation analysis depends most heavily on the identity of the sequential slot "question" – arguing that whatever follows what is heard as a question will have sequential relevance as an answer. I briefly mention these two other approaches just because the Gricean approach stands in such stark contrast: what matters for the Gricean approach is not the identity of the discourse slots (and the basis of this identity can certainly differ depending upon approach), but the cooperative principle. (8) illustrates (this is Levinson's 1983: 102, example 18).

(8) A: Where's Bill?
     B: There's a yellow VW outside Sue's house.

Levinson argues that B's utterance violates the maxims of quantity and relevance. Because we try to interpret B's utterance as cooperative at some level, however, we infer that Bill may be at Sue's house, i.e. we interpret B's utterance as an answer to A's question. Thus, it is because people assume cooperation (at the level of either the general CP or specific maxims) that an utterance can be heard to occupy a particular sequential position. Put another way, the sequential identity of an utterance emerges from (is a product of) the cooperative principle: an utterance is heard as an "answer," and can thus be a constituent in a question/answer structure, only because interlocutors share an underlying assumption of cooperation.

In sum, the Gricean approach to discourse is basically a functionalist approach to language: explanations for language structure are sought in a general cooperative principle that rests ultimately upon human rationality. Both the constituents of discourse structure and their orderly arrangement as coherent text thus arise because of the impact of communicative principles on the linguistic realization of speaker meaning at different points in time.

3 Comparisons among approaches: from utterance to discourse

Although we differentiated a structural from a functional definition of discourse in chapter 2, our review of how different approaches to discourse incorporate both structure and function within their analyses suggests that this is by no means as absolute a distinction in practice as it is in principle: many discourse analysts end up trying to bridge or somehow combine the two analytical worlds. Before concluding this chapter, I more directly compare the way different approaches combine structure and function.

A convenient way to begin our comparison is in terms of how different approaches relate what is said within individual utterances to structures holding across utterances. We will see that the aspects of a constituent utterance that have an impact on discourse structure vary for different approaches: some structures are based more on the functions of individual clauses than others. Similarly, the functions that are proposed vary: not only is there a different range, but some are more situated in ongoing talk than others, some more abstract than others. Finally, both structures and functions are more or less grounded in text, or in an interplay between text and context.

We noted earlier that *conversation analysis* assumes a structural framework: relationships between utterances are structurally organized. CA subordinates the analysis of function to the analysis of structure: the function of an item can be discovered only by analysis of its location relative to other items in talk, i.e. its sequential distribution. CA also relates properties of utterances to regularities across utterances. Turns are exchanged, for example, because of a distribution system that holds across different parties' utterances. Yet what enables turn-taking is not just a set of context-free sequentially applicable and recursive rules, but the fact that the rules are context-sensitive (Sacks et al. 1974): the rules apply at particular locations (turn-transition spaces) defined *within utterances*. Preference structures provide another example of how CA relates properties of utterances to structures across utterance boundaries. Preference structures are defined across turns at talk: one second-pair part (e.g. an agreement) is preferred over another (e.g. a disagreement). Evidence for a preference, however, is found in the distribution of items (e.g. particles, pauses) within an utterance (an utterance located as the second part of a two-part pair). Thus, what occurs within utterances facilitates the emergence, and the discovery, of structures across utterances.

We also noted earlier that CA distrusts generalizations that are not empirically grounded, and that this distrust extends to the analysis of functions and structures (both across and within utterances). Although this need not preclude *linguistic* structure from serving a function in a text, CA itself makes absolutely no assumptions about linguistic structure and how it may be related to structure across utterances.

In sharp contrast, *variation analysis* is the approach to discourse that incorporates linguistic structure and methodology most extensively. Variation analysis considers how surface features of utterances, and actions performed by utterances, build structures across clauses; these structures lead to coherence. Our analyses of particular text-types (e.g. narratives, lists) in chapter 8 showed that one way the surface features of utterances contribute to coherence is by realizing functions associated with that text-type, at a particular location within that text. Recall, for example, how the distribution of active and stative predicates differs across narratives and lists: we said that this reflects the differential provision of temporal and descriptive information within the two text-types. Surface features of utterances are also sometimes analyzed as variables: alternative realizations of referential or functional equivalents. Different realizations of a variable may be sensitive to location in a text. Again, as we saw in chapter 8, pronouns and nouns in lists are sensitive to the category level of a list-item and to the location of a next-mention of that item within the list. Whereas speakers use pronouns to evoke a general category (X) regardless of its location in the list, they do not use pronouns to evoke a specific list-item (X1) if a different list-item (X2) was mentioned *after* a prior mention of the item (X1). The use of one variant (e.g. a full noun) rather than another (e.g. a pronoun), and the way such variants are conditioned by textual constraints, helps build the overall coherence of a discourse.

We also noted in chapter 8 that the linguistic variables focused upon by Labovian variation analysis, and the abstract speech actions focused upon by Labov's method of comprehensive discourse analysis, seem very different at first. Both constructs, however, rest upon a single assumption about discourse coherence: coherence depends upon the sort of complex hierarchical organization that "is plainly derived from the linguistic analysis of phonology and grammar" (Labov and Fanshel 1977: 350).

Of course variables and abstract speech actions do differ: they contribute to coherence in different ways, and at different locations in the complex hierarchical organization on which coherence depends. Traditionally defined linguistic variables are segments of underlying representations that are encoded in surface forms of language: it is possible (in fact, necessary) to view a variable as a closed set of options. Abstract speech actions are quite different. Not only are they not encodable in language alone, but they are not a closed set of options. Labov and Fanshel (1977: 358) point out that the existence of a closed set of options for speech actions seems unlikely because of their contextual dependence: "A very large portion of the social structure enters into the construction of such speech actions, and, at the present time, a comprehensive grammar of [higher level speech actions, such as] insults or challenges seems to be out of the question." However, the degree to which social context (including prior utterances) enters into the formulation of speech act rules varies for different actions. Labov and Fanshel (1977: 93–7) suggest, for example, that a repeated request is a challenge when H fails to comply with a prior request whose appropriateness had been assumed by S because of S's beliefs about H's social competence. Unlike the CA assumption that *all* talk is sequentially relevant and sequentially implicative, then, variationists weigh and measure the importance of sequential embedding. (We see in chapter 10 that variationists treat both text and situation as "optional" contextual constraints on language use.) The quantitative methodology used by variationists segments environments into factors that act as probabilistic constraints on variants. Even the abstract speech actions that figure in sequencing rules can be more or less dependent on the talk whose sequences they are helping to construct: the rule for challenges noted above (but not for requests), for example, relies upon assumptions about role-related competence.

We have seen thus far that variationists use two different constructs (variables, abstract speech actions) to relate what is said within individual utterances to structures holding across utterances; both of these constructs depend on the assumption that the hierarchical organization of language contributes to discourse coherence. Abstract speech actions, however, are not linguistic constituents within a hierarchy: they are language functions. *Speech act theory* also focuses on actions. However, the finite set of actions upon which it focuses are more narrowly, and less socially, defined than those focused upon by variationists (and other scholars who take a more social interactional approach to speech acts: Ciccourel 1980; Schegloff 1987). Furthermore, speech act theorists do not group together surface features of utterances into the construct of "variable," e.g. they do not say that the range of illocutionary force indicating devices that can be used to realize a single speech act are alternative ways of "filling" an underlying speech act "slot." (As we note in chapter 10, however, speech act theorists do use the constructs of "rules" and mapping relationships among encoded (and encodable) meanings.) Thus, variation analysis and speech act theory both assume that it is text–context relationships encoded within an individual utterance that create structures across utterances.

We noted earlier that the initial task (and one of the key tasks) of a structural analysis is the discovery and identification of constitutents. But as both variation and speech act theory make clear, units cannot be identified by linguistic criteria alone. The shift to a level of action, however, threatens the most basic assumption of all structural analyses: structural units are linguistic units, not units defined by what a speaker does and intends to do through language. Thus, once we begin to search outside language itself for criteria by which to identify structural units, we are forced to deal with the relationship between language and the contexts of which it is a part – precisely the text–context relationship that structural analysts purportedly ignore (see chapter 10).

Like conversation analysis, variation analysis, and speech act theory, the *ethnography of communication* also focuses on sequential structures across utterances. Like speech act theory, the constituents of these structures for ethnographers are often functionally labelled speech acts, whose identity is related to linguistic features of clauses. Unlike speech act theory, however, little is assumed about universal inventories of such acts. More crucially, such acts are not separable from the larger speech events in which they occur: what seems like the very same utterance may realize radically different acts depending on the communicative structure of its speech event. Thus, both functions and functional alternatives are grounded in communicative structures.

The ethnographic approach thus seems similar, in some ways, to the conversation analytic approach. Both situate functions (actions and meanings) within sequential structure. Neither CA nor ethnography assumes the relevance for one particular speech event of any *a priori* categories. Furthermore, both approaches are built upon particularities and the discovery of generalizations that account for each particular case.

Despite these similarities, some important differences between the two approaches remain. Whereas CA does not venture beyond what is displayed in a transcript itself (seeking evidence only in participants' conduct), ethnography depends on "thick interpretation" (Geertz 1973) of cultural meanings – interpretation that requires not only extensive fieldwork and participation in a community, but also the use of knowledge about a wide matrix of beliefs and actions in a particular culture. The ethnography of communication also makes more explicit a two-way relationship between structure and function. This interdependence is assumed to hold across "unit" size: just as the communicative structure of a speech event reveals the function of constituent acts, so too does the function of the act contribute to the structure of the event. This interdependence is also assumed to hold across "levels" and conventional compartments of grammar: just as linguistic structure can reveal social functions, social functions can reveal new levels of structural organization (e.g. Hymes 1981). Thus, the ethnography of communication assumes a two-way mapping between the functions of utterances (and their linguistic properties as clauses) and discourse structure.

We have been focusing thus far on how functions of language can serve as constituents in discourse structure. However, not all functions can be neatly chunked and arranged. We noted in our discussion of interactional sociolinguistics, for example, that Jan's *Are you free for lunch today?* (7) can function as a display of solidarity. Although this function sets limits upon what follows next in an interaction, we might not want to segment and label this function as a speech act. This is not to say, of course, that *Are you free for lunch today?* would not lead to a particular kind of response. It would be inappropriate to follow a display of solidarity with just *no*, for example: a more appropriate response would draw from the same strategic repertoire, e.g. propose another time for lunch, convey appreciation, explain one's non-availability.

Our analysis of "speaking for another" (chapter 4) also illustrated the interactional socioliguistic reluctance to always segment and label utterance functions. Although we did consider this an act that one person takes in relation to another, it is not an act that can be defined in terms of illocutionary force or conventional formulae. One reason is that it is an act that is always overlaid on another act, e.g. one provides an "answer" or an "account" for another. In addition, the expressive meaning of this act is always relative to its context, including the sorts of institutional and interactional contexts whose interpretive relevance can be indexed by contextualization cues. Put in still stronger (but perhaps overly simple) terms, the act itself is dependent on the interpretive contexts in which it is situated. But, again, this is not to say that speaking for another would not lead one to expect a particular kind of response – a response dependent on its interactional meaning.

I have been suggesting, then, that the acts considered by interactional sociolinguists are contextualized functions that set up expectations about what comes next: they do not delimit a closed set of well-formed structures whose constituent acts have autonomous identities. Although some of these expectations do seem to result in structures similar to those posited by Labov's comprehensive discourse analysis (see e.g. Goffman 1971a, b; Merritt 1976, 1984) or speech act approaches, not all sequential regularities in talk can be chunked into discrete, functionally based actions that can be mapped onto utterances.

The interactional sociolinguistic view of structure differs in another way from the speech act view: the role of rules. A speech act approach to discourse relies upon three kinds of rules: constitutive rules that create the act *per se*, mapping rules that relate an utterance to the constitutive rules, sequencing rules that relate the actions that result from the mapping rules (rather than the surface linguistic details of each utterance in the text). Instead of constitutive and mapping rules, interactional sociolinguistics speaks of norms of conduct (Goffman 1959, 1963), strategies (Brown and Levinson 1987; Gumperz 1982a), and principles (Tannen 1981). When interactional sociolinguists do speak of rules (e.g. Goffman's 1963, "traffic rules"), the focus is on the patterns of conduct created by norms, and the social meaning of conforming to (or deviating from) such norms. Furthermore, instead of the fixed knowledge states (constitutive rules) assumed to underlie speakers' meanings, the interactional view of speakers' meanings is that they are situated, inherently flexible, and multifaceted. Instead of hearers mapping from text/context to constitutive rules, the interactional view of hearers' inferences relies upon many different aspects of an utterance, including the situated meanings and implications of acts (e.g. chapter 4, section 3.2.2).

Note, also, that implied through the speech act construct of rule is a more deterministic view of human behavior than that with which most interactional sociolinguists would be comfortable. By assuming that human behavior is guided by norms of conduct, strategies, or principles, interactional sociolinguistics allows human behavior – both unintentional conduct and intentional communication (see chapter 11) – not only to be probabilistic, but to have meanings and interpretations that can shift from user to user and context to context (cf. Gricean principles, chapter 6). This view of human action also frees interlocutors from a dependence upon a fixed inventory of speech act types (as usually assumed by speech act theorists). Rather, a range of acts (and act types) can emerge from the particular expectations and obligations that arise during an ongoing interaction.

We noted above that speech act theory is wed to a relatively deterministic identification of a limited set of functions whose identity is shared by interlocutors. This assumption means that a process that is important to functional approaches – the process of locating functions in many different aspects and types of contexts of an utterance – creates a danger for a speech act approach to discourse because it creates a sense of "indeterminacy." It creates no such danger for interactional sociolinguistics, however. Not only does this approach assume that meaning is more protean, but the underlying model of communication that is assumed does not require symmetry between speaker intention and hearer interpretation (chapter 11).

A final point. Interactional sociolinguistics is less eager than the other approaches to rely upon structure either within or across clauses (but see discussion of pragmatics below). As noted above, rather than discover well-formed structures across clauses, such researchers account for sequential expectations. And such expectations emerge not from interlocutors' reliance upon grammatical (i.e. "core") structures of what is said, but from both verbal (e.g. prosodic, phonological, morphological, syntactic, rhetorical) and nonverbal (kinesic, proxemic) aspects of what is said. These qualities serve as cues used by participants to infer an interpretive framework in which to identify relationships between utterances. Thus, interactional sociolinguistic analyses of relationships across utterances do not depend upon linguistic structures *within* clauses. Rather than assume that speakers' meanings depend upon knowledge of a stable system of shared, context-free rules (cf. discussion of intersubjectivity in chapter 11), interactional sociolinguistics assumes that interlocutors' knowledge is situated: principles and strategies (not rules) underlie language use. Such principles are inherently flexible and multifaceted, and as noted above they do not always lead to actions with conventional labels. (This is similar to the Gricean pragmatics view; see below.) Hearers are assumed to make inferences by relying upon many different aspects of an utterance, including the situated meanings and implications of acts, and crucially the contextualization cues that may signal those meanings.

Like interactional sociolinguistics, *pragmatics* rejects the assumption that what lead to regular structures across utterances are stable, shared rules that allow interlocutors to encode meanings within utterances. The principles of communication captured by Grice's cooperative principle are similar to norms. Although norms are a type of rule (cf. Taylor and Cameron 1987), norms are more like conventional expectations for behavior than formal algorithms that map linguistically encoded forms from one level of representation to another. Furthermore, although the Gricean approach seeks to explain structural facts of language, these facts are often part of the syntax and semantics of individual clauses – not structures that hold across clauses. Thus, unlike variation and speech act approaches to discourse, Gricean pragmatics does not map from surface form to any higher level functionally labelled unit at all. Like interactional sociolinguistics, Gricean pragmatics views speakers' meanings as flexible and situated (although what "situates" meanings is a very different type of context; see chapter 10). Such meanings need not be realized in sequentially defined slots in a text.

4 Conclusion

We observed in chapter 2 that the availability of two different perspectives – one structural, one functional – is partially responsible for the tremendous scope of discourse analysis. If we focus on structure, our task is to identify and analyze units, determine procedures for assigning utterances a constituent status, discover regularities underlying combinations of units, and make principled decisions about whether or not particular arrangements are well formed (or whether they conform to, or violate, sequential expectations). If we focus on function, on the other hand, our task is to identify and analyze actions performed by people for certain purposes, interpret social, cultural, and personal meanings, and justify our interpretations of those meanings for the participants involved. Dealing with both structure and function is a delicate and difficult task – one that requires stepping into two different analytical worlds.

We have seen that each approach discussed in this book depends upon both structure and function. This means that each approach inherits the strengths and the weaknesses of both perspectives (although in sometimes different ways) – but also that the strengths of one might complement, or at least partially compensate for, the weakness of the other.

As just noted, structural approaches face an "identification" problem: it is difficult to find the right criteria to use to decide upon the identity of units. Nor can we be absolutely sure that particular units (or the criteria by which we chose them) are the ones that participants in the interaction would actually rely upon (or even that there is one set upon which all people consistently rely).[1] Functional analyses can sometimes provide an antidote for structural problems such as these. Several of the approaches discussed view units in discourse through a functional lens: what does an utterance "do" for interlocutors? Yet functional solutions are far from perfect and themselves raise other problems. Functional analyses are built on a process of progressive contextualizing: the addition of more information about the contexts (both general and specific) of a single form allows the induction of more functions of that form. As necessary as this process is for the interpretation of function, it creates a danger: the more we learn about the many different contexts in which a single form is embedded, the less sure we are that any single interpretation (based on any single context) is correct. In fact, our entire notion of what it means to "be correct" – and whether there is a single correct analysis of something – becomes open to skepticism. Thus, our identification of functionally based units, and the structures that they form, may also end up being uncertain and unstable.

Consider, also, that discourse organization and structure is emergent: discourse emerges over time (it is constructed on an utterance-by-utterance basis). This means that discourse is continually imposing its own contexts and hence its own sources of indeterminacy. What is said is always in response (in some way or another) to what was said before and in anticipation of what comes next (cf. the CA idea of context-shaped and context-renewing). Thus, the function of an utterance (and hence its identity) must be defined in relation to (and as appropriate to) a context that is not static, but dynamic, and even more critically, a context that is still in the process of being interactively formed. This has an impact on the structural side of analyses of discourse: as Bateson (1955) points out, we cannot always see an outline of a conversation when we are in the middle of it as clearly as when it is finished.

The emergent structure of discourse makes it difficult to know from what set of response options (what "system") a response will be selected until that choice has been made (Schiffrin 1987a: 23). Once a response is issued, however, we know more about the structure being built, and more about the functional repertoire from which a response has selected. In some ways, then, this is another way that we can draw upon the strengths of one type of analysis to compensate for the weaknesses of the other. Just as we may try to identify units through their functions, we may also try to discover (and thus limit) functions by seeing which function seems to be attended to and receive a response.

To summarize, the approaches to discourse analysis described in this book suggest that what is appropriate "is to examine structure in the light of functional requirement and function in the light of structural requirement" (Sadock 1984: 142). Thus, neither radical structural nor radical functional analyses are appropriate. Rather, combining facets of both types of analyses may help to balance the weaknesses of one mode of analysis with the strengths of another.

Note

1 Despite the difficulties of identifying structural units of discourse, there seems to be a fundamental assumption in all analyses of language, and of social life, that people categorize the world that surrounds and informs them. Such categorizations not only enable people to inform others about that world: they also help people make sense out of what would otherwise be a steady stream of stimuli from sources of information that are often simultaneously available. Put another way, we routinely and automatically segment our environment and relate those segments to one another in ways that capture both their similarities and their differences. There is no reason to expect that we – in our capacity as speakers and hearers engaging in social interaction – stop doing this when we produce and interpret utterances. And there is no reason to expect discourse analysts to stop trying to categorize those utterances (parts of utterances, or combinations of utterances) as units of some kind, to try to identify the "stuff" of which they are made, and to analyze relationships among units. Like other categories of experience, such units would seem to help people make sense out of their interactive world and the utterances that are produced and interpreted within that world. (Also like other categories, we might find that some utterances are "better" examples of a category member than others.)

10　Text and Context

1　Introduction

The focus of this chapter – how different approaches to discourse view text and context – provides a bridge between chapter 9 (on structure and function) and chapter 11 (on communication). In chapter 9 we discussed how discourse has been viewed as structure (a unit of language that is larger than the sentence) and as the realization of functions (the use of language for social, expressive, and referential purposes). We saw that all the approaches discussed in this book incorporate both structure and function into their analyses: the structures analyzed in discourse lead to the identification of functions, and the functions analyzed in discourse are linguistically realized in ways that create structures.

In chapter 11 we turn to linguistic assumptions about communication. Linguists often assume that messages are created through an interaction between two different types of information. The first type of information is often called "semantic": a stable core of propositional meanings conveyed through the language (i.e. the linguistic code) itself. The semantic information presented in units larger than a clause is often thought of as textual information.[1] The second type of information is contextual information. Context is more difficult to define than text. Contextual information is always information that is identified in relation to something else that is the primary focus of our attention. This means that it is impossible to talk about context in a vacuum: context cannot exist unless we are thinking of "something else" (e.g. an image, a smell, a sound, a word, an utterance, a sequence of utterances) that is located relative to it. The identity of that "something else" (and what kind of sense we are trying to make of it) influences our decisions about what counts as context and about what "parts of" context we find important. Thus, although it seems possible to find a single source of "text" (i.e. in the linguistic system), the source of contextual information is necessarily more varied:

context has multiple sources that can be quite different from one another and can shift depending on our focus of attention. (See, for example, Becker 1984.)

The belief that messages are created through an interaction between text and context implies a procedure by which to identify the communicative content of an utterance: combine linguistic meaning with context to derive inferences about messages. Identifying the communicative content of an utterance is important for discourse analysis: it can help us understand coherence relations across utterances. Actually using the procedure noted above to identify either the communicative content of an utterance or relations across utterances, however, is more complicated than it seems. First, it is often difficult to decide whether it is linguistic or contextual information that is responsible for communicative content. Such difficulties are illustrated by debates about the meaning and function of the conjunction *and*, i.e. it is not clear how to account for the added meanings (e.g. temporal, causal) that use of the word *and* seems to convey (Posner 1980; Schiffrin 1986a). Second, it is not always clear how text and context interact to allow inferences about communicative content. For example, it is not clear whether the directive function of *I need these papers typed by 2 p.m.* is inferred through recipients' use of linguistic information (e.g. Searle 1975), contextual information about social role and setting (e.g. Ervin-Tripp 1976), and/or contextually based inferences about communicative strategies (Brown and Levinson 1978). Third, since interpretive contexts are continually being created through what is said, inferences about communicative context are dynamically situated; thus, whatever one infers about a particular utterance can be modified (or even cancelled) through later utterances. Finally, it is difficult to even be sure about what should count as communicative content. Levinson (1983: 131), for example, classifies different types of communicative content that all contribute to meaning-nn (chapter 6), i.e. what a speaker intends to convey by means of a hearer's recognition of that intention. But other scholars focus less exclusively upon intention as a basis for communicative content (chapter 11).

Despite such difficulties, the discovery and use of some kind of procedure for identifying the communicative content of utterances is an important goal for discourse analysis. The current chapter focuses on the way different approaches to discourse view the two types of information that contribute to communicative content: text and context.

In order to compare different views of text and context, we need to define both terms in a way general enough to apply to all the approaches. As noted earlier, I will use the term "text" to differentiate linguistic material (e.g. what is said, assuming a verbal channel) from the environment in which "sayings" (or other linguistic productions) occur (context). In terms of utterances, then, "text" is the linguistic content: the stable semantic meanings of words, expressions, and sentences, but not the inferences available to hearers depending upon the contexts in which words, expressions, and sentences are used. Put another way, text is the propositional meanings that are linguistically realized (e.g. that might constitute the "semantics" of a grammar) in grammatically definable units such as clauses, and through the relations that are conveyed between (and among) such units. Context is harder to define in a way that covers all the approaches to discourse that we have described: in fact, we will see that it is precisely their consideration of context that most clearly differentiates the approaches. We can provide an initial definition of context, however, in terms of utterances: if we say that text provides for the "what is said" part of utterances, then it is context that combines with "what is said" to create an utterance. Context is thus a world filled with people producing utterances: people who have social, cultural, and personal identities, knowledge, beliefs, goals and wants, and who interact with one another in various socially and culturally defined situations.

All the approaches discussed in this book consider both text and context as interdependent contributions to utterance meaning and to discourse coherence across utterances. Yet they also make assumptions about text and context, and about their relationship, that are not always clearly articulated and that differ quite surprisingly from one another. At first glance, structurally motivated approaches (conversation analysis, variation analysis; chapter 9) might seem to be "text" based – to focus upon the propositional meanings that are linguistically realized through units such as clauses or sentences, and through the relations conveyed or implied between such units. We saw in chapter 9, however, that although variation analysis (chapter 8) does focus upon textual structures based (partially) on relationships between clauses, conversation analysis (chapter 7) does not consider the linguistic structures underlying clauses, sentences, and texts at all. We might also assume that functionally motivated approaches are more concerned with context: the non-linguistic environment (be it cognitive, social, and/or cultural) in which texts are produced and interpreted. However, there are also differences among these approaches. Pragmatics (chapter 6) assumes a relatively clear distinction between text and context as two autonomous sources of information.[2] But the ethnography of communication (chapter 5) intentionally obviates the distinction between what is text and what is not: recall, for example, the inclusion of both verbal and nonverbal "instrumentalities" in the etic grid through which the communicative components of different events can be comprised. Thus, whether an approach is structurally or functionally motivated does not necessarily predict either its theoretical or methodological emphasis on text or context, or how it incorporates text and context into theory and method.

We noted above that what most clearly differentiates approaches to discourse is their treatment of context: scholarly attention to context can focus upon knowledge, situation, and/or text itself (section 2). Approaches to discourse also differ in their view of "text" in relation to "context" and in terms of the unit of analysis (i.e. single or multiple utterances) upon which they initially focused (section 3). Section 4 summarizes.

2 What is context?

The approaches to discourse discussed in this book make different assumptions about what aspects of context are relevant to the production and interpretation of utterances. Speech act theory (2.1.1) and pragmatics (2.1.2) view context primarily as "knowledge"; although a key part of such knowledge is "knowledge of situation," "situation" is largely unanalyzed by these approaches. Interactional sociolinguistics (2.2.1) and the ethnography of communication (2.2.2) also view context as "knowledge," and they, too, include "knowledge of situation"; these approaches, however, propose frameworks and constructs through which to analyze "situation" as part of "knowledge." Speech act theory also depends partially upon the kinds of concrete situations analyzed by interactional sociolinguistics and the ethnography of communication (2.2.3). Variation analysis (2.3) views context as "situation," without explicitly incorporating it into "knowledge"; it also categorizes "text" as part of context. Conversation analysis (2.4) focuses on how text is a means of displaying "situation," and on how text creates knowledge including, but not limited to, knowledge of "situation."

2.1 Context as knowledge

Speech act theory and pragmatics both view context in terms of knowledge: what speakers and hearers can be assumed to know (e.g. about social institutions, about others' wants and needs, about the nature of human rationality) and how that knowledge guides the use of language and the interpretation of utterances.

2.1.1 Speech act theory and context

People can use language to do things – to perform speech acts – because the rules through which speech acts are realized are part of linguistic competence. Although the rules specify both textual and contextual conditions underlying language use, a central goal of speech act theory is to characterize our knowledge of those rules (rather than, for example, the range of forms and situations in which the rules take effect). What this means is that the social circumstances that might help to define a particular act are incorporated into the description of "what we know" when we speak. This abstract knowledge of text and context is what allows us to identify different types of speech acts at both a general level (e.g. directives, commissives) and a specific level (e.g. questions, offers).

An emphasis on knowledge pervades the application of speech act theory to discourse. Although this application requires the analysis of actual utterances, the analysis of how those utterances perform speech acts assumes that linguistic competence includes speaker and hearer mastery of constitutive rules. Such rules are part of mutual knowledge and have an important role in governing language use: it is mutual knowledge of these rules that allows hearers to discover a speaker's intended speech act, and mutual knowledge of abstract rules that makes possible a sense of coherence across utterances.

Note that not all approaches to discourse rely so heavily upon mutual knowledge as a path to, or locus of, coherence (see chapter 11). The ethnography of communication, interactional sociolinguistics, and conversation analysis, for example, avoid the assumption of mutual knowledge by relying upon the actual utterances produced in response to a given utterance as a way to discover the *hearer's* interpretation of a speaker's intention – an interpretation that may or may not coincide with the speaker's actual intention. Thus, in contrast to speech act theory (which, as noted above, locates coherence in the linguistic rules that are part of speaker/hearer mutual knowledge), the other approaches just noted search for coherence in a behavioral context: they examine a speaker's own utterance and the utterance issued by someone else in response to that utterance. In brief, very different kinds of contextual assumptions can be said to provide a route to coherence.

I have suggested thus far that context for speech act theorists is a specific kind of background knowledge called "constitutive rules," i.e. knowledge about what conditions need to hold if an utterance is to count as a particular speech act. Although people draw upon constitutive rules much as they might draw upon other contextual information that is used to make inferences about meaning (e.g. Grice's cooperative principle), constitutive rules also have another role. Recall that constitutive rules *create* speech acts (in contrast with regulative rules, which regulate pre-existing behavior). This means that the rules appropriate to a given utterance have to be cognitively "activated" in order for a given utterance to count as a realization of a particular speech act. Put another way, constitutive rules provide the organized framework of knowledge in which to discover a solution to the problem of speech act identity. Thus, constitutive rules can be seen as a kind of cognitive context in relation to which what is said may be interpreted and found to be meaningful.

We noted above that our knowledge of speech act rules – the cognitive contexts that underlie how we use language to do things – includes both linguistic and social information about what constitutes a particular speech act. This means that social contexts, such as social institutions, others' wants and needs, and so on, do contribute to the definitional framework for speech act interpretation. Our discussion of Austin (chapter 3, section 2.1), for example, mentioned contextual conditions ("circumstances") and textual conditions (e.g. the availability of explicit performative formulae) that allow an utterance to have a certain illocutionary force. Like Austin, Searle's rules and conditions for speech acts draw upon both context and text: they also elevate intentions and other psychological states as conditions enabling a speech act, by assigning to them their own type of rule. (Also like Austin, Searle classifies conditions and rules according to their necessity for the act.) But in contrast to Austin, Searle classifies different kinds of conditions (and rules) according to what aspect of text and context is focused upon in the condition or rule. The different conditions also overlap (partially) with different components (i.e. locutionary, illocutionary) of a total speech act.

In sum, the central contribution of context to utterance interpretation in speech act applications to discourse is its contribution to the knowledge (i.e. the conditions and rules) underlying the successful performance and interpretation of speech act types. The abstract knowledge of text and context just noted is what allows us to identify different types of speech acts. Abstract knowledge of context, however, is only one way that context figures in speech act applications to discourse. The actual social circumstances during which an utterance is produced also provide a framework in which an utterance is successfully realized as a token of a particular type of act. Thus, context is not just a matter of knowledge: context is also a set of social circumstances in which utterances can be produced and interpreted as realizations of their underlying constitutive rules. I discuss this in section 2.2.

2.1.2 Gricean pragmatics and context

Gricean pragmatics also views context as a cognitive contribution to utterance interpretation. The context that is proposed, however, is quite different from that assumed by speech act theory. The context proposed by Gricean pragmatics is a general principle that participants assume one another to believe and observe: "Make your conversational contribution such as is required, at the stage at which it occurs, by the accepted purpose or direction of the talk exchange in which you are engaged." It is this principle that is called the cooperative principle (CP).

The CP allows the inference of speaker meaning – meaning that can go well beyond (or even substitute for) semantic meaning. Such inferences (called "implicatures") are calculated with the use of the following information:

(1) the conventional meaning of the words used, together with the identity of any references that may be involved; (2) the CP and its maxims; (3) the context, linguistic or otherwise, of the utterance; (4) other items of background knowledge; and (5) the fact (or supposed fact) that all relevant items falling under the previous headings are available to both participants and both participants know or assume this to be the case. (Grice 1975: 50)

Item (1) is what someone "says" (the semantic meanings of propositions). Although Grice mentions context only briefly (as item (3) "the context, linguistic or otherwise, of the utterance"), context is actually critical to implicature calculation. We can extrapolate from Grice's division of context into "linguistic" and "otherwise" (in item 3), and his notion of "linguistic" as what someone "says," to define two types of context. First is a linguistic context: the *text* within which the utterance is linguistically encoded (see section 3.1). Second is the "otherwise" context: the *situation* during which the utterance is produced. These contexts bear on inferencing only because they contribute information that can be used as mutually known *background knowledge*. That contexts are akin to mutual knowledge is suggested by Grice's item (4), noting *other* items of background knowledge (presumably, information about the world not provided from text or situation), and by Grice's item (5), the availability of mutual knowledge.

Calculating implicatures also requires the cooperative principle (item 2). Despite the central role played by the CP and its maxims in inferencing, however, the CP is actually quite similar to the other contexts listed: it, too, is background knowledge that participants assume one another to share. This similarity allows us to suggest that what allows hearers to calculate implicatures and infer speaker meaning is conventional meaning (item 1) and background knowledge from a number of different sources, i.e. assumptions about human nature (item 2), text (item 3), situation (item 3), and the world (item 4).

Despite the importance and diversity of the "otherwise" and "background knowledge" contexts, Gricean pragmatics offers no suggestions about how to analyze those contexts. Some of the issues raised in our sample analysis in chapter 6 illustrate the kinds of contextual analyses that might be needed, at least for a Gricean analysis of referring sequences. Background knowledge is pertinent to the identification of referents (e.g. the use of metonymic references) and the forms used for first-mentions (e.g. initial definites) and next-mentions. We might analyze this background knowledge as a schema (frame, or script) that provides structured expectations about what kinds of people and things typically appear in a given setting, and what kinds of actions typically occur there. The analysis of text itself is also important (3.1). Text can reinforce expectations about the relevance of schematic knowledge for interpretation of a particular referent. Analyses of text can also help to explain shifts from explicit first-mentions to inexplicit next-mentions and the dependence of inexplicit forms on different descriptive frameworks (e.g. story world versus conversational world) that are textually created. Finally, the circumstances of talk itself can provide a framework of expectations relative to which cooperation is geared: the actual situations in which language is used include speakers and hearers, whose needs, goals, and wants are tailored to a particular socially and culturally defined communicative situation. Thus, interactional and ethnographic analyses of different communicative situations are also relevant: they might suggest, for example, that how much information we provide is tailored to our socially and culturally based conceptions of what our interlocutors need for the purposes of a particular social exchange.

In sum, a Gricean pragmatic approach to discourse analyzes the way speaker meaning is dependent upon a cognitive context of shared beliefs and assumptions. Although this view of context is similar in some ways to that of speech act theory, there are also important differences. Speech act theory compartmentalizes context into different aspects of social circumstances, and associates different clusters of conditions (both textual and circumstantial) with specifically labelled functional units (i.e. speech act types). Gricean pragmatics, on the other hand, compartmentalizes context into different sources of background knowledge (assumptions about human nature, text (see section 3.1), situation, the world) without grouping specific types of knowledge into labelled units (see Sperber and Wilson 1986: 243–54).

2.2 Context as situation and knowledge

Both approaches to discourse discussed thus far include knowledge of the social circumstances framing an utterance as part of the cognitive context in which utterances are produced and interpreted. Yet neither approach guides the analysis of the actual circumstances in which utterance tokens (not abstract utterance types, i.e. speech act types (2.1.1)) are embedded. This section considers the way two other approaches to discourse – interactional sociolinguistics (2.2.1) and the ethnography of communication (2.2.2) – incorporate situational analyses into their view of context. In so doing, however, they also alter the cognitive contexts considered by speech act theory (from linguistic to either communicative competence (Hymes 1974a) or situated competence (Gumperz 1985), and pragmatics (from inference to situated inference). This section also considers the way speech act applications to discourse need to incorporate analyses of context as situation as well as knowledge (2.2.3).

2.2.1 Interactional sociolinguistics and context

Context as "situation" is critical to interactional sociolinguistics. In fact, one of the main features of this approach is that it provides a richly textured view of social interaction and social situations, including the way participation frameworks and presuppositions arise from situated interaction. Language and context constitute one another: language contextualizes and is contextualized, such that language does not just function "in" situated interactions, language also forms and provides for these interactions (Duranti and Goodwin 1991).

The contexts upon which interactional sociolinguistics focus are both internal and external to the individual. Nowhere is this better illustrated than in a well-known formulation from one of the sociological "fathers" of interactional sociolinguistics: "if men define situations as real, they are real in their consequences" (Cooley 1902). Although Cooley's notion of the definition of a situation focuses on inner subjectivity (that need not be shared by others, however; chapter 11), it also focuses on one's perception of social circumstance and on the real social consequences of that perception. This means that a definition of a situation can probably not be formed in complete isolation from the social "here and now," and, furthermore, that its material consequences in that "here and now" are very concrete. (Note that these links to the external world allow definitions of the situation to escape the problem of infinite regress faced by Gricean pragmatics' dependence on mutual knowledge: Smith 1982). Thus, even the cognitive contexts that are considered by interactional sociolinguists (e.g. frames: Goffman 1974; Tannen 1979) are socially grounded: knowledge is knowledge of social circumstances or expectations about social conduct.

Interactional sociolinguistics also provides a way to analyze social context and to incorporate those contexts into the procedures through which we infer meaning. Goffman's sociological research focused attention on the interactional order that underlies social occasions, situations, and encounters. Knowledge of this general organization leads to appreciation of the socially constituted "moves" that help create a sense of "reality" in a particular interaction (i.e. a definition of the situation). This sense of reality is intimately related to Gumperz's ideas about contextualization cues, contextual presuppositions, and situated inferences.

Recall that situated inferences are interpretations at two levels of inferencing: what is going on in the "here and now" (i.e. are we teasing? arguing?) and what typically happens during this kind of situation (i.e. what usually characterizes teasing? arguing?). Recall, also, that contextualization cues are aspects of language and behavior that relate what is said to contextual knowledge. These cues signal contextual presuppositions: assumed background knowledge about the different situations in which we act. The contextual presuppositions signalled by contextualization cues inform us about our current activity by tying it to a more general framework of expectations about situated activity-types, of which our current activity is but one specific example. Contextual presuppositions are strikingly similar to definitions of a situation: what we know about, and what we expect to find, in a particular activity (or situation) provides the framework through which we characterize and define that activity (or situation). Thus, we draw situated inferences about speakers' messages through the use of contextualization cues that signal our contextual presuppositions, i.e. our definition of the situation.

In sum, interactional sociolinguistics provides a way to identify different kinds and levels of contexts, to conceptualize the organizational and interpretive role of contexts, and to describe how utterances and parts of utterances have a contextualizing role that allow us to draw situated inferences.

2.2.2 *Ethnography of communication and context*

The ethnography of communication combines other approaches within a larger framework of inquiry into cultural knowledge and the social and linguistic practices for which it provides. It views context as both cognitive (what we know, embedded in our communicative competence) and social (the social and cultural components that combine to define communicative events). The ethnography of communication also provides a way to discover the organization of context: the SPEAKING grid segments social context into different components that not only define a particular communicative situation (event, and act) as a closed and bounded unit (Hymes 1972b: 56), but also provide a way to systematically differentiate from one another those situations (events and acts) that comprise the communicative repertoire of a given community.

Ethnographically motivated analyses of context provide an important supplement to the interactional sociolinguistic focus on contextual presuppositions and definition of the situation. Above we noted that contextualization cues are clues by which we retrieve knowledge (i.e. contextual presuppositions) about what is expected to occur during a particular activity (or situation). We use this knowledge to draw situated inferences about what others mean. We noted that these inferences are "situated" in two ways: they are located in the "here and now" of an ongoing interaction; they depend upon our general knowledge of social situations. An important way to discover the knowledge that allows situated inferences is an ethnographic analysis of communicative situations, events, and acts. Suppose, for example, that we wanted to say that a particular phrase or intonation served as a contextualization cue by which to signal participants' definition of a situation as a reference interview in a library (chapter 5): we would need to know what typically occurs during such an interview in order to describe the contextual presuppositions evoked by the contextualization cue. It is in this way that the ethnography of communication can provide us with the contextual presuppositions upon which interactional sociolinguistics relies as a basis for situated inferences about speakers' meanings.

In sum, the ethnography of communication makes the role of context central to the analysis of communication – to the meaning of specific speech acts, to the intentions underlying a specific utterance, to the relationships assumed to hold between utterances, to the organization of acts within events, and events within situations. What we say and do has meaning only within a framework of cultural knowledge – not linguistic, but communicative, competence. The ways that we organize and conduct our lives through language are thus ways of being and doing that are deeply embedded within the particular contexts – cultural frameworks – by which we make sense out of experience. The detailed analyses of context that this approach provides sometimes make it difficult to propose generalizations about language functions apart from the contexts through which they arise. However, it is just such detailed knowledge about situations, events, and acts that provides the contextual presuppositions needed by interactional sociolinguists, and that forms a key part of our communicative competence.

2.2.3 *Speech act theory: context as situation*

In section 2.1 we noted that context plays a dual role for speech act theorists: it is the abstract knowledge underlying speech act types; it is a set of social circumstances in which utterances can be produced and interpreted as realizations of their underlying constitutive rules. The relationship between the cognitive contexts underlying the general production and interpretation of speech act types, and the actual circumstances during which a specific utterance serves as a token of a particular speech act, is complex. To make this point more concretely, let us consider the following hypothetical examples. In (1a), a text produced by one speaker seems to state all the underlying conditions of a particular speech act.

(1a)   DORIS: I just noticed that we're out of milk. We'll need some tomorrow
                  morning. I won't have a chance to buy any today. You can pass
                  the grocery store on your way home from work later. Even
                  though I know that you didn't plan to buy milk there, I want
                  you to buy some milk there. Will you do that?
        ANDY: Okay.

Requests like (1a) rarely occur in conversational interaction simply because at least some of the information needed to understand such a text as a request can be assumed to be either already known or easily inferrable by a listener. That is, Doris may very well be able to assume that Andy knows the conditions and the constitutive rules for requests without stating them explicitly.

   Contrast the hypothetical (1b):

(1b)   DORIS: Uhoh. [looking in the refrigerator]
        ANDY: Okay.

Although what Doris says in (1a) and in (1b) is linguistically different, her utterances are functionally equivalent in some ways: they both issue a request. Thus, the same abstract conditions and the same constitutive rules underlie these two different realizations of the "same" speech act type. More specifically, the same abstract constitutive rules hold for Doris's act in both (1a) and (1b): S predicates a future act A of H (the propositional content rule); S assumes that H is able to do A and S believes H is able to do A; it is not obvious to both S and H that H will do A in the normal course of events of his own accord (preparatory rules); S wants H to do A (the sincerity rule); S's utterances count as an attempt to get H to do A (the essential rule). However, the way the utterances in (1a) and (1b) realize this act is dramatically different. What Doris says in (1a) requires little attention to the physical context in which it occurs. (1b) is the opposite: interpreting *uhoh* as a request relies almost entirely upon how that remark is situated in its physical context. Regardless of the way the "texts" in (1a) and (1b) are bound to their actual situational contexts, the request receives the same response: Andy agrees to comply with the request to buy milk.

   The contrast between (1a) and (1b) bears in several ways on the role of context in speech act applications to discourse. First, (1a) and (1b) show that the relationship between text and context is basic not only to an understanding of messages, but also to an analysis of relationships across units of discourse. Second, (1a) and (1b) suggest that the text–context relationship is not fixed: although some utterances in a text can be analyzed as relatively autonomous from their physical context (as in 1a), others must be analyzed as totally dependent on their context (as in 1b). Third, (1a) and (1b) illustrate a kind of trade off between text and context: in fact, as both Austin and Searle note, it is possible to perform an act "without invoking an explicit illocutionary force-indicating device where the context and the utterance make it clear that the essential condition is satisfied" (Searle 1969: 68). These points all bear on our main concern here: the role of context as situation in speech act applications to discourse. Although social circumstances always have a role in the abstract knowledge underlying speech act types, their role in the interpretation of actual speech act tokens may be diminished (as in 1a) or enhanced (as in 1b) depending upon the actual situation in which an utterance is issued. Similarly, uncovering the basis for sequential coherence across utterances may require supplementing abstract speech act knowledge with understandings about social proprieties and interactive norms (chapter 4, section 3.2.2). Thus, although cognitive context (mutual knowledge of speech act rules) is critical to the production and interpretation of speech acts in general, the circumstances during which an utterance is produced (and the social meaning of those circumstances) cannot have a theoretically fixed (or *a priori*) relationship with the utterances through which speech acts are realized.

I have suggested in this section that abstract knowledge of context is only one way that context enters speech act applications to discourse: social circumstances also provide a framework in which utterances are successfully realized as particular acts. Context has this extra "situated" role simply because the linguistic form and content of an utterance rarely provide a guide sufficient to the task of identifying its speech act. Situated context gains special importance in the analysis of those acts for which no performative verb exists and those acts that are often labelled "indirect." Thus, although the linguistic form and content of an utterance do give clues to its speech act function, such clues must work with contextually provided information. What is said works with information available from actual circumstances to allow utterances to do things. More specifically, social situations and their meanings provide the clues that allow hearers to infer the illocutionary force of specific utterances: they help hearers find the "right" constitutive rules by which to interpret the function of, and formulate a response to, an utterance.

2.3 Context as situation and text: variation analysis

We have seen that several approaches to discourse consider context in two different, but interrelated, ways: context as knowledge (incorporated in linguistic or communicative competence) and context as situation (including knowledge of both the "here and now" situation, and knowledge of general "types" of situations).

Variation analysis also considers context as situation, but in a way somewhat different from the approaches discussed thus far. Like the ethnography of communication, variation analysis divides situation into separate components. Such components are a subset of those in Hymes's SPEAKING grid: the social situation (setting and scene), the participants (their social identities, such as gender, age, ethnicity), and the key (formal or informal, careful or casual style of speaking). Unlike ethnography, however, variationists view situational factors like setting, identity, and key as discrete and mutually exclusive factors that can be coded, counted, and compared across different circumstances (cf. chapter 5, section 3.4).

The variationist view of context differs even more dramatically from the interactional sociolinguistic view of context. Let us compare, for example, the views of social identity from both perspectives. Variationists typically treat identities as social and cultural categories that we "step into": our identities are not easily open to our own control or to alteration by another (cf. Eckert and McConnell-Ginet 1992). This view of identity underlies the variationist practice of coding identity as a categorical variable: a speaker is coded as a white, middle class, middle-aged male from Philadelphia, for example, and he is assumed to maintain that very same identity regardless of the activity or interaction in which he is engaged. A very different view of social identity is provided by interactional sociolinguistics. This perspective suggests that identity is locally situated: rather than an identity being maintained throughout an extended period of time (be it a speech activity, a situation, a span of life, or even a lifetime), different facets of identity may be highlighted or submerged during different periods of time. This more dynamic view suggests that identity is open to intentional manipulation by self, and to interpersonal negotiation between self and other. Thus, identity is less amenable to the "once and for all" coding used by variationists.

A similar difference appears in the interactional and variationist views of situation itself. In the interactional approach, participants' sense of "what is happening" is not supplied when an activity begins, but is molded and re-molded during different phases of the activity, such that definitions of the situation emerge at the same time as the situation itself. Thus, a situation is open to definition and redefinition. Variationists do not consider a situation *in toto* to change once a definition of that situation is established. However, variationists do conceive of different parts of a situation as open to change. This is revealed somewhat indirectly through the methods by which variationists code the variable "speaking style." Labov (1972c) differentiates styles (e.g. careful, casual) according to the amount of attention paid to speech. Since attention to speech is difficult to measure, variationists rely upon indirect clues of style shifts. Whereas some of these clues concern the way a speaker produces an utterance (what Labov speaks of as "channel cues"), other clues are situational. A shift in addressee, for example, can accompany a shift in style: if an interviewee speaks to someone other than the interviewer, that utterance is coded as "casual." Thus, although the different components of a situation can shift, the situation itself is viewed as relatively static.

Another difference between the variationist, and ethnographic and interactional, approaches to context concerns the necessity of bringing situation into an analysis of text. Our sample analysis in chapter 8, for example, considered the textual structure of lists without saying anything at all about the purposes of the lists, the situations in which they were presented, the speakers, and so on. This is in stark contrast to the ethnographic and interactional analyses in which the form and function of even a single utterance could not be considered apart from its situation (e.g. as part of a speech event, a participant structure, or in relation to contextual presuppositions). That situation can be an *optional* part of a variationist analysis reflects the variationist view of discourse as an autonomous unit whose internal parts stand in systematic relationships with one another. When compared to most of the other approaches to discourse being discussed in this book, then, variationists' assumptions about text – and language – are closer to a key assumption of formal grammarians: language has a modular structure with interacting, but autonomous, components. (In many other respects, of course, variation analysis is firmly within a functionalist paradigm; see chapter 2.) This assumption is responsible for the variationist practice of separating language structure *per se* (not only at textual levels, but at syntactic and phonological levels) from social and communicative function (e.g. Labov 1987). Function and context are relevant only when structural explanations fail to account for the range and distribution of linguistic variants.

In addition to viewing components of "situation" as context, variationists also view "text" as context. Let us briefly return to the analysis from chapter 8 to illustrate. Recall that we were interested in how a referring term (call it R-3) in a particular location in a list (call it clause-3, C-3) was constrained by its location in the structure of the list. One part of our procedure was to characterize the structure of the list, and the location of both R-3 and C-3, in that structure. Note, however, that what this amounted to was treating the other clauses in the list (C-1, C-2), and the other referring terms (R-1, R-2) as part of the environment in which R-3 and C-3 were located. Put another way, we treated the text in which an option (R-3), and its containing clause (C-3), were located as a context – as information to be considered only in relation to something else that was the primary focus of our attention. Thus, text itself became a context (cf. Brown and Yule's 1983: 46–50, term "co-text") that could be compartmentalized, coded, and counted.

Note, then, that the same kind of approach is applied by variationists to both text and situation: both are divided into discrete and mutually exclusive factors that can be coded, counted, and compared. The compartmentalization of text is easily understandable given our earlier observation (chapter 9) that variation analysis is a structurally motivated approach. Not only do variationists define discourse as a unit of language larger than a single sentence (chapter

2, section 3), but variationists analyze how that unit is comprised of smaller units (whether those units are conceived of as clauses, sentences, turns, utterances, and so on) that are systematically related to one another. Given the focus upon text as comprised of smaller units, and the analysis of the relationship of those units with one another, the segmentation and categorization of text into units that have systematic effects upon each other is not surprising. It is this basic structuralist methodology that also seems to be applied to variationist analyses of situation.

In sum, variationists consider both situation and text to be context. They segment and categorize both aspects of context, viewing different facets of its form and content as discrete and mutually exclusive factors that can be extracted from *their* surroundings (e.g. their broader cultural frameworks) to be coded, counted, and compared across different circumstances. The different components into which variationists divide and classify situation and text are defined as "constraints" on the variant being focused upon: they are contextual influences on linguistic realizations in a particular sequentially defined slot.

2.4 Context as knowledge, situation, and text: conversation analysis

At first glance, conversation analysis seems to combine the way other approaches view context: context is knowledge (speech act theory, pragmatics), situation (interactional sociolinguistics, ethnography of communication), and text (variation analysis). But a very particular view of knowledge – and its relationship to action and language – differentiates the CA view of context from the others.

As we discussed in chapter 7, CA is an approach to discourse that inherits from ethnomethodology the goal of accounting for the common-sense knowledge that members have for constructing talk. The knowledge on which members rely is treated by them as part of the same setting that it also makes orderable (Garfinkel 1974: 17). Thus, knowledge *is*, in a sense, context (cf. the speech act (2.1.1) and pragmatic (2.1.2) views). But knowledge cannot be considered apart from either the situations in which, or the actions for which, it is used. Knowledge and situation are mutually constitutive: participants' understandings of their circumstances, and participants' role in constructing those circumstances through actions, are all intertwined. Activities serve to publicly display an emergent sense of order: activities provide a practical basis, and a sense of intersubjectivity, through which other activities (and the situation that they help to create) can be sustained. Social action thus not only *displays* knowledge (cf. the speech act view), but is critical to the *creation of* knowledge: one's own actions produce and reproduce the knowledge through which individual conduct and social circumstance are intelligible.

Not only does this relationship differentiate the CA view of knowledge from the speech act and Gricean pragmatics views (in which knowledge seems to exist even when it is not knowledge "in use"), it also has an important bearing on the study of language and on the relationship between text and context. As we noted in chapter 7, members produce "typifications": categories that are continuously adjusted according to whether the anticipation of an actor (an anticipation on which the actor's own conduct was based) is confirmed by another's actions. Language (and action through language) is a situated product of rules and systems that provide actors an ability to "make continuous sense of their environments of action" (Heritage 1984a: 292). Language serves as a medium through which common-sense categories (typifications) are constituted. Language also enters into the mutually constitutive relationship between action and knowledge: speakers produce utterances assuming that hearers can make sense out of them by the same kind of practical reasoning and methodic contextualizing operations that they apply to social conduct in general.

I have been suggesting thus far that the CA view of context is built upon the ethnomethodological view of language, action, knowledge, and situation. What CA analyses show is that the sequential progression of interaction – the positioning of utterances – is critical to members' display of their understandings (including their knowledge about situation) through language. Each utterance in a sequence is shaped by a prior context and provides a context for a next utterance: "the significance of any speaker's communicative action is doubly contextual in being both context-shaped and context-renewing" (Heritage 1984a: 242). From a speaker's point of view, next-position thus offers a location in which to find the recipient's analysis of the utterance – to see whether an anticipated response is confirmed. From a recipient's point of view, next-position offers an opportunity to reveal aspects of the understanding of prior talk to which own talk will be addressed. It is not surprising that two constructs central to CA reflect the doubly contextual role of utterances. Adjacency pairs are organized patterns of stable, recurrent actions that provide a normative framework in which actions are accountably implemented (Heritage 1984: 249). The exchange of turns allowed by turn-taking rules provides for "next-position," and thus for the emergence of sequentially ordered displays of understandings to which actors are mutually accountable.

The terminology used above – an utterance is context-shaped and context-renewing – clearly shows that CA views "text" as "context." This terminology does not mean, however, that the CA view of text-as-context is the same as the variationist view (2.3). The CA view of text-as-context as both retrospective and prospective reflects the ethnomethodological view that meanings (and knowledge) are continually adjusted and sequentially emergent. In sharp contrast to variation analysis, then, utterances are not positioned relative to one another because of their underlying linguistic properties (or speech actions) or their abstract textual relations. Rather, utterances are positioned because they provide frameworks of understanding and meaning for both past and upcoming utterances.

We noted above that interactional sociolinguistic and ethnographic approaches to discourse do not readily separate what is said from the situation in which it is said; the variationist view, on the other hand, resorts to situation-as-context when structural (text-based) explanations cannot fully account for the range and distribution of linguistic variants. The CA treatment of situation-as-context bears a surface similarity to the variationist view – since situation-as-context is not *assumed* to be relevant – but again, it differs in a critical way. Although CA assumes that utterances always have contextual relevance for one another, not all aspects of situation-as-context are assumed to have so constant a relevance. Although CA transcripts (and analyses) of talk pay a great deal of attention to the productive details of utterances (e.g. pauses, inbreaths, overlaps) they pay little attention to components of situation, e.g. participants, setting. By intentionally ignoring what are often assumed to be static features of a social world (e.g. the occupation of a participant), CA reflects still again the ethnomethodological avoidance of premature generalizations and idealizations. Categories of social life and conduct cannot be assumed apart from the activities in which (and through which) they are realized: like knowledge and language, the definition of the situation is subject to locally emergent interpretive activity. The relevance of a social identity, for example, can be no more presumed to hold across different times and places than can the relevance of a one second pause. Thus, although CA is an approach to discourse that emphasizes context, context-as-knowledge and context-as-situation are grounded in – and can only be discovered by – context-as-text.

2.5 *Summary: different approaches to context*

We have seen in this section that different approaches to discourse make different assumptions about what aspects of context are relevant to the production and interpretation of utterances. Whereas speech act theory and pragmatics view context primarily as "knowledge," interactional sociolinguistics and the ethnography of communication view context as "knowledge" and as "situation." Variation analysis views context as "situation" and "text." Conversation analysis focuses on the reflexive relationship among "knowledge," "situation," and "text." The next section briefly considers the way different approaches view "text," and how their analyses of text are related not only to their view of context, but also to the unit of analysis (i.e. single or multiple utterances) upon which they initially focused.

3 What is text?

Earlier in this chapter we defined "text" as the linguistic content of utterances: the stable semantic meanings of words, expressions, and sentences, but not the inferences available to hearers depending upon the contexts in which words, expressions, and sentences are used. Text provides for the "what is said" part of utterances; context combines with "what is said" to create an utterance. Although all the approaches to discourse that we discussed are concerned with language and with the "utterance," not all the approaches are explicitly concerned with text and "utterances." Speech act theory and Gricean pragmatics, for example, are *applicable* to discourse, but they were not initially concerned with relationships across utterances (3.1). Virtually all the other approaches, on the other hand, were initially interested in utterances, whether that interest stemmed from the contextual or textual contribution to coherence across utterances (3.2).

3.1 Text and context for "utterance" based approaches

Both speech act theory and Gricean pragmatics focus on single utterances. Given this focus, it is not surprising that these approaches offer no way to analyze text either as part of context (cf. sections 2.3, 2.4) or as its own unit of analysis: neither approach considers how to analyze multiple utterances, the relationship between utterances, or how adjacent utterances contribute to the communicative content of one another. I suggest here, however, that both approaches can extend their view of how language and context are related within one utterance to an analysis of multiple utterances.

Let us begin by recalling that both Austin and Searle differentiate the propositional meaning of an utterance from its illocutionary force: a locutionary act is the utterance of sounds and words with meaning (sense and reference). Searle (1969: 22–33) goes on to argue that the propositional content of an utterance (a part of the locutionary act) can remain constant despite variation in the illocutionary act. Propositional content can have a role in speech act interpretation: what is said and how it is said plays a key role in making particular background knowledge relevant to the interpretation of illocutionary force. Even in the most direct speech acts, for example in the performative *I promise*, use of the verb "promise" is the cue that accesses the relevant knowledge about the conditions underlying the speech act "promise." In addition to performative verbs, sentences have illocutionary force indicators as varied as verbs, syntactic form, and intonation. Recall, for example, our discussion of intonation and the semantics of the verb "want" in the identification of Henry's *Y'want a piece of candy?* (chapter 3) as a question. Our discussion of *Y'want a piece of candy?*, and a librarian's *May I help you?* (chapter 5), showed that analyses of indirect speech acts also consider "what is done" (despite the fact that syntactic form itself may not be a direct reflection of the multiple functions of an utterance). Thus, linguistic form and meaning can provide clues to the rules (and the knowledge that they represent) that are responsible for illocutionary force.

One way to extend speech act analyses from "utterance" to "utterances" is to extend the distinction between propositional content and illocutionary force from sentence to text. For example, we might analyze how the linguistic form and meaning of a story contributes to its communicative function: this was an essential part of our analysis of how Irene's "diet" story served as an account (chapter 3). However, we might also need to consider how each sentence within a text has its own illocutionary force, and how (or if) those embedded speech acts contribute to a text-level illocutionary force. We might also need to add an analysis of propositional meanings *across* utterances (e.g. the rhetorical predicates identified by Thompson and Mann 1987) or the macro-level propositions that texts produce (e.g. van Dijk 1977).

Another possibility is to find that not all sentences in a text perform their own autonomous speech acts. As we noted in chapter 3, text can enter the constitutive rules of a speech act somewhat surreptitiously through the felicity conditions for a specific act: an act may require a response to be felicitous (e.g. S's bet requires H's uptake; Austin 1962: 37) or require prior utterances to be felicitous (e.g. a conclusion has to follow prior evidence; Searle 1979). Similarly, one utterance can provide information about the speech act being performed by another utterance. Conversation analysts, for example, have proposed that a speaker may anticipate the speech act to be performed in an upcoming utterance through a prior utterance that engages an interlocutor in a "pre-sequence," e.g. a speaker may issue a pre-request, pre-announcement, and so on (Levinson 1983: 345–64; Schegloff 1980, 1988a). For example, I might not ask you to take me to the train station (a request) unless I have first checked to see whether you are free at the time I need to go (a preparatory condition, i.e. whether you have the ability to perform the act). Thus, what is said by one utterance (e.g. "What time do you have to be at work tomorrow?") can prefigure the illocutionary force of a later utterance (e.g. "Can you take me to Union Station in time for a 9:05 train?").[3] However, it is not just the propositional (cf. locutionary) meaning of a prior utterance that helps perform an upcoming act: it is how that prior utterance represents the felicity conditions of the upcoming act. Thus, multiple utterances can create the very same context-as-knowledge necessary for interpretation of an act as a single utterance. Put another way, the representation of a knowledge base through which to interpret the illocutionary force of a speech act may be not only a sentential task, but a textual task.

Gricean pragmatics also differentiates propositional meaning (what speakers "say") from communicative meaning (i.e. meaning-nn, speaker intention). Recall that propositional meaning is one type of information that we use when we calculate implicatures: implicatures are allowed, in part, by the conventional meaning of words (2.1.2). But implicatures also rely upon the context, "linguistic or otherwise" (Grice 1975: 50), of the utterance.

Our sample analysis in chapter 6, for example, showed that "linguistic" context can provide information appropriate in quantity to the use of a referring term in a later clause. Put another way, one could implicate the referent evoked by a referring term by integrating the linguistic content of prior text into assumed knowledge. Likewise, "linguistic context" can also provide information to which a later referring term can be relevant: again, one could infer the referent evoked by finding the assumed knowledge to which it was relevant. In addition to showing how "linguistic context" (text) could figure in implicatures, our sample analysis also suggested that the situation (the "otherwise context") could figure in implicature calculation. Consistent with the idea that quantity of information is suited to the current purposes of an exchange, we suggested that ambiguous expressions (e.g. *they*) might be perfectly well suited for the telling of a story (or part of a story) to one kind of audience, but not to another. Thus, the use of actual utterances in their "linguistic and otherwise" contexts forces us to attend to how speakers' and hearers' needs, goals, and wants are tailored not just to the conventional meanings of prior text, but also to particular socially and culturally defined communicative situations.

We have seen in this section that, although speech act theory and Gricean pragmatics are two approaches to discourse that do not begin from the analysis of utterances, the insights that they offer for the analysis of a single utterance can be extended to multiple utterances.

3.2 Text and context for "utterances" based approaches

In contrast to the two approaches to discourse that began in philosophy (speech act theory, pragmatics), the approaches to discourse analysis that began in anthropology, sociology, and linguistics all began with a focus on utterances. These approaches offer more explicit concepts and methods by which to relate what is said in a text to the context in which it is said.

Interactional sociolinguistics is an approach to discourse that views all language as inherently contextualized and contextualizing. Aspects of language as varied as rhythm, repetition, and syntactic structure, and units as small as single expressions or as large as texts, all reflect (and construct) the participation frameworks, identities, encounters, situations, occasions, and so on in which a single message is situated. To return to the terms used above, language (including text) is contextualized: relationships between utterances come to be interpreted as coherent by virtue of the contexts in which they are situated. But language is also contextualizing: one utterance constructs an interpretive context (in part, by providing information about background expectations associated with a given activity or situation) in which the meaning of a next utterance can be inferred.

The contextualizing processes noted above are achieved through links between language and participants' knowledge of situation. Language provides connections to context through contextualization cues. We are able to convey and interpret meaning because we use core (e.g. phonology, syntax) and marginal (e.g. prosody, rhythm) features of language to signal relationships between what we say and contextual knowledge. The knowledge signalled by these features is crucial to the accurate inferencing of what we mean. Because core and marginal features both provide contextualization cues, interactional sociolinguists sometimes collapse the distinction between language as grammar (abstract rules) and language as use (performance features). Thus, contextualization cues (in "text") signal contextual presuppositions (knowledge about "situation") that allow the inferencing of a speaker's meaning.

The ethnography of communication is also a contextual approach to text. This approach assumes that language is always constitutive of some portion of social and cultural life. Consistent with the comparative and relativistic premises of this approach, however, few *a priori* assumptions are made about the degree to which language (or which aspect of language) is constitutive of context. Thus, the relative autonomy (context-dependence or context-independence) of text from context cannot be assumed: it must be discovered through empirical investigation.

Ethnographers do believe that language is a system that is firmly located within a system of cultural beliefs and understandings that work together to define communication and communicative events. The fact that language is so deeply embedded in culture means that the ethnographic study of language is broader than the study of grammar *per se*. Furthermore, the aspects of language that do mesh with context – and the linguistic functions that can be discovered through contextual analyses – are due to the fact that context itself has a communicative structure comprised of a variety of components that co-occur and alternate with one another. It is the higher level structures provided by the communicative events defined through these components to which language itself accommodates. However, ethnographers also believe that some aspects of language (including aspects of text) may very well be part of a system comprised of smaller systems that are not only partially autonomous from one another, but also perhaps independent of context. The point is that all fundamental concepts – including the relationship between text and context, structure and use, code and performance – are to be taken as problematic and to be investigated (Hymes 1974a).

Finally, as we saw earlier, both conversation analysis and variation analysis include text as a type of context. We also noted, however, that the CA view of text-as-context is not the same as the variationist view. The CA view of text-as-context reflects the ethnomethodological belief that meanings (and knowledge) are continually adjusted and sequentially emergent. This belief is also responsible for the idea that whatever aspects of situation-as-context are relevant to relations between utterances are manifested in utterances themselves. Variation analysis, on the other hand, attributes the sequential positioning of utterances to their underlying linguistic properties or abstract (functional or structural) relations. Variation analysis also separates text-as-context from situation-as-context; the former are linguistic constraints, the latter non-linguistic constraints, on linguistic realizations in a particular textually defined slot. Thus, variationists allow linguistic variants and textual segments more autonomy relative to their sequential location in a text than do explicitly contextualizing approaches like interactional sociolinguistics or the ethnography of communication, or sequentially based approaches like conversation analysis. (We see in chapter 11 that this separation of text from situation-as-context is more consistent with the code model of communication than the interactional model of communication.)

It is important to note, however, that although variationist analyses of discourse seem reluctant to mesh text and context as two mutually constitutive systems (cf. interactional sociolinguistics, ethnography of communication, conversation analysis), variationist analyses of two-party discourse (in which speakers exchange turns) rely more upon considerations of social meaning and context than do analyses of narratives. Although Labov (1972e: 252) proposes that the "fundamental problem of discourse analysis is to show how one utterance follows another in a rational, rule-governed manner," he also notes that "there is no formal basis in sentence-grammar to explicate our reaction" to many everyday exchanges as coherent and well-formed (Labov 1972d: 299).

4 Conclusion

All the approaches to discourse discussed in this book consider both text and context as crucial to the analysis of utterances. The approaches vary, however, in their definitions of context and in their views of how text is related to context. These differences mean that although all the approaches assume an interdependency between text and context, they differ in their understanding of the processes by which speakers/hearers rely upon text and context to construct/discover the meaning of an utterance and the coherence relations across utterances.

We noted at the outset of this chapter that context is difficult to define. We suggested that one reason for this difficulty is that contextual information is always information that is identified in relation to something else that is the primary focus of our attention: the identity of that "something else" influences our decisions about what counts as context. We have seen in this chapter that different approaches to discourse define context quite differently. One reason for this may be that each approach began by focusing on a variety of issues and questions (on a different "something else") that then defined the sort of context likely to be of interest. Those approaches that began by focusing on the meaning of a single utterance, for example, were less likely to offer an explicit way to focus on text *per se* as a source of background information – simply because text itself was not already included as an object of inquiry. However, if discourse analysts hope to use such perspectives to analyze utterances – whether it is the relationship between utterances, or how adjacent utterances contribute to the communicative content of one another – then the inclusion of text-as-context seems unavoidable.

In conclusion, I would like to suggest – in keeping with the eclecticism reviewed in this chapter – that text and context cannot be related in any simple or single way. Not only can context be conceived of very differently, but the interpretation of "what is said" cannot rest upon a fixed interdependency with the contexts (whether context as knowledge, situation, or text) in relation to which an utterance is issued. Put another way, contexts can impose themselves upon texts (or aspects of texts) to different degrees and in different ways (see Duranti and Goodwin 1991; Schiffrin 1987a: chapter 10, 1990a).

Our constructed example from an earlier section in this chapter can help make these points. Compare (1a) and (1b) again:

(1a) DORIS: I just noticed that we're out of milk. We'll need some tomorrow morning. I won't have a chance to buy any today. You can pass the grocery store on your way home from work later. Even though I know that you didn't plan to buy milk there, I want you to buy some milk there. Will you do that?

      ANDY: Okay.

(1b) DORIS: Uhoh. [looking in the refrigerator]

      ANDY: Okay.

Analyzing the text/context relationship in Doris's utterances is important if we want to explain how it is that Andy's *Okay* seems coherent in relation to what Doris has just said. To be more specific: Andy can use *Okay* as a coherent response to Doris's utterances in either (1a) or (1b). In either case, *Okay* can convey Andy's willingness to undertake the action that Doris has requested (see also Merritt 1984). But it is precisely in understanding the basis for the coherence of *Okay* as a response that we need to consider the text/context relationship: we cannot possibly understand how Andy's *Okay* fits into the dialogue structure, or how it functions as an agreement to comply with Doris's request, without first analyzing the way that text and context worked together to create Doris's message.

Earlier I suggested that (1a) is a text that can be understood almost completely apart from a context, i.e. it relies very little upon its context-as-situation. (1b) is a text that cannot be understood without its situation-as-context. We might thus say that (1a) and (1b) illustrate that text and context intertwine with one another to different degrees.

However, (1a) and (1b) actually illustrate more complexities in the text/context relationship than I previously suggested. We said earlier that (1a) is independent of its context in that the request ("I want you to buy milk") can be interpreted without the use of situational information. However, the reason this message is so easily retrieved is that (1a) encodes all the background conditions typically assumed to underlie the formulation of felicitous requests (chapter 3). If we allow background conditions (and background knowledge in general) to be a part of context (a cognitive part), we then get quite a different picture of the text/context relationship. Since (1a) displays a great deal of background information in its text, it can actually be seen as a reflection of context, and thus totally dependent on (rather than independent of) context.

There is still another way to analyze text/context in (1a) and (1b) – in terms of conditions of use. Ways of speaking vary according to their situational appropriateness, such that what sounds right in one situation would sound very wrong in another. Although (1a) and (1b) are appropriate under very different circumstances, each way of formulating a directive *is* appropriate in some situation. In this sense, both (1a) and (1b) are equally bound to their contexts: their difference lies in the type of situational context to which they are bound.

I have used (1a) and (1b) to suggest some of the difficulties of trying to formulate a single view of the text/context relationship. It is beginning to seem that we get different views of this relationship depending upon what facet of text we focus on, what aspect of context, and what kind of relationship we are examining. If we focus on interpretability of a text, an elliptical utterance (such as 1b) can be seen as heavily dependent on context; if we focus on background knowledge, very explicit and detailed utterances (such as 1a) can be seen as heavily dependent on context; if we focus on appropriate conditions of use, all texts can be said to depend on their contexts. Variation such as this suggests not only that the text/context relationship may be impossible to analyze in any single way, but that describing the text/context relationship may require empirical analyses of different aspects of texts, different aspects of contexts (drawing here, from the contextual analyses offered by the approaches most explicitly interested in context as "situation"), and the ways they are bound to one another.

Notes

1 The term "text" has been used in various ways, including a cognitive sense in which it refers to a mental representation of what is said (e.g. Webber 1979), and a linguistic sense in which it refers to passages of sentences that "form a unified whole" and exhibit semantic cohesion (Halliday and Hasan 1976). Briggs and Bauman (1992) and Bauman and Briggs (1990) discuss how our cultural conceptions of "text" are intertwined with genre, social power, context, and intertextuality.

2 Note, however, that the availability of implicatures can constrain the structure of the lexicon. Horn (1972), for example, suggests that a concept will not be directly lexicalized if it is generally implicated through an existing word.

3 Rather than analyze my question about your availability as an indirect request (see chapter 3), we might analyze it as a pre-sequence to my upcoming request (see chapter 7).

11 Discourse and Communication

1 Introduction

Discourse is used for communication: people use utterances to convey information and to lead each other toward an interpretation of meanings and intentions. This role greatly increases the scope of discourse analysis, simply because one has to address how the language of utterances is related to aspects of the communication process (such as knowledge or intentions) that bear an indirect (and controversial) relationship to language *per se*.

Some of the approaches to discourse analysis that we have discussed are quite explicit in relating their frameworks to communication. Speech act theory, for example, locates the speech act as the basic unit of human linguistic communication. Interactional sociolinguistics aims to integrate what we know about grammar, culture, and interactive conventions into a general theory of verbal communication. The ethnography of communication seeks to discover how communication (including, but not limited to, language use) is culturally organized. Gricean pragmatics begins with a general principle that underlies not just language use, but communication in general. Although conversation analysis and variation analysis are less openly concerned with communication, they too end up addressing issues that bear on how people produce and interpret language during interactions with one another. It seems, then, that what discourse analysts learn about utterances has to do with what we know about communication and that the products of discourse analyses can be integrated with our knowledge of communication.

As I discuss in this chapter, however, the approaches to discourse reviewed in this book differ quite surprisingly in terms of what model of communication they assume: variationist approaches assume a *code model*; pragmatic and speech act approaches assume an *inferential model*; interactional, ethnographic, and conversation analytic approaches assume an *interactional model*. Before discussing these models in detail, I first describe some aspects of communication that are differently conceived by the models, incorporating some comparisons among the six approaches to discourse within this description (section 2). Section 3 is devoted to a more focused comparison among the different models of communication assumed by different approaches to discourse. Section 4 summarizes.

2 Aspects of communication

Although virtually all models of communication identify at least three components as pertinent to the exchange of information, those components are neither labelled nor conceived of in the same way. Smith (1977: 14), for example, refers to a communicator, a signal, and a recipient, but Martinich (1984: 17) refers to a sender, a message (something with considerably more "meaning" than the signal), a medium (e.g. the code in which signals are conveyed), and a receiver. Most models also assume that participants are capable of sharing knowledge and experience, or at least of reaching similar interpretations, i.e. of intersubjectivity. Indeed, as Taylor and Cameron (1987: 161) note, a principle of intersubjectivity is "so central to the study of verbal communication in modern times that it might be called its fundamental principle" (see also Taylor 1992). However, models differ in terms of how extensively they assume participants to rely upon intersubjectivity, and at what point in the communication process intersubjectivity is salient.

Let us begin our general discussion of communication with *participants*: how do we speak of those who communicate and what do we imagine them doing when we say that they are communicating? Although scholars agree that the process of communicating involves at least two participant roles, they disagree on the nature of those roles and their contribution to the process of communicating. This disagreement pervades even so basic an issue as the choice of terms through which to refer to participants. For example, the terms that are often used, "sender" and "receiver," are borrowed from information theory: they stress the "transmission" aspect of communication, whereby a message is assumed to be created at one end of the process and sent to the other end of the process along a channel (cf. the familiar conduit metaphor; Reddy 1979). Many linguistic analyses of communication often label "sender" and "receiver" as "speaker" and "hearer" respectively. However, this choice of terms is also theoretically implicative and consequential: use of "speaker" and "hearer" conforms to a tacit assumption that communication is typically verbal and dyadic, and that communicative roles can be neatly segregated as to relatively active versus passive roles (i.e. speaking versus hearing). Even the use of the more seemingly neutral terms "individual," "self," and "person" reflect different ways of conceptualizing human beings, e.g. as a member of the human kind, as a locus of experience, and as an agent-in-society respectively (Harris 1989), thus conveying different assumptions about how human beings are oriented toward participation in the communication process.

Note that we made implicit assumptions about participant role in each chapter in part II – each time we presented an example and each time we had to label the identities of participants. In the speech act chapter I often used the names of participants (since they were familiar to me), but I also referred to S (for speaker) and H (for hearer) in the discussion of general speech act rules. This is consistent with the notion that speech act rules apply across various situations and situated identities, despite the fact that other aspects of social context may enter into the choice of linguistic forms by which to realize the acts. Pragmatics maintained a focus on S and H. In discussion of the story in the sample analysis, however, I used the speaker's name – to reflect the personal basis of the experience being reported. The interactional sociolinguistic approach is concerned with social and personal identities of interactants: hence, the use of personal names in the examples, and the extensive discussion of social identities and personal relationships in explicating the examples. The examples in the ethnography of communication chapter labelled the identities bestowed by the speech event: L for librarian and P for patron; S for sociolinguistic interviewer and R for respondent. The implication here is that participant identity is couched within normatively guided events for the use of speech. Conversation analysis might rely upon similar labels of situated identity – if it can be shown that those identities are relevant to, and displayed through, what is being said. Since the data being used for the CA analysis were from sociolinguistic interviews, I labelled them that way – although perhaps just S and H would have been more appropriate since not all talk seemed bound to the interview *per se*. Variationist examples elsewhere in the literature usually use informants' names to capture their identity as real people with actual identities, as opposed to hypothetical idealized speakers. However, I also relied upon IVer and IVee for the variationist examples just to reflect the speech situation in which the lists being focused upon were produced.

It is not only the choice of a particular pair of terms for participants that has theoretical consequences: the use of *any* two-part division that is expected to hold for all communicative domains necessarily ignores the ways in which participation rights may be socially and culturally allocated for particular speech acts, events, or situations (chapter 5). The use of a two-part division also implies that no more than two participation roles are available, thus ignoring the many ways that participants both create and display multiple participation statuses depending upon their (productive or receptive) orientation to what is said (see chapter 4).

During an act of communication, one person is assumed to make something available to another – a *message* – that the other did not have before. Receipt of a message can possibly alter the other's course of action, even if that alteration is no more than the creation of a shared piece of information that is stored for reference or use in the indefinite future (Smith 1977: 15). The source of a message is differently conceived. For some analysts, for example, messages are essentially thoughts that are externalized and made available to others through their representation in a shared code. For others, messages are communicative intentions, e.g. what a speaker believes or wants. Even when the content of a message is assumed to be referential (i.e. to say something about the world), messages can be said to accomplish this referential function in ways that are relatively code-dependent or context-dependent. Furthermore, the basically referential meaning of a message can be said either to exhaust its communicative function or to work along with other types of information (e.g. social, expressive) that may or may not be conveyed in the same manner or through the same channel.

The production and interpretation of messages depends upon the availability of a *medium of communication*. Some models of communication are very code-dependent: they place much of the communicative burden for the receipt of messages on the signals conveyable in the code, such that messages are said to be encoded and decoded. But other models depend much less on the code, assuming that a code is an imperfect and incomplete guide to a communicator's intentions. Such models reduce the import of the code by becoming more context-dependent: without denying the importance of the code, they assume that codes can convey messages only in relation to the way an utterance is situated in time, place, and so on, and in the way it is related to what other messages have already conveyed and what other information is potentially available for interpretation.

Despite the usual tendency of linguists to focus primarily on language as a medium of communication, then, many scholars focus on both verbal and nonverbal channels as mediums of communication. Even among linguists who focus on the verbal channel, scholars make different assumptions about how information is made available. As noted above, information may be seen as codified through the grammatical resources of a language, e.g. a meaning can be mapped onto a sentence and represented through a sequence of sounds. But participants may also make inferences (grounded in context and contextual assumptions) that supplement the content of a verbal-based message with meanings that could not be conveyed through the grammar. Linguists differ tremendously on the proper way to describe such a grammar (e.g. as *a priori* or emergent; Hopper 1988) and on the number and content of contextually derived principles.

We noted earlier that a principle of *intersubjectivity* is central to the study of communication (Schiffrin 1990a; Taylor 1992). Simply put, intersubjectivity has to do with the sharing of knowledge or experience. According to many scholars, intersubjectivity is seen as relevant to communication at the two ends of the communicative activity itself: its inception and its completion. That is, it is often assumed that in order for communication to proceed at all, people must share certain basic knowledge, e.g. knowledge about the world, about the language to be used, and so on. It is also assumed that one of the main purposes of communication is the transmission of information from one person to another. This means that one product of communication is shared knowledge: a key part of the communicative process involves person A sending to person B a message (sometimes seen to originate as a thought or representation of the world) that goes from his own mind to then reside in the other's mind. In short, intersubjectivity is often assumed to have a dual role: it both *allows* communication, and is achieved by communication.

At first glance, it might seem as if discourse analysts cannot help but believe in intersubjectivity: certainly, communication does both require and create shared knowledge. To take a simple example, suppose you are my neighbor, you own a dog that is barking late into the night, and I want you to get your dog to stop barking. There are a number of ways that I can try to convey this intention to you: I can buy a muzzle and send it to you anonymously, I can complain to you that I am tired because I have not been sleeping well, I can ask you if you know whose dog has been barking at night, and so on. Suppose I choose a relatively direct route, and during the course of a conversation with you, I say the following: "I want your dog to stop barking." Now, if this message is to be understood, I must assume that you share certain world knowledge with me (e.g. dogs bark, owners have some control over dogs) and certain linguistic knowledge (e.g. when I say "I," I am referring to myself, when I say "stop barking," the change of state verb "stop" leads to the inference that barking has occurred). All this knowledge – and of course other knowledge as well – is assumed by me to be shared with you in order for our communication to proceed at all. Once I actually present my utterance, and assuming that it is understood, what have I accomplished? Regardless of what you decide to do about your dog (and regardless of what you may think of my rather direct tactics in making my request), what I have accomplished is the transformation of my previously private intention to communicate something into a publicly shared piece of information.

It is because communication does have so intimate a relation with shared knowledge (which is of course more intricate than my example suggested) that intersubjectivity seems to play so necessary a role in communication. However, intersubjectivity is actually an extremely problematic notion, in part because it dwells at the complicated crux between what is private experience and/or knowledge (and known just to an internal self) and what is public (and available for others to witness and/or share).

Now that we have reviewed four aspects of communication (participants, message, medium, intersubjectivity), let us go on to describe how different approaches to discourse adopt different perspectives on the nature of communication. In so doing, we will be speaking of three different models of communication that define and treat the aspects just discussed (both individually and together) quite differently.

3　Discourse analysis and models of communication

In this section, I describe three different models of communication: a code model (3.1), an inferential model (3.2), and an interactional model (3.3). The approaches to discourse discussed in this book are more or less aligned with one of these models: variationist approaches assume a *code model*; pragmatic and speech act approaches assume an *inferential model*; interactional, ethnographic and conversation analytic approaches assume an *interactional model*. I begin description of each model by considering the participant role of the person who initiates communication: differences in participant role are related to different conceptions of the message and the medium, and to assumptions about intersubjectivity. My discussion of each model includes the way different approaches to discourse are more or less wed to the assumptions of that model.

3.1　Code model

The main participant role assumed by the code model of communication is a sender. Examined a bit more closely, a sender has three sequentially ordered roles. First, a sender has an internally represented proposition (perhaps we can think of this as a "thought") that she intends to make accessible to another person. Second, a sender transforms a thought into a set of externally and mutually accessible signals, here drawing upon knowledge of a code that is shared with an intended recipient of the message. Finally, a sender transmits that thought (a transmission allowed by conversion of the thought into code-derived signals) to its intended recipient; the recipient then relies upon essentially the same procedures to decode the signal, retrieve the message, and thus access another's thought.

The code model of communication is "entrenched in Western culture" (Sperber and Wilson 1986: 6): it is said to trace back to Aristotle and it underlies many contemporary linguistic theories. For example, as stated by Katz (1966: 104–104):

> The speaker's message is encoded in the form of a phonetic representation of an utterance by means of the system of linguistic rules with which the speaker is equipped. This encoding then becomes a signal to the speaker's articulatory organs, and he vocalizes an utterance of the proper phonetic shape. This is, in turn, picked up by the hearer's auditory organs. The speech sound that stimulates these organs is then converted into a neural signal from which a phonetic representation equivalent to

the one into which the speaker encoded his message is obtained. This
representation is decoded into a representation of the same message that
the speaker originally chose to convey by the hearer's equivalent system
of linguistic rules.

Various scholars (Sperber and Wilson 1986; R. Harris 1981) argue that Saussure's development of a theory of signs in the early twentieth century helped
to guarantee the code model of communication a prominent place in linguistics. In part, this is because the translation of internally represented propositions about the world (thoughts) into a format accessible to another person
can be assumed to be greatly facilitated by the use of a shared and fixed code
– a code in which sounds (signifiers) are conventionally (and stably) linked
with meanings (signifieds). What this means for our current purposes is that
the view of the sender (as someone with the three sequential roles noted
above) is not only associated with a particular view of the message (as an
internal proposition), but is also deeply dependent upon a particular view of
the medium used to communicate, i.e. a view that language is a fixed code
(R. Harris 1981). That is, the originator of a message is assumed to map the
thought onto (or realize the thought through) a set of paradigmatic and
syntagmatic choices provided through the code, that are then interpretable by
the receiver because that receiver has access to the same code.

Note that this model of communication restricts messages to thoughts that
the speaker *intends* to convey, i.e. what sets the whole process in motion is
not a thought *per se*, but an intention to convey a thought. In fact, various
scholars (e.g. Ekman and Freisen 1969; MacKay 1972) have argued for the
need to make a clear-cut distinction between material that is communicative
(because of its intentional basis, or in MacKay's terms "goal-directed") and
material that is informative (that may be interpreted regardless of whether or
not it is intended to be so). Critically, it is only signals encoding a thought
that the speaker intends to transmit that end up being communicative – just
so long as the receiver decodes the signals (relies upon the code) in such a way
as to create in his own mind a thought matching the content of the sender's
own thought.

Intersubjectivity plays a critical role in the code model of communication.
Not only is the goal of communication to achieve a shared message, but the
process by which that goal is achieved rests upon the prior existence, and use,
of a shared code, i.e. shared units, rules, and so on. Thus, it is no surprise that
Taylor and Cameron (1987: 161) call intersubjectivity the "fundamental principle" of verbal communication – for it is the code model of verbal communication that is so often being assumed.

Variation analysis is an approach to discourse that is wed to the code model
of communication. Many of the variationist concepts discussed make sense
only if we assume that sender and recipient encode and decode a code. Take
the notion of variable, for example. Not only does a variable link together
surface forms at a deeper level of representation within the code, but what

provides the basis for the link (i.e. the relationship of referential equivalence) resides in a shared and fixed code. Put another way, the reason we identify different ways of speaking as variants is because we assign them the same conventionally based link between sound and meaning. Furthermore, it is because meaning is attached to the linguistic code that variationists can analyze discourse units (e.g. narratives, lists) apart from the way they are locally situated in talk.

We also noted that the source of coherence across exchanges in talk is often located at levels other than the surface forms and meanings of utterances: this certainly seems to de-emphasize the role of the code. Recall, however, that the processes by which coherence is created (i.e. by which utterances are produced and interpreted) are viewed as similar to the encoding and decoding procedures underlying linguistic rules: the only difference is that they map form to action, instead of form to meaning. (Recall, also, the point in chapter 9 that the abstract speech actions (focused upon by Labov's method of comprehensive discourse analysis) rest upon an assumption that discourse coherence depends upon a complex hierarchical organization derived from the linguistic analysis of phonology and grammar.) Finally, although social context is clearly important to the variationist approach, context is viewed as a constraint on the way people use the code – not as something that pervades the definition of categories in the code.

3.2 *Inferential model*

Even though the view of the communicator, the message, and the code are quite different in the inferential model than in the code model, the inferential model of communication also depends upon a principle of intersubjectivity. Let me begin again with a description of the person initiating a communicative act.

As we saw in section 3.1, the code model of communication focuses only upon those thoughts that a sender intends to transmit. A considerably more restricted, and differently defined, set of intentions figures in the sort of meaning pertinent to communication in the inferential model, and critically those intentions are not directly concerned with propositions or thoughts *per se*. The description of those intentions owes much to the philosopher Grice (1957, 1968), and it is from his description that we can create a picture of a communicator as one whose primary role in communication is to display intentions (see fuller discussion in chapter 6). As we noted earlier, the Gricean view of communication involves three intentions:

(a) S's utterance of x to produce a certain response r in a certain audience A
(b) A to recognize S's intention (a)
(c) A's recognition of S's intention (a) to function as at least part of A's reason for A's response r.

We viewed these intentions as cycling back upon one another: intention (c) is that intention (b) function as at least part of the reason for the fulfillment of intention (a). We also noted that it is only when the three intentions are activated that an individual is acting as a communicator; it is only when the three intentions are realized (cf. recognized by an audience, see below), that communication has occurred. Thus, the inferential model assumes that the initiator of communication is not one who transmits thoughts, but one who makes manifest (displays) the sort of reflexive intentions described above.

Although I have done no more than sketch the different intentions claimed to be crucial to communication, it should be obvious from my description that a particular capacity of the individual as actor is being focused upon: the capacity of the individual to make intentions obvious to others. Such a focus has a striking consequence. Once we view "having and displaying intentions" as the central means by which individuals communicate, we also have a means by which to differentiate behavior which is communicative from behavior which is not communicative, and, even further, what it is we communicate when we do communicate. In other words, our view of the person provides a way to define what we communicate when we send a message to our audience; that is, we communicate our intentions. And the way we do so is through utterances: "a modification of the physical environment designed by a communicator to be perceived by an audience" (Sperber and Wilson 1986: 29).

Nothing that I have said thus far implies that speakers' intentions need be limited to referential information: for example, one may intend an utterance to communicate an understanding that its speaker has a feeling of gratitude (expressive information), or one may intend an utterance to produce a feeling of interpersonal solidarity in its audience (social information). And in another sense, intentions are not propositional (i.e. descriptive of the world) at all: they are more akin to attitudes or beliefs. However, analyses of communication that focus on intentions tend to focus almost totally on how utterances produce understanding of the speaker's intention to convey a proposition, i.e. the referential content of a message. Thus, messages are essentially propositions (properties or actions predicated of entities) that the speaker intends to convey.

Let me use a brief example to illustrate this point. Suppose I invite you to a party that I'm having on June 16 at 8 p.m. One intention in doing so is to convey a feeling of good will toward you; another is to include you in a celebration of a particular event; still another is to reciprocate for a dinner that I had at your house in May. Now, although these may all be my intentions, in models of communication in which the actor's primary role is to display intentions, it is only the purely propositional content of the message that is the critical intention. My speaker meaning (Grice 1957, 1968), in other words, would be something like the following: "I want you to come to a party at my house on June 16 at 8 p.m."

The role of the addressee in this process is surprisingly simple in some ways, yet complex in others. As I described above, the communicator's intentions are reflexive. Although these intentions are formulated from the speaker's point of view, the recipient is assumed to act as a mirror-image of the speaker: the recipient recognizes intention (c), thereby recognizing intention (b), which is that the speaker intended recognition of intention (a) which is that an utterance produce a certain response.

Now, what would the recipient in our hypothetical example above do? My invitation would produce a certain response (intention (a)) – a response that amounts to no more than the recipient's recognizing my intention and thus understanding the referential meaning of the message that I intended to convey. The way that such recognition was achieved would have involved recognition that I had intended this understanding.

An additional feature of the inferential model of communication – one with consequences for its view of message and recipient – is that messages may be communicated by way of information that is not itself propositional information. In other words, although a communicator's intention may focus on the communication of propositional information, that information may be conveyed in ways other than the referential means encoded in the semantics of the language *per se*.

Although I discussed this more in chapter 6, recipient recognition of a communicator's intentions can be achieved somewhat independently of shared reliance on (and decoding of) conventional signs. What supplements a shared code is a shared set of communicative principles: added information about communicative intentions is inferrable through joint reliance on a set of maxims concerning the quality, quantity, relevance, and manner of information. The analysis of implicatures thus allows one to account for how people convey considerably more than is provided through their shared linguistic code, in particular, through the stable semantic content of their words. Since messages can be inferred despite reduced attention to the linguistic code, individuals need not be assumed to rely solely on their shared knowledge of the sound–meaning correspondences assigned so central a role in the code model of communication (2.1). But, as I noted above, individuals are assumed to rely on shared knowledge of another sort – shared knowledge of communicative principles – for it is these principles that also allow the inference of communicators' intentions.

Our discussion thus far has led to the role of intersubjectivity: despite the considerable shift in our view of the message (from "thoughts" to "intentions") and the medium (from "code" to "code plus general communicative principles"), intersubjectivity has as pervasive a role in the inferential model of communication as it did in the code model. First, the goal of communication is the achievement of intersubjectivity, i.e. one person's recognition of another's intentions. Second, intersubjectivity is achieved through a procedure in which recipient recognition of intentions mirrors the communicator's display of intentions. Third, procedures for achieving intersubjectivity are based in prior knowledge: people share the same linguistic code, as well as the same principles of communication. Thus, intersubjectivity remains a fundamental principle of verbal communication.

Since the inferencing of speaking meaning is central to Gricean pragmatics, it is not surprising that this perspective assumes the inferential model of communication. The Gricean view, however, also incorporates the code model. We saw above that conventional meaning plays a role in the construction of messages: what people "say" is "closely related to the conventional meaning of the words (the sentence)" (Grice 1975: 44); in addition, what is "said" figures in the processes by which implicatures are calculated. Of course Grice adds to these "explicit" meanings (Sperber and Wilson 1986: 21–38) the more "implicit" and code-independent meanings created through the cooperative principle. But it is the role of implicated meanings that alters Grice's model of communication from being merely a code-based model to an inferential model of communication.

Even though we have not dealt with this at length in chapter 6, still another feature of the Gricean view of communication has to be mentioned. The implicatures created through utterances are inherently more open ended than code-based meanings: not only can different assumed contexts lead recipients toward different implicatures, but the lack of grounding in what is actually said can lead to the cancellation of an implicature. A well-known example is that an utterance like *Marge has one child* leads to the implicature "Marge has only one child." This implicature, however, can be cancelled (since *one* does not mean "only one"): if we are discussing the availability of financial assistance which requires that a person have one child, for example, I might then quite reasonably say *Marge has one child, in fact, she has several*. That implicatures can be cancelled is critical to the Gricean view of communication – for it presents a view of communication as flexible and indeterminate (Levinson 1983: chapter 3).

Finally, we have repeatedly stated that speakers display intentions that are intended to be recognized by recipients, and that although one part of such a display is code-based, another part rests on the cooperative principle and the other contexts that figure in the calculation of implicatures. This means that two kinds of knowledge must be assumed to be shared by communicators: one is shared knowledge of the linguistic code; the other is shared knowledge of the contexts that help create implicatures (Schiffrin 1990a). That the CP has status as shared knowledge means that people communicate not just by relying on linguistic rules (formal grammatical rules that are part of linguistic competence; Chomsky 1965), but also by relying on a very general set of rationally based principles that apply not just to language use, but to behavior in general. And these principles do not have the formal algorithmic nature of linguistic rules, but are more like norms (Taylor and Cameron 1987), simply because they are socially shared (in fact, supposedly universally shared) expectations about behavior whose violations also have the ability to convey meaning.

The model of communication implicit in speech act theory also combines the code and inferential models (but as I note below, there are some similarities with the interactional model). Although Gricean principles are assumed to play a role in inferencing (e.g. of indirect speech acts; Searle 1976), speech act theory also allows the code a central contribution to meaning (Searle 1969: 42–50; but also Recanati 1987; Martinich 1984). Communication proceeds when people recognize and classify others' speech acts. The way they do so is by matching their knowledge of certain linguistic devices (illocutionary force indicating devices), along with their knowledge of context, intentions, and so on, with a particular speech act label. The ability to make such "matches" – regardless of their code-based or context-based source – is part of linguistic competence. Thus, speech act identities (indicated partially by the code) are critical in the communication of intention in the speech act view: we recognize an utterance as a promise not only by knowing the underlying conditions for promising, but by knowing the labelled category "promise." But in the neo-Gricean inferential model proposed by Sperber and Wilson (1986: 243–54) communicative intentions (including intentions to perform certain actions) can be inferred without the use of such categories.

Although speech act theory stresses speaker intentions (albeit intentions more limited to illocutionary force than the Gricean view), it also makes a place for effects upon recipient other than the recognition of speaker intention, i.e. what we described earlier as perlocutionary effect. Perlocutionary effect is not the focus of much attention in orthodox speech act theory (although Austin (1962) and Searle (1969) both note that it cannot always be easily separated from illocutionary force). But the fact that it is identified as one type of meaning or act (along with locutionary and illocutionary) does suggest that the speech act view of communication is also somewhat of an *interactional* model. I do not want to overemphasize this similarity, however: like interactional models of communication, speech act theory assigns a role to unintended meanings and acts; but unlike interactional models, speech act theory assumes that intentional meanings play a role much more central to communication than unintentional meanings.

In sum, both Gricean pragmatics and speech act theory assume a model of communication that is centered on the inferencing of speaker meaning, while also allowing the code a role in such inferencing. Inferences about speaker meaning are allowed not only by conventional meanings that are linguistically encoded (either at a sentential or textual level), but also by the operation of the cooperative principle – a particular kind of cognitive context – in conjunction with background and situational knowledge.

3.3 *Interactional model*

The interactional model of communication shifts our view of participant roles (the communicator and the recipient), the message, and the medium; it also places less emphasis on the principle of intersubjectivity. Put most simply, this model assumes that what underlies communication is behavior – regardless of whether that behavior is intentional or not. As we will see, this belief shifts much of the responsibility for communication from initiator (one who displays information) to recipient (one who witnesses and interprets information); it is this shift that diminishes the role of intersubjectivity.

Let us begin, again, with the communicator. Some scholars believe that communication can occur regardless of a person's intentions, and regardless of whether an utterance is designed to be perceived by a recipient. Such scholars view an individual as one who communicates not by transmitting a thought or manifesting an intention, but by displaying information – information which may not even be designed for perception by an audience (cf. Sperber and Wilson's definition of utterance, quoted on p. 394). Consider, in this regard, a key observation from Watzlawick et al. (1967: 48–9):

> First of all, there is a property of behavior that could hardly be more basic and is, therefore, often overlooked: behavior has no opposite. In other words, there is no such thing as nonbehavior or, to put it even more simply: one cannot *not* behave. Now, if it is accepted that all behavior in an interactional situation has message value, i.e. is communication, it follows that no matter how one may try, one cannot *not* communicate. Activity or inactivity, words or silence all have message value: they influence others and these in turn, cannot *not* respond to these communications and are thus themselves communicating. (emphasis in original)

Thus, as long as an individual is in an interactive situation (i.e. as long as behavior is available to others' observations), that individual communicates information: even efforts *not* to communicate would be, by default, communicative.

This view of what is involved in communication is often characteristic of those whose focus is the situated nature of all behavior (not just verbal behavior). Poyatos (1983), for example, argues that both physical reactions (e.g. sweating, blushing) and paralinguistic qualities of verbal utterances (of which an individual may be unaware) may convey messages – even if such behavior is neither intentional nor conscious. That such behavior is considered potentially communicative is a radical departure from the view described earlier, not only because it is not intentional behavior, but also because it is behavior which is not necessarily designed for perception by an audience (see Schiffrin 1987b).

In some analyses of the individual as one whose communicative role is to display information, an actor is assigned two different capacities by which to display information. For example, Goffman's (1959) distinction between information given and information given-off clearly differentiates the intentional from the non-intentional role. Information given is information intentionally emitted by a person and received by another in the manner intended by the actor; information given-off, on the other hand, is information which is interpreted for meaning by a recipient even if it has not been intended to convey that meaning. Because either type of information may be interpreted by a recipient, either type is communicative. Furthermore, communicative primacy may be accorded to information either given or given-off: individuals at both the productive and receptive ends of the communication process may become quite adept either at manipulating the supposedly unintended meanings of their own displays or at interpreting the unintended meanings of others' displays (Goffman 1959; see also Goffman 1963).

How does this portrait of the communicator alter the role of other parts of the communication process? Above I quoted Watzlawick et al.'s (1967) view that one cannot *not* communicate. I will use the examples with which they continue to illustrate how our conceptions of message and recipient also change.

> The man at a crowded lunch counter who looks straight ahead, or the airplane passenger who sits with his eyes closed, are both communicating that they do not want to speak to anybody or be spoken to, and their neighbors usually "get the message" and respond appropriately by leaving them alone. This, obviously, is just as much an interchange of communication as an animated discussion. (p. 49)

Note that in these examples, individuals may very well wish to be left alone, and may even wish to convey that message to others. But it is not critical that they intend their gaze *per se* – or their lack of gaze – to convey that message. Thus, behaviors such as silence, gaze, and so on can communicate messages even if they are not intended to do so.

Or take my earlier example of an invitation to come to a party on June 16 at 8 p.m. I suggested that a number of intentions may underlie such an invitation, e.g. a desire to convey a feeling of good will toward you, to include you in a celebration of a particular event, to reciprocate for a prior meal. We noted earlier that for those who view a speaker's role as primarily to display intentions, the meaning would be something like "I want you to come to a party at my house on June 16 at 8 p.m." For those who view the speaker's role as centered around the display of information, however, any of those above-mentioned intentions could be communicated. Even more strikingly, those same meanings could be interpreted even if they were not my intentions.

One question that arises from these examples is how unintended meanings – meanings that may, in fact, not even be verbal or representational – are created. In both examples, what we need to assume is that an audience uses its background knowledge to draw inferences about social and expressive meanings of the particular information to which they have access (either nonverbal actions such as gaze direction, or verbal actions such as invitations). Now, such knowledge may indeed be conventional, e.g. interpretations of gaze are based on socially and culturally created conventions. However, it is probably not knowledge that is code-based in the same way (or, more weakly, to the same degree) as linguistic knowledge – if only because the interpretation of the information is so dependent on how that information is situated.

The notion of "situated" information leads us to another point critical to understanding the interactional model of communication: it is less code dependent and more context-dependent than either the code or the inferential models. As Smith (1977: 14–15) notes, analyses may very well begin with the signals emitted in a code, but "many more sources of information than one signal have a significant effect on a recipient's behavior. Expanding the minimal description to accommodate these other sources of information is vital to understanding the process of communicating." Suggested as other sources of information are not only those typically found in a "context" (e.g. Hymes's SPEAKING grid, chapter 5), but also the information that recipients themselves bring to communication, e.g. their own background knowledge, psychological states, etc.

Let me take an example of a simplified greeting sequence to illustrate how bringing the notion of "situated information" into a model of communication can alter our consideration of this process by complicating our analysis of the meaning of a message. Greetings provide a good example: they rely upon a limited set of items from the linguistic code to do a great deal of social and expressive work in a well-circumscribed set of occasions (Schiffrin 1977). Suppose I enter a room where you are sitting and having a conversation with someone else. I do not interrupt you, but when you look up and see me, you say "Hi"; I then respond "Hi."

How do we analyze the two utterances of "Hi?" We can easily say (as would the code model) that each utterance is a conventionalized greeting signal; or we can say (as would the inferential model) that each "Hi" is recognized as an intention to greet. What the interactional model offers, however, is the possibility of quite different analyses for each "Hi" – simply because of our notion of situated information. For example, we might view the initial "Hi" as a response to the situation itself: you and I have entered a setting that offers increased mutual access to one another; once you have exhausted a current involvement and you notice the increased access, you mark that increase with a relatively informal greeting (that not only reveals something about our social relationship, but also displays that our prior contact was not all that long ago). We might also say that the second "Hi" is responding to the same situation of increased mutual access to which you responded. Alternatively, we might say that the second "Hi" is responding to the situation that the initial "Hi" has created – a situation in which the increase in mutual access has already been marked (and must thus be responded to as a display of that access) and in which certain possibilities for our upcoming contact have been created. Regardless of which description we adopt, the point is that once we allow "situated information" into a model of communication, we can argue that an utterance is a response not only to information conveyed in a prior utterance, but to the situation in which the prior utterance is located, or to the situation that the prior utterance helps create.

Another change in our view of how messages are created arises from the diminished role assigned to intentions, and relatedly, changes in our conception of participant role. Since we are allowing two kinds of information to be communicative (information intentionally designed to be perceived as communicative, and information not so designed) we are, in effect, allowing two sources for messages – one residing in that aspect of a person emitting information, the other in the person receiving information. Thus, in contrast to both the code and the inferential models, the recipient in the interactional model is assigned a much more active role: the recipient finds meaning in another's situated behavior and tries to assign possibly multilevelled interpretations (referential, emotive, social) to whatever information becomes available. This means that the message that is communicated need not be rooted in either thoughts or intentions: it is just as likely to emerge from interactions among information intentionally emitted by an actor and unintentionally emitted by an actor, the way that information is situated, and the interpretations that the recipient assigns to that information.

Finally, the principle of intersubjectivity in this view of communication has a role less pervasive than that described for other models. First, communication need not rest upon the achievement of intersubjectivity; as Watzlawick et al. (1967: 49) state, we cannot "say that 'communication' only takes place when . . . mutual understanding occurs" (cf. Smith 1977: 15). Rather, the goal of communication is recipient achievement of an interpretation of displayed information. Second, the procedures used to interpret others' displays need not mirror those used to produce displays. A related point is that what a recipient of a message knows may lead to an interpretation that diverges from what was intended by its producer. The one place where intersubjectivity does play a role is in the realm of prior linguistic knowledge: shared knowledge allows decoding of linguistic information. But because the interactional model places more emphasis on how information is situated, it is less code-dependent and thus less dependent on the intersubjectivity assumed to underlie a shared code.

The interactional model of communication underlies three approaches to discourse discussed in this book: interactional sociolinguistics, ethnography of communication, and conversation analysis. Since it is these approaches that pay most attention to social context (chapter 10), it is not surprising that they rely upon the model that provides context with a role that is more than cognitive.

Consider, first, interactional sociolinguistics. Analyses from this approach often reveal that a single exchange can have multiple interpretations, interpretations that may be associated with different social identities and the use of different background knowledge. This suggests that what is communicated is inherently situated, and often situated (in an interpretive sense) in different ways for different people. Situated interpretations are made possible by contextualization cues: it is this construct that also closely links interactional sociolinguistics to the interactional model of communication.

As we discussed in chapter 4, contextualization cues are signalling mechanisms (such as intonation, speech rhythm, lexical, phonetic, syntactic, and textual options) that affect the expressive quality of a message (Gumperz 1982a: 16). Not only can these cues be core or marginal features of language, they can also be nonverbal, e.g. facial expression, physical posture. Thus, the verbal/nonverbal, and core/marginal, distinction evaporates once the significance of contextualization cues as indicators of contextual presuppositions is recognized. Since these cues are not always based in the linguistic code, there is obviously no place for them in the code model of communication. Rather, the reliance of these cues upon a great variety of behaviors to contextualize the meaning(s) of a message fits within a model of communication in which the code works along with other information sources, and in which all of that information has meaning only by being interpreted in context.

The nature of messages and the contribution of contextualization cues to those messages also belong firmly within the interactional model. Contextualization cues themselves are information given-off: they are almost never consciously noted or assigned conventional meanings. But by helping to signal contextual presuppositions, contextualization cues influence *both* the expressive quality of a message and its basic (propositional) meaning (Gumperz 1982a: 131). Thus, contextualization cues facilitate the inferencing of information given as well as information given-off: they contribute to the linguistic and expressive components found in messages (Goffman 1963: 16).

Contextualization cues are a construct that reflects the assumptions of the interactional model of communication in still other ways. Consider their cognitive and social functions, and how these functions bear on participation in communicative exchanges. We said above that contextualization cues are information that is given-off. The proposal that people utilize contextualization cues to make inferences (as Gumperz calls them, situated inferences) means that the ability to rely upon information given-off is part of the cognitive capacity through which interactants interpret what is going on. Contextualization cues also have the social function of displaying social identity and definition of situation. Recall our discussion of footing: "the alignments we take up to ourselves and the others present as expressed in the way we manage the production or reception of an utterance" (Goffman 1981c: 128). One way that interactants indicate shifts in footing and alignment is through contextualization cues (Goffman 1981c: 126–7). Thus, the social and expressive functions of contextualization cues are to convey the capacity in which someone who produces an utterance is acting and how that person is relating to the recipient of the utterance. This function fits comfortably within the interactional model of communication in which the main capacity of a speaker is not necessarily to emit information (cf. the sender in the code model) or to display intentions (cf. the inferential model): a message can be dissected into different parts for which different aspects of a self might be responsible. The central role of contextualization cues in interactional sociolinguistics is also consistent with the added contribution of the recipient in the interactional model of communication: the recipient finds meaning in another's situated behavior and tries to assign possibly multi-levelled interpretations to information both given and given-off. Likewise, contextualization cues reflect the interactional view that communication is situated: cues help to convey the expressive meaning and the illocutionary force of a message, in part by indicating in what "frame" (e.g. what speech activity, what key) the recipient should locate an utterance.

Consider, finally, another way that the participant role assumed by interactional sociolinguistics is embedded in the interactional model of communication. We noted earlier that speaker intention is the foundation of communication for both pragmatics and speech act theory. Interactional sociolinguistics supplements the construct of speaker intention with discourse strategy. Whereas speaker intention is essentially internal to the individual, discourse strategy is directed from the speaker to a recipient and its presence becomes inferrable through an observable effect on the recipient. This balance between what is observable (a recipient response) and what is not (an intention, a strategy) arises from the interactional sociolinguistic insistence upon building generalizations from repeated observations of behavior, and from a willingness to posit constructs that go beyond what can only be seen or heard (cf. conversation analysis). Interestingly, however, the willingness to propose unobservable constructs such as "strategy" returns interactional sociolinguistics to a more static assumption of intersubjectivity than proposed by conversation analysts (see below), i.e. intersubjectivity would be based on shared discourse strategies.

The ethnography of communication also assumes an interactional model of communication. However, the status of the code, the nature of a message, the importance of context, and the role of participants are all open to empirical and comparative investigation. In Hymes's (1972b: 12) words, "just as what counts as phonemic feature or religious act cannot be identified in advance, so with what counts as a communicative event." Nor can one assume the constant relevance of the code or the context for any particular communicative event, not only across cultures but also within a single culture. Also not warrantable apart from empirical investigation is the assumption that messages are constructed along identical principles, and that participants have constant roles in producing and interpreting messages.

Like interactional sociolinguistics, the ethnographic approach views communication as a process that revolves around a single construct – not contextualization cue, but the considerably broader construct of culture. We saw how culture provides the fundamental lens through which behavior is interpreted in our very first example of the ethnographic approach in chapter 1, in which an Ojibwa Indian reacted to the sound of thunder in the same way that he would respond to a human being whose message had not been clear. Culture defines not only what counts as communication ("no phenomenon can be defined in advance as never to be counted as constituting a message": Hymes 1974b: 13), but also how communication is chunked and labelled as speech acts and speech events. These meaningful units provide contexts in which messages are produced and interpreted. Thus, an utterance is always culturally situated (and culturally relative) as a message only through its relationships with other utterances and within an encompassing framework of actions, beliefs, and situations.

As we discussed in earlier chapters, the linguistic code – so central to communication in the code model – is also part of culture. Communicative competence assumes a relationship between code and culture in which culture encompasses linguistic knowledge; communicative competence is cultural knowledge that includes social and psychological principles governing the use of language, as well as abstract "grammatical" rules pertaining to the linguistic code.

Just as culture allows us to "make sense" of experience, so too does language: "the communicative event is the metaphor, or perspective, basic to rendering experience intelligible" (Hymes 1974b: 16). In a way, then, language "allows" the interpretations, the sense-making, and the tacit assumptions that embody culture. To a certain degree, it is the design features of the linguistic code that provide language with its sense-making capacity (the capacity so critical to our notion of culture): "Of codes available to human beings, language, as the one more than any other capable at once of being explicitly detailed and transcendent of single contexts, is the chief beneficiary under many circumstances of the primary centrality of communication" (Hymes 1974b: 16). Yet it is not only the code-like properties of language that allow people to "render experience intelligible". Hymes (1981: 9) adopts Cassirer's (1961: 113) point to make this clear: "individuals do not simply share what they already possess; it is only by virtue of the sharing process that they attain what they possess, constructing a 'shared world' of meaning within the medium of language." It is not just the code *per se* that enables experience to be intelligible: it is interactions between human beings that allow language to have a sense-making capacity – the capacity so central to culture itself. Thus, the linguistic code serves communication by allowing the potential construction of a shared world of meaning (i.e. intersubjectivity, culture).

Finally, the fact that "the sharing process" is so central to communication, to sense-making, and to culture has an important consequence for the view of participant role in communication. Hymes (1974b: 13) observes that the communicative status of approaching footsteps, or the setting of the sun, "is entirely a question of their construal by a receiver." The elevated status of the recipient is completely in keeping with the interactional model of communication. Yet, consistent with the ethnographic approach, even the status of the recipient is particular and relative: one cannot assume that participant roles, whether they are senders' intentions or receivers' interpretations, have a constant role in the process by which meanings come to be shared.

Although conversation analysis also assumes the interactional model of communication, it does so almost by default: the code and inferential models make too many assumptions about stable systems of representations (in the linguistic code) and single goals underlying communication (whether those goals are information transmission or recognition of intention) to provide a framework of assumptions compatible with the practice of CA. Unlike interactional sociolinguistics and the ethnography of communication, CA has no central construct in relation to which different aspects of communication are defined. This lack of a central construct is intentional: to assume any single construct as central to communication would be to work with just the kind of idealization that Sacks believed would misrepresent what happens in specific sets of events. In keeping with the idea that meaning and action are both context-shaped and context-renewing, however, CA obviously assumes that context is important during communication. Of course, what is "in" context cannot be assumed: its relevance must be made manifest through what is said (chapter 10). The stable and determinate meanings assumed present in a linguistic code are similarly suspect to generalization. Similarly, intersubjectivity cannot be assumed: it must be displayed in next-turn or immediately afterward (Schegloff 1992). Finally, since recipient response is methodologically and theoretically critical to CA, the fact that an interactional model of communication provides a wider communicative role for a recipient is compatible with CA.

4 Summary

In this chapter, I described three different models of communication. The code model assumes that an individual transmits a message, through use of a shared code, to a receiver. The inferential model assumes that an individual displays intentions that are inferred by a recipient who relies upon both a shared code and a shared set of communicative principles allowing the use of inferencing strategies. The interactional model assumes that an individual displays situated information that is interpreted by a recipient. We have seen that although all discourse analyses (indeed, all linguistic analyses) assume some underlying model of communication, the approaches to discourse discussed in this book differ quite surprisingly in terms of which model they assume.

12 Conclusion: Language as Social Interaction

1 Introduction

I noted at the outset of this book that discourse analysis is one of the most vast and least defined areas in linguistics. What I have tried to accomplish in this book is the description and comparison of six different approaches to the linguistic analysis of discourse: speech act theory, interactional sociolinguistics, ethnography of communication, pragmatics, conversation analysis, variation analysis. As I noted initially, my aim was not to reduce the vastness of discourse analysis, but to clarify the scope of discourse analysis in such a way that it can continue to deal with a wide range of problems and phenomena, but hopefully in a more systematic and theoretically coherent way.

In this closing chapter, I summarize the approaches to discourse that we have discussed (section 2). I also suggest, despite the sometimes substantial differences among the approaches, some general principles of discourse analysis that emerge from all of the different approaches (section 3). Section 4 concludes the book.

2 Starting points: differences among approaches

Each approach to discourse that we discussed began by noting a different issue, problem, or phenomenon, sometimes from the vantage point of very different frameworks of inquiry and traditions of research. Despite these different starting points, I have tried to show that each approach can be used to address some of the same general problems of discourse analysis (e.g. how one utterance contributes to the communicative content of another, how utterances are related to one another) and some of the same specific problems (e.g. question–answer sequences, referring sequences).

Speech act theory began with the observation that language could be used not just to describe the world, but to perform actions: its focus was communicative acts performed through speech. What speech act theory offers to discourse analysis is a set of constitutive rules by which particular labelled speech actions can be defined. Speakers and hearers are assumed to share these rules and to use the rules to produce and interpret a variety of actions (regardless of whether those actions occupy one, or more than one, utterance). The particular action defined through the rules provides expectations for a next-action. Thus, discourse coherence emerges on a local, action-by-action basis; the sequential relationships between actions are derived from the knowledge that we use to relate an utterance to an action.

A speech act approach to discourse leads to a particular view not only of structure (chapter 9), and of the text/context relationship (chapter 10), but also of coherence (the overall sense of a discourse: Schiffrin 1985a, 1987a: 21–9, 326–30; see also Dorval 1990) and the processes by which coherence is found. Coherence is the result of underlying mapping rules (relating an utterance to the rules defining it as a speech act) and sequencing rules that relate not the surface linguistic details of what is said, but the actions that have resulted from the mapping rules. Thus, the speech act approach to coherence is rule-centered: not only does it require constitutive rules for the very definition of speech acts, but it requires mapping rules to link an utterance (or utterances) to an act, and sequencing rules to link utterance–action correlations to one another (cf. Labov and Fanshel 1977). We can thus say that coherence is created by the application of rules. The status of the three different rule types, however, deserves further analysis. Although mapping and sequencing rules seem more normative (and thus regulative) than constitutive, deviations from all three types have similar results, i.e. behavior that seems inappropriate, rather than ungrammatical, and that often can be made appropriate by being relocated in a different context.

Interactional sociolinguistics began with the social and linguistic meanings created during interaction. Compared to speech act theory, interactional sociolinguistics thus offers a framework in which utterances can be analyzed not just as actions, but also as indicators of social, cultural, and personal meaning. Utterances are situated in both local and global contexts of interpretation. Any one utterance is assumed to be sequentially relevant to what came before (its local context) and to a general framework of understandings about a particular "type" of situation (its global context). Contextualization cues are aspects of language that evoke both of these contexts – signalling the relevance of frameworks within which messages are to be understood. Discourse can thus be seen as a contextualized and contextualizing vehicle for the construction of different levels of meaning. Utterances contextualize, and are contextualized by, one another: each utterance is itself linked to a broader framework of assumptions to which it provides ongoing indices.

The verbal and nonverbal cues that are part of cultural repertoires for signalling meaning are important not just to interactional sociolinguistics, but also to the ethnography of communication. The ethnographic approach began with observations of a gap in traditional anthropological and linguistic theory: a lack of analytical attention to "ways of speaking." The focus of the ethnography of communication is communication as cultural behavior: language is part of a matrix of meanings, beliefs, and values that extend beyond knowledge of grammar.

A key concept in the ethnography of communication is communicative competence. This concept integrates linguistic competence into cultural knowledge: communicative competence is cultural knowledge that includes social and psychological principles governing the use of language, as well as abstract "grammatical" rules pertaining to the linguistic code. But language is more than an individual possession, capability, or "instrument" that represents experience (cf. the code model of communication, chapter 11). Language allows us to "make sense" of experience ("the communicative event is the metaphor, or perspective, basic to rendering experience intelligible"; Hymes 1972b: 16) not only because of its design features as a code, but also because its use creates the potential for a shared world of meaning. Thus, discourse is constitutive of a larger social or cultural reality only because of the properties of language and because of the ability of human beings to use language to create, if not intersubjectivity itself (Taylor 1992), at least a belief in intersubjectivity.

Like interactional sociolinguistics, the ethnography of communication also offers a contextual approach to the analysis of utterances. As just noted, what is said is always constitutive of a larger social and cultural reality. This means that the analysis of any single aspect of form or function can only be part of the overall framework of understanding and interpretation through which actions and beliefs are created. The communicative units studied by ethnographers are also believed to constitute one another. Events and situations stand in a dependency relationship with acts: just as the communicative structures of speech events and situations reveal the function of constituent acts, the function of the act itself contributes to the structure of the event and the situation. Thus, discourse (and language in general) is a part of culture: because culture is a framework for acting, believing, and understanding, culture is the framework in which communication (and the use of utterances) becomes meaningful.

Pragmatics began with a focus on a very different kind of meaning than the contextual approaches just discussed – not social and cultural meaning, but individual, intention-based meaning that could supplement the logical, propositional, and conventional meanings representable through a linguistic code. Despite its focus on a different level of meaning, pragmatics also offers another broad contextual framework for the analysis of utterances. Its contextual focus is not situational or cultural contributions to utterance meaning, however, but the very general assumptions that speaker and hearer bring to each and every occasion of speaking – assumptions about one another's cooperative nature. These assumptions work with textual and situational information to allow very particular inferences about speaker meaning. Because what is said in one utterance can contribute to the inference of speaker meaning in another utterance, discourse can be seen a chain of inferential relationships whose links are based in relationships that arise from the operation of the maxims (e.g. quantity, relevance) as they apply across utterances.

Conversation analysis began by searching for ways to discover our ordinary, everyday procedures for constructing a sense of social and personal reality. Its main focus is the way language is shaped by context, and, in turn, the way language shapes context. The contexts upon which conversation analysts focus, however, are only those that can be empirically attested through actual speech or behavior. Likewise, inferences about language (or textual) structure, about speaker intention, about relationships across utterances, and so on, must be grounded in actual doings and sayings. Conversation analyses thus end up offering very close and detailed analyses of the workings of specific devices or structures in the construction of talk. The contribution that utterances make to one another's meanings has to be attested in what is actually said. Similarly, relations between utterances cannot be assumed (except in next position; Sacks 1971: lecture 4, 11–12): interdependency between utterances (cf. coherence) must be demonstrated through the way recipients orient toward talk.

Whereas conversation analysis began with a general interest in the local construction of social order, variation analysis began with an attempt to find order in areas of language structure and behavior whose patterns seemed to defy traditional means of discovery. Variation analysis offers an approach to discourse that applies some of the same tools and concepts to texts as are applied to lower level (phonological, syntactic) variation. Text and situation are both divided into discrete and mutually exclusive factors that can be coded, counted, and compared. Not only do variationists define discourse as a unit of language larger than a single sentence, they also analyze how that unit is comprised of smaller units that are systematically related to one another. Given the focus upon text as comprised of smaller units, and the analysis of the relationship of those units with one another, the segmentation and categorization of text into units that have systematic effects upon each other is not surprising. Thus, discourse is a unit of linguistic analysis whose coherence arises because of systematic relationships between the units (whether these are words, meanings, clauses, or actions) that comprise a text.

My initial differentiation of approaches to discourse was according to what I still believe is their most significant characteristic: they have very different origins. The origin of an approach provides different theoretical and meta-theoretical premises that continue to influence assumptions, concepts, and methods. For example, different origins may be responsible for different assumptions and beliefs about how human beings engage in meaningful discourse. Both approaches originating in philosophy, for example, make assumptions about the role of speaker intention that are not shared by those approaches

that begin from social scientific or humanistic directions. Interactional sociolinguistics, the ethnography of communication, and conversation analysis all
downplay the role of speaker intention by constructing more sociogenic explanations for human behavior, by allowing for the empirical discovery of
culturally diverse concepts of the self (and allied notions of human responsibility and will), or by subjugating the discovery of speaker intention to empirical confirmation in hearer response. Despite their specific differences, these
approaches all view human behavior as part of the interactive construction of
meaning. Not only is each utterance actually (rather than hypothetically)
interpreted by a recipient, but each utterance is part of a larger framework of
social and cultural meaning. Thus, utterances can be assigned a level of
particularity (and potential diversity) not at all possible if one relies solely on
constructed, hypothetical utterances as data.

Different origins are also responsible for different conceptions of language
– including assumptions about the stability of linguistic meaning, the contribution of linguistic meaning to interactive meaning, and the degree to which
language is designed for communicative purposes. Several approaches (interactional sociolinguistics, ethnography of communication, conversation analysis)
view communicative meaning as inherently contextualized and contextualizing. Some interactional sociolinguistic analyses propose that language is not
only inherently contextual, but communicatively designed. This suggests that
linguistic structures emerge not from the static rules of abstract grammar, but
from a process whereby strategies for constructing texts get "sedimentized" into
seemingly stable forms (DuBois 1987b; Hopper 1987; Hopper and Thompson
1980, 1984). This belief is carried still further in the conversation analytic
distrust of idealizations – a distrust that means that idealization has no role
as a basis for research in social science, as the grounds for ordinary human
action, or as the structural scaffolding upon which the construction of an
utterance depends.

The contextual approaches just noted allow utterances to be less context-
independent (cf. the view that language has a modular structure with autonomous components, chapter 2) than does the approach most grounded in the
linguistic analysis of text – variation analysis. We can trace this difference to
one of the initial motivations of variation analysis: a desire to solve traditional
problems of linguistic theory using new methods of analysis.[1] Similarly, we
can trace Searle's belief about the value of idealization in speech act theory to
his interest in abstract grammatical theory and linguistic competence. Searle
(1969) argues that our intuitions provide "idealized models" (p. 56) of the
conditions necessary and sufficient for the utterance of a given sentence as a
successful, non-defective performance of a given act, and that we cannot hope
to be systematic if we do not engage in idealization (p. 55).

Other differences that can be at least partially traced to different origins
include beliefs about methods for collecting and analyzing data. For example,
some approaches focus intensively on interpretation of a few fragments of talk
(e.g. interactional sociolinguistics); others focus on distributions of discourse

items across a wide range of texts (e.g. variationists). Some approaches avoid quantitative analysis. The ethnographic approach to discourse, for example, does not assume either the mutual exclusivity of categories or the ability to extract one function of an utterance from the myriad functions that are realized by an act of speaking. Both of these are prerequisites to the kind of coding, counting, and comparing that quantitative analyses (such as those carried out by variationists) would require.

Some approaches to discourse (e.g. ethnography of communication, interactional sociolinguistics) require a great deal of social, cultural, and personal information about interlocutors and may use interlocutors as informants in analysis of their own talk. Other approaches (e.g. pragmatics, speech act theory) assume an idealized speaker/hearer whose specific social, cultural, or personal characteristics do not enter into participant strategies for building text at all. Conversation analysis requires that whatever aspects of participant identity are relevant to the production or interpretation of a particular utterance have to be revealed in locally situated interpretive activity: "it is only within organizations of sayings and doings that assignably 'personal' attributes are made manifest" (Coulter 1989: 103).

Methodological differences such as these are due, partially, to different theoretical assumptions – assumptions that are based in the different origins noted above. If it is assumed, for example, that linguistic meaning is less important to interactive meaning than are sequential structures of talk (as in conversation analysis), then an analyst would pay little attention to linguistic form and structure *per se*. But if it is assumed that linguistic form and meaning are constrained by context (i.e. that one is embedded in the other, as in the variationist approach) then one needs to pay a great deal of attention to form and function at many different levels of analysis. Or, if it is assumed that many different features of language provide clues to the contextual presuppositions by which we interpret personal, social, and cultural meanings (as in interactional sociolinguistics), then one has to devote attention to the aspects of language (rhythm, prosody, and so on) that are often overlooked by more structural analyses. In short, no methodological preferences are reached in a vacuum: they are all the product of more general beliefs in what constitutes data and what counts as evidence and "proof."

Although each approach to discourse has a different starting point – complete with interest in a different set of problems, a different motivation, and different assumptions – I have tried to show in this book that each approach can be used to address some of the same problems of discourse analysis. In chapters 9 to 11, and thus far in this chapter, I have been discussing how each approach addresses relatively general problems concerning relationships between utterances. I return now to some of the specific problems on which our sample analyses in each chapter concentrated.

We considered question–answer sequences in chapters on speech act theory, interactional sociolinguistics, and ethnography of communication. Our speech act analysis began with the conditions underlying questions and how they

applied to one particular utterance. It then considered the conditions underlying two other speech acts – requests, offers – that this utterance also seemed
to perform. Next-utterances were then considered only in relation to how they
provided sequentially appropriate acts defined in relation to an initiating
utterance. Our interactional sociolinguistic analysis of question–answer sequences (chapter 4) was quite different. Although we began with the same
utterances (implicitly acknowledging their multiple functions and sequential
relationships), we considered how different people participated in the three-
part exchange initiated by the question–request–offer. We focused upon the
social meaning created when one person provided a response sequentially
available to another person ("speaking for another"). To do so, we drew upon
other data as a way of proposing that this particular interactional move could
have larger social meanings and could be related to participant identity. Thus,
whereas chapter 3 began with individual knowledge of speech acts, chapter 4
went on to the social meanings created by self/other participation in a speech
act sequence. Our ethnographic analysis (chapter 5) then located "participants
in a speech act sequence" in a still broader framework of analysis. In chapter
5, we considered questions and answers in different speech events (reference
interview, sociolinguistic research interview), showing how the form and function of questions could be part of two different communicative events, defined
not only in terms of who participated in each, but also in terms of participant
goals, act sequences, and norms for interaction and interpretation. Thus, what
chapter 5 added to the analysis of question–answer sequences was a concern
for the social and cultural meanings that provide a shared framework for
participation in a communicative event.

Although the shift in framework in chapters 3, 4, and 5 led to a shift in
issues and data, there were some phenomena that were addressed (or could
have been addressed) in each chapter. In chapter 3, for example, we discussed
final rising intonation as an illocutionary force indicating device. By showing
that final rises (in particular types of exchanges) could satisfy some of the
conditions underlying the speech act "question," we were able to propose that
this intonation could lead to the identification of a declarative statement as a
question. Although we did not explicitly address final rises in chapter 4, this
is an issue that could easily be considered in the interactional sociolinguistic
framework: final rising intonation is a contextualization cue that helps to
trigger a situated inference about a particular speech action. Chapter 5 did
consider final rising intonation – not in relation to abstract speech act conditions, but in relation to actualized speech acts in speech events. Our ethnographically motivated discussion of final rises was less wed to the abstract
meaning of this intonation than to its concrete and particular uses within a
communicative event.

The topics of the sample analyses in chapters 6, 7, and 8 were different, yet
the transitions between the framework of inquiry in each chapter were surprisingly consistent. In our chapter on pragmatics (chapter 6), we focused on
the way one person told a story, and on how that person presented the

characters in his story. But our focus upon an individual telling a story had significance beyond the choice of data: it reflected the pragmatic focus upon speaker meaning, and the kind of knowledge upon which a hearer would need to rely in order to interpret speaker meaning. Thus, our focus in the pragmatics chapter was somewhat similar to our focus in the speech act chapter: we were interested in how an individual relies upon a particular kind of knowledge to produce and interpret language.

Our conversation analysis (in chapter 7) moved the analysis of speaker meaning into the analysis of how speaker and hearer construct a conversation. Here we concentrated on the way a particular linguistic construction fit into the mechanics of conversation: we focused upon "there + BE + ITEM" in relation to adjacency pairs, turn-taking, topic transitions, and repairs. We also considered the role of this construction in relation to first-and next-mentions of a referent – allowing some comparisons with the Gricean pragmatic approach from chapter 6. But rather than address individual knowledge, we addressed the way self and other – joint participants in talk – used a construction to organize mentions in talk, and how that organization was related to the other tasks facing people who are jointly engaged in the construction of conversation.

Our variation analysis (in chapter 8) located the analysis of referring sequences in a textual structure (the "list") whose organization contrasted with that of another text (the "narrative"). We said little about the interactions in which lists (and their referring terms) are presented, focusing instead on how the underlying organization of the list could influence the use of one form rather than another. In this sense, we moved from an analysis in which one person's interactional mission is to interpret the other's intention (by drawing upon shared assumptions about cooperation), to an analysis of how the structures of conversation are jointly achieved, and finally, to an analysis of how norms for constructing a text-type are assumed to underlie the production of each text-token, in some sense superseding the particular instance in which each text appears.

As I noted above, although a shift in framework sometimes leads to a shift in issues and data, there are some phenomena that can be addressed through different frameworks. Chapters 6, 7, and 8, for example, all addressed the use of definite noun phrases for first-mentions of a referent, i.e. initial definites. Our pragmatic analysis (chapter 6) viewed initial definites in relation to the way the quantity and relation maxims help hearers to use background knowledge to draw inferences: situational or textual information can allow a hearer to infer the existence of a referent by providing a framework within which the existence of such a referent is expected. Our conversation analysis (chapter 7) suggested that first-mentions – whether definite or indefinite – in *there* constructions are integrated into the turn-taking and adjacency pair structure of conversation. Our variation analysis analyzed the alternation between initial indefinites and definites in terms of the textual structure of lists – showing that initial definites were a reflection of the category organization underlying lists.

In sum, the order in which I discussed each approach, and the type of inquiry for each area of empirical focus (each sample analysis), was not random. They reflected a broadly based transition from a focus upon individual actions, knowledge, or intentions (speech act theory, pragmatics) to a focus upon how self and other interactively construct what is said, meant, and done (interactional sociolinguistics, conversation analysis) to a focus upon the semiotic systems shared and used by self and other during their interactions (to make sense of utterances, the ethnography of communication draws upon culture and the structure of communicative events; variation analysis draws upon the linguistic structure of texts). It is difficult to allow and account for transitions from self to self/other to shared semiotic systems in one's analysis of discourse – even more challenging to incorporate such transitions into a theory of discourse. But such a goal seems to be a crucial part of a discourse analysis that seeks to integrate what so many different approaches can offer both individually and together to the analysis of utterances. In the next section, I offer a preliminary attempt to bring together some general principles of discourse analysis from the particular approaches we have been discussing.

3 Principles of discourse analysis: language as social interaction

The subtitle of this section matches the subtitle of this chapter: "language as social interaction." I have done this because I believe that it is this formulation that best unites (at a very general level) the different approaches to discourse that we have discussed.[2] Each approach somehow incorporates this insight into its specific methods and concepts. Speech act theory focuses upon the linguistic actions that we perform toward another person – the actions that initiate (or continue) interaction. The cooperative principle so crucial to Gricean pragmatics is a principle applicable to human interaction: it is this assumption that governs the way people interpret one another's meaning during interactions with one another. Interactional sociolinguistics and conversation analysis are quite clear in their beliefs that social interaction is the locus of language use: what we know and understand about interaction complements our ability to use language. The ethnography of communication focuses upon communicative situations, events, and acts: these are "units of analysis" that can be realized only if one assumes that human beings are interacting with one another. Variation analysis takes as one of its central goals the analysis of "language as it is used in everyday life by members of the social order, that vehicle of communication in which they argue with their wives, joke with their friends, and deceive their enemies" (Labov 1972f: xiii). It is within everyday speech – or, as I would say, the speech used in everyday social interactions – that one can find the "basis of intersubjective knowledge in linguistics" (Labov 1972f: xiii).

Saying that each approach to discourse views "language as social interaction" has two important consequences. First is to focus discourse analysis on praxis and process. To be more specific: social interaction is a process whereby one person has an effect on another. To be involved in a social interaction is to be involved in an interchange in which our own activities are directed to other people and others' activities are directed to us. Ochs (1988: 15) has stated that "activity mediates linguistic and sociocultural knowledge and that knowledge and activity impact one another." (She attributes this view, more generally, to Piaget 1952; Vygotsky 1962; Bourdieu 1977; Giddens 1979.) What I would like to add to Ochs's view is that the activity most pertinent to our understanding of discourse is interactive activity: activity that is directed to another person and has a potential for affecting that other person. Discourse analysis, then, views language as an activity embedded in social interaction. It is thus interactive activity that mediates linguistic and sociocultural knowledge.

This view of language as an interactive activity mediating linguistic and sociocultural knowledge has a consequence for the paradigmatic school of linguistics into which discourse analysis fits. In chapter 2, we reviewed two different paradigms within linguistics: formalist and functionalist. We noted that definitions of discourse can be framed within the assumptions of either paradigm: "discourse is language above the sentence" is more formalist; "discourse is language use" is more functionalist. We proposed an alternative definition of discourse as "utterances" in an effort to avoid the problems noted with the other two definitions. If we take "language as social interaction" as the core shared assumption of all the approaches reviewed, however, we can say that discourse analysis studies not just utterances, but the way utterances (including the language used in them) are activities embedded in social interaction. Although this view of the domain of discourse analysis does not preclude formal analyses of linguistic or interactional structures, it does place discourse analysis squarely within a functionalist paradigm as described by Leech (1983: 46), but with some slight modifications. According to Leech, language is regarded "primarily as a societal phenomenon." I am proposing here that the language of discourse is primarily a social interactional phenomenon. Linguistic universals tend to be derived from "the universality of the uses to which language is put in human society." Here we can substitute the idea that discourse universals are derived from the universality of uses to which language is put in human interaction. And as Leech concludes: "formalists study language as an autonomous system, whereas functionalists study it in relation to its social function." Again, we can say that discourse analysts study the language of utterances in relation to its function in social interaction.

In addition to suggesting that all the approaches to discourse view language as social interaction, and all are more compatible with a functionalist than a formalist paradigm, I want to also propose several general principles of discourse analysis. These principles are not intended to supplant those aspects of theory and methodology which differentiate the specific approaches. Nor do I want to imply that all the assumptions of one specific approach are necessarily shared by others; for example, assumptions about the stability of linguistic meaning, about whether particular features can be studied in isolation from other features, and so on. Despite such differences, I propose that all the approaches to discourse share a single set of underlying principles (see also Schiffrin 1988b, 1990d).

1 Analysis of discourse is empirical.
   Data come from a speech community: data are about people using language, not linguists thinking about how people use language.
   Analyses are accountable to the data: they have to explain the data in both sequential and distributional terms.
   Analyses are predictive: they produce hypotheses that can be falsified or modified by other data.
2 Discourse is not just a sequence of linguistic units: its coherence cannot be understood if attention is limited just to linguistic form and meaning.
3 Resources for coherence jointly contribute to participant achievement and understanding of what is said, meant, and done through everyday talk. In other words, linguistic forms and meanings work together with social and cultural meanings, and interpretive frameworks, to create discourse.
4 The structures, meanings, and actions of everyday spoken discourse are interactively achieved.
5 What is said, meant, and done is sequentially situated, i.e. utterances are produced and interpreted in the local contexts of other utterances.
6 How something is said, meant, and done – speakers' selection among different linguistic devices as alternative ways of speaking – is guided by relationships among the following:
   (a) speaker intentions;
   (b) conventionalized strategies for making intentions recognizable;
   (c) the meanings and functions of linguistic forms within their emerging contexts;
   (d) the sequential context of other utterances;
   (e) properties of the discourse mode, e.g. narrative, description, exposition;
   (f) the social context, e.g. participant identities and relationships, structure of the situation, the setting;
   (g) a cultural framework of beliefs and actions.

It is important to note that these principles are both empirically and theoretically motivated. For example, the cumulative results of analyses of actual

talk are what motivate the principle of sequentiality. Another equally important source is the assumptions implicit in individual approaches to discourse.
For example, the focus on "interactive achievement" is based on conversation
analysis and interactional sociolinguistics. And the focus on how speakers
select among different linguistic devices (in the sixth principle) stems from
variation analysis, specifically the assumption that heterogeneity of form can
be explained by attention to function and to (linguistic and social) context.

I also want to note that there are individual differences in the way these
principles actually guide analyses. Take the second principle: coherence cannot be understood if attention is limited just to linguistic form and meaning.
How discourse analysts go beyond language – what they add to language to
explain coherence – clearly differs. Gricean pragmatics, for example, posits
communicative maxims which allow speakers to express intentions beyond
what can be conveyed in the semantic meanings of their words, and allow
hearers to recognize those intentions. Speech act theorists propose multiple
mapping relationships – and rules – linking utterances into sequences, and
linking what is said to what is meant and done. Interactional sociolinguistics
proposes that the process of conveying meaning requires speaker and hearer
to share underlying interpretive schemata whose relevance for the interpretation of a particular message is signalled through the use of specific verbal and
nonverbal devices. Despite the differences among these three approaches, each
adheres to the general principle, simply because each is an attempt to account
for discourse coherence by supplementing semantic meaning with contextualizing factors.

Finally, approaches to discourse may be united not only by the shared
principles noted above, but also by the way specific analyses jointly contribute
to three overall research questions. First, how do social and linguistic resources
differentiate a discourse from a random sequence of sentences? The answers
given to this question can contribute to the goals of discourse analysis noted
initially in this book (p. 41). Sequential analyses seek to discover the principles
underlying the order in which one utterance, or one type of utterance, follows
another; semantic and pragmatic analyses seek to describe how the organization of discourse, and the use of particular expressions and constructions
within certain contexts, allow people to convey and interpret meaning. The
general goal of differentiating discourse from a random sequence of sentences
(or utterances) – sequentially, semantically, and pragmatically – underlies all
discourse analysis: the solution suggested by the approaches that view "language as social interaction" is that both social and linguistic resources are
responsible for discourse.

Second, how does our understanding of utterances in discourse contribute
to our knowledge of language? This question has traditionally been posed in
relation to syntactic structures and their semantic interpretations: how does
our knowledge of how a particular construction is used in discourse contribute
to our knowledge of the form and meaning of that construction? But it can
also be asked in relation to areas often considered as part of phonological

theory, e.g. what does the use of intonation as a contextualization cue (or as an indicator of illocutionary force) tell us about the role of intonation in language? Can phonological variation serve discourse purposes, and if so, what does that tell us about the reasons for alternating between two different ways of saying the same thing?

Third, how are social and linguistic resources distributed throughout a speech community and across speech communities? This is basically a comparative question that focuses on distribution within a speech community (but across speakers, situations, styles), as well as distribution across speech communities. What do "unequal" distributions tell us about the way our human ability to use language becomes valued as symbolic capital? Can access to social and linguistic resources change over time?

Of course, not all analyses of discourse need to focus specifically on these questions. Some focus on the linguistic resources differentiating text-types (narratives versus descriptions) or modalities (spoken versus written). Some focus on the social and linguistic strategies by which actions are performed (e.g. how direct and indirect requests are performed). And there are of course other specific goals. But the answers provided by such studies can be pulled together in a common effort to answer these three broad research questions. And like the principles stated above, this is still another means of synthesizing different approaches to discourse.

4   At the borders of different disciplines

In this book, I discussed six different approaches to discourse analysis that began in different disciplines. I also considered three issues which greatly expand the scope of discourse analysis: structure and function, text and context, discourse and communication. Now I am suggesting, despite the internal diversity among the approaches and despite the external expansiveness of discourse analysis, that these approaches share some very general principles.

In closing, however, I want to suggest that discourse cannot be analyzed – even if one considers one's analysis linguistically motivated and linguistically relevant – through one discipline alone. Consider the issues about which all discourse analysts make assumptions: structure and function, text and context, discourse and communication. In each pair of concepts, the first member is the one that fits most comfortably into the realm of linguistic inquiry. To be specific: structures can be identified at many levels of linguistic organization (sounds, sentences), but functions are usually seen as non-linguistic (e.g. cognitive, social); texts are linguistic, but contexts include non-linguistic situations and people; even discourse, although rarely seen as confined to language *per se*, is certainly more language-centered a concept than communication (which involves people, intentions, and knowledge).

In a sense, then, the need to combine the study of structure with that of function, to understand the relationship between text and context, and to make clear how discourse is related to communication, is actually a single need. This need bears directly on the interdisciplinary basis of discourse analysis. I have said that it is difficult to always know how to separate (and relate) structure and function, text and context, discourse and communication. But what I am really saying is that it is difficult to separate language from the rest of the world. It is this ultimate inability to separate language from how it is used in the world in which we live that provides the most basic reason for the interdisciplinary basis of discourse analysis. To understand the language of discourse, then, we need to understand the world in which it resides; and to understand the world in which language resides, we need to go outside of linguistics. When we then return to a linguistic analysis of discourse – to an analysis of utterances as social interaction – I believe that we will find that the benefits of our journey have far outweighed its costs.

Notes

1 Labov (personal communication) has contrasted this *modus operandi* of variation analysis with that of ethnography of communication, which seeks to use traditional methods of analysis (i.e. participant observation) to discover and resolve new problems (e.g. patterns of communication).

2 It is important to note that researchers in one tradition have also drawn quite explicitly from the insights of other traditions. One particularly rich area of interaction is between conversation analysis and ethnography of communication (Moerman 1988); areas whose connections have also been explored are pragmatics and conversation analysis (Bilmes 1993; Levinson 1983; chapter 6).

Appendix 1 Collecting Data

Given the vastness and variety of topics and issues that fall under the label "discourse analysis," it should not be surprising that a wide range of data can be used to illustrate how to go about doing an analysis of discourse. In order to apply the approaches discussed in this book, e.g. by replicating the sample analyses, using the exercises suggested at the end of each chapter, or finding other ways to illustrate the approaches, I suggest having available one or more of the following types of data:

1 A taped conversation between two or three personal acquaintances. This can be collected during a variety of gatherings or occasions, e.g. a dinner, a study session, a discussion, a phone conversation. A section of the conversation should be transcribed (see appendix 2), preferably a section with more than one "main" speaker, more than one "text type" (e.g. a story, an explanation, a description), more than one "exchange type" (e.g. question–answer, repairs, clarifications), and more than one topic (or subtopics). If there is some section that seems especially interesting for some reason (e.g. maybe it seems puzzling, maybe there was a misunderstanding, maybe the topics are interesting), this section might also (or alternatively) be a good choice for transcription.

2 One (or more) instances of some type of institutional talk (e.g. service encounters in stores) – although these may be more difficult to tape. Encounters between people of institutionally differentiated statuses may be helpful, e.g. professor and student, barber and customer, head of a division and assistant(s). Again, these should be transcribed: although some such encounters are short, it is difficult to remember enough details of the utterances for analyses illustrating all the different perspectives.

3 Family conversations between parents and children of different ages, or interactions among children. Again, these should be transcribed (but see Ochs 1979).

4 Sociolinguistic (or other research) interviews (see chapter 5) can provide a varied group of text-types. They can also be supplemented by other types of interviews (e.g. television talk shows, news interviews), publicly accessible

discussions (e.g. radio call-in shows), or conversational data (as noted in point 1). Again, these should be transcribed.

5 Written discourse from a variety of sources: news articles, academic articles, letters to the editor, instructional texts (e.g. recipes, home repairs), etc.

Describe for whatever data you collect as much as possible about the participants and the setting (cf. chapter 5 on the ethnography of communication), including personal background knowledge about the participants (if available).

Suggested readings are: Labov (1984), Milroy (1987), Ochs (1988: chapter 2), Schiffrin (1987a: 41–8), Stubbs (1983: chapter 11), Tannen (1984: chapter 3), and Wolfson (1976).

Appendix 2   Transcription Conventions

From DuBois (1991)

Symbols for discourse transcription

Units
       Intonation unit   *{carriage return}*
       Truncated intonation unit   —
       Word   *{space}*
       Truncated word   -
Speakers
       Speaker identity/turn start   :
       Speech overlap   [ ]
Transitional continuity
       Final   .
       Continuing   ,
       Appeal   ?
Terminal pitch direction
       Fall   \
       Rise   /
       Level   —
Accent and lengthening
       Primary accent   ^
       Secondary accent   '
       Booster   !
       Lengthening   =
Tone
       Fall   \
       Rise   /
       Fall-rise   \/

Rise-fall	∧
Level	–
Pause	
Long	...(N)
Medium	...
Short	..
Latching	(0)
Vocal noises	
Vocal noises	( )
Inhalation	(H)
Exhalation	(Hx)
Glottal stop	%
Laughter	@
Quality	
Quality	⟨Y Y⟩
Laugh quality	⟨@ @⟩
Quotation quality	⟨Q Q⟩
Multiple quality features	⟨Y⟨Z Z⟩Y⟩
Phonetics	
Phonetic/phonemic transcription	(/ /)
Transcriber's perspective	
Researcher's comment	(( ))
Uncertain hearing	⟨X X⟩
Indecipherable syllable	X
Specialized notations	
Duration	(N)
Intonation unit continued	&
Intonation subunit boundary	|
Embedded intonation unit	⟨| |⟩
Reset	*{Capital Initial}*
False start	⟨ ⟩
Codeswitching	⟨L2 L2⟩
Non-transcription lines	
Non-transcription line	$
Interlinear gloss line	$G
Reserved symbols	
Phonemic/orthographic	,
Morphosyntactic coding	+ * # { }
User-definable	" ~ ;

Synopsis of Transcription Design Principles

Category definition: *define good categories*

  1 Define transcriptional categories which make the necessary distinctions among discourse phenomena.

 2 Define sufficiently explicit categories.
 3 Define sufficiently general categories.
 4 Contrast data types.

Accessibility: *make the system accessible*

 5 Use familiar notations.
 6 Use motivated notations.
 7 Use easily learned notations.
 8 Segregate unfamiliar notations.
 9 Use notations which maximize data access.
 10 Maintain consistent appearance across modes of access.

Robustness: *make representations robust*

 11 Use widely available characters.
 12 Avoid invisible contrasts.
 13 Avoid fragile contrasts.

Economy: *make representations economical*

 14 Avoid verbose notations.
 15 Use short notations for high frequency phenomena.
 16 Use discriminable notations for word-internal phenomena.
 17 Minimize word-internal notations.
 18 Use space meaningfully.

Adaptability: *make the system adaptable*

 19 Allow for seamless transition between degrees of delicacy.
 20 Allow for seamless integration of user-defined transcription categories.
 21 Allow for seamless integration of presentation features.
 22 Allow for seamless integration of indexing information.
 23 Allow for seamless integration of user-defined coding information.

From Jefferson (1979)

Transcript notation

1 Simultaneous utterances

Utterances starting simultaneously are linked together with either double or single left-hand brackets:

```
        Tom:      I used to smoke a lot when I was young
[[                [[
        Bob:      I used to smoke Camels
```

2 Overlapping utterances

When overlapping utterances do not start simultaneously, the point at which an ongoing utterance is joined by another is marked with a single left-hand bracket, linking an ongoing with an overlapping utterance at the point where overlap begins:

[Tom: I used to smoke ⌜a lot
         Bob: ⌞He thinks he's real tough

The point where overlapping utterances stop overlapping is marked with a single right-hand bracket:

]   Tom: I used to smoke ⌜a lot⌝ more than this
         Bob: ⌞I see⌟

3 Contiguous utterances

When there is no interval between adjacent utterances, the second being latched immediately to the first (without overlapping it), the utterances are linked together with equal signs:

=   Tom: I used to smoke a lot=
         Bob: = He thinks he's real tough

The equal signs are also used to link different parts of a single speaker's utterance when those parts constitute a continuous flow of speech that has been carried over to another line, by transcript design, to accommodate an intervening interruption:

Tom: I used to smoke ⌜a lot more than this=
Bob: ⌞You used to smoke
Tom: = but I never inhaled the smoke

Sometimes more than one speaker latches directly onto a just-completed utterance, and a case of this sort is marked with a combination of equal signs and double left-hand brackets:

         Tom: I used to smoke a lot=
= [[Bob: = [[He thinks he's tough
         Ann: [[So did I

When overlapping utterances end simultaneously and are latched onto by a subsequent utterance, the link is marked by a single right-handed bracket and equal signs:

         Tom: I used to smoke ⌜a lot⌝=
]=   Bob: ⌞I see⌟=
         Ann: = So did I

4   *Intervals within and between utterances*

When intervals in the stream of talk occur, they are timed in tenths of a second and inserted within parentheses, either within an utterance:

(0.0)   Lil: When I was (0.6) oh nine or ten

or between utterances:

Hal: Step right up
       (1.3)
Hal: I said step right up
       (0.8)
Joe: Are you talking to me

A short untimed pause within an utterance is indicated by a dash:

-     Dee: Umm - my mother will be right in

Untimed intervals heard between utterances are described within double parentheses and inserted where they occur:

((pause))   Rex: Are you ready to order
                   ((pause))
            Pam: Yes thank you we are

5   *Characteristics of speech delivery*

In these transcripts, punctuation is used to mark not conventional grammatical units but, rather, attempts to capture characteristics of speech delivery. For example, a colon indicates an extension of the sound or syllable it follows:

co:lon   Ron: What ha:ppened to you

and more colons prolong the stretch:

co::lons   Mae: I ju::ss can't come
           Tim: I'm so::: sorry re:::ally I am

The other punctuation marks are used as follows:

.   A period indicates a stopping fall in tone, not necessarily the end
        of a sentence.

, A comma indicates a continuing intonation, not necessarily between clauses of sentences.

? A question mark indicates a rising inflection, not necessarily a question.

¿ A combined question mark/comma indicates a rising intonation weaker than that indicated by a question mark.

! An exclamation point indicates an animated tone, not necessarily an exclamation.

- A single dash indicates a halting, abrupt cutoff, or, when multiple dashes hyphenate the syllables of a word or connect strings of words, the stream of talk so marked has a stammering quality.

Marked rising and falling shifts in intonation are indicated by upward and downward pointing arrows immediately prior to the rise or fall:

↓ ↑ Thatcher: I am however (0.2) very ↓ fortunate
(0.4) in having (0.6) a   ↑ mar:vlous
dep↓uty

Emphasis is indicated by underlining:

Ann: It happens to be <u>mine</u>

Capital letters are used to indicate an utterance, or part thereof, that is spoken much louder than the surrounding talk:

Announcer: an the winner: ↓iz:s (1.4) RACHEL ROBERTS
for Y↑ANKS

A degree sign is used to indicate a passage of talk which is quieter than the surrounding talk:

°° M: ˙hhhh (.) °Um::°'Ow is yih <u>mother</u>
by: th'<u>wa</u>:y.h̄

Audible aspirations (hhh) and inhalations (˙hhh) are inserted in the speech where they occur:

hhh Pam: An thi(hh)s is for you hhh
˙hhh Don: ˙hhh O(hh) tha(h)nk you rea(hh)lly

A 'gh' placed within a word indicates gutturalness:

gh J: Ohgh(h) h hhuh <u>huh</u> <u>huh</u> ˙huh

A subscribed dot is used as a "hardener." In this capacity it can indicate, for example, an especially dentalized "t":

dot J: Was it ↑la:s' night.

Double parentheses are used to enclose a description of some phenomenon with which the transcriptionist does not want to wrestle. These can be vocalizations that are not, for example, spelled gracefully or recognizably:

(( )) Tom: I used to ((cough)) smoke a lot
      Bob: ((sniff)) He thinks he's tough
      Ann: ((snorts))

or other details of the conversational scene:

      Jan: This is just delicious
            ((telephone rings))
      Kim: I'll get it

or various characterizations of the talk:

      Ron: ((in falsetto)) I can do it now
      Max: ((whispered)) He'll never do it

When part of an utterance is delivered at a pace quicker than the surrounding talk, it is indicated by being enclosed between "less than" signs:

> < Steel: the Gua:r:dian <u>newspaper</u> <u>looked</u> through >the
          manifestoes< la:<u>st</u> ↑week

6 *Transcriptionist doubt*

In addition to the timings of intervals and inserted aspirations and inhalations, items enclosed within single parentheses are in doubt, as in:

( ) Ted: I ('spose I'm not)
    (Ben): We all (t-   )

Here "spose I'm not," the identity of the second speaker, and "t-" represent different varieties of transcriptionist doubt.
  Sometimes multiple possibilities are indicated:

Ted: ₁(spoke to Mark)
 I (’spose I’m not)

Ben: We all try to figure a (tough angle) for it
 (stuffing girl)

When single parentheses are empty, no hearing could be achieved for the string of talk or item in question:

Todd: My (   ) catching
(   ): In the highest (   )

Here the middle of Todd’s utterance, the speaker of the subsequent utterance, and the end of the subsequent utterance could not be recovered.

7 Gaze direction

The gaze of the speaker is marked above an utterance, and that of the addressee below it. A line indicates that the party marked is gazing toward the other. The absence of a line indicates lack of gaze. Dots mark the transition movement from nongaze to gaze, and the point where the gaze reaches the other is marked with an X:

```
Beth:   . . . . ₁X_____
         Terry- ˡJerry’s fa ₁scinated with elephants
Don:             . . . . . . . . ˡX_____
```

Here Beth moves her gaze toward Don while saying “Terry”; Don’s gaze shifts toward and reaches hers just after she starts to say “fascinated.”

If gaze arrives within a pause each tenth of a second within the pause is marked with a dash:

```
Ann:                       . . . . ₁X_____
         Well (--- ₁-) We coulda used ˡa liddle, marijuana.=
Beth:          ˡX_____
```

Here Beth’s gaze reaches Ann three-tenths of a second after she has said “Well-,” and one-tenth of a second before she continues with “We coulda used. . . .”

Commas are used to indicate the dropping of gaze:

```
Ann:     _____
         Karen has this new hou:se. en it’s got all this
Beth:    _____, , ,
```

Here Beth’s gaze starts to drop away as Ann begins to say “new.”

Movements like head nodding are marked at points in the talk where they occur:

```
Ann:    _____
        Karen has this new hou:se. en it's got all this
Beth:   _____, , ,                    ((Nod))
```

Here Beth, who is no longer gazing at Ann, nods as the latter says "got."

Asterisks are used in a more ad hoc fashion to indicate particular phenomena discussed in the text. In the following fragment, for example, Goodwin uses them to indicate the position where Beth puts food in her mouth:

```
Ann:    _____
        = like- (0.2) ssilvery:: g-go:ld wwa: ⌈llpaper.
Beth:                            * * * * * *  . . . ⌊X____
```

8   *Applause*

Strings of X's are used to indicate applause, with lower- and uppercase letters marking quiet and loud applause respectively:

Audience: xxXXXXXXXXXXXXXxxx

Here applause amplitude increases and then decreases.

An isolated single clap is indicated by dashes on each side of the x:

Audience: -x-

Spasmodic or hesitant clapping is indicated by a chain punctuated by dashes:

Audience: -x-x-x

A line broken by numbers in parentheses indicates the duration of applause from the point of onset (or prior object) to the nearest tenth of a second. The number of X's does *not* indicate applause duration except where it overlaps with talk, as in the second of the following examples:

```
Speaker:    I beg >to supp↓ort the m↓otion<=
            |————————(8.0)————————|
Audience:   =x-xxXXXXXXXXXXXXXxxxx-x

Speaker:    THIS ↓WEEK ⌈SO > THAT YOU CAN STILL MAKE ⌉=
Audience:              ⌊xx-XXXXXXXXXXXXXXXXXXXXX      ⌋=
Speaker:    = ⌈⌈YEAR MINDS UP<
Audience:   = ⌊⌊XXXXXXXXXXXXX ((edited cut))
```

9 *Other transcript symbols*

The left-hand margin of the transcript is sometimes used to point to a feature of interest to the analyst at the time the fragment is introduced in the text. Lines in the transcript where the phenomenon of interest occurs are frequently indicated by arrows in the left-hand margin. For example, if the analyst had been involved in a discussion of continuations and introduced the following fragment:

    Don: I like that blue one very much
→ Sam: And I'll bet your wife would like it
    Don: If I had the money I'd get one for her
→ Sam: And one for your mother too I'll bet

the arrows in the margin would call attention to Sam's utterances as instances of continuations.

Horizontal ellipses indicate that an utterance is being reported only in part, with additional speech coming before, in the middle of, or after the reported fragment, depending on the location of the ellipses. Thus, in the following example, the parts of Don's utterance between "said" and "y'know" are omitted:

Don: But I said . . . y'know

Vertical ellipses indicate that intervening turns at talking have been omitted from the fragment:

Bob: Well I always say give it your all

    .
    .
    .

Bob: And I always say give it everything

Codes that identify fragments being quoted designate parts of the chapter authors' own tape collections.

From Schiffrin (1987a)

Transcription conventions

Key to transcription conventions

        falling intonation followed by noticeable pause (as at end of declarative sentence)

?	rising intonation followed by noticeable pause (as at end of interrogative sentence)
,	continuing intonation: may be slight rise or fall in contour (less than "." or "?"); may be followed by a pause (shorter than "." or "?")
!	animated tone
...	noticeable pause or break in rhythm without falling intonation (each half-second pause is marked as measured by stop watch)
-	self interruption with glottal stop
:	lengthened syllable
italics	emphatic stress
CAPS	very emphatic stress

When speech from A and B overlap, the starting point of the overlap is marked by a left-hand bracket, and the ending point of the overlap is marked by a right-hand bracket.

```
A:  Do you know what time the party's supposed ⌈ to start?  ⌉
B:                                             ⌊ Six o'clock.⌋
```

When lack of space prevents continuous speech from A from being presented on a single line of text, then '=' at end of A1 and '=' at beginning of A2 shows the continuity.

```
A1:   Do you know what time the party's supposed ⌈ to start?=  ⌉
B:                                               ⌊ Six o'clock.⌋
A2:   = Because I have to work late tonight.
```

When speech from B follows speech from A without perceptible pause, then z links the end of A with the beginning of B.

```
A:  Do you know the time?
B:  Six o'clock.           ᶻSix o'clock.
```

When speech from B occurs during what can be heard as a brief silence from A, then B's speech is under A's silence.

```
A:  I can't wait to go to the party!          It'll be fun.
B:                                  Oh yeh!
```

From Tannen (1989a)

Transcription conventions

The following transcription conventions are used.

.	indicates sentence final falling intonation
,	indicates clause-final intonation ("more to come")
?!	indicates exclamatory intonation
...	three dots in transcripts indicate pause of 1/2 second or more
..	two dots indicate perceptible pause of less than 1/2 second
...	three dots show ellipsis, parts omitted in quotations from other sources
´	accent indicates primary stress
CAPS	indicate emphatic stress
Í	Accent on words already in CAPS shows emphatic stress
[	Brackets (with or without top flap) show overlap. Two voices going at once. ⌐ Simultaneously.
	Brackets with top flap reversed show latching. No perceptible inter-turn pause
:	colon following vowel indicates elongated vowel sound
::	extra colon indicates longer elongation
-	hyphen indicates glottal stop: sound abruptly cut off
" "	quotation marks highlight dialogue
	Underlining highlights key words and phrases
→	Left arrows highlight key lines arrow at right of line indicates → speaker's turn continues without interruption → so look for continuation on succeeding line
A	upper case "A" indicates pronunciation of the indefinite article ("a") as the diphthong /ey/. (Note that distinguishing between the unstressed form of the article "a" and the hesitation marker "uh" is always an interpretation, as they both have the same phonetic realization (/ʌ/).
/words/	in slashes show uncertain transcription
/?/	indicates inaudible utterance
( )	Parentheses indicate "parenthetical" intonation: lower amplitude and pitch plus flattened intonation contour

Suggested readings are: DuBois (1991), Edwards (1991), Edwards and Lampert (1992), Macaulay (1991), Ochs (1979), and Preston (1982).

Appendix 3 Sample Data

HENRY:	(1)	That's what I was tellin' Deborah.
	(2)	Your children have t'*earn* what they want.
	(3)	I once talked to a wise man, his name happened to be un m-Nixon.
	(4)	The man was a very smart man.
	(5)	And I was working very hard,
	(6)	and I told him, I said "I must save money t'send my children t'college."
	(7)	Y'know what he told me for an answer?
	(8)	He says, "Henry, children find their *own* way t'go t'college if they want to."
	(9)	He says, "*They* make better children."
IRENE:	(10)	I agree with [that.=
HENRY:	(11)	[And I never forgot what he said.=
IRENE:	(12)	=[I agree with that.
HENRY:	(13)	=[Absolutely.
DEBBY:	(14)	Yeh. I think it's much better t'[raise your children-
HENRY:	(15)	[Yes. You have- you don't give- you won't- you f-
	(16)	I'll tell y'somethin' else,
	(17)	them real wealthy people, in most cases their children have t'work.
DEBBY:	(18)	Yeh it's [the middle
IRENE:	(19)	[That's right.
HENRY:	(20)	It's the *middle class* . . .
IRENE:	(21)	It's the middle class [that gives their kids everything.
DEBBY:	(22)	[Yeh.
HENRY:	(23)	[I got-=
DEBBY:	(24)	Yeh.

HENRY: (25)   =I got mo[n:ey, and I'll give y'this, and I'll=
IRENE: [That's right!
DEBBY: (26)   ⌐ yeh
HENRY: (27)   =give y'[that. And not-
DEBBY: (28)   [Yeh.
IRENE: (29)   But it's not a [matter of- even- Hen if they have=
HENRY: (30)   [And there is *less respect*=
IRENE: (31)   =money- even if they don't have mo[ney-
HENRY: (32)   [But today there is less
                respect for the mother, and the father of the
         (33)   house. The father's not the kingpin in his own=
DEBBY: (34)   ᶻum
HENRY: (35)   =house.   And *this* is one of the bad things *also*.=
DEBBY: (36)   ᶻHmmm.
HENRY: (37)   =The fac- that's basically *every*thing in America.
         (38)   Y'don't have the father, as the kingpin of the house.=
DEBBY: (39)   Hmmm.
HENRY: (40)   He is the *shluf* today!=
IRENE: (41)   It depends on [the house.
HENRY: (42)   [He is not the- he is not the kingpin.
DEBBY: (43)   Why d'y'think that happened?
HENRY: (44)   *Why?*
DEBBY: (45)   Yeh.
HENRY: (46)   Because the- well then- this is the- this is-=
IRENE: (47)   ᶻThe=
HENRY: (48)   =[*this* came out-   this came out-
IRENE: (49)   =[mothers went t'work.   ᶻIt's a=
HENRY: (50)   [*No!* This came about-
IRENE: (51)   financial situa[tion that t'live the mothers had=
HENRY: (52)   [*No!* This came about-
IRENE: (53)   =t'go t'work.
HENRY: (54)   *Right*. You're right you're right you're right.
         (55)   This came about, before the second world was when most of
                the mothers were home.
         (56)   When their children went t'school, they came home,
         (57)   and they fou- the mother was waiting for their children.
         (58)   But then we had the war,
         (59)   and the women applied,
         (60)   and they done a *won*derful job,
         (61)   there's no question to it.
         (62)   Eh, the women done the job,
         (63)   they got- they carried on with the country,
         (64)   and a lot of them held it,
         (65)   and the money was *good*.
         (66)   Because the needs were greater,

	(67)	and the more money, the better that you lived.
	(68)	Y'spend more, you live better than ever.
	(69)	So then the man and wife worked,
	(70)	and the kids were running around.
	(71)	Well you know if you get a sixteen- seventeen year old kid and the mothers' workin,
	(72)	and she's got a boyfriend,
	(73)	they're gonna play!
IRENE:	(74)	[They're gonna play anyway.
HENRY:	(75)	=[They're gonna play. They're gonnna make babies!
	(76)	And this is what happened, [because you got more-
IRENE:	(77)	[They're gonna play=
HENRY:	(78)	=[babies than y'ever had. [That are not married.=
IRENE:	(79)	=[regardless [It's the morality.
HENRY:	(80)	=And y'can't blame 'em. Look, their nature.
	(81)	They're eh people!
	(82)	[They're full of- full of eh Heh?
IRENE:	(83)	[The standards though are different today.
	(84)	The standards are different today.
HENRY:	(85)	Standards are different.
	(86)	But I'm *tell*in' y.
	(87)	If the father is respected, [an:d eh
IRENE:	(88)	[Henry, lemme ask you question.
	(89)	Lem- you made a statement that the mothers: run the house. Right?
	(90)	All right how many fathers today, hold down two jobs, because they can't afford t'live, and are never around.
HENRY:	(91)	This is bad. Well [this is the society that we're in.
IRENE:	(92)	[Look, my husband holds down one job.
	(93)	He's not home now. [He hasn't been home since=
HENRY:	(94)	He [works hard.
IRENE:		=seven thirty this morning.
	(95)	Basically, I run that house yes.
	(96)	Because who's gonna run it?
HENRY:	(97)	You can run a hou- [whatcha- now whatcha you can=
IRENE:	(98)	[you mean he can't- I mean any kinda-
HENRY:	(99)	=ran a house- you can run a house a- and *do* the job,
	(100)	=which is important, y' can't y- a man can't do it himself, and a woman can't do it himself w- if y' want it to be successful. In most cases.
IRENE:	(101)	Why do [they: even, the Jewish people from *years* ago,=
HENRY:	(102)	[But eh-
IRENE:		=where- where- where there *were* intermarriages,
	(103)	why was the point left to being, that whatever the mother is, *that's* what the child is.=

HENRY: (104) Well this is [debatable that (   )
IRENE: (105)   =[Because the mother is the one that raises: the child.
         (106) And *makes* the child go t'Hebrew, or go t'church or go here, or go there.
HENRY: (107) But- well this is because she's home t'see that the child *does* it.=
IRENE: (108) ^{z}Right!
HENRY: (109) =But the child- the mother's not there, so the kid plays hooky. The kid is playin' hooky.
IRENE: (110) Right but there's plenty of mothers that are home, and the kids play hooky.
HENRY: (111) Heh?
IRENE: (112) There are plenty of mothers that are home, and [the=
HENRY: (113)   [But=
IRENE: =[kids play hooky.
HENRY: =[in most cases eh eh percentage wise, it will work better that way.
         (114) It wor- Irene, you gotta remember one thing.
         (115) You cannot put yourself in that category, because you are in a different circumstance.
         (116) You know you went through, and you went through something else.
         (117) T'catch up.
         (118) Y'know you got a lot t'catch up.
         (119) An:d you're both working hard,
         (120) but it ain't always gonna be like *that*,
         (121) it's gonna pay, it's gonna be different.
IRENE: (122) But [I could never-
HENRY: (123)   [But you still have a family structure.
IRENE: (124) Right. [But I could never go back to the point wh-=
HENRY: (125)   [Right? Y'still have a family-
IRENE: =where I didn't work.
         (126) Give it up now that I have been exposed to it for a year and a half,
         (127) and feel   [being home=
HENRY: (128) ^{z}Because the- [the goodies are there.=
IRENE: (129) =and just   [Money-Not so=
HENRY: (130)   = ^{z}Because the goodies are [there!
IRENE: =much the [goodies yo-
HENRY: (131)   [But if Jay made a livin', do you think it would be *right* for you to work?
         (132) Would your-would your [fam-=
IRENE: (133)   [YES. ^{z}NO. Y'know why?=

HENRY:	(134)	*Absolutely not.* [I'm dea- dead against it.
IRENE:	(135)	^{z}=Because [I don't think a woman today is content to be the stagnant housewife of cooking, and cleaning,
	(136)	and you feel like your brain, is- gets to a point, and it stops.=
HENRY:	(137)	Then have [more babies. That'll keep y'busy.
IRENE:	(138)	=[It stops. Oh that's a-
	(139)	Y'can't go on havin' babies for the rest [of your life.=
HENRY:	(140)	[Why not?
IRENE:	(141)	=There's other things t'do.
HENRY:	(142)	These women are bored because they [( )
IRENE:	(143)	[If I'm not allowed t'work, so I go around t'department [stores and spend=
HENRY:	(144)	[All right maybe=
IRENE:		=money.
HENRY:	(145)	=that's a foolish statement.
	(146)	But let's put it this way.
	(147)	A woman is needed in the house,
	(148)	t'clean the house,
	(149)	and t'cook the hou- uh cook the meals,
	(150)	and clean the clothes,
	(151)	there is- there is a tre*mendous* amount of work for a [woman.
IRENE:	(152)	[( ) You're ( ) Henry.
HENRY:	(153)	You don't think there's a d-a lot of work for [yourself?
ZELDA:	(154)	[You can get- you can get anybody t'come in an' clean: [the=
HENRY:	(155)	[All week?
ZELDA:	(156)	=house. *That is not the point.*
IRENE:	(157)	That's not r- No=
ZELDA:	(158)	[That's off. No. That's off, [Henry.
IRENE:	(159)	=[That's not true.
HENRY:	(160)	[You say that's wrong?
ZELDA:	(161)	Yep. That's not a mother's duty. Just t'clean and cook and clean.

Bibliography

Abbott, B. (1993) A pragmatic account of the definiteness effect in existential sentences. *Journal of Pragmatics*, 19(1): 39–56.

Aries, E. and Johnson, F. (1983) Close friendship in adulthood: Conversational content between same-sex friends. *Sex Roles*, 9: 1183–96.

Ariel, M. (1990) *Accessing Noun-phrase Antecedents*. London: Routledge.

Athanasiadou, A. (1991) The discourse function of questions. *Pragmatics*, 1(1): 107–22.

Atkinson, M. and Heritage, H. (eds) (1984) *Structures of Social Action*. Cambridge: Cambridge University Press.

Austin, J. (1962) *How to Do Things with Words*. Cambridge, MA: Harvard University Press.

Bach, E. (1981) Tenses and aspects as functions on verb phrases. In C. Rohrer (ed.), *Time, Tense and Quantifiers*. Tübingen: Niemeryer, 19–37.

Bach, K. and Harnish, R. (1982) *Linguistic Communication and Speech Acts*. Cambridge, MA: MIT Press.

Bamberg, M. (1991) Narrative activity as perspective taking: The role of emotionals, negations, and voice in the construction of the story realm. *Journal of Cognitive Psychotherapy*, 5(4): 275–90.

Bamberg, M. and Marchman, V. (1991) Binding and unfolding: towards the linguistic construction of narrative discourse. *Discourse Processes*. 14(3): 277–306.

Basso, K. (1972) "To give up on words." Silence in Western Apache culture. In P. Giglioli (ed.), *Language and Social Context*. Harmondsworth: Penguin, 67–86.

Bates, E. and MacWhinney, B. (1982) A functionalist approach to grammar. In E. Wanner and L. Gleitman (eds), *Language Acquisition: the State of the Art*. New York: Academic Press, 167–214.

Bateson, G. (1955) A theory of play and fantasy. American Psychological Association Psychiatric Research Reports, II. Reprinted in *Steps to an Ecology of Mind*. New York: Chandler (1972), 177–93.

Bauman, R. (1974) Speaking in the light: the role of the Quaker minister. In R. Bauman and J. Sherzer (eds), *Explorations in the Ethnography of Speaking*. Cambridge: Cambridge University Press, 144–61.

Bauman, R. (1986) *Story, Performance, and Event*. Cambridge: Cambridge University Press.

Bauman, R. and Briggs, C. (1990) Poetics and performance as critical perspectives on language and social life. *American Review of Anthropology*, 19: 59–88.

Becker, A. (1984) Biography of a sentence: a Burmese proverb. In E. Bruner (ed.), *Text, Play and Story: Proceedings of the American Ethnological Society*, 135–55.

Becker, A. L. (1988) Language in particular: a lecture. In D. Tannen (ed.), *Linguistics in Context*. Norwood, NJ: Ablex Publishing, 17–35.

Bennett, A. (1978) Interruptions and the interpretation of conversation. *Proceedings of the Fourth Annual Meeting of the Berkeley Linguistics Society*, 557–75.

Berko-Gleason, J. and Weintaub, S. (1976) The acquisition of routines in child language. *Language in Society*, 5: 129–36.

Berlin, B. (1976) The concept of rank in ethnobiological classification: some evidence from Aguaruna folk botany. In R. Casson (ed.), *Language, Culture and Cognition: Anthropological Perspectives*. New York: Macmillan.

Berlin, B., Breedlove, D. and Raven, P. (1974) *Principles of Tzeltal Plant Classification*. New York: Academic Press.

Besnier, N. (1989) Information withholding as a manipulative and collusive strategy in Nukulaelae gossip. *Language in Society*, 18(3): 315–42.

Biber, D. (1988) *Variation across Speaking and Writing*. Cambridge: Cambridge University Press.

Bilmes, J. (1985) "Why that now?" Two kinds of conversational meaning. *Discourse Processes*, 8: 319–55.

Bilmes, J. (1988a) The concept of preference in conversation analysis. *Language in Society*, 17(2): 161–82.

Bilmes, J. (1988b) Category and rule in conversation analysis. *Papers in Pragmatics*, 2 (1/2): 25–59.

Bilmes, J. (1993) Accounting practices as an ethnomethodological and linguistic pragmatic concern: the case of response priority. Paper presented at International Pragmatic Association Meeting, Kobe, Japan.

Blakemore, D. (1987) *Semantic Constraints on Relevance*. Oxford: Basil Blackwell.

Blakemore, D. (1988) The organization of discourse. In F. Newmeyer (ed.), *Linguistics: the Cambridge Survey*, 299–350. Cambridge: Cambridge University Press.

Bloomfield, L. (1933) *Language*. New York: Henry Holt and Company.

Bolinger, D. (1977) *Meaning and Form*. London: Longman.

Bolinger, D. (1982) Intonation and gesture. In *Papers from the Parassession on Nondeclaritives*. Chicago: Chicago Linguistic Society, 1–22.

Bourdieu, P. (1977) *Outline of a Theory of Practice*. Cambridge: Cambridge University Press.

Boxer, D. (1993) Social distance and speech behavior: the case of indirect complaints. *Journal of Pragmatics*, 19(2): 103–26.

Briggs, C. (1986) *Learning How to Ask*. Cambridge: Cambridge University Press.

Briggs, C. and Bauman, R. (1992) Genre, intertexuality, and social power. *Journal of Linguistic Anthropology*, 2(2): 131–72.

Brown, G. (1977) *Listening to Spoken English*. London: Longman.

Brown, G., Currie, K. and Kenworthy, J. (1980) *Questions of Intonation*. London: Croom Helm.

Brown G. and Yule, G. (1983) *Discourse Analysis*. Cambridge: Cambridge University Press.

Brown, P. and Levinson, S. (1987) *Politeness*. Cambridge: Cambridge University Press.

Bruner, J. (1986) *Actual Minds, Possible Worlds*. Cambridge, MA: Harvard University Press.

Bruner, J. (1990) Autobiography as self. In *Acts of Meaning*. Cambridge, MA: Harvard University Press, 99–138.

Button, G. (ed.) (1991) *Ethnomethodology and the Human Sciences*. Cambridge: Cambridge University Press.

Button, G. and Casey, N. (1984) Generating topic: the use of topic initial elicitors. In J. Atkinson and J. Heritage (eds), *Structures of Social Action: Studies in Conversation Analysis*. Cambridge: Cambridge University Press, 167–90.

Cameron, D., Frazier, E., Harvey, P., Rampton, B. and Richardson, K. (1991) *Ethics, Advocacy and Empowerment: Issues of Method in Researching Language*. London: Routledge.

Carlson, L. (1981) Aspect and quantification. In Tedeschi and Zaenen (eds.) *Syntax and Semantics 14: Tense and Aspect*. New York: Academic Press, 31–64.

Carlson, L. (1984) *"Well" in Dialogue Games*. Amsterdam: John Benjamins Press.

Cassirer, E. (1961) *The Logic of the Humanities*. New Haven, CT: Yale University Press.

Chafe, W. (1974) Language and consciousness. *Language*, 50: 111–13.

Chafe, W. (1976) Givenness, contrastiveness, definiteness, subjects, topics, and point of view. In C. Li and S. Thompson (eds), *Subject and Topic*. New York: Academic Press, 25–56.

Chafe, W. (1980) The deployment of consciousness in the production of a narrative. In W. Chafe (ed.), *The Pear Stories: Cognitive, Cultural and Linguistic Aspects of Narrative Production*. Norwood, NJ: Ablex Press, 9–50.

Chafe, W. (1987) Cognitive constraints on information flow. In R. Tomlin (ed.), *Coherence and grounding in discourse*. Amsterdam: John Benjamins Press.

Chafe, W. (1992) Prosodic and functional units of language. In J. Edwards and M. Lampert (eds), *Talking Data: Transcription and Coding in Discourse Research*. Hillsdale, NJ: Lawrence Erlbaum Associates.

Chatham, S. (1978) *Story and Discourse*. Ithaca, NY: Cornell University Press.

Cherry, R. (1990) Politeness in written persuasion. *Journal of Pragmatics*,

Chomsky, N. (1957) *Syntactic Structures*. The Hague: Mouton.

Chomsky, N. (1965) *Aspects of the Theory of Syntax*. Cambridge, MA: MIT Press.

Christian, D. (1973) What do you mean by request for clarification? In R. Fasold (ed.), *Variation in the Form and Use of Language*. Washington, DC: Georgetown University Press, 26–74.

Ciccourel, A. (1972) Basic and normative rules in the negotiation of status and rule. In D. Sudnow (ed.), *Studies in Social Interaction*. New York: Free Press, 229–58.

Ciccourel, A. (1980) Language and social interaction: Philosophical and empirical issues. In D. Zimmerman and C. West (eds), *Language and Social Interaction*. Special issue of *Sociological Inquiry*, 50 (3/4): 1–30.

Clancy, P. (1980) Referential choice in English and Japanese narrative discourse. In W. Chafe (ed.), *The Pear Stories*. Norwood, NJ: Ablex Publishers.

Clark, H. (1979) Responding to indirect speech acts. *Cognitive Psychology*, 11: 430–77.

Clark, H. and Carlson, T. (1981) Context for comprehension. In J. Long and A. Baddeley (eds), *Attention and Performance IX*. Hillsdale, NJ: Lawrence Erlbaum, 313–30.

Clark, H. and Carlson, T. (1982) Hearers and speech acts. *Language*, 58: 332–73.

Clark, H. and Haviland, J. (1977) Comprehension and the given-new contract. In R. Freedle (ed.), *Discourse Production and Comprehension*. Norwood, NJ: Ablex Publishers, 1–40.

Clark, H. and Marshall, C. (1981) Definite reference and mutual knowledge. In A. Joshi, B. Webber and I. Sag (eds), *Elements of Discourse Understanding*. Cambridge: Cambridge University Press, 10–63.

Clark, H. and Murphy, G. (1982) Audience design in meaning and reference. In J. LeNy and W. Kintsch (eds), *Language and Comprehension*. Amsterdam: North Holland Publishing Company.

Clark, H., Schreuder, R. and Buttrick, S. (1983) Common ground and the understanding of demonstrative reference. *Journal of Verbal Learning and Verbal Behavior*, 22: 245–58.

Clark, H. and Wilkes-Gibbs, D. (1986) Referring as a collaborative process. *Cognition*, 22: 1–39.

Cole, P. (ed.) (1981) *Radical Pragmatics*. New York: Academic Press.

Cole, P. and Morgan, J. (1975) *Speech Acts (Syntax and Semantics, Volume 3)*. New York: Academic Press.

Collett, P. (1983) Mossi salutations. *Semiotica*, 45 (3/4): 191–248.

Comrie, B. (1985) *Tense*. Cambridge: Cambridge University Press.

Cooley, C. H. (1902) *Human Nature and the Social Order*. New York: Scribner.

Corsaro, W. (1979) "We're friends, right?": children's use of access rituals in a nursery school. *Language in Society*, 8: 315–36.

Coulter, J. (1989) *Mind in Action*. Atlantic Highlands, NJ: Humanities Press International.

Coulthard, M., Montgomery, M. and Brazil, D. (1981) Developing a description of spoken discourse. In M. Coulthard and M. Montgomery (eds), *Studies in Discourse Analysis*. London: Routledge and Kegan Paul.

Coupland, N. (1983) Patterns of encounter management. *Language in Society*, 12(4): 459–76

Craig, R. and Tracy, K. (1983) *Conversational Coherence: Form, Structure, and Strategy*. Beverly Hills, CA: Sage Publications.

Cumming, S. (1984) The sentence in Chinese. *Studies in Language*, 8(3): 365–95.

Davison, A. (1975) Indirect speech acts and what to do with them. In P. Cole and J. Morgan (eds), *Speech Acts (Syntax and Semantics, Volume 3)*. New York: Academic Press, 143–86.

Deakins, A. (1989) Talk at the top: topics at lunch. Manuscript William Patterson College, New Jersey.

Dil, A. (ed.) (1971) *Language in Social Groups*. Stanford, CA: Stanford University Press.

Dines, E. (1980) Variation in discourse: "And stuff like that". *Language in Society*, 9(1): 13–33.

Donnellan, K. (1978) Speaker reference, descriptions, and anaphora. In P. Cole (ed.), *Pragmatics (Syntax and Semantics 9)*. New York: Academic Press, 47–68.

Dorval, B. (ed.) (1990) *Conversational Organization and Its Development*. Norwood, NJ: Ablex.

Downing, P. (1980) Factors influencing lexical choice in narrative. In W. Chafe (ed.), *The Pear Stories: Cognitive, Cultural and Linguistic Aspects of Narrative Production*. Norwood, NJ: Ablex Press, 89–126.

Dowty, D. (1986) The effects of aspectual class on the temporal structure of discourse: semantics or pragmatics? *Linguistics and Philosophy*, 9: 37–61.

Dry, H. (1981) Sentence aspect and the movement of narrative time. *Text*, 1: 233–40.

Dry, H. (1983) The movement of narrative time. *Journal of Literary Semantics*, 12: 19–53.

DuBois, J. (1980) Beyond definiteness: the trace of identity in discourse. In W. Chafe (ed.), *The Pear Stories*. Norwood, NJ: Ablex Press, 203–74.

DuBois, J. (1987a) Meaning without intention: lessons from divination. *Papers in Pragmatics*, 1(2): 80–122.

DuBois, J. (1987b) The discourse basis of ergativity. *Language* 63(4): 805–55.

DuBois, J. (1991) Transcription design principles for spoken discourse research. *Pragmatics*, 1(1): 71–106.

Duncan, S. (1972) Some signals and rules for taking speaking turns in conversations. *Journal of Personality and Social Psychology*, 6: 341–9.

Duranti, A. (1984) The social meaning of subject pronouns in Italian conversation. *Text*, 4: 4.

Duranti, A. (1988) Intentions, language, and social action in a Samoan context. *Journal of Pragmatics*, 12: 13–33.

Duranti, A. (1989) Ethnography of speaking: toward a linguistics of the praxis. In F. Newmeyer (ed.), *Linguistics: The Cambridge Survey*. Cambridge: Cambridge University Press.

Duranti, A. and Brenneis, D. (1986) The audience as co-author: an introduction. In A. Duranti and D. Brenneis (eds), *The Audience as Co-author*, special issue of *Text*, 6(3): 239–47.

Duranti, A. and Goodwin, C. (1991) *Rethinking Context*. Cambridge: Cambridge University Press.

Durkheim, E. (1893) *The Elementary Forms of the Religious Life*. Glencoe, IL: Free Press.

Durkheim, E. (1895) *The Rules of Sociological Method*. New York: Free Press.

Eckert, P. and McConnell-Ginet, S. (1992) Communities of practice: where language, gender, and power all live. In K. Hall, M. Bucholtz and B. Moonwomon (eds), *Locating Power*, Proceedings of the Second Berkeley Women and Language Conference, University of California, Berkeley, 89–99.

Edwards, J. (1991) Transcription. In W. Bright (ed.), *Oxford International Encyclopedia of Linguistics*. New York: Oxford University Press.

Edwards, J. and M. Lampert (eds) (1992) *Talking Data: Transcription and Coding in Discourse Research*. Hillsdale, NJ: Lawrence Erlbaum Associates.

Ehrlich, S. (1990) Referential linking and the interpretation of tense. *Journal of Pragmatics*, 14: 57–75.

Ekman, P. (1979) About brows: emotional and conversational signals. In M. von Cranach, K. Fopa, W. Lepenies and D. Ploog (eds), *Human Ecology*. Cambridge: Cambridge University Press, 169–249.

Ekman, P. and Freisen, W. (1969) The repertoire of nonverbal behavior: categories, origins, usage and coding. *Semiotica*, 1: 49–98.

Erdmann, P. (1976) *There Sentences in English*. Munich: Tuduv.

Erickson, F. and Shultz, J. (1982) *The Counselor as Gatekeeper: Social Interactions in Interviews*. New York: Academic Press.

Ernst, T. (1983) *Towards an Integrated Theory of Adverb Position in English*. Bloomington: Indiana University Linguistics Club.

Ervin-Tripp, S. (1976) Is Sybil there? The structure of American English directives. *Language in Society*, 5: 25–66.

Fairclough, N. (1989) *Language and Power*. London: Longman.

Fasold, R. (1990) *Sociolinguistics of Language*. Oxford: Blackwell.

Feld, S. (1982) *Sound and Sentiment: Birds, Weeping, Poetics, and Song in Kaluli Expression*. Philadelphia: University of Pennsylvania Press.

Ferguson, C. (1983) Sports announcer talk: syntactic aspects of register variation. *Language in Society*, 12(2): 153–72.

Ferrera, A. (1985) Pragmatics. In T. van Dijk (ed.), *Handbook of Discourse Analysis, Volume 2: Dimensions of Discourse*. New York: Academic Press, 137–157.

Figueroa, E. (1990) Sociolinguistic metatheory: an utterance based paradigm. PhD, Dissertation, Georgetown University.

Fillmore, C. (1968) The case for case. In E. Bach and R. Harns (eds), *Universals in Linguistic Theory*. New York: Holt, 1–88.

Firbas, J. (1964) On defining the theme in functional sentence analysis. In *Travaux Linguistiques de Prague, Volume 1*. University of Alabama Press, 267–80

Fishman, P. (1983) Interaction: the work women do. In B. Thorne, C. Kramarae and N. Henley (eds), *Language, Gender and Society*. Newbury, MA: Newbury House, 89–101.

Fleischman, S. (1990) *Tense and Narrativity*. Austin: University of Texas Press.

Ford, C. (1993) *Grammar in Interaction: Adverbial Clauses in American English Conversation*. Cambridge: Cambridge University Press.

Ford, C. and Thompson, S. (1986) Conditionals in discourse: a text-based study from English. In E. Traugott, C. Ferguson, J. Snitzer Reilly and A. ter Meulen (eds), *On Conditionals*. Cambridge: Cambridge University Press.

Ford, C. and Thompson, S. (1992) Projectability in conversation: grammar, intonation and semantics. Manuscript, University of Wisconsin, Madison.

Foucault, M. (1982) *Power/Knowledge: Selected Interviews and Other Writings by Michel Foucault, 1972–1977*. New York: Pantheon.

Fox, B. (1987) *Discourse Structure and Anaphora*. Cambridge: Cambridge University Press.

Fox, B. and Thompson, S. (1990) A discourse explanation of the grammar of relative clauses in English conversation. *Language*, 66(2): 297–316.

Fraser, B. (1988) Motor oil is motor oil: an account of English nominal tautologies. *Journal of Pragmatics*, 12: 215–70.

Freeze, R. (1992) Existentials and other locatives. *Language*, 68(3): 553–95.

Garfinkel, H. (1967) *Studies in Ethnomethodology*. Englewood Cliffs, NJ: Prentice Hall.

Garfinkel, H. (1974) On the origins of the term "ethnomethodology". In R. Turner (ed.), *Ethnomethodology*. Harmondsworth: Penguin.

Geertz, C. (1973) *Interpretation of Cultures*. New York: Basic Books.

Gees, J. and Michaels, S. (1989) Discourse styles: variations across speakers, situations, and tasks. *Discourse Processes*, 12(3): 263–6.

Geluykens, R. (1987) Intonation and speech act type: an experimental approach to rising intonation in queclaratives. *Journal of Pragmatics*, 11: 483–94.

Geluykens, R. (1988) On the myth of rising intonation in polar questions. *Journal of Pragmatics*, 12: 467–85.

Geluykens, R. (1989) Raising questions: question intonation revisited. *Journal of Pragmatics*, 13: 567–75.

Giddens, A. (1979) *Central Problems in Social Theory: Action, Structure, and Contradiction in Social Analysis*. Berkeley and Los Angeles: University of California Press.

Gilligan, C. (1982) *In a Different Voice: Psychological Theory and Women's Development*. Cambridge, MA: Harvard University Press.

Givón, T. (1979) *On Understanding Grammar*. New York: Academic Press.

Givón, T. (ed.) (1983a) *Topic Continuity in Discourse: Quantified Cross-language Studies*. Amsterdam: John Benjamins Press.

Givón, T. (1983b) Introduction. In T. Givón (ed.) *Topic Continuity in Discourse: a Quantitative Cross-language Study*. Amsterdam: John Benjamins Press.

Givón, T. (1983c) Topic continuity in discourse: a quantitative cross-linguistic study. In T. Givón (ed.) *Typological Studies in Language*. Amsterdam: John Benjamins Press.

Givón, T. (1983d) Topic continuity in spoken English. In T. Givón (ed.), *Topic continuity in Discourse: a Quantitative Cross-language Study*, Amsterdam: John Benjamins Press.

Givón, T. (1989) *Mind, Code, and Context: Essays in Pragmatics*. Hillsdale, NJ: Lawrence Erlbaum Associates.

Givón, T. (1992) The grammar of referential coherence as mental processing instructions. *Linguistics*, 30(1): 5–56.

Godard, D. (1977) Same setting, different norms: phone call beginnings in France and the United States. *Language in Society*, 6: 209–19.

Goffman, E. (1959) *The Presentation of Self in Everyday Life*. New York: Anchor Books.

Goffman, E. (1961) The medical model and mental hospitalization. In *Asylums*. New York: Anchor Books, 323–86.

Goffman, E. (1963) *Behavior in Public Places*. New York: Free Press.

Goffman, E. (1967a) On face work. In *Interaction Ritual*. New York: Anchor Books, 5–46.

Goffman, E. (1967b) The nature of deference and demeanor. In *Interaction Ritual*. New York: Anchor Books, 49–95.

Goffman, E. (1971a) Supportive interchanges. In *Relations in Public*. New York: Basic Books, 62–94.

Goffman, E. (1971b) Remedial interchanges. In *Relations in Public*. New York: Basic Books, 95–187.

Goffman, E. (1974) *Frame Analysis*. New York: Harper and Row.

Goffman, E. (1981a) Introduction. In *Forms of Talk*. Philadelphia: University of Pennsylvania Press, 1–4.

Goffman, E. (1981b) Replies and responses. In *Forms of Talk*. Philadelphia: University of Pennsylvania Press, 5–77.

Goffman, E. (1981c) Footing. In *Forms of Talk*. Philadelphia: University of Pennsylvania Press, 124–59.

Goffman, E. (1981d) Radio talk. In *Forms of Talk*. Philadelphia: University of Pennsylvania Press, 197–330.

Goffman, E. (1981e) Response cries. In *Forms of Talk*. Philadelphia: University of Pennsylvania Press, 78–123.

Goodwin, C. (1979) *Conversation Organization*. New York: Academic Press.

Goodwin, C. (1984) Notes on story structure and the organization of participation. In M. Atkinson and J. Heritage (eds), *Structures of Social Action*. Cambridge: University Press, 225–46.

Goodwin, C. and Heritage, J. (1990) Conversation analysis. *Annual Review of Anthropology*, 19: 283–307.

Goodwin, M. (1990) Tactical uses of stories: participation frameworks within girls' and boys' disputes. *Discourse Processes*, 13: 33–71.

Goodwin, M. (forthcoming) Byplay: playful rendering of talk in stories. In J. Baugh, G. Guy and D. Schiffrin (eds), *Towards a Social Science of Language*.

Goody, E. (1978) Towards a theory of questions. In E. Goody (ed.), *Questions and Politeness*. Cambridge: Cambridge University Press, 17–43.

Gordon, D. and Lakoff, G. (1975) Conversational postulates. In P. Cole and J. Morgan (eds), *Speech Acts (Syntax and Semantics, Volume 3)*. New York: Academic Press, 83–106.

Greatbatch, D. (1988) A turn taking system for British news interviews. *Language in Society*, 17(3): 401–30.

Green, G. (1975) How to get people to do things with words. In P. Cole and J. Morgan (eds), *Speech Acts (Syntax and Semantics, Volume 3)*. New York: Academic Press, 107–41.

Green, G. (1989) *Pragmatics and Natural Language Understanding*. Hillsdale, NJ: Lawrence Erlbaum Associates.

Grice, H. P. (1957) Meaning. *Philosophical Review*, 67: 377–88.

Grice, H. P. (1968) Utterer's meaning, sentence-meaning, and word-meaning. *Foundations of Language*, 4: 1–18.

Grice, H. P. (1975) Logic and conversation. In P. Cole and J. Morgan (eds), *Speech Acts (Syntax and Semantics, Volume 3)*. New York: Academic Press, 41–58.

Grice, H. P. (1981) Further notes on logic and conversation. In P. Cole (ed.), *Radical Pragmatics (Syntax and Semantics, Volume 9)*. New York: Academic Press, 113–28.

Grimes, J. (1975) *The Thread of Discourse*. The Hague: Mouton.

Grimes, J. (ed.) (1978) *Papers on Discourse*. Dallas, TX: Summer Institute of Linguistics.

Grimes, J. (1982) Topics within topics. In D. Tannen (ed.), *Analyzing Text and Talk*. Washington, DC: Georgetown University Press.

Grimshaw, A. (1981) *Language as Social Resource*. Stanford, CA: Stanford University Press.

Grimshaw, A. (ed.) (1990) *Conflict Talk*. Cambridge: Cambridge University Press.

Grosz, B. (1981) Focusing and description in natural language dialogues. In A. Joshi, B. Webber and I. Sag (eds), *Elements of Discourse Understanding*. Cambridge: Cambridge University Press, 84–105.

Gumperz, J. (1957) Some remarks on regional and social language differences in India. (Reprinted in A. Dil (ed.), *Language in Social Groups*. Stanford, CA: Stanford University Press, 1–11.)

Gumperz, J. (1958) Dialect differences and social stratification in a North Indian village. (Reprinted in A. Dil (ed.), *Language in Social Groups*. Stanford, CA: Stanford University Press, 25–47.)

Gumperz, J. (1964) Linguistic and social interaction in two communities. *American Anthropologist*, 6: 137–53.

Gumperz, J. (1981) The linguistic bases of communicative competence. In D. Tannen (ed.), *Analyzing Discourse: Text and Talk*. Washington, DC: Georgetown University Press, 323–34.

Gumperz, J. (1982a) *Discourse Strategies*. Cambridge: Cambridge University Press.

Gumperz, J. (1982b) *Language and Social identity*. Cambridge: Cambridge University Press.

Gumperz, J. (1985) In D. Schiffrin (ed.) *Meaning, Form and Use: Linguistic Applications*. Washington, DC: Georgetown University Press.

Gunter, R. (1974) *Sentences in Dialog*. South Carolina: Hornbeam Press.

Guy, G. (1992) Explanation in variable phonology: an exponential model of morphological constraints. *Language Variation and Change*, 3(1): 1–22.

Guy, G., Horvath, B., Vonwiller, J., Daisley, E. and Rogers, I. (1986) An intonational change in progress in Australian English. *Language in Society*, 15(1): 23–52.

Halliday, M. (1967) Notes on transitivity and theme in English. Parts 1 and 2. *Journal of Linguistics*, 3: 37–81, 199–244.

Halliday, M. (1973) *Explorations in the Functions of Language*. London: Edward Arnold.

Halliday, M. (1974) The place of "functional sentence perspective" in the system of linguistic description. In F. Danes (ed.), *Papers on Functional Sentence Perspective*. The Hague: Mouton.

Halliday, M. (1975) *Learning How to Mean: Explorations in the Development of Language*. London: Edward Arnold.

Halliday, M. (1978) *Language as a Social Semiotic*. London: Edward Arnold.

Halliday, M. and Hasan, R. (1976) *Cohesion in English*. London: Longman.

Hallowell, A. (1964) Ojibwa ontology, behavior and world view. In S. Diamond (ed.), *Primitive Views of the World*. New York: Columbia University Press, 49–82.

Hanks, W. (1990) *Referential Practices*. Chicago: University of Chicago Press.

Hannay, M. (1985) *English Existentials in Functional Grammar*. Dordrecht: Foris Publications.

Harris, R. (1980) *The Language Makers*. London: Duckworth.

Harris, R. (1981) *The Language Myth*. London: Duckworth.

Harris, R. and Taylor, T. (1991) *Landmarks in Linguistic Thought*. London: Routledge.

Harris, Z. (1951) *Methods in Structural Linguistics*. Chicago: University of Chicago Press.

Harris, Z. (1952) Discourse analysis. *Language*, 28: 1–30.

Harris, Z. (1988) *Language and Information*. New York: Columbia University Press.

Heath, S. (1982) What no bedtime story means. *Language in Society*, 11: 49–76.

Herbert, R. (1990) Sex based differences in compliment behavior. *Language in Society*, 19(2): 201–24.

Heritage, J. (1984a) *Garfinkel and Ethomethodology*. Oxford: Basil Blackwell.

Heritage, J. (1984b) A change-of-state token and aspects of its sequential placement. In J. Atkinson and J. Heritage (eds), *Structures of Social Action: Studies in Conversation Analysis*. Cambridge: Cambridge University Press, 299–345.

Heritage, J. (1989) Current developments in conversation analysis. In D. Roger and P. Bull (eds), *Conversation: an Interdisciplinary Perspective*. Clevedon: Multilingual Matters, 21–47.

Heritage, J. and Atkinson, J. (1984) Introduction. In J. Atkinson and J. Heritage (eds), *Structures of Social Action: Studies in Conversation Analysis*. Cambridge: Cambridge University Press, 1–16.

Hinrichs, E. (1986) Temporal anaphora in discourses of English. *Linguistics and Philosophy*, 9: 63–82.

Hockett, C. (1958) *A Course in Modern Linguistics*. New York: Macmillan.

Holker, K. (1989) Con and co: continuity and marqueurs in oral discourse. In M. Conte, J. Petofi and E. Sozer (eds), *Text and Discourse Connectedness*. Amsterdam/Philadelphia: John Benjamins Press, 83–92.

Holmes, J. (1989) Sex differences and apologies: one aspect of communicative competence. *Applied Linguistics*, 10: 194–213.

Holmes, J. (1990) Apologies in New Zealand English. *Language in Society*, 19(2): 155–200.

Hopper, P. (1987) Emergent grammar. *Proceedings of the Thirteenth Annual Meeting, Berkeley Linguistics Society*. Berkeley: Berkeley Linguistics Society, 139–157.

Hopper, P. (1988) Emergent grammar and the *a priori* grammar postulate. In D. Tannen (ed.), *Linguistics in Context: Connecting Observation and Understanding*. Norwood, NJ: Ablex Press, 117–34.

Hopper, P. and Thompson, S. (1980) Transitivity in grammar and discourse. *Language*, 55: 251–99.

Hopper, P. and Thompson, S. (1984) The discourse basis for lexical categories in universal grammar. *Language*, 60(4): 703–52.

Horn, L. (1972) *On the Semantic Properties of the Logical Operators in English*. Indiana University Linguistics Club.

Horn, L. (1985a) Metalinguistic negation and pragmatic ambiguity. *Language*, 61(1): 121–74.

Horn, L. (1985b) Toward a new taxonomy for pragmatic inference. In D. Schiffrin (ed.), *Meaning, Form and Use in Context: Linguistic Applications* (Georgetown University Round Table on Languages and Linguistics). Washington, DC: Georgetown University Press, 11–42.

Horvath, B. (1987) Text in conversation: variability in story-telling texts. In K. Denning et al. (eds), *Variation in Language: NWAV-XV at Stanford*. Stanford, CA: Stanford University, Linguistics Department, 212–23.

Houston, A. (1989) The English gerund: syntactic change and discourse function. In R. Fasold and D. Schiffrin (eds), *Language Change and Variation*. Amsterdam/Philadelphia: John Benjamins Press, 173–96.

Hurford, J. and Heasley (1983) *Semantics: a Coursebook*. Cambridge: Cambridge University Press.

Hymes, D. (1961) Functions of speech: the evolutionary approach. In F. Gruber (ed.), *Anthropology and Education*. Philadelphia: University of Pennsylvania Press, 55–83.

Hymes, D. (1972a) Toward ethnographies of communication: the analysis of communicative events. In P. Giglioli (ed.), *Language and Social Context*. Harmondsworth: Penguin, 21–43 (excerpts from Hymes, D. (1966) Introduction: toward ethnographies of communication. *American Anthropologist*, 66(6): 12–25).

Hymes, D. (1972b) Models of the interaction of language and social life. In J. Gumperz and D. Hymes (eds), *Directions in Sociolinguistics: the Ethnography of Communication*. New York: Holt, Rinehart and Winston, 35–71.

Hymes, D. (1973) Speech and language: On the origins and foundations of inequality in speaking. *Daedalus*, Summer: 59–86.

Hymes, D. (1974a) Toward ethnographies of communication. In *Foundations in Sociolinguistics: an Ethnographic Approach*. Philadelphia: University of Pennsylvania Press, 3–28.

Hymes, D. (1974b) Why linguistics needs the sociologist. In *Foundations in Sociolinguistics: an Ethnographic Approach*. Philadelphia: University of Pennsylvania Press, 69–82.

Hymes, D. (1974c) Linguistic theory and functions in speech. In *Foundations in Sociolinguistics: an Ethnographic Approach*. Philadelphia: University of Pennsylvania Press, 145–78.

Hymes, D. (1974d) Linguistics as sociolinguistics. In *Foundations in Sociolinguistics: an Ethnographic Approach*. Philadelphia: University of Pennsylvania Press, 193–209.

Hymes, D. (1981) *In Vain I tried to Tell You*. Philadelphia: University of Pennsylvania Press.

Hymes, D. (1984) Linguistic problems in defining the concept of "tribe". In J. Baugh and J. Sherzer (eds), *Language in Use: Readings in Sociolinguistics*. Englewood Cliffs, NJ: Prentice Hall.

Jacoby, S. and Gonzales, P. (1991) The constitution of expert–novice in scientific discourse. *Issues in Applied Linguistics*, 2(2): 149–82.

Jakobson, R. (1960) Closing statement: linguistics and poetics. In T. Sebeok (ed.), *Style in Language*. Cambridge, MA: MIT Press, 350–77.

Jefferson, G. (1972) Side sequences. In D. Sudnow (ed.), *Studies in Social Interaction*. New York: Free Press, 294–338.

Jefferson, G. (1974) Error corrections an interactional resource. *Language in Society*, 3: 181–99.

Jefferson, G. (1978) Sequential aspects of storytelling in conversation. In J. Schenkein (ed.), *Studies in the Organization of Conversational Interaction*. New York: Free Press, 219–48.

Jefferson, G. (1979) A technique for inviting laughter and its subsequent acceptance/ declination. In G. Psathas (ed.), *Everyday Language: Studies in Ethnomethodology*. New York: Irvington, 79–96.

Jefferson, G. (1980) On "trouble premontory" response to inquiry. *Sociological Inquiry*, 50: 153–85.

Jefferson, G. (1984) On the organization of laughter in talk about troubles. In J. Atkinson and J. Heritage (eds), *Structures of Social Action: Studies in Conversation Analysis*. Cambridge: Cambridge University Press, 346–69.

Jefferson, G. (1989) Preliminary notes on a possible metric which provides for a "standard maximum" silence of approximately one second in conversation. In D. Roger and P. Bull (eds), *Conversation: An Interdisciplinary Perspective*. Clevedon: Multilingual Matters, 166–96.

Johnstone, B. (1983) Presentation as proof: the language of Arabic rhetoric. *Anthropological Linguistics*, 25: 47–60.

Kalcik, S. (1975) ". . . like Ann's gynecologist or the time I was almost raped": personal narratives in women's rap groups. In C. Farra (ed.), *Women and Folklore*. Austin: University of Texas Press, 3–11.

Kamp, H. and Rohrer, C. (1983) Tense in texts. In R. Bauerle, C. Schwarze and A. von Stechow (eds), *Meaning, Use and Interpretation of Language*. Berlin: W. de Gruyter, 250–69.

Kaplan, R. and Bresnan, J. (1982) Lexical-functional grammar: a formal system for grammatical representation. In J. Bresnan (ed.), *The Mental Representation of Grammatical Relations*. Cambridge, MA: MIT Press, 173–281.

Katz, J. (1966) *The Philosophy of Language*. New York: Harper and Row.

Kay, P. (1975) Synchronic variability and diachronic change in basic color terms. *Language in Society*, 4: 257–70.

Keenan, E. (1979) Universality of conversational postulates. *Language in Society*, 5: 67–80.

Keenan, E. and Schieffelin, B. (1976) Topic as a discourse notion. In C. Li and S. Thompson (ed.), *Subject and Topic*. New York: Academic Press, 335–84.

Kipers, P. (1987) Gender and topic. *Language in Society*, 16(4): 543–58.

Kreckel, M. (1981) *Communicative Acts and Shared Knowledge in Natural Discourse*. New York: Academic Press.

Kroeber, A. and Kluckhohn, C. (1952) *Culture: a Critical Review of Concepts and Definitions*. New York: Vintage.

Kronfeld, A. (1990) *Reference and Computation*. Cambridge: Cambridge University Press.

Labov, W. (1966) On the grammaticality of everyday speech. Paper presented to the Linguistic Society of America.

Labov, W. (1972a) The study of language in its social context. In *Sociolinguistic Patterns*. Philadelphia: University of Pennsylvania Press, 183–259.

Labov, W. (1972b) The transformation of experience in narrative syntax. In *Language in the Inner City*. Philadelphia: University of Pennsylvania Press, 354–96.

Labov, W. (1972c) The isolation of contextual styles. In *Sociolinguistic Patterns*. Philadelphia: University of Pennsylvania Press, 70–109.

Labov, W. (1972d) Rules for ritual insults. In *Language in the Inner City*. Philadelphia: University of Pennsylvania Press, 297–353.

Labov, W. (1972e) The social stratification of (r) in New York City department stores. In *Sociolinguistic Patterns*. Philadelphia: University of Pennsylvania Press, 43–69.

Labov, W. (1972f) Introduction. In *Sociolinguistic Patterns*. Philadelphia: University of Pennsylvania Press, xiii–xviii.

Labov, W. (1978) Where does the linguistic variable stop? A reply to Beatriz Lavandera. *Working Papers in Sociolinguistics*, 44. Austin, TX: Southwest Educational Development Laboratory.

Labov, W. (1981) Speech actions and reactions in personal narrative. In D. Tannen (ed.), *Analyzing Discourse: Text and Talk* (Georgetown University Round Table). Washington, DC: Georgetown University Press, 219–47.

Labov, W. (1984) Field methods of the project on linguistic change and variation. In J. Baugh and J. Sherzer (eds), *Language in Use*. Englewood Cliffs, NJ: Prentice Hall, 28–53.

Labov, W. (1987) The overestimation of functionalism. In R. Dirven and V. Fried (eds), *Functionalism in Linguistics*. Philadelphia/Amsterdam: John Benjamins Press, 311–32.

Labov, W. and Fanshel, D. (1977) *Therapeutic Discourse*. New York: Academic Press.

Labov, W., Karen, M. and Miller, C. (1991) Near-mergers and the suspension of phonemic contrast. *Language Variation and Change*, 3(1): 33–74.

Labov, W. and Waletzky, J. (1967) Narrative analysis. In J. Helm (ed.), *Essays on the Verbal and Visual Arts*. Seattle: University of Washington Press, 12–44.

Ladd, R. (1978) *The Structure of Intonational Meaning*. Bloomington: Indiana University Press.

Lakoff, G. (1987) *Women, Fire and Dangerous Things*. Chicago: University of Chicago Press.

Lakoff, G. and Johnson, M. (1980) *Metaphors We Live by*. Chicago: University of Chicago Press.

Lakoff, R. (1973) The logic of politeness: or minding your p's and q's. Proceedings of the Ninth regional meeting of the Chicago Linguistics Society, University of Chicago, 292–305.

Lakoff, R. (1975) *Language and Woman's Place*. New York: Harper and Row.

Lavandera, B. (1978) Where does the sociolinguistic variable stop? *Language in Society*, 7: 171–83.

Leech, G. (1983) *Principles of Pragmatics*. London: Longman.

Lefebvre, C. (1989) Some problems in determining syntactic variables: The case of WH questions in Montreal French. In R. Fasold and D. Schiffrin (eds), *Language Change and Variation*. Philadelphia: John Benjamins Press, 351–66.

Levinson, S. (1983) *Pragmatics*. Cambridge: Cambridge University Press.

Levinson, S. (1987) Minimization and conversational inference. In M. Papi and J. Verschueren (eds), *The Pragmatic Perspective*. Amsterdam: John Benjamins Press, 61–129.

Levi-Strauss, C. (1967) *Structural Anthropology*. New York: Anchor Books.

Linde, C. and Labov, W. (1975) Spatial networks as a site for the study of language and thought. *Language*, 51: 924–39.

Lucy, J. (1992) *Language Diversity and Thought*. Philadelphia: University of Pennsylvania Press.

Lyons, J. (1977) *Semantics*. Cambridge: Cambridge University Press.

Macaulay, R. (1991) "Coz it izny spelt when they say it": Displaying dialect in writing. *American Speech*, 280–91.

McHoul, A. (1987) Why there are no guarantees for interrogators. *Journal of Pragmatics*, 11: 455–71.

MacKay, D. (1972) Formal analysis of communication processes. In R. Hinde (ed.), *Nonverbal Communication*. Cambridge: Cambridge University Press, 3–26.

MacLaury, R. (1991) Social and cognitive motivations of change: measuring variability in color semantics. *Language*, 67(1): 34–62.

Maitland, K. and Wilson, J. (1987) Pronominal selection and ideological conflict. *Journal of Pragmatics*, 11: 495–512.

Martinich, S. (1984) *Communication and Reference*. Berlin: Walter de Gruyter.

Mathesius, V. (1924) Some notes on the function of the subject in modern English. CMS 10: 244–8.

Matthiessen, C. and Thompson, S. (1987) The structure of discourse and "subordination". *ISI Reprint Series*, 87–183.

Mead, G. (1934) *Mind, Self and Society*. Chicago: University of Chicago Press.

Merritt, M. (1976) On questions following questions (in service encounters). *Language in Society*, 5: 315–57.

Merritt, M. (1984) On the use of "okay" in service encounters. In J. Baugh and J. Sherzer (eds), *Language in Use*. Englewood Cliffs, NJ: Prentice Hall, 139–47.

Milroy, L. (1987) *Observing and Analyzing Natural Language*. Oxford: Blackwell.

Moerman, M. (1988) *Ethnography and Conversation Analysis*. Philadelphia: University of Pennsylvania Press.

Morgan, J. (1975) Some interactions of syntax and pragmatics. In P. Cole and J. Morgan (eds), *Speech Acts (Syntax and Semantics, Volume 3)*. New York: Academic Press.

Morris, C. (1938) Foundations of the theory of signs. In O. Neurath, R. Carnap and C. Morris (eds), *International Encyclopedia of Unified Science*. Chicago: University of Chicago Press, 77–138.

Muhlhausler, P. and Harré, R. (1990) *Pronouns and People*. Oxford: Blackwell.

Murray, S. (1985) Toward a model of members' methods for recognizing interruption. *Language in Society*, 13: 31–41.

Myhill, J. (1988) A quantitative study of future tense marking in Spanish. In K. Ferrara et al. (eds), *Linguistic Change and Contact*. Austin: The University of Texas, Linguistics Department, 263–72.

Newmeyer, F. (1983) *Grammatical Theory*. Chicago: University of Chicago Press.

Newmeyer, F. (1991) Functional explanation in linguistics and the origins of language. *Language and Communication*, 11 (1/2): 3–28.

Ochs (Keenan), E. (1976) The universality of conversational implicature. *Language in Society*, 5: 67–80.

Ochs, E. (1979) Transcription as theory. In E. Ochs and B. Schieffelin (eds), *Developmental Pragmatics*. New York: Academic Press, 43–72.

Ochs, E. (1985) Clarification and culture. In D. Schiffrin (ed.), *Meaning, Form and Use: Linguistic Applications*. Washington, DC: Georgetown University Press.

Ochs, E. (1988) *Culture and Language Development*. Cambridge: Cambridge University Press.

Ochs, E., Taylor, C., Rudolph, D. and Smith, R. (1991) Storytelling as a theory-building activity. *Discourse Processes*, 15(1): 37–72.

Partee, B. (1984) Nominal and temporal anaphora. *Linguistics and Philosophy*, 7: 243–86.

Perlmutter, D. (ed.) (1983) *Studies in Relational Grammar*. Chicago: University of Chicago Press.

Philips, S. (1974) Warm Springs "Indian time": how the regulation of participation affects the progression of events. In R. Bauman and J. Sherzer (eds), *Explorations in the Ethnography of Speaking*. Cambridge: Cambridge University Press, 92–109.

Piaget, J. (1952) *The Origins of Intelligence in Children*. New York: Norton.

Piaget, J. (1970) *Structuralism*. New York: Basic Books.

Pike, K. (1967) *Language in Relation to a Unified Theory of the Structure of Human Behavior*. The Hague: Mouton.

Polanyi, L. (1978) False starts can be true.

Polanyi, L. (1979) So what's the point? *Semiotica*, 25: 207–41.

Polanyi, L. (1982) Linguistic and social constraints on storytelling. *Journal of Pragmatics*, 6: 509–24.

Polanyi, L. (1985) Conversational storytelling. In T. van Dijk (ed.), *Handbook of Discourse Analysis. Volume 3. Discourse and Dialogue*. London: Academic Press, 183–201.

Polanyi, L. (1988) A formal model of the structure of discourse. *Journal of Pragmatics*, 12: 601–38.

Pomerantz, A. (1984) Agreeing and disagreeing with assessments: Some features of preferred/dispreferred turn shapes. In J. Atkinson and J. Heritage (eds), *Structures of Social Action: Studies in Conversation Analysis*. Cambridge: University Press, 57–101.

Pope, E. (1976) *Questions and Answers in English*. The Hague: Mouton.

Posner, R. (1980) Semantics and pragmatics of sentence connectives in natural language. In F. Kiefer and J. Searle (eds), *Pragmatics and Speech Act Theory*. Dordrecht: D. Reidel and Co., 87–122.

Potter, J. and Wetherell, M. (1987) *Discourse and Social Psychology: Beyond Attitudes and Behavior*. London: Sage Publications.

Poyatos, F. (1983) *New Perspectives in Nonverbal Communication*. London: Pergamon Press.

Preston, D. (1982) 'Ritin fowklower daun 'rong: folklorists' failures in phonology. *Journal of American Folklore*, 95: 304–26.

Preston, D. (1985) The Li'l Abner syndrome: written representations of speech. *American Speech*, 60(4): 328–36.

Prince, E. (1978) On the function of one *this* and this really weird *one*. Presented at the LSA Summer Meeting, Urbana, IL.

Prince, E. (1981) Toward a taxonomy of given-new information. In P. Cole (ed.), *Radical Pragmatics*. New York: Academic Press, 223–56.

Prince, E. (1984) Topicalization and left-dislocation: a functional analysis. *Annals of the New York Academy of Sciences*.

Prince, E. (1985) Fancy syntax and "shared knowledge". *Journal of Pragmatics*, 9: 65–81.

Prince, E. (1988) Discourse analysis: a part of the study of linguistic competence. In *Linguistics: the Cambridge Survey*. Cambridge: Cambridge University Press, 164–82.

Pufahl, I. (1988) How to assign work in an office: a comparison of spoken and written directives in American English. *Journal of Pragmatics*, 10: 673–92.

Quirk, R., Greenbaum, S., Leech, G. and Svartvik, J. (1972) *A Grammar of Contemporary English*. London: Longman.

Rains, C. (1992) "You die for life": on the use of poetic devices in argumentation. *Language in Society*, 21(2): 253–76.

Rando, E. and Napoli, D. J. (1978) Definites and *there* sentences. *Language*, 54(2): 300–13.

Recanati, F. (1987) *Meaning and Force: the Pragmatics of Performative Utterances*. Cambridge: Cambridge University Press.

Reddy, M. (1979) The conduit metaphor. In A. Ortony (ed.), *Metaphor and Thought*. Cambridge: Cambridge University Press, 284–324.

Reed, S. (1972) Pattern recognition and categorization. *Cognitive Psychology*, 3: 382–407.

Reichenbach, H. (1947) *Elements of Symbolic Logic*. London: Macmillan.

Reichman, R. (1985) *How to Get Computers to Talk Like You and Me*. Cambridge, MA: MIT Press.

Rickford, J. (1987) The haves and have nots: Sociolinguistic surveys and the assessment of speaker competence. *Language in Society*, 16(2): 149–78.

Robert, H. (1992) *Telephone Conversations*. Bloomington: University of Indiana Press.

Romaine, S. (1981) On the problem of syntactic variation: a reply to B. Lavandera and W. Labov. *Working Papers in Sociolinguistics*, 82. Austin, TX: Southwest Educational Development Laboratory.

Rosch, E. (1973) Natural categories. *Cognitive Psychology*, 4: 328–50.

Rosch, E. (1978) Principles of categorization. In E. Rosch and B. Lloyd (eds), *Cognition and Categorization*. Hillsdale, NJ: Laurence Erlbaum, 27–48.

Rosch, E., Mervis, C., Gray, W., Johnson, D. and Boyes-Braem, P. (1976) Basic objects in natural categories. *Cognitive Psychology*, 8: 382–449.

Sacks, H. (1971) Lecture notes. School of Social Science, University of California at Irvine.

Sacks, H. (1972a) Lecture notes. School of Social Science, University of California at Irvine.

Sacks, H. (1972b) On the analyzability of stories by children. In J. Gumperz and D. Hymes (eds), *Directions in Sociolinguistics*. New York: Holt, Rinehart and Winston, 325–45.

Sacks, H. (1984) Notes on methodology. In J. M. Atkinson and J. Heritage (eds), *Structures of Social Action*. Cambridge: Cambridge University Press, 21–7.

Sacks, H. and Schegloff, E. (1979) Two preferences in the organization of reference to persons in conversation and their interaction. In Psathas (ed.), *Everyday Language: Studies in Ethnomethodology*. New York: Irvington, 15–21.

Sacks, H., Schegloff, E. and Jefferson, G. (1974) A simplest systematics for the organization of turn-taking in conversation. *Language*, 50: 696–735.

Sadock, J. (1985) Whither radical pragmatics? In D. Schiffrin (ed.), *Meaning, Form, and Use in Context: Linguistic Applications* (Georgetown University Round Table on Languages and Linguistics). Washington, DC: Georgetown University Press, 139–49.

Sankoff, D. (1988) Sociolinguistics and syntactic variation. In F. Newmeyer (ed.), *Linguistics: The Cambridge Survey*. Cambridge: Cambridge University Press, 140–61.

Sankoff, D. and P. Thibault. (1981) Weak complementarity: tense and aspect in Montreal French. In B. Johns and D. Strong (eds), *Syntactic Change* (Natural Language Studies, 26). Ann Arbor: University of Michigan.

Sapir, E. (1933) Communication. *Encyclopedia of the Social Sciences*, 4: 78–81.

Saussure, F. de (1959) *A Course in General Linguistics*. New York: Philosophical Library (originally published 1916).

Saville-Troike, M. (1982) *The Ethnography of Communication*. Oxford: Blackwell.

Schegloff, E. (1972a) Sequencing in conversational openings. In J. Gumperz and D. Hymes (eds), *Directions in Sociolinguistics*. New York: Holt, Rinehart and Winston, 346–80.

Schegloff, E. (1972b) Notes on a conversational practice: Formulating place. In D. Sundow (ed.), *Studies in Social Interaction*. New York: Free Press, 75–119.

Schegloff, E. (1979a) The relevance of repair to syntax-for conversation. In T. Givon (ed.), *Syntax and Semantics, 12: Discourse and Syntax*. New York: Academic Press, 261–88.

Schegloff, E. (1979b) Identification and recognition in telephone conversation openings. In Psathas (ed.), *Everyday Language: Studies in Ethnomethodology*. New York: Irvington, 23–78.

Schegloff, E. (1980) Preliminaries to preliminaries. In D. Zimmerman and C. West (eds), *Language and Social Interaction*. Special issue of *Sociological Inquiry*, 50 (3/4): 104–52.

Schegloff, E. (1981) Discourse as an interactional achievement: Some uses of "uh huh" and other things that come between sentences. In D. Tannen (ed.), *Analyzing Discourse: Text and Talk*. Washington, DC: Georgetown University Press, 71–93.

Schegloff, E. (1984) On some questions and ambiguities in conversation. In J. Atkinson and J. Heritage (eds), *Structures of Social Action: Studies in Conversation Analysis*. Cambridge: Cambridge University Press, 28–52.

Schegloff, E. (1987a) Between micro and macro: contexts and other connections. In J. C. Alexander et al. (eds), *The Micro–Macro Link*. Berkeley: University of California Press.

Schegloff, E. (1987b) Confirming allusions. Talk presented to Linguistics Society of America Summer Institute, Stanford University.

Schegloff, E. (1988) Presequences and indirection: applying speech act theory to ordinary conversation. *Journal of Pragmatics*, 12: 55–62.

Schegloff, E. (1992) The last site for intersubjectivity. *American Sociological Review*.

Schegloff, E., Jefferson, G. and Sacks, H. (1977) The preference for self-correction in the organization of repair in conversation. *Language*, 53: 361–82.

Schegloff, E. and Sacks, H. (1973) Opening up closings. *Semiotica*, 7 (3/4): 289–327.

Schenkein, J. (ed.) (1978) *Studies in the Organization of Conversational Interaction*. New York: Academic Press.

Scherer, K. and Giles, H. (eds) (1979) *Social Markers in Speech*. Cambridge: Cambridge University Press.

Schieffelin, B. (1990) *How Kaluli Children Learn What to Say, What to Do and How to Feel*. Cambridge: Cambridge University Press.

Schiffrin, D. (1977) Opening encounters. *American Sociological Review*, 42(4): 671–91.

Schiffrin, D. (1981a) Tense variation in narrative. *Language*, 57(1): 45–62.

Schiffrin, D. (1981b) Handwork as ceremony: the case of the handshake. In A. Kendon (ed.), *Nonverbal Communication, Interaction, and Gesture*. The Hague: Mouton, 237–50.

Schiffrin, D. (1984a) Jewish argument as sociability. *Language in Society*, 13(3): 311–35.

Schiffrin, D. (1984b) How a story says what it means and does. *Text*, 4(4): 313–46.

Schiffrin, D. (1985a) Multiple constraints on discourse options: a quantitative analysis of causal sequences. *Discourse Processes*, 8(3): 281–303.

Schiffrin, D. (1985b) Conversational coherence: the role of "well". *Language*, 61(3): 640–67.

Schiffrin, D. (1986a) The functions of *and* in discourse. *Journal of Pragmatics*, 10(1): 41–66.

Schiffrin, D. (1986b) Turn-initial variation: structure and function in conversation. In D. Sankoff (ed.), *Diversity and Diachrony*. Philadelphia: John Benjamins Press, 367–80.

Schiffrin, D. (1987a) *Discourse Markers*. Cambridge: Cambridge University Press.

Schiffrin, D. (1987b) Toward an empirical base in pragmatics. Review article of Stephen Levinson, *Pragmatics. Language in Society*, 16(3): 381–95.

Schiffrin, D. (1988a) Conversation analysis. In F. Newmeyer (ed.), *Linguistics: the Cambridge Survey*. Cambridge: Cambridge University Press, 251–76.

Schiffrin, D. (1988b) Sociolinguistic approaches to discourse: Topic and reference in narrative. In K. Ferrera et al. (eds), *Linguistic Contact and Variation*. Austin: University of Texas Press, 1–28.

Schiffrin, D. (1990a) The management of a cooperative self in argument: the role of opinions and stories. In A. Grimshaw (ed.), *Conflict Talk*. Cambridge: Cambridge University Press, 241–59.

Schiffrin, D. (1990b) Between text and context: deixis, anaphora and the meaning of *then. Text*, 10(3): 245–70.

Schiffrin, D. (1990c) The principle of intersubjectivity in conversation and communication. Review article of Talbot Taylor and Deborah Cameron *Conversation analysis* (1988), and Lauri Carlson, *"Well" in dialogue games* (1987). *Semiotica*, 80: 121–51.

Schiffrin, D. (1990d) Conversational analysis. *Annual Review of Applied Linguistics*, 11: 3–19.

Schiffrin, D. (1992a) Gender displays among family, friends, and neighbors. In K. Hall, M. Bucholtz, and B. Moonwomon (eds), *Locating Power*, Proceedings of the Second Berkeley Women and Language Conference, University of California, Berkeley, 515–27.

Schiffrin, D. (1992b) Anaphoric *then*: aspectual, textual and epistemic meaning. *Linguistics*, 30(4): 753–92.

Schiffrin, D. (1992c) Conditionals as topics in discourse. *Linguistics*, 30(1): 165–97.

Schiffrin, D. (1993) Research talk *on, for*, and *with* subjects. Peer commentary on Cameron (et al.) *Ethics, advocacy and empowerment: Issues of method in researching language. Language and Communication*, 13(2): 133–6.

Schiffrin, D. (forthcoming). The transformation of experience, identity, and context. In J. Baugh, G. Guy and D. Schiffrin (eds), *Towards a Social Science of Language*.

Scott, M. and Lyman, S. (1968) Accounts. *American Sociological Review*, 33: 46–62.

Searle, J. (1962) What is a speech act? In M. Black (ed.), *Philosophy in America*. Ithaca, NY: Cornell University Press, 221–39.

Searle, J. (1969) *Speech Acts*. Cambridge: Cambridge University Press.

Searle, J. (1975) Indirect speech acts. In P. Cole and J. Morgan (eds), *Syntax and Semantics. Volume 3: Speech Acts*. New York: Academic Press, 59–82.

Searle, J. (1979) A taxonomy of illocutionary acts. In *Expression and Meaning*. Cambridge: Cambridge University Press.

Searle, J. (1989). On conversation. In J. Searle (ed.), *(On) Searle on Conversation*. Amsterdam: John Benjamins Press.

Segal, E., Duchan, J. and Scott, P. (1991) The role of interclausal connectives in narrative structuring: evidence from adults' interpretations of simple stories. *Discourse Processes*, 12(1): 27–54.

Sells, P. (1985) *Lectures on Contemporary Syntactic Theories*. Stanford, CA: Center for the Study of Language and Information.

Selting, M. (1992) Prosody in conversational questions. *Journal of Pragmatics*, 17(4): 315–45.

Sheldon, A. (1990) Pickle fights: gendered talk in preschool disputes. In D. Tannen (ed.), *Discourse Processes: Special Issue on Gender and Conversational Interaction*, 13(1): 5–32.

Sherzer, J. (1983) *Kuna Ways of Speaking*. Austin: University of Texas Press.

Sidner, C. (1986) Focusing in the comprehension of definite anaphora. In B. Grosz, K. Jones and B. Webber (eds), *Readings in Natural Language Processing*. Los Altos, CA: Morgan Kaufman Publishers, 363–94.

Sifianou, M. (1989) On the telephone again! Differences in telephone behavior: England versus Greece. *Language in Society*, 18: 527–44.

Silva-Corvalan, C. (1983) Tense and aspect in oral Spanish narrative. *Language*, 59: 760–80.

Simmel, G. (1911) The sociology of sociability. *American Journal of Sociology*, 55: 3. (Reprinted in 1950 in K. Wolff (ed.) *The Sociology of Georg Simmel*. New York: Free Press, 40–57.)

Sinclair, J. and Coulthard, M. (1975) *Towards an Analysis of Discourse: the English Used by Teachers and Pupils*. London: Oxford University Press.

Slobin, D. (1991) Learning to think for speaking: native language, cognition, and rhetorical style. *Pragmatics*, 1(1): 7–26.

Smith, N. (1982) *Mutual Knowledge*. London: Academic Press.

Smith, W. (1977) *The Behavior of Communicating*. Cambridge, MA: Harvard University Press.

Sperber, D. and Wilson, D. (1986) *Relevance*. Cambridge, MA: Harvard University Press.

Stenstrom, A. (1984) *Questions and Responses in English Conversation*. Stockholm: CWK Gleerup.

Strawson, P. (1964) Intention and convention in speech acts. *Philosophical Review*, 73: 439–60.

Stubbs, M. (1983) *Discourse Analysis*. Chicago: University of Chicago Press.

Tannen, D. (1979) What's in a frame? Surface evidence for underlying expectations. In R. Freedle (ed.), *New Directions in Discourse Processing*. Norwood, NJ: Ablex Publishing, 137–81.

Tannen, D. (1981) Review of Labov and Fanshel, *Therapeutic discourse* in *Language*.

Tannen, D. (1984) *Conversational Style*. Norwood, NJ: Ablex Press.

Tannen, D. (1989a) *Talking Voices: Repetition, Dialogue, and Imagery in Conversational Discourse*. Cambridge: Cambridge University Press.

Tannen, D. (1989b) Interpreting interruption in conversation. Papers from the 25th annual regional meeting of the Chicago Linguistics Society, Chicago, 266–87.

Tannen, D. (1990) *You Just Don't Understand!* New York: William Morrow.

Tannen, D. (ed.) (forthcoming) *Linguistic Framing in Conversation*. Oxford: Oxford University Press.

Tannen, D. and Saville Troike, M. (eds) (1985) *Perspectives on Silence*. Norwood, NH: Ablex Publishing.

Tannen, D. and Wallat, C. (1986) Medical professionals and parents: a linguistic analysis of communication across contexts. *Language in Society*, 15(3): 295–312.

Taylor, T. (1992) *Mutual Misunderstanding*. North Carolina: Duke University Press.

Taylor, T. and Cameron, D. (1987) *Analyzing Conversation*. New York: Pergamon Press.

Terasaki, A. (1976) Pre-announcement sequences in conversation. Social Science Working Paper 99, School of Social Science, University of California, Irvine.

Thompson, S. and Mann, W. (1987) Rhetorical structure theory: a framework for the analysis of texts. *Papers in Pragmatics* 1(1): 79–105.

Tomlin, R. (1985) Foreground–background information and the syntax of subordination. *Text*, 5 (1/2): 85–122.

Tomlin, R. (1987) Linguistic reflections of cognitive events. In R. Tomlin (ed.), *Coherence and Grounding in Discourse*. Philadelphia: John Benjamins Press, 455–79.

Trudgill, P. (1974) *The Social Differentiation of English in Norwich*. Cambridge: Cambridge University Press.

Tsui, A. (1989) Beyond the adjacency pair. *Language in Society*, 18(4): 545–64.

Turner, R. (ed.) (1974) *Ethnomethodology*. Harmondsworth: Penguin.

van Dijk, T. (1972) *Some Aspects of Text Grammars*. The Hague: Mouton.

van Dijk, T. (1977) *Text and Context*. London: Longman.

van Dijk, T. (1985) Introduction: discourse as a new cross-discipline. In T. van Dijk (ed.), *Handbook of Discourse Analysis, Volume 1: Disciplines of Discourse*. New York: Academic Press, 1–10.

Varenne, H. (1984) The interpretation of pronominal paradigms: speech situation, pragmatic meaning, and cultural structure. *Semiotica*, 50 (3/4): 221–48.

Vendler, Z. (1967) *Linguistics in Philosophy*. Ithaca, NY: Cornell University Press.

Vincent, D. (1983) Les ponctuants du langage. Dissertation, Université de Montreal.

Virtanen, T. (1992) Issues of text typology: narrative – a "basic" type of text? *Text*, 12(2): 293–310.

Vygotsky, L. (1962) *Thought and Language*. Cambridge, MA: MIT Press.

Ward, G. (1990) The discourse functions of VP preposing. *Language*, 66: 742–63.

Ward, G. and Birner, B. (1993) *There*-sentences and information status. Presented at LSA Annual Meetings, Los Angeles, CA.

Ward, G. and Hirschberg, J. (1991) A pragmatic account of tautological utterances. *Journal of Pragmatics*, 15: 207–20.

Ward, G. Sproat, R. and McKoon, G. (1991) A pragmatic analysis of so-called anaphoric islands. *Language*, 67: 3.

Watzlawick, P., Beavin, J. and Jackson, D. (1967) *The Pragmatics of Human Communication*. New York: Norton.

Webber, B. (1979) *A Formal Approach to Discourse Anaphora*. New York and London: Garland.

Webber, B. (1988) Tense as discourse anaphor. *Computational Linguistics*, 14(2): 61–73.

Wierzbicka, A. (1987) *English Speech Act Verbs: a Semantic Dictionary*. New York: Academic Press.

Wierzbicka, A. (1987) "Radical semantics" vs. "radical pragmatics". *Language*, 63: 95–114.

Wolfson, N. (1976) Speech events and natural speech: some implications for sociolinguistic methodology. *Language in Society*, 5: 189–209.

Wolfson, N. (1979) The conversational historical present alternation. *Language*, 55: 168–82.

Wolfson, N. (1988) The Bulge: a theory of speech behavior and social distance. In J. Fine (ed.), *Second Language Discourse: a Textbook of Current Research*. Norwood, NJ: Ablex, 21–38.

Wong, M. (1990) Referential choice in spoken Cantonese discourse. PhD Dissertation, Georgetown University.

Wootton, A. (1989) Remarks on the methodology of conversation analysis. In D. Roger and P. Bull (eds), *Conversation: an Interdisciplinary Perspective*. Clevedon: Multilingual Matters, 238–58.

Wright, S. and Givón, T. (1987) The pragmatics of indefinite reference. *Studies in Language*, 11(1): 15–31.

Zimmerman, D. (1988) On conversation: the conversation analytic perspective. In *Communication Yearbook 11*. Beverly Hills, CA: Sage.

Ziv, Y. (1982) Another look at definites in existentials. *Journal of Linguistics*, 18: 73–88.

Index